EX LIBRIS

Child Psychology

Child

FIFTH EDITION

Psychology

Arthur T. Jersild
Teachers College, Columbia University

Englewood Cliffs, N. J.
PRENTICE-HALL, INC.

Child Psychology,

FIFTH EDITION

Arthur T. Jersild

Fourth printing.......*April, 1962*

Designed by Harry Rinehart

Photographs from
Monkmeyer Press Photo Service:
Pinney, 1, 12; Statile, 3; Gregor, 30; Censer, 64; Luoma, 94;
Hayes, 113, 115, 127, 155, 171, 199, 233, 235, 255,
287, 299, 301, 332, 352, 373, 401, 423, 440.

to Catherine, Alice, and John

Foreword

In this fifth edition of *Child Psychology* I have emphasized certain themes that were expressed in the fourth, but my main effort has been to re-examine my earlier material in the light of new findings and such seasoning as I have acquired through the passing years.

While again emphasizing the concept of the self as an essential feature in the study of all aspects of a child's development, I have tried to inquire more deeply into the interplay between the subjective and objective dimensions of a child's life—his "inner" and his "outer" world. In so doing, I have given more attention than in the preceding edition to the beginnings of self-awareness, the importance of the child's perception of things, and to overt and covert currents in his life and in his view of himself.

I have expanded my discussion of parent-child relationships throughout the book and in two new chapters, seeking to give a balanced account of ways in which parents and children mutually influence one another. The effort I have devoted to this topic will be well repaid if it helps parents and prospective fathers and mothers (and those who sit in judgment on them) to take a more humane view of both the child *and* his parents.

In assessing the role of parents, other adults, and peers in a child's development I have also given more attention to the interaction between a child's heredity and his environment.

As in earlier editions, I have drawn most heavily on the research literature in child psychology. I have also made extensive use of the contributions of psychoanalysis.

In writing this edition I have become increasingly impressed by the vast network of forces in the child himself and in his environment that shape the fortunes of his life. I have found again that each new edition is more absorbing but also harder to write than the one before. The longer I study children the more I realize how much I have yet to learn. When I try to cover new writings about children and to reconsider the old I feel as one who is climbing a mountain which becomes higher the farther he ascends. I also face anew the pressing question: What is the personal meaning of the things I observe and read and write?

Many persons have helped me in preparing this book. I am grateful to my own children and to other children I have had the privilege of knowing; to the many instructors who have commented on the earlier edition; to my own students and to students in other institutions who have taken the trouble of writing to me.

In the text and in the Bibliography at the end of the book, I have named the persons whose writings are cited. This is intended both to acknowledge their contributions and to guide students who wish to read original sources.

I appreciate the kindness of colleagues who assisted by providing reprints from foreign journals and drafts of studies that were unpublished when the book went to press. Valuable materials were sent to me by Professor Millie Almy, Dr. Philip Kraus, Professor Wayne Dennis, Dr. Harriet Rheingold, Professor Dorothy H. Eichorn, Dr. R. L. Debus, Dr. R. Meili, Mr. Abraham Tannenbaum, Professor Mary Cover Jones, and Professor S. R. Jayaswal.

I want to express warm thanks to my friends at Prentice-Hall. I am especially indebted to Mr. Edgar P. Thomas for his counsel and encouragement and to Miss Nancy O'Donohue who edited the manuscript.

I am deeply grateful to my close associates who have aided me in writing the book, locating references, and checking countless items. I have received devoted help from Miss Marlene Miller, Mrs. Lilly Sprecher Dimitrovsky, Mrs. Adele Brodkin, and Miss Eve Allina. I am very pleased that Dr. Wanda Walker has prepared an instructor's manual to accompany the text.

In preparing this book I have again been sustained by my wife's and my children's patience and support.

A. T. J.

Contents

ix

Contents   **xi**

INFLUENCE OF OTHERS ON A CHILD'S VIEW OF HIMSELF

SELF AS IS COMPARED WITH THE "IDEAL SELF"

Maintenance of the self-image. Conscious and
unconscious processes underlying attitudes pertaining to self.

The importance of parents' attitudes and personality trends.

ACCEPTANCE, REJECTION, AND OVER-PROTECTION

The accepting parent.

CONSEQUENCES OF BEING ACCEPTED

THE REJECTING PARENT

Factors underlying rejection and over-protection.
Consequences of rejection. Rejection and self-
repair.

FORMS OF ATTACHMENT TO PARENTS

Mixed emotions.

HOW DOES THE CHILD PERCEIVE THE PARENT?

The idealized parent.

SELF-ASSERTION IN A CHILD'S RELATIONSHIPS WITH PARENTS

PREVAILING UNDERTONES

RESPONSES OF CHILDREN
TO CHILD-REARING ATTITUDES AND PRACTICES

FACTORS INVOLVED IN THE ASSESSMENT
OF PARENT-CHILD RELATIONSHIPS

VARYING ROLES AND RELATIONSHIPS WITHIN THE FAMILY

INFLUENCE OF OTHERS ON THE CHILD

CULTURAL INFLUENCES ON PARENTAL PRACTICES

Changing fashions and philosophies in child-
rearing. Child-rearing in various cultures.

xiv   *Contents*

Contents **xv**

P A R T   F O U R

Expanding Horizons

page 299

factors limiting recall of early experiences.
Emotional quality of early memories. "Memory
optimism" and "memory pessimism." Memories
from childhood as compared with childhood
behavior as viewed by others. Conditions that
influence forgetting and facilitate recall. Influence of present moods and personality trends
on recall of the past. Residual effects of early
experiences. Significance of early memories.

FROM EXPERIMENTATION TO PLANNING

EARLY MANIFESTATIONS

THEMES OF MAKE-BELIEVE

EMOTIONAL CONTENT OF MAKE-BELIEVE

Make-believe as a kind of thinking. Make-
believe as a means of dealing with emotional
problems. Facing the future through fantasy.
Make-believe undercurrents in seemingly unreasonable behavior.

USES OF MAKE-BELIEVE IN SOCIAL RELATIONSHIPS

DAYDREAMS AND FANTASIES

IMAGINARY COMPANIONS

THEMES IN DAYDREAMS OF OLDER CHILDREN

OTHER FORMS OF VIVID IMAGERY AND ASSOCIATION OF IMAGES

CHILDREN'S DREAMS

Early signs of dreaming. The dream as related
to the dreamer.

PROJECTIVE METHODS

Interpretation of projected responses.

THE GROWING WORLD

Awareness of people. Widened range of response to world at large. Increased capacity
for generalizing.

Contents   xiv

PART ONE

A Child Is Born

Entering
a Child's World

CHAPTER ONE   Birth means the coming of a human being who forty weeks earlier was no more than a single cell. He looks helpless and many of his activities seem to be aimless. But he quickly comes to grips with life.

Soon his movements will be fashioned into countless skills. Within a few weeks or even hours he will display characteristics that set him off as a unique personality, different from all other people. In a year or two he will be able to speak. As a social creature he soon will be deeply involved in the fortunes of his fellows. While yet an infant he will feel the surge of most of the emotions that pervade the life of an adult. And as time passes, the horizons of his world will greatly expand.

Why should we study this child as he moves from infancy through childhood years? The an-

swer is that to understand human beings we must study their beginnings. It is necessary to enter the child's world if we wish to understand others, or ourselves.

When we study the infant or young child we must rely on what we can observe in his behavior, for he cannot tell us about himself, and most of us can recall very little from our own infancy. Much happened in our childhood before we were able, through lasting memories, to pick up some of the threads that form the fabric of our mental life.

As the child grows older we can observe his actions and we can also listen to what he tells about himself. This is helpful. But there probably is no child who is able or willing fully to reveal his feelings and his thoughts. Also, as we study the older child we can draw on the larger store of impressions which we formed concerning ourselves and other children as we grew older. These impressions from our earlier years were important in shaping our outlook on life. Many of them do not stand out as distinct memories. Others, again, can be revived in some detail as we recall, for example, our first day at school, or a happy birthday, or a fight with a playmate. Recollections from childhood are a link between our present and our own childhood and the childhood of others. And this is a helpful link. However, our recollections of what happened when we were children will be colored by our unique perception of happenings as they occurred and by the influence which later fortunes in our lives have on our interpretation of what has gone before.

So, in a sense, we come as strangers when we seek to enter the world of a child or try to re-enter the world of our own childhood. But we do not come as complete strangers. We cannot read the child's mind but we can go far in judging the nature of his strivings, thoughts, and feelings as compared with our own. In the sphere of emotion, for example, the feelings expressed by a child when he is only a few weeks old are made of the same raw material as our own. Moreover, the child each one of us once was still resides in us. Even if we try to abandon him by turning our minds to other things he will never abandon us. He is an essential part of *my* existence as I write, and of *your* existence as you read. And nothing comes closer to the essence of life than our own existence. For this reason, so the writer believes, it is a rewarding task to endeavor to understand children as they now are and the children we once were.

Stages in the birth of a personality

In the process through which a person comes into being, three steps are especially significant. The first is *conception*. A person's life as a distinct organism begins when he is conceived. *The process of being born* is a second step; it sets each one of us apart physically from others. *The development of selfhood* is a third step, involving all the experiences through which each of us becomes aware of his existence as a person, distinct from all others.

Signs of self-awareness appear during the first year of a child's life and they increase quickly as he grows older. Evidence of self-awareness that others can detect appears earlier than the web of experience we ourselves can remember in later years.

THE PASSIVE PHASE

The baby who in time will actively strive and plan to take the affairs of his life into his own hands is passive at first. At the moment he was conceived a good part of what he might ever become was decided by the nature of his biological inheritance. His heredity was handed to him. He did not ask for it. He could not ask for it, nor could he ask to be conceived, or request that he might or might not be born. Life was thrust upon him. This is a simple fact and yet profoundly significant for understanding a child. The equipment a child will use as he faces his future is, to a large degree, determined in advance. He cannot change it. There still is room, of course, for a tremendous range in the ways he might use this equipment and in the extent to which his environment helps or hinders him in realizing his potentialities as he grows older. Yet there is something final about it when a person has been conceived and born. There is no going back and only one certainty remains—he will die. The main probabilities of existence have been laid down.

BEGINNINGS OF THE ACTIVE PHASE

The third phase, during which a child begins to assert himself and comes into being as a person with an awareness of himself, does not have this finality. This phase of his life is not, as we ourselves see it, so completely determined by forces beyond our control. Neither is it fixed in point of time, for in the process of self-discovery we not only live in the present but also anticipate the future and incorporate the past. Even the past is not entirely unchangeable, for the effect of what has gone before may be changed by what is now and what is yet to be. Our past asserts itself, for example, when something we now face makes us afraid because of an earlier unpleasant experience with it, but this effect, reaching out of the past, is modified when we now discover that we can overcome this fear.

In the development of the self there is no chance to be unborn, but there is, according to the experience of the person himself, a chance of being "reborn." As viewed from the standpoint of our own thoughts and feelings we have some freedom to change and to choose. We are also aware that much unexplored and untried ground still lies ahead. In this phase of development there is, then, an added dimension; whereas the story of what is *probable* already has been told, the chronicle of what seems *possible* has only just begun.

Two approaches to the understanding of children

There are two major approaches that can be made in studying children. One is to observe or to measure the *objective* dimensions of a child's make-up and conduct. The other is to inquire into the *subjective* aspects of his personal experience.

We use an objective approach when we measure a child's size, his abilities and overt behavior, and record his language, and the like. We use the subjective approach when we not only take account of what can be seen and measured but also go on to ask: What is the nature of his inner life? What is his world from his point of view? What might be his private thoughts and feelings?

From an objective point of view we are interested in knowing that a three-year-old child is three feet tall. From the subjective point of view we are interested not solely in this statistic but in what it might mean to him. Objectively, the child is near the average in height. Objectively, also, he is a big child as compared with his one-year-old brother and he is a little child as compared with his ten-year-old sister. But the subjective dimension as viewed from the child's standpoint may be something else. He may perceive himself as a rather large child if all his playmates are shorter than he, or he may be acutely aware of the smallness of his size when he notices that bigger children have privileges that are denied to him. A child's perception of his size and his feelings about his size are, from a psychological point of view, more important than his physical stature as such.

The subjective view a child has of his experience and of circumstances in the world about him may or may not be in keeping with the view held by others. For example, a child may feel that his mother favors a younger brother. From the point of view of the mother or from the point of view of a visitor this may not be true at all. But this does not alter the significance of the fact that the child himself feels unfairly treated.

Similarly, let us take three older boys who are running a race. Henry comes in first, Billy second, and Sammy third. Henry was the victor but he does not feel victorious; he knew in advance that he could win. Billy, although he only came in second, has a feeling of triumph. He isn't as sure of himself as Henry and from his point of view it was an achievement to be in a race with Henry and to come in ahead of Sammy. And Sammy, too, although he came in last, and in that sense was a failure, may feel very good about the race for, although he did not win or place, the other boys at least let him in on the race, and that is very gratifying to him.

We could multiply examples of this sort. Paralleling the external or objective facts about a child's development, his behavior, his ability as compared with others, or his emotions as viewed in the light of his actions, are the child's private perceptions, feelings, and motives. These may or may not correspond to the objective facts others can see.

This subjective aspect of a child's world constitutes part of what we call the *self*. The self begins to come into being from the time of early infancy, and it is in process of becoming as long as a person lives. The child's self includes all that he calls "I"; it is all that he calls "mine." It is his world as experienced by him.

To understand children it is necessary to be concerned about both the objective and the subjective dimensions of their development. In the research literature in child psychology there is a huge accumulation of findings dealing with development primarily from an objective point of view. These findings show, in quantitative terms, the normal characteristics of children at various stages of growth. In the physical sphere there are tables which show the "norms" of physical growth indicating, for example, the average height of children at age three as compared with age four and the "normal distribution" of height—the range from the tallest to the smallest and the proportion of children who measure one or two or more centimeters above or below the average. There also are norms of mental growth. Similarly, there are findings showing in quantitative terms what is characteristic of children at various age levels when a study is made of their social behavior, their joys and problems, their display of anger, their fears, and so on. Such findings, based largely on objective measurements and records, are quite impersonal when set forth in a table. But they supply information which is significant when we try to understand a child from a more subjective or personal point of view. When a certain two-and-a-half-year-old child is rather obstinate, or wets his bed, or mispronounces many of his words, or sometimes has "bad dreams," we might view him as having unique behavior problems if findings did not show that the same holds true for a large proportion of children at his age.

THE SPECTATOR AND THE PARTICIPANT OBSERVER

When we try to assess the meaning of a child's behavior at a given age it is essential to view it in the perspective of development as revealed by impersonal data based on the study of many children. However, to understand a child it is necessary also to look into the personal aspects of his experience. We do not understand him simply by noting his behavior and comparing it with the norm. It is necessary not only to observe and compare but also to interpret.

He chortles, and we infer that he is full of glee. He stamps his foot and we infer that he is angry. We do more, however, if we are trying to understand him: We try to appreciate his joy and to understand what his anger stands for in his experience, even though, as we see it, he really has nothing to be angry about. When we try to understand what a child's experience might mean from his point of view, we must do so in part through the medium of our own experience. We have no other anchor or reference point. We draw upon our own thinking when we judge what the child thinks and upon our own feelings when we try to understand how he might feel. The greatest difficulty we, as older persons, have in dealing with a child is to view things from his standpoint. To overcome this difficulty we not only have to observe a child as a *spectator* might but also as a *participant*.

A spectator observes or measures the child's characteristics in an impersonal way. A participant observer, on the other hand, is not just a detached onlooker: he is involved; he endeavors to fathom the personal meaning of what he sees. Both of these methods of observation are important in the study of children.

As spectators we measure the IQ's of a group of children and record these as objective facts. As participants we are interested in the child's intelligence rating as compared with that of others and also in the bearing a child's IQ might have within the realm of his own experience—his success or failure and the view he has of himself. When we do this, we have to draw upon the meaning of the experience of success and failure in our own lives.

According to this view, we can better appreciate a child's laughter or his tears if, while observing him, we can also listen to the echo of our own laughter and taste the salt of our own tears. Similarly, to appreciate a child's fears—the meaning these have for him—it is necessary to face the personal meaning of our own fears. When we do this we are, as participant observers, to a degree sharing his fear. Instead of viewing it dispassionately we respond to it compassionately, seeking to encompass the child's emotion through a fellowship of feeling.

However, even as participant observers we have to remain detached to some degree: When we try to understand a child's fears in the light of our own this does not mean that at the moment we must become as frightened as he. If we became that scared we would be so absorbed in our own fears that we would lose sight of the child's.

HAZARDS CONFRONTING THE PARTICIPANT OBSERVER

Whenever we try to assess what a child's experience might mean to him we face the hazard that our observations may be distorted and confused by the bias of our own ideas and attitudes. For example, as an observer I am being misled by my own feelings if, when annoyed, I take it for granted that a child who grins is being sarcastic.

The participant observer's perceptions may, indeed, be quite false. In view of this we face the question: Is it not better to avoid this kind of observation? Would it not be safer to cling to the role of being a spectator?

One answer is that if we use the participant approach it is necessary to use safeguards, such as will be described below. Another answer is that the choice as to whether we will view the child as an object or try to see him as one with whom we share a common humanity depends on the kind of information we seek and the role we desire to play. The practical demands of life help to decide. A person cannot be equally involved as a participant observer of all children. He may with some be deeply involved, with others very little. Even in his dealings with his own pupils or with his sons and daughters, a person's role may from time to time range all the way from that of a passive spectator to that of a deeply involved participant.

SAFEGUARDS IN OBSERVATION OF CHILDREN

One means of discovering and guarding against the effects of our own bias when we observe children is to compare our perception with that of others. In formal research studies this is a standard procedure. In the informal observations of day-to-day life it often is not possible to use this procedure, but many opportunities for applying it do occur. When, for example, a father and a mother or a parent and a visitor, or two or more teachers compare their separate versions of a child's behavior each has an opportunity to take a look at himself.

Another safeguard lies in an effort to understand one's self. To understand another, a person must be in a mood to grow in self-understanding—to face his own feelings, and to deal with emotional currents that begin to flow in his own life as soon as he enters into a relationship with others.

According to the position taken in this book, two basic principles are involved in the study of human psychology. First, a person's knowledge about himself determines to an important degree what he can perceive *in* others and what he will be able to learn *about* them. Secondly, knowledge gained *from* others can contribute to an important degree to a person's understanding of himself. The process of gaining understanding of others and the process of self-discovery are interdependent. The interplay between self-understanding and understanding of others can be noted, for example, when we study a child's anger. In order to appreciate the significance of a child's anger from his point of view we have to draw upon what we can learn from our own experience of anger. But the reactions produced in us by the child's anger may also, at the moment, or on second thought, give us a deeper understanding of our own anger.

More will be said about the interplay between self-understanding and understanding of others in later chapters.

As stated earlier in this chapter, to understand children and to understand ourselves, it is essential that we try, as far as possible, to understand the child who still resides within us. It is important to take stock of the child we remember and also of the child whom we can't remember. A person old enough to write or to read a book, such as this, cannot recall occasions in his early life when he trustingly counted on the good will of others, or when (if such is what happened) he cried himself to sleep again and again, or would have cried had he not learned to be silent to avoid a greater hurt. Yet such happenings and many other happenings may have a bearing on the way he now feels about himself and others. An attitude of willingness to explore and to accept the implications of our own childhood experiences makes a great difference in what we can learn from studying a child. A person cannot attain maturity unless he is willing to try to accept and incorporate into his present existence all that he is and has been—which means all that belongs to his past that might now be operating in the present. Unless one as an older person can, in a sense, be a child, and seek to comprehend what it is to be a child, or what it might mean to have been a child, one cannot be comfortable in one's understanding of children nor can one comfortably accept oneself.[1]

The concept that a healthy and emotionally mature person can accept and integrate his past with his present without blinding himself or harshly blaming himself or others is implicit in most full-scale theories of the psychology of the personality, and in psychoanalytic theory. It is expressed in the ancient admonition, "Know thyself."

Recommended Readings

Wayne Dennis's "Historical Beginnings of Child Psychology" (1949) gives a succinct, informative account of pioneer studies in developmental psychology. Most of the chapters in the *Manual of Child Psychology*, a compendious volume edited by Leonard Carmichael (1954), include historical sketches of research dealing with various facets of a child's development.

John E. Anderson's "Methods of Child Psychology" (1954) describes the research procedures that have most commonly been used in the

---

[1] This position is in keeping with the Scriptural saying that unless one becomes as a little child he cannot enter the kingdom of heaven (Matthew 18:3).

study of children and offers a thoughtful discussion of safeguards that are necessary in designing an investigation and in interpreting the results.

Millie Almy's *Ways of Studying Children* (1959) contains excellent descriptions of methods teachers and others in charge of groups of children can use to increase their understanding of children and, in the process, gain deeper understanding of themselves. The writer's book, *When Teachers Face Themselves* (1955), discusses the interplay between self-understanding and understanding of others. The annual volume of *The Psychoanalytic Study of the Child*, edited by Ruth S. Eissler, Anna Freud, Heinz Hartmann, Marianne Kris, and others (1958) presents a variety of studies based on a psychoanalytic approach to developmental psychology. Summaries of research and references to new developments in the psychology of childhood and adolescence appear regularly in chapters on "Developmental Psychology" in the *Annual Review of Psychology*, edited by Paul R. Farnsworth. The most recent of these excellent reviews was written by George R. Thompson (1959). Many outstanding studies in child psychology are reproduced, in whole or in part, in books of readings by Wayne Dennis, *Readings in Child Psychology* (1951); by William E. Martin and Celia Burns Stendler, *Readings in Child Development* (1954), and by Jerome M. Seidman, *The Child: A Book of Readings* (1958).

Principles
of Development

CHAPTER TWO   When we study children it is instructive to look at facts regarding particular phases
of growth and also to consider principles that
help us to see the process of development in a
larger perspective. It is helpful also to view the
child in the light of a conception of humanity and
a philosophy of growth. In the preceding chapter,
two principles, which the writer regards as basic
to the study of children, were discussed. One
stressed the need to look at both the objective and
the subjective dimensions of a child's life. The
other dealt with the interplay between understanding of others and self-understanding. This
chapter sets forth a number of principles regarding the process of development; some of these are
well established, but others are more theoretical.

Life as a form of striving

What is the mainspring in human conduct and what is the dynamic force underlying the activities and experiences that constitute the child's way of life? There are two main views. According to one, a child's actions consist primarily of efforts to overcome conditions that block his desires and needs. He acts to overcome frustrations, problems, irritants, or other conditions that upset his equilibrium. Irritants may be such things as hunger and other unsatisfied "primary needs"; or obstruction in the physical environment; or friction that arises between the child and others. The main motive in life is to relieve, to be rid of, and then to get back to a state of equilibrium.

According to a different view, living involves a positive striving. The organism is endowed with an impulse to mobilize its resources and put them to use. According to this position the child is not just trying to maintain a state of equilibrium—he invites a state of disequilibrium—he seeks to put potential abilities to use, to enter into experiences that employ his capacities for doing, thinking and feeling, and for sharing with others. The position taken in this book is that there is a positive, forward impetus in growth which does not consist solely in an effort to achieve riddance, relief, and escape. The healthy child, like the healthy youth and oldster, is constantly involved in a process of self-realization. This does not mean, however, that he is free from frustrations. The main point is that the growing child has an impulse to reach beyond the here and now, to discover, to explore, to venture into the untried.

SPONTANEOUS USE AS A FEATURE OF GROWING ABILITY

As a child's capacities for doing, thinking, and feeling mature, he has an impulse to put them to use. For example, when the mechanics involved in creeping have been established, a child will creep of his own accord even without an external lure such as a toy, or an annoyance from which he wishes to creep away. When his legs become capable of supporting him, he repeatedly tries to stand, despite unpleasant falls. When he has matured to the point where he is able to begin to use language, he coos, babbles, and prattles; in time, he will practice words and phrases over and over again. As he becomes able to imagine, he plunges into make-believe. As his intellectual abilities develop, he exhibits a lively curiosity; he comes forth with a barrage of questions; he experiments, he seeks to know. From early infancy onward, the child reaches for the possibilities that lie ahead. He is an active agent in furthering his own development.

These examples illustrate one principle of development, *indigenous motivation*: An integral feature of the development of a capacity or power

is a tendency to use that capacity or power. The machinery of development is equipped with a self-starter.

STRUGGLE AS A FEATURE OF HUMAN DEVELOPMENT

Many predicaments are linked to the process of development. When a
child ventures into life he faces gratifying possibilities but he also faces
conflicting impulses and demands. Some of these are thrust upon him.
Some of them arise as an outcome of his own striving toward maturity.

In his relations with his parents, it is comforting for a child to be dependent, but he also has a powerful urge to become independent. As a
dutiful child he would like to obey his parents but he also has an impulse
to assert himself, even to the point of being rebellious. He feels affection
for his parents, but they also arouse his anger. Moreover, under the best
circumstances he is likely to make demands which they either cannot or
will not fulfill. And he has desires which his parents, representing the
larger society in which he lives, forbid.

As a member of a peer group it is necessary for a child to conform to
the ways of his fellows, yet it is also essential for him to preserve his
individuality. In his relationships with his peers the enterprising child
makes many ventures and runs risks. When he seeks acceptance he runs
the risk of being rejected. When he reaches out to others he faces the
possibility of tasting the sweetness of a close companionship and also the
bitterness of loneliness and loss. When the child applies his abilities in
meeting demands and opportunities of everyday life he faces the prospect
of joy in successful achievement but also the possibility of not succeeding.
The typical school situation, for example, is so arranged that large numbers of children will have a taste of failure.

In connection with the affairs of his inner life the child faces many
possibilities that have to be reconciled with the pressures of reality.
Through his imagination he can take off into realms of glory but he must
also keep his feet on the ground. He has a noble inborn capacity for anger,
but he has to learn to subdue it. He has an inborn capacity for joy, curiosity, and fear, but in the process of being socialized he must learn to
subdue his spontaneous feelings. In doing so he builds up walls which
separate him from others—this in spite of the fact that one of the most
common fears in early childhood is the fear of separation.

A growing person cannot reach his full development without encountering difficulties, and somewhere along the road to maturity he is bound
to be hurt. There are even some possibilities in his nature he cannot tap
unless he has suffered. One of the greatest achievements of the mature
person is a capacity for compassion, and probably no one can realize
compassion unless he himself has suffered.

But we must distinguish between suffering that produces growth and suffering that hinders growth. The healthy person is not one who is never tense or worried or hurt. It is not the absence of adversity that marks the healthy life. Rather, it is the ability to venture forth even though the going may be painful, and the ability to draw something constructive from the venture.

SOCIAL ORIGINS OF THE INDIVIDUAL

A philosophy of growth must take account of both the individual and the society in which he lives. It is in a social setting that the child finds elements that are essential for his own self-fulfillment. A child standing all alone, completely divorced from society and from the developments that come through fellowship with others, would not be a child (except in the sense of being one who is yet young). He would not be a human being in our usual sense of that term. Humanity is not an individual possession, but rather something held in common with others. A child finds himself through his relationships with his fellows, but he loses himself and his dignity as a human being if, in the name of social adjustment, he simply becomes a conformer, an "organization man."

THE HEALTHY INDIVIDUAL AND THE HEALTHY SOCIETY

The child's development may take a healthy or an unhealthy turn and the society in which he lives may also be healthy or unhealthy. A state of health prevails when the influence in society combined with the impetus of a child's own growth help him to realize his potentialities. An unhealthy condition prevails when a child's development is distorted by forces in a society which imposes stifling stereotypes. "Social adjustment" is not synonymous with healthy development. For example, in a given community, adjusting to a society may mean that a child must suppress his capacity for being friendly by yielding to the prejudices that prevail or by bending all his energies toward being competitive. This form of adjustment reflects an unhealthy state both in him and in the society to which he belongs.

Heredity and environment

Everything in a child's development is a product of an interplay between his heredity and his environment. Often, in discussing these two factors, people have a tendency to take sides, as they do in a political debate, sometimes even using the phrasing, heredity *vs.* environment. Obviously, it is important to recognize both of these factors and the *interaction* between the two.

In the literature on child psychology there usually is a heavy emphasis on the influence of the environment, and this emphasis also appears in the present book. When we study children it is with the hope that the knowledge we gain will help us to be more thoughtful and wise in our dealings with them. Whenever we try to apply our knowledge of children to promote their welfare we are using an environmental approach. As parents, child psychologists, teachers, nurses, social workers, and others who have children in our care we are, in a sense, environmentalists by profession.

It is important, however, in the process of providing for a child's nurture, that we also give heed to his original nature. Each child's development is determined to an important degree by the seed from which he sprang. This is no more than a simple truism, yet it needs to be stressed. To be alert to a child's welfare it is essential as far as possible to assess his inherent potentialities and limitations. It is essential also to be on guard against demands or hopes which require more of him or of ourselves than ever can be fulfilled. The most prudent approach to a child is to combine a concern about his environment with a deep respect for his heredity.

This view of the child is important not only when we consider his situation but also when we assess the role of his parents, and especially when we try to understand what has happened when things go wrong. In recent decades there has been a rash of writings which blame the world's ills on parents. Mothers, especially, have received a beating from people who take an extreme environmentalist position. They have been told that if their infant is anxious, it is they who made him so; if he has colic, it is their fault; if, as an older child, he has trouble in learning to read or in meeting any of the stresses of life it is because they have failed.

The view that the child's development is shaped by all-powerful parents appears in the pronouncement that there are no "problem children," rather, all human difficulties are due to "problem parents." Such a view has value if it calls attention to conditions in the environment which a child's elders are able to correct. However, a pronouncement such as this probably does more harm than good, for it does not express a scientific principle but a form of moral condemnation. It is true, of course, that parents are powerful figures in the child's environment, but they do not hold the "whole wide world in their hands." The child's inborn qualities make a difference in what parents can and cannot do. From the time of birth, a child's nature influences the way in which he responds to the nurture he receives.

Evidence relating to the operation of heredity and environment will be considered in later sections of this book, so at this point only a few general statements will be made.

The influence of heredity can be seen most clearly in children's physical characteristics—their appearance, stature, eye-color, and body-build.

In the *psychological* sphere some of the most impressive findings concerning the effects of the environment have come from studies of children reared under adverse conditions in institutions that provide only a bare minimum of physical care. The development of such children is often impaired. Evidence concerning the effects of the environment also appears in studies of foster children. In one of the most carefully conducted long-term investigations in this area, foster-children were studied before the age of two and then re-examined from time to time until they had reached an average of thirteen and a half years (Skodak and Skeels, 1949).[1] The development of many of these foster-children was more favorable than would be predicted from the facts regarding the background of their biological parents. However, the influence of heredity also stood out prominently. There was practically a zero correlation between the intelligence ratings of the foster-children and the educational status of their foster-parents, and there was a comparatively high correlation between the children's intelligence in early adolescence and the intelligence of their "true" mothers from whom they had been separated as infants. (The correlation was .38 on the basis of one test and .44 on the basis of another, as compared with a correlation of .50 that usually is found when comparisons are made between parents and their own children, sharing the same environment.)

Some of the most impressive findings concerning the role of heredity have come from studies of identical twins (who presumably come from the same fertilized egg and therefore share the same heredity). Such twins often resemble one another to a remarkable degree in many of their characteristics, whether they have been reared apart or in the same home environment. In a large-scale investigation of mental illness diagnosed as schizophrenia it was found that if one member of an identical-twin pair suffered from the illness the chances were about 86 in 100 that the other member of the twin pair would also have the illness; if one of a pair of non-identical (two-egg or fraternal) twins had the illness, the chances were about 14 in 100 that the other would suffer from it, too (Kallman, 1953).

When identical twins resemble each other to a high degree in the fortunes and misfortunes of their development the similarity is not necessarily due to heredity alone. The very fact that they are twins means that their environment, both before and after birth differs from the environment of children who are born singly. Moreover, even though there usually are marked similarities between identical twins there are some one-egg twins who are very dissimilar.

At any rate, findings from many lines of investigation (including

---

[1] This reference and others mentioned in the text are listed in the bibliography at the end of the book.

studies of the effects of environmental stresses and of inbreeding in animals) underscore the position that in trying to understand development it is essential to take account of both heredity and environment, and the interaction between these forces. To consider both is not only wiser but also more humane than to place all responsibility for human welfare or distress on one or the other of these factors. It is desirable, as Kallman puts it, to refrain from "gross exaggeration regarding the presumed utopian powers of one or the other of two artifically separated formative forces in man. . . ." The more we can learn about the role of one of these factors the more necessary it is to consider the other. If, for example, it is evident that a child has inherited high potentialities it is also evident that he needs an environment that will help him to realize his potentialities. If his inborn resources are below average it is important to help him to use these resources to best advantage rather than to place demands on him that can only result in failure and self-reproach. If he has inherited weaknesses it is necessary, as far as possible, to be alert to signs of these weaknesses, to protect him and to enlighten his parents, and to look for ways of correcting or surmounting these weaknesses.

Early signs of individuality

Almost from the moment of birth infants show distinct individual characteristics. Some are decidedly more mobile, active, robust, hungry, and on the go than others. One baby is inclined to be irritable, or restless, or "fussy," while another is more placid and serene. The individual characteristics of infants tend to a strong degree to persist as they mature, although there are changes in the way in which these characteristics are expressed. For example, a child who is vigorous in asserting his demands for attention may do so by crying when he is an infant, through his speech when he has learned to talk, and through more subtle forms of self-assertion as he grows older.

Development as a product of learning and growth

In a child's development two processes are operating: growth and learning. These factors are interdependent; they cannot be isolated in pure form, yet they can be separated for purposes of discussion. In everyday speech we make this distinction when we note that a child has *grown* two inches in height since we saw him last and that he has *learned* to recite "Jack and Jill." When we say a child has grown in a physical and physiological sense we refer to changes that normally occur in a healthy child with the passage of time. As a result of growth, there is an increase in height, weight, length of bones, and changes in bone structure and in the structure of parts of the nervous system. "Learning" represents a modification of behavior that has come about by virtue of experience, use, or exercise.

"Maturation," an important term in the discussion of development, denotes the process of ripening, of moving toward a fuller unfolding of the potentials of the organism. Growth and maturation have a meaning in common. However, "maturation" denotes not solely a change in the physical equipment of the organism but also a change in *function, in capacity to perform* through the use of this equipment.

Although growth, learning, and maturation are interwoven it is useful, for practical reasons in connection with the rearing and education of children, to make a distinction between changes affected by learning and those occurring as a consequence of growth and maturation. The child's education begins at birth, if not before. Much of this education is not planned; but from the very beginning many experiences are definitely designed to promote his development. The huge budget involved in the formal schooling of children represents only a small fraction of the total outlay of time and means devoted to training children from early infancy. To make this investment yield the best returns, to prevent the discouraging effects of failure, and to make the best use of the stimulus of accomplishment, it is important to try to adapt the child's training to his growing abilities.

GROWTH FACTORS IN ESTABLISHMENT OF BASIC COORDINATIONS

During the first two years of life the growth factor plays a predominant role in the development of the basic coordinations involved in locomotion (such as creeping, standing, and walking) and in prehension (such as reaching, grasping, and apposition of thumb and fingers in handling an object). This does not mean that these accomplishments simply thrust themselves upon a passive organism, for the healthy child spends much of his waking time in exercising his powers. Yet the impetus for these early developments springs largely from within; there is not much that an ambitious adult can do to hasten them.

By recording the movements and manipulations of infants with a motion-picture camera, Ames (1940) noted that new and often complex behavior patterns can appear for the first time in a form so complete that several weeks—often several months—of exercise do not appreciably change either their form or speed.

In one study (Dennis, 1938), two infant girls were kept in a restricted environment until they were seven months old. They spent their time in separate individual enclosures; they received no toys; no one played with them; and the only attention they received occurred in connection with caring for their routine needs. Yet, in many aspects of their behavior, the progress of these children did not differ substantially from the progress made by children who receive much more attention from adults. (The retarding effects of deprivation would probably become increasingly apparent if the experiment had been continued well beyond the age of seven months.) As far as they go, the findings indicate that the small infant is not a creature whose development stands still unless he is prompted and encouraged to try out his powers. The impulse to grow is strong, and if a young child has freedom to exercise his growing talents in his own way he will do so.

In another study (Dennis and Dennis, 1940), it was found that the infants of Hopi Indians, who were bound to cradle boards—rigid structures on which they spent many of their waking hours—during much of their first year of life, did not differ substantially in their early motor development from infants whose mothers did not use cradle boards.

The findings in the Dennis studies indicate that many of the developments normally shown by infants will appear even though the infants have less stimulation and less freedom of action than infants usually enjoy. These findings do not mean, however, that a child will develop in a normal way if his freedom to exercise his growing powers is seriously curtailed. A later study by Dennis (1959) of institutionalized children bears on this point. Infants in a crowded institution who spent most of their time on their backs in small cribs were distinctly retarded in the development of their ability to sit alone, creep, stand, and walk. Dennis points out that when a child is placed in a prone (face down) position or is free to work himself into this position he has an opportunity to "raise his head from the surface, push with his arms, raise his chest, pull his arms and legs beneath his body—in other words, he can practice acts employed in creeping." Dennis observed that few of the institutionalized babies who were placed on their backs in small cribs on soft bedding were able, under their own power, to change from a supine to a prone position. His observations show that a baby cannot become a creeper simply by lying supinely on his back.

EFFECTS OF TRAINING IN RELATION TO MATURITY

It is not possible to get a child to skip a grade in his development by giving him additional or unusual opportunities. In many studies it has been found that the gain a child gets from opportunities to practice, use, or exercise a particular skill is determined by his level of maturity. In a number of motor performances, a relatively short period of practice when a child is somewhat older will yield as much competence as a longer period of practice begun when the child is younger. Studies of the effect of practice have covered such activities as playing with blocks, stair-climbing, buttoning, and cutting with scissors.[2] The fact that added maturity may increase the individual's capacity to profit from practice has been noted also in studies of certain intellectual operations, including early language development (Strayer, 1930), memorization of numbers (Gates, 1928), and understanding the concept of historical time (Pistor, 1940).

Benezet (1935) found that children whose formal training in arithmetic was postponed to the sixth grade rapidly gained as much competence as children who had struggled with formal arithmetic in earlier grades. The growth factor is important in determining readiness to learn other school subjects; this has been emphasized in studies by Olson (1943, 1959) and Olson and Hughes (1943, 1944). A study by Millard (1940) indicates that children differ considerably in the course they follow in learning to read. Some children are "fast starters" in school subjects, while others— who eventually may be able to catch up—are "slow starters."

Studies such as these strongly suggest that many children would find education far less frustrating and far more fruitful if schools scaled requirements to the pace of growth. In dealing with intellectual development, as in dealing with many other aspects of development (notably in the emotional sphere), most school people have been backward and bound by academic traditions.

When the growth pattern of particular children is not in gear with the standard school program, these children face difficulties not at the school alone but in other situations. The child who is a "late starter" in reading, for example, is likely to feel that there is something wrong with him at school; if he goes to Sunday school and is asked to read, he also feels ill at ease there; if he goes to a birthday party where there are place cards with reading matter, he also feels at a loss there. He may develop a dislike for school (where he is failing), and for the church (where he again is reminded of his shortcomings), and even for social affairs (where he may not only fail but be teased, besides). However, it is probably at school that such a child has his most bitter and damaging experience of being an unworthy person.

NATURE AND QUALITY
OF LEARNING AS RELATED TO MATURITY LEVEL

The child's level of maturity, in addition to affecting his ability to profit from practice at a particular time, will also affect the nature or quality of what he learns. A child who is still in the creeping stage can

---

[2] See studies by Gesell and Thompson (1929), Gates and Taylor (1926), and Hilgard (1932, 1933).

learn to climb, but he will climb like a creeper (McGraw, 1935); that is, he will push himself upward and forward by gripping with his toes. The practice he receives from pushing with his toes may not be of much benefit to him when, at a later stage of growth, he depends more on his arms than on his toes in climbing.

Some skills learned at one level of maturity may need to be relearned or readapted to the child's growth pattern at a later stage of maturity. This does not hold true for all skills, however. A study by McGraw (1939) illustrates this point: A pair of twins had experience with roller skating, tricycling, and other activities before the age of two years and a further study was made of the children at the age of six years, about four years after the main experiment ended. Both twins maintained their proficiency in riding a tricycle. As neither had a tricycle at home, it appears that this type of skill does not have to be relearned as the body matures. Roller-skating showed a different picture. Partly because of changes in bodily proportions as they grew older (including relatively longer legs and a shift in the center of gravity), the twins—who had learned to roller-skate when they were about two years old—had difficulty in maintaining their balance on skates at the age of six.

VARYING TIMELINESS IN RELATION TO MATURITY

A youngster at a certain level may be unready for learning one form of activity and ripe for learning another activity. In McGraw's study (1935) it was found, for example, that a child was able to make phenomenal progress in learning to roller-skate, beginning when he was little more than one year old; but it was not until many months later that he was able to make progress in learning to propel a tricycle. Two studies (Jersild, 1932, and Updegraff, Heiliger, and Learned, 1937) have shown that children of preschool age are able to make spectacular gains in singing of musical tones, intervals, and phrases, while, at the same age level, children have been found to make little or no gain in keeping exact time to music while walking or in beating time with their hands (Christiansen, 1938, and Jersild and Bienstock, 1935).

Unfortunately, studies dealing with the maturity level at which it would be most timely and strategic for a child to learn the countless things that he eventually must learn at home or at school are too limited to provide an outline of how all the details of an educational program might best be scaled to a normal child's maturing capacities. However, such data as are available indicate that if the entire educational program were examined from the maturity-level point of view, there would be important changes in what we expect of a child at home and in school, and very great improvements in the range of accomplishments that children could learn to master and enjoy.

Critical periods in the process
of development

The concept of the "critical phase" has a great deal in common with the adage: Strike while the iron is hot. A phase of growth may be "critical" because what happens during this phase may have a marked effect on the later course of development. It appears that certain types of behavior may especially be influenced by what happens at a particular time in the sequence of development and that there are times when the organism is especially vulnerable to harm.

Much of the research dealing with the critical phase has been done in experiments with animals. Studies by Hunt (1941, 1947) indicate that laboratory rats who early in life went through periods of being deprived of food were more likely as adults—during periods when they alternately had little or ample food—to become hoarders than rats who had not been deprived as infants.

Studies of animals show that the social experiences they have at a particular juncture of their lives may leave a lasting imprint on their behavior. According to Scott (1957), in every species of animal there is a short period in life, usually fairly early, during which primary social bonds are formed. After this period it becomes difficult to change these bonds or to form new ones. Lambs, ducklings, and goslings that have been reared with people and that lack contact with sheep, ducks, or geese may continue as they grow older to seek the company of human beings, rather than their own kind.

Puppies reared with cats may never learn to enjoy the sport of chasing cats. Kittens reared with mice may never become mousers. A chimpanzee reared with human beings may hesitate, later, to mix with other chimps. A Mallard duck reared with tame ducks may grow up tame, unlike his wild brothers and sisters.

In relationships with creatures of their own kind, the things animals learn when young may also have important outcomes. As described by Scott, two puppies in the same litter may be on an equal footing, but if one pup happens to win a fight, he may get an edge, becoming the agressive one or attacker, while the other becomes the submissive one who (with this pup, at least) runs away. According to a study by Kahn (1951, 1954), when young mice are attacked and defeated by a mouse that previously has been trained to fight, the younger the mouse is at the time of the first defeat the more likely he is to be a withdrawing non-fighter as an adult.

A German shepherd puppy, brought into a home where there is a canny adult terrier, may allow the little dog to be the boss even after he has grown to be several times larger and more powerful. In a litter of pigs, one pig which has a slight edge in aggressiveness (or good luck) may get hold of a good teat several times while another does not. The first little pig will thrive and grow strong while the other becomes a runt.

Quite apart from the question, "Is there a critical period beyond which a new mode of conduct is difficult or impossible to establish?," is the more general principle that behavior that is *once* learned is likely to persist over a period of time unless there are strong forces within the organism that induce a change (such as those which impel a child who eagerly learned to creep to be just as eager, when more mature, to learn to walk). As Beach and Jaynes point out, there are several reasons why habits acquired early in life will be especially persistent. A response, once acquired, may block other possible responses. Moreover, the happenings befalling a younger animal perhaps have a more absorbing and intense effect than similar happenings at a later time: hunger may be more intense, the effect of fear more traumatic, the effect of losing a fight more overwhelming. In a review of studies of animals, Beach and Jaynes (1954) state that additional carefully controlled investigations are needed in order to explore fully the effects of early experiences on later behavior and to determine what accounts for these effects.

Evidence of the "critical phase" can also be seen in the development of children, although usually not so clearly or in so simple a form. Several writers have reported, for example, that a baby who is not properly mothered during the second half-year of life may receive a setback that is hard to remedy. Also, a difference in social relationships that at first is rather small may have large consequences. In a pair of identical twins, for example, the one who is a bit lustier and hungrier may become the dominant twin.

In daily life we can observe examples of what might be regarded as a critical period. A person who does not learn the accents of a language before the age of eight or ten, for example, may have great difficulty in mastering these accents at a later time. We can also observe evidences of what might be called a "snowballing effect." A child who is slow in learning to read, and who is pressured or ridiculed, may become discouraged about school and about himself, and what began as a moderately slight handicap may become a very serious one. A youngster who early in life becomes suspicious and distrustful of others because of neglect or abuse may develop attitudes which make it hard for him, as time goes on, to develop friendly relations with friendly people. An adolescent boy who is an "early maturer" at a time when size and athletic ability have a strong influence on a boy's popularity may continue, even after others have caught up with him in their physical development, to harvest the benefits of greater self-confidence and poise (Jones, 1949).

The "critical phase" of development is probably most *critical* in connection with the growing child's view of himself, his attitudes toward himself, his ability to feel confident concerning his own worth. Here, as in other aspects of development: Large oaks from little acorns grow. However, although the concept of the critical phase is a very important one for understanding the way in which a child's present condition may have been favored or blighted by conditions in the past, children—unless severely damaged—have a potentiality for undoing or reshaping the effects of fortunes or adversities of their earlier experiences.

Other principles of development

"WHOLEHEARTEDNESS AND GRADATION" [3]

The child's tendency to put his growing power to use frequently means that he will be intensely absorbed for a time by any new mode of behavior or phase of development. When on the brink of a new accomplishment the child may seem to exaggerate or overdo. He may be so engrossed that other things are neglected. When the child, for example, first knows the thrill of walking, he may demand to be fed on his feet or he may find it almost impossible to sit down long enough to finish a meal. When he first discovers that he can ask questions and receive answers he often goes on a binge of asking questions.

Examples of this tendency may be seen in other aspects of a child's development. Now in this experience, now in that, a child frequently goes "all out" in his enthusiasm. Then, as time passes, what was new and absorbing tends to lose its separate fascination, and becomes a feature of the larger context of behavior.

The child's wholeheartedness in new ventures sometimes becomes trying to an adult, especially if the adult has forgotten the thrill he himself derived as a child from venturing into new experiences.

ANTICIPATION

Development is not simply geared to the needs of the time but also to the needs of the future. The corneal reflex, for example, is present at about seven months, long before a child normally will be called upon to blink.

The principle of anticipation illustrates the margin of safety with which the organism is endowed. Normally a child is not called upon to endure the rigors of independent life before about 40 weeks, but he may be able to survive if thrust from the womb as early as 26 weeks. This is one of

---

[3] The wording is from H. L. Hollingworth (1927).

many safety factors in development that equip the child almost from the time of conception with a large degree of resiliency.

CAPACITY FOR SELF-REPAIR

Another factor that adds greatly to the growing child's ability to face physical misfortune is his great capacity for self-repair. Tissues may be wounded and yet show a remarkable capacity for healing. With help, broken bones are able to mend. A child may go through a normal growth pattern even though his nutrition is not the best.

Is there a similar capacity for repair in the psychological sphere? This question as to psychological hardihood—how much a human being can take—is of supreme importance. Assumptions and conclusions bearing on this question underlie a vast amount of what has been said or written about the origin of behavior disorders, emotional disturbances, and mental illness. There is a lot of theory on this subject but not very much good research. In the psychological sphere as in the physical sphere there probably is a breaking point, a point beyond which damage cannot be repaired, but this breaking point is hard to define.

In the physical area the margin of tolerance before irreparable injury occurs is fairly well established. If the blood supply is cut off from a hand or finger beyond a certain period of time the tissue will not revive. On the other hand, in the psychological area it seems possible to withhold "intellectual" nourishment or "emotional" nourishment for a more variable period of time before irreparable harm is done. The capacity for psychological self-repair appears to be very great. The literature dealing with the care and treatment of disturbed human beings abounds in illustrations of this.

Children can suffer deep emotional wounds and yet respond to healing. The child who, under adverse circumstances, has become suspicious, can with help acquire a degree of trust. The child who has been burdened with fear can learn to shake off some of his burden. The child who was sorely rejected may still be able to learn to love. An injury that has been treated may, of course, leave a scar behind, but a scar is obviously much better than an open wound.

The idea that each growing person possesses a large capacity for healing and repair does not condone a policy of neglecting children or abusing them. It does, however, underscore a note of optimism and hope which, this writer believes, is an essential feature of a philosophy of growth and is amply justified by what we know of the process of development. Such a note of hope is not just a comforting sentiment; it has practical value for everyone who is responsible for the rearing of children and everyone, whatever his age may be, who still is building the structure of his own life.

DEVELOPMENTAL REVISION OF HABITS

At every level of maturity children show behavior which they will change or abandon in their own good time. At a given level of his development a child may use certain behavior over and over again, but this does not necessarily mean it will remain fixed. Behavior that is suited to one level of maturity and frequently repeated does not necessarily establish a habit that will carry over to a later level. Exercise of the grasp reflex, over and over again, does not fix the reflex forever; reflex grasping gives way to voluntary use of the hand. The young infant sucks; later he bites and chews. The child creeps, but later abandons creeping for walking.

Similarly, in his early language development the child has difficulty in articulating or pronouncing many words, but "muvver," even though repeated again and again, becomes "mother," and "dat" becomes "that."

As a child's abilities mature and as he becomes capable of new and different interests, he will not only revise, but completely reverse, many of his earlier forms of behavior. The youngster who awoke at an ungodly hour in the morning at three years may be hard to rout out of bed at ten. The child who was unkempt at ten years may become, if anything, too much of a dandy at eighteen years.

This phenomenon, which we call *the developmental revision of habits*, has an important practical implication in the rearing of children. Parents would be spared much worry and children much bother if it were generally realized that many forms of behavior will be abandoned by the child himself in his own good time. While this is true, it is also true that we do not precisely know all the forms of behavior that fall in this category or just when it might help to push the process of revision.

PERSISTENCE OF ARCHAIC BEHAVIOR TRENDS

It sometimes happens that the youngster, instead of revising his behavior, retains an older habit even though a newer way would be more appropriate. When this occurs we have the phenomenon of persistence of archaic behavior tendencies. These may range from mildly burdensome habits to complex behavior patterns that disturb the child's entire personality. A child at the age of six or eight, for example, may show many forms of dependence on others that were quite appropriate at the age of three or four. By virtue of overprotection or some other misfortune, he may retain not only a habit but also an attitude of dependency, and he may shrink even from an effort to strike out for himself. Again, a child who lives for a time in an environment in which he is mistreated may continue, even when his lot improves, to react to others with a certain amount of defensiveness and suspicion. In dealing with siblings or peers, he may acquire very strong competitive tendencies which he will carry into situations that do not call for competitive behavior.

When behavior thus persists beyond its proper season, it usually means trouble. The child who shows immature dependency on others may build up an elaborate system of wiles, ruses, and rationalizations to support his dependency. In an older person immature behavior may be rationalized to such an extent that the individual refuses or is unable to see his weakness.

At the adult level, curious or queer and irrational conduct often illustrates the principle that a childish form of behavior may persist beyond its appropriate time.

GROWTH AS A PROCESS OF BECOMING

Human development has its roots in an organism that is always in the process of coming into being. The organism as a living system is "open" (as Dale Harris, 1956, has expressed it); it is never completely static. Development emerges from what has been transmitted through heredity and through the influence of the environment, but a child is never completely a creature of what has gone before: The changes that occur in him also produce changes in his environment.

When he is able to walk, he moves in a world that is different from the world in which he previously lived. When he is able to talk, to ask, argue, protest, and persuade, he can give a new structure to the ideas others had about him. When he is able to imagine, he can build a world that combines elements of the old with images of a future that is yet to be. When he is able in his thinking to deal with abstractions, he is able to move from the sod into the realm of symbols. He can detach himself from things as they are in his physical environment; he can take a backward look at what has gone before, form new ideas, lay plans for the future. By way of thoughts, he can encompass time, space, and countless things; he can weigh alternatives, without having to pursue them in the flesh. He is able to select, to choose, and, having chosen, to retain the thought that he might have chosen something else.

Through this ability to make choices and to sit in judgment upon the choices he has made he exercises what, as seen from his point of view, is a kind of *freedom:* the freedom to say yes or no, to go or come, to follow one path instead of another. In exercising this freedom a person becomes, at least in part, in his own view, the author of what he is and what he will become.

If a person is forthright he will of course recognize that this freedom, no matter how real it seems, is fettered in many ways by his heredity, and by the past and present circumstances of his life.

The idea of freedom may be frightening—one writer has referred to it as "dreadful freedom." A person may try to escape from it by deliberately placing himself under the dominion of others. He may try to explain it away—and in doing so he joins company with a host of scientists and philosophers who have a deterministic view of things.

We may ask: "Is there really a margin of free choice or is the idea of freedom an illusion?" To go into the *pros* and *cons* of this question would require a different book than the one here intended. We can say, however, that the *experience* of being free, at least to some extent, to choose is one that all children seem to have. The ability to make decisions, or at least the conviction that one can make some decisions, seems to be an inevitable one; this, from the point of view of the individual himself, is a concrete reality no matter what scientists or philosophers might say about it from an abstract point of view. A person's conviction that he can make decisions carries with it a train of responsibility, pride, and shame, and a tendency to praise and blame.

Recommended Readings

The Concept of Development, edited by Dale Harris (1957), discusses theories and concepts underlying an approach to the study of development. Franz J. Kallman's *Heredity in Health and Mental Disorder* (1953) gives an account of the mechanics of heredity and reports evidence concerning the role played by heredity in determining some of the fortunes and misfortunes that befall human beings. In the final section of his book Kallman gives a thoughtful and humane discussion of the implications of human genetics for educators and social scientists. The second edition of Willard C. Olson's *Child Development* (1959) contains very informative sections on principles of development.

During recent years, increasing numbers of the author's students have chosen to supplement their readings in developmental psychology with books that inquire into the nature of human striving and the possibilities and predicaments that confront all human beings—parents, older children, and adolescents. Books that many of these students have found especially thought-provoking are Paul Tillich's *The Courage to Be* (1952), Erich Fromm's *Man for Himself* (1947), and Jean Paul Sartre's *Being and Nothingness* (1956).

Birth
and Early Infancy

CHAPTER THREE   The development of behavior begins long before a child is born and well in advance of the time when his mother first begins to detect his movements within her womb. At the end of the second month the child can be recognized as human in form. Before this, some bodily activity has begun. The heart begins to beat by the end of the third week. At the twenty-fifth week the child is equipped with practically all the machinery necessary for him to survive as a separate creature, although most of this machinery requires further maturation.

In this chapter we shall consider developments that take place before the child is born and conditions before and after birth that influence the course of his growth. We will also note changes that take place during early infancy as the child becomes increasingly active and more alert to the happenings in the world in which he lives.

Development before birth

A great deal of information regarding the beginnings of behavior has been obtained by studying fetuses that have been removed from the mother's body at various stages of development, due to accidents or other misfortunes.

Hooker (1943) observed a reaction in a fetus at about eight-and-a-half weeks, when it was stroked with a hair in the region of the mouth. During the third month of fetal life, and increasingly thereafter, responses involving the transmission of nerve impulses from one part of the body to another have been observed.

Before birth "the forehandedness of development," which we discussed in the preceding chapter, is strikingly illustrated. The capacity for many functions is established well in advance of the time when normally there is a need to use these functions. One result of this forehandedness is that even though babies normally are born about 280 days after conception, it is possible for a child to survive after having spent only about 180 days in the mother's body. According to some accounts even younger fetuses have survived.

DIRECTION OF EARLY DEVELOPMENT

Development before birth tends to proceed in a *cephalocaudal* direction (Scammon and Calkins, 1929)—that is, growth and differentiation progress from the head to the tail region. During the earlier stages of growth, development in the head region is far in advance of development in the posterior part of the body, although this does not mean that development is complete at one end before it begins at the other. Illustrating this tendency is the fact that the head is well developed before the legs assume their final form and that the arms are budding before leg buds appear. After the child is born, he can make good use of his arms and hands in reaching and grasping before he can use his legs in standing and walking.

In the development of segments of the body, there is a parallel to this cephalocaudal trend in the body as a whole. Development is in a *proximodistal* direction: The structures that lie nearest the main axis of the body mature earlier than those that are more removed. After birth, this is illustrated by behavior. For example, gross movements of the arms and forearms precede more refined movements of the wrists and fingers.

Factors influencing prenatal development and behavior

The course of a child's growth before birth is determined primarily by his heredity. However, even during the period before birth, he is not completely beyond the reach of conditions in the environment. We will first take a brief look at the physical basis of heredity, even though this information may already be familiar to some readers.

THE PHYSICAL BASIS OF HEREDITY

In the cell with which the child's life begins there are structures known as *chromosomes* and these chromosomes contain thousands of substances known as *genes*. The genes are too small to be seen through a microscope, but their existence is inferred from indirect evidence. It is through the action of the genes that a person's hereditary (genetic) potentialities are generated.

According to recent studies the fertilized germ cell contains forty-six chromosomes, consisting of twenty-three pairs (earlier accounts put the number at forty-eight). The germ cells of each parent contained the same number of pairs of chromosomes, but only one from each pair is passed on to the next generation. The process by which the number of chromosomes in the sperm and in the egg cell is reduced by half is known as *reduction-division* or *meiosis*.

Varieties of possible combinations of chromosomes. In the process of meiosis, many different combinations of chromosomes may emerge. Each parent similarly receives half of *his* or *her* chromosomes from the father and half from the mother. So, when the father's cells undergo meiosis, it is possible, by chance, that all chromosomes in a certain sperm cell might have come from his mother's side, or all from his father's side, or all but one from his mother or from his father, and so on through all the other possible combinations. The seminal fluid released by the father in the process of mating may contain millions of spermatozoa, carrying a great variety of combinations of chromosomes, but (in the usual instance) only one of these will find its mark.

In the case of the mother the ripe egg that is waiting to be fertilized may include any one of a great number of combinations of the chromosomes transmitted to her by her parents. The combination residing in a particular ovum may be very different from that in the ovum that ripened in the previous menstrual cycle, or from the one that will ripen in the next cycle.

Variations in the operation of genes.   The fact that the fertilized egg contains two sets of chromosomes also means that it includes a double set of genes—one contributed by the father and the other by the mother. These genes act and interact in a great variety of ways. A trait may arise from a *single-factor* mode of inheritance through the operation of a single gene, sometimes referred to as a *major* gene. Again, a characteristic may result from the interaction of several genes, producing what has been called the *multifactor* or *polygenic* type of inheritance. It has been assumed that characteristics which show a normal range of variation (such as gradations in height) are based on polygenic inheritance (Kallman, 1953).

The genes contributed by the two parents may be alike in their effects, as would be the case if both parents contributed genes producing blue eye-color. Or they may be unlike; for example, if one parent contributed genes for blue eye-color and the other for brown. In many such combinations one gene, called the *dominant* gene, is more potent; it overshadows or suppresses the effect of the other, known as the *recessive* gene. In the example we have used, eye-color, the genes that determine dark eye-color are generally dominant over those producing lighter eye-color. So a child may be born with brown eyes yet possess recessive genes that could produce blue eyes. He can transmit either the dominant or the recessive genes to the next generation. When a brown-eyed man with recessive "blue-eyed" genes mates with a brown-eyed woman who also has recessive "blue-eyed" genes the result may be a blue-eyed baby. The baby has inherited blue eyes from brown-eyed parents.[1]

In view of the many chance combinations of chromosomes that may occur, and in view of operation of multiple, dominant, and recessive genes, it is exceedingly unlikely that a child will be a duplicate of either of his parents, or that the combination of traits inherited by one child will be the same as that inherited by a sibling. On the basis of heredity alone, two siblings may differ greatly in many traits even if they could, by some magic, be reared identically in the same environment.

Genotypes and phenotypes.   The terms *genotype* and *phenotype* have been used to distinguish between what is manifest and what is inherent in an individual. The genotype consists of all the elements that belong to an individual's inheritance—his total endowment of genes. The phenotype is the totality of an individual's observable qualities and characteristics: *pheno* + type, as in *phenomenon:* that which shows, is visible or apparent.

---

[1] There are many other intricacies in the operation of genes which will not be discussed here. Readers who wish to pursue this topic are referred to Ausubel (1958), Boyd (1953), and Kallman (1953).

The genotype embodies a person's inherited potentialities; the phenotype represents the ways in which or the extent to which these potentialities are realized or revealed. A person's phenotype is a product of (1) the particular genes and genic patterns which happens to be combined in the fertilized cell when he is conceived; (2) the interaction between these elements such as occurs, for example, when dominant genes are ascendant over recessive ones; and (3) the influence of his environment, before and after birth.

The genotype and the phenotype may correspond to each other in varying degrees. Normal human beings invariably have two legs, for example, and in this respect the genotype and phenotype are the same. On the other hand, the two do not correspond if, for example, a person with a certain leg *length* has genes which might produce offspring with shorter or longer legs. The genotype and phenotype are dissimilar also when an individual displays a dominant trait (as in the example of the brown-eyed parents) but in his germ plasm carries recessive genes which can produce a different trait. Further, the two are dissimilar if the environment has interfered with the development of an individual's genetic potentialities. This occurs, for example, if a child with an excellent inheritance is listless and seems to be stupid as the result of neglect or abuse.

There is a rather close correspondence between the genotype and phenotype in "pure-bred" strains of animals. Such animals resemble each other closely from one generation to the next. The similarity appears not only in physical but also in psychological characteristics, as when members of one strain of laboratory rats, contrasted with another, are superior in their ability to run a maze, or show a disposition to be vicious or gentle, or a tendency to be very active or quite inactive.

Prenatal influences

The unborn child is highly protected but he is not completely insulated from happenings in the world about him. While most of the movements of the child before birth seem to be in response to internal conditions it is possible also sometimes to elicit movements by external means. One observer noted, for example, that a kick and other movements were exhibited by a child (thirty-one days before birth) when the sides of the bathtub in which the mother was lying were struck with a metal rod (Forbes and Forbes, 1927). During the late stages of pregnancy, some mothers have reported that a musical concert may lead to increased fetal activity.

Influence of the mother's condition. Conditions in the life of the mother may lead to greater than normal amounts of fetal activity (Sontag and

Richards, 1938).[2] There may be more fetal movement when the mother is emotionally excited than during moments of calm. Mothers have reported that they sense more fetal activity when they are fatigued than when they are rested, although this may be due to greater sensitivity on the mother's part. Changes have been noted also in the heart-rate of the unborn child. In some instances, the rate has been higher after the mother climbed a flight of stairs than some minutes later, and higher after she had smoked a cigarette than just before or some time later.

Can circumstances in the child's environment before birth influence his character and disposition and the later course of his development? Superstitions and theories about prenatal influences have lived on through the centuries. A typical tale is that if a pregnant woman is frightened by a rabbit her child later will show a birthmark in the shape of a rabbit's foot. Then there is the theory that the unborn child is able to respond to "psychic" influences—that is, he can sense whether he is wanted or unwanted by his mother.

Actually, there is no medium through which the psychological state of the mother can be communicated directly to the child, but the effects of a mother's psychological condition might be communicated indirectly. When a mother is emotionally excited or disturbed, for example, secretions from the ductless glands are released into her blood stream, and these hormone substances may be carried to the child in the fluid interchange between mother and child. It is conceivable then that the unborn child might indirectly, through chemical means, be affected by conditions affecting the mother. Sontag and his associates (1935, 1944a, 1944b) have observed that fetuses show a greater than usual amount of activity when mothers are undergoing severe emotional stress.

HAZARDS CONNECTED WITH GROWTH BEFORE BIRTH

Fortunately, most children who are conceived develop satisfactorily as embryos and fetuses, and come lustily into the world at the time of birth. Nature takes great care of an unborn child. If minerals and hormones essential to growth are in short supply, for example, the child may get his share at the mother's expense. But sometimes the story is different. The unborn child and the mother face many hazards. There are limits to what a mother can give and what a child can take. Defective heredity or misfortunes that arise during pregnancy or childbirth result in many casualties and heartaches.

Some of these are starkly apparent: A fetus may be so lacking, or the mother so lacking, in what it takes to sustain healthy growth that the

---

[2] See also other studies by Sontag and his associates dealing with fetal behavior, including Sontag and Wallace (1934, 1935).

little creature is cast out as a stillbirth before his time, or dies at the time of birth. Unfortunate prenatal conditions may not be so radical as to cause death and yet may result in serious impairments. Many investigations have shown that brain damage may be inflicted before or about the time of birth by toxins in the blood supply (toxemia of pregnancy), bleeding during pregnancy, or an undersupply of oxygen (anoxia). The effects of such brain damage may be apparent at birth or may not be particularly noticeable until later when the child begins to have difficulty at school.

Notable among the investigations in this area are those of Pasamanick and his associates. Pasamanick's studies lead him to postulate that there is a "continuum of reproductive casualty, consisting of brain damage incurred during the prenatal and paranatal periods as a result of abnormalities during these periods." Such damage may lead to a "gradient of injury" extending from death (during the fetal stage or at the time of birth) "through cerebral palsy, epilepsy, mental deficiency, reading disability and behavioral disorder." [3]

Evidence supporting this theory was obtained in separate studies of the medical histories of persons afflicted with cerebral palsy and epilepsy. Pasamanick and his associates also found that the medical histories of children with behavior disorders showed significantly more complications of pregnancy and prematurity than their matched controls. Behavior disorders were less often associated with mechanical difficulties during labor than with non-mechanical abnormalities, such as toxemia. This was notably observed in the case of children who were "hyperactive, confused and disorganized." The investigators point out that there are obviously many factors in addition to abnormalities of pregnancy and childbirth that cause behavior disorders.

These findings suggest that some of the troubles children encounter at school, such as difficulty in learning to read, may be due in part in some instances to brain injuries that were too small to have a distinctly noticeable effect on their previous behavior but large enough to make a difference when they face a critical test. The need for further research in this area is apparent. But it also is apparent from studies of the interplay between biochemical and psychological influences that when children have "problems" or difficulty at school, a more humane and sensitive diagnosis is required than that expressed by such moralistic language as: "Child does not exert enough effort" or "Child should do more homework."

Boys seem to encounter more difficulties in being born than girls. There are more stillbirths among boys than girls, more deaths following child-

---

[3] This quotation is from Pasamanick and Kawi, 1956. Other references to Kawi and Pasamanick (1959) and to Pasamanick are listed in the general bibliography.

birth, more mental defectives, cerebral palsied, epileptics, and more boys who are hyperactive, confused, and disorganized (Rogers, Lilienfield and Pasamanick, 1955).

Organization of behavior

What is the general pattern by which new forms of behavior emerge as development goes on before and after birth? Discussions of this subject have been based largely on observations of lower animals. In studies of amblystoma (a salamander), Coghill (1929, 1936) took the position that reactions of the total organism precede separate movements of parts of the body. The primary state is one of integration, and partial movements become *individuated* out of larger movements. Swimming movements in the salamander, for example, are movements involving the whole body. Before the limbs can move independently, they are tied in with, and are an integral feature of movement of, the body as a whole.

Coghill says that the act of seeing involves at first a total bodily response. As an object moves from left to right through the salamander's field of vision, the animal does not sit like a sphinx with roving eyes that can follow the object while the rest of its body stays put. Instead, the whole organism of the young salamander participates in the act of seeing. It is not until a later stage of development that eyes can move more or less independently. (A partial analogy in human beings occurs when a child first tries to wink one eye. At first there may be movements of the other eyelid and the child's head may bob up and down—there may even be movement of the shoulders and trunk.)

Coghill implies that these observations of the salamander and other lower animals hold true for animals in general as well as for man. On this point, however, investigators are not in full agreement. In experiments by Carmichael and others [4] with the fetuses of mammals, it has not been found that all observed movements conform to the concept of a gradually expanding total pattern, completely integrated from the beginning. While individuation of specific movements out of previously larger activities accounts for a good part of the development of behavior, a full description would have to go many steps further. Various activities are differentiated at different rates. New relationships between some specific responses are established before specialization has gone far in other activities.

After birth, behavior develops through a refinement and increasing

---

[4] For a review of studies in this area see Carmichael's chapter in the *Manual of Child Psychology* (1954).

specialization of specific movements, as well as through integration of movement systems that were not tied together at the start.

Through the generations and in various cultures there have been many superstitions connected with pregnancy. Many of these are patently false, but one thing certain is that pregnancy and childbirth have profound emotional meanings to the mother.

There have been theories to the effect that a woman during pregnancy is likely to become a little odd, that she is more susceptible to insanity, that she may develop peculiar cravings and make irrational demands. Actually, a pregnant woman is likely to show a continuation of the psychological tendencies and traits which she possessed before she became pregnant.

Pregnancy may, however, give added intensity or a new emphasis to emotional tendencies that already exist. The mother who has a zestful approach to life may be in her element once she is pregnant. She has a glow and is exuberant in the knowledge of her fertility. If the pregnancy is her first she may have a feeling of self-fulfillment and prepare herself to make a more or less peaceful departure from an old into a new state of existence.

But even if the mother has a warm welcome for motherhood, and is a realistic person with healthy attitudes toward herself and others, pregnancy will be quite a trial at times. If there are such special difficulties as financial problems, heavy duties in the home, complications due to the fact that other members of the family become "difficult," the test will be a very severe one. Pregnancy—like any venture in life that involves a process of growth, and which means taking a chance with one's own role in life and with the destiny of other persons (a chance a woman very definitely takes when she brings a new human being into the world)—is likely to be accompanied by some struggle and apprehenshion and pain. It is unlikely that any sensitive woman who is honest with herself could go into such a fateful undertaking without some fear and foreboding. But in contrast to this fear, there is also something challenging and rewarding in the experience and in the prospect.

A moving and enlightening account of the feelings mothers undergo during pregnancy and delivery, and after a child's birth, has been written by Hamilton (1955). In her study, Hamilton had the cooperation of fourteen mothers of first-born children. These women confided many intimate details of their experiences to her—their fears, their discomforts, their need for emotional support, their reactions to superstitions and "old wives' tales" about the hazards of bearing and begetting a child.

If a mother has a relatively healthy and matter-of-fact attitude regarding herself, without a compulsion to be perfect, or to hold herself up to impossible standards she probably will view her pregnancy in much the same spirit. But she is likely to have fears. In Hamilton's study all but one of the mothers reported that there were times when they were afraid. Nine of the fourteen mothers feared that they might lose the child or that the child might be malformed.

If the expectant mother is the kind of person who ordinarily blames herself quite severely, one who suffers from feelings of guilt, she quite likely will have guilt feelings in connection with pregnancy. She may worry for fear she has not done the right thing. She may have forebodings that the child will be malformed because of something she has or has not done. Her misgivings about herself may lead her to imagine that disaster will strike her or her child as a kind of punishment. Such feelings of guilt are likely to be more intense if the mother actually has misgivings about having a child, even though she is already pregnant, and if she resists the idea of being a mother. Feelings of guilt might also lead her to be apprehensive about the prospect of taking anesthetics during the child's delivery for fear that she might, while in a drugged state, reveal carefully guarded secrets about herself.

The time of pregnancy brings added burdens if the mother is very prudish and squeamish about the physical properties of her body and if she shrinks from the prospect of being naked and exposed in the care of doctors and nurses.

If she has difficulty in accepting herself as a female, or feels that, as a woman, she has been cheated by nature and not given her just rights, her protests against womanhood may take the form of a recognized or unrecognized (unconscious) protest against motherhood. But if the mother who bears a child is content with her role as a woman and accepts herself as a woman, the bearing of a child is a way of confirming and expressing her womanhood.

Pregnancy may add a happy quality to good relationships that already exist between husband and wife or aggravate difficulties that already prevail. According to one view, the period of a wife's pregnancy is a time when some husbands seem to think that they have the right to stray into intimate relations with other women. The likelihood is that if a husband does stray it is not something brought about by the pregnancy. But pregnancy can aggravate tensions and difficulties that already exist in the intimate relations between husband and wife. According to the study by Hamilton referred to above, if a wife normally enjoys sexual relations with her husband she will probably continue to do so during pregnancy, but if there is friction on this score pregnancy may be used as an excuse for avoiding physical intimacy.

The more fully a woman accepts herself and the more fully she and her husband accept each other, the more the pregnancy will be welcomed—in spite of the apprehensions it creates and the inconveniences it involves.

The "birth ordeal"

Poets, doctors, and psychologists have all speculated about the meaning of the birth process to the child. Obviously the fact of being born is a drastic upheaval and a tremendous change. The child is thrust from the warmth and protection of the womb, where nourishment flowed through him and where he was not even called upon to breathe. He now must exert effort to obtain food, draw his own breath, and, at times, gasp and cough and struggle to obtain it. He is exposed to changes in temperature, rays of light that strike his eyes, and sound waves that beat upon his ears. Instead of floating in a fluid within confines that are yielding yet firm he now lies loose, naked and unenclosed, free to move as his limbs thrash in empty space. His head sags if not supported. His body falls if not held. If the child who is being born had the ability to sense these changes—to take note of the tremendous contrast—we might expect that the process of moving from the womb into the world would have a staggering psychological effect.

There have been many conjectures about this situation. It has been said, for example, that the birth cry is not just a noise mechanically brought about by the first intake of air, but a cry of pain or protest or sorrow or fear. It has also been proposed that the process of being uprooted and cast from the womb causes a psychological shock and produces in the child, as long as he lives, an unconscious yearning to return to the protection and security of the womb.

This theory of the drama of birth is questionable, however. The child who is being born is a very immature and a very unfinished creature. His higher brain centers and the rest of his nervous system are not capable of functioning as those of an older person. His equipment for sensing and feeling is not fully developed. Moreover, the process of being born is a part of a larger total process of growth. The machinery with which the mother cares for the child as an embryo and fetus, providing oxygen, nourishment, and the room for the child's growing size, is not designed to care for him indefinitely. If we were to attribute wishes, hopes, and fears to this little child, we probably would have to assume that toward the end of pregnancy he hopes to be born even more than he desires not to be born. If we judged simply from what his mother says about his turning, squirming, jerking, wrenching, and kicking before he is born, we probably must assume that he is more eager to get out of the womb than he ever will be to get back in.

Birth is part of a larger process by which a child comes into being, a process which continues after birth as the child, with the passage of time, strives to creep, to walk, to pursue the untried with eager feet, and to plunge into the unknown with a curious mind. In the developmental process from birth to the end of life there is striving and struggle, but it is unlikely that in any feature of this process of development a healthy child will spontaneously seek completely to retire into the past. It is probably only an adult who has suffered a cruel loss of hope who would claim that a healthy child wishes, after birth, to retreat into the shadows of an earlier phase of life.

The world surrounding the newborn child

Many environmental influences surrounding a newborn child are obvious to the eye, but there are also many that cannot be seen. The infant lies in a visible cradle, surrounded by an invisible environment consisting of the thoughts and feelings, attitudes, desires, hopes, and expectations of members of his family. If all is well, this composite of thoughts and feelings will offer the child a comfortable place. His mother will be drawn to him with feelings of pride in her role as one who has brought forth a child, and she will feel a strong impulse to protect him. His father will be drawn to him with sentiments which he might never have discovered until he became a father. Also, if all is favorable, older brothers and sisters will be prepared to welcome him, even though they may be disturbed by the events surrounding his birth and perplexed as to what it will mean in their own lives to have a new person in the household.[5]

On the other hand, this environment may not be so hospitable. For one cause or another, the child may come unwanted into a troubled home. If so, the effects of such unfriendly or conflicting emotions will soon be felt in his own life.

Although there are differences, such as the foregoing, in the setting into which the child is born, the child is not entirely at the mercy of conditions as they are. From the beginning, he is not merely a creature of his environment; he helps to create his environment. Even in his weakness there is strength, for his helplessness draws others to him. Through his appearance and all his ways he commands attention, makes impressions, and, without so intending, influences the attitudes of his elders, whatever they may have thought or felt beforehand. So, a woman who vowed that she could never become "crazy" about a baby may find when the baby comes that he has completely taken her over. A father who was secretly

---

[5] For a discussion of psychological connotations and practical arrangements in connection with childbirth and early infant care, see Grantly Read's *Childbirth Without Fear* (1953) and a volume edited by Jackson and Trainham (1950).

convinced that he could not love a second child as much as the first may discover that it is quite a different story when the new youngster nestles in his arms.

The tide may, of course, run in the other direction if the parents have nurtured a glorified image of a baby-to-be and then find that the real baby is quite somebody else; if they fear the responsibilities which the child places upon them; or if they are rather mechanical and detached people who shrink from him not just because he is so small but because they have never learned to come into close emotional contact with any other human being.

Behavior at birth

Although there are many more or less clearly defined acts in the flow of the newborn infants' activity, an outstanding feature of his early behavior is a vast amount of diffuse and seemingly uncoordinated movement.[6]

GENERALIZED MOVEMENT

Even in connection with apparently simple reflex activities, or in response to stimuli applied to a limited area of the body, there may be a variety of associated movements in other parts of the body. For example, when an object is brought into contact with the infant's mouth, he is likely to begin to suck, but there may be many additional movements in other parts of his body that don't have much to do with sucking. Some activities seemingly have little revelance to the conditions that produced them. One investigator noted that infants made sucking movements when their hair was pulled, when they were dropped, and when someone pinched their big toes (Jensen, 1932). However, even though the child exhibits a great deal of generalized movement, there is some specialization of behavior from the beginning. Offer the healthy child a nipple when he is hungry and he will do a fine job of sucking, regardless of other activities that may accompany it. Pinch his toe, and his response is likely to be more pronounced in the limb that is pinched than in more remote areas of the body.

It is possible to detect quite a repertory of accomplishments in the child. He sucks, swallows, excretes, defecates, vomits, salivates, hiccoughs, sneezes, yawns, stretches, kicks, waves arms and legs, trembles, shivers, turns his head, grimaces, moves his eyes, blinks, cries, grunts, and sighs. He can meet the world more than halfway in making his presence known.

---

[6] For a review of studies of the newborn child, see Pratt (1954).

The term "reflex" is used to designate an involuntary reaction that is rather specific and fixed. Actually, however, reflexes are somewhat less fixed and specific when they are first exhibited by the newborn child than they become with the passage of time.[7] Sucking, for example, is a response that is ready for business when the child is born. But, as we have seen, sucking may be set off by happenings that have nothing to do with feeding. The act of sucking, itself, changes and becomes more efficient during the days following birth (Gesell and Ilg, 1937).

In the course of development some reflex activities wane, or are displaced by other forms of behavior. As the child's nervous system matures he is able to check or inhibit some movements that occurred first as reflex actions. One reflex that shows an interesting course is the Moro *Umklammerungs* reflex, also called the clasping or embrace reflex (Fruedenberg, 1921). This reflex may be elicited by striking a sharp blow on the surface on which a child is lying on his back. The infant throws out his arms and then brings them together as if in an embrace. At the same time, his legs are thrown out and then flexed. This reaction was believed by its discoverer to be an atavistic or primitive fright reaction in response to the jarring of the body. In a primate, such movements might enable the young creature to grab hold of his mother's body or the limb of a tree. Another investigator (Schaltenbrand, 1925) terms it a "readiness-to-jump reaction, ensuring a safe landing." This reflex undergoes changes during the first months of life. McGraw (1937) found that at about three or four months the gross movements had diminished considerably. At about seven months, overt movements had further waned, so that merely a weak body jerk accompanied by blinking remained. The changes from the grosser to the more refined and subdued response parallels certain developments in the infant's nervous system, according to McGraw. She states that the cerebral cortex is not functioning in the first phase of the response. As the cortex develops and comes into action, the primitive kind of movement over which the infant seems at first to have little or no control gives way to a more calculated act.

The grasp reflex, which occurs when an object is brought into contact with the palms of the hands of a young infant, also changes with time. This grasp may be so powerful at first that the infant, clinging to a bar as it is lifted, can support his own weight for many seconds. But this act of grasping, which seems involuntary at first, vanishes as the child matures and becomes increasingly capable of voluntary control of his hands.

---

[7] For a discussion of studies dealing with this topic, see Anderson (1936).

Special senses

What impressions does the newborn child receive? This question is difficult to answer. Any sign that he can see, hear, smell, and taste gives us a glimpse of what the content of his early experience might be. The infant's response must be judged by observing his overt actions and these are influenced by many conditions, such as being wet or dry, hungry or sated, asleep or awake.

There is a problem of how to adjust our observations of the child to his own ways. The newborn infant is unable to do much to cooperate, so it becomes the observer's job to cooperate with the infant. Suggestive in this connection is a study dealing with infants' ability to fix their gaze on an object and follow it with their eyes (Beasley, 1933). The experimenter tried to meet the infant at least halfway: he moved the stimulus (such as a light) into the child's line of vision until he found the point at which the child's eyes seemed to be fixed upon it. Only after fixation had thus been procured did the experimenter proceed with the next step: finding how far and how long the infant would continue to keep his eyes on the object as it was moved about in the field of vision. The results indicated that when this procedure was used the children were more capable of following a visual stimulus than would be apparent if a more arbitrary procedure had been followed.

Sight. Almost from the time of birth the average infant behaves as though he can see. When he is able to fix his eyes on an object and follow it as it moves through space, it is reasonable to infer that he is seeing or obtaining glimpses of one sort or another, although we have no way of knowing just what kind of impression he has. Infants vary considerably in their apparent ability to fix their eyes on an object. In some children, for a time after birth, movements of the eyes are not coordinated. Normally it is not until many weeks after birth that eye coordinations are fully established in pursuing an object that moves up and down or from side to side in the field of vision.

Hearing. A child may be responsive to the physical vibrations that produce sound even before birth, but we cannot surmise from this just what the child hears. Some investigators have claimed that infants are deaf at birth, but many studies show that a majority of babies respond in some way to sounds within the first days of life.

Other sensory responses. It has been found that the average infant responds positively to milk and to sweet solutions, and negatively to solutions that are strongly salt, sour, or bitter.[8]

When babies have just been fed they are likely to make finer taste discriminations than when they are very hungry (Jensen, 1932). We notice the same thing in older children and in adults—the hungrier a person is the less fussy he is likely to be about his food. Since children discriminate in this way even during the first weeks of life, it adds to the difficulty of studying their capacities. If a child is not hungry, he may reject both sweet and sour food, not because he cannot taste the difference but because he desires neither. In studying his ability to taste, as in studying his ability to see, it is important to approach him in the right way at the right time.

In studies of the infant's sense of smell, such odors as ammonia and acetic acid, which are powerful enough to cause discomfort to adults (perhaps by virtue of pain rather than olfactory stimulation), also produce reactions in newborn infants, while milder odors, which adults are able to detect, appear to have little effect. Infants react to temperatures that are hotter or colder than the normal temperature of the body, and they appear to react more to extreme cold than to extreme heat (Pratt *et al.*, 1930).

From birth, infants are responsive to the stimulus of pressure or contact. During the first days of life infants also show a variety of responses to changes in their bodily positions. Righting responses of a sort that are eventually involved in maintaining an upright posture can be observed during the first days of life.

The emotions of the newborn child

What capacity for feeling and emotion does an infant have during the first days and weeks of life? This is a difficult question yet it is a crucial one, for while a person's awareness of his existence comes partly through the sensory experiences—sight, sound, touch, taste, and other sensations—feelings comprise an essential element in his awareness of himself.

Most infants (even the serene ones) manifest what seems to be a great deal of emotion. They cry, squirm, wiggle, kick, and thrash about. If an adult were so animated we would have to assume that he was having a stormy time. There have been many opinions given and a great amount of research done on the child's emotional capacity, but unfortunately both the opinions and the research leave large question marks.

---

[8] For reviews of studies in this area, see Pratt (1954).

The view that the young infant is subject to profound emotional experiences has been set forth by Freud, and many of his followers have added views of their own.[9] Freud spoke of the danger which confronts a child because of his helplessness, giving rise to a need to be loved, which a human being is destined never to renounce. Isaacs (1936) maintains that wants and wishes, fear and anger, love and hate are there from the beginning. According to Despert (1946), a child comes into the world lonely, and he is afraid.

Against these views are findings suggesting that the child is just as unfinished, as far as capacity for emotional experience is concerned, as he is in other respects. We shall look later at some of these findings.

We cannot *prove* whether or not a child is capable of intense emotional experience during the first few days after birth. But for two reasons, the writer judges it much better to lean too far toward assuming that the child *is* capable of varied emotional experience (despite the lack of objective proof) than to lean in the other direction. First, if we heed a child's cries and his other expressions of emotions by going to him, caring for him, comforting him, probably no harm will be done; we will most likely accomplish some good; and harm might be done if we did *not* give heed. Better to lean on the side of solicitude and compassion. Second, only by assuming that the child does feel, and assuming that it is possible to detect the emotion that he is experiencing and seeking to communicate, can we be alert to his feelings, learn the signs of emotion, learn to feel with him, and to have a kind of communication with him.

But what is said here does not pertain alone to relationships with young infants. It applies to relationships with children at all age levels, and with adults. The broad principle is that the more we seek to respond to the humanity of others and to draw upon our own humanity, the more alert we will be to the feelings of others and to feelings within ourselves.

HUNGER

The newborn child shows his hunger by means of cries and restless movements. When fed, he tends to quiet down. Healthy babies demand food about every three hours, but there is wide variation from child to child.

If the child is not fed when he announces his hunger, his crying and activity are likely to increase. Similarly, if a youngster has been fed on a regular schedule for several days after birth and his feeding is then delayed beyond the usual time there is likely to be a sharp increase in crying, fussing, and general activity.

What are the feelings associated with this cycle of hunger and its

---

[9] See Freud (1936), Isaacs (1936), and Sharpe (1950).

satisfaction. There are times when a baby will cry as though his inner-most being was in torment. Is he swept by a vague fear of annihilation because his need for food is not satisfied? Is he consumed with rage because his desires are not being met? Do the softer notes that appear among his more strident outcries mean that his terror and rage are blended with feelings of gloom—the gloom of one neglected by elders whose withholding of food means also the withholding of love? We cannot confidently answer yes or no to these questions. But it is obvious that the infant at times throws his whole being into his quest for food.

EXPERIENCES INVOLVED IN PERSONAL CONTACTS

Being hungry and being fed have a relatively greater prominence in the life of the young infant than they have later on, and the same seems true of the infant's contacts with others when any of his wants are being cared for. These contacts are interwoven with his well-being and his survival from day to day. Within a few days after birth, he will cease his crying, at least for a time, if only he is held in someone's arms, while earlier it required not only holding but also food to pacify him. Within another few days, he will cease fussing simply in response to the sight or sound of a person who is coming to him. Later comes a time when he wants someone to be near him, even though he is comfortably warm and dry and well fed, as though he desired company for its own sake.

Soon after birth infants thus seek attention beyond what is required for feeding and other aspects of their physical care. They want human companionship, and usually they receive it by being held in the arms, and by being spoken to, hummed to and sung to, and by being rocked, stroked, squeezed, patted and petted, nuzzled, cuddled, and fussed over in countless ways. Acts of this sort that involve affectionate, comforting, tender and playful contacts are known as "mothering." The typical infant soon after his birth craves mothering. We might argue that this desire for mothering is a secondary desire, acquired by associating the satisfaction in being fed with the lifting, handling, and holding that accompanies feeding. Or we might argue that the infant's desire for being mothered is something primary, representing a need that is just as primitive and unlearned as the need for food. Actually, it would not pay to debate this question. For whether this desire for contact with other human beings is inborn, or whether it is learned, it appears early in most children, and it is strong, and as time passes it is of great importance in the child's development as a person. From his crib in early infancy the child confirms the saying that it is not good for man to be alone.

With the passage of time, the child welcomes contact with a friendly parent not only as a source of apparent satisfaction in itself but also as a help in stimulating his own efforts and in bearing the hurts and bruises of everyday life. Little children often exert themselves most—in their chatter, their handling of objects, their first articulation of a recognizable word—when another is in physical or psychological contact with them. As the child becomes older, pain from a fall, anger from the loss of a toy, rage from having been struck by another child become easier to bear if he is picked up and held in a parent's arms. He derives psychological support from such contacts just as he derived life and physical well-being from the body of his mother before the time of his birth.

PAIN

Infants seem relatively insensitive to certain forms of pain stimulation. We cannot determine how soon or how deeply an infant feels pain as compared with an adult, but it is undoubtedly true that an adult's pain is frequently more intense because of past experiences. If pain stimulation could be stripped of tensions and fears that grow out of past experiences, many agonies experienced by older people would, no doubt, be less severe.

It is interesting to observe how the infant's apparent insensibility to certain pains is reflected in medical practice. Circumcisions performed upon a child under two weeks of age without the use of an anesthetic, and other forms of surgical treatment, do not customarily produce signs of suffering as acute as one would expect if an older person received similar treatment. However, we cannot be certain that absence of outward signs denotes a similar absence of feeling.

CRYING

Crying is one of the most important accomplishments of the young child, and it has a vastly complex set of functions and meanings. Through his crying the child expresses his needs, his wants, his discomfort, and, in time, his desire for company, his wish to be noticed, his hurts and bruises, his annoyances, his impatience, and his grief. Crying becomes not merely a sign of distress but also a kind of self-assertion. Crying serves the child as a means of calling his friends to his side, and also very early in life (although not intentionally at first) it becomes a weapon which the infant can use as a protest against those who ignore, neglect, or abuse him.

From an early age all healthy babies cry lustily, but even in this primitive means of expression there are many marks of individuality. In similar circumstances some babies cry far more than others.

Some causes of crying. Often the cause of crying seems clear, but often it does not. In observations by Aldrich, Sung, and Knop (1945a, 1945b), it appeared that hunger and being wet or soiled accounted for a large proportion of instances of crying; but in about a third of the instances the cause could not be ascertained by those who were watching the baby.

Crying and colic. In young infants, notably during the first three months, "colic" is a frequent cause of crying. Medical literature gives many definitions and describes many forms of colic. As applied to infants, the term usually denotes a condition of loud crying combined with symptoms of acute distress in the digestive tract. In a study of infants who cried "excessively" as compared with other infants, it was noted that the former showed "excessive" gas in the gastrointestinal tract and a more rapid stomach emptying than babies in a low-crying group (Stewart *et al.*, 1954).

Theories regarding the causes of colic range from the view that it arises mainly from the immaturity of the nervous system or some kind of inadequacy in the child's physical equipment to the view that it might arise out of a disturbed psychological relationship between the mother and the baby. Among those who have stressed the psychological effects of the mother is Harry Stack Sullivan. According to Sullivan, the mother-infant interaction is disturbed when a mother is notably anxious. The mother's anxiety induces anxiety in the infant and this interferes with the infant's normal functions. Others who have dealt with the effect a mother's emotional state might have on a child's physical well-being are Escalona (1945), Stewart and associates (1954), and Lakin (1957). In the last two studies, mothers of colicky babies, as compared with other mothers, seemed to be less accepting of their roles as mothers; they appeared more uncertain about themselves, and showed other evidences of being less secure and less in harmony with other people.

It seems reasonable to believe that conditions ranging from weaknesses in the make-up of the infant himself to stresses stemming from the emotional relationship between the mother and the child may lead some children to cry much more than others. In many instances the physical and psychological factors are interwoven. We cannot explain the situation simply by saying that if a crying, colicky baby has gas in his gut it is his bad mother who put it there! An infant's prolonged crying—whatever the cause—is bound to have a serious effect on the mother-child relationship. Even the best mother is likely to become anxious and to have doubts about her adequacy as a woman and as a mother if her child cries for long periods in an agonized way and is unsoothed by anything she does to comfort him.

Qualities of children's crying. Children vary not only in the extent but also in the manner and style of their crying. One baby's crying tends to be sharp and staccato while another's is characteristically more smooth and connected. Some babies have loud cries while others have softer tones, moaning low as an adult might if he were weary or wished to weep without calling too much attention to himself.

By the time he is a few months old, a child's crying acquires characteristic qualities of tone and rhythm and cadence. We might gain a deep insight into this young person if we knew how to interpret his cries. For example, a motherless child who has been passed from hand to hand during a period of foster care, shifting again and again to strange cribs, and to unfamiliar arms, might develop a bedtime cry which seems to express a protest against sleep and a fear of waking up once more in a strange place.

Adult response to crying.   The crying of young infants has received much attention in research studies, but there remains much about it that is baffling yet fascinating. In the crying of young babies there are sounds that seem to have distinct meanings and yet it is difficult to tell what these meanings might be. Here, as in studying other aspects of a young baby's behavior, the listener's interpretation will be colored by his own mood and feelings toward the child. His interpretation of the crying of someone else's child is likely also to be colored by his attitudes toward parents—his tendency to blame parents or to sympathize with them.

A child's crying often is disturbing to adults because it arouses sympathy, or annoyance, or it reactivates buried hurts so much that it is hard for adults to listen to a child's crying without being threatened by it. One who views the child in the aloof manner of a spectator probably is less likely to confuse the child's crying with feelings of his own, but he might also by virtue of his detachment fail to perceive anything. The dilemma here is that one who is genuinely interested in the child and has a fellow-feeling for him may hear too much and one who is not concerned will only hear an unpleasant noise.

ABSENCE OF CLEARLY DEFINED EMOTIONAL RESPONSES

Although the child during the first weeks of life shows general excitement by crying and bodily activity his emotional reactions are more diffuse, less specific and defined than will be true at a later time. Even in an older person these patterns are none too clearly differentiated, but as a person grows older there are times when his expressions have unmistakable earmarks of anger, fear, or joy.

In studies of emotional behavior following birth, children have been observed when exposed to conditions that might produce pain, anger, or fear. To study "anger" responses, such tactics as compressing the child's nostrils, restraining the use of his arms, interfering with his head movements by pressure against his chin have been used. In a majority of instances, infants who have been subjected to such treatment for brief periods during the first two or three weeks after birth have not shown anything resembling the classic picture of rage. Indeed, many infants bear treatment of this sort as though it were meant in a friendly, or at least neutral, spirit.

Before many weeks have passed the story will be different, of course. Physical restraint and thwarting of movement become quite effective in arousing anger. But even when the child has become able to put on a show of anger, what constitutes restraint or interference will not depend solely on what another person does to him. If he is quiescent, or if he seems to be in the mood for a little horseplay, he will allow his arms to be held to his sides for a time and will even patiently accept the indignity of having his head pushed back by pressure on his chin. On the other hand, anger is likely to ensue if the thwarting is real from the standpoint of the child—if, for example, his arms are forcibly restrained just as he is in the act of using them, or if his feeding is delayed after he has seen the bottle and is all set to take his milk.

At birth, the infant will react with crying and restlessness to any form of intense and enduring stimulation, of which rough restraint may be one form (Dennis, 1939). At a later age the infant will react in the same way, with crying and restlessness, when his accustomed ways of behaving are interfered with.

A sharp, shrill, or loud noise may cause an infant during the first days of life to start, kick, squirm, and perhaps cry. Such behavior has the appearance of fear. But other forms of stimulation, which a sympathetic adult would not regard as particularly fear-inspiring, may produce similar bodily movements and similar cries. On the other hand, infants often seem undisturbed by rather drastic treatment. In one study (Irwin, 1932), each of twenty-four infants under one month of age was raised in a supine position above the experimenter's head, was dropped, and was caught after he had fallen a distance of two feet. In eighty-five trials of this sort, crying resulted only twice. In 12 per cent of the trials the infant made no detectable overt response. In half the number of instances in which the children did react to this treatment, their movements were confined to the arms alone.

From the viewpoint of emotional expression, the child's reactions during the first weeks of life group themselves roughly, on the one hand, as reactions of apparent withdrawal or rejection, such as squirms, twists, tension, movements of the trunk and the arms and extremities, turning of the head, and crying. On the other hand, there are reactions of apparent acceptance, quiescence, passivity, and a rudimentary form of pursuit, such as is found when the child turns his head and opens his mouth to suckle when an object is moved toward his lips.

Other functions

The newborn child's heart beats more rapidly than an older child's; his normal breathing rate is higher, and his blood pressure is lower. [10]

When fed according to their own demands, infants vary considerably in their feeding rhythm but they probably will seek to be fed considerably more often than the six feedings per twenty-four hours which sometimes have been regarded as the standard (Marquis, 1941, and Simsarian and McLendon, 1942, 1945).

The average infant voids his bowels about four to five times a day and his bladder about nineteen times in twenty-four hours, but there is great variation in these matters (Halverson, 1940).

The premature child

The average child is born approximately 280 days after he is conceived, but there are wide differences, especially in the direction of shorter periods of gestation. Precise records of the "age" of children at birth are difficult to obtain, but the age can be determined at least approximately. It is possible also to apply an objective criterion, such as weight at birth. For example (in order to have a fixed and arbitrary criterion), it has been assumed that a child weighing less than 5½ pounds at birth has been born before the full normal term of forty weeks (Scammon and Calkins, 1929).

Children at birth vary considerably in "maturity." Gesell and Amatruda (1945) have estimated that the range in age of newborn babies who are capable of living is as wide as from twenty-six to forty-six weeks. These figures indicate the vast leeway of chance and possibility within which life proceeds. Although the average birth weight is a little above 7 pounds for girls, and a little under 7½ for boys, babies have survived who weighed as little as 1½ pounds or even less (Hoffman, *et al.*, 1937). However, it is unlikely that a child weighing less than about 2½ pounds will survive, and the chances of survival increase with added weight up to 4 or 5 pounds.

Children who are born well before full term are usually known as "premature" babies. This label is a useful one, but it is somewhat lacking in precision. Actually, two children may be born at exactly the same fetal age, yet one may be more "mature"—more fully developed—than the other (Blatz and Millichamp, 1937). Or a child may be "premature" in the sense of being born in advance of the average of forty weeks and yet be more

---

[10] Feldman (1920); Sontag and Richards (1938).

"mature" in the sense of being more advanced in his development than another child who has been born at full term. Differences in rate of growth, which are so conspicuous after birth, appear also in growth before birth.

The "premature" child has the characteristics of an "immature" child; he has not had time to complete the developments that usually occur between the period of his untimely delivery and the period when babies normally are born. [11] Accordingly, the younger he is, the less fully is he equipped to carry on the business of living an independent life. As a result, the premature child has less chance than the full-term baby to live, and if he does survive he is more subject to weakness and impairments of many kinds. These may be an outgrowth of the conditions that caused him to be born prematurely or they may arise from the hazards he faces after birth.

The premature child obviously requires special attention. Care must be taken to keep him warm, partly because he lacks the deposits of fat that normally accumulate during the later stages of fetal growth; it may be necessary to aid his respiration by feeding him oxygen; he may need help in taking nourishment because of weak sucking or swallowing reflexes, or inadequacies in his digestive processes.

The premature child looks like a tired, little old man. He is so near life's beginning yet he looks as though he were near its end. If not artificially warmed, his temperature will fall, breathing cease, and the heart which has been beating steadily from the time he was about one month old will stop.

He is cadaverous, with a huge head out of proportion to the size of his body, less handsome even than a full-term baby; but who would call him ugly? Not his mother, if she has yearned for a baby, nor his father, for he will see this imperfect creature as the tentative and uncertain fulfillment of a hope.

So this child who was sent too soon into the world is placed in an incubator, and continues to grow and to mature. It is almost as though he were still in his mother's womb. The incubator in which he is kept alive is a mechanical thing, but it is a kind of motherly care—one step removed. Only in a civilization which values the life of every human being could it have been contrived. [12]

---

[11] See studies by Rogers, Lilienfeld, and Pasamanick (1956); Bibace, Caplan, Hughes, and Rabinovitch (1958); and Dunham (1955).

[12] The care shown for a premature child, and usually for newborn children in general, is inspiring. Yet it is depressing to note that human beings whose sympathies are so readily aroused by the obvious physical helplessness of an infant often are quite impervious to the less obvious signs of psychological helplessness in the same child when he is older. Ten years hence, if the tenderly cared for premature child happens, like so many other children, premature and full-term, to be having trouble at home or at school—trouble springing from the fact that he has become frightened, anxious, hostile, or bewildered in the struggle of life—he usually cannot expect the same tenderness he received as a helpless newly born premature child. But if we could see his inner

The premature child's course of development. Being born prematurely does not mean that the child "skips a grade" in his development. If he is born at six months he has the characteristics of a six-month fetus. "He remains faithful to his fetality, even when birth has made him an infant" (Gesell and Amatruda, 1945). However, even though he does not leap into a later phase of development, he is likely to set a faster pace in many aspects of his development, from the time of his birth until the time when he normally would have been born, than the pace set by the child who is spending this same period in his mother's womb. A healthy child who is born six months after conception is likely to be more competent and alert to his environment three months later than a full-term baby who is newly born nine months after conception. However, the full-term baby, three months from the time of his birth (or almost twelve months from the time of conception), is likely to be further advanced in his development than a six-month premature child born at the same date as he.

When age is calculated from time of birth, the average premature child is likely, at the start, to be backward in his development as compared with full-term children. As time passes, the premature child tends to "catch up" (although there are exceptions, especially if the child also suffers from organic defects). Investigators differ in their estimate of when the premature child is likely to have caught up; indeed, the estimates have varied from a matter of months to a matter of several years. Prematurely born children, in common with full-term babies, eventually show an enormous range of individual differences in mental and physical characteristics and in temperament and personality traits.

Some investigators have maintained that certain mannerisms and characteristics are peculiar to prematurely born youngsters during the first years of life and perhaps even later. For example, prematurely born children in one study were found to be relatively more advanced in "personal-social" behavior (smiling, noticing people, and so on) than in motor ability (Shirley, 1938). In another study, prematurely born children proved to be relatively more alert in the use of their senses than in coordinated use of their muscles; they were sensitive to sights, colors, moving objects, and sounds, while remaining somewhat backward in such motor performances as sitting upright or manipulating objects (Shirley, 1939).

Apart from factors in his heredity and prenatal environment there are special factors in the environment after birth that may influence the development of the premature child. Since he begins life even more helpless than the normal child, he must have extra care and attention. His parents may be overanxious at first, and look even more eagerly than other parents

---

personality, we would know that he is now as much in need of tenderness as he was when he was born.

for signs of progress in the child's development. Later, according to Shirley (1938), parents may shift from their policy of shielding the child to one of urging him on, in order to accelerate his development. In this way, the lot of the premature child can be less easy-going and "natural" than that of a baby born at full term.

Learning during
the first days and weeks of life

As soon as a child is born the stage is set for him to begin his career as a learner. How early does this process of learning begin? Probably from the time of birth, if not before.

Mothers sometimes report signs of learning within a week or so after birth when a hungry, crying baby ceases crying as soon as he is picked up and held in his mother's arms. Previous to this he became quiet only when actually fed. It is as though the child accepts the picking up and holding as a signal of feeding. If the child thus responds to a signal, where previously he actually had to have a sip, it seems that he has "learned." However, observations such as these do not necessarily prove that learning has taken place. The experience of being picked up and held would probably at the later age have a quieting effect in itself, even if it was not previously associated with the experience of being fed. The evidence of learning becomes more convincing if the child resumes his crying more vigorously than ever, if there is a longer than usual delay between the time when he is picked up and the moment he is fed.

Many interesting studies have dealt with the subject of learning in early infancy. Some of these have raised the question—is it possible for a child during the first days of life to acquire a "conditioned" response? In one experiment (Marquis, 1931), eight infants were bottle-fed from the time of birth, and at each feeding a buzzer was sounded. After three to six days, seven of the eight infants showed feeding activities, such as an increase in sucking and mouth-opening, a lessening of general activity and crying, in response to the buzzer alone. Since an infant's response to any sort of stimulus may be quite generalized, some of these effects might possibly have occurred even if feeding had not been used as a "conditioning" stimulus.

A clearer picture emerges in a study (Kantrow, 1937) of sixteen infants whose ages when the experiment first began ranged from one month and fourteen days to three months and twenty-seven days. In this study a buzzer was sounded for five seconds, and then continued to sound during fifteen additional seconds as the nipple of a milk bottle was inserted in the infant's mouth and the infant proceeded to feed. Here it was found that sucking in response to the buzzer alone was established in from three to nine feedings (during the course of which the buzzer and the bottle had been presented together from sixteen to fifty-three times).

An interesting feature of the findings was that the infants would give the sucking response to the buzzer when they were hungry but not when they were sated. Even though a connection had been established between sucking and the buzzer, it required the motive of hunger to call it forth.

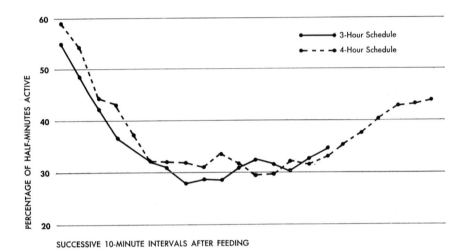

FIGURE 1 *Comparison of activity between feedings of babies fed on a three-hour and a four-hour schedule. Average of all subjects, days 2-8. Figs. 1 and 2 are adapted by permission from D. P. Marquis, "Learning in the Neonate: The Modification of Behavior Under Three Feeding Schedules." Journal of Experimental Psychology, 1941, 29, 270 and 273.*

Apparently, the infants used what they had learned only when there was good use for it. In addition, it was found that the conditioned response to the buzzer disappeared when, in a second part of the experiment, the buzzer was sounded repeatedly without the accompaniment of feeding after the infants were partially sated. While still less than four months old, these infants were thus demonstrating "intelligent" behavior in two ways: (1) They learned to respond to significant signals (buzzing as a signal of food) and, (2) they learned to discard false signals (buzzing that no longer betokened food). [13]

Another approach to this problem was made in an investigation of whether infants adapt to (that is, "learn") a feeding schedule within the first ten days of life (Marquis, 1941). A record was obtained of the gen-

___

[13] See also Wenger (1936), and Wickens and Wickens (1940).

eral bodily activity of sixteen babies who were fed on a three-hour schedule until they were eight days old and then, on the ninth day, changed to a four-hour schedule. A record was also made of the activity of another group of newborns who were on a four-hour schedule, and of a third group fed on a self-demand schedule, that is, fed whenever they seemed hungry. Activity was recorded mechanically by a device that supported the bassinets in which the infants lay.

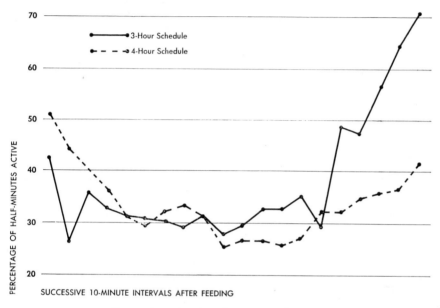

FIGURE 2 *Comparison of activity between feedings of babies on a four-hour schedule and babies previously fed on a three-hour schedule but now changed to a four-hour schedule. Average of forenoon and afternoon periods for all subjects on Day 9.*

Figure 1 gives a picture of the activity of the three-hour and four-hour groups during selected between-feeding periods from the second through the eighth day. Both groups show a falling off in activity after a feeding, as though the infants were gradually settling down. At the end of three hours, the three-hour group is relatively quiet, while the four-hour infants thereafter show a rising rate of activity. Contrast this with the curves in Figure 2, which shows what happened when the three-hour group was put on a four-hour schedule. At the end of the third hour, when they usually had been fed, the activity of these infants increased abruptly, and by the end of the fourth hour it reached a level higher than at any previous time. It also quite exceeded the level shown by the children who had been fed on a four-hour schedule from the beginning.

Birth and Early Infancy

This high level of activity was frequently accompanied by crying. Moreover, the increased rate of activity continued even after the infants had been fed. It might have been expected that the infants, when changed from a three-hour to a four-hour schedule, would have become so fatigued by the excess activity during the extra hour's wait that they would settle down after at last having been fed and would go to sleep sooner than before. Instead, the opposite occurred. During the periods following the shift to a four-hour schedule the infants continued to be more active than usual and again, at the end of three hours, there was an abrupt rise in activity.

These observations indicate that the infants on the three-hour schedule had "learned" to expect food at the end of three hours. Their vigorous reaction when this expectation was denied is vividly shown in Figure 2.

In this same study, there was evidence, although not unmistakable, that the infants on a four-hour schedule were "learning" to wait four hours. As we have seen, they showed an increase in activity between the third and fourth hours; but as the days went on, this activity tended to lessen rather than to increase.

During the period of the study the infants who were on a self-demand schedule appeared to be hungry and were fed approximately every three hours on the average. In other words, while other infants of the same age sought food about every three hours, the four-hour babies seemed to be on the way toward accepting the four-hour schedule. Already the "four-hour" babies were adapting themselves to a mode of life (as far as feeding was concerned), even though this did not conform to what many of them would have chosen for themselves. Thus during the first days of life, a child reveals a resiliency, a capacity to adapt to what the environment demands or affords. As time goes on he will continue to show this capacity as he adapts to countless demands, whether these be arbitrary or inevitable, wise or foolish. However, as we shall see in later chapters, there are limits beyond which a child cannot be pushed, and there are demands he is unable to sustain.

Personal and social aspects of development in infancy

The healthy newborn child quickly plunges into development tasks that lie before him. As time goes on, there is a fascinating interaction between abilities belonging to various spheres of his development. His use of his mind depends in important ways on the development of his muscles; some of his most notable feats as an individual are linked to his social relationships with others; and his growing intellectual and physical attainments are interwoven with his emotions, ranging from delight to anger and from a passionate kind of seeking to timidity and fear.

Each person who observes the development of an infant is impressed in his own way by what he sees. In the writer's opinion, there are some features of early growth that are especially impressive. The early evidence of the child's individuality, referred to earlier in this book, is one of these features. Very soon after birth, the baby may be recognized as not just another baby but as a child with distinct characteristics of his own.

Another and even more noteworthy feature is the fact that, very early in life, all healthy infants show a remarkable range of responsiveness to people and things. It is impressive to observe how rich are the resources of an infant's humanity when he is only a few weeks old. Long before he is able to creep or walk or talk an infant takes notice, explores, distinguishes between people, actively communicates with others, expresses many nuances of feeling. In their reactions to adults infants usually show far more "positive" than "negative" behavior (Bühler, 1930). In a study of sixteen infants who lived in an institution and who were given a series of tests at weekly intervals for eight weeks, beginning when they were about six months old, Rheingold (1956) kept a record of "negative" responses—such as frowning, or a worried look, whimpering, crying, turning the head away, rolling or crawling away from the adult, and of "positive" responses—such as smiling, laughing, and rolling or reaching toward the adult. In their response to a total of 527 social contacts the infants reacted negatively in only 65 instances. Even some of these were debatable, for in many instances an infant would show the "negative" response of rolling away from the experimenter but would also smile and laugh and promptly roll back.

A third outstanding characteristic is that the infant's mental abilities in many respects develop more swiftly than his physical abilities. The reach of his senses goes far beyond the reach of his body. He follows the activities of members of his family even though he cannot join in these activities. Judging from the way he pays attention and addresses himself to things in his surroundings, he seems to have many intentions before he is able to carry them out. Gesell and Ilg (1943) say, in speaking of a sixteen-week-old infant, "It is interesting to note that he can 'pick up' a small object with his eyes long before he can pick it up with his fingers!"

POSTURAL CONTROL, USE OF EYES AND HANDS

For a time after birth a baby continues to assume the curled-up posture of the fetus. When he is lifted, his head—large in proportion to the rest of his body—will sag if not supported. At about the age of three weeks, while lying on his stomach, he is able to lift his head and raise his chin clear of the surface which supports him. During ensuing weeks, he develops further postural control, including the ability to hold his head erect, to balance and turn it, and to sit without support. As the child gains increasing mastery over his movements, he is able to exercise other abilities that are developing apace.

Coordinated eye movements in watching and following persons and things. Among the muscle systems that quickly come into service in early infancy are those involved in the use of the eyes. The newborn child responds to light. At the beginning, his eye movements are not well coordinated and his gaze is fleeting, but within a few weeks he becomes able to control the movements of his eyes, and to fix his gaze upon an object.

In a study by Shirley (1933a) of the development of twenty-five babies from birth to two years, the following achievements were shown by 50 per cent or more of the babies as time went on: following a light with the eyes at five days; watching an object one or two times at three weeks; following an object (a tape) moved in a horizontal direction at five weeks, and in a vertical direction at nine weeks.

On the basis of her observations, Shirley concludes that by the time he is two, a child can probably see with his naked eye anything that an adult can see. He will, of course, see things from a different angle and fail to notice many things that an adult would notice, such as the words on a printed page.

Gazing and smiling. Many examples of the interplay between physical and other aspects of development appear in connection with the muscular control of eye movements. In Shirley's study, smiling at a person is recorded both as a feature of the development of eye coordination and as a feature in the sequence of *social* development. Smiling at a person appeared at about eight weeks. Shirley comments that smiling is definitely more than an eye reaction, "but the visual element certainly plays a part in it." It differs from just watching an object or person, for when an infant is smiling at a person his gaze is definitely focused on the face.

Watching and exploring. Eye coordination likewise comes into play in various later aspects of *intellectual* development—for example, when the child actively explores his environment with his eyes or, in searching for an object that was in view and now is out of sight, shows that he retains (or "remembers") an earlier impression.

Reaching and manipulation. The infant is actively taking a hand in the affairs of the world about him when he is able to reach out, grasp, and manipulate things. At first, as we have noted, the reach of the eye seems to surpass the reach of the hand. Reaching or waving in the direction of objects appears earlier than a deliberate effort to lay hold of them. As time passes, the infant reaches, touches, and momentarily grasps objects. In the process, he is likely at times to catch hold of one hand with the other, and play with his own hands and fingers.

The infant's ability to grasp, with seeming intent, develops before he is adept at letting go, but he has taken quite a step when he seems to realize that it is he who can make an object move, that he can grasp it, handle it, release it, and pick it up again. He is now producing an effect, asserting a kind of mastery over things. This ability to manipulate things involves a coordinated use of eye and hand, which is greatly improved when he is able not only to grasp by curling his fingers around an object but also by opposing his thumb to the rest of his fingers, using his hand as though it were a sensitive pincer.

The babies in Shirley's study made tentative reaching movements at a median age of seven weeks and attained thumb opposition at fifteen weeks. In the ensuing weeks and months many other skills emerged, such as grasping a dangling object, ringing a bell, and opening a box. With such movements at his command, even though they may be imperfect at the start, the child is able to explore the heft and feel of things, to bring objects to his mouth, to shift objects from hand to hand, to fit them into open spaces, and to pile one object upon another.

In connection with the development of his ability to manipulate things, the infant spontaneously throws himself into a great amount of activity as he grasps, snatches, scratches, pounds, pulls things apart, tries to put them together, knocks them down, and piles them up again.

Other signs of mental activity.   During the first year of life, and increasingly during the second year and later, there are countless further signs of mental activity. Before the end of the first year, the child makes searching movements for objects that have fallen or that have been laid away by an adult—as if these objects, though out of sight, are not "out of mind." Before the end of the first year, many children seem able to anticipate, to pretend an action, as when a youngster makes a display of intending to grab a toy or other object and then stops his action mid-way, laughing as he does so.

Evidences of mental activity appear conspicuously in the child's language development many months before he speaks his "first word." The youngster calls to attract attention. He "talks," using many inflections of speech before he is able to put his talk into recognizable words. In Shirley's study, speech became a social reaction sometime between the second and sixth month. The child usually comprehends the meaning of many words before he can use them: When asked "Where is Mama?" he turns and looks at her before he can begin to phrase the answer.

Rudimentary experiences with the sequence of cause and effect. When an infant puts things in motion, as though deliberately intending to do so, he produces a sequence of cause and effect. He has many other experiences in which he is, in a sense, a cause producing an effect, such as when he cries and his mother comes, when he points to an object, as though desiring it, and someone gives it to him.

Many such experiences occur long before he can clearly formulate the idea of cause and effect and express this idea in words. Some investigators have stated that the child is several years old before he understands the concept of cause and effect. Certainly, by comparison with an adult's abstract thinking, a young child is not a sharp logician. However, we cannot judge the child's rudimentary notions about cause and effect by testing him solely according to the logic of an adult mind. As far as possible, we must observe how he operates within his own world if we wish to conjecture about the nature of his earliest thoughts. From this point of view, it is apparent that a child, at an early age, is quite a "thinker" in his own way.

Response to people. When only a few weeks old, the infant follows others with his eyes. As stated by Bühler (1930), "In the second month the glance of the child allows itself to be enticed by the glance of the grown-up—one can observe a slight quiver of genuine smiling in response to the voice and glance of the human being." The infant returns the glance, turns his head and body and stretches out his hands toward the grown-up. Many children, through their behavior, give signs of "recognizing" their fathers and mothers when only ten or eleven weeks old, or even younger (Shirley). At a median age of fourteen weeks the children in Shirley's study seemed to notice the difference between strangers and their own kinfolk.

The infant's emotions. In the emotional sphere, as in others, the infant undergoes rapid change. At birth, most of his emotional reactions occurred as a rather general form of excitement. Within a few weeks, his emotional behavior becomes more differentiated; many nuances are added; and the range of conditions that affect him is greatly increased. According to Gesell (1928), a child at one month gives different cries for hunger, pain, and discomfort. He also shows signs of active displeasure, and "displeased astonishment" (1930), at about this time. At two months, Bühler detected evidence of "function pleasure"—pleasure in carrying out an activity. At about two or three months, the child expresses what appears to be delight and pleasure through his smiles and the sounds he makes (Bühler, 1930, Gesell, 1928). When about four months old, many children laugh loudly when played with. In the meantime, also, the youngster gives many signs of anger and fear.

The fact that the child when only a few weeks old is responding actively to others, and continues to do so in an increasing variety of ways and with many emotional undertones as he develops from month to month, has important implications when we seek to piece together the meaning, to him, of his experiences during early childhood. In his social and emotional behavior the normal infant, while yet very young, shows a high degree of sensitivity to other people. He is eager, responsive to their actions, he shows delight, fear, anger, and disappointment. This sensitivity does not necessarily mean that we must regard him as an especially fragile creature, completely at the mercy of the passing whims and moods of those who have him in their care. But it does help us to understand some of the current theories with regard to how a child might be affected by his dealings with others early in his life—the effect, for example, of being warmly accepted or rejected and ignored; the effect of being separated from his mother and placed in unfamiliar hands; the effect of living in an institution where he receives little individual attention.

Recommended Readings

Leonard Carmichael's "The Onset and Early Development of Behavior" (1954) gives a detailed review of findings in studies of development during the embryonic and fetal stages of growth. Karl C. Pratt's "The Neonate" (1954) discusses the behavior of the newborn child. Revealing accounts of the development of behavior after birth and the emergence of distinct individual characteristics in babies can be found in the following books written a number of years ago (which probably can be found in many libraries): Charlotte Bühler, *The First Year of Life* (1930); W. Preyer, *The Mind of the Child* (1888); Arnold Gesell and Helen Thompson, *Infant Behavior* (1934); Mary M. Shirley, *The First Two Years*, Volumes I-III (1933). A more recent account is Dorothy Burlingham's *Twins: A Study of Three Pairs of Identical Twins* (1952).

Everyday Needs
and Demands
in Early Childhood

CHAPTER   FOUR   This chapter deals with developments during early childhood that play an important role in the practical day-to-day relationships between the child and the adults who care for him. We will discuss feeding, sleeping, elimination, and the beginnings of sexual behavior.

Psychological meanings of physical care

The child's bodily contacts with his mother and others who care for him, when counted one by one, run into the tens of thousands. To pick up an infant, to hold him, feed him, bathe him, and play with him mean far more than just physical manipulation: In connection with each event of this sort there is a communication between the adult and the child, and an interpersonal relationship is established.

EMOTIONAL INTIMACY

The adult brings to these interpersonal relationships his own emotions, moods, and mannerisms. Physical contact is the surest means of attaining emotional intimacy with a child, provided the adult has the capacity for it.

Many, and perhaps most, of the experiences that occur in the child's contacts with people early in life are infused with feeling. The child has much at stake. He is desperately hungry, for example, even though he was well fed only a few hours before. Emotion is bound to come into play when something for which he is so eager is supplied or withheld. Again, he is lying in an uncomfortable position, or a pin bothers him, or he is wet and fidgety; relief from any discomfort is pleasant. Even if all his physical needs are cared for, he is pleased to have company and disappointed when the company leaves him (provided he's alert and in the mood). Meanwhile, many of the child's own undertakings are accompanied by eagerness or annoyance and an obbligato of sounds with emotional overtones as he cries, coos, trills, smiles, gurgles, yawns, sighs, and belches.

LINES OF COMMUNICATION

It is frequently easy to see that an adult is communicating something from within himself in his dealings with children, especially the older ones. What the adult says or does may clearly show that he has a human touch or that he is unsure of himself, or is plodding through his job in a mechanical way. But what about the subtler interchanges that take place, especially when the baby is quite young? An interesting theory relating to this question has been proposed by Harry Stack Sullivan (1947, 1953).

According to Sullivan, there is a kind of emotional linkage, involving emotional contagion or communion, between the baby and other significant people (the mother or the nurse). Sullivan calls this emotional linkage *empathy*. He maintains that communication exists between the child and the significant adult through empathy before the child is mature enough to perceive overt expressions of emotion, such as smiling, pallor, or a "worried" look.

In discussing the kind of communication that takes place between the mother and the child, Sullivan states that if the mother hated the pregnancy, and deplores the child, "it is pediatric commonplace that there are feeding difficulties" with the child. Likewise, according to this theory, if a mother who is otherwise deeply attached to the infant is seriously disturbed or worried by something at the time of nursing, the infant will have indigestion or some other kind of feeding difficulty.

Sullivan says there are indications that empathy endures throughout life, at least in some people. But he assumes that the time of its greatest importance is in later infancy and early childhood—perhaps from the age of six months to twenty-seven months.

This concept of a kind of emotional communication between an adult and an infant through signs and symbols different from those older people usually notice touches upon an area in which there has been much speculation but little systematic research. There are studies which indicate that babies in the care of mothers who are obviously anxious cry more than the babies of mothers who are not so obviously anxious. Such studies support the view that a mother's emotional state affects her child. However, to make a conclusive test it would be necessary not only to study the characteristics of mothers but also of children, since some babies are more serene or cry more than others no matter who is caring for them. The idea that there are subtle communications between babies and adults squares with what can be observed in everyday life when it appears that babies are definitely more fretful or at ease with some people than with others. Hospital workers have maintained, for example, that there are some nurses who seem to have a soothing effect on babies, while the same babies tend to fuss and cry when in the care of other nurses on the ward. The actions of a nurse who likes children and welcomes them into her arms may vary from those of another well-trained nurse in ways that make a difference to a baby even though these actions are too subtle to be measured.

CHILD CARE AND THE PROCESS OF SELF-DISCOVERY

To the extent that the practices a person uses with children are an expression of his own inner tendencies, he has something of a reflection of himself in his dealings with children. If he has the courage to look and the insight to see, he may be able to learn something profoundly significant about himself.

In order to see themselves as reflected in their relationships with their children most parents probably could profit from the help of friendly and perceptive counselors. The value of such help was noted in an outstanding long-term study of problems faced by a group of mothers in rearing their children, by MacFarlane, Allen, and Honzik (1954). They cite findings which indicate that the mother's "self-assurance and poise" or the lack of these are important, supporting "the conviction of the clinic staff that major benefits accrued to young children when the mothers were helped to be more understanding and at ease with themselves so that they were freer to handle wisely the rearing of their children." The idea of understanding, of being at ease with oneself, of having a kind of inner freedom, places the emphasis on the *parent as a person,* and underscores the position that self-knowledge and a healthy attitude of self-acceptance are more basic to the parent's role than a set of practical rules or an intellectual notion as to whether a parent should be strict or lenient, permissive or authoritarian.

Everyday activities and everyday care

Obtaining food and rest and eliminating waste are essential to the welfare of the child, and parents usually keep close watch over these worthy occupations.

The young infant spends a large part of his time sleeping. When he reaches school age he still sleeps about half of every twenty-four hours. By the time he is eighteen and for the rest of his life he devotes about one-third of his time to sleep. In the meantime, his sleeping habits have received a good deal of attention, first from his parents and later from himself.

Even more demanding of attention during early infancy are the functions involved in getting nourishment and eliminating waste. The child makes periodic demands for food. He frequently voids his bladder and bowels. In due time, this natural flow of events is drastically changed. Where before, the child had only to suck for a living, he now has to chew and take a more active part in the feeding process, and even when he is very young his eating becomes regimented in countless ways. The processes of elimination, completely involuntary at the start, are also brought under control, often with considerable prompting from the child's parents. Much of the youngster's earliest education revolves around activities connected with feeding, sleeping, and other "routines"; by way of these activities he is first introduced to many of the demands and taboos of the society in which he lives.

Feeding and
behavior associated with feeding

We might expect that establishing good feeding habits would be the easiest feature of a child's training, for the drive to obtain nourishment is one of the strongest drives in living creatures. However, children's feeding behavior often gives a good deal of trouble. The more a child's diet and eating routines can be based on natural wants rather than on a conglomeration of rules and formulas, the smoother the road is likely to be. Likewise, the more nearly changing demands (such as the introduction of solids, weaning, the use of skills involved in handling cups and other utensils), can be scaled to the child's growing capacities, the better the outcome is likely to be.

SUCKING

In the newborn child the impulse to suckle usually is strong enough to enable the child to take food if he is given the breast or the bottle. Some babies need help to begin the process, but sucking is something most infants can do very well. As Feldman (1920) has pointed out, the mechanism involved in sucking is well protected against physical damage. The so-called suction cushion in each cheek, composed of a pad of fat, can be found even in very emaciated babies when fat has disappeared from other parts of the body.

The newborn's suckling and swallowing movements are closely merged, so that unswallowed milk runs out of his mouth when he releases the nipple. During the act of nursing, he swallows a good deal of air, and feeding must then be interrupted so that he may belch. This ritual is sometimes referred to as "burping the baby." As the child grows older and becomes more proficient at nursing, he swallows less air and his need for belching diminishes.

SUCKING ACTIVITIES APART FROM FOOD GETTING

Although sucking and mouthing are important for food getting, these activities come into use apart from the process of feeding at an early age. The baby sucks, even though his appetite for food is sated. Many babies do a certain amount of sucking, apart from nursing, from birth. The act may be most prominent when the child is hungry or immediately after he has been fed. A case has even been reported of an infant who apparently had sucked his thumb before he was born (Gesell and Ilg, 1937). The baby's thumb was swollen on delivery, and soon after the birth cry he placed the swollen thumb in his mouth.

All babies are likely to suck their fists, fingers, or thumbs at some time during infancy and early childhood, especially during teething—but this is not the only occasion. A child may cease to suck for a time and then do so again more vigorously than before. Many children, as is well known, continue the finger or thumb-sucking habit for several years. And many adults also have sucking, biting, and mouthing habits. For instance, we see one who, like a beaver, gnaws at pencils; one who is a lip biter; another one who sucks on a dry pipe; and still another whose tongue and lips fondly caress a juicy cigar.

Adults are often disturbed by a child's thumb-sucking for they think there is something unbecoming about it, and some worry about the possibility that such sucking, if continued, will cause the jaw to be malformed and produce a fine set of buck teeth.[1] There is an interesting sex difference in thumb-sucking: in several studies it has been noted that girls do more thumb-sucking than boys (Honzik, 1959).

Many theories have been proposed to account for finger sucking. The most obvious, of course, is that the child sucks his fingers because he wants to, but there are other more learned theories.

SUCKING AS A RESPONSE TO AN ORAL DRIVE

One view is that the child sucks his thumb or fingers because his need for exercise of the sucking mechanism is not completely satisfied in the process of sucking to obtain food (Levy, 1937). According to this theory, a bottle-fed child is more likely to continue to suck if the nipple hole is large, permitting the milk to flow freely, than if the aperture is small and the child must work harder and longer to obtain the same amount of milk.

By way of analogy, Levy gives the example, familiar to one who has been raised on a farm, of the behavior of young calves. A dairy calf who is not allowed to suckle his mother but is taught from the start to feed from a pail is likely, for some time after his first feedings, to suck an accommodating finger or the ear or tail of another calf or any other object that is handy. Such sucking may be inspired by the fact that the pail-fed calf probably gets smaller rations than a calf who has a whole cow as a source of supply. At any rate, the pail-fed calf continues to suck when even he must realize there is not much nourishment in it. (Technically this is known as "non-nutritive sucking.") Such sucking by the calf seems to correspond, at least in some respects, to thumb sucking in the child, although the child's sucking is likely to last longer and to be influenced by many psychological factors that do not bother the average calf.

Lack of sufficient sucking exercise in connection with food getting probably accounts for some finger-sucking but this theory alone cannot account for all finger-sucking in childhood (Blau and Blau, 1955). Some children suck their fingers even though they are allowed to nurse at their mother's breast as much as they seem to want (Simsarian, 1948).

SUCKING AS A PLEASURABLE ADJUNCT
TO THE DRIVE FOR FOOD

The situation in which sucking occurs—the alleviation of hunger—is one of the earliest and most profound satisfactions in a child's life. When a

---

[1] Many children who suck persistently for extended periods and then drop the habit show no harmful dental defects. Moreover, in some cases where malformation has taken place, it appears that the deformity may be corrected in the process of growth after the sucking is stopped. Apparently, the chances of malformation are greater if the practice is continued vigorously after the child has his secondary teeth (Lewis, 1937) and if a child already has a poor bite (Sillman, 1951).

child goes through the motions of sucking, the reason may be that it has become pleasurable in itself by virtue of being originally a part of a pleasurable situation.

EXPLORATORY FUNCTIONS
OF MOUTH AND LIPS IN EARLY LIFE

The child's use of tongue, lips, and mouth play a very important part in his early ventures in life, representing not simply a means of food getting, or (if we accept the theory) a kind of striving for sensuous pleasure, but a means through which the child expresses himself and explores the world in which he lives. In this respect a young child's lips, tongue, and mouth serve much the same function as his eyes and ears. When we interfere with the child's oral activities we are depriving him, to some degree, as we would deprive him with blinders on his eyes or sound-plugs in his ears.

Even after a child has become alert to sights and sounds he continues for a long time to use his mouth and lips to investigate the world about him. Once he is able to grasp objects with his hands, there is a period when he tries to carry almost everything to his mouth. The infant explores contours and surfaces, tests the taste, temperature, hardness, and softness of things with his lips and teeth. This exploration may include cramming a block into his mouth, and mouthing balls of lint, bits of earth, crayons, and even morsels of food that he discovers on the floor (after he has refused what remains on his plate).

SUCKING AND MOUTHING AS RELATED TO SEXUALITY

According to Freud (1938b) stimulation of the inner membranes of the mouth brought about by sucking and mouthing yields a kind of sensuous pleasure related to the pleasurable sensations arising from stimulation of the genital organs. Satisfactions connected with stimulation in the mouth region (oral satisfactions), described from this point of view, are a feature of the child's sexuality. When a child is preoccupied with such satisfactions he is said to be manifesting a kind of *oral eroticism,* and the period of his preoccupation has been called an *oral* phase or stage of sexual development. (It has similarly been proposed that children go through an *anal* and a *urethral* phase in the development of sexuality during which they are absorbed by sensuous experiences associated with stimulation of the tissues of the anus and urethra.) According to this same theory of sexuality, the focal point of erotic stimulation in a later and more mature phase is mainly in the genital area. Also according to this theory, the child's progress from one phase of development to the next may become distorted if his natural interests are severely interfered with and if he is subjected to abuse during the oral and anal phases of his development. The frustration may lead to emotional complications and give rise to character traits which carry over into later years. According to Fenichel (1945), the deprivation of oral satisfaction, caused by early weaning, may create a craving for such satisfaction, resulting in a pessimistic or sadistic character. On the other hand, late weaning, which denotes fuller and longer satisfaction of oral drives, results in self-assurance and optimism (Fenichel, 1945).

Actually, the accumulated research data do not support anything so simple and categorical as this. It has not been established, for example, that the earlier the weaning occurs the greater will be the evidence of a drive to meet unfulfilled needs for oral satisfaction. As a matter of fact, there is some evidence that the child's desire for oral activity, rather than diminishing, increases the longer he is allowed to go unweaned and suck freely at the bottle or breast during the first year or so (Sears and Wise, 1950).[2]

How important are these views for understanding the young? In the writer's judgment, there are three answers. First, references to the *anal* and *oral,* to *oral* and *anal* eroticism, and to *oral* deprivation appear in writings about children so frequently that we need to be acquainted with these terms. Secondly, whether sucking and mouthing have an erotic or sexual significance depends on our definition of sexuality. If we wish we can define sexuality so broadly that it includes these oral activities.

Third, and the main consideration: anything that commands the child's attention and absorbs his energies to the extent that oral activities do must be viewed as important in the economy of his life, whether or not these oral activities are related to sexual development. When we use punishment or other harsh measures against these activities, we are punishing something in the child. We are rejecting *him,* in a sense, and that is a larger consideration than whether in the process we are interfering with his sexual interests.

Observations by Newton (1951) suggest that breast feeding or a flexible or rigid handling of the feeding schedule are not *per se* the important factors; the mother's attitude toward the child as expressed in the total feeding situation is more important than any one isolated factor in the manner of feeding. Similar overt procedures in feeding can have psychologically different meanings, depending on the attitude of the mother.

---

[2] Orlansky (1949) has reviewed theories and findings dealing with this subject up to about the year 1949. In a study by Sewall and Mussen (1952), in which information was obtained from mothers and personality tests were administered to children, the results did not show a significant relationship between abrupt or gradual weaning and personality adjustment. In another study (Thurston and Mussen, 1951), questionnaires and the Thematic Apperception Test (described in Chapter Fifteen) were used with college students to explore the relationship between early oral gratification and later traits. The results were conflicting and no clear relationship was found.

Everyday Needs and Demands   **71**

CHEWING

Biting is usually not noted until about the fourth month, although it may appear considerably earlier. Gesell and Ilg (1937) observe that occasionally children even at the time of birth show "surprising strength of bite," and they add that "this strength is not only unseasonable but unsuitable to normal sucking." Likewise, chewing movements may appear even before a child has any teeth and may precede by a considerable time the actual chewing of food.

Many children go through the motions of chewing before they have a practical need for it in feeding. They "chew" on milk, applesauce, puréed vegetables, and the like, as though they were practising for the future. This is another illustration of the developmental principle of anticipation as set forth in Chapter Two.

SPONTANEOUS FOOD DEMANDS

To what extent can a healthy child's demands be trusted as a guide for determining when, what, and how much he should be fed? This is a significant question, for if a child's appetite for food is trustworthy, both he and his parents could be spared much trouble.

When babies are placed on a "self-demand" breast or bottle feeding schedule (fed whenever and as much as they want), there are fluctuations in the number of feedings they demand per day and yet also a considerable degree of consistency. In one study (Simsarian and McLendon, 1942) it was found that in the interval between the second and the tenth day of life there was one day when a child demanded to be fed only six times and another day when the same child demanded eleven feedings. However, there were five days out of nine when the baby demanded nine feedings. This study and others suggest that if a fixed rather than a self-demand schedule is used immediately after a child is born it probably is better to feed him approximately every three hours than to use a four-hour schedule.

A further observation has been that as the infant grows older he reduces of his own accord the number of feedings demanded per day.

Still another observation is that the amount of food intake varies widely from day to day and from feeding to feeding. A child might, on one occasion, demand a large meal and on another, when his mother expects that he will be quite hungry, take only a sip. But in his day-to-day and week-to-week demands there is likely to be a larger pattern of consistency if the baby is in good health.

The findings in these studies also indicate that infants seem to be well nourished when on a feeding schedule geared to their own demands.

There has been no evidence that any of the infants who were so fed suffered any ill effects. Some mothers maintain that the self-demand schedule is, if anything, psychologically more satisfying both to the infant and to the mother than is a fixed schedule.

The systematic findings bearing upon this problem in early infancy are limited but it is interesting to note that those available are in agreement on the main points mentioned above.[3]

Self-selection of formulas in early infancy. Infants have shown a wisdom and logic of their own, not only when allowed to choose when and how much they should eat, but also when given a choice of food.

In one experiment (Davis, 1935) three infants, beginning at or before the tenth day of life, were offered, in rotation, four different formulas at each feeding and were permitted to take as much of each as they wished. The children showed unmistakable preferences almost from the beginning. As the children grew older (the experiment was continued until they were about eight months old), they would sometimes reject the bottle with the unfavored formula without even tasting it—apparently responding to odor, appearance, or some other cue. There were large differences among the babies in patterns of choice. At the end of the experiment the nutritional status of the infants was reported to be "excellent in every way."

Spontaneous food selection and consumption in later infancy. When a child's diet includes solids, his feeding increasingly involves questions of what he should be fed as well as when and how much. To what extent can a child now be trusted to make good choices?

Davis (1928, 1933) observed children who were free to select their own diets. The children had several choices at each meal, but all the items in the total menu were not presented at any single meal. At a particular feeding, a tray consisting of twelve items (selected from a list of thirty which were variously combined at different meals) was placed before each child. It included, among other things, whole milk and lactic milk, raw and cooked meat, raw and cooked vegetables. Each child was free to choose; food was not offered to him or suggested; a nurse sat nearby and helped the child to get what he wanted, as he indicated his wants by pointing, and in other ways. So far as they desired or were able, the children were permitted to feed themselves by means of their fingers and to wield their own spoons.

There were wide variations in the self-selected menus of the same child from time to time and in the menus selected by different children. The

---

[3] Other studies of infants on self-demand schedules have been reported by Gesell and Ilg (1937), Trainham *et al.* (1945), Simsarian (1948), and Simsarian and McLendon (1945).

selections often were thoroughly unorthodox and sometimes startling from an adult's point of view. But physical examinations and measurements seemed to show that the children made wholesome choices and thrived.

When the experiment was begun—with three newly weaned infants who had had no experience with solid foods—each infant at first chose some foods which he spat out. After the first few meals, however, the infants chose foods promptly without regard to their position on the tray, and there was no more spitting out. A youngster would often select a bizarre diet, including as many as seven eggs at a single sitting (in another series of observations, a two-and-a-half-year-old ate ten eggs at one meal!), or as many as four bananas. Salt was taken only occasionally, and then often the infant would splutter, choke, and even cry, but would keep it in his mouth and swallow it.

The infants frequently ate certain foods in waves: After eating moderate amounts of fruits, eggs, or cereal, there would be a period when larger and sometimes "astonishingly large" amounts were eaten, followed by a decline to the previous level. Symptoms of overeating did not appear in connection with such "jags," nor were they followed by periods of disgust. The children were omnivorous, and their preferences were unpredictable. They showed no consistent preferences for cooked or raw food, but some items were definitely preferred cooked and others raw. Dunking of hard crackers in milk or water was observed, especially at periods when a new tooth was erupting. The infants tended to take their foods "straight" rather than to mix foods or even to pour milk over cereals. One infant who had active rickets when the study began spontaneously consumed large quantities of cod-liver oil, and then later left it untouched when this active condition had been overcome, as revealed by blood tests and X-ray examinations.

In another study, Davis (1931) reports observations made of fourteen children in a hospital ward, each of whom selected his own diet from the various foods prepared for the day. The findings in this series of observations conformed to those noted above, and the children, for all the vagaries of their appetites, and occasional grotesque selections, seemed to choose wisely as far as could be determined by records of their digestive balance, health, energy, and growth. There was also less food wasted than under the usual system.

The evidence in Davis' study, as well as in other observations, indicates that a young child has more sense about eating what is good for him than he often is credited with, granted that he has wholesome articles of diet from which to choose. A nutritionally balanced diet need not be achieved by an arbitrary package of so much of this and so much of that at every meal.

A self-selection program in the average home would involve many complications and, to be properly safeguarded, would require some knowledge about nutrition (Roberts, 1935). In view of the vast variety of conditions and circumstances that may affect the feeding situation, the findings with regard to self-demand (in timing and amount of feedings) and self-selection (in choice of foods after the child can begin to choose) should not be, and cannot be, adopted too literally or rigidly. The underlying concept in these findings is not that we should substitute one absolute system of control (what is demanded by the child) for another absolute system (what is demanded by the mother). The idea, rather, is to encourage an attitude of respect for a child's needs and wants, and to underscore the point that "mother knows best" only if what she "knows" is determined to a large degree by what she can learn from her child.

SELF-HELP IN EATING

Many of the child's earliest efforts to try out his abilities and to assert himself are expressed as he tries to feed himself with his fingers. At a later phase, some of his sturdiest battles for self-determination are fought with a fork and a spoon.

Gesell and Ilg (1937) have studied many of the steps a child takes in developing the ability to feed himself. They noted a sequence, such as the following, in a child's use of a cup. At twelve weeks, the average child will notice the cup but will be unable to grasp it; his movements are jerky, gross, and lacking in direction. At sixteen weeks the normal child makes contact with the cup; at twenty weeks he makes a "corralling" approach upon the sides of the cup; at twenty-eight weeks he grasps and lifts it, usually with both hands; at thirty-two weeks he grasps the handle; it is not until thirty-six weeks that his manner of lifting the cup in an upturned position, grasping the handle, and mouthing the rim, approximates the true raising of a cup to the lips for drinking purposes. Although he can manipulate the cup at thirty-six weeks, his concept of the cup as a utensil and a receptacle is still in a very rudimentary state, according to Gesell and Ilg. Well-defined self-management of the cup is not observed in the typical child until about sixty-five weeks. He now tilts the cup as it empties, but by means of his palms; later on his fingers will assume the main role in tilting.

The child is likely to do a good deal of finger feeding during the second year, while he is developing ability to use the cup and spoon. Unless he is curbed, his hands and fingers will come into play for a long time thereafter. Use of a blunt fork may be expected at about two to three years, of a blunt knife between the ages of three and five, and of the knife for cutting at about five to six. However, as in other matters, there are wide variations among children.

The period during which a child is learning to handle table utensils is trying for many parents. Even if a parent is not finicky or squeamish, he is likely to become impatient at times with the spilling and messing, the clumsy tipping of food containers, and the child's insistence on doing some things for himself when it is obvious that he cannot succeed. The child has quite a job also; not only must he cope with new skills, but he must often put up a struggle for permission to try them out.

Food preferences

As we have said, children have food preferences at an early age. Factors connected with the food itself can influence these preferences, such as the appearance of the food and its taste, texture, and consistency, or the way it is served (Borgeson, 1938). In some cases there may be an organic aversion to a food, as in allergic conditions. As noted earlier, a child will show shifts in his preferences from time to time. It also has been observed that a child may show dislike for a new article of diet and then spontaneously acquire a liking for it if it is made available from time to time and no effort is made to coerce him.

Often it seems that a child's tendency to like or dislike various foods, his tendency to eat almost anything (or to try any food item at least once), or to be choosy and conservative in what he will eat is not an isolated characteristic. A child who eats everything in sight, eagerly cadging his full share or more, may also be watchful to make sure that he gets his share of other things—gifts, attention from his parents, and so on. A child who tends to be critical of food that is served may be similarly inclined to faultfinding in other ways. In individual cases a child who is finicky about food may also be finicky about his clothes. The conservative child who won't eat an unusual food such as frogs' legs when he has a chance, may also refuse to wear a cap which differs from those his playmates are wearing.

Feeding problems

Many of the so-called "behavior problems" that arise in connection with the rearing of children represent problems of feeding, sleeping, and elimination. In one study (Jersild et al., 1949) in which five hundred parents took part, difficulties with "routine care" constituted the second largest group of problems reported by the parents. Most frequent among the problems under the heading of everyday care were problems of feeding. Second in frequency were problems of sleep; "dress, grooming, personal adornment" stood third in frequency; this was followed by a category containing problems of elimination (most of these had reference to bladder control). Concerns pertaining to feeding are frequently expressed by mothers of young infants when they consult their pediatricians (Blum, 1950).

In the study by Macfarlane and her associates (1954), referred to earlier in this chapter, over half the children in the age range from twenty-one months to six years had varying degrees of "food finickiness," according to their mothers. Fewer children were reported as being finicky in the age range from seven to fourteen years. "Finickiness," denoting an active aversion for many or several specific articles of food, was reported as a problem considerably more often than insufficient appetite for food in general.

In some cases parental concern over a child's feeding behavior is complicated by the fact that children who had voracious appetites at the age of one or two seem to want proportionately less food at the age of three or four. Moreover, as a child grows older he may revise the timing of his food intake. A child who is just beginning to go to school, for example, may take very little breakfast but eat heartily at suppertime. Many children react to the tensions aroused at school by eating light breakfasts.

In dealing with "feeding problems" several considerations must be kept in mind. It is wise first to ask whether there really is a problem. To answer this question it is necessary to take account of the child's level of development. A child of two or three obviously cannot be expected to have the skills and manners of an older child. Further, if the child seems to be finicky about his food, it is well to remember that children differ greatly in the strength of their appetites, their food preferences and food intake. A child's finickiness may be a harmless idiosyncrasy.

If there seems to be a good reason to believe that a feeding problem really exists it is important to inquire into its nature and meaning. Feeding difficulties may be due to physiological factors (such as specific allergies, digestive weaknesses). Or they may spring from psychological factors, and express a variety of concerns in the child's life. If so, the difficulty probably cannot be remedied by efforts aimed simply at correcting specific food habits.

When we ask what the concerns underlying feeding difficulties might be we face the fact that food and the process of eating have many psychological meanings. Food is a symbol of intimacy and sharing. It can be used to satisfy cravings that run deeper than physical hunger. According to observations by Bruch (1947), some persons use food as a means of satisfying needs for security and other yearnings that are unfulfilled. Over-eating and under-eating apparently also at times are symptoms of anxiety.

A child's feeding difficulties may be an expression of anger (as when, for example, he takes revenge by refusing to eat); or of fear (as when, for example, he dreads the thought of going to school and has no appetite for breakfast). A child's feeding problems may also serve as a means by which he asserts himself or calls attention to his needs. Macfarlane and her associates, in the study cited earlier in this chapter, state: "It appears to us that food-finickiness is a pattern in boys associated with the dependence-independence struggle."

Sleeping

In the newborn child, periods of complete wakefulness and periods of complete sleep are considerably briefer than they are later on. As time passes, periods of wakefulness increase in length, especially during the daytime hours, and periods of uninterrupted sleep likewise increase. The total amount of time spent in sleep also diminishes, although with many fluctuations. If placed on an arbitrary schedule of feedings, the child often must be awakened to be fed; sometimes a child will refuse to nurse or take the bottle, or will do so while remaining in a rather sleepy state.

Table 1 shows the average amount of time spent in sleep by a number of children at various age levels from one month to eight years as reported by their parents. The averages are based on results for all seasons combined and are therefore approximate, since the amount of sleep varies with the seasons, being greater in winter and smaller in summer. The table is based on studies by Foster, Goodenough, and Anderson (1928).

TABLE 1 | AVERAGE AMOUNT OF SLEEP PER DAY AT VARIOUS AGE LEVELS *

(The values represent averages for all seasons combined)

Age	Hours	Minutes
1-6 months	15	3
6-12 months	14	9
12-18 months	13	23
1½-2 years	13	6
2-3 years	12	42
3-4 years	12	7
4-5 years	11	43
5-6 years	11	19
6-7 years	11	4
7-8 years	10	58

* From J. C. Foster, F. L. Goodenough, and J. E. Anderson, *The Sleep of Young Children* (Minneapolis: University of Minnesota, Institute of Child Welfare, 1930), Circular No. 4, 11 pp. Reproduced by permission.

The records on which Table 1 is based showed large individual varia-tions at all age levels. Below the age of one year, there was a difference of more than three hours between the 10 per cent of children who slept most and the 10 per cent who slept least. Up to the age of four years, the corresponding difference was more than two hours; from four to eight years, the difference was more than an hour. The differences between individual children at the two extremes were decidedly larger.

It is well to remember that children show wide differences in the amount of sleep they require. A difference of two hours in the sleep needs of two children who get up at the same time in the morning, and who have similar naps, would mean that if one child is put to bed at seven in the evening, the other might stay up until nine. Again, it may mean that a two-year-old, who happens to require less sleep than the average, can get along with less sleep than a four-year-old, who happens to require more than the average. It would be hard to judge just what a child *requires* and just what would be optimum, but the practical importance of recognizing individual differences still remains.

Many difficulties are involved in obtaining measurements of time spent in sleep as a basis for practical recommendations. Even a careful observer will have difficulty in telling whether a child whose eyes are closed actually is asleep.

There is difficulty, too, in determining "natural" sleep needs. A healthy infant, left free to sleep uninterruptedly whenever he wants, does not present a problem on this score; but the problem arises as a child grows older. Some children apparently are prevailed upon to stay in bed longer than is necessary, but it is no simple matter to let the runabout child control his sleep schedule according to his own "natural" demands. Many elements in his environment (such as boisterous play and excitement) may conspire to keep him awake when he normally would become drowsy and to wake him before he becomes "slept out" (such as the bustle of the household in the morning). As children grow older they desire to stay up later in the evening; at the same time, more of them have to be called in the morning. The difficulties of "natural self-regulation" of sleep are even greater in the case of children whose equilibrium is disturbed by mal-nutrition, illness, digestive difficulties, or other bodily disorders. Such disturbances may make a child wakeful even when he badly needs sleep.

Lacking full information about a given child's natural sleep needs, conscientious parents generally feel that the more sleep a child can conveniently get the better it is for him and, usually, the easier it is for them. However, in trying to make sure that the child gets plenty of sleep, parents sometimes invite needless trouble. If they insist that the child go to bed early, they may simply be depriving themselves of sleep—for the earlier the child goes to sleep the earlier he is likely to awaken them in the morning.

Studies of children's sleep demands have yielded certain results that parallel their spontaneous food demands in some respects. Reynolds and Mallay (1933) observed thirty-four children who lived at a nursery school for several weeks during the summer; the children showed wide variations in amount of sleep from day to day. When results were computed in terms of longer periods, however, such as two or three weeks, there was a high degree of constancy in the amount of sleep. This phenomenon, it may be noted, corresponds to children's eating patterns—a child may show wide short-term fluctuations in the times when he is hungry and in the amount of his food intake, and yet show a high degree of stability when trends are measured in terms of weeks rather than hours or days. Also it was observed that if a child lost a good deal of sleep during one day, he did not promptly counterbalance it by sleeping that much more the following day; rather, he made it up over several ensuing days.

Daytime naps. The total amount of sleep during a twenty-four hour span is reduced, even during the first weeks after birth, mainly by cutting the amount of time spent in sleep during the daytime hours. The length of uninterrupted sleep at night increases at the same time. In many children, the early morning nap, which followed a feeding early in the morning, and the late evening nap, which they once took, become merged with nighttime sleep.

An afternoon nap is usually a part of the child's daily schedule at about the age of two. Many children continue during the next year or two to sleep during this period; others become more and more wakeful during part or all of it, but remain in bed: as described by Sherman (1930), "The child learns to stay in bed a certain amount of time." Reynolds and Mallay (1933) found that many children abruptly drop the daytime nap instead of gradually tapering off.

Sleeping, restlessness, and dreaming. "To sleep: perchance, to dream; ay, there's the rub." Macfarlane and associates (1954), in a long-term study of children from twenty-one months to fourteen years old, classified sleep problems under two headings: "restlessness in sleep" and "disturbing dreams." Restlessness (such as tossing and turning, kicking off covers, waking at a slight noise) was most common at the youngest level (38 per cent of the boys and 27 per cent of the girls), less common at three years (18 and 22 per cent), and then diminished further for a time. "Disturbing dreams" ranged from nightmares, with screams of panic, or "terrible dreams" almost every night, to less frequent and less intensely disturbing unpleasant dreams. At all age levels from about two up into the teens a rather sizable proportion of children had disturbing dreams (at twenty-one months 16 per cent of the boys, 13 per cent of the girls;

at age three, 29 and 29 per cent respectively; corresponding percentages from age three and a half through eleven ranged from 20 to 47).

In the lives of most children, sleep comes as a cozy means of rest and renewal of the energies that are needed for waking hours. For them, " . . . the night shall be filled with music, and the cares that infest the day shall fold their tents, like the Arabs, and silently steal away." But for many children (and adults) sleep does not offer this sweet relief. The concerns of the day spill over into the sanctuary of the night. These concerns may cause sleeplessness or come, garbled and distorted, in a dream more stark and more frightening than experiences during the day.

Children's sleep is, of course, affected by anything in their everyday lives that disposes them to be excited or relaxed, tranquil or disturbed. Their sleep is affected by their fears. A child's willingness to go to bed and to slough off his daytime preoccupations may be affected by his ability to make peace with himself and with other members of the household. It is not only the painful or hostile emotions that may make inroads on sleep. An alert, interested child, happy in his surroundings may also try to remain awake as long as he can.

Bedtime as a time of communion. Many children establish quite a bed-going ritual. There may be stories that must be told; songs that must be sung; verses that must be said. The child may need not one but several drinks of water; the shade must be adjusted just so; dolls or other possessions must be settled in the right place; for good measure, the child may demand "a little more scratching." When all this has been done, the parent may be called back for another round on the plea that a detail has been forgotten or that the youngster has a new bit of information to relay or a new question to ask. Some children have a fertile supply of serious ideas requiring discussion just when bedtime arrives. Even though the day is over, and the child (so the parent thinks) should be weary, bedtime can become the most important period of the day.

Tactics such as these, which delay the last goodnight, have many meanings for the child. The child and parent may be most warmly and comfortably responsive to each other at bedtime. If a child is afraid, this ritual may stave off the moment when he will be left to himself. He seeks to assure himself of the companionship and friendliness of his parent. If there are several children in the family, and each is tucked in separately, bedtime may be the only occasion when the child feels he has the parent all to himself. Sometimes confidences are shared, sins are confessed, fears are revealed, pains which have worried the child are described, and much else that has been hidden is brought to light. The older child, who long since has outgrown his crib and who sturdily objects to being babied during the day, may now allow himself to be babied.

After the age of five or six, bedtime provides the main opportunity (and maybe the only opportunity) for some children to communicate intimately with their parents. Children use this time in different ways. One wishes to talk. Another desires a story. One begins to drowse at the end of the bedtime prayer, another at the end of a lullaby. Still another asks, as a final goodnight gesture, that his father or mother get him a snack from the icebox. But the words that are spoken, the details of the ritual are not so important as the feelings they are charged with. [4]

Before falling asleep some children rehearse skills they are currently acquiring. They practise their speech and their ability to carry on a conversation. When they are able to sing and memorize songs, they may go through their repertoire at bedtime.

As a child grows older, especially after learning to read and becoming interested in radio and television programs, he may desire a very different type of bed-going routine. Instead of seeking to prolong the attention he receives from his parents, he may try to discourage it.

Elimination

It would be nice if infants were housebroken at birth. The fact is that bladder and bowel control develops relatively slowly, entailing labor on the parent's part and frequently some emotional complications for the child. To control elimination it is necessary to inhibit processes that are completely involuntary at the start. An infant lacks the nervous mechanism for voluntary control and would be unable to control his urination or bowel movements, even if, by some freak of nature, he had a desire to do so. When training in bladder and bowel control is timed and adapted to the growth pattern, some children require hardly any "training." Unless other complications arise (such as illness, or chronic emotional disturbances), the child is eager, in his own good time, not to wet or soil himself.

PROGRESS IN THE CONTROL OF ELIMINATION

Gesell and Ilg (1937) draw an interesting parallel between control of bladder and bowel and the development of voluntary control of other movements. They point out that a child acquires the power deliberately to release an object held in his hand rather slowly. In early infancy a child is not able, at will, to release his grasp and let go of an object. They further point out that an equivalent control of the tonus of the bladder

---

[4] Many children continue to cherish and recite rituals and lullabies of early childhood long after they put aside other childish things. Even when they are adults, these echoes of childhood may recur when they are deeply moved, filled with gratitude, or about to undertake a solemn task, such as going under ether for a serious operation.

sphincter is in some respects more difficult. So a child's failure to respond to "training" may be due to the fact that his sensorimotor mechanism is immature, and not at all a sign that he is stubborn.

During the first part of the second year, while the mechanism for control of the bladder is being perfected, the child is also establishing postural control, and complications may arise in coordinating the two. Being placed on the toilet seat may produce postural tensions, so that the child withholds his urine and then promptly urinates when removed from the seat.

When a child is approaching the stage of being able to assume voluntary bladder control, he may show this by many signs (McGraw, 1940). He may notice the tinkle, seem to realize that the sound effects originate with him, show interest in puddles, and begin to learn a word or sound for the act of urination. "Even a glint in his eye may reveal his awareness of the act" (although the glint is more likely to be found in the eyes of his parents).

But the first flush of success does not necessarily mean that the triumph is complete. There may be regressions arising from other circumstances that are not connected with the bladder. The child may become so interested in play that he does not want to be diverted. Even if he heeds the call of nature, he may wet himself because he does not allow enough time. He may be so absorbed in trying out his motor skills that he can't be bothered with other things.

A definite statement about when the child may be expected to assume full responsibility in these matters cannot be made because of individual differences in children and because of differences in their training. Some who turn out to be fine citizens do not achieve full control until the age of three or even four or five. The "norms" for bladder control, as reported by different investigators, show much variation.

Daytime control usually precedes nighttime control. A large proportion of children have pretty well acquired the "dry habit" during the day by about the age of two and a half, but it may be another year before the same youngsters are equally in control at night.

After the child has established control, it may be some time before he is capable of self-help in going to the toilet and in managing his clothes. This is especially true if the fixtures and his clothing are not suited to his limited abilities.

Control of the bowel usually is established more readily. In the healthy child, bowel movements are more regular and considerably less frequent; they can be anticipated more accurately and at an earlier age than can voidance of the bladder, and this helps the learning process. But again, there are large individual differences. Bowel control, and attitudes associated with defecation, may be complicated by the parents' attitudes and practices, such as disgust, compelling the child to sit on the pot for long periods, or using suppositories and laxatives excessively.

Lapses in bladder control are so common that they should be regarded as a normal feature of growth. The child's performance is likely to be affected variously by such factors as teething, illness, temperature, and consumption of liquids. Even after several years of consistent control a child may relapse under trying conditions. Some children, for example, again wet their beds when they begin to go to school, apparently as a symptom of emotional strain. The fact that stresses in a child's life may produce a greater than usual amount of incontinence has been reported in investigations of British children who were evacuated from city to country places during World War II (Burt, 1940).

A child will sometimes revert to incontinence when a new baby arrives in the family; his motive sometimes, it seems, is to draw attention to himself, although this is probably not the only explanation. Parents sometimes become discouraged when a child who seems well on the way to complete control of the eliminative functions backslides. The child himself may feel ashamed, so that when accidents occur, he tries to conceal them, or lie about them, blaming the mess on others. Children have been known to blame their puddles on Grandma or the family dog.

ATTITUDES WITH REGARD TO ELIMINATION
AND GENITAL ORGANS

In our culture, the process and the organs of elimination become enveloped in furtiveness, secrecy, and shame. To an older person, the excrements are unpleasant and wetting and soiling are uncomfortable. A young child is not squeamish about contact with his urine and feces, but in time he also shows distaste. He probably would acquire this distaste even if not vigorously taught by others. (It may be noted that many animals, whose manners are not too delicate in other respects, become quite fastidious about contact with their own waste products: The pig carefully deposits his in a separate part of his pen; the grazing calf leaves a little ring of uncropped grass around droppings in the pasture—unless grass is quite sparse.)

It is seldom, however, that the child is left alone to acquire an aversion to waste products or an attitude of modesty with respect to the processes of elimination. Adults and older children usually are very alert to hasten the development of such attitudes. The processes of elimination become, for many children, associated with uncleanness, with the shame which in many families is connected with nakedness, and with the guilt which quite widely in our society is connected with sex. The tendency to regard the process of elimination and the organs connected with elimination as obscene is so strong that even the children whose parents are least prudish and rather free and outspoken at home pick up some of the prevailing attitudes in the community. As they become older, such children sometimes admonish their parents not to use "dirty" words, not to be so shameless about nakedness and not to go to the bathroom so openly. The attitudes of disgust that some children acquire extend far beyond what is required or justified on practical counts of cleanliness or on moral grounds.

ELIMINATION PROCESSES
IN RELATION TO ATTITUDES TOWARD SELF

The attitudes parents show toward the process of elimination and express during a child's toilet training are bound to have an important influence on the attitudes a child acquires concerning his own bodily functions. Moreover, a parent's views concerning toilet-training are likely to reflect attitudes he has regarding himself and his child. If he is harsh in dealing with a child who is in the process of establishing bladder and bowel control, he probably also will be harsh in other ways. If he is strongly competitive in his approach to child rearing, he is likely to be impatient for the child to acquire the dry habit and prove himself—in this humble enterprise, as in other activities—better than the next fellow. On the other hand, if he is able to abide the demands of his own nature, without deploring the "lower" part of his nature, he is likely to view the operations of his child's bladder and bowels in the same light.

Bladder and bowel activities are a channel of significant communication between the parent and the child. To punish the child for wetting or soiling is a way of rejecting the child. To call him dirty and smelly and view his excrements with abhorrence is, in effect, a way of telling the child that *he* is a shameful character.

Bladder control and soiling are frequently mentioned by parents as "problems" when children are quite young (Macfarlane *et al.*, 1954). To regard a child under the age of two as a "problem" if he wets or soils himself when he is still too immature to control his elimination is much the same as viewing a child in the creeping or babbling stage as a "problem" because he is still too immature to walk or talk.

When parents thus regard a child as a problem and try to "train" him out of it, the youngster is bound to feel the pressure. If the pressure is severe he will feel that his parents disapprove of him and, in his own way, he may feel that *he* has failed and should disapprove of himself. A child who feels disapproved of by others and then disapproves of himself *for not achieving something which he does not have the power to achieve,* is measuring himself against an impossible standard. He is measuring himself *as he is* (one who is unable to control his bladder at times) against an ideal of *what he should be* (one who *ought* always to be able to control his bladder).

THE CONCEPT OF THE "ANAL PHASE" OF DEVELOPMENT

According to Freud and his followers, young children go through a phase during which the sensations connected with voiding the bladder and bowel are erotic in nature and play an important role in the child's sexual development. According to this theory, unfavorable character traits may result if the child's efforts to satisfy his anal interests are severely frustrated, as when parents put severe pressure on the child, try to hurry him, or treat him coercively while he is in the process of developing voluntary control. It has been claimed that a child who has been frustrated in this way may acquire a tendency to limit all his primitive pleasure-seeking activities. He may be tight-lipped and stingy. In extreme cases he may lose spontaneity and regard freedom as dangerous. Or he may become saddled with restrictive character traits, which follow him into adulthood, such as acquisitiveness, or a tendency to be meticulous and to assume a punitive attitude toward himself or toward others.[5]

In the writer's opinion, this theory of "anal eroticism" should be viewed according to the position taken earlier in this chapter with regard to "oral eroticism". We can recognize that the young child goes through periods when he is intensely interested in the process and products of elimination and he undoubtedly gets pleasure from voiding himself. When we ask whether this pleasure should be regarded as erotic, linked to the development of sexuality, we may note that the linings of the mouth, rectum, and sex organs have grown from the same primitive tissue and so these regions have at least that much in common. The important issue, however, is that anything which occupies the child's time and attention, and absorbs his interest and energies, is significant in his development, whether or not we choose to say that it is erotic in character. [6]

---

[5] For a discussion of this subject, see Freud (1930, 1938b), Fenichel (1945), Despert (1944), Huschka (1942), Fries (1947), and Orlansky (1949).

[6] Horney (1939) explains so-called "anal" character traits in terms of the total social situation in which the child lives. According to her, "anal" traits must be understood as a response not simply to erotic frustration but to the sum total of experiences in the early environment. A person does not have tight lips because he has acquired a tight sphincter; if both are tight it is not that one has caused the other but that both express a more pervasive tendency in a person's character, namely, to hold onto what he has and never to give anything away. Observations by Bostock (1951) are in keeping with the position that the type of toilet training a child receives will be influenced by the extent to which he is wanted and accepted.

Early phases of sexual development

The child's sexual develop-
ment begins before birth and his sexual behavior begins soon after birth.
The view that sexuality appears in infancy was emphasized by Freud
in his classic theories of the role of sex in human development. Many
investigators have found that children display sex activities and interests
at an early age, although there is disagreement among investigators on
whether the child's sexual development conforms to the stages described
by Freud. (We have already, in preceding pages, discussed Freudian
theories regarding oral and anal aspects of sexuality.)

In a study by Halverson (1940) of nine male infants aged three to
twenty weeks, tumescence (erection of the penis) occurred at least once
daily in at least seven of the nine; in individual children it occurred from
four to over thirty times during an eight hour period. Tumescence was
accompanied by restlessness while detumescence was associated with a
more relaxed state. This does not necessarily mean that the young boy
has erotic sensations similar to those of an older person, but it does mean
that the genital organ is active at an early age. (Spitz (1949) observed
that some kind of genital play occurred quite generally during the first
fifteen months in children living in a normal home environment. Genital
play in the first year of life is apparently one of the normal activities of
the young child. Manipulation of the genitals at the infancy level, and
similar behavior—sometimes accompanied by other signs of interest in
sex, at the pre-school level (Issacs, 1933; Koch, 1935; Levy, 1928)—may
be transitory, or it may persist for an extended period of time; it may
occupy a child many times during a day, or it may occur at widespread
intervals. In this behavior, as in all other aspects of development, there
are wide individual differences among normal children.

In a study of two groups of nursery-school children, Dillon (1934)
recorded children's sex play and attitudes toward the genital organs. In
the younger group (median age of thirty-five months), handling of the
genital organs was less frequent than in the older group (median age of
fifty-one months); it was shown by fewer children, took place more
openly, and in most cases was more fleeting than in the older group.
Such play was shown by seven of the twenty-two younger children and
eight of the sixteen children in the older group. The children who gave
more than passing attention to this play tended to show more tenseness
in other aspects of their behavior than the other children. Interest in sex
did not seem to be aroused materially by nakedness, the presence of the
opposite sex, or elimination. Several of the children showed an interest
in the genitalia, the anus, breasts, navel, and other organs, much as

they might show an exploratory interest in other things that caught their attention.

Through failure to recognize that interest in sex and sex play are common and normal features of development, some parents become unduly alarmed. If parents apply severe restraint or punishment, or obviously show squeamishness or revulsion, they may have a very unwholesome effect on the child. By their own irrational attitudes, parents may stimulate the child's interest or induce unwholesome feelings of anxiety, and impulses which the parents deplore may become stronger rather than weaker.

Actually, a large proportion of children who stimulate themselves abandon the practice of their own accord or after a few matter-of-fact promptings; just as a large proportion of children suck their thumbs for a time and then stop. Many children have an active interest in matters relating to sex for a time, then seem to lose interest, and later, show a renewed interest.

Recognizing differences between male and female anatomy. Sooner or later children will notice anatomical differences between the male and the female. Some writers have maintained that the child's discovery of the differences between the genital organs of the two sexes produces a severe emotional shock and leads to feelings of anxiety or hostility or a mixture of both (Levy, 1940). This view has been disputed (Conn, 1940), but it is apparent that many youngsters, once they have noticed the difference between the sexes, are quite interested. If the child is hindered from pursuing his interest by the prudery of his parents, he may—even at the early age of two or three—become quite furtive in his efforts to satisfy his curiosity by peeking or other stealth to obtain a view of the naked human body.

The children in the nursery group aged twenty-seven to forty-two months, mentioned above, gave little evidence of a clear differentiation between the sexes, but children in the older group all showed some consciousness of sex differences. Not all the older children, however, had a clear recognition of physical differences. Some recognized differences in clothing and costumes, never failed to apply the words "boy" and "girl" correctly, and yet apparently regarded the male sex organ as an incidental possession which girls did not have rather than as an essential distinguishing characteristic.

Apart from the foregoing, the early appearance of certain forms of behavior relating to sex is an interesting illustration of the developmental principle of anticipation which was noted in Chapter Two. Developments relating to sex are so forehanded that even as an infant in his crib, more than a dozen years in advance of the time when he will be able to procreate, the child first begins to manifest forms of behavior and interests that anticipate his role as one destined by nature to reproduce his kind.[7]

Discipline

Infancy and early childhood have been called the period of domestication. This is rather a prosaic way of looking at the dramatic tasks of development during the early years of life, yet it is true that one important aspect of a child's early development consists in acquiring many of the skills, habits, and manners that distinguish a more or less polite civilized human being from other creatures. Some of the change comes about in the process of growth. But the young child soon is under pressure to conform to certain external standards of conduct. These pressures may be imposed on him with a heavy hand or through a series of gentle nudges. But they do operate, and they constitute the beginnings of discipline.

THE NATURE OF DISCIPLINE

Discipline, broadly speaking, is any kind of influence designed to help the child to learn to deal with demands from his environment that go counter to demands he might wish to make upon his environment. Discipline arises from the need to bring about a balance between what the individual wants to do, what he wants of others, and the limitations and restrictions demanded by the society in which he lives or by the hazards in the physical environment. What the child does, and abstains from doing, by virtue of the discipline he receives is something he would not at first do of his own accord. He spontaneously will try to feed himself, but usually it is as a result of discipline that he eats with his spoon instead of his fingers.

THE NEED FOR DISCIPLINE

The aim in discipline is not to curtail freedom but to give the child greater freedom within manageable limits.

A parent must be both permissive and restrictive, and a failure to strike a fairly good balance between the two or, better yet, an integration of the two, will have unfortunate effects. For, if a child has more freedom than he is able to handle he is likely to get into trouble. A child needs freedom to grow and to learn in his own way, but he cannot thrive on unlimited freedom. He needs discipline. This is one of many parodoxes

---

[7] The role of sex in parent-child relationships and the theory of the Oedipus complex are discussed in Chapter Seven. Sex as related to emotional development is discussed in Chapter Eleven, and Freud's theory of the Oedipus complex as related to anxiety is discussed in Chapter Twelve.

in development. A child cannot fully enjoy the fruits of freedom without surrendering some of it. A parent cannot help a child to learn how fully to enjoy his freedom without in some ways curtailing that freedom.

Without discipline it would be hard for a child to survive and, if he did survive, he probably would be a wreck. Through restrictions and controls, a child is spared from dangers which he might otherwise run into at an age when he is too young to perceive the consequences of his actions, as when he plays with fire, or runs into heavy traffic, or ventures into deep water before he can swim.

Other circumstances that require discipline are regulations tied to the public interest, convenience, and necessity, such as traffic regulations, time schedules, everyday amenities of life, and cleanliness.

The need to share limited goods, when there is rationing of food or fuel on a national scale, for instance, is one form of discipline. So too is the rationing which continually takes place in the home: one child does not get all the steak while another gets nothing but spinach. Discipline is also involved when the mother and father avoid giving all their attention to the most demanding child in the family while the other children receive no attention.

In a sense, discipline must be imposed upon a person either by others or by himself as long as he lives. As a young person grows up, he must learn to accept many rules and regulations even if they seem meaningless to him. He must learn to bow to some of the facts of life or he will wear himself out by futile resistance.

If children have not learned to curb their expectations, they are due for some hard jolts as they move on in years. They may have a vague notion of omnipotence and illusions concerning their own rights, which will clash sooner or later with the realities of life. Even the most angelic parent eventually will be tried beyond endurance if his child, as he grows older, continues to make such demands as we usually allow only a young child to make or demands such privileges as only an older person can win by his own efforts.

BENEFITS OF DISCIPLINE

Discipline, as such, is neither good nor bad. Its value depends on its appropriateness. Good discipline is scaled to the child's maturity level. It protects the child from his own imprudence. It relieves the child of the responsibility for deciding matters over which he has no choice and thus frees his energies for action where he does have a choice. Good discipline provides the child with a foundation for healthy self-discipline.

Discipline is unhealthy when it is unduly severe, restrictive, or coercive, or when it is administered unfairly in a situation where there are several children. Unduly restrictive and unhealthy discipline occurs when we insist on a level of cleanliness that is impossible for a young child to achieve; or insist that he accomplish, punctually and perfectly, tasks that are not geared to his maturity level; or insist that he sit still for hours when his organism is geared to be active; or insist that he do his arithmetic lesson not only correctly but within an arbitrary and tension-producing time limit (as often is done at school); or insist that he not only restrain his temper but even perform the impossible feat of not feeling angry when someone offends him.

Whenever children are subjected to discipline merely for its own sake, they eventually are likely to rebel, either openly or by devious means.

DISCIPLINE AND GRIEVANCE

Discipline is often frustrating and it may leave a child with lingering grievances. Some grievances are probably inevitable, no matter how wise the discipline may be. Parents who always shrink from doing anything that might produce a grievance are in a difficult spot: If they fail to insist on some rules, their child is likely to try to rule them and, then, sooner or later *they* will feel a grievance.

Under fortunate circumstances, a child recovers from his frustration, and learns to take his discipline in stride. However, his grievances may mount to such an extent that he has a continuing feeling of being abused. When such a feeling prevails, other complications often follow. The child, already on the alert against what he regards as unfair treatment, is more likely than ever to perceive further disciplinary acts as unfair, whether they are or not. He is also more likely to take offense. This can start a vicious circle which is painful both for the child and his parents.

Children differ greatly in their tendency to feel abused—one takes correction in a friendly spirit while another child, similarly corrected, becomes annoyed. It is more likely, however, that discipline will leave a grievance if it is unfair or accompanied by severe punishment.

It is not just children of two or three, but young people in their twenties and older people who face questions of discipline. Many adults have failed to resolve personal problems that arose from the kind of discipline they received when they were small. In studies conducted with the co-operation of teachers, for example, the writer and his associates (Jersild *et al.*, 1955; and Jerseld and Allina, 1960) found that a large proportion (almost half) of these adults still had problems stemming from their attitudes toward "authority figures"—parents, principals, or colleagues—whom they tried to domineer or who tried to domineer them.

PUNISHMENT

The aim of punishment is (or should be) to enforce discipline by *deterring* the child who has broken a rule from breaking it again. Such punishment is meant to be *remedial* and sometimes is. Punishment may also be used (and often is) as a means of taking revenge. Such punishment is *punitive*. It gives the punisher an outlet for his anger, but it is not likely to do much good for the one who is punished or the one who punishes. The punished child may, it is true, become so afraid of future hurt that he mends his ways. He may also, however, become more defiant, either openly or secretly.

When a parent (or teacher or society at large) punishes in anger in order to make a child suffer, the effect may be favorable if the act of punishment clears the atmosphere, relieves the feelings of the punisher and the guilty feelings of the child. Such punishment does not help anyone, however, if it is simply an expression of chronic hostility in the adult, producing a wave of counter-hostility in the child. (Such hostility appears when irate citizens, during a "delinquency wave," rail against "coddling" the young and insist that the police make active use of their night-sticks. Many of these citizens probably would be the first to be angry at "police brutality" if the police followed their advice.)

When we, as adults, face the subject of punishment, we are dealing with an extremely difficult issue. No parent (or teacher or court officer) has found a perfect solution. On the one hand, there is evidence (much of it stemming from the work of E. L. Thorndike) which shows that praise and reward are far better incentives to learning than punishment and reproof. On the other hand, it is impossible to bring up a child without punishing him. Even if parents try to avoid spanking or sharp scolding they are bound to punish at times in other ways. They do this directly when, in a moment of anxiety of danger, they sternly warn their child in threatening tones. They do it also by deliberately depriving the child of what he wants, or by showing their disapproval of him, either subtly or openly. Punishment of this sort cannot be avoided and sometimes it is necessary.

While there is no perfect solution to the problem of punishment, a few general rules, such as the following, can be laid down:

Punishment is more useful as a *deterrent* than as a *corrective:* Through punishment we can deter a child who, in anger, smashed a plate from breaking another plate; but the punishment won't cure his anger.

As a deterrent, also, punishment through restraint (as when a fighting child is isolated from others or when a dangerous criminal is put in jail) is sometimes necessary to protect others.

Punishment is likely to be most effective when it comes as a direct consequence of a child's misdeed and is so perceived by the child (for example, when the child who threatened to injure others is forcibly restrained, as mentioned above).

Punishment should have a terminal point—the more clear-cut it can be, the more effective it is likely to be. It is better to scold or slap and be done with it than to stretch reprisals over a period of time.

It is better also to punish on the spot than to build up a list of accusations and then "crack down." This rule (like the others) is not easy to follow. Frequently a child is punished when an adult's patience has worn thin, with the result that a little misdeed, which by itself does not deserve punishment, triggers off the wrath aroused by a string of previous misdeeds.

A final word about *corporal* punishment. It is direct, emphatic, and it helps to relieve the feelings of the punisher. If the child feels a need for punishment, it may also relieve him. But it is also an assault, a form of violence, which people are much more likely to use against the young than against persons their own size. When a big person strikes a little one he usually is taking advantage of his superior strength, not his superior wisdom. He is also taking advantage of his superior legal power: When an older child strikes his parent or his teacher it is usually considered a more serious offense than if they strike him, even though justice may be on the child's side. Custom and law gives adults more right than children to be bullies. In view of this, an adult should be wary of using corporal punishment. But he should be even more wary of punishing the child through such means as sarcasm, belittling, constant nagging, and a continual undertone of disapproval.

Recommended Readings

Benjamin M. Spock's *The Common Sense Book of Baby and Child Care* (1946) and *Infant and Child in the Culture of Today* (1943) by Arnold Gesell and Frances L. Ilg are helpful books for parents and others who have young children in their care. The United States Children's Bureau regularly issues excellent booklets on child-rearing; two recent publications by the Bureau are *Infant Care*, Revised Edition (1955), and *Your Child from One to Six*, Revised Edition (1956). *Discipline for Today's Children and Youth* by George V. Sheviakov and Fritz Redl (1956) offers a very thoughtful treatment of discipline. Sections dealing with aspects of child care in various cultures are included in the books of readings, cited in Chapter One, edited by Wayne Dennis (1951); William E. Martin and Celia Burns Stendler (1954); and Jerome M. Seidman (1958). Reports of conferences on problems of infancy and childhood under the auspices of the Josiah Macy, Jr., Foundation contain excellent papers dealing with various aspects of child growth and care. The seventh conference report, edited by Milton J. Senn, was published in 1954.

Motor Development

A child moves from the helplessness of early infancy toward self-help and independence largely through his motor development. Motor activities also play a crucial role in many of his earliest intellectual enterprises as he explores the world about him with his eyes and his hands, and they provide the means for a large proportion of his social contacts with other children. Throughout life a person's view of himself is influenced by his perception of his body and its properties, his strength and skill in physical activities.

In this chapter we will consider general characteristics of motor development and single out certain achievements for more detailed examination. In the preceding chapter, the account of self-help in eating illustrated one aspect of motor development.

Trends in physical growth

The average newborn child is about 20½ inches long. During the first year, his length increases by over a third, and by the age of five he will be about twice as tall as he was at birth. During the period of physical growth, there are continuing changes in the proportions of the body. The head, for example, is comparatively very large at birth and does not increase nearly as much in size as other parts of the body. There is a considerably larger increase in the length of the trunk, and even greater increase in the length of the arms, and, by the time full stature is attained, a still greater increase in the length of the legs. These trends are generally in keeping with the cephalocaudal (head-tail) direction of development.

The parts of the body grow at different rates and reach their maximum size at different times during the period from early childhood to maturity. This is also true of the internal organs. Not only is there a differential course of growth for the various parts of the body, but the pattern of growth differs from individual to individual.

INFLUENCE OF HEREDITY
AND ENVIRONMENT ON PHYSICAL GROWTH

There is a high degree of correspondence between the height of children and their parents. This is shown in Table 2, which is based on Bayley's long-term study of the same group of children who were measured over a period of years. "Mid-parent" heights were computed by means of a formula which expressed, in one figure, the heights of both

TABLE 2	CORRELATION BETWEEN MID-PARENT HEIGHTS AND HEIGHTS OF THEIR CHILDREN *

| | Boys | | Girls | |
Age	Number	Correlation	Number	Correlation
6 months	32	.35	29	.61
2 years	27	.36	23	.66
10 years	24	.60	24	.59
18 years	21	.58	17	.76
18 years	21		17	
	(father-sons)	.52	(father-daughters)	.64
	(mother-sons)	.44	(mother-daughters)	.52

* Adapted in abridged form from Nancy Bayley, "Some Increasing Parent-Child Similarities During the Growth of Children." *Journal of Educational Psychology*, 1954, 45, 1-21. Reproduced by permission.

parents. The table includes father-child and mother-child correlations at the eighteen-year level.[1]

Table 3, based on a study by Eichorn (1959), gives information of a kind that has not been available until recently: It shows correlations between height measurements of children and of the children's parents when *they* were children. It also shows comparisons between the adult height of the parents and their children's height, and the height of the parents as children and as adults.[2]

| TABLE 3 | TWO-GENERATION SIMILARITIES IN HEIGHT DURING THE FIRST FIVE YEARS * | | | |

Age in Months	Number	Correlation: Children and Parents as Children	Correlation: Children and Parents as Adults	Correlation: Parents as Children and as Adults
3-8	30	.18	.29	.61
9-14	29	.19	.12	.66
15-20	17	.52	.49	.69
21-30	24	.31	.40	.65
31-42	27	.27	.40	.66
43-53	18	.22	.39	.68
55-66	18	.67	.67	.83

* Adapted from Dorothy H. Eichorn, "Two-Generation Similarities in Weight, Height and Weight/Height During the First Five Years." Reported at Twenty-fifth Anniversary Meeting, Society for Research in Child Development, National Institutes of Health, Bethesda, Md., March 10, 1959. Reproduced by permission.

Eichorn's study shows that there is a far higher than chance resemblance between a person's adult height and his height as a young child

---

[1] The paper from which this table is adapted gives more detailed comparisons and an account of the formula used in computing "mid-parent" height.

[2] Table 3, and Table 2 from Dr. Bayley's study, are based on a long-term investigation at the Institute of Child Welfare, University of California. Table 3 includes a combination of father-child and mother-child pairs. The measurements of the two sexes were converted into "standard scores" based on measurements of a large population. (This meant, for example, that a woman of average height received the same height score as a man of average height even though the man is taller than the woman.) Because of a number of considerations mentioned by Dr. Eichorn it is difficult to tell to what degree her findings would hold for children in general. The number of persons represented in Table 3 is small (although large when viewed against the difficulty of getting repeated measurements of two generations). Members of the first generation were more homogeneous in height (taller, on the average) than adults in the population at large: Statistically this would tend to lower the parent-child correlations, but genetically it might raise them, since people do not mate entirely at random (there is more than a chance likelihood that a tall woman would select a tall man). Moreover, the second generation, in most instances, contained several children from one family.

(correlations ranging from .61 to .83 as compared with a correlation of zero if the two measurements were completely unrelated). Bayley's and Eichorn's studies both indicate that heredity is an important factor in determining height. The resemblance between children and parents, in practically all comparisons, is far higher than a chance one. According to Bayley's findings, parent-child similarities are likely to be greater when children move into late childhood and adolescence than when they were infants.

The fact that height is influenced by heredity does not mean that it is unaffected by the environment. In the United States and some other countries, recent generations of children are taller than their forebears, presumably because of better nutrition. In a study of British children (Clements, 1953), significant increases in both height and weight were noted over the past seventy years. These gains were greater between wars than during wartime. The increases also were greater in the lower than in the upper income groups, suggesting that the lower income groups have most to gain in physical growth from a generally improved standard of living.

Locomotion

A child's ability to walk is the climax of a long series of developments. The groundwork for the ability to walk is being laid many months before the child is able to stand or walk alone. Locomotion begins not with the legs, but with the muscles of the upper trunk and arms.

Although children differ considerably in the *rate* at which they learn to walk, they usually are quite similar in the *order* in which various accomplishments appear. Shirley (1931) describes several stages that lead to walking: First, postural control in the upper regions of the body, including the ability to lift the head, and then the chest; control of head movements; and ability to sit on a lap, with some support. Later skills include the ability to sit alone for a moment, and then for a longer interval. The child is likely to achieve the power of moving his body forward or backward by hitching, pulling or pushing or "swimming" motions, many weeks before he can creep. In Shirley's study, the median child was able to stand while holding on to furniture at forty-two weeks; to creep at forty-four and a half weeks; to walk when led at forty-five weeks; to stand alone at sixty-two weeks; and to walk alone at sixty-four weeks.

A youngster may be quite resourceful in covering ground well before he can walk. For example, if he has strong arms and a lot of determination he may be able to hoist himself over the bars of his crib, and reach the floor without injury. He may then come clattering downstairs, with whoops of triumph, alerting his mother who thought he was quietly napping.

The ability to walk alone is part of a larger, continuing process of motor development. As soon as the child is able to walk, he launches upon other skills that incorporate elements of walking into larger activity patterns.

Impact of walking

Walking is an important milestone in a child's life. It affects all other aspects of his development. He is able now to increase his contacts with other people and with things. But while able to walk into new areas of interest, exploration, and adventure, he is also able to walk into mischief and danger. It is harder now for his parents to keep an eye on him. The beginning of walking ushers in a period that lasts until the child is about four years old—a period that is strenuous for the child, strenuous also for the parent. The child's ability to get about and to get into things far exceeds his judgment and awareness of danger.

In the first year or two after a child begins to walk, he makes great demands on his parents' time, energy, and patience. It is delightful to watch a child during this period and to stroll along with him; but he looks most beautiful to his tired mother when he finally closes his eyes in sleep at the end of the day. If not carefully watched, he will pull books off shelves; make off with scissors and knives; lay hold of cigarette butts; jerk the tablecloth off the table; fall off chairs; make his way up stairs and then come tumbling down; drain the last dregs from a beer can left by a careless guest; eat from the dog's food-bowl; drink from the bird-bath; stroll off into brambles and poison ivy; creep under parked cars; toddle into the path of traffic; raid the ice box; and make forays on the garbage pail.

Many clashes of purpose are in store for the walk-about child—he is not only testing his legs but also trying out his ability to do things with his hands, to assert himself, and to pursue matters in his own way. Many parents experience considerable anxiety when a child enters the runabout stage, especially if they already have a tendency to be anxious. But the anxiety is not just the product of their imaginations, for many children at this age do get into serious accidents. In many neighborhoods, adults have vivid memories of hearing or reading about two-year-olds who wandered off into traffic or into woods and swamps. It is true that parents fear for the safety of their children far more often than danger actually strikes. But parents' apprehensions are not relieved by knowledge of the actual statistical probabilities. And it would be difficult for children if the ratio between fears and fatalities were reversed.[3]

Use of arms, hands, and fingers

When an adult picks up and devours a peanut, no one watching him is likely to admire his consummate act of skill. The person himself is only half aware of his performance, for he is so sure in his aim, so expert in grasping the nut with thumb and forefinger and in conveying it to his mouth. But back of this little act lies a long story of development, beginning when the infant was unskilled in eye-hand coordinations.

At first the child's reaching consists of crude shoulder and elbow movements (illustrating the proximo-distal direction of development noted in Chapter Three). His aim is poor and his approach clumsy. In time, he becomes able to make selective movements with his wrist, to aim more accurately, and to rotate his hands. In his first attempts at grasping, he makes practically no use of his thumb, but closes in upon the object with a scooping or corraling movement of palm and fingers. This, in time, yields to a deft and well-aimed grasping with the thumb and the tip of the forefinger. Until he is about twenty-four weeks old, the infant's approach seems to consist of three distinct acts: the raising of the hand, a circuitous and forward thrust of the hand, and then a lowering of the hand. Finally, at about forty weeks, the act is coordinated into a single performance, bearing little trace of the separate acts (Halverson, 1931).

These observations illustrate just a few of the steps involved in the seemingly simple act of reaching, grasping, and handling an object. The age at which children achieve the performances described above will vary, of course, with different individuals.

Table 4 shows the median age at which various performances with arms, wrists, and fingers were achieved by infants in a study by Bayley (1935) The items in this table have been selected from a larger list.[4]

DEVELOPMENTAL CHANGES IN INTEREST AND ATTITUDE IN CONNECTION WITH MOTOR ACTIVITIES

All aspects of motor development during early childhood illustrate the principle that a child seeks spontaneously to make use of his growing

---

[3] A discrepancy between fear of what might happen and the actual occurrence of accidents, injuries, and illnesses is common among parents (Jersild, Woodyard, and del Solar, 1949).

[4] Studies dealing with motor activities that are reviewed in Chapter Two in the discussion of the role of learning and growth in development will not be reintroduced here.

power. This tendency will show itself in different ways and with varying intensity at different stages of development. To illustrate: Damann (1941) studied the responses of a child who was given an opportunity to climb an inclined board. The first observations were made at eight months when the youngster had just begun to creep. At this time the opportunity to climb was not in itself a strong attraction, apparently, for the child was lured on by means of a toy. But his attention span was short and he was easily distracted, so he would pause to examine a knot in the wood, a speck of dust, or a scratch in the varnish. At a later phase he sometimes became overstimulated by the toy used as a lure. In his eagerness to secure it he would raise his head and shoulders, which shifted his center of gravity and threw him off balance. As his ability to climb matured, the performance of climbing the board became satisfying in itself: The youngster frequently went up and down the slide several times even though there was no lure. When he had mastered the skill of climbing,

TABLE 4 | ADVANCES IN PREHENSION *

Motor Performance	Age Placement in Months
Retains red ring (retains a ring, designed for the test, when placed in his hand)	0.7
Arm thrust in play (when lying in a dorsal position, makes vertical arm thrusts in random play)	1.7
Hands predominantly open (hands predominantly open even though not grasping an object)	3.6
Beginning thumb opposition (beginning evidence of use of thumb in opposed manner in grasping a cube)	4.1
Partial thumb opposition (opposes thumb to fingers in a partial, but not complete, manner, using the palm of the hand, as well as thumb and fingers in picking up the cube)	5.1
Unilateral reaching (tends to reach and manipulate with one hand more often than bimanually)	6.4
Rotates wrist (rotates wrist in manipulating toys)	6.7
Complete thumb opposition (picks up the cube with thumb and fingers completely opposed, and without the use of the palm)	7.6
Partial finger prehension (picks up a small pellet with several fingers opposed to thumb and not with a scooping into the palm with the fingers)	7.8
Fine prehension with pellet (picks up a small pellet precisely with thumb and forefinger)	9.3

* Adapted from Nancy Bayley, *The Development of Motor Abilities During the First Three Years,* Monographs of the Society for Research in Child Development (1935), No. 1, 26 pp. Reproduced by permission.

the inclined board no longer seemed to offer a challenge in itself. Now, again, the child was distracted, apparently because he was bored. To make things more interesting, he would vary his methods of climbing.

Later features of motor development

After the child has achieved the ability to walk alone, his progress in specific motor skills depends more on special opportunities than it did earlier. However, within broad limits, children reared in similar environments exhibit a good deal of uniformity in their progression from one level of performance to the next and in adding new skills to their repertory. Studies show that children who have not had the opportunity to acquire a certain skill will tend to pass through stages similar to those exhibited by children who acquire the same skill at an earlier age. However, when the older child does get an opportunity, he is likely to pass through the preliminary stages more rapidly.

Walking, running, and jumping. Table 5 on page 102 summarizes children's progress in certain locomotor skills after they have learned to walk.

Use of wheel toys. An account by Jones (1939) of the development of children's uses of wheel toys (doll carriage, wagon, dump truck, kiddie car, and tricycle) offers many insights into changing motor reactions as children become older. The study involved observation of twenty-four children from the age of twenty-one to forty-eight months. The following account illustrates a change in the uses made of vehicles, and shifts in interests as the child's ability increases.

At ten months, David crept to a small doll carriage which was in the room. He looked inside it, then held on to the side as he raised himself a little, and ran his finger along the rough surface. He started to creep away, but turned and gave the carriage a small push. His interest span was thirty-five seconds.

At twelve months, Barbara, who could walk only a few steps alone, saw her older brother, aged thirty months, climb into a large doll carriage. She rose to her feet and pushed the carriage with her brother in it across the floor. At other times she was unable to push it because it slipped away from her. (This item illustrates the fact that small children will often, at first, try to make use of a carriage as a support in walking; a relatively heavy, sturdy carriage, which has a low center of gravity and which does not move at a light touch, is more suited to the child's pur-poses at this age than is a flimsy or easily pushed vehicle.)

TABLE 5 | ADVANCES IN LOCOMOTION *

Motor Performance	Age Placement in Months
Walks sideways	16.5
Walks backward	16.9
Stands on one foot with help	19.9
Walks upstairs with help	20.3
Walks downstairs with help	20.5
Walks upstairs alone, marks time	24.3
Walks downstairs alone, marks time	24.5
Jumps off floor; both feet	28.0
Stands on left foot alone	29.2
Stands on right foot alone	29.3
Walks on tiptoe	30.1
Stands on walking board with both feet	31.0
Walks on line; general direction	31.3
Jumps from chair	32.1
Walks upstairs, alternating forward foot	35.5
Walks tiptoe three meters	36.2
Jumps from height of 30 cm.	37.1
Distance jump—36 to 60 cm.	39.7
Jumps over rope less than 20 cm. high	41.5
Distance jump—60 to 85 cm.	48.4
Hops on right foot less than 2 meters	49.3
Walks downstairs—alternating forward foot	50.0

* Adapted from Nancy Bayley, *The Development of Motor Abilities During the First Three Years,* Society for Research in Child Development Monographs (1935), No. 1, 26 pp. Reproduced by permission.

At later ages, as would be expected, the children became more adept at using the doll carriage for pulling and pushing on the level floor or up an incline or under an arch. At twenty-one months, 15 per cent of the children used the carriage as a conveyance for other materials; at thirty-six months, 55 per cent of them did this.

The following statements describe the use made of a wagon at successive age levels; the records are much abridged:

Twenty-one months: Starts to climb in; walks away; returns and looks at wagon; pushes it forward from behind; leaves; examines other material in the room; manipulates a light fixture on the wagon; pushes wagon back and forth; plays with other material in the room, and so on. (During ten minutes, he has gone to the wagon and left it again three times.)

Twenty-four months: Gets into wagon with right knee in and left foot on floor; leans over and examines light; sits and shakes handle (note that there is no propelling, although he is in a position to propel); touches trademark on side; he examines wheels, touches various parts, makes one attempt to pull handle up, lays the handle down and says: "I want to go home and see Charlie" (this after five minutes spent entirely in or with the wagon); observer suggests that he use the wagon; he makes a few passes at the wagon, pulls it briefly, then wanders about.

Thirty months: Gets into wagon with right knee, with left foot on floor, and propels the wagon, first forward and then backward; gets out and asks for doll carriage (apparently desires to combine other materials with wagon, for when asked to continue to use wagon, he gets a small wagon and puts it into the larger one); pushes and pulls; sits astride and tries to propel with both feet, but cannot reach the floor, then propels with one leg as before; continues pushing, pulling and the like.

Thirty-six months: Propelling with one foot now established; a new performance is to pull wagon empty to the top of an incline and coast down; the child also hauls dirt with the wagon.

Forty-eight months: Pulling, pushing, propelling, coasting, and use of wagon to haul things continues, with two notable additions: (1) uses in make-believe game ("I'm playing moving van"); and (2) stands up in wagon, steering it by means of the handle, as his sister pushes him on request, saying, "Look everybody, I'm standin' up riding," and later telling another boy "Did you ever stand...? It's lots of fun.... Can you hold your balance?"

When a child had mastered an activity so well that it did not require his full attention he often proceeded to merge it with another performance. In other words, the progress was from work with a separate movement toward a combination of several movements into one activity. But later, at about forty-eight months the children centered their attention mainly on predominating ideas which they were attempting to put into practice. As a result, the performance of any one skilled movement was usually secondary to the project as a whole.

Increase in speed and strength. Changes in speed, accuracy, and power in certain athletic performances are shown in Table 6. This table is based upon findings obtained by Jenkins (1930) in measurements of fifty boys and fifty girls at each level from five to seven years. The original study should be consulted for information concerning the children who were tested and concerning the spread of scores at each age level.

Integration of skills with social and intellectual enterprises. As motor skills become established, they tend more and more to be incorporated into larger projects and enterprises that combine physical activities with social or intellectual activities. In her study of the development of children's uses of wheel toys, Jones found that children would concentrate all their attention on a certain motor performance as a project sufficient in itself while they were still in the process of mastering the performance (Jones, 1939). But once the children had mastered the basic operations (such as riding the tricycle, propelling the Kiddie Kar with good control of direction), they tended to spend less time on the activity as an occupation in itself and merged it with a more extensive enterprise, such as a make-believe game of transportation.

TABLE 6	AVERAGE SCORES OBTAINED BY FIVE-, SIX-, AND SEVEN-YEAR-OLD CHILDREN IN VARIOUS MOTOR PERFORMANCES *					

| Activity and Measure Used in Scoring | Age Groups | | | | | |
| | 5-year-olds | | 6-year-olds | | 7-year-olds | |
	Boys	Girls	Boys	Girls	Boys	Girls
35-yard dash—timed in seconds	9.30	9.70	8.52	8.84	7.92	8.02
Hop 50 feet without error—timed in seconds	10.82	10.33	9.20	8.89	8.81	7.59
Baseball throw at target— 10-foot distance—error in inches	8.87	16.90	5.40	13.17	4.20	8.50
Baseball throw—distance in feet	23.60	14.50	32.80	17.80	41.40	24.40
Soccer kick—distance in feet	11.50	8.00	18.40	10.10	25.40	15.00
Standing broad jump —distance in inches	33.70	31.60	39.30	38.00	42.20	41.00
Running broad jump —distance in inches	34.40	28.60	45.20	40.00	58.80	50.80
Jump and reach —vertical distance in inches	2.52	2.22	4.02	3.48	4.98	4.28

* Adapted from L. M. Jenkins, *A Comparative Study of Motor Achievements of Children at Five, Six, and Seven Years of Age*, Contributions to Education (New York: Teachers College, Columbia University, 1930), No. 414, 54 pp. Reproduced by permission.

The fact that a child has become skillful in a performance does not mean, however, that the performance no longer has any appeal in its own right, for the child may go on to perfect and enlarge his skill, to add hazards and "embroideries" to his performance, as when he takes his tricycle over the bumps or rides it along ledges or down steep grades, or when he goes down the slide backward, or endeavors to make a one-hand or running catch after he has become adept at catching a ball with both hands while standing still. Some skills that can be used satisfactorily even by a small child still afford almost limitless opportunity for further refinement and improvement as he grows older. Examples are such activities as playing marbles, roller skating, swimming, bicycling, and ball play of various sorts. Ball play is a good illustration of an activity which offers so wide a range of possibilities that it is challenging to a clumsy beginner and to a major leaguer.

Motor and artistic activities

Motor operations play an important role in the field of the arts. Activities such as using modeling clay, or building houses with blocks, aesthetic dancing, or playing a musical instrument require manual skill as well as the ability to conceive and plan. Observers have noted that children progress through fairly regular stages in these activities. Although a child of four has had the same opportunity to work with clay as an average child of six, he will not perform like a six-year old. And if a six-year-old child is introduced to clay for the first time, he is likely to perform like a younger child in the beginning, but he probably will progress fairly quickly to a higher level of performance. This observation suggests that it is best for a rank beginner to begin at the beginning—even if it means performing initially at the level of a young child.

An interesting account of children's progress in block-building is offered by Johnson and her associates (1933). They observe that at first a child simply handles and carries the blocks and piles them into irregular masses. Between the age of two and three, he begins to make simple designs by placing the blocks in a row or one on top of the other or forming a tower. He can begin to experiment with the spacing of alternate sizes, and attempt to build a structure, such as a bridge or an enclosure. Further development will be shown in his attempts to devise patterns and by his improved technique in handling the blocks. By the ages of four and five years, the children used the blocks for dramatic representation; and at five or six years, attempts were made to reproduce actual structures. Individual children vary considerably with respect to timing and sequence. It was noted, however, that children who had had no previous experience with blocks at the age of four or five years tended to repeat the stages exhibited by children who began their block play at the age of two, but then passed through the various stages at a more rapid rate.

Table 7, based upon results obtained by Slater (1939) in observations of nursery-school children's spontaneous uses of blocks for building purposes, shows the frequency of various structures at different age levels. The children's handiwork was graded according to a four-point scale, as indicated in the summary.

In children's attempts to draw, a general pattern of progress has been noted. Biber (1934) observed that the child passes through a stage of

TABLE 7 | BLOCK-BUILDING ACTIVITIES *

Levels of Performance in Block-Building	Number of Children Showing the Various Levels of Performance						
	2 years	2½ years	3 years	3½ years	4 years	4½ years	Total
Crude, unsteady towers (which toppled over on their own accord or were "joyously demolished by their maker"	3	9	4	—	—	—	16
Towers, carefully done (primitive, but blocks fitted so they would stand with some apparent joy in workmanship)	1	5	7	9	3	—	25
Some imaginative elaboration (a definite plan, such as a train or house, somewhat recognizable)	—	1	6	1	4	2	14
Careful, symmetrical construction (houses with windows, trains on tracks, etc.)	—	2	2	1	2	2	9

* Adapted from E. Slater, II. *Types, Levels, and Irregularities of Response to a Nursery School Situation of Forty Children Observed with Special Reference to the Home Environment*. Studies from the Center for Research in Child Health and Development, School of Public Health, Harvard University, Monographs of the Society for Research in Child Development (1939), 4, 2, 148 pp. Reproduced by permission.

exploration, followed first by acquisition of some manual control, then by efforts to make designs, and finally by the beginnings of representative drawing at about the age of three and a half and four years. In their first attempts to draw, many children make vertical lines before they are able to make horizontal lines; they also find it easier to imitate a drawing made by another as they watch than to imitate a finished copy.

Interrelations in motor development

From early childhood into adult years, motor achievement represents a combination of many factors. Among the more obvious determining factors are strength and speed, size, and anatomical build. Among the more elusive factors that influence motor performance are interest, self-confidence, a tendency to be intrepid or fearful, willingness to take a chance, and self-consciousness and its opposite.

A child may be quite unskilled at one performance and still do well in others. Studies show relatively little correlation between ability in various specific motor performances (Gates and Scott, 1931; Wellman, 1937). Low correlations,[5] usually ranging below 0.30, have been found between scores in separate activities, such as throwing, climbing, and jumping. While correlations between various tests of strength tend to be considerably higher (ranging from 0.40 to above 0.80), there may be relatively little relationship between strength and speed. Because of this lack of interrelation, Wellman (1937) concluded that we should be hesitant in speaking about "the motor ability" of the child. Rather, we should think of "motor abilities" as a series of skills that are not closely related. Further study is necessary in order to determine how much of this lack of interrelation is due to chance factors in the environment and how much to general factors of ability.

Relation of physical and motor characteristics to other traits

The general finding has been that there is a low positive correlation between the mental and the physical status of children. In a study of the relationship between mental and physical characteristics of children and of college men and women, Abernethy (1936) compared measures of standing and sitting height, carpal development, chest girth, lung capacity, records of pubescence and other physical data, with scores on mental tests. Abernethy found, as have other investigators, that there was a positive correlation between mental and physical measurements, but that this correlation was relatively low. Jones (1949) found that there was practically a zero relationship between intelligence and motor performance in a group of adolescents.

In a study of young children, Bayley (1933a) found that during the first fifteen months there was a relatively high correlation (0.50) between "motor" and "mental" abilities, as far as these could be differentiated and separately measured. Success in one sphere seemed to be associated with success in the other. However, after the age of fifteen months the correlations were low although positive. This suggests that the operations labeled as mental and motor during early infancy were not well differentiated.

The low correspondence between mental and motor abilities means that many children who have a hard time in intellectual tasks may be able to do very well in practical arts and crafts and in several athletic activities. If the school program calls for only one kind of ability, there are many children whose main experience in school is failure or humiliation or boredom. Where the program calls for, and honors, varied abilities in

---

[5] For a description of correlation and an illustrative computation, see pages 376-377.

children, more children will have a chance for achievement in some field. The personal satisfaction that a child derives from being able to do something well is an important factor in his growing conception of himself. In other words, motor development—as well as mental development—is vital from the standpoint of mental health. In the opinion of the writer, the people in the school and in the community who prescribe how schools are to be equipped and what the curriculum shall be have greatly underrated the role of motor development.

MOTOR ABILITY IN RELATION TO SOCIOECONOMIC STATUS

Ability in the common athletic skills (and probably also in common mechanical skills) is not tied to socioeconomic status or what some authors refer to as social class. In studies of adolescents and near-adolescents, Jones (1949) found little or no correlation between children's performance in various physical feats and their socioeconomic status. This differs from measurements of intelligence and scholastic achievements, in which children of higher socioeconomic status usually tend to have an advantage.

So here is an additional facet of the role of motor abilities in the larger affairs of life: They provide, to a degree, a democratizing influence. The child who might be discriminated against when appraised in terms of his intelligence quotient or academic grades, may be able to make the grade in other important matters if he is given a chance to develop his motor potentialities. It does not follow, of course, that the poorer child will be the better performer in mechanics or sports—that is not the nature of the relationship. But it does follow that children who do not "rate" on the basis of IQ or school grades or family background are about as likely as their brighter and more affluent playmates to possess athletic competence that has a high value in the eyes of their peers. This finding emphasizes the importance of viewing the child's motor abilities in the light of the total perspective of his development and in the light of the assets and limitations he brings to his relationships with his peers.

Motor performance as a personality manifestation. A child's motor activity often seems congruent with other features of his makeup (Frauquier, 1940). While the factors of maturation and opportunities to practice are important, as we have seen, something more is involved, for children of the same maturity level and with equal opportunities for practice differ very widely in their choice of activities and the way in which they pursue them. For example, a child who is aggressive and competitive in his day-to-day conduct is likely to display these characteristics in his motor activities. Again, a child who is intrepid and enterprising is likely to reveal these qualities also in his choice of games and sports. Many other personality traits may appear in a child's actions. One child persists in a motor activity in spite of difficulties and failure while another gives up quickly. One child braces himself to catch a hard-hit baseball or risks a rough tackle in football, while another shrinks from being hurt, yet has his own favorite list of less rugged sports. One child does not hesitate to try his hand at a competitive sport, even if he is not good at it; it doesn't seem to bother him that he is inept and that he probably cuts a poor figure in the eyes of the spectators. Another has a higher standard for himself, is less able to let himself go or to run the risk of looking foolish, and, if he does enter in and misses an easy catch or a close shot, he blames himself bitterly and says he feels like kicking himself.

When one youngster shrinks from a sport or a game or test of skill because he fears ridicule and the possibility of making a poor showing, while another is uninhibited, each reveals traits that go beyond the sphere of motor development. Something more pervasive is involved, something tied to the child's attitude regarding himself and others, and the role he should play.

Handedness

Handedness exemplifies the way in which a given form of behavior may represent an interplay of many factors, including conditions within the organism, circumstances in the environment, the child's relationships with others and his views concerning himself.

Theories of handedness. It has been variously assumed that handedness is inherited; that it is caused by physical differences between the two sides of the body, such as dominance of one hemisphere of the brain or dominance of one eye over the other; that it arises through chance; that it is due to direct or indirect training imposed by others who have grown up in a traditionally right-handed world.[6]

Varying degrees of handedness. Although a majority of children eventually become predominantly right-handed, a definite hand preference is not usually established until several months after birth. Even when apparently well established, hand preference may be less clear-cut than it seems. A person may use his left hand in writing, throwing, and eating, but use a right-handed approach to some other performances, like batting a ball or digging with a spade; and he may perform additional acts equally well with both hands.

―――――――――

[6] For a review of studies of the development of hand preference, see Martin (1952).

There are three major questions that can be raised when we seek to understand left-handedness as it affects the individual child. First, how did he get that way? If his own natural bent toward left-handedness was so strong that it won out against the pressures of a right-handed world, it is a good thing for him that he is left-handed. There probably are many such "naturals" among left-handers. The situation may not be so favorable, however, if he is left-handed by reason of neglect or if he had to put up a sharp struggle to remain left-handed.

Second, what practical handicaps, if any, does the child's left-handedness impose on him? There are bound to be some inconveniences even if no busybodies point a finger at him. There may be a subtle psychological effect that operates when an adult and a child have different hand preferences: one or the other may become discouraged because the model set by the adult cannot be followed precisely by the child. Many performances are difficult for a right-handed person to demonstrate to a left-handed child—drawing, knitting, tying a necktie, tying a bow, managing a musical instrument. The left-handed child may learn to write in a crab-like fashion, holding his hand so that it smudges what he already has written; this often means that his schoolwork has an untidy look. He may be handicapped in using sports equipment—for example, he cannot share the baseball gloves other boys use (at least not without some awkwardness).

Third, apart from any important practical handicaps that might go with it, how does the left-handed person himself feel about his handedness? He is bound to feel a bit "different" if others call attention to his handedness, and there usually are people who will. He might feel a bit ashamed so that he makes a special effort not to be conspicuous. For example, he may be self-conscious when there is company at mealtime, trying to avoid a collision between his left elbow and the right elbow of the hearty feeder next to him.

These details are small in themselves and may not mean much, but anything that hinders communication between the child and others will, at least to a small degree, curtail his spontaneity and freedom. However, handedness *as such* is likely to have a very small impact on the child's personality and his view of himself if other circumstances in his life and in his relationships with others are favorable. The difficulties faced by a child who might have been a right-hander but turns out to be a left-hander are likely to be minor compared with the plight of the child who has a strong natural bent toward left-handedness, or who gets a long start in learning to prefer the left hand, and then is compelled to shift to the right hand.

Other practical considerations. That children who have been compelled to change from the left to the right hand may show a tendency to stutter, at least for some time, has been observed in some cases, but the cause-

and-effect relationship here is not entirely clear. It is difficult to determine whether the stuttering is directly due to the change in handedness or whether it is due primarily to the methods that are used and the atmosphere that prevails when the child is being forced into using his right hand. The stuttering, in other words, may be a symptom of the tension and confusion produced by the pressures that are brought to bear rather than a direct result of the change itself. Furthermore, while stuttering sometimes occurs, it by no means occurs in all cases in which a child is prevailed upon to change to the right hand; in addition, stuttering appears in cases in which there is no clear evidence of difficulty with regard to hand preference. To sum up, a change in hand preference as the result of pressure from others may, in individual cases, have unwholesome consequences. Risking such consequences is certainly not worth while.

Considerably more frequent than efforts to change an established preference for the left hand are the efforts parents exert while hand preference is still in its formative stages. In a great many cases, youngsters seem spontaneously to develop a preference for the right hand, without parental intervention. But many parents take pains to cultivate right handedness—favoring the child's right side in placing toys and tools within his reach; placing the spoon, cup, or pencil always in his right hand; and gently transferring operations to the right hand if the child seems in a random way to have started with the left. There are numerous little things parents can do to encourage the use of the right hand, and in most cases the child turns out to be the fine little right-hander his parents intended him to be.

The left-hander is bound to face inconveniences in a right-handed world. To some extent these inconveniences may be offset by the greater degree of ambidexterity some left-handers acquire. There is room for more systematic study in this area. Handedness is important enough to deserve the attention of parents when the child is developing hand preference. But right-handedness is not so important in itself that parents should interfere if the child shows a strong inclination to lead with his left as he squares off for the battle of life.

Recommended Readings

Volume I of Mary M. Shirley's *The First Two Years* (1931) gives a detailed account of motor development in infancy and early childhood (excerpts from this volume are reproduced in Jerome M. Seidman's book of readings, 1958). "Physical Growth" by Helen Thompson (1954) reviews a wide range of studies dealing with physical development from the fetal stage through adolescence. Many aspects of motor development as reflected by children's play are described by Ruth E. Hartley and Robert M. Goldenson in *The Complete Book of Children's Play* (1957).

PART TWO

Self and Others

Social
and Individual Origins
of the Self

From the time when his life begins, each child is very much a social creature. As a young infant strong ties are being established between him and other human beings. Interwoven with the child's earliest experiences and expectations, and intimately connected with his survival from day to day, are associations with others. These accumulate during the ensuing weeks and months as he grows more and more alert to what is happening about him. The child's experience with the humanity of others helps to shape his own humanity.

In the normal course of events a child becomes more actively *social* as he grows older, builds relationships with other persons, and acquires values and aspirations that others share. But from the beginning he has a streak of individuality of his own and as time passes he becomes increasingly aware of himself as a separate being.

The structure of the self

That which we call the *self* comes into being as the child, with all that is inherent in his make-up, comes to grips with the experiences of life. The self, as it finally evolves, is made up of all that goes into a person's experiences of his individual existence. It is a person's "inner world." It is a composite of a person's thoughts and feelings, strivings and hopes, fears and fantasies, his view of what he is, what he has been, what he might become, and his attitudes pertaining to his worth. As James (1902) puts it, a person's self is the "sum-total of all that he can call his."

The self includes, among other things, a *perceptual* component: the way a person perceives himself—the image he has of the appearance of his body, the picture he has of the impressions he makes on others. It also includes a *conceptual* component: his conception of his distinctive characteristics, his abilities, resources, assets, lacks, and limitations, his conception of his background and origins, and of his future. There is also an *attitudinal* component of the self, including the feelings a person has about himself, his attitudes concerning his present status and future prospects, his tendency to view himself with pride or shame, his convictions concerning his worthiness or unworthiness and his attitudes (which may be mixed) of self-esteem and self-reproach. As a person reaches maturity, these attitudes relating to self include also the beliefs, convictions, ideals, values, aspirations, and commitments that comprise what we speak of as a person's philosophy of life.

Although the self is a subjective phenomenon it is possible for a person to regard aspects of himself both as a subject and as an object. When a person says, "This is what I think and how I feel," he expresses a state which only he directly experiences. But he can also view himself objectively. He can (to a degree) examine his feelings and ask why he feels as he feels. He can also view his thoughts and examine his beliefs as though they were objects: he can review and question them. So when a person says, "This is me," he speaks both as a knower and something known, a perceiver and something perceived.

Development of the self

When we try to assess the process through which a child becomes aware of himself we do so largely by inference: we cannot directly assess the nature of his awareness. From his behavior we can reasonably infer that soon after he is born a flood of sensations pours in upon him; sensations from within his own body that probably are there when he cries in hunger; sensations from the surface of his body, such as occur when he withdraws his foot or hand from contact with a cold cloth while being bathed; sensations that reach him through his eyes and ears and probably also sensations of taste and smell. Judging from the diffuse nature of his earliest reactions, he is not at first able to make a clear distinction between these sensory experiences and the stimuli which give rise to them. The dawn of self-awareness probably occurs when a child begins to make a distinction between his sensations and the conditions which produce them.

The development of the self involves, among other things, a process of differentiation. The child begins life as though he were part of his mother's body. For some time after birth he continues to be helpless and dependent. Very soon, however, he is active in trying out his capacities. He cries and people come. He turns and gets another view. In time, he explores the boundaries of his person and his environment. He tests the limits of his reach.

In the development of a child's emerging view of himself as he grows older all of his capacities are mobilized; his senses; his ability to perceive and to think; his ability to learn; his ability to imagine and to embroider the happenings of his life with the glamour or the menace of a dream; his bodily appetites; his desires, which often conflict; his striving; his capacity for joy; his capacity for fear and rage which at first is freely expressed and then driven underground; his capacity for loving and need for affection; his ability to choose, and, in time, his experience of being free to make choices.

Beginnings of self-awareness

When does the child become aware of himself as a distinct individual? Many conjectures have been made about this, and one estimate is that it is sometime during the first year that the infant "discovers himself" and "finds a place in, yet apartness from, the outside world" (Ames, 1952).

The development of self-awareness does not occur in an all-or-none fashion which would enable us to assume that up to this point the child does not possess it but beyond this point he does. It is more likely that a child perceives different aspects of what he eventually calls himself with varying degrees of clarity at different times (Sarbin, 1952). His awareness of his distinctness from others seems to take place while he still has not gone very far in his perception and conception of many of the characteristics that eventually comprise what he calls himself. Moreover, the process of self-discovery is actively going on at least as long as the child is developing or discovering new potentialities, and in a healthy person the discovery of self continues as long as he lives.

Among the early signs of self-awareness are those appearing when a child begins actively to control things in his environment. In his explorations, the child notices and manipulates things that are apart from him. At first he seems almost to proceed by accident, but later he does so by design. At first when objects are placed in his hand he is able to grasp them but not able, at will, to release them or throw or move them about. Soon, however, he is able to grasp and to release, to reach for things and place them in a certain spot. When he uses this ability he probably has a dim awareness of himself as one who can produce effects by his own actions. An account of a five-months-old child illustrates this point. The youngster seemed to discover, while tearing a page from a journal, that it was he who produced the sound and the severing. He then patiently proceeded to tear page after page as though gaining satisfaction from being a cause of change and from seeing "that the remarkable alteration of an entire journal into little scraps [was] due to his own activity" (Preyer, 1888, 1890).

Awareness of the body

An important feature of a child's eventual view of himself is his "body-image," the picture he has of the physical properties of his body, his appearance, including (as he perceives the situation) the figure he cuts in the eyes of others. This body image is not just a photographic impression; in common with all other aspects of the way in which a person views himself, it is likely to be colored by feelings and attitudes.

When we ask how a child at first perceives his body we can answer only by conjecture. There is good reason to believe, as we have noted, that sensations play an important role in defining the boundaries of a child's image of his body. It also appears, however, that the child does not at first have anything approaching a clear perception of his body as a whole, or even a clearly defined awareness of the parts of his body. This can be seen, for example, when he fingers his hand in play or inspects his hand, gazing upon it as he might gaze upon another object. Some babies at first seem to treat their bodily parts almost as though they were separate objects. This appears, for example, when a baby bites his fingers and cries without seeming to realize that he is biting himself.

One approach to the study of self-awareness is to note the way infants respond to a mirror image of themselves. It has been observed that children recognize others (such as the mother) in the mirror and in pictures before they recognize themselves.

Five children who took part in a study of the development of "self-recognition" showed distinct changes with age in response to the mirror and the order of these changes was remarkably similar in all five infants (Dixon, 1957). At first the infants regarded their reflections "briefly and soberly" but showed no sustained interest, even though, at this stage, they readily recognized their mothers' reflection in the mirror (this was also observed by Zazzo, 1948). At a later phase the children became more sociable with their images, smiling, talking, and trying to make contact with the image in the mirror. Dixon calls this the "playmate stage"—the child reacts to the mirror image in much the same way as he reacts when placed before another infant. Then came what Dixon calls the "Who dat? Who do dat when I do dat?" stage in which the child seems to be connecting the mirror image with himself—keeping his eye fixed on the changing image, the child repeats certain acts (such as opening and closing his mouth, raising his arm and moving his fingers) as though he were trying to "master and work his new-found puzzling discovery."

At this stage "an apparent attempt at conversation-testing, as though expecting an echo," was observed a few times but soon died out, as did pointing at the image while asking a portentous question such as "Dah?". Sometime between the age of twelve and eighteen months the children entered what Dixon calls the "coy" stage. When confronted with his mirror image, the child now "instead of basking in reflected vanity" might turn his head away, or cry, or smile coyly, or kiss the image after refusing for some time to approach it. Such coyness also has been noted by others.

EMOTIONAL UNDERTONES
OF THE PROCESS OF SELF-DISCOVERY

As noted above, a child's growing awareness of himself has emotional overtones. When he first recognizes himself in a mirror it is not as though he were merely eyeing a portrait. Some children show a great deal of animation in connection with this discovery. One investigator was especially impressed by the emotional coloring of this development, noting the "jubilant interest" shown by an infant at the sight of his own image in a mirror, and of the child's ecstasy when he saw that the movements in the mirror corresponded to his own movements. There appeared to be a real affective

Social and Individual Origins of the Self   **119**

value in having a vision of the whole body as distinguished from knowing it in bits and pieces (Lacan, 1953).

Emotional experiences such as those connected with a child's recognition of his body can also be noted in connection with other forms of self-discovery. A child lets forth a jubilant cry, for example, when he discovers how to ring a bell or how to take the lid off a box. A detailed record of joyful episodes in the life of a young child would probably show that a large proportion of these are connected with experiences in which he tries himself out and realizes, in a new way, the reaches of his own strength and ability. If we grant this, we still have the question, why, then, do some babies not only show an eager interest but also coyness, as though they were embarrassed when they first seem to realize that the image in the mirror is their own? And why should a child cry? Perhaps the child who cries is somewhat apprehensive, as though this new-found creature were both a stranger and a familiar figure.

Another approach to the study of early self-identification has been to note how children think of themselves with reference to their bodies. In one study (Horowitz, 1935), two-, three-, and four-year-olds and students in psychology were asked to "localize" themselves (e.g., the experimenter would ask, while pointing to a leg, head, and so forth: "Is this Joan?"). One child located herself in the abdomen and lower thorax; another localized herself in her lower right jaw; another in the mouth region of the face. The students mentioned a variety of localization points, including the head, brain, eyes, face, heart, and genitals.

An important step in children's self-awareness occurs when they recognize the bodily differences between boys and girls and clearly identify the sex to which they belong. Many youngsters show a keen interest in the anatomical differences between the sexes in connection with this aspect of self-discovery. According to some writers, this discovery may be quite disturbing. One theory is that girls are especially likely to have feelings of inferiority or envy when they realize the difference between themselves and boys. However, the discovery of differences between the genital organs of the two sexes does not produce an emotional shock in the typical, healthy child (Conn, 1940), although children usually are greatly interested (this topic was discussed in Chapter Four).

Other evidences
of increasing self-awareness

After a child has learned to talk, signs of self-awareness become increasingly apparent, as when, for example, he correctly distinguishes between "I" and "you" and "mine" and "yours"; or is able to distinguish between dreams and actual happenings;

or he is able to acknowledge feelings as his own, saying (as one four-year-old did) "Don't bother me, I'm in a bad mood"; or when he takes pains to conceal his feelings, saying, "I'm not scared," in spite of signs to the contrary.

SELF-ASSERTION AND COMPARISON OF SELF WITH OTHERS

A notable phase in the development of the self occurs when a child begins to assert himself in opposition to others. As will be noted more particularly in a later chapter, many children go through a phase when they are especially obstinate or "negativistic," beginning at about the age of two. During this phase a youngster seems to be testing his powers of self-assertion in his relationship with others.

Another important phase in the development of a child's view of himself occurs when he is able to compare himself with his peers and to test his powers in competition with them. When a child knowingly competes he is using others as a standard against which to measure himself. Still another significant sign of self-scrutiny occurs when a child is openly critical of his own work.

AWARENESS OF SELF
AS BELONGING TO A PARTICULAR ETHNIC OR SOCIAL GROUP

Sometime during childhood a youngster is likely to form a more or less clear conception of his family's socioeconomic status or social class. He also becomes aware, in time, of his religious affiliation, the nationality of his parents and the ethnic stock from which he came. Children's awareness of social class differences does not usually appear to be well established until they are well along in the elementary school years (Stendler, 1949).

The age at which children realize the ethnic group to which they belong (whether Negro or white, for example) depends in part on circumstances in the environment in which they live. A child who associates only with his own ethnic group during early years of life does not particularly have reason to notice his ethnic identity. On the other hand, a youngster in a community which includes a mixture of ethnic groups or nationalities is likely to be reminded of his background at an earlier age. This will especially hold true if there are distinct cleavages within the community or if he is a member of a minority group against which there is a prejudice. Among the most moving accounts of childhood are those given by older children and adults of their first remembered encounter with prejudice. A child who is abused because of his ethnic origins bears an extra burden in the process of forming ideas and attitudes pertaining to himself, especially if he is made to feel ashamed of his background.

In a study in which Negro children aged three to five were asked to identify themselves by pointing to pictures they regarded as most nearly like themselves (Clark and Clark, 1940) it was found that light-skinned Negro children chose a white child as being most like themselves more often than did Negro children with darker skins, suggesting that children identify themselves in terms of skin color, which is to them a "concrete reality," before they identify themselves in terms of "race," which apparently is a more sophisticated concept. Pictures were also used in a study by Horowitz (1940) who noted that a child who seemed to be aware of being a member of a minority group might still choose a picture of a majority group member as being most like himself.

Influence of others
on a child's view of himself

Among the earliest experiences which influence the development of the child's view of himself are those with other people. The position that the child's attitudes pertaining to himself are influenced by "significant" people, notably at first by his mother or mother substitute, has been expressed most strongly by Sullivan.

According to Sullivan the "self-system" has its origins in interpersonal relationships and it is influenced by "reflected appraisals." If a child is accepted, approved, respected, and liked for what he is he will be helped to acquire an attitude of self-acceptance and respect for himself. But if the significant people in his life—at first his parents and later his teachers, peers, and other persons who wield an influence—belittle him, blame him and reject him, the growing child's attitudes toward himself are likely to become unfavorable. As he is judged by others, he will tend to judge himself. Further, according to this position, the attitudes concerning himself which he has thus acquired will, in turn, color the attitudes he has toward other persons. He judges himself as he has been judged and then, in turn, judges others as he judges himself.

In assessing the influence of interpersonal relationships in the development of a child's view of himself it is essential, however, not to lose sight of the fact that the relationship is *inter*personal. It includes the child as well as others, and the child's own qualities play an important role in the relationship. As noted in other sections of this book, children differ from the time of birth in temperament and disposition, in their demands and in their response to the treatment they receive from others, and in the response they evoke from others. Infants, for example, differ in the extent to which they are active or passive, irrespective of the social environment in which they are reared (Bühler, 1933). Similarly, parents who have reared two or more children report, for example, that almost from the day of birth one child was more sensitive than another and that as the youngsters grew older, one would show "hurt feelings" when mildly scolded while the other would take the scolding in stride or even strike back. Unfortunately, in the research literature there is no systematic account of the way in which the natural bent of children and the treatment they receive from others interact in the development of children's ideas and attitudes pertaining to themselves.

Self as is compared with the "ideal self"

When older children and adults are asked to describe themselves most of them are able to make a distinction between what they think they are and what they would like to be or think they ought to be. A person's view of what he aspires to be or believes he ought to be is sometimes referred to as the "ideal self." In most persons there is some discrepancy between self-as-is and the ideal self. Such a discrepancy occurs, for example, when a child says he *never* studies hard, but *should always* study hard, or when he says he *often* loses his temper but he *ought never* to lose his temper. In some persons, the difference between what they say they *are* and what they *should be* is very marked.

When a child's view of what he is corresponds quite closely to what he believes he ideally ought to be he expresses what seems to be a rather comfortable view of himself. When there is a marked difference between the self-picture and the ideal picture it appears that the child, in his own eyes, is failing to live up to the mark and he is, in that sense, a self-rejecting person. However, there are several reasons why it is necessary to be very cautious in labelling a person as self-accepting or self-rejecting on the basis of what he tells about himself as-is and as he thinks he ought to be. What a person reports about himself depends upon: (1) what he is consciously *able to recognize* as qualities belonging to his make-up, (2) what he not only recognizes but also is *willing to admit*, (3) what he feels impelled to *deny*, and (4) what he feels impelled to *claim* about himself.

There is a low discrepancy between an item pertaining to self-as-perceived and the "ideal self" if, for example, a child claims that he studies hard (whether or not he really does) and also claims that ideally he should study hard. Again, there is a low discrepancy between these two measures if he freely admits that he doesn't study hard and then (in describing the ideal) sets a low "aspiration level" for himself, claiming that he doesn't think he should work any harder than he does. Due to the fact that it is possible thus to manipulate the answers, it is necessary to know more about a child than can be gained from a self-rating inventory if we are to be reasonably sure of what might be his conception of himself.

In describing themselves, children differ greatly in the extent to which they are able to recognize or willing to admit even minor childhood foibles. In one study (Taylor and Combs, 1952) children were asked to respond to a list of statements which were regarded as "probably true" of all children (e.g., "I sometimes disobey my parents"; "I sometimes say bad words or swear"). The youngsters who had been rated as least well-adjusted according to an earlier measure (a test of personality) less fre-quently admitted common faults than those rated as well-adjusted. Such results raise a question as to the reliance that can be placed on self-rating inventories. Information supplied by such measures is interesting as far as it goes, but it is likely that a child will give a far more genuinely re-vealing account when talking about himself over a period of time to some-one in whom he is willing to confide than when he responds to a quick paper and pencil check-list. It is also likely that children will reveal many facets of themselves when they tell about their fantasies and dreams or respond to projective techniques (described in Chapter Fifteen) which they will not disclose when asked point-blank to describe themselves.

MAINTENANCE OF THE SELF-IMAGE

While still in the process of making new discoveries concerning his properties as an individual the growing child has a strong tendency to preserve ideas and attitudes he already has formed. He strives in the pres-ence of others and in his own eyes to be himself (as he sees himself) and to live in accordance with his concepts or attitudes regarding himself, whether these be true or false. He tries to be consistent with himself (Lecky, 1945). He is likely to resist anything that is inconsistent with his own view of himself. It may even be difficult for him to see or hear or grasp the meaning of anything, favorable or unfavorable, that goes coun-ter to his picture of himself. His perception of new events in his life will be colored by views he already has established.

CONSCIOUS AND UNCONSCIOUS PROCESSES
UNDERLYING ATTITUDES PERTAINING TO SELF

The foregoing sections have dealt with various aspects of *self-awareness* and with the characteristics which a person is clearly able to *recognize* as part of his make-up. These constitute a person's *phenomenal self* (the self which, as a *phenomenon*, appears, shows, is perceptible). There also are facets of a person's make-up which influence his ideas and attitudes per-taining to himself but which are *unconscious* in the sense that he does not consciously recognize them.

The term *unconscious* has a vast variety of meanings and interpretations which we do not here need to explore. But it is necessary to take account of some of the meanings of the concept of the unconscious when we seek to understand children. There are many currents in a child's life concerning which he is not consciously aware. A child does not comprehend the roots of his experience, when, for example, he has fears springing from happenings which he has forgotten or has a phobia arising from conflicts which he does not grasp. Likewise, a child is not conscious of what is occurring when, for example, he warms up to a teacher without realizing that he does so because the teacher touches off sentiments he has for his mother, or if he is deeply wounded by a mild criticism without realizing that the criticism triggers off feelings of self-reproach springing from earlier experiences in his life.

What has frequently been referred to as "the unconscious" is also at work if a child who has learned to suppress his anger gamely grins and feels no rage when someone abuses him but then later, for no apparent reason, feels a pain in his gut and throws up his dinner. In later sections, notably those dealing with emotion and the devices a child uses to defend his pride, there will be other illustrations of the way in which motives which a youngster does not recognize influence his actions and his endeavor to maintain a cherished view of himself.

A condition which a person is not consciously aware of occurs when he has an "idealized image" of himself that is not in keeping with the realities of his life. An idealized image of self containing elements which a person does not knowingly perceive occurs when he adopts a pose or facade and then somehow loses sight of the fact that he is posing. Such a condition occurs, for example, if an adult sees himself as a cold-hearted cynic when actually his cynicism is only a veneer, covering warm-hearted impulses. It occurs if an older child, with a powerful, competitive drive, views himself as a disinterested scholar, eager to learn for the sake of learning, without recognizing that he is using his scholarly efforts as a vehicle for competing with others.

> The "idealized self" is discussed again in later sections of this book dealing with anxiety and personality problems. For a more complete discussion of the concept of the idealized image the reader is referred to the writings of Horney (1937, 1939, 1945, 1946, 1950). Horney describes the idealized self as a kind of pseudo-identity. The "idealized self," containing elements which a person is not consciously aware of, has a different meaning than the "ideal self" which a person describes when he knowingly tells about his aspirations. The idealized self is not, from a person's own point of view, an ideal toward which he is striving but something he actually has attained—it is his "real self" as he sees it.

When we use an inventory to measure a person's ideas about himself as he thinks he really is, or measure his ideas concerning his ideal self—the kind of person he thinks he ought to be—we cannot be sure to what extent one or the other account reflects unrecognized elements of an idealized image of self. Moreover, as pointed out earlier in this chapter, neither can we know, without deeper inquiry, to what extent a person is revealing aspects of his inner life which he consciously recognizes but is unwilling to disclose.

In view of all this we might ask: Is it not futile for parents or teachers or any of us, with our ordinary minds, to apply the concept of the self in trying to understand children? The answer is no. Inquiry into the self is a complicated business, but it is far from futile for several reasons. One reason is that regardless of what might be hidden the typical child consciously harbors many thoughts and feelings about himself which he usually keeps secret but would willingly confide to someone whom he trusts. He is most likely to reveal himself to a person who does not view him solely in terms of his overt behavior. He is also more likely to reveal himself to a person who desires to understand him and who does not immediately pronounce a moral judgment on him. Further, even though a child may be impelled by motives which he cannot consciously perceive it is often possible for a sympathetic observer to look beneath the surface. We are inquiring into "unconscious" reaches of the child's life when, for example, we begin to look for clues in an effort to understand what might be the nature of a child's ideas and attitudes regarding himself when he plunges happily into things, or is shy, or shows off, or is withdrawn, or is extremely "good," or becomes angry on slight provocation, or is extremely competitive or afraid to compete.

Recommended Readings

William James's chapter on "The Consciousness of Self" in Volume I, *Principles of Psychology,* published in 1890, is a classic, interesting both from an historical and a contemporary point of view.

Writings on the subjective dimensions of experience reflect, to a large degree, an endeavor to reconstruct childhood experiences from the thoughts and theories of adults rather than from first-hand study of children. The literature contains many writings on ego psychology, most of which have been influenced by Freud, several of whose writings are listed in the bibliography at the end of this book, and writings that use the terminology of the self. Important books on the theory of the self have been written by Carl Rogers, *Counseling and Psychotherapy: New Concepts in Practice* (1942); Prescott Lecky, *Self Consistency: A Theory of Personality* (1945); Arthur W. Combs and Donald Syngg, *Individual Behavior: A Perceptual Approach* (1959); George H. Mead, *Mind, Self and Society* (1934); Karen Horney, *Our Inner Conflicts* (1945) and *Neurosis and Human Growth* (1950), and Harry Stack Sullivan, *Conceptions of Modern Psychiatry* (1947).

In the middle of the 19th century Sören Kierkegaard wrote movingly about the search for selfhood. His *Sickness Unto Death* and *Fear and Trembling* are combined in a paperback edition (1954).

Children
and Their Parents

CHAPTER SEVEN   When we look at the fortunes of family life it will be useful if here and there we can see a glimpse of ourselves. To a large degree we are the product of the kind of rearing we received as children and we have an added stake: Every adult who deals with children occupies the role of a parent, whether the children are his own or belong to someone else. In the span of life there probably is no satisfaction more rewarding than to be a "successful" parent and no tragedy more poignant than to be an "unsuccessful" one.

THE IMPORTANCE OF PARENTS' ATTITUDES AND PERSONALITY TRENDS

Parents are called upon to make countless decisions every day and a great deal has been written to guide them in making these decisions. Such advice may be helpful but it may miss the mark,

since the role of a parent involves more than a succession of separate acts. The parent's qualities as a person have an important bearing on what he does and leaves undone. On the basis of a detailed study of the way in which two mothers brought up their first-born children, Shirley (1941) maintains that the attitudes and the personality of the mother determine the manner in which she administers each phase of child care, even in such matters as bathing and dressing her child. From a study of twenty-five mothers, Behrens (1954) concludes that a child's upbringing is influenced more by the quality of the mother's "character structure" and its effect on the "total mother-child interaction" than by specific child-rearing practices and techniques. According to this principle, it is important, in assessing the role of the parent, to inquire into underlying attitudes rather than to concentrate only on methods and techniques. The same principle probably also applies to teachers and all others who, to a greater or lesser degree, have a parental role.

When a parent's dealings with a child reflect his "personality," this does not mean that a parent's personal qualities operate in a mystic way. Whatever the personality of the parent might be, it is expressed or communicated through what the parent is and does. But the concept of "personality" does not offer a simple formula, for personality is very complex and has many facets; and even though some traits are very durable, no personality is completely fixed or unchanging.

This concept that a parent's activities reflect qualities in his make-up opens the way for a larger and more meaningful view of the parent and of the child. It means that when we examine the details of child-rearing—such as the way in which the parent feeds the child or puts him to bed, or answers his questions—we look beyond the separate practices for the underlying personal characteristics which they might reflect: a tendency, say, to be patient or impatient, cheerful or dour, decisive or vacillating, responsive to the child's wishes or unresponsive.

To understand the parent-child relationship it is necessary to consider not only the parent's characteristics but also the child's: his tempo, his demands, his tendency to be responsive or unresponsive. As we have seen, children show marked individual traits almost from birth. Even one of a pair of identical infant twins may, from the beginning, be more hungry, robust, and demanding than the other (Burlingham, 1952). Regardless of a mother's personality or character structure, she is likely to deal differently with a rugged baby than with a very fragile and sensitive baby. In discussing this point, Coleman, Kris, and Provence (1953) point out, for example, that a child who readily accepts cuddling will elicit a different response from the mother than the child who does not. The fact that the parent-child relationship is interpersonal, and cannot be fathomed simply by looking at it from the point of view of one or the other of the individual persons involved, has been overlooked in much of the research dealing with this relationship.

Acceptance, rejection, and over-protection

In the discussions of parents, many of the labels used have a connotation of approval or disapproval. There is a note of strong approval when we speak of a parent as accepting and loving, and of disapproval when we speak of the "rejecting" parent. All parents have their share of human foibles and frailties, but the "rejecting" parent is usually regarded as the chief among sinners.

THE ACCEPTING PARENT

Each parent accepts his child in his own way and therefore one cannot draw a portrait of *the* accepting parent. There are, however, many qualities that are interwoven with an attitude of acceptance. These are described below, although no parent possesses all of these qualities to the same degree. Moreover, it is also well to bear in mind that acceptance involves many paradoxes: The accepting parent is both gentle and firm, sentimental and realistic. He loves his child but, if he is honest with himself, he will admit there are times when he is angry with his child. He feels close to his child, yet there are times when he wishes the youngster would get out of his hair.[1]

Affection for the child. The accepting parent has a feeling of tenderness toward the child even though, at times, other less loving feelings arise. Intermingled with the tenderness are feelings of completeness and fulfillment. In the words of Thorndike (1913): "To a woman who has given birth to a child, a baby to see, to hold and suckle is perhaps the most potent satisfaction that life can offer; its loss, the cause of the saddest yearning."

The loving parent finds much in an infant that will arouse his tender feelings—the warm, tight clutch of little fingers, the lingering gaze, the weary sigh, the morning smile, the eager gobbling of the first mouthsful of food. As the child grows older, the parent's fondness for the youngster is aroused and expressed in countless ways.

Sensitivity to the child's needs. The accepting parent is responsive to the child's needs, to the extent he can perceive them. He will notice signs of eagerness, discomfort, fear, or pain. He will protect the young child from

---

[1] An instrument for measuring parental acceptance has been prepared by Porter (1954). Results from the use of this instrument have been reported by Hawkes *et al.* (1956).

needless hurt. As the child grows older he will continue to be a protector, realizing, however, that in the world beyond the home the child will face many predicaments that are beyond the reach of a parent's protecting hand.

Ability to enjoy the child.   Linked to affection for the child is an ability to enjoy him. The parent gets pleasure from being with the child (except when one or both are cranky and tired). He shares a great deal of fun with his child. He enjoys the child's individual ways, and gets satisfaction from observing the child's growth. The accepting parent can relish the child's individuality without feeling compelled to mold the youngster in his own image.

Respect for a child's individuality and the ability to enjoy him are closely linked. This fact appeared in a study in which parents told about the satisfactions they derived from their children (Jersild, Woodyard, and del Solar, 1949). Parents frequently mentioned that their children gave them delight even when they showed characteristics which, in themselves, were not particularly pleasing (such as a streak of stubbornness). Many of the same parents also admitted, however, that their ability to enjoy the child's individuality had its limits: They could admire a child for having a will of his own and yet become exasperated by his wilfulness.

Respect for the child's pace of learning and growth.   An accepting parent seeks to respect the tempo of his child's development. This means resisting the temptation to *hurry* the youngster who is doing the best he can. It means an attitude of patience (which sometimes is sorely tried and breaks down) when the child, in the process of learning to do things for himself, fumbles, and seems to move at a snail's pace. The accepting parent recognizes that it takes time for a child to learn and to grow. The child may be slower in getting his first tooth, or in walking, or in learning to talk or to read than the child next door, but he is still an acceptable child. Respect for the child's individual rate and pace of development is not easy in a highly competitive society.

The accepting parent is eager to have a child do well in all things, but he does not put a price tag on his love, giving it only when the child excels or lives up to expectations, and withholding his love when the child does not.

Accepting the consequences of the child's immaturity.   The accepting parent, while endeavoring to help his child to "grow up," does not look upon the child's immaturity as a kind of stupidity or as a moral offense. When the child unintentionally spills his food, vomits, or has a vagrant bowel movement, the parent does not welcome the mess but he will try not to treat the child as an offender. He does not regard his child as a liar when the youngster is unable to distinguish what is true and what is not. The accepting parent does not regard his child as "bad" when the youngster, in his make-believe, does extravagant things (such as "spanking" a doll).

Acceptance and spontaneity.   The accepting parent is more likely than the unaccepting one to be spontaneous with his child—to laugh and to be gay and also to let other emotions show. The parent who has this ability does not have to put on an act of being a good parent. He does not have to pretend that he is bubbling with mirth when he is not, or pleased when he actually isn't, or free from annoyance when the youngster really annoys him. Depending on the child's age and fortitude, he probably will, at times, show less anger or anxiety than he feels. He will not deliberately hurt a child but neither will he feel it necessary always to use kid gloves.

Acceptance of children and self-acceptance.   The accepting parent, while loving his child, also accepts his responsibilities as a parent. He will not just be an easy mark, a pushover, unable to draw a line between the child's wishes and his own, or unable to distinguish between the child's wishes and the rights and duties of an older person. While granting his child the right to be himself, he remains convinced of his own rights—the right to say yes or no, the right to have and to assert his own beliefs, the right to be devoted to his child without becoming the child's slave. This aspect of the parent-child relationship presents difficulties to many parents. Frequently it is easier to shower a child with gifts and to indulge him (until his demands become unbearable) than to set limits, to deny the child something when, in the long run, it would be best to do so.

Acceptance of rejection.   We often hear about "rejecting parents," but there are also "rejecting" children. All parents probably have a feeling of being rejected when their children are grossly disobedient, and seem callous, or to want to hurt them. In adolescence, for example, a youngster may say he is ashamed of his parents or his home, or he may shift his loyalties to peers whose standards differ from those of his parents. Actually, in seeming to reject his parents the youngster may be seeking a kind of independence which, in the long run, will be to the good. The child's striving for independence may basically be a tribute to his parents rather than a kind of rejection. But at the time his parents are likely to feel that he is turning against them.

Conduct that seems rejecting is often most disturbing at the adolescent level, but children at all ages can be rejecting. The infant who cannot tolerate his mother's milk is, in a sense, rejecting his mother, although that is not his attention. The child who, in a phase of rugged "resistance" or negativism goes out of his way to oppose his parents, seems to be doing his share of rejecting. The child who does not respond to any of the interests which his father tries to pursue with him, but turns instead to interests which his father cannot share, may look like a rejecting child. A youngster who does poor work at school, perhaps in a perverse effort to detract attention from a brother or sister who is doing good work at school, is, to a degree, rejecting his parents who are trying to encourage him to do better work.

None of these illustrations need be regarded as actual rejection, but parents from time to time will have a taste of being pushed aside and ignored as each child in a family strives to hammer out his own distinctive way of life.

Experiences of this kind test the mettle of an accepting parent. The parent is called upon to accept his child, even though the child, in one way or another is rejecting him. This is not only a test of the parent's acceptance of his child, but, even more basically, of the parent's acceptance of himself. A parent is fortunate if he still can feel worthy even though his best intentions seem to have been defeated and even though he is sharply reminded that he does not have the power to be the ideal parent of an ideal child.

Acceptance and realism.   According to the thought expressed above, the more accepting a parent is, the more realistic he is likely to be. He will not attempt the impossible. He will not always be plagued by guilt if something in his role as a parent seems to go wrong. We use the word "always" advisedly here, for (so the writer is convinced) many "good" and accepting parents have feelings of guilt. Preliminary results in an exploratory study by the writer and Eve Allina support this view. When parents really feel free to "let down their hair," it appears that most of them (probably all of them) will express feelings of guilt about something they have done or failed to do.[2]

Our culture cherishes the belief that if a parent really wills it he can be loving, patient, thoughtful, and wise enough to solve all problems. There probably is no human being who can be *that* loving, patient, thoughtful, and wise.

One mark of realism is to recognize that, no matter how glorious it is to have children, parents often have feelings and thoughts about them that are very inglorious. This is brought out in a study by Le Masters (1957).

---

[2] In an earlier study by the writer and his associates (Jersild, Woodyard, and del Solar, 1949) in which parents were interviewed, but not "in depth," a large proportion spontaneously expressed feelings of self-reproach for what they had done or left undone.

When Le Masters interviewed forty-six young couples, thirty-eight (83 per cent) reported that they had faced an "extensive" or "severe" crisis in adjusting to their first child. Some of the experiences that made adjustment difficult (as reported by mothers) were loss of sleep, chronic fatigue, confinement to the home, having to give up social contacts and income from outside employment, guilt at not being a "better" mother, and worry over change in appearance. Fathers echoed most of what the mothers said and added items of their own, such as a decline in the wife's sexual response, worry about a second pregnancy, and a "general disenchantment with the parental role." According to Le Masters, the crisis was not a result of not wanting children. It occurred in a large number of marriages which were rated "good" both by the couples themselves and their close friends. Most of the couples also said that they were able to work out a good adjustment as parents, although the transition was difficult.[3]

Another mark of realism is to recognize that there are limits to what a loving parent can do. He cannot spread his love over the entire landscape. He cannot always be there to assuage a child who falls into the hands of cruel playmates, or unfeeling teachers, or adults who have no love for children. Regardless of the firm foundation of confidence and trust built by parents in their relationships with children at home, they cannot spare their children from the possibility of being rejected outside the home.

Consequences of being accepted

The child who has been reared in a climate of acceptance is likely to have many advantages, even though there are limits to what even the most accepting parent can do for a child. While still helpless and weak the child can count on protection. He does not have to fight battles that he is not strong enough to win. In an atmosphere of affection the child has an opportunity to acquire an an attitude of confidence and trust in those who rear him; as he grows older he will be in a better position to develop his own capacity for affection for others. In a climate of affection and understanding he will have a kind of freedom which a rejected child is unlikely to possess—freedom to grow, to venture, to try and fail and then to try again, without always having to prove his worth or defend himself. He will be freer to express his feelings. He will have more freedom to be open and frank in his relations with others than is the youngster who is tolerated only

---

[3] When parents report difficulties in getting used to their first child, this does not necessarily mean that the first child has a rougher time than later born children. Lasko (1954) found that some mothers are less warm emotionally and more restrictive with their second-born than with their first born children.

when, as a "good" child, he does the right thing in a polite way. He will have more freedom to reveal his fears without the risk of ridicule. He will have less need to fear his own anger and to drive it underground.

Probably the greatest advantage of being an accepted child is that the growing youngster will have a better chance to learn to accept himself. He will be less likely to feel guilty about the fumbling and errors which a youngster inevitably makes in the process of growing up.

The rejecting parent

When we speak of the rejecting parent we deal with the tragic side of the drama of family life. The tragedy becomes compounded when we use the concept of rejection to accuse and condemn.

The writer recalls an instance of this in work some years ago with a group of students in clinical psychology. The case history of a harassed "rejecting" mother was being read when a student remarked, "Why doesn't she shoot the kid and be done with it?" Some students endorsed this remark with laughter. Apparently without realizing it, they were rejecting this mother—perhaps as much as the mother had rejected her child—and they were not alone in this. In many writings dealing with "rejecting" parents it is difficult to determine who is most rejecting—the parents or the writers.

The lot of a rejected child is bitter. But the possibility exists (while he is still growing up) that someone, somewhere will accept him. The lot of a rejecting parent is also bitter. His attitude is rooted in the tragedies of his own life. And, as an adult, he probably is less likely than the rejected child to discover that someone, somewhere, will view him with compassion.

It is important to lean a bit to the compassionate side in applying the concept of rejection. Accepting and rejecting attitudes are often intermingled. A parent may seem to be rejecting even if he is deeply devoted to his child. Moreover, the press of everyday life and the need for setting limits on what a child can expect or be allowed to do inevitably means that every parent is quite often seen by the child as a rejecting parent. According to Anna Freud (1955) the concept of the rejecting mother has been used too loosely by child welfare workers. She distinguishes between various types of rejecting behavior and points out that no matter how devoted a mother might be she cannot meet all the boundless demands made on her by her child.

Among the more extreme signs that a parent is rejecting his child, as described by one of the earlier writers on this subject (Fitz-Simons, 1935) are the following: The parent deserts the child or puts him into an institution (such as reform school or military school) to discipline him or avoid being bothered by him; the parent is able to see only the child's faults, and uses very severe punishment. Other items listed as signifying rejection are frequent criticism, threats to evict, locking the child up (in closet or basement), or deliberately frightening him. Still other signs of rejection, rated as somewhat less severe, include nagging, spanking, paying no attention to the child, failing to provide him with money or toys or advantages, comparing the child unfavorably with others, making no effort to improve his condition through the help of doctors, teachers, and other trained adults.

One of these milder items by itself does not mark the parent as "rejecting," but if a parent habitually uses many of them, with no off-setting friendly ways, it seems highly probable that he not only lacks affection for his child but actually feels hostile toward him.[4]

There are many other ways of rejecting a child. One can reject him by not caring enough and so failing to detect signs that he is afraid or is being mistreated at school. One can reject a child by promising to love him only if he is good or if he keeps clean or does superior work. One can reject a child by over-indulging him, giving in to him and giving him almost every thing he desires in order to quiet him and be rid of him.

Over-indulgence may appear to be a form of over-protection, which on the surface looks very different from rejection. But over-protection is in many respects a way of rejecting a child by not giving him the opportunity to develop his own strength and ability to fend for himself. To develop his own potentials, as he grows older, the child must act for himself, think for himself, and assume some of the risks of everyday life.

Behavior such as the following has been regarded as a sign of an "over-protecting" attitude, as contrasted with a "rejecting" attitude: excessive contact of mother with child (sleeping in same bed, continually keeping within sight); infantile care prolonged far beyond infancy; lack or excess of parental control; indulging the child or caring for his physical needs to an excessive degree.

FACTORS UNDERLYING REJECTION AND OVER-PROTECTION

A common element in rejection and over-protection can be seen when a parent over-does his protecting role without permitting the child to venture out on his own. He may, for example, go to great lengths to protect his child from the ordinary dangers of everyday life, carefully standing by whenever the youngster rides a bicycle or goes swimming or sledding.

---

[4] For writings dealing with the effects of parental attitudes, including rejection, nonrejection, and overprotection see Fitz-Simons (1935), Levy (1943), and Symonds (1938), and a series of studies initiated by Levy, published in several numbers of the journal *Smith College Studies in Social Work* during the years 1930 and 1931.

When a parent constantly hovers over a child we may suspect that perhaps he is an anxious parent who, in seeming to care too much, is trying to make amends for an uneasy feeling that he has not cared enough. Over-protection in some aspects of the child's life may be linked with rejection in other aspects. For example, a parent who is neither willing nor able to respond to the child's psychological needs may overdo his concern about the child's physical needs. We see this when a parent refuses to listen to the child when he is frightened or angry, but then showers the child with attention when he has a slight cold or bellyache.

A parent's tendency to reject or to over-protect may be influenced by many conditions. According to Levy (1943), an over-protecting attitude may be the result of disappointment or frustration prior to having a child (due, for example, to miscarriage or death of another infant); of conditions that threatened the child's life, such as severe illness; of unsatisfactory marital relationships; or of an unsatisfied hunger for affection. Any condition in a parent's life which makes him anxious, withdrawn, unable freely to feel and to express emotion will interfere with his ability to love his child.

CONSEQUENCES OF REJECTION

The child who is reared without affection faces a hard life. While young and weak he cannot count on the protection and help he needs. He is thrown on his own resources when his resources are very limited. He may be left for long periods, hungry, uncomfortable, angry, frightened, friendless, and alone.

The child who is not only ignored but actively abused (as some children are even in infancy) does not have the strength to defend himself. His main weapon is crying. But when he cries in anger, grief, or fear his cries are likely to evoke complaint instead of compassion. Under conditions of severe rejection a child is like a warrior who is wounded even before he has a chance to fight.

The older child carries a large burden if there is no friendly adult at home to blunt the edge of assaults which he receives from unkind playmates or teachers, or other members of the community who have a cruel streak. He is constantly driven back on his own defenses. If he withdraws within himself, he cuts himself off from the friendliness he might somewhere find. If he fights back, he is likely to meet with further rejection.

A child whose faults are noticed while his merits are ignored is constantly failing in the eyes of others, and no one can thrive on a diet of failure. The child who receives no love will have difficulty in learning how to bestow it. He will lack a model of love and good will that would help him to trust others, to count on their mercy, and to acquire love for others. Having received no affection he learns not to expect it. He learns to expect nothing, or to expect the worst, and having learned that, his guard is up against all who come. But the more he guards himself the more he erects a wall between himself and those who might befriend him. The flow of fellow-feeling, so important in healthy relationships with others, is cut off. There is a rift between him and other people. But more, there is a rift also within him. Under a regimen of rejection and failure it will be hard for him to develop confidence in his own worth. If no one esteems him it will be difficult for him to learn to esteem himself.

Response to neglect and deprivation. In some situations it is possible to distinguish between the circumstances of a *rejected* child and of a child who is *neglected.* In its severest form, rejection means that a child is treated unkindly by persons who view him with distaste or are openly hostile toward him. Such a child's position differs in some respects from that of a child who—while not openly abused—is not given the care which children need and normally receive.

Accounts of children whose development has been impaired by deprivation, neglect, and lack of "mothering" make a deep appeal to the sympathy of the reader. They also produce anxiety in parents who wonder if *they* perhaps are guilty of not having mothered their babies properly. Much of the evidence regarding the effects of deprivation is based on studies of babies who have been separated from their mothers and reared in foundling homes or orphanages. The conclusions reported in studies of such children have varied greatly. Apparently, this is partly a result of the different kind of care provided by different institutions (Dennis [1959] found, for example, that children in two institutions that were seriously understaffed were severely retarded in their early motor development, while children in a third institution which provided more individual attention showed little retardation). The varied conclusions drawn from studies of institutional babies are apparently due also to differences in the age level of the children at the time they were studied, their biological background, their experiences before and after they were placed in institutions, and the amount of time they spent under institutional care.

Some studies have reported that babies suffer dire and tragic consequences from lack of adequate mothering, showing such symptoms as emotional shock, apathy, anxiety, and *marasmus*—a form of wasting that cannot be traced to any specific physical cause but may be due to severe emotional disturbance. Among the investigations that report the most damaging consequences of lack of mothering is a series of studies by Spitz (see Spitz, 1951, and references in this study to earlier reports).

In a study by Rheingold (1959) careful techniques were applied to measure the attention five infants received from their mothers at home and the attention five babies received from caretakers in an institution.

The babies ranged in age from 3.2 to 3.8 months. The home infants had many more contacts with their mothers than institutional infants had with their caretakers. The infants differed widely in their activities, as measured and recorded in this study, but as a group the home-reared infants did not differ materially from the institution-reared infants. According to Rheingold, "That no differences of statistical significance were found in the infant activities recorded suggests the possibility that wide as the differences in caretaking were, they were still not wide enough to produce differences in infant behavior." (There is still the possibility, Rheingold suggests, that differences in the behavior of the babies might be found if they were older, or that there might have been differences in forms of behavior that were not measured in her study.)

Dennis and Najarian (1957) compared babies reared in an institution "in which 'mothering' and all other forms of adult-child interaction are at a minimum because the institution is seriously understaffed" with home-reared children who were brought to a Well Baby Clinic. The institutional children's average "developmental quotient," as determined by standardized tests, was approximately 100 (normal) at two months, but between the ages of three and twelve months the average was about 63. Dennis and Najarian conclude that "the retardation prevailing between three and twelve months seems to be due to lack of learning opportunities in situations comparable to the test situations." (The babies spent most of their time on their backs during this period, with little opportunity, in a sitting position, to practice various skills, such as following objects with their eyes or manipulating them with their hands.) However, when tested at the 4½- to 6-year levels, the average developmental scores were about 90, leading to the conclusions that "Retardation in the last nine months of the first year . . . does not result in a generally poor performance at 4½ to 6 years, even when a child remains in a relatively restricted environment."

From their observations of the children's emotional reactions (such as crying, smiling, friendliness, tendency to show fear) Dennis and Najarian found "nothing to suggest that emotional shock, or lack of mothering or other emotion-arousing conditions, were responsible for behavioral retardation." They believe that their findings pertaining to the retarding effects of being reared in an institution which provides a minimum of individual care "can be interpreted in terms of specific kinds of restrictions on infant learning."

Rheingold and Bayley (1959) made a study of sixteen babies living in an institution during approximately the first nine months of their lives. From the sixth through the eighth month half of them, known as the experimental group, were cared for by one person for seven-and-a-half hours a day. These children received a considerable amount of personal attention. They became more socially responsive than the children in the control group who were cared for under the usual institutional routine. The two groups did not differ significantly, however, on various standardized tests while the experiment was under way. After the experiment, fourteen of the babies were tested again at the age of nineteen months, after they had returned to their homes or had been placed in boarding or adoptive homes. On the retests, the children who had received special mothering while in the institution were more vocal than members of the control group, but apart from this the two groups did not differ significantly in their developmental progress or social responsiveness. The children in both groups were friendly, and they did not resemble the emotionally disturbed and mentally retarded children described in some of the studies that have been made of the effects of institutional life or separation from the mother.

Striking findings concerning the effect of deprivation and neglect on children living in an orphanage which did not provide adequate child care have been reported by Skeels, Updegraf, and associates (1938). These children were more on the defensive, less free to reach out for friendly care than normal children who have been cared for at home. They were backward in nearly all aspects of their development—in ability to handle the physical environment, in language ability, in ability to enter into the give and take of social interaction.

When a special nursery school was set up in the orphanage the children did not at first respond as nursery children normally do. Although they had been left to shift for themselves, they were less able to care for their physical needs than normal children. They did not know how to use equipment, such as blocks and wheel toys; they destroyed a good deal of property; their attention span was short; they tended to lose control of themselves when crossed by others. One of the first necessities was to help each of these children to develop "consciousness of himself as an individual," capable of achievement and able to receive consideration from others. It took about six months to bring them to the point where they were able to profit from the educational opportunities which the nursery school provided but which had been lacking in their orphanage environment. But as a cheerful note, it should be added that the children who were placed in the nursery school, in the hands of devoted teachers, made great progress after a time.

The experiment by Skeels, Updegraf, and their associates is one of the most impressive in the literature of psychological research. The drama of the study resides not so much in spectacular deeds as in the attention it calls to the earthy aspects of a child's development. In order to have the freedom to be curious, to explore, and to fully enjoy the opportunities for learning which the environment affords, a child needs the support of friendly adults.

A study by Goldfarb (1943) indicates that children in an institution where the usual intimacy of affection between parent and child does not exist may be penalized severely in their development. The findings indicate that a person who has not had affection may later lack the kind of intellectual freedom and enterprise necessary for dealing with large concepts or abstractions.[5] According to this line of thought, a person who has not been accepted emotionally may be more constricted in his mental operations, more tied to the literal, the exact data, the detailed facts. The ability to think big thoughts is not solely a product of rigorous intellectual discipline. It apparently involves a kind of emotional freedom, coupled with intellectual acuity, that makes it possible to see the details in a larger synthesis. On the other hand, the less freedom there is, the more tendency there will be to stay with the given facts—to see the trees but not the forest.

Findings in some studies indicate that the degree of cordiality that existed between a child and his parents affects the child's moral development (Zucker, 1943) and his attitudes—his tendency to be conservative or radical as a young adult, for example (Stagner et al., 1944).

The importance to the child of security in his accustomed ties and contacts with adults has been emphasized in several studies dealing with the effects of wartime happenings, notably evacuation, upon the behavior of children (see Issacs et al., 1941; and Burt, 1941). Some children seemed to be emotionally more affected by leaving home and living in a new place with strange people than by being exposed to air raids at home.

REJECTION AND SELF-REPAIR

In our schools and in the community at large we can see many persons who appear to bear the marks of having been rejected by others and who show symptoms of a rejecting attitude toward others. The child at school who is unresponsive and sullen is quite probably one who has been neglected or rejected or feels rejected. His feeling of rejection may stem from his home, or it may have arisen from his experience at school. Such a child is baffling and hard to reach. It is difficult for him to respond to a friendly approach. Such a child is exasperating, but teachers who have little feeling for other human beings will find him especially exasperating. They may respond to his rejecting attitude by rejecting him, using some of the many weapons at their command—ignoring him, giving him failing grades, making him the butt of sarcastic remarks, complaining to his parents, or indirectly attacking him by complaining about his parents. So the youngster most in need of understanding and sympathy receives the least.

---

[5] For a discussion bearing on this, see Goldfarb (1943), and for a discussion of some of the underlying theory, see also Goldstein and Scheerer (1941).

However, an unresponsive child may come under the influence of a teacher who is able to reach out to those whom others reject. Such a teacher can sometimes make a remarkable difference. The child who was a surly brat may soften and become friendly under the influence of a teacher who cares and seeks to understand. While working with teachers the writer has had an opportunity to observe great improvements in children who once were hostile or apathetic. The literature contains many reports of children who have benefitted from specialized psychological help (and also of children who did not). Knowing that some children at least can be helped adds a hopeful note to the saga of the rejected child. Usually we know so little about him, his past and his possibilities, yet this (the writer believes) we do know: Even a child who seems beyond repair may possess potentialities for health and growth. A child who has suffered rejection may still retain, within the desert of his life, a small green patch that can be cultivated.

Many psychologists view the greatest human hunger as a hunger for love. The normal child will take all he can get and then ask for more. We do not know how much affection from others is needed to keep a child's capacity for affection alive, but this capacity is hard to destroy.

The rejected child is a challenge to our humanity. And to the degree that he has a capacity to survive despite adversity we can view him with hope and not as a symbol of despair.

Forms of attachment to parents

A child's attachment to his parents expresses itself in many ways. The youngster may, for example, prefer to romp and play with his father but demand the company of his mother when he is sick or when he awakens from a bad dream.

Attachment to parent of the opposite sex. Among children, as among adults, one sometimes finds individuals who are very strongly attached to the parent of the opposite sex. A boy's devotion to his mother, and a girl's to her father, may be so strong that each (consciously or unconsciously) looks for the image of the beloved parent when choosing a mate. The boy, knowingly or unconsciously, wants a girl just like the girl that married dear old Dad.

It is not strange that this should be so. The boy gets his first impression and probably his most enduring conception of womanhood from his mother. The girl is likely to get her primary image of a strong and lovable man from her father.

As described by Freud, children go through an *Oedipal* phase, during which they are sexually attracted by the parent of the opposite sex. This creates difficulty for the boy who wants to possess his mother and displace his father, and for the girl who wants to possess her father. Feelings of jealousy and hostility toward the rival parent arise and produce anxiety and guilt.[6] Those who accept orthodox Freudian theory maintain that one of the most difficult hurdles of childhood is to resolve this complex. According to less orthodox views, now widely held by many psycho-analysts, anthropologists, and psychologists, an Oedipal attachment to the parent of the opposite sex may occur, and perhaps often does occur, but it should not be regarded as something inevitable.

In any event, no one can question the importance of the child's emotional relationships with the people (usually the parents) who have his physical and psychological well-being in their hands. This relationship, whether or not it involves a classical Oedipus complex, is of great significance in the child's early development and will influence his relationships with others and his developing ideas and attitudes concerning himself.

MIXED EMOTIONS

The full range of human emotions enters into the parent-child relationship—anger, fear, and sorrow, as well as love and joy. Parents are likely to feel anger, or a combination of anger, regret, and self-reproach, for example, when a child disobeys or angrily tries to hurt their feelings. Children frequently feel anger when, for example, they are denied things. Grievances and feelings of being abused which arise in connection with a child's discipline are described in Chapter Four.

Frequently the feelings of children for their parents and of parents for their children are mixed. When children and parents have strong feelings that clash with one another, such as anger and love or fear and love, they face a conflict within themselves. The label "ambivalence" or "ambivalent feelings" has been used to identify mixed feelings of this sort.

Ambivalence as revealed by children's fantasies. Ambivalent feelings toward parents often appear in children's make-believe. In doll-play, for example, a girl, acting the part of a mother, spanks one of the babies unmercifully, or pets one baby while pushing another aside, or "feeds" one baby while letting the other go hungry. Here, on a make-believe level, the mother is portrayed as a punitive and unfair person. The actual mother, watching this, may dismiss it as childish play. Or (as the writer has observed in discussion with some mothers) she may secretly feel hurt, and perhaps openly protest against what the child is doing. One

---

[6] Freud's theory of the Oedipus complex as related to anxiety is discussed in Chapter Twelve.

mother asked, for example, "Why does my daughter treat her dolls so brutally? She beats them. I have never given her that kind of beating."

In assessing the meaning of make-believe play in which a child takes the part of a punishing parent, portraying the parent as a hostile person and indirectly showing hostility toward his own parent, three things must be borne in mind. First, a child's make-believe does not just happen—it probably reflects something very significant in his experience. Second, a child's make-believe often, from an adult point of view, seems exaggerated: In spanking a doll he perhaps uses a more severe kind of physical punishment than he himself has received. But spanking may be the child's way of acting out, in a crude way, punishments which he has received (or might wish to give) in a more subtle way. Third, a youngster who acts out his aggressive impulses is not necessarily more hostile or browbeaten than one who doesn't. Without additional information we cannot tell whether the mother of a child who spanks a doll is a more punishing kind of person than the mother of a child who never spanks a doll.

Many illustrations of the way in which children, in their make-believe and fantasies, seem to express mixed or ambivalent feelings toward parents and other members of the family were recorded in a study by Griffiths (1934). In her work with five-year-old children in London and Brisbane, Griffiths obtained her data by means of stories, drawings, an "imagery test," accounts of dreams, and an ink blot test. She states that children's "daydreams and subjective ideas" differ from the "objective crust of current thought" and reveal significant insights into their emotional life.

Children's imagery and make-believe relating to parents express both negative and positive attitudes. "Crude and brutal imagery occurred not only in the records of children from poor and overcrowded homes but also in those of children from better homes." According to Griffiths, ambivalence is expressed not only toward the least-liked member of the family (such as a rival sister) but it is "usually towards the most beloved individual that the ambivalence is most strikingly expressed."

As an illustration Griffiths describes a London boy who greatly admired his father (a carter skillful with horses), but also feared him. The boy spoke of an "old man—some old man, any old man what's gonna catch me —he takes yer to his house and cooks yer and eats yer up. If he did that to me I would push the pot up and hit him and run away. . . . It is a bit like my dad when he gonna hit me . . . (but) my dad not really like that." Another boy was devoted to two babies in his home, but he also had many images such as "a baby fell downstairs . . . a baby got killed by the soldiers." Yet another boy, a "gentle" child, apparently well cared for in a superior home, played happily at "mothers and fathers" yet also showed antagonism, as, for example, in telling a story about a man who "fell out of a window and was dead. And a 'copper' came along, and got a big pail o' crabs, and he dropped it on the man, and they eatin' the man all up."

Discomforts of mixed emotions. It is very uncomfortable to feel angry, frightened, or guilty. And anger is often frowned upon as unseemly. As a result, parents and children alike try to evade the meaning of these raw and unpleasant emotions. One way of dealing with uncomfortable emotions is to pretend they don't exist, or at least to play them down. If we ask a parent, "Does your child love you?" he is likely to say, "Yes, I think so, at least I hope so." But when asked, "Does your child hate you or fear you?" the typical parent is tempted to evade the question or to say that while his youngster does get angry at times and may even be afraid at times, these feelings are transient ripples. It would, of course, be easier if all concerned could face the fact that unpleasant as well as pleasant emotions are intermingled in parent-child relationships, and frankly acknowledge this condition not as a glaring fault but as one of the simple facts of life.

How does the child perceive the parent?

To probe the meaning of the parent-child relationship we need to ask not only what the parents do and what they intend but also how the child perceives the situation. The child's view, of course, may be very different from what the parents have in mind. Ausubel and his associates (1954) have expressed this matter in the following assumption: ". . . although parent behavior is an objective event in the real world, it affects the child's ego development only to the extent and in the form in which he perceives it. Hence, perceived parent behavior is in reality a more direct, relevant and proximate determinant of personality development than the actual stimulus context to which it refers." [7]

Differences in viewpoint. The differences between the parents' view of their actions and the child's view stand out sharply when parents say no, and the child regards them as mean and unreasonable; or when they punish, and the child, aware of his own hurt, is unable to understand why he was punished; or when the child for various reasons has a strong need to see his parents as more noble and generous than they really are. The child's view may differ from that of the parent (or of a visitor in the home)

---

[7] Other studies dealing with the ways in which children and parents perceive one another have been reported by Connor *et al.* (1958), Davidson *et al.* (1958), Henry (1957), Jackson (1956), and Kagan (1956).

even when parents openly express their fondness for him. Willie's parents affectionately call him Willikins, but Willie resents this pet name, especially if his parents use it when there is company. When Willie goes to kiss Daddy goodnight, Daddy gives him a hug and presses his cheek against Willie's, but what does Willie experience? The father's cheek, unshaved since morning, is rough and grating. So the father's caress is not, to Willie, a loving touch but something unpleasant. (In an instance reported to the writer, a son, now middle-aged, while listing the unpleasant things his father had done, recalled the grating touch of his father's stubbly cheek. Then he felt a wave of affection when it occurred to him that what he had perceived and remembered as something unpleasant actually was a mark of his father's tenderness.)

Many instances of a changed view of parents were reported in a study (Jersild and Allina, 1960) in which adults reviewed various aspects of their lives. Some who, for example, as children and young adults, had favored one parent now were convinced that it was the other parent who really was the "good" parent. When an adult thus revises his view of his parents we cannot conclude that his present perception is more accurate or less accurate than the one he had before. It is clear, however, that the perception a person has of his parents reflects something in his own subjective experience and is not simply a mirror reflection of what his parents actually felt or did.

Each child has a perception of his parents (and each parent has his unique perception of his child and of himself) that may or may not reflect what they "really" are. Therefore it is no wonder that research workers usually find low correlations between ratings of the behavior or personalities of parents and the personality traits of normal children.

Differences in perception arise even in matters that seem obvious from an objective point of view. Janet's mother is never regularly absent from home, except for volunteer work in a hospital on Wednesday afternoons. But Janet, demanding much and resenting her mother's absence, says, "Mother is 'almost never' home." Mabel's mother is regularly absent every workday of the week but her daughter may report "Mother is 'almost always' home." Of course, both daughters may, in a sense, be right. Janet's mother, who is almost always physically at home may be a detached mother who, in a psychological sense, is almost never at home; and Mabel's mother, who spends forty hours a week on her job may, pscho-logically, be a person who is close and near at hand. But when we simply count the hours, collecting the objective "facts," we do not catch this distinction. Even in the dimensions of time, which can be measured so precisely by the hands of the clock, there is a great difference between the objective and the subjective spheres. To one, an hour of waiting is like eternity; to another, an hour, a day, a week, a year, is like a fleeting moment, well worth the time of waiting. To the child who is passionately hungry, a moment's delay is agony—and anger. To another, less hungry, a delay in feeding does not matter much.

In many situations the difference between the child's and the parent's view of things is not brought out into the open. If a child could tell and parents could know how a child perceives their actions, all might be spared a good deal of misunderstanding. As the poet Robert Burns has said:

> Oh wad some power the giftie gie us
> To see oursels as others see us!

Sometimes, of course, the child's view will come out in an explosive way. Once while two parents were reprimanding their child (in a very reasonable way, so they thought), the child cried out "Why don't you just go ahead and shoot me!" The parents had had no idea that the child felt so violently abused.

While, in theory, it would probably be a good thing if parents and children could see one another in the same light, there are times when it would be impossible to achieve such mutual understanding. In some phases of his development it is perhaps best for the child not to perceive his parents' actions as they perceive them. While going through a phase of resistance or negativism children often stubbornly refuse to see the point, but it may be a good thing for them to learn to assert themselves even though, from the point of view of their parents, they are very unreasonable. Again, at adolescence, there are many times when a robust youngster and his parents definitely do not see eye to eye. The youngster, influenced by his peers, and swept along by his desire for freedom and independence, demands privileges which, from his parents' point of view, he should not have. Parents regard the restrictions they place on the youngster as reasonable and necessary; but the youngster sees his parents as forbidding and stiff, or just plain foolish. (According to Mark Twain, "When I was a boy of fourteen my father was so stupid I could scarcely stand to have the old man around. But by the time I got to be twenty-one I was astonished at how much he had learned in the last seven years.")

If parents had the courage and interest to inquire and children the freedom to respond frankly, most parents would probably be quite surprised by the picture the children paint of them. In one instance a father asked his adolescent boy, "When you think back, what's the worst thing I ever did to you?" The father, remembering times when he, as he thought, had been too severe or too impatient, thought the boy would speak of one of these episodes. But the boy's reply was, "When I started school the teacher was strict, but at home you would talk things over with me, and in school the teacher wouldn't. So it was very hard for me to get used to school. And that is the worst thing you have done to me."

THE IDEALIZED PARENT

In perceiving his parents a child may view them as worse than they are but he may also see them as being much more noble, saintly, and reasonable than they are. In either event, the misconception makes it difficult for parents and children to communicate with each other. In one of the writer's studies, a record tells of a boy who confessed to his mother that the teacher had punished him that day. Why? He had used bad words. "What words?" The boy shrank back, "I can't tell those words to you—they are not fit for a woman's ears!" The words apparently were not unfit for the coarse ears of the woman who was his teacher, but they were not suited to the image he had of his mother as an especially sensitive and refined person.

The more idealized the child's picture of his parents, the more difficult it will probably be for him to go to them with some of his concerns. If he sees his parents as being especially virtuous he may carry a sin on his conscience, unwilling to confess to parents who are so good and he is so bad. Here we have an interesting paradox. In theory, parents should set a good moral example for their children. But, when parents set an example of uprightness they may create a barrier between themselves and their children. There probably is no child who has not committed at least a small theft or had an impulse to steal. But his parents—they are not thieves! If they ever stole or had an impulse to steal he does not recognize this fact. So he is psychologically separated from them. He cannot openly go to them, as one thief might go to another. There probably is no healthy child who, even while quite young, has not been involved in sex play, or has not had fantasies about forbidden sex behavior. But if he sees his parents as being sexually pure, not only in their actions but also in their thoughts, he is separated from them. Of course, matters may be even more difficult for the child if his parents are known thieves or openly involved in sexual misconduct. But the child faces a perplexing situation whether he mistakenly perceives his parents as rigidly righteous or sees them as moral derelicts.

Keeping the image alive. A child will perceive his parents' behavior as something to admire or rebel against depending on his interests and desires at the moment and also—as time passes—by his need, once he has taken a position, to cling to it and even to justify it. Consequently, an older child or an adult in telling about the kind of treatment he received from his father or mother may be consistent with the view that he has taken but not consistent with the happenings that took place, as seen by another. At the adult level it appears that many persons find it very important to protect and defend an image they have of their father or mother. The father who was harsh may be seen as a strong Olympian character who is admirable in every way, or the image a person has of his father may make him out to be much harsher or much less considerate than he really was. Similarly, the mother may be seen in a glowing idealistic light or in the opposite light.

The perception we retain of our parents, as we grow older, will not only color our memories of childhood but it is likely also to color our perception of others who are father and mother figures, such as teachers. Partly because of perceptions carried over from childhood a certain instructor is a wonderful person in the eyes of one student while another student regards him as a lout.

Perceptions carried over from childhood and a desire to preserve these are likely to influence the meaning we derive from studying child psychology and even the studies on which child psychology is based. When, for example, scholars have differing theories about parent-child relationships or report conflicting research findings, the main reason probably is that conflicting forces actually are at work and the relationship is hard to untangle. But part of the reason may be that each scholar is influenced by his individual perception as he theorizes, defines the nature of his problem, sets up the design for his study, and interprets his results. (This is one of several reasons why, in the study of child psychology, it is necessary not only to look at the theories and objective facts but also at subjective meanings. In accounts of parent-child relationships something more than a purely objective approach is at work when one person, for example, places all the emphasis on heredity, another on the environment, or when one adopts an extreme Freudian or anti-Freudian point of view, or when one stresses the mechanics of learning while another places all the stress on underlying motives.)

Self-assertion in a child's relationships with parents

In their striving for independence many young children go through a phase when they are especially resistant or "negativistic." [8] From an adult's point of view there are times when a child's self-assertion is a nuisance, and counter to his own best interests, but his efforts to assert himself are an essential feature of healthy growth. In asserting himself a child cannot avoid some opposition to others.

---

[8] Self-assertion in relationships with other children is discussed in Chapter Nine.

In many children, resistance in relationships with their elders becomes most noticeable at about eighteen months, with a peak at about the age of four (Reynolds, 1928). This is the time when many children are busy acquiring and asserting that we call "a will of their own."

Resistant behavior as related to the larger context of growth. Some children, while going through a "negative" or "resistant" phase launch a campaign in which they almost seem to be stubborn just for the sake of being stubborn. However, resistant behavior is related to the larger sweep of the child's development. When a child begins to be notably resistant at about the age of two, he is in a phase of growth in which great things are happening. His "life-space," the world in which he lives, has expanded greatly beyond that of infancy. He is able to walk and has far more ability than before to get into things. He is able to understand a great deal of what others say and he can judge, better than before, what they expect of him, and what they intend for him to do or not to do. He has begun to talk, and he is advancing rapidly in his language development. One word he uses frequently is "I" (or "me" or "mine") and he also often uses the word "no." These words mark him as one who is strongly preoccupied with his own undertakings.

Also, if he has an opportunity at the time of the negative phase, he is in the process of establishing brief give-and-take relationships with age-mates outside the home.

He is also plunging into make-believe play, and while his legs carry him into a larger "outer world," his imagination carries him into an expanding "inner world."

The "negativistic" child is, in many ways, a little baby yet his sphere of action is very large. Many paths of self-assertion are open to him. He lives in a big kingdom, but as a child he is still a little king, with many restraints placed on him. He not only resists many of these restraints but he also is testing the limits, testing his ability and right to have a say of his own. Viewed in this perspective, the "resistant phase," while trying to his elders, can also be seen as a fascinating expression of a child's impulse to venture into the possibilities of life.

When a child openly and actively resists, it shows that he has the spunk and the guts to stand up for himself. Resistance may be overdone. But the child who resists his elders at home is at least putting up a struggle. Likewise, the older child who resists a domineering teacher at school is probably a healthier child than one who meekly surrenders to such a teacher but fails to swallow his resentment.

Apart from the developments that are taking place in his own career, conditions in the environment also contribute to resistance. As a child moves from infancy into early childhood there not only is an increase in what he can demand of others but often there is an increase in what others demand of him. As an infant with a loving parent he could cry, soil himself, expect quick attention to his needs. Now, as a walker and a talker he is entering the "you must be a big boy (or girl)" stage. He is expected more and more to take care of himself—to control his bladder, to help in dressing and undressing, to fall in with the household mealtime routine, to share toys with others.[9]

Some effects of resistance on parents. A child's resistance is in many ways a threat to the self-esteem of those who care for him. A parent who likes to think of himself as a reasonable person faces quite a test when his child rejects his nice reasoning. Even when the parent is convinced that it is the child, not he, who is headstrong, it still may be a blow to his pride to realize that one so reasonable as he should have so unreasonable an offspring. Similarly, if the adult likes to think of himself as an unusually generous and forbearing person, his child's sturdy stubbornness will threaten this cherished self-image, and such a threat is tough on any parent. On the other hand, a child's resistance, although not in itself easy to take, may give parents a great deal of satisfaction. If they are not unduly hampered by a compulsion always to be right and to look right they may get quite a thrill out of their child's self-assertiveness.

Forms of resistance. In the young child, resistance frequently takes the form of failure to carry out a request he quite apparently understands, or seeming not to hear or understand a request, or showing stubbornness in connection with eating and the daily routine, or many other little acts of self-assertion. Children sometimes carry their resistance to the extreme of refusing to urinate until they no longer can retain themselves, or refusing to take food or to swallow, or vomiting, or holding their breath until they are blue in the face.

Resistance may also take the form of bickering and argumentativeness and continuous questioning after an answer has been given. An example of this appeared in the case of a two-and-a-half-year-old child who had become extremely disputatious. One day his father was telling this boy and two other children about a chicken farm once owned by the boy's grandfather. Some of the chickens on this farm, the father related, were black and some were white. The boy interrupted to say: "Naw, they were not black and white, they were blue." This form of bickering, after a

---

[9] For a discussion of these and other aspects of resistance and some unfortunate outcomes of conditions that aggravate resistance see Benjamin (1942).

short time, disappeared almost as suddenly as it had come. There un-doubtedly were many factors underlying this behavior, but it appeared that it was, in part, at least, a form of experimentation which coincided with the child's growing ability to question others and to voice his own opinions.

Resistance may also take the form of refusing to accept reality or re-fusing to bow to the inevitable. Thus, a child still hungry for pudding may refuse to accept the fact that there is no pudding even though the empty dish is there for him to see.

Varying degrees and areas of resistance. In a study by Reynolds (1928) "negativism" (resistance), defined as refusal to comply with understood requests, was approached from several angles. Children were rated by their parents and by nursery-school teachers and were also observed under experimental conditions. The experimental situations afforded thirteen opportunities to be resistant (such as refusing to repeat numbers and continuing to play with blocks when asked not to). In this situation "resistance" scores ranged from zero (compliance with every request) to 12 (resistance to all but one of the requests). The average score was 4.38.

There was no significant resemblance between the negativism scores in the experimental situations and negativism at home or in nursery school as rated by parents or teachers of the same children. In everyday observa-tions one can verify this. A child may be very stubborn with one person and not with another, in one situation but not in another. A child who is stubborn and headstrong at home may be quite compliant and cooperative at school, or when visiting a neighbor. Accordingly, a parent and a teacher might have quite different views concerning a child's tendency to be compliant or resistant. What sometimes seems to happen is that a child discovers where and when and with whom he can safely assert himself.

A child whose purposes have been thwarted by one person may express his resistance with another. Some children show a sharp, stubborn streak when they come home from a day in nursery school in which they have been out-maneuvered by clever teachers and overwhelmed by the climate of group conformity which some schools succeed in creating.

The fact that youngsters are quite resistant in some situations and not in others sometimes leads to erroneous conclusions. If a child behaves like a little angel with a teacher or relative, and like a little devil with his own father or mother, the relative and teacher may feel that the youngster is a fine character, that they really know how to get along with him and that there must be something wrong with the parents. If, however, the child were theirs, and the person who is now the parent came and took over (within the nice protection of being an occasional visitor or within the bulwark of the school), it might be the parent who would look "good." [10]

Resistance to the adult is frequently encountered when intelligence tests are being administered to young children. A child's resistance may mean that he is unable to do what is requested of him, but often lack of ability is not the cause. This appeared in a study (Rust, 1931) of resistance during mental tests. About 58 *per cent* of the test items initially refused by the children were passed successfully on subsequent presentations, even though the children received no further help.

Some contributing factors.   There are, of course, many conditions that influence resistance aside from the child's own endeavor to assert himself. He is likely to resist if he is often needlessly interfered with, if he is jerked or forced abruptly while already trying to obey a command, if he is frequently caressed and fondled against his wishes, if he is frequently teased or given contradictory commands, or if he is coerced in any way, whether roughly or by a person who is an expert at gentle coercion. Moreover, if he meets the same person or similar advances in many situations, he may come to resist this person and such advances in other situations as well.

Resistant behavior is sometimes aggravated by the fact that people do not take proper account of the child's limited capacity for concentration. In playing with a child, adults often are tempted to overdo their attentions. If a child is just beginning to talk, for example, an adult may be tempted to coax him to repeat words or to speak new words. Such urging soon becomes tedious.

Sometimes, too, resistance is a bid for attention, as when a youngster who is left to care for himself while his mother is attending to a younger child dawdles, procrastinates, or demands help in what he actually is able to do for himself.

Even in the best home the young child is subject to numberless "no's" and "don'ts," many of them spoken, many of them expressed through restraining gestures and other techniques that keep a child away from forbidden ground. If these could be tallied, it no doubt would be found that the "no's" and "don'ts" to which a child is exposed are far more frequent

---

[10] The fact that children in struggling to assert themselves often choose their own battleground can also be observed at later age levels. One result is that a child's "adjustment" may be viewed very differently by different adults. In a long-term study of school children (Kraus, 1956) it was noted that a rather large proportion of children who were rated as not well-adjusted at home were rated as well-adjusted at school and a large proportion of those rated as not well-adjusted at school were rated as well-adjusted at home. Some children, of course, have difficulty both at home and at school, but many of them, it appears, choose where they will assert themselves or act out their problems.

than the "no's" and "I won'ts" with which he retorts. The fact that a great many rules and restraints are not only inevitable but reasonable from an adult point of view means little to the child. When we consider the amount of regimentation to which children are exposed at home and at school the remarkable thing is not that they resist but that they resist so little.

Resistance at later age levels.   As children become older they usually show less resistance in the somewhat crude forms described above, but there are exceptions to this, notably as they approach or enter the adolescent years. A decline in open resistance may be due to many circumstances. The older child understands better what is expected of him, is better able to comply, and has learned that he will be more comfortable if he complies with the wishes of others whether or not he really feels like it. Open resistance also is likely to decline when a child has learned to express himself better by means of words or when he has acquired other more subtle means of asserting his independence. A decline in resistance is also likely to occur because of learning on the parents' part; they may be more wary or better able to handle issues that are likely to provoke resistance.

Continuing symptoms of rebellion.   Although overt resistance usually declines after the fourth year, it persists in one form or another throughout life. As the child grows older, his methods of resisting become more subtle. The child pretends he does not hear or understand, refuses to see the point, persists in referring to a topic that has been closed, carelessly executes commands, teases, resorts to indirect recriminations, and employs a number of other devices. At adolescence, many youngsters show a new upsurge of resistance, sometimes called the "second negative phase" and sometimes referred to as just plain mutiny. The "resisting" adolescent, like the child of two or three, is waging his own struggle for independence, sometimes in a way that brings him into serious trouble.

Resistant tendencies resembling those of children often can be seen in otherwise normal adults, as when an adult chronically "rises" against suggestions, goes out of his way to eat or to wear what he has been advised against, or persists in mannerisms for no apparent reason other than the fact that he has been urged not to.

Recommended Readings

The Happy Family by John Levy and Ruth Monroe (1938) is an earthy, readable (and, in spots, controversial) account of the satisfactions and frictions that arise in relationships between parents and children. Hilde Bruch's *Don't Be Afraid of Your Child* (1952) is a "guide to perplexed parents" who are bewildered by the deluge of advice, often conflicting, to which modern parents are exposed. Other recommended readings on the subject of parent-child relationships are listed at the end of Chapter Eight. References to studies of parent-child relationships appear regularly in the chapter on "Developmental Psychology" in the *Annual Review of Psychology*. Several papers dealing with parent-child relationships and the role of the family are presented in the three books of readings, recommended in Chapter One, edited by Wayne Dennis (1951); William E. Martin and Celia Burns Stendler (1954); and Jerome M. Seidman (1958).

Patterns
of Parental Behavior

If we observe parents over a period of time we can probably detect in many of them certain patterns or trends in the way they deal with their children. This does not mean that parents can be separated into clear-cut types nor that they will always run true to form. In this chapter we will examine some of the patterns of child-rearing and review studies of the relationship these have to the personality development of children.

Most of our information about the interaction between parents and children has been obtained by observing parents and children or by questioning them. When the method of direct observation is used, the investigator goes to the home and records what the parents and children do and say in their interaction with one another. The observer may simply go with pencil and paper

and, during a set period of time, write down details as they occur, later classifying these under various headings—such as "coerces," "scolds," "praises," "shows affection," "answers questions." Or he may record what he hears and sees on a form or check-list, prepared after preliminary study. The procedures used when parents and children themselves describe their behavior and attitudes include interviews, and questionnaires, check-lists and self-rating scales which parents or children respond to in writing.

Prevailing undertones

Twenty-one mothers obligingly invited one investigator (Lafore, 1945) into their homes where she recorded the practices the parents used and the behavior of their children. No parent consistently used a single approach, but Lafore was able to classify parents into four groups as follows:

"*Dictators.*" Parents who usually made a dictatorial approach with emphasis on authority and obedience.

"*Cooperators.*" Parents who were predominantly friendly, who seemed to deal with the child on a basis of mutual respect and who appeared to feel that if things could be explained, and if there could be joint action, unquestioning obedience was not necessary.

"*Temporizers.*" Parents whose approach seemed to be preponderantly "situational." These parents followed no consistent pattern of behavior, but seemed to fall into one situation after another. If the situation was pleasant the parent was pleasant; if the situation got out of hand the parent became confused, without seeming to know what she should do, what she had done, or what she would do.

"*Appeasers.*" Parents whose approach was predominantly conciliatory and who seemed somewhat afraid of the child, as though he was in control. These parents tended to avoid issues and tried to circumvent problems that arose. Their apparent aim was to prevent trouble rather than to face an issue.

When we call a parent a "dictator" or an "appeaser" we are giving him an unpleasant name, and if the parents in Lafore's study read her account it is likely that some of them would see themselves and not feel complimented. Yet all the parents in this study were "good" parents and they very definitely were cooperative parents; they were interested enough to allow an investigator to come into their homes and to see them as they were. Lafore speaks feelingly about these parents and their children, recognizing the strains and perplexities that arise in every family. In her visits to the homes she became convinced that each parent and each child was trying his best, yet she also noted ("with a feeling of pity") that they often worked at cross-purposes.

Further evidence about patterns of parental behavior comes from studies by Champney (1931) and Baldwin and his associates (1945, 1949) who devised and applied a form for recording the interaction between parents and children in the home. They noticed syndromes or clusters of behavior in the ways in which parents dealt with their children. Some parents, for example, showed a preference for "democratic" practices. Other parents could be classed as "indulgent"—parents who seemingly were unable to separate their own personalities from the personalities of their children and who tended to give them too much care and protection. There also were parents classed as *actively rejectant* and *nonchalantly rejectant;* these were parents who sought to avoid their responsibilities by ignoring their children and then punishing them, or by demanding strict compliance. (In a later study, Crandall and Preston (1955) used this same instrument and added a new category—"coercive control.")

Evidence that the way an adult deals with children reflects certain motifs also comes from observation of teachers (H. H. Anderson *et al.*, 1937a, 1937b, 1945). Some teachers used what the investigators called "dominative" approaches to children while others used "socially integrative" approaches. The characteristics of the teachers seemed to persist from one year to the next even though the teachers were dealing with different groups of children. In other words, whether a teacher is peremptory and bossy, or whether she enters into a relationship with a thoughtful kind of give and take, depends not only on the characteristics of the pupils but also upon tendencies within the teacher herself.

In a study of patterns of child-rearing, Sears and his associates (1957) used a carefully developed interview form to obtain information regarding the way in which parents dealt with aspects of child care such as cleanliness, aggressiveness, sex behavior, care of property, noisiness, and toilet training. Comparisons were made between parents differing in socioeconomic status.[1]

Sears and his associates found that mothers tended to express attitudes that were similar in dealing with various aspects of child care. Mothers who reported a permissive attitude toward aggressiveness, for example, also were more likely to express a permissive rather than a severe approach to such matters as sex, cleanliness, care of property, noisiness, toilet training, and use of physical punishment as a means of discipline. The correlations between ratings of attitudes shown in various aspects of child care

---

[1] For other instruments that have been developed for assessing parental attitudes, see: Shoben (1949); Schaefer and Bell (1955); and Markley (1958).

were not high but most of them were positive. An exception to this occurred in attitudes toward quarreling and other forms of aggression directed against others and directed against the mother herself. There was "virtually no correlation between permissiveness of aggression toward them (the mothers) and toward other siblings or other children." Many mothers applied one set of standards to interaction between children and another to interaction between children and themselves.

While the Sears study (in common with others cited here) demonstrates certain prevailing trends in the attitudes of parents, we cannot conclude that knowledge of one facet of a parent's personality will enable us safely to infer what another facet might be. Sears and his associates found, for example, that a permissive mother "was not necessarily a warm and affectionate one."

In a study of the way in which parents carry out their roles, G. B. Watson (1957) undertook to locate parents who were "permissive" and parents who were "strict" in their discipline with a view to examining the effects of such discipline on the personalities of children. Watson and his associates worked in a suburban community in which most of the parents were above average in income and education; they selected only parents of "normal" children living in "good" homes where children were "wanted, loved, and well cared for." Watson used a questionnaire designed to show how parents managed each of thirty-five fairly common situations, such as feeding, sleeping, dressing, toilet training, and cleanliness. To each situation the questionnaire provided three possible responses, ranging from clearly permissive to strict standards. Weights were assigned to the responses so that the total possible score ranged from 35 (meaning the choice of the "strict" response to every one of the thirty-five items) to 175 (meaning the choice of the "permissive" response in every instance).

No parent according to his or her own report was consistently either "strict" or "permissive." The range in scores was from 55 to 158.

Watson then undertook to make a special study of parents who were distinctly permissive as compared with others who were not. This part of the undertaking was not easy, for, as Watson says, "the first surprise of the study was our difficulty in finding parents who were fairly consistently permissive."

Response of children
to child-rearing attitudes and practices

How do children respond when their parents show certain predominant trends in their behavior?

In Lafore's study, which classified parents as "dictators," "cooperators," "appeasers," and "temporizers," it was found that the parents who most frequently dictated to and interfered with their children received the largest number of expressions of hostility from their children. Parents who showed numerous instances of blaming, hurrying, punishing, threatening, and interfering had children who presented many instances of crying. Children who were frequently threatened tended to show a good deal of fearfulness. Children who were cautioned most often tended to be low in resourcefulness.

Lafore describes Michael, an enterprising child of three years whose mother was labeled a "cooperator" but whose father was more of a "dictator." First we see Michael and his father:

> Michael and a friend are playing happily, sitting at a small table talking about eggs. Michael says "Eggs are pink." Tom, the friend, adds "Eggs are purple." Michael continues "Eggs are green." Michael's father interrupts. "Since when is an egg green? Michael, what is the color of an egg?" Tom says "Eggs are green, blue, and red." Michael's father says "No, Michael, what *is* the color of an egg?" At this point the father notes Michael's face and interrupts himself to say, "Did you get paint on your lips? Come here and let me see. Stand up. Did you put this in your mouth? Open your mouth." Michael says "No," but allows his father to pull him to his feet and wash out his mouth. When he is released, the situation is changed. Michael begins to nag and to ask plaintive questions, and after he and his friend sit down to painting once more the father again interrupts with instructions not to use so much water, not to get the paper wet, not to use a cup but a jar, not to take so much water, not to use a certain brush but another. When Michael calls attention to a painting the father scolds him for the "mess" he has made. . . . The record continues to show repeated interruption, interference, and commands, and after a time the two boys begin to throw clay at each other and the father orders the visiting boy to go home. Michael cries. Michael and his father argue, first about putting some blocks away, then about closing a door, and then about the father's order that Michael should play with blocks. Following this the father tries to undress Michael who kicks and scratches. The family cat approaches the bed on which they are sitting and the father pushes it away. Michael says to his father "I don't like you any more." His father replies, "I don't like *you* any more."

Another record shows Michael with his mother:

> The mother gave few commands, offered no interference, and instead entered into a good deal of give and take. Michael several times wanted to do things his own way but at no time did he say, "No, I won't." An example of how the two worked things out together appears in the following excerpt: His mother says, "Now let's see. How are the hands? I would wash them." Michael (who insists on doing things for himself) says, "I want to wash." His mother replies, "All right and try not to soil your clothes. Just wash the hands and that's all." Michael says, "I can do it myself." His mother says, "Of course you can. Now rinse them off. That's a very good job."

During the periods when the parents and Michael were together, the father *interfered* with the boy thirteen times; the mother three times. The father *dictated* fourteen times; the mother once. The father *praised* twice; the mother six times. The father *hurried* the child three times; the mother showed no instance of hurrying. The father *blamed* three times; the mother showed no instance of blaming. The father *offered a reason* four times; the mother seven times. Both father and mother showed a number of other practices in which they were more alike than different in their treatment of the child.

Sears and his associates found that mothers who were anxious about the job they were doing in child rearing tended to have more aggressive children than mothers whose anxiety was low. Similarly, there was some tendency for children to be more aggressive if mothers were dissatisfied with the way in which child rearing interfered with their free time, if they had low esteem for their husbands, or if they disagreed with their husbands to a considerable extent about child rearing.

In Watson's (1957) study, children reared permissively did not differ significantly in most of the personality traits that were explored, but in some characteristics there was substantial difference between the two groups.

Children from permissive homes, who were allowed greater freedom, showed "(a) more initiative and independence (except, perhaps, at school tasks); (b) better socialization and cooperation; (c) less inner hostility and more friendly feelings toward others; and (d) a higher level of spontaneity, originality, and creativity." There was also "a marked tendency for greater freedom in the home to show itself in greater independence in the child's behavior outside the home." Children from permissive homes were also on the whole more effective in their social relationships. No significant difference between the two groups was found in teacher ratings of "initiative," "independence," or "ability to withstand frustration." Watson's findings do not support the view that strict parental control interferes with the development of the child's self control. The children did not differ significantly in their tendencies to be energetic or passive, but children who had been strictly disciplined showed more hostility than those permissively reared.

When rated with respect to a tendency toward happiness or sadness there was a slightly larger proportion of children from permissive homes in both the "happy" and the "unhappy" categories, but the differences were unreliable. When rated with respect to "security-anxiety" there were no clearly distinct differences between the two groups. Half a dozen children from strict homes and half a dozen children from permissive homes showed "marked evidence of anxiety" while another half dozen from each category seemed to be easy and secure. Watson states that what makes for

anxiety in a child must be something other than the usually strict or unusually lax parental control.

In summing up the results, Watson points out that none of the personality differences found in this study appeared in all cases. "Some children
from strict and some from permissive homes may be found at every level
on every characteristic tested." Watson also states that "It is impressive,
however, to find no clear personality advantage associated in general with
strict discipline in a good home. Where differences do emerge, these are
consistently to the credit of the more permissive upbringing."

The complicated interplay of factors in the development of personality
as related to parental practices is noted by Watson who says, "This study
cannot distinguish the extent to which the advantages associated with permissiveness are due to that procedure alone and the extent to which more
permissive parents may convey hereditary or cultural assets with which
the permissive attitudes happen to be correlated. . . . Perhaps the kind of
parents who choose the permissive role transmit, via heredity or via associated cultural influences, a different temperament or pattern of living. It
should not be assumed that if parents who have heretofore practiced strict
discipline were simply to change over to great permissiveness, their children would thereby become more independent or cooperative. They might
or might not. A correlational study cannot satisfactorily answer questions
of causation (Watson, 1957).

So far in our discussion we have noted that it is possible, to some degree,
to detect certain prevailing attitudes and tendencies in the way in which
parents deal with their children. We have also reviewed findings which
indicate that the behavior patterns of parents may have an influence on
certain personality characteristics of their children. The relationships between parental attitudes and personality traits of children, as measured by
ratings and statistical computations are not, however, outstanding or consistently in one direction or the other.

In a large accumulation of other studies dealing with the effects of parents' attitudes and child rearing practices on the personality development
of children, the findings have varied greatly. Some investigators have
found little or no relationship between measurements of parental behavior
and their children's scores on personality adjustment. Others have found
what appears to be a very important relationship.[2] On the whole, evidence
of the effects of parental attitudes has been less clear-cut in studies of
normal children in relatively good homes than in studies of children from
distinctly unfavorable environments. Apparently, within a reasonably
"good" home, there is great leeway in what parents can do without giving

---

[2] See Hess and Handel (1956), Burchinal *et al.* (1957), Highberger (1955),
Sewall (1952), Itkin (1955), Mummery (1954), and a review by Roth (1950).

children a marked advantage or disadvantage that can be disclosed by the methods of study that generally have been used. (If more exacting methods were used the story might be quite different; this subject will be discussed shortly.) When studies are made of an atypical group—such as delinquents—the evidence regarding the effects of home conditions is likely to be more emphatic. The histories of many of these unfortunate persons show a record of broken homes, neglect, rejection, and other unfavorable conditions (Koppitz, 1957).

The histories of persons who become mentally ill also frequently give evidence of very unfavorable parent-child relationships. When it is possible to verify a record of ill treatment at home in the history of a seriously disturbed person it seems obvious that his development was impaired by the kind of upbringing he received. When the evidence is not so clear it is necessary to be guarded in evaluating the record. Case histories are frequently taken at a time of distress, after serious trouble has occurred. A person's distress at the moment is likely to color his report of what occurred many months or many years prior to that time (the effect of present moods on recollections of the past is discussed in Chapter Fourteen). It is necessary also to bear in mind that the way in which a person perceived events in his childhood and responded to them cannot be determined entirely by looking at the happenings themselves. Prout and White (1956) compared records of the childhood experiences of persons who were mentally ill with records of brothers and sisters who were not ill. Those who became sick and siblings who remained well did not seem to differ so much in the nature of the adversities they had met as children as in their ability to cope with these adversities.

Factors involved in the assessment of parent-child relationships

We face many questions when we try to assess a parent's influence on his child. What does the parent actually do? A record of his behavior gives a partial answer, but such a record does not always answer the question: What were his intentions and underlying attitudes?

How does the child perceive what the parent is doing? In the preceding chapter we noted that the actions of the parent *as perceived by the child* may be more decisive than the actions themselves, as seen from an objective point of view by someone else.

How does the parent perceive himself in his dealings with his child? We can ask the parent to tell us, through interviews or in response to questionnaires and check-lists such as those mentioned earlier in this chapter, but how does the parent's perception of his actions and attitudes compare with the judgment someone else would make about him? In one study (Crandall and Preston, 1955) mothers rated themselves and were rated by a clinical psychologist who observed them in their homes. There was "only moderate agreement between mothers' self-ratings and the Home Visitor's ratings of the mothers' overt behavior." Correlations computed for twenty-two characteristics that were rated ranged from .59 to −.16 (half of the correlations ranged from .23 to −.16 and half of them from .26 to .59).

When a parent and an outside observer show little agreement regarding many aspects of a parent's behavior, we cannot be sure whose judgment to accept. A parent (in common with others) may conceal as much as he reveals, and both the parent and the observer may be misled. In the handling of anger and hostility, for example, one parent may "let himself go" when angry, openly showing his feelings, while another angry parent shows a smooth and unruffled surface. The parent who "lets go" may see and describe himself as a rather cantankerous person and an outside observer may put him down as a punitive parent. The parent who cloaks his hostility may look on himself as forbearing and patient, and an observer may also see him in that light. But the parent who shows anger may, in the long run, be a more comfortable person to live with than the one who works hard to conceal it. Similarly, a parent who seems fretful and freely admits it may produce less tension in the home than a parent who uses a great store of energy to keep his anxiety concealed from himself and from others.

Similarly, a parent who always seems to be unaggressive may be very aggressive but in ways that will not show on a self-rating instrument or in the records of an occasional observer in the home. His aggressiveness may be expressed, for example, in an "I can top that" approach: Before his son can finish telling about playing in a close baseball game, the father begins to tell about games *he* played as a child. He may also seem to be very permissive: he does not beat or scold his son for neglecting to mow the lawn, but at suppertime he tells about the large lawn he so faithfully mowed when he was a boy. Similarly, a parent may be anxious in ways that a self-rating form or the records of an occasional observer will not reveal. He makes philosophical comments about the weather, but after a week with no rain he ominously says, "We probably won't have any crops this year." The parent's anxiety may be aroused when a troubled child makes a brave attempt to tell about his fears or his bitterness toward a teacher, but the record may only show a breezy, "Cheer up, things will get better."

Other questions arise, especially when we try to determine what is cause and what is effect in the interplay between parents and children. When parents and children show similar excellent characteristics is this due to a common heredity or a common environment? If a child is troubled, is it because a troubled father or mother made him so? Or did the parents become troubled as a result of the child's difficulties? Or were both parents and the children swept along by the same tide of good or bad fortune?

From the foregoing account of parent-child relationships it is clear that professional workers should be cautious in drawing conclusions concerning the influence of the home on the children with whom they deal from day to day. It would be nice (in theory, at least) to be able to label a parent as a "pure" dictator and then to say that the child of a dictator either will become a broken-spirited cringer or an aggressive little dictator. It would be neat, from a practical point of view, if we could say that the child of a firm but "permissive" parent is very likely to become a "well-adjusted" person. It would also be convenient, when we work with children who have difficulties at school, to place all responsibility for the difficulties on the parents. But things are not that simple. The child, his parents, and all the rest of us are creatures of a combination of forces: heredity, conditions within the home and the school, the influence of our peers, and circumstances in the larger society in which we live.

There are three factors that frequently operate when we interpret the behavior of others, or our own: *our desire for certainty,* such as is offered by a simple explanatory theory which we *know* is true (heredity or the home environment, or an Oedipus complex); *our desire to find a hero* whom we can applaud when things go well (the hero may be oneself) *and a scapegoat* whom we can blame when they don't (the scapegoat may be parents, or ourselves, or someone else); and *our desire* in appraising ourselves or others, *to confirm our own notions* concerning what happened, for better or worse, in our own childhood.

The fact that conditions in the child's world, and in our own inner world, are very complex adds to our difficulty when we try to understand children. But when we deal with children we are constantly making judgments about them whether it is easy to do so or not, and our judgments are likely to be truer and more humane if we recognize the complex nature of their world, and our own.

Varying roles and relationships within the family

As we have seen, children differ greatly in their response to the kind of upbringing they receive whether their parents are lenient or strict, gentle or stern. An illustration of the role played by the child in influencing relationships within the family was given in an earlier reference to a study by Burlingham (1952) of identical twins and it is interesting, in the present connection, to note a few additional details from this study. Burlingham noted that the twin who emerged from the prenatal environment as the more robust and healthy of the two demanded food "more impatiently and with greater energy" than the other twin. In a pair of twin boys, the hungrier of the two became the more aggressive. In a pair of twin girls, Bessie and Jessie, Bessie "screamed for her food hungrily" and "became the more passionate twin from then onwards." Moreover, "the difference in behavior, which was initiated in the feeding situation," continued to express itself in her relationship with her mother and with her twin sister and in her stubbornness. According to Burlingham, "In the case of Jessie and Bessie it was possible to observe their mother-relationship in minute detail and to feel satisfied that the behavior of the mother towards the children was equal except when the greater demandingness of Bessie enforced differences."

Following are three further illustrations of differences in the response of children, drawn from the writer's observations:

In a family with two sons the father had many of the characteristics of a "dictator" as described in Lafore's study. One son, as a child, meekly obeyed his father. The other son defiantly stood up against him. As he grew toward adulthood the meek son resented his father and he in turn became a father who seemed to combine the spirit of the Cooperator and Appeaser (as described by Lafore). The defiant son, as an adult, greatly admired his father, perhaps with a touch of guilt about having been defiant, and he adopted many of his father's authoritarian traits.

At a railroad station a family, coming from a religious convention, walked by, wearing the habit of their faith. There was a girl who was smiling and gay, apparently not perceiving (or not caring about) the fact that she and her mother, with their bonnets and long skirts, were conspicuously different from other mothers and girls in the station. Then came the father and his son, in black clothes and black hats, the father striding resolutely, the boy slinking, and seeming to cower under his black hat, as though keenly aware that his father and he were "queer." What had happened in the earlier history of these children no watcher could know. But it was apparent that one child took a very different view of the situation from the other.

When riding in the family car, Adele as a little baby cheerfully sat in a child's elevated car seat. Two years later her baby brother, Jonathan, refused to use the seat, insisting on sitting, adult-wise, on the regular seat, or standing on the floor of the car. To Adele the car-seat was all right, but Jonathan protested, as though it were an effront. Several times, when the brakes were applied, Jonathan was protected just in time, from bashing his face into the dashboard, and once while driving with a friend of the family the door swung open and he fell out. The parents, for his safety, wanted him to use the little seat as his sister had done, but the child refused to do so.

Within a family consisting of two or more children, each child has a role of his own which will be influenced by and also will have an influence on the role played by each of the other members of the family. Even identical twins (as we have noted) are not likely to play identical roles. One may be a bit more enterprising than the other, and this slight edge will make a large difference in determining who leads and who follows, who yields and who resists. The effects of such a difference may be so subtle that a visitor does not detect it: The twins look and act so much alike that he cannot tell them apart.

In a large family there may be a very complicated network of roles and relationships. An older brother who is a bitter rival of the brother next in line may "adopt" a younger brother and with him play the part of a kind, big brother. The last-born child, if considerably younger than his brothers and sisters, may be treated in a parental way by his brothers and sisters so that instead of having two parents he has a whole houseful of parents.

Within a large family there may be differences even in the names children give one another. The youngest girl, for example, is called Ann by everyone except her oldest sister, to whom she is "Baby" or "Honey." Little Sam may be Sammy to everyone except an older brother who affectionately calls him "Tootsie"—until "Tootsie" gets older and begins to object.

The varying roles that might be played by children in a family have been examined by Bossard and Boll (1957). One may take the part of a responsible child, taking life seriously and being somewhat bossy with the other siblings. According to Bossard and Boll, such a youngster is often the first child, especially if a boy. Another role is that of the sociable, well-liked child—who may be the second child. Some of the other roles children may assume are: the social butterfly, the isolate, the irresponsible child, the sickly one, or the spoiled one.

No parent can predict the effect a second child will have on the first child or on the total family situation, or what effect a third child will have on the fourth, and so on. What the parents do with one sibling will be influenced by the presence of other siblings. The way they perceive each child in the family, and the way the parents are perceived, will be influenced by each of the other children.

Influence of others on the child

The influence a parent can exert is modified, as the child grows older, by the influence of peers, teachers, and other members of the community. A study by McGuire (1953) is one of several which discuss this aspect of personality development. A child and his parents face an especially complicated situation if the standards established in the home strongly conflict with those of other parents and children in the community. In dealing with this situation children sometimes adopt one line of conduct at home and another when with their peers. One boy who had learned to use "correct" English at home acquired a second set of speech habits (he called it his "dialect") when he went to school in a community where most of the families used poor grammar. For example, the expression "I don't have any" was changed to "I ain't got none" when he talked to his pals.

The influence of a child's teachers on the development of his personality is also largely beyond the control of the parent. Amatora and her associates (1954) rated teachers and pupils on twenty-two elements of personality such as kindness, sympathy, dependability, and thoughtfulness of others, and found a positive correlation between the personality ratings of teachers and of children on all of the scales that were used. Amatora concludes that while a similarity between the personality of teachers and children does not necessarily prove that the teachers have caused the traits children display, the findings at least indicate that care should be taken to employ teachers who possess well-adjusted personalities. The interplay between the personalities of teachers and the behavior of children has also been brought out in a study by H. H. Anderson and his associates (1946), and by Herrick (1945); they observed, for example, that when a teacher is peremptory, or uses a cooperative approach, pupils are likely to respond in kind.

Cultural influences on parental practices

Regardless of their own personality leanings, parents are bound to be influenced by the customs of their community. Various sections of society use somewhat different child-rearing practices, and even within a particular social group there may be changes from one generation to the next—or even from one decade to the next—in ideas about the right way to bring up children.

CHANGING FASHIONS AND PHILOSOPHIES IN CHILD-REARING

These changes may occur so swiftly that parents face one set of pressures in rearing their first-born child and a different set in rearing a later child.[3]

---

[3] For an account of changes in emphases in recommended child-rearing practices see Wolfenstein (1953). In a book with the title, *Don't Be Afraid of Your Child,* Bruch (1952) writes sympathetically about modern parents who "have been exposed to a flood of advice on how to be 'good' parents." This advice comes to them through mass communication media "whether they ask for it or not." But despite all these instructions, according to Bruch, "modern parents are beset with the most amazing number of questions and worries" and it is they who take the blame if the child falls short of fulfilling all the expectations placed upon them.

During the past two or three decades there have been significant changes in views relating to discipline, with a swing in "progressive" circles toward a permissive kind of child-rearing, followed (so it appears) recently by a swing back in the direction of firmer discipline.

Apart from such shifts in general theory, there have been changes in specific practices that are recommended. Some years ago it was the accepted thing for mothers to bottle-feed their babies. Then came a back-to-nature drive, and mothers were exhorted to breast-feed. Then (at least in some circles) the good word was that it is the quality of the affective relationship between the mother and baby that counts, whether the feeding is by bottle or breast.

There is, of course, no law that compels parents to do a certain thing just because an "expert" recommends it or because neighbors do it. However, parents with firm notions regarding one or more aspects of child-rearing often find that it is not easy to carry them out. Even when parents try not to be influenced by other *parents* in the neighborhood they are likely to be influenced by their neighbor's children. They may discover, for example, that their ideas about modesty and their child's sex education have repercussions in the community if other parents have different views.[4]

Parents who would prefer not to have a TV set (because it interferes with homework and other activities) may find that their children insist on visiting neighbors who do have a set. In spite of their strong views on the subject, they may give in to the pressure and buy a TV set of their own.

Parents are sometimes swayed by fads and fashions in child-rearing and then regret it. Among a group of mothers interviewed in a study by the writer and his associates (1949) there were some who had their first children when pronouncements made by the behaviorist, J. B. Watson (1928), were still very much in the air. (Watson had warned parents against the dangers of too much love. He admonished parents not to be demonstrative with their children.) Two parents stated regretfully that they had taken these pronouncements to heart in bringing up their first baby. By virtue of changing fads and their own spontaneous impulses they used a different philosophy in bringing up their second child.

CHILD-REARING IN VARIOUS CULTURES

The effects of child-rearing practices pose an interesting question not only when we consider practices used by parents belonging to the same culture (as in studies of American families) but also when we compare the members of one culture with those of another.[5]

---

[4] Sears and his associates (1957) have discussed this subject.

[5] Among the anthropologists whose studies of cultural differences have received much attention are Mead, Benedict, Gorer, and Kluckhohn. Studies in this area have been discussed by Whiting and Child (1953), and Kerlinger (1953).

Some aspects of child-rearing differ considerably in different cultures, and some writers maintain that as a consequence there are characteristics of temperament and personality which distinguish members of one culture from those of another. Such observations raise this question: Are the characteristics shown by children in any particular group "natural" or are they a product of the particular culture in which the children are reared? When we observe that most of the children in a typical American community are rather competitive and show a good deal of aggressiveness, it is easy to conclude that these common characteristics are a natural and inevitable feature of development. But when anthropologists maintain that children in some other cultures do not display these characteristics, we may wonder whether these simply reflect the way of life prevailing in a particular culture.

In assessing the influence of cultures that seem quite different it is necessary to inquire whether the difference (in the display of friendliness, competition, aggressiveness) is genuine or real. People in various cultures probably differ considerably more in their customs and overt actions than in their underlying attitudes. A person who visits another culture can easily be misled by the surface appearances. An example of cultural differences that are more apparent than real is given by Hallowell who observed Indians of the Saulteaux society living in a region east of Lake Winnipeg (1940). According to Hallowell "to the casual observer, cooperation, laughter, harmony, patience, and self-control appear to be the key notes of Saulteaux interpersonal relations." These people seldom show anger, seldom fight, show a spirit of mutual helpfulness, and on the surface every thing seems almost idyllic. Yet, Hallowell points out, this picture "does not expose the deeper psychological realities" of Saulteaux life. On closer acquaintanceship, Hallowell found powerful currents of hostility and aggressiveness in this society, but these are expressed indirectly in ways that often seem more vicious and harmful than an open show of hostility. For example, the Saulteaux resort to gossip (such as saying scandalous things behind a person's back). They also use covert insults instead of direct assault. Another indirect expression of hostility was by way of sorcery and magic. Hallowell points out that while there are no *official* records of murder among the Saulteaux, murderous intentions have been and are expressed through sorcery and magic.[6]

---

[6] The position that an outsider can be led into faulty generalizations about the character of people in a certain culture from a superficial evaluation of child-rearing practices in that culture is also set forth by Kerlinger (1953), who takes issue with generalizations that have been made by Gorer, La Barre, and Meadow regarding characteristics of the Japanese. The writer's own observations while residing in Japan similarly led him (after a time) to question the validity of much he read in books about the difference between the character of Japanese and Americans. On the surface, the differences were impressive. But these differences vanished more and more when

Recommended Readings

Patterns of Child Rearing by Robert R. Sears, Eleanor E. Maccoby, and Harry Levin (1957) combines a wealth of research findings obtained from carefully designed parent interviews with a lucid interpretation of these findings from a practical and theoretical point of view. Sears and his associates question many popular clichés concerning attitudes toward child-rearing as related to socioeconomic status. John W. Whiting and Irvin L. Child in *Child Training and Personality: A Cross-cultural Study* (1953) have compiled findings regarding child-rearing practices in various cultural groups. David P. Ausubel's *Theory and Problems of Child Development* (1958) discusses many facets of the parent-child relationship, emphasizing the principle that to understand this relationship it is necessary not only to examine the parent's conduct and attitudes but also to consider the characteristics and perceptions of the child. Gertrude G. Lafore's monograph, *Practices of Parents in Dealing with Preschool Children* (1945), reports a research project that is somewhat limited in scope but wise and humane in its discussion of the predicaments faced by parents and children. The annual volumes of *The Psychoanalytic Study of the Child,* mentioned at the end of Chapter One, contain many articles dealing with parent-child relationships. The readings recommended in Chapter Seven are also recommended in connection with this chapter.

---

the author threw away some of the preconceived notions he had derived from books and tried to communicate with the Japanese as one ordinary human being with others. The writer believes that the closer we come to the emotional currents in human existence—love, anger, anxiety, and attitudes toward self—the more we will find that people are similar even though their surface customs differ greatly. In a discussion of cultural factors in the personality adjustment of children, Klineberg (1953) expresses the view that we know little about the child's reaction to many cultural experiences, and that the different behavior shown by people with almost identical cultural backgrounds has never fully been explained.

Children
and Their Peers

First Steps in the Social World

The usual child is skillful in dealing with older persons before he learns to play a role with children his own age. Even after establishing comfortable relations with his age-mates, the youngster frequently comes to adults, as though using them as a base from which to make excursions into the world of his peers. He is likely to step out among his age-mates with more assurance if he has a secure footing in his relationships with adults.

Long before he can walk or talk a child takes notice of other children. He begins to throw in his lot with his own generation at an early age. It is, of course, with this generation that he eventually will share the responsibilities of adult life.

In order to trace the child's social responses from the beginning, we will briefly review some of the observations made in Chapter Three.

Beginnings of social response

Many infants during the first two months of life will fix their eyes upon the mother's face and smile in response to her smile. By about three months, children show many signs of social awareness, such as ceasing their crying when a person comes, making searching movements to locate an approaching adult, turning their gaze to a person, giving heed to another's voice, smiling in response to another's gaze, and whimpering or crying when a person leaves their presence.

Until the age of five months an infant is as likely to smile whether a person speaks to him in friendly or angry tones or looks. at him with a stern or a kindly expression. But at about five months, and thereafter, the infant begins to show more discrimination of tone and expression (Bühler, 1930). Likewise, at about five months the infant becomes more active in his advances toward others by way of vocalizations and attempts to grasp and touch.

Between about five and seven months, most children become able to distinguish strangers from familiar persons. Some children, at this time, begin to show signs of timidity or fear of strangers. In one study (Shirley, 1933a), six of a group of twenty-five babies, whom the investigator had visited time and again, showed fear of her for the first time during the last part of the fourth month or between five and six months. A half-year-old child in a study by the writer and Holmes who had begun to notice differences between members of his family and others shrank and cried when approached by a maid who worked for the family since he was born. Babies differ greatly in the way they accept or shrink from strangers. Some babies seem to be naturally predisposed to shyness while others are spontaneously outgoing and eager to welcome all comers, but the experience babies have had with other people probably also make a great difference. Parents differ noticeably in the amount of freedom they encourage others to assume with their babies. Some shield the baby from contact with others; other parents freely let others hold the baby, play with him, and care for him.

Normally a child's timidity with strangers in the home soon wanes, although other periods of shyness will come later. Voices and faces that were once unfamiliar soon blend into the realm of the known.

After the first half-year of life, as one would expect, the number and complexity of social reactions increases. Between the ages of six and ten months, babies learn to participate in social interplay in such activities as peek-a-boo, rock-a-bye, waving bye-bye, and they ask for attention by means of yells, laughter, squeals and grunts.

RESPONSE TO OTHER CHILDREN

A child begins to notice another child his own age at about the age of six months, and during the following months his interest in other children becomes more active. Before the age of one year, many children pay brief attention when another child cries. Some babble to gain attention, or actively attempt to exclude another child from their sphere of activity. It usually is not until considerably later that cooperative play with another child occurs.

WHEN BABIES MEET

A "baby-party" technique, by which two or more children are placed together, has been used to investigate young children's reactions to one another. In one such study (Maudry and Nekula, 1939) children showed relatively little social interchange or response to one another up to the age of about nine months. From nine to fourteen months, the children continued to give more attention to their surroundings and to play materials than to one another, and when they did interact they frequently pushed one another aside.

From fourteen to eighteen months, there was a gradual transition to a more positive sort of social response. By the age of twenty-five months, social responses and interest in play materials became more closely integrated. At this time, also, friendly and cooperative interchanges predominated over negative responses.

At about the age of two years, some youngsters are quite sensitive in their dealings with other children. In Maudry and Nekula's study, some children were especially sensitive if others excluded them. There also were some who showed a distinct preference for particular children. After children become active group members they are likely to show strong affinities, but it is instructive to note that even before the age of two a youngster may be drawn to one child and not to another. At the adult level it is common for a person to feel more comfortable and relaxed with certain persons than with others; individual A "hits it off" better with B than with C, but this does not mean that C is a generally unlikable person, for he (or she) may feel drawn to D. This aspect of human relationships has not been thoroughly explored, yet in the life of an older person, and probably also in the life of a young child, it is very important. The qualities that make a congenial relationship seem far more subtle than the gross features we commonly measure in tests of "social adjustment" or "popularity."

BEGINNINGS OF GROUP BEHAVIOR

At about the age of two, normal children are definitely sociable with other children, but the give-and-take exchanges between two or more children are likely to be brief. When several children of this age occupy the same play space they take notice of one another, tend to gather in the same place a good deal of the time, and make contacts with one another. Much of the time, however, the children's activities will be *parallel* and adjacent—with occasional interchanges—rather than merged into a joint, continuing activity (Parten, 1932).

After the age of three there is an increase in group activities, and such activities stretch over longer periods of time. By the age of five or six, children will sometimes play in groups of five or six members or more, but they usually prefer groups no larger than three (Green, 1937b). At this age, children will sometimes play with youngsters they don't particularly like in preference to spending all their time alone; they would rather have an uncongenial companion than have no companion at all. The six-year-old undertakes a wide range of social behavior, including cooperation, friendliness, sympathy, competition, fighting, and quarreling.

As a child progresses from relatively little social interchange to participation with more and more children, lapses into earlier forms of behavior are likely now and then to occur. A child may return to solitary behavior if, for example, he faces a problem at home or if difficulties arise between him and other members of his group. He may be a participator in one group and an onlooker in another. He may return to solitary or hermit-like behavior if, as sometimes happens, he begins to mature more rapidly than his associates or acquires special interests of his own. At any stage of growth, when a child faces a new group in a new social situation, his first tentative approaches may roughly reproduce the sequence in his early behavior (such as watching, parallel play, brief contacts with a few children) until he begins to feel at home.

Early social relationships and the process of self-discovery

Beginning at the preschool level other children play an important part in defining for the child who he is and what he can do. Children receive support and a great amount of discipline from one another. A child may be reminded again and again that others approve of him or he may be told that he is "messy," "dumb," a "cry-baby," or a "brat."

If we could peer into the child's thoughts and feelings as he ventures into the social world of his age-mates we would probably see much that does not appear on the surface. There is probably a distinct thrill of discovery, and a great deal of pleasure in being accepted in give and take relations with others. On the other hand, it is probably a very painful and bitter experience for a child to be the butt of jeers and name-calling, as he sometimes is.

"Natural" and acquired aspects of social behavior

The new forms of social behavior that emerge in early childhood are influenced both by learning and changes that take place within the child in the process of growth. Buhler (1933) noted that at about the age of six weeks the babies in her study began to respond differently to the human voice and gaze and to other noises and visible objects: The babies smiled. Buhler recognizes that this smile may possibly be a response carried over from the satisfaction of being fed, but she also points out that adults are present in many other situations, comforting as well as painful, in which the satisfaction of hunger is not a factor. She considers it more likely that the smile is an "original and primary reaction to the human voice and look" (Bühler, 1933). A pair of infant twins in a study by Dennis (1938) were reared in a restricted environment until they were seven months old. They were well cared for, but in a stolid way: no one smiled at them or cuddled or fondled or played with them. But when they reached the age when babies usually begin to smile at adults, these babies smiled. When they reached the age when babies usually laugh, they laughed, and they also showed signs of affection for their attendants. Such observations do not, of course, prove that these forms of behavior will occur without stimulation from the environment (the Dennises, even when unsmiling and unfrolicsome, were still very human people!), but they do indicate that a child has a potentiality for being responsive to human contacts at an early age and that he will attempt to make contact with others even though he receives little specific stimulation or encouragement from them.

On the basis of continuing observations and tests of infants during the first two years of life, Shirley (1933a) concluded that children show a sequence of development in the sphere of social behavior just as they do in the sphere of motor development. She reports, for example, that manifestations of shyness and self-consciousness during the second year of life appeared consistently enough to suggest that they were not due to learning alone but were a normal outcome of growth. Observations such as these do not, of course, mean that social responses spring forth full-fledged, apart from environmental influences. Without a social environment and the stimulation it affords there obviously could be no social behavior. But the child's capacity for acquiring various forms of social behavior changes as he matures.

Beginnings of cooperation

Young children are likely to be more cooperative and friendly than competitive and hostile. The proportion between friendly and unfriendly responses will vary, of course, with different children and in different situations, but it is significant that in studies of young children the balance has run strongly in favor of the friendly forms of behavior.

After a child has begun to mingle actively with members of his own age group, friendly contacts are likely to be more frequent than unfriendly ones. (As noted in Chapter Three, children prior to this time give far more positive than negative responses in their reactions to adults.) In a study of two-year-olds, Mengert (1931) found that friendly actions outnumbered unfriendly ones by over four to one. In a later study of three-, four-, and five-year-olds, Walters and his associates (1957) noted that at all of these levels children were more affectionate than aggressive in their dealings with one another. Wright (1942) observed that children gave toys more frequently to strangers who were introduced into the experiment than to their own established friends. According to this and other studies, a young child does not subscribe to a philosophy of "war of all against all."

These findings suggest that the potentialities for friendly, coooperative behavior are as strong as, and probably stronger than, the potentialities for self-assertive behavior at the expense of others. It might, of course, be maintained that the rather high level of cooperative behavior in young children is deceptive because they are urged and trained to act cooperatively and politely. However, as we will note in the next section, even when young children are left to work out their relationships with one another, with a minimum of exhortation from adults, they are able to achieve a remarkable amount of cooperation.

GROUP LOYALTIES

The power of group loyalties can be seen notably in the club and group formations of children of adolescent or near-adolescent age. However, something resembling a closely-knit society of age-mates has been observed also in younger children. A fascinating account of the way in which children at an early age can form a social structure of their own is given by Freud and Dann (1954). They describe six young German-Jewish orphans, whose parents had been killed during the Hitler regime. These youngsters, after being passed from hand to hand during the first year of their lives, lived together as a group (instead of being placed with families) in a reception center and later in a refuge called Bulldog's Bank in England during their second and third years.

These children "were without parents in the fullest sense of the word, not merely orphaned at the time of observation, but most of them without an early mother or father image in their unconscious minds." Instead of having parents as objects of love, "their companions of the same age were their real love objects." At first, when moved to a settled refuge they centered their attention on each other, treating the adult staff members with cold indifference or with active hostility. They insisted on being together and became upset when separated, even for short moments. Although members of the group had individual preferences, they spontaneously shared and took turns. They were "a closely knit group of members with equal status, no child assuming leadership for any length of time, but each one exerting a strong influence on the others." After several weeks in the refuge they began to show individual personal attachments to adults, but during their stay at Bulldog's Bank the ties of these children to the adults "in no way reached the strength of their ties to each other."

These children "bypassing as it were the parent relationship which is the normal way to social attitudes" apparently found nurture in their relationships with each other. They showed impairments in their development (and improved very notably in many ways when, in time, adults played an important part in their lives) "but they were neither deficient, delinquent, nor psychotic." Originally they spoke German with an admixture of Czech words, but in the new environment they learned English. According to Freud and Dann, "That they were able to acquire a new language in the midst of their upheavals bears witness to a basically unharmed contact with their environment."

The "experiment" into which fate thrust the children in the study by Freud and Dann is different from most of the experiments in child psychology. The things we contrive in our studies usually are not made of such stern stuff. What of the future of these children? Perhaps a later report will tell. But it is impressive to observe that—according to the records, at least at this moment—these children, denied the nurture a parent usually gives, were able to draw so freely upon each other for emotional support.

Other observations of ways in which children respond when their upbringing is, so to speak, left in the hands of their age-mates at a very early age are reported by Freud and Burlingham (1944). These children were uprooted from their families and lived together in an institution, where, for a time, they received only routine attention from adults. At an age when most children have an anchorage in the home, these youngsters were thrown into a world consisting mainly of their own age group. They had to "become social" at an age "when it is normal to be antisocial."

According to the authors, "Under pressure of these circumstances they developed a surprising range of reactions: love, hate, jealousy, rivalry, competition, protectiveness, pity, generosity, sympathy, and even understanding." After a time, these children were divided into small units and placed in artificial families under the care of one adult acting as a foster mother. In this situation, their behavior changed: The adult rather than the peer group became the center of attention. The family arrangement had a very positive effect on the children's development, but for a time it introduced "disturbing and complicating elements" into their lives. "Children who have shown themselves adaptable and accommodating under group conditions suddenly become insufferably demanding and unreasonable." Their jealousy, and, above all, their possessiveness of the beloved grown-up seemed to be boundless.

The studies we have just reviewed, dealing with children who were not living under typical conditions, definitely do not imply that a fatherless and motherless child can obtain from his own age group all that he demands and all that he receives from a parent or a parent substitute. They do, however, reveal that children, even when very young, have a great capacity for giving support to one another, and for influencing and being influenced by their peers.[1]

Friendships among young children

As soon as children actively begin to notice and play with others many of them show preferences among their playmates. Before the age of two, a child is likely, if there is occasion, to begin to show that he has preferences among the children with whom he has a chance to play, and by the age of three or four years strong attachments between two children often occur.[2] Such attachments may last only a few days or weeks, but sometimes close friendships persist over a period of months and even years, although in the meantime each child has dealings with many others. One of the greatest fortunes of childhood is to have a close friend in whom to confide; one of the greatest sorrows is to lose such a friend.

In connection with one of his studies the writer had occasion to observe two boys who had a warm friendship, which had begun when they were two years old. At the age of six, one of the boys moved with his family to another locality, and the two saw each other only once in a long while. When they met after periods of separation there were no effusive greet-

---

[1] The influence age-mates wield on the course of a child's social development and personal characteristics is discussed further in Chapter Ten.

[2] For discussions of friendships between young children, see Challman (1932), Fite (1940), Green (1933b), Hagman (1933), Koch (1944), and Lippitt (1941).

ings; they scarcely even smiled; yet they slid at once into an effortless kind of companionship, as though they had been together all the time.

Friendships among young children are influenced by such obvious factors as similarity in age, intelligence, sociability and interests, resemblance of one child to a previous companion or a sibling of the other, and resourcefulness in enlisting cooperation. But each friendship or apparent friendship has its own characteristics and may represent a wide range of relationships. A friendship may be based on real affinity between two people or it may be based on a more opportunistic relationship. For example, a child who joins a new group may at first attach himself to the most approachable youngster and then, as he feels more sure of himself, he will break away and seek other friends. Sometimes friendless children in a nursery school try to win the loyalty of a newcomer or a timid child by such techniques as hovering near the child, smiling, patting, giving invitations, and suggesting games that might be played.

Apparent friendships among young children take other forms, too. One of the friends may be dominant, the other submissive. Or one may be a "big wheel" and the other a "social climber." We cannot gauge the nature of the relationship, or its meaning or value (or harm) simply by noting how much time children spend together or even by noting how much energy they pour into their dealings with each other.

In companionships between young children, the relationship may also be that of leader and follower. One child may be a leader partly because he is very voluble, mobile, and able to cover much ground. Another child may select and dominate the play activities of a group by virtue of aggressive methods and coercion. Still another child leads because he is resourceful in seeing new and original possibilities and in establishing friendly relations with other children.

Perhaps the most warmly accepted leader is the one who makes it pleasant to be a follower. Here is an example of resourceful leadership: Kirk had the knack of making another child feel important, while he himself was running things. On one occasion, he initiated a make-believe game of running a boat, using a big box. Kirk approached another child and asked him to be the captain, saying, "The captain is the big boss, you be the captain. I'll be the engineer." When the "captain" was installed in all his glory on the deck, the humble engineer, from below, ran both the captain and the ship.

THE FRIENDLESS ONE

Occasionally we can observe a young child who seems to have no particular friends. This child may behave in a manner that makes others reject him. He may be ill at ease with other children and seek rather to associate with adults. He may be interested for the time being in following his own solitary pursuits. Or he may have interests that others don't share.

One such solitary child, who was observed by the writer, was unusually precocious in his language development; he used words that other children could not understand. When he approached the other children, they did not actively rebuff him but merely gave him an uncomprehending look and went on with their own affairs.

Sometimes, of course, a child is friendless because he has characteristics that other children find unpleasant. For example, a boy spent two years in a nursery school without ever, as far as could be ascertained, being warmly received by any other member of the group. This boy had a habit of poking about, edging up now to one group, now to another, and always announcing his presence by asking, in a somewhat whining tone, such questions as: "What's that you're making?" "Why do you do that?" "What's that for?" He was not an alluring playmate, but he was trying in his own way to be accepted by others.

Loneliness in early childhood. In early childhood (as in later years) a person's endeavor to find a friend and to be a friend cannot be gauged by the ordinary signs of social adjustment. The difference between outward appearances and the child's own inner situation is illustrated by a boy who felt out of things and who was actually lonely, even though he had several brothers and sisters near him in age, and many companions in the community in which he lived. His father was preoccupied with his own ambitions and anxieties, and his mother was busy keeping the family in order. Instead of offering companionship to him his many brothers and sisters were competing with him for affection. So this boy fell back on his own resources. In his search for friendship, he constructed a set of imaginary companions—a whole family, consisting of a father, a mother, and two children. With lonely courage he endowed his imaginary family with the friendliness he could not find in actuality, and he tried to draw from its members the intimacies he could not gain from his fellows. He was about three and a half years old when he invented his companions, and they served him well for a time. But as he grew older others grinned when they saw him at play with his "family," and so he cast the imaginary companions aside, even though he had found no one to take their place.

BEGINNING OF SYMPATHY FOR PEERS

An important element in the social relationships of older children and adults is the capacity for sympathy and fellow-feeling. Unless a person eventually becomes sensitive to the joys and sorrows, hurts and satisfactions of others he will not be able to enter into any degree of close relationship with them.

When a child sympathizes with another the experience combines *perception, feeling,* and *action* (or an impulse to act). The child must be able to perceive the signs of another's distress. He must be able to allow his own feelings to come into play. And he must be able to communicate his feelings through what he does or says.

A child's ability to perceive the misfortunes of others expands as his mind matures and as he learns, through his own experience, to appreciate the meaning of misfortune. In a study of nursery-school children aged two to four years, Murphy (1937), observed that the older children responded to a wider range of distress situations: they noted, for example, that another child had a bruised hand even though he did not wear a bandage. The older ones also more often actively tried to comfort, help, or defend a troubled child while the younger children were more inclined to stare or to ask anxiously about the distress of others.

A child's ability to feel sympathetic depends on many factors (Murphy, 1937). If he is deeply absorbed in his own concerns he may not be able to respond to those of others. If he is frightened by another's distress (as when another child is crying because of ill-treatment from a person whom the youngster himself is afraid of) he may be so absorbed in his own need to defend himself that he is unable to sympathize with the one who cries.

In observations of pairs of sisters, McFarland (1938) noted that a child's tendency to sympathize with another youngster depended not simply on the degree of distress shown by the sufferer, but upon the child's relation to this distress. For example, a child would sympathize with her sister if the sister herself got into trouble or if her distress was caused by someone else, but would fail to sympathize when she herself was the cause of distress. Children who were responsive to the misfortunes of their sisters tended also to be sympathetic toward others who were in trouble. (This observation suggests that sympathy, like charity, begins at home.)

A child's sympathies are likely to vary, depending on what he has at stake. He may have a strong streak of sympathy but show just the opposite response if the other child's demands conflict with his own desires. Again, if a child's effort to be sympathetic is rebuffed, he may switch from a friendly to a hostile approach. (This change in attitude may also be seen in a child's dealings with animals: If a child tries to befriend a hungry kitten, the youngster's mood may change to anger when the kitten won't eat.) One child may be sympathetic when he himself is somewhat afraid and insecure and then grow less sympathetic as he gains in confidence, while another child may show the reverse tendency.

Expressions of sympathy in young children cover a wide range (Murphy, 1937), such as helping, removing or attempting to remove causes of distress, comforting, punishing the cause of distress, protecting and defending the distressed person, warning, telling an adult that another child is having trouble, questioning to discover the cause of trouble, suggesting or effecting a solution. When children are conscious of another's distress but don't quite know what to do about it they sometimes show their concern by disorganized responses such as watching anxiously, head shaking, frowning, compressing the lips, and crying and whimpering.

When two groups of nursery-school children were observed by Murphy (1937), the following frequencies of sympathetic response were recorded:

	Hours of Observation	Number of Sympathetic Responses	Number of Unsympathetic Responses
Group A	188	318	195
Group B	234	398	60

The children in group B represented a wider age range and a higher average age than the children in Group A. The B group also had a larger playground than the A group. The ratio of sympathetic to unsympathetic responses, initiated and received, varied considerably from child to child. In the older group some children, when faced with another child's distress, almost always sympathized, while others of the same age seldom did so. Likewise, although intellectual ability contributes to the quality of sympathetic responses and to the insight a child might have into another's distress, the factor of intelligence was less influential than other factors, such as a child's interests and responsiveness to other children.

Youngsters who are active socially tend to show a larger number of both "positive" (friendly, cooperative) and "negative" (quarrelsome, rivalry) forms of behavior. This interesting aspect of social behavior has been observed in many studies. When the children in Murphy's study were rated with respect to sympathy and aggressiveness, the scores showed a positive relationship: The children who most often sympathized tended also most often to be aggressive. There were notable exceptions to this trend, however; one child, for example, stood near the bottom in his tendency to be sympathetic and near the top in his tendency to be aggressive.

> If we studied older children and adults we would find also among them great differences in their sympathies. Sympathy requires that a person be sensitive to the condition of another, and that he also possess an extra emotional capacity which enables him to feel for the other one. It is not necessarily the poor who are best able to sympathize with the poor, or those who have been most sick or frightened or broken on the rack of experience who are most likely to sympathize with others whose plight is like their own.

Persons who have undergone pain and stress differ in unpredictable ways in the effect this will have on their fellow-feeling for others. This is apparent in the attitudes parents take toward other people's children. No parent can rear a child without facing the predicaments others face— illnesses, accidents, hurt feelings, fears, tempests of anger, misbehavior, and all the rest. Some parents become mellow and sympathetic (to them, "Sweet are the uses of adversity"); some are quick to condemn when the children of other parents run into trouble. An attitude of hostility toward the children of other parents is difficult to understand.

Unless a person has known distress he cannot grasp the meaning of another's misfortune. But suffering alone does not beget sympathy, nor does pain by itself produce compassion.

Rivalry and the beginnings of competition

A child's first experience with competition usually occurs within the home. He may be the rival of one or both of his parents, demanding that he receive the affection and attention of one or both at the other's expense. If there are two or more children in the home, it is inevitable that some sibling rivalry will occur. Rivalry between siblings can be relatively mild or can attain an almost shattering degree of intensity and bitterness.

When a condition of intense rivalry exists it is sometimes openly displayed, sometimes not. It shows directly when a youngster tries to harm a baby brother or sister by smothering him, or by pushing him down the stairs, or by giving him a sharp knife to play with. It may appear indirectly as when a child in make-believe play with a "baby" doll sticks pins into the doll or threatens to put it on the stove and burn it. Sometimes, however, children suppress feelings toward a sibling rival and even convince themselves that no rivalry exists. There are adults who will say, for example, that they had no inkling of the intensity of their bitter feelings toward a brother or sister until they reached adult years. An adult who has acknowledged only a mild rivalry situation in his childhood may, in discussing early experiences (as in the course of therapy), come forth with an outburst of rage and a flood of tears.

Many circumstances in the total family situation will intensify or partly relieve rivalry and jealousy in relationships between siblings (see Foster, 1928; Sewall, 1930; Smalley, 1930; and Neisser, 1951).

Parental attitudes toward children's rivalries will be influenced by their own experiences. In a series of three case studies Hilgard (1951) illustrates how a mother's childhood rivalries may persist in her life as a mother and cause her to treat her children as potential rivals. Hilgard states that a woman who has not resolved her own feelings of rivalry toward her siblings when she was a child "will in all probability set the stage for the reliving of the old drama, once she becomes a mother." She may relive her own childhood competitive struggles in the competitive struggles among her children.

If parents (or other adults) are obviously unfair or openly favor and admire one child more than another it is quite understandable that the unfavored child might feel hurt. However, sibling rivalry illustrates the fact that we cannot understand what will happen in a *social* situation simply by studying the separate characteristics of each *individual* involved in the situation. Nor can the rivalry situation be averted simply by a process of manipulating the environment. In a study of relationships between pairs of sisters McFarland (1938) noted, for example, that a policy of providing "two of everything" (two swings, two sand-boxes, two tricycles, two pairs of similar galoshes) did not prevent rivalry. Such things may not touch on the real sources of rivalry. The tricycle or swing may be the battleground but not the cause of conflict.

Rivalry becomes an especially acute problem if one or all the siblings in a family happen to have a strong streak of possessiveness, or if the children are especially demanding. Some youngsters seem much more inclined than others to want to establish a monopoly—to have everything for themselves, all the attention, all the care, all the favors. Others, even at an early age, seem to find it easier to share.

The *proportion* a child receives may to him be far more important than the *amount*. A youngster with a strong appetite and a sharp eye may be less satisfied by a slightly smaller fraction of a large pie than by a larger fraction of a small pie.

EARLY MANIFESTATIONS OF COMPETITION

Competition for prestige and accomplishment usually comes later than competition for the affections of parents, but many children at the age of two, and more thereafter, show awareness of what another child is doing, and of their own showing compared with that of another. Such expressions as "I am older," "I am bigger," "Mine's nicer" are among the milder signs. One nursery-school child, on learning that today was the birthday of a playmate, proceeded not only to claim that today was *his* birthday, too, but also to go the rounds inviting children to his birthday party.

In verbal "I-am-better-than-you" battles, the child with a superior vocabulary may have an advantage, as illustrated in the following encounter between two children:

> *John:* I can count up to a hundred.
> *Frank:* I can count up to a thousand.
> *John:* I can count up to a million.
> *Frank:* I can count up to a billion.
> *John:* I can count up to a trillion.
> *Frank:* I can count up to infinity.

Competition among peers is likely to be more prominent at the age of four and thereafter than at the age of three. In a study by Leuba (1933), children aged two to six were observed in an experimental room, singly and then in pairs, where they had an opportunity to play with a peg board. In the two-year-old group, the presence of another child did not seem to have much influence on what a child did or said. The children did not compete but were interested mainly in the materials before them. Three-year-old children showed they were aware of what the other child was doing. At four to six years, a majority of children revealed a desire to excel and an increased understanding of the idea of excelling. At six years, some of the children were also more critical in judging their own work than they had been before.

A similar increase in competition was found in a study by Greenberg (1932) of children aged two to seven years, observed while playing with blocks. Children aged two to four usually picked up blocks as they needed them, but four- to seven-year-olds more often cornered a supply. There was an increase with age in children's favorable remarks about their own work and a steady increase from one year to the next in the percentage of children who showed signs of competition (the percentages at three, four, five, and six years were, respectively, 42.6, 69.2, 75.4, and 86.5).

Competition at the kindergarten level has been noted when children are faced with a difficult task (Wolf, 1938). The children stayed longer with a task, on the average, when competing than when working alone. Some children, however, responded much less to competition than others.

Many instances of rivalry were noted in a study by McFarland (1938) of twenty pairs of sisters. Individual children were aroused to rivalry by different types of situations. An interesting finding was that pairs of sisters who showed rivalry most frequently were about as companionable as those who showed less rivalry. From this study, as we will note more particularly in dealing with cooperation and competition in older children, it is apparent that competition—while it may take the form of "going against" others—may be a part of a larger cooperative relationship.

Fights and quarrels among young children

The healthy preschool child not only cooperates, sympathizes, and establishes friendly relationships, but he also bickers, quarrels, and fights.[3] Children's fights and quarrels usually attract a good deal of attention from adults, especially if a

---

[3] Debus (1953) in a study of aggressive behavior in young children reports original findings and reviews some of the other studies dealing with this subject.

youngster is in danger, or is very combative, or is a helpless target of the aggressiveness of other children.

Adult attitudes toward aggressiveness in children as related to attitudes toward their own aggression.   When a child fights (or cringes when attacked), he is likely to touch off deep feelings adults have regarding their own aggressiveness. Adults differ greatly in the way they handle their own aggressive impulses. Some openly attack (occasionally with fists but more often with the tongue) when in a fighting mood; others carefully control their aggressiveness and among these there are some who have succeeded in persuading themselves that they really don't have aggressive tendencies; some cringe under the assault of aggressive persons and then go off with hurt feelings, muttering in their beards; some manage to divert or detour their aggressiveness into socially acceptable channels, such as intense competition. The reaction of adults to children's aggressiveness ranges from a rather tolerant view to a very determined and even anxious policy of demanding that the child squelch it or at least hide it from the public eye.

EVIDENCE OF AGGRESSION

Usually we judge a child's aggressiveness or lack of aggressiveness by his actions. When a child comes out fighting, clawing, or breathing fire it is obvious that his intentions are not very peaceable. Such a youngster may not, however, be basically more aggressive than one who, at an early age, has learned to smother his anger. In understanding aggressiveness in children we must also consider the child who seldom fights openly, but who engages covertly in rather polite but hostile forms of make-believe play or in savage fantasies that he keeps to himself. Even at the nursery-school age (as Fite, 1940, has shown) there may be a vast difference in the extent to which children display and express their aggressive impulses. In educating children, we are likely to "do something" about the youngster whose anger flows out into a clenched fist. But we are likely to ignore the child whose anger turns inward (unless he is obviously timid, anxious, and withdrawn). Here we have another illustration of the difference between overt behavior and what is happening in the child's hidden feelings and thoughts.

DEFINITIONS OF OVERT AGGRESSION
AS SHOWN IN FIGHTS AND QUARRELS

In a study of children's conflicts with one another Debus (1953) defined aggressiveness as "the directed expression of hostile feeling." To supplement this definition, the investigator adopted one used in a study of children's fights and quarrels by the writer and Markey (1935). An act of aggressiveness was defined as occurring in any situation in which one child "attacks another person, or by word or deed interferes with another, or threatens by word or gesture to do so, or tries by force or spoken demands to direct another's activities or to possess another's things in opposition to the apparent desires of the person against whom the aggression is made."

VARYING MOTIVES AND CAUSES

Aggression in young children ranges from tussles that arise in the general flow of activity when two children want to use the same toy or occupy the same space or accidentally collide, to acts in which there is an apparent intent to injure. Aggressive acts with a harmful intent range from those that are directly provoked on the spot to those which spring from a residue or carry-over of hostility from earlier experiences. Aggressive acts in the last-named category may, in turn, be a delayed retaliation against an offender (as when a child bides his time and hits or grabs a toy from a youngster who, in another situation had hit him or grabbed his toy) or they may take the form of displaced aggression; for example, if a child is in a bad mood he may strike out at a youngster who had nothing to do with arousing this mood. When a youngster is angered by a strong, aggressive child (or by a parent or teacher) whom he cannot subdue, he may "take out" his anger on a mild youngster who won't fight back.

CONFLICTS ARISING
IN THE GENERAL COURSE OF GIVE AND TAKE

The more a child "gets around" and the more contacts he makes, the more he is likely to have collisions with others. Quarrels are likely to be frequent among children who spend much or their time together. According to one study (Green, 1933a) "mutual friends are more quarrelsome, and mutual quarrelers are more friendly than the average," and "quarreling is part of friendly, social intercourse at these ages." (This is in keeping with the positive correlation between aggressive and sympathetic behavior mentioned on an earlier page.) Children who are most sociable are likelier than the inactive ones to get into situations where they notice another's hurt and sympathize with him, or bump into another and fight with him. But there are, of course, many exceptions to this.

Among the circumstances that give rise to fights and quarrels are: a desire for possessions, intrusions by an unwanted playmate, a desire to be the boss, and disagreement about what should be done and how it should be done. As we have seen, conflicts also sometimes arise from a seemingly unprovoked attack by one child upon another. Many currents of feeling flow into such attacks, including jealousy, ill-will carried over from an earlier time, a desire to annoy, or resentment aroused by others and now displaced on a handy victim.

Sometimes children get into a tussle for no apparent cause and with no obvious sign of resentment. On the surface, at least, it seems that the children are merely experimenting and testing out their strength. The participants in such a fracas seemingly had no initial intention either of stirring up a fight or of gaining anything in particular by it.

COMBATIVENESS AS A FEATURE OF IMPROVED OR DISTURBED SOCIAL RELATIONSHIPS

Combativeness may be a sign of healthy enterprise or of distress. This is illustrated by the records of two nursery-school children who showed a notable increase in the frequency of their conflicts during the course of the school year (Jersild and Fite, 1939). The first child, at the beginning of the school year, had spent much of his time with a companion whom he dominated, but with the help of the teachers, the dominated child was able to establish ties with other children. When the boy discovered that his hold over his companion had been broken, he tried to find new associates. Partly because of his aggressive techniques and his small size, he met rebuffs from the other children whom he tried to join. They would tell him to go away; he would then tell them to shut up, and they would tell him to shut up; he would hit and they would hit; and thus there was an increase in his warfare. This boy resorted to fighting as a means of meeting his difficulties, but his fighting actually increased his difficulties, at least for a time.

The second child who showed an increase in frequency of conflicts was a girl who, at the beginning of the year, was dominated by a playmate. As the weeks went by, this girl became more and more sociable in her relations with other children, but as this happened she had to fight off her dominating companion. In this case, an increase in conflicts was connected with an improvement in the child's social relationships within the group as a whole.

HEALTHY AND UNHEALTHY FORMS OF COMBATIVENESS

Although combativeness in children is frowned upon, and often arouses anxiety in parents and teachers, it is possible to make a rough distinction between relatively "healthy" and "unhealthy" forms. Aggressiveness can of course be overdone, and some writers make a point of maintaining that an emotionally "mature" person is one who has come to grips with his aggressive impulses. But if a growing child, and especially a preschool child, were to avoid clashes with his peers he would have to move to another world. There are times when others invade his rights and it is healthy for him to stand up and fight. There are other times when friction arises simply because children get in each other's way. A child who fights to ward off unprovoked attacks is probably, under the circumstances, doing the most healthy thing he can. Moreover, a child who behaves aggressively in order to achieve or to protect a goal that he regards as important is showing a healthier attitude than a youngster who simply vents his anger on an innocent bystander.

FREQUENCIES AND FORMS OF COMBATIVE BEHAVIOR

At the preschool level there is a vast range in the extent to which children are openly involved in fights or quarrels. In a study by the writer and Markey (1935) fifty-four children who were between two and four years old were observed over a period of time, during ten-minute intervals, for a total of two hours. Conflicts occurred, on the average, once every five minutes, although most of the conflicts were brief (lasting less than half a minute).

At one extreme was a child who engaged in 141 conflicts during the course of the observations, while at the other extreme was a child who took part in only 17. One child made a personal attack on another (hitting, pushing, throwing things at, holding, making threatening gestures toward) 87 times; another child did not lay hands on anyone or threaten to do so a single time.

In a somewhat similar study of Australian children (Debus, 1953) found that a conflict occurred every six or seven minutes, but most of these, also, were quite brief. One child in this study took part in 132 aggressive situations; two children took part in only 6. One child was the aggressor 59 times during the period of observation while, at the other extreme, there were three children who were never observed to take the initiative in starting a squabble. The two studies just cited yield similar findings on the frequency of encounters and the differences between the most aggressive and least aggressive children. This similarity may be a coincidence (in the study by the writer and Markey far less aggressive behavior was observed in two of the groups than in the third). The exact frequencies are not so important as the fact that children differ markedly in how much initiative they take in aggressively opposing one another. (When we note such wide extremes of behavior it occurs to the writer to wonder—and it might occur to the reader—what his own "score" on agressiveness might have been if he had been observed as a three- or four-year-old.)

CHANGES WITH AGE IN AGGRESSIVE BEHAVIOR

Between the ages of two and four, the most notable change occurring in children's aggressive behavior is in the techniques they use. In the groups cited above there was a decline in screaming, weeping, and cries for help, and in hitting and other forms of physical attack. There was an increase in the use of language during conflicts. As children grow older they become more adept at using language as a weapon, and in many adults such use of language has been developed into a fine art. It would make quite a spectacle if the polite verbal battle between two dinner guests could suddenly be transformed into the hitting and biting of a pair of three-year-olds.

As children grow older their conflicts tend to last longer. In one study it was noted that when two-year-olds fought with one another, only 40 per cent of their conflicts extended beyond one stage or "round," while 67 per cent of conflicts between four-year-olds went two rounds or more (Appel, 1942).

Sex differences in aggressiveness. The common finding (and expectation) is that boys are, on the whole, more openly aggressive than girls. This difference, however, is more likely to appear when children are older than when they first begin to join in group activities. At the age of two, for example, boys and girls in a study cited above (Jersild and Markey, 1935) were quite similar in the frequency of their screaming and crying. But with increased age, the boys cried relatively less, hit relatively more, and were aggressive more often than the girls. In an investigation in which a doll-play situation was used, Sears (1951) found that boys showed more aggression than girls and that girls were more likely to inflict psychological harm than to make a physical attack.

Conflicts between children as related to background. Large group differences appear when children's conflicts are studied (Jersild and Markey, 1935). Children in a day nursery, representing a somewhat underprivileged economic and educational background, entered into more conflicts than did children in a nursery school, representing a relatively higher socioeconomic background.[4] Group differences were noted also in the study by Appel cited above. Children representing homes of relatively low socioeconomic status showed more conflicts over possession of material objects than did children of higher socioeconomic status.

ADULT RESPONSES TO CHILDREN'S COMBATS

In about a third of the children's conflicts in one study (Jersild and Markey, 1935), the teachers took steps to stop or settle the disputes. In a

---

[4] At the adult level we likewise can observe that people in some groups of low socioeconomic status are quite free to use their fists when they fight, while in more highly educated circles people are expected to fight it out with words. Feelings of anger may run just as high in the latter group as in the former, however, and the aftereffects of bitterness and resentment may be just as intense.

majority of such instances the teachers decided the issue against the children who were most aggressive and who "won" a high proportion of their conflicts when left to themselves. Frequently this seemed justified, but such favoritism toward the less aggressive child sometimes went so far as to leave him the winner in a dispute in which he was not the guileless one. It has also been noted that an adult, coming abruptly upon a fracas between children, can easily make a wrong judgment concerning the underlying issue (Fite, 1940). Two children are involved, for example, in a tug of war over a small box. On the surface, it seems that only the box is at stake and that a reasonable solution can be found; actually, however, the struggle for the box may be only incidental to an effort by one of the combatants to get even with the other.

Adults differ considerably in the methods they commonly use when dealing with children's fracases. Some nursery-school teachers repeatedly use what Appel called "ending" techniques, while others more often used "teaching" techniques. Those who used the latter were not trying just to stop a fight but to help children learn ways of getting along together.

Adults can do much to help children to learn socially approved ways of getting along with one another. In one study (Chittenden, 1942), domineering children who were inclined to use force, threats, commands, and criticism in dealing with other children were singled out for special attention. Play situations (in which dolls were used to represent preschool children in typical social situations) were arranged to help the children understand and interpret social situations and to learn cooperative techniques. The children in the group studied were able to learn more effective ways of dealing with others. But we cannot assume that young children will learn to use more socially acceptable ways of handling their difficulties simply by being restrained from bickering or told not to fight. In one group included in a study by the writer and Markey, the teachers interfered more than did teachers in another group. In addition, there was more passive interference since three or four teachers were usually in charge, as compared with only one or two in the other group. During the year, when these conditions prevailed, the much-interfered-with children fought less often than did the children who had more freedom to settle their disputes in their own way. But the following year, when children from both groups moved on to two kindergartens, in both of which the teachers interfered relatively little with the children, the reverse was true. The previously little-fighting and much-interfered-with children doubled the frequency of their conflicts (despite the fact that normally, if anything, there is a decline with age in open aggressiveness). On the other hand, the previously little interfered-with and much-fighting children, instead of fighting even more when allowed a greater degree of freedom, actually did slightly less fighting than during the preceding year.

A finding such as this does not mean that a child of three or four has within him a certain amount of fight which he must get out of his system: rather it suggests that an aggressively-inclined child will learn more polite ways of expressing aggression if he has had a chance, at some point in his life, to show his aggressiveness openly.

Influence of skills on social behavior

Whether a child is young or old, his ability to take part in the games and other activities favored by his group will greatly affect his social relationships. A child who lacks motor skill is restricted in his social activities. When his playmates dash across the playground on tricycles or down the street on roller skates, he is left behind or must follow on foot; when they climb, he is left watching on the ground. In countless ways he is "out of it," although occasionally a child who is inept at using his limbs will be able to make extra use of his wits and direct the play into channels where he can hold his own.

The way in which increased ability in handling situations can influence a child's dealings with others is shown in an investigation by Jack (1934). A number of children were first studied to note their tendency to be ascendant or non-ascendant in their relations with others—the extent to which they asserted themselves or failed to assert themselves in securing play materials, in defending their possessions, and in directing or taking directions from others.

Then five children who were least ascendant were given special help in certain performances, including fitting mosaic blocks into a frame, fitting together the parts of a picture puzzle, and repeating a story that was read to them. After the children had mastered these performances each of the five was observed when paired with another child and confronted by these tasks. As a result of the special help, the five children now more often showed a tendency to lead, to assert themselves, to direct the other child, and to exhibit "ascendant" behavior than in the initial series of observations.

When an adult helps a child to improve his practical skills something more than just a mechanical operation is involved. The experience of working with a friendly adult, tasting companionship with the adult and success in the relationship, can significantly influence the child's attitudes toward himself and others.

Effects of nursery-school experience

The child who goes to nursery school has a splendid opportunity to further his own growth. At the beginning of the nursery-school period the youngster is ready to make some of his first ventures into work and play with his peers. By the end of this period, the typical youngster has the capacity for a wide range of social activities, including cooperative play with small groups, showing sympathy, and competing, and he is able to use a large variety of techniques in dealing with other children.

The nursery-school experience comes at an important juncture in the child's social development and it offers many special advantages. He lives, works and plays with children his own age under adult supervision. The nursery-school teacher is frequently a woman who has chosen to work with young children even though she could earn more as a teacher of older children. In a well-planned nursery school the physical equipment (ranging from sandboxes, blocks, wheel-toys, and painting materials to child-sized chairs and little toilets) is especially designed for young children. Many of the restraints imposed at later levels are missing; there are no mid-year examinations, no demands from above that all pupils meet certain academic requirements. Here is a small world that seems made to order for a small child.

GROUP TRENDS

Many studies have been undertaken to assess what children gain from nursery-school experience. Among the trends indicated by studies [5] in this area are the following: an increase in participation in group activities, and a decrease in "onlooker" behavior; an increase in poise and spontaneity in social participation, and a decrease in fear of other people, attempts to shrink from notice and to hover near adults; an improvement in self-help in eating, dressing, toileting, with resulting increases in freedom of action and diminished dependence upon adults.

Nursery-school attendance can help to dilute tensions between a child and others in the home environment. Indeed, one very important, although little publicized, function of the nursery school is to free the mother for a little while from the child's continuing demands. Although no study has been made of whether the respite helps the mother to put more verve and patience into her dealings with the child during the rest of the day, the likelihood is that it does.

Gains have been noted, as we might expect, in children's skill and resourcefulness in using the play materials and equipment provided by the school. Some of these gains may be only temporary, to be sure, or restricted largely to the nursery-school environment.

One noteworthy finding is that when a child shows a gain in sociability

---

[5] Among the studies that deal directly or indirectly with this problem are investigations by Cushing (1934), Hattwick (1936), Jersild and Fite (1939), Kawin and Hoefer (1931), Murphy (1937), Thompson (1944), and Bonney and Nicholson (1958).

in the nursery school it does not mean that his personality is being submerged more and more by the group. Rather, along with an increase in sociability, it is likely that there will be an increase in the child's tendency to exercise independence, to assert himself as an individual, to stand up for his interest and his rights as he sees them. In one study, for example, children's scores on "resistance" (the number of times they refused by word or deed to carry out the demands of others, to yield ground to another, and so on) were somewhat more closely related to the length of time they had spent in nursery school than to their chronological age (Caille, 1933). In another study, Ezekiel (1931) observed that children who were rather unaggressive at the beginning of the school year showed an increasing tendency to make themselves the center of activity. On the other hand, children who had been aggressive when the school term first began continued to retain this characteristic with the passage of time.

Individual variations.   The foregoing statements describe general trends; many children do not conform to the general trend. A study by the author and Fite (1939) revealed that while the group as a whole showed a sharp increase in frequency of social contacts, some children showed relatively little change, and two children seemed to suffer a setback. To appraise the value of nursery-school experience would require an intensive study of the individual child. From such a study we would probably discover that experience in a nursery-school group is better suited to some children than to others.

Children respond in their own individual way to the nursery school. Table 8 is based on a study of a group of children who were observed individually in the fall, soon after the beginning of the school term, and again in the spring, near the end of the school year. Some of the children had previously attended nursery school (labelled "old" children) while others were attending for the first time (labelled "new" children). A count was made of "social contacts"; the child received a tally of one for each half-minute period during part or all of which he engaged in social interchanges with other children.

The "old" children entered into more than twice as many social contacts, on the average, at the beginning of the school year as did "new" children who had never before attended nursery school. But by spring, the two groups were practically equal. Indeed, computations not shown in the table indicated that "new" children began to gain rapidly on the "old" ones during the first few weeks of school.[6]

---

[6] It is not here taken for granted that the more "social contacts" a child exhibits the better off he is, although an increase in sociability, as measured by the present techniques, usually represents a wholesome trend.

The "old" children did not have a lasting advantage over the newcomers. Even though not attending nursery school, the "new" children had been maturing and gaining experience and, when given a chance, they quickly made up for lost time. This does not mean, of course, that by waiting a year a child can gain as much from nursery school as he would gain had he attended the year before as well. It would require a more intensive investigation to measure the values that are gained from earlier attendance.

TABLE 8 | PERCENTAGE OF INTERVALS
DURING WHICH SOCIAL CONTACTS OCCURRED

(Chronological ages in years and months, in the fall, are shown in parentheses) *

"New" Children (without previous nursery-school experience)			"Old" Children (with one or more preceding years of nursery-school experience)		
Name	Fall	Spring	Name	Fall	Spring
Alice (3-6)	42.0	82.5	Holden (2-11)	67.3	45.0
Thelma (3-8)	25.7	58.8	Dennison (3-0)	64.0	81.3
Dick (3-9)	25.7	64.5	Nancy (3-6)	58.3	83.8
Sally (2-10)	25.7	43.8	Evan (3-6)	53.3	71.3
Morris (3-10)	14.0	47.5	Kirk (3-5)	46.3	71.3
Nell (3-1)	10.0	61.3	Joyce (2-10)	21.7	42.5
Sammy (2-10)	6.0	21.3	Bernard (3-8)	19.3	12.5
Average	21.3	54.2	Average	47.2	58.2

Children "new" to the group but with one year of previous experience in other, separate, schools:

Jerry (2-10)	50.3	73.8
Carter (3-6)	36.7	71.3

* Adapted from Jersild and Fite, *The Influence of Nursery-School Experience on Children's Social Adjustments,* Child Development Monographs (New York: Teachers College, Columbia University, 1939), No. 25, 112 pp. Reproduced by permission.

Children differ in their response to the nursery-school group. (This was noted earlier in discussions of sympathy, negativism, and children's conflicts with one another.) One child is actively aggressive, another is seldom, if ever, aggressive. One child is almost constantly involved in social activity (see, for example, Nancy and Alice in Table 8) while other youngsters seem to be involved only because they are placed in the same space as other children (see, for example, Sammy and Bernard in Table 8).

As seen from the pupil's standpoint, we cannot speak of *the* nursery-school situation as though it were the same environment for all the pupils.

Although all the youngsters go to the same school, the school represents about as many different situations as there are children.

Influence of type of nursery-school program. The effect of nursery-school experience or of any organized play group will depend, of course, upon what the school or the play group offers. A school that has clearly formulated educational objectives may have quite a different effect on the child's behavior than a school which lacks well-defined policies. This was brought out impressively in a study in which a comparison was made between children in two nursery-school groups with differing policies (Thompson, 1944). In both schools (designated A and B) the teachers were instructed to be responsive to the children, but in school A the teacher was told to make only minimal contacts with the children on her own initiative and to let them work out their own plans and activities, assisting only when asked. In school B the teacher was told to participate more actively, to try to become a warm friend of each child, to guide the children's thinking and activities into productive channels *not* by telling the children what to do but by her own interested participation and willingness to supply information, to cooperate, to supply and arrange materials in the most constructive manner. At the beginning of the experiment the children in groups A and B were equivalent in various measurements of their behavior. At the end of the experiment (eight months later) they differed in many ways. Group B, in which the children received teacher guidance, excelled group A, which had little teacher guidance, in *constructiveness* when faced with possible failure, in *ascendant behavior*, in *social participation*, and in *leadership*. Group B also showed fewer *nervous habits*, but the difference between the groups in this respect was not statistically significant. There was no significant difference between the two groups in IQ.

Thompson's study indicates that the educational policy of a nursery school may have pronounced effects on the behavior of children. Further studies of these children would be needed to discover how much of the benefit they appeared to have gained carried over into their out-of-school conduct or into their later lives.

What effect does nursery-school experience have on children as they move on to the elementary school? The answer to this question depends on the characteristics we measure and how we measure them. According to one carefully conducted study (Van Alstyne and Hattwick, 1939), elementary-school children who had attended nursery school were given more favorable ratings—on the whole—than children who had not attended nursery school, in qualities such as leadership, independence of adult approval and adult help, and ability to react in a constructive way to failure. It was noted, however, that many of the former preschool youngsters who were having difficulties in the elementary school had had similar difficulties in the nursery school. Likewise, the children who were most adaptable in the elementary school had, on the whole, shown greater adaptability in the nursery school. In commenting on their findings, these investigators point out that one aim in nursery education should be to help children deal with difficulties which are likely to follow them into later years.

In another study (Bonney and Nicholson, 1958), elementary-school children who had had preschool experience (nursery school or kindergarten or both) did not have any decisive advantage over non-preschoolers when rated by teachers and tested by sociometric techniques. It is possible, of course, that a youngster might receive benefits from preschool experience which cannot be measured by elementary school standards—such as whether he conforms to the demands of elementary-school teachers or fits into the prestige system of typical elementary-school children. If a child, before the first grade, has gone to schools which encourage initiative, spontaneous self-assertion, and the development of unique talents, there probably is no reason to expect him to be more adept than others in falling in with the formal routines and social conformities characteristic of most elementary schools. To throw light on this question, we need a deeper appraisal of the child than the usual rating methods provide and also we need to look critically at the values by which children are judged in the elementary school.

To judge the long-term effects of nursery-school experience it would be necessary also to study more decisively just what the nursery-school teachers intend to accomplish for individual children and to what extent these intentions are achieved. As noted by the writer and Fite (1939), we cannot assume that children will benefit simply from being thrown together as a group in a nursery school. A well-superintended group undertaking will not necessarily provide individual youngsters with what they need.

Influence of the nursery-school teacher. The benefits children derive from nursery school will probably be influenced to a large degree by the personality and competence of the teacher.

A revealing account of what a nursery-school teacher does in her moment to moment and hour to hour contacts with children has been given by Rigney (1952). A record was made of all the practices used by several experienced and several less experienced teachers. The most conspicuous finding was the vast amount of attention given to "routines"—helping children with wraps, picking up, arranging materials, and so forth. These duties constituted about a third of all practices. The second largest emphasis was on duties and rules governing the use, care, and protection of materials and property. In other words, much attention was given to the external aspects of the environment and external characteristics of behavior as distinguished from helping children to gain in understanding of others or to gain in awareness of their own interests, purposes, and feelings. Rigney questions whether this emphasis is inevitable: "In wiping noses, buttoning pants, everlastingly washing, tidying, 'resting,' keeping objects in their place and handling them just so, are we evading rather than meeting up with realities in the lives of children? In coming closer to children's physical and material needs, do we, whatever the reason may be, leave little time and emotional energy for deeper psychological involvement with children?"

Nursery-school teachers might profitably re-examine not only the curriculum they provide for children but also their own attitudes and goals as teachers. But if this applies to nursery-school teachers (who in many ways are far closer to the feelings and concerns of children than teachers of older children), it probably presents an even greater challenge to kindergarten, elementary, and high-school teachers. (We mercifully leave college teachers out of this!) [7]

Recommended Readings

Harold H. and Gladys L. Anderson's "Social Development" (1954) is a thoughtful review of studies with social development, sprinkled with refreshing Andersonian observations. Charlotte Bühler, one of the pioneers in the study of early social development, has a chapter in Carl Murchison's *Handbook of Child Psychology* (1933), now about thirty years old, which offers many insights and poses many questions that still remain unanswered. Susan Isaac's *Social Development in Young Children* (1933) discusses the socialization of the child from a psychoanalytic point of view. *Readings in Child Development* by William E. Martin and Celia Burns Stendler (1954) contains a large selection of papers dealing with social development in various cultural groups and it includes also a report of the study by Anna Freud and Sophie Dann referred to in the text.

---

[7] Differences in the attitudes and practices of different teachers are shown in studies by Landreth *et al.* (1943), and by Nesbitt (1943).

Peer Relationships
in Later Childhood

CHAPTER TEN   In this chapter we will consider the child's social development from the late preschool years into adolescence. During this time the child's life becomes less centered in the home and his fortunes are more and more in the hands of age-mates and adults in the community at large, notably his teachers. In our discussion of the social sphere we will note developmental trends in group behavior; we will also consider qualities within the child himself and characteristics of the social structure in which he lives which influence his lot as a member of society at large.

A growing child enters into a tremendous variety of social situations. The range of children's activities is shown vividly in a study by Barker and Wright (1954) of the "psychological habitat" of children in a town of about 700 inhabitants (designated as "Midwest, U.S.A."). Barker and

Wright identified a total of 2030 "behavior settings" that were open to some or all of the children. Of these, 1445 were located within the home (these were "family behavior settings" such as meals, festive occasions) and 585 were found in the town community (such as school classes, clubs, grocery stores, service stations, churches, the movies). Even the children of preschool age covered a wide territory. When one of the observers expressed astonishment at seeing a four-year-old boy "on his own so far from home" the boy said, "I go over the whole world." Wright (1956) reports that "something like this was true for Midwest children of every age."

Off to school

For many children, the beginning of their school career in the first grade or kindergarten marks a radical departure from their previous way of life. The youngster is now legally and psychologically in the custody of someone outside the home several hours of the day. All children are probably deeply impressed with the important step they are taking. Some children move eagerly into this new phase of existence; some have looked forward to school for a long time; but for many children it is a time of stress. Quite a few show the strain openly through an increase in "behavior problems" (McFarlane, et al., 1954), or by clinging to their parents, crying, or making a scene, during the first day or even during the first few weeks of school. We cannot, however, judge a child's feelings, whether of joy or of distress, at this juncture of his life simply by noting his smiles or his tears.

In one investigation in which the same children were studied as they moved from kindergarten into the elementary-school grades, the children who were most explosive in showing their feelings about entering school made as good an adjustment and, if anything, a better adjustment to school in the long run than those who seemed to take the venture calmly (Kraus, 1956). This finding may have other meanings, but it suggests that children who seem distressed when entering school may be no more deeply stirred than those who remain outwardly calm; the difference may be that some youngsters freely express their emotions while others keep them hidden. As we have noted in several sections of this book, it is quite common for children to feel deeply moved when they enter a new phase in their careers. And it is not the children alone who are moved, for many parents also feel a surge of emotion. When a child sets off for school, his departure is a symbol of a larger undertaking. The child is taking an important step on a long road; at the end of the road, if all goes well, he will no longer be a child but an independent adult. It is no wonder, therefore, that many parents, while pleased that their child is growing up, also feel a tightening at the throat as they watch him leave home for his first day at school.

Group formation and teamwork

At the age of six, a child's capacity for work with groups is still quite limited, but he is beginning to show an interest in games that involve several children. The games in which he joins are likely to be loosely organized, such as tag and hide-and-seek or to involve make-believe themes that allow for a good deal of individual freedom.

A typical class of twenty or thirty six-year-old first-graders is a *group* only in the formal sense that they are kept together in the same room. When they work as a unit on a common project it is not by virtue of a cohesive group organization of their own but by virtue of the teacher's leadership.

At the first-grade level, the children who are leaders are likely to lead small groups rather than the entire class. It is not until about the fourth grade or later that a class is likely to act as a whole, united under a common leader, on a common project, originated and directed by the children themselves. When the older children operate as a cohesive unit it is often because one or two or more youngsters are able to take the lead (Bühler, 1933).

At the beginning of the elementary-school years, children are not only limited in their ability to act as a total group but also in their intellectual comprehension of the group situation in which they find themselves. If asked to describe his classmates as persons, a first-grader is likely to show that he has a distinct impression of some members of his class but a rather vague and indistinct notion about some of the others. According to one investigator (Reininger, as reported by Buhler, 1933) at age ten children are able to rank all their classmates in order of their importance (as perceived by the child who is doing the rating). Younger children cannot do this so successfully. Even the ten-year-old is likely to have a more distinct picture of the youngsters he ranks high and low than of those he ranks in the middle.

DEVELOPMENT OF TEAMWORK AND GROUP RULES

As children grow older, they are increasingly able to identify themselves with the fortunes of a team or club, and they show increased ability in following complex rules of action. In their own activities, children in time establish complicated regulations governing procedure, the roles of individual members, taking turns, and the like. However, when children of a wide age range play together, they frequently will adapt their procedures to the varying capacities of the players. Thus, when ten-year-old boys play ball each is expected to take a regular position and to follow a definite order in batting. But, if a six-year-old is in the game he may be given a roving commission as backstop for both teams, with freedom to drop in and out of the game; he may even be indulged with irregular turns at bat; he and other less able players may be allowed four strikes instead of three; and the poorer team may be allowed more than three "outs" before losing its turn at bat. Similarly, in a game of "cops and robbers," the older child is expected to stay "dead" when he is shot until the rules of the game permit him to revive, while a younger child may be permitted to peek when he is supposed to be dead.

INCREASE IN INTELLECTUAL TEAMWORK

During the elementary-school period the child develops increasing ability to exchange ideas with other persons. This line of development is illustrated in Table 9, based on a study of children's contributions during class discussions in school. In the second grade only 12 per cent of the contributions made by the children in their class discussions continued a line of thought that had been brought up by a previous speaker. At the sixth grade, in contrast, well over two-thirds (77 per cent) of the contributions dealt with an idea that someone else had previously introduced. Conversely, most of the contributions at the second-grade level represented "new topics"—that is, the child was simply giving voice to something that happened to occur to him. He made no effort to link his statement to what had been said before or to merge it into the treatment of a common topic.

TABLE 9 | PERCENTAGE OF CHILDREN'S CONTRIBUTIONS IN CLASS DISCUSSIONS IN ELEMENTARY SCHOOL THAT CONTINUED AN EARLIER TOPIC OR BROUGHT IN A NEW TOPIC *

Contribution	Grade 2 (62 pupils)	Grade 4 (54 pupils)	Grade 6 (45 pupils)
New Topic, not obviously related to what earlier speaker had said	87%	33%	23%
New Topic, but apparently suggested by something said by a previous contributor	8	24	33
Logical Continuation of a topic previously introduced	4	43	44

* Adapted from H. V. Baker, 1942, *Children's Contributions in Elementary-School Discussion*, Child Development Monographs, No. 29. New York: Teachers College, Columbia University. Reproduced by permission.

An important aspect of a child's social development is his growing perception or awareness of the feelings, moods, and intentions of others. Awareness of others may take the form of a clearly defined perception, such as occurs when a child correctly concludes that a playmate is enjoying himself or is ill at ease. A child can also be responsive to the moods of others even though he is not able, at a moment's notice, to formulate in words the cues on which his response is based. It is likely that the more genuinely a child is in communion with himself in the sense that he is free to feel the surges of anger, fear, joy, sorrow, liking, and disliking that arise in him, the more responsive he can be (if he so chooses) to subtle communications from others. This theory that self-awareness and awareness of others are related has not, however, been explored adequately in studies of children.

Awareness of expressions of emotion. In a study by Gates (1923, 1925), children ranging in age from three to fourteen years were shown photographs of an actress expressing joy, anger, surprise, fear, scorn, and pain. Adults are usually able to identify the emotions which these pictures are intended to show. At the kindergarten level 70 per cent of the children recognized laughter but less than half of them recognized expressions of pain, anger, and fear. None of the children of kindergarten age could interpret the pictures showing surprise and scorn. In tests of older children it was found that more than half of them could identify anger at the age of seven, fear at ten, and surprise at eleven. In daily life, with familiar, living faces before them, these children undoubtedly would recognize moods which they could not identify in a photograph of a stranger, but it is nonetheless instructive to note how far some children lag behind adults in recognizing the conventional signs of emotion.

Awareness of qualities liked or disliked in others. During the elementary-school years, children become increasingly able to formulate in words the traits and characteristics of others that they like or dislike. In a study in which children were asked, among other things, to describe what they disliked in the world about them, an increasing percentage of children from the age of five and upward named people or undesirable traits in people. Six per cent of the answers at five to six years, and 22 per cent at eleven to twelve, fell into this category (Jersild, Markey, and Jersild, 1933) although the question was not phrased in a manner that would turn their attention to people.

Peer Relationships in Later Childhood **203**

Recognition of own status as compared with others.   As he becomes increasingly able to take an active part in complex social enterprises, the child becomes more aware of social relationships and of his own status as compared with that of others. As noted in Chapter Nine, a child of school age is likely to understand the meaning of competition and to appreciate how he compares with others in many fields of activity. Children at this age are also capable of a certain amount of self-criticism in the light of their own aspirations and on the basis of their appreciation of the standards set by others, and many of them are sensitive to ridicule, failure, and loss of prestige. As one result, a child may become shy and self-conscious about performances that earlier were quite spontaneous, such as singing before a small group.

THE DESIRE TO BELONG

A child's desire to be noticed and accepted, which first appeared in his relations with his parents, follows him as he moves into the larger social world. Some children go to great lengths to attract notice by clowning or "showing off," or by misbehaving.

Attitudes toward substitute parents.   In his relationships with adults outside the home, the child has a need for an emotional anchorage. Adults who are in a position of authority, such as the teacher at school or the playground director, are, to a large degree, reacted to as substitute parents. Most children desire the approval and affection of these substitute parents even when their conduct seems to belie it. It is probable that some of the most incorrigible children, who seem inspired by the devil himself, wish to be liked by their teachers. A teacher who is harassed by many duties and by the "problem" children in her group will find it hard, of course, to realize this. When a child is spurned in his crude efforts to get attention he may really begin in earnest to rub his teacher the wrong way.

The child who gets a good or a bad start when he begins school often acquires a reputation that follows him from class to class and from teacher to teacher. The child with a good reputation is fortunate, but the youngster with a poor reputation is more likely to do things that will keep him in bad repute than to change for the better. To break through the crust of hostile attitudes which a child in this plight has acquired is the most difficult task that confronts a teacher. When such a child is rude and defiant the teacher, like any other human being, is bound to feel threatened or angry and this makes it all the harder for her to perceive the pathos hidden beneath the child's nasty ways.

The child's desire for status appears also in his relations with other children. Behavior that is baffling to adults often is motivated by the child's desire to please his peers or to gain their attention. His feelings when rebuffed or ridiculed by his peers may range from grief and despair to intense rage. It is difficult for a youngster to express such feelings, and the reasons for them, to adults, for to do so he must admit to himself the bitter fact that persons whose good will he desires actually do not like him. Instead of directly expressing his feelings he may reveal them through symptoms such as fault finding, fighting back, complaining, and other responses of the "sour-grapes" variety. As a consequence, his elders may not realize that when he is telling how much he detests certain children he actually may be expressing how much he would like to be liked by these same children, or how deeply he feels contempt of himself.

The following account shows how one child reacted to rejection by her peers and how her parents tried to help her:

> Isabel was six years old and in the first grade. On two occasions her parents, while driving past the school during recess, happened to notice that the girl stood by herself while the other children were playing. This was puzzling, for she was quite gregarious. A few days later Isabel happened to mention that she had played that day with some "big boys from the third grade." Some days later she again mentioned that she had played with one of the big boys and had pulled his shirttails out of his pants. That evening, as though troubled, she asked her mother at bedtime, "Have I been a good girl today?" In answer to this unusual question the mother said yes, and then added rather lightly that she thought it would be better if Isabel did not pull shirttails out of boys' pants. At this she burst into tears. She sobbingly asked, "Then who shall I play with? When I eat lunch I sit alone, and out on the playground the other girls don't play with me." The difficulty, in part, was that Isabel was a newcomer among girls who had been playmates before coming to school.
>
> Isabel's parents now tried to help. Two schoolmates chosen by Isabel were invited to the home by the mother and this may or may not have been partly responsible for the fact that the girl soon became accepted by the group.

When children have troubles of this sort and do not reveal them, it is difficult, of course, for adults to understand or to try to help. Through lack of understanding the adult may even make things harder for the child. In the instance above, for example, it might have made matters worse if the mother through ignorance of the situation had scolded the child for rough play with older boys when actually this play, from the child's point of view, was a poor substitute for play with girls her own age.

Peer Relationships in Later Childhood　　**205**

Measurement of social acceptance

To understand a child it is important to know how he rates with other children, and why. We ask, "Why," not only to learn about the qualities of the child but also to learn the values and standards held by the children who rate him.

Among the most widely used methods for assessing children's acceptance of one another are "sociometric techniques." [1] These techniques are relatively simple; in many situations, a trained investigator can make practical use of information obtained from them.[2] In school, children might be asked, for example, to name one or two or three pupils whom they would like most to work with, or to have as seat-mates, or as their favorite out-of-school companions. In institutions where children spend all their time, sociometric techniques have been used to find out whom the residents would prefer as table-mates or as cottage-mates. It is possible also to ask a variety of other questions, such as whom the youngster wishes to play with, go to a picnic with, or have as a companion on an overnight camping trip.

Some of the methods of obtaining sociometric ratings are as follows: (1) Having the children write down the names or point to the photographs of one or two or more children whom they prefer. (2) Giving each child a list of the names of every member of his group and asking him to rate each child on a scale (ranging, say, from "like very much" to "dislike very much"). (3) Giving the child a list on which each child is paired with each of the other children and asking him, in connection with each such pairing to name which of the two he prefers. (4) Asking the child to rank each child in his group in order of preference, placing the most preferred first, the next preferred second, and so on.[3]

Negative opinions may be obtained by asking youngsters to name persons whom they would not especially care to have as friends, or as seat-mates, or as study companions. This approach has not been used as commonly as the positive approach, for there are children who are reluctant to speak unfavorably about others. Some negative information can be inferred from the positive approach. For example, if a child is not named by anyone when children choose their seat-mates, it is evident that he is

---

[1] Research in this area received a great impetus from studies published in 1934 by Moreno. For an account of "old and new trends in sociometry" see Moreno (1954).

[2] A study by Cunningham in collaboration with a number of classroom teachers (1951) gives revealing findings obtained when teachers use sociometric techniques as a first step in an effort to understand their pupils.

[3] A widely used booklet by Cunningham (1947), "How to Construct a Sociogram," offers time-saving suggestions on how to compile the results of sociometric ratings.

not especially popular. It does not follow, however, that he is actively rejected.

A simple example of results obtained by means of a sociometric method applied to fourteen boys in a fourth-grade group is shown in Table 10 on page 208. The children were asked to name the person or persons in their class whom they would like best to have as a friend. They were also asked to name the person or persons in the class whom they did not especially care to be friends with. The diagram on page 209 is a simple illustration of a *sociogram;* it portrays only the positive responses represented in Table 10. As shown in Table 10, the children named more persons when choosing whom they liked than when naming whom they disliked. One boy (Duval) both chose and was chosen by four other boys, while several boys were not named as a choice by the youngsters whom they preferred.

The information obtained by sociometric methods answers a variety of questions: Who is chosen most? Who is chosen least or not at all? Who is chosen by whom, but does not reciprocate? To what extent are choices associated with various factors such as age, sex, socioeconomic status, and nationality? Some findings obtained with this technique may simply confirm what is already known from observation of the group; but the findings may also yield important new information, and sometimes the findings with respect to individual children are quite surprising.

The information that is gained by sociometric methods can have many practical implications (see Jennings, 1950a, 1950b). In one study (Kerstetter and Sargent, 1940), the sociometric results in a fifth-grade class revealed an isolated clique of five boys. Further observation showed that as time passed there was a greater and greater cleavage between these boys and the rest of the group. On the basis of this information it was possible to take steps to overcome this isolation and to improve the attitudes of the five boys by such methods as new seating arrangements, assignment of the five children to various small study groups, coupled with other efforts to understand the boys and to gain their cooperation. In another study, sociometric techniques were used in conjunction with other methods to study children who were repeating a grade in school (Sandin, 1944). The findings showed that the nonpromoted children, more often than their classmates, mentioned children in higher grades when they named their friends.

As we can see from the limited examples given above, the sociometric technique yields results that are interesting from a research point of view and also impressive from a personal point of view. In Table 10 there is one boy (Harper) whom four classmates pointedly named as one whom they did not care to have as a friend, and no one in the group named him as a friend. As far as we can tell from the sociometric results, Harper is an outcast (in the language of sociometry, Harper is called an "isolate"), but

it would require a more personal kind of inquiry to discover how vigorously he is rejected by the boys who name him as one they don't care for,
or why he is unchosen by anyone else, and what all this means to Harper.
In Sandin's study of nonpromoted children mentioned above, it similarly
appeared that these youngsters were, in a sense, stranded in an alien
group, cut off from age-mates whom they would prefer because they had
not lived up to the standards for promotion which the school required.[4]

			DISTRIBUTION OF CHOICES AND REJECTIONS AMONG BOYS—				

TABLE **10** — DISTRIBUTION OF CHOICES AND REJECTIONS AMONG BOYS— MADE BY FOURTEEN BOYS IN A FOURTH-GRADE CLASS *

Name and Number	Sex	Age	Chooses	Chosen by:	Rejects	Rejected by:	Mutual Choices
1. Don	B	10	2, 8, 12	—	4	5	—
2. Duval	B	9	5, 6, 8, 12, 13	1, 3, 5, 6, 8, 12	—	—	5, 6, 8, 12
3. Henry	B	10	2, 8, 12	2, 5	10	—	—
4. Harper	B	9	—	—	—	1, 6, 7, 8, 10	—
5. James	B	10	2, 3, 11, 12	2, 11	1, 7	—	2, 11
6. Jasper	B	9	2, 8, 13	2, 11, 12	4	—	2
7. Jacob	B	9	10, 11	11	4	5, 9	11
8. Luke	B	8	2	1, 2, 3, 6	4	—	2
9. Matthew	B	9	14	11	7	—	—
10. Porter	B	9	12	7, 11	4	3	—
11. Philip	B	9	5, 6, 7, 9, 10	5, 7	12	—	5, 7
12. Ramos	B	9	2, 6, 13	1, 2, 3, 5, 10	—	11	2
13. Tom †	B	—	—	2, 6, 12	—	—	—
14. Fritz †	B	—	—	9	—	11	—

* In this group there was no instance in which two children mutually rejected each other, or in which
a child chose a youngster who had rejected him, or in which a child rejected a youngster who had
chosen him.
† Absent but either chosen or rejected.

STABILITY OF SOCIOMETRIC RATINGS

While the sociometric method is simple to apply and sometimes requires only that children, on the spur of the moment, write or check the
names of youngsters whom they prefer (or don't prefer), it usually pro-

---

[4] From an academic point of view, the school was perhaps justified in requiring the
youngsters to repeat a grade, although on the basis of all the information Sandin could
obtain it is doubtful whether the youngsters, or the classmates from whom they were
separated, or the younger group of classmates to whom they were assigned, received
any benefit from this.

vides information that is reliable and significant, as far as it goes. Even at the preschool level, it was observed in one study (Biehler, 1954) that children's choices of companions were very similar when measured by records of their actual behavior and when measured by a sociometric technique (children indicated their choices by means of photographs). In studies at the preschool level, and in numerous studies of older chil-

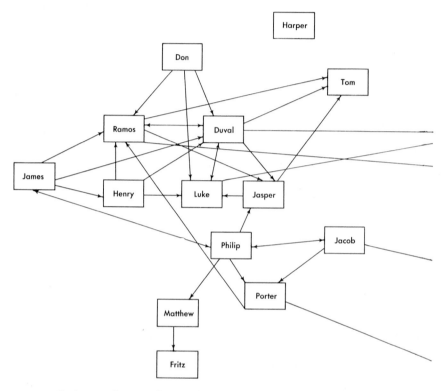

Sociogram showing choices (but not rejections) by boys represented in Table 10.

dren, it has been found (in most instances) that children's choices show a high degree of stability, when a sociometric test is applied and then applied again after a few months or (at later age levels) after a year or more.[5]

In some studies it has been found that children's "social acceptance

---

[5] For studies dealing with this subject, see Bonney (1943a, 1943b); Dunnington (1957); Murray (1953); Laughlin (1953); Riley (1953); and a review by Witryol and Thompson (1953).

scores" remain almost as constant from year to year as their scores on intelligence tests. An investigation of children who were first tested in various elementary schools showed a high degree of stability in their sociometric ratings when re-tested after they had moved on to a junior high school, with a considerable reshuffling of the population (Laughlin, 1953).

QUALITIES ASSOCIATED WITH ACCEPTANCE AND NON-ACCEPTANCE

Numerous qualities make a child appealing or unappealing in the eyes of one or more of his fellows, but certain qualities have been found in several studies to stand out.[6] Children who win a high degree of acceptance have been described by their associates as active and alert and interested (but not restless or obviously out to get attention), good looking, cheerful, and friendly. Popular children tend, if anything, to be above average (but not necessarily a great deal above the average) in intelligence, scholastic standing, and health, more dependent on themselves and less dependent on adults, sensitive to the thoughts and interests of others. There are however, notable individual exceptions.

The factors associated with unpopularity are also quite varied. Among children who are low in acceptance there are some who have no apparent interest in the general environment and little interest in other persons, or who are quiet or shy, or "socially ineffective," or who are noisy, rebellious, boastful, or obviously seeking attention. Children who appear to be anxious, as shown by restlessness and other signs, are frequently in the non-accepted group.

The child who is deeply preoccupied with problems of his own is not likely to be appealing to others. Troubled children who have benefited from therapy have shown an improvement in their social relationships along with an improvement in their emotional state (Cox, 1953).

Children who are most accepted by their peers possess qualities such as those we have just noted, but there are many undisclosed nuances of need, self-interest, and interest in others which influence the choice of one child by another particular child. To be accepted socially a youngster must, in general, have certain qualities but not to excess: he is interested in others, but does not too obviously seek attention; he is active, but not hyper-active; he is confident but not boastful.

If we could look more deeply into social acceptance "scores" we would probably find that they have many different meanings. When a certain youngster names three children as his favorites, one of these may be a

---

[6] For studies dealing with this subject, see Bonney and Powell (1953); Northway (1944a, 1944b); Laughlin (1953); Dunnington (1957); McCandless and Marshall (1957); Marshall and McCandless (1957); and Trent (1957).

child whom he intensely likes while the other two may be "also-rans." One youngster may choose another because he genuinely likes him and another because he stands high in prestige in the group and belongs to the proper set. A youngster may be chosen because he has prestige rather than because he is especially liked (Keislar, 1953).

The preferences and affinities children reveal in their relationships with one another show that the factor of IQ has less weight when school children are appraised by each other than when they are appraised by the school (Laughlin, 1953). At the adolescent level, H. E. Jones (1949) also found little correlation between intelligence test scores and popularity.

FACTORS INFLUENCING CONSISTENCY AND CHANGE IN PEER-GROUP STATUS

We might expect a high degree of consistency from year to year in a child's status with his peers since his qualities tend to remain stable as time goes on. In addition the values by which he is judged by his peer group, at least until the time of adolescence, are also likely to remain fairly stable (unless he moves from one group to another with different standards). The standards by which adults judge him, notably at school, usually are stable, too. Whether well-deserved or not, the child's reputation is likely to follow along with him. A child's reputation with his teachers is likely to be rather consistent from year to year, especially if he has become earmarked as a "problem child" (Tucker, 1937).

Still another factor tends to harden a child's position within his group: being accepted or rejected is likely to strengthen the qualities which, originally, influenced acceptance or rejection. The accepted child thrives on acceptance. Unless he has won by being a sycophant he is likely to grow in the kind of poise and self-confidence that helped him to be accepted originally. The rejected child, on the other hand, is likely to feed on his rejection; the experience of being rejected is more likely to strengthen rather than remove the qualities that led him to be rejected in the first place.

When we consider the forces that, in a sense, render acceptance or rejection a self-perpetuating condition it appears that there is a kind of fatalism in a child's life as a member of his peer group. The child's fortunes (or misfortunes) with his age-mates often seem to follow the rule that to him that hath shall be given and from him that hath not shall be taken away even that which he has. We might ask, is the wheel of fate, after its first few rounds, destined to move in the same course, to high ground for some and into a deeper rut of misfortune for others? The answer will depend in part on the mood and philosophy of those who reply. We might take the view that when a child leaves the confines of the home and is thrown upon the mercies of his peers and his teachers his fate is already pretty well determined by the combined forces of his heredity and the kind of upbringing he has received. However, there are at least four factors that make the child's status less fixed than it otherwise might be.

First, even when things are left to take their own course, there is a considerable amount of change, as time passes, in the way in which individual children are regarded by members of the group. This is illustrated by the fact that while the correlations between sociometric scores one year after the next are relatively high, they are not in the order of +1. A correlation of about .60 or even .70 between scores at one time and at a later time means that there have been changes in the status of individual children. The change is more likely to mean a shift in rank rather than a complete reversal of position (such as would occur if a youngster who is at the top at one time falls to the bottom, or vice versa). But it does mean that the social situation, while relatively fixed, is still quite fluid.

Second, adults, if interested, can often do a great deal to change the circumstances of children who are rejected by other children.[7]

Third, changing conditions in a child's life as he moves to young adulthood may alter his situation.

Fourth, changes that occur in the process of development may produce a change in a child's status. For example, a youngster who is a "slow starter," slow in finding a place for himself as a member of a group, may show a spurt of growth which changes his role. Again, changes in outlook that occur as children grow older may also make a difference. In one school community two girls who belonged to a minority Protestant group received rough treatment from some of the boys belonging to the dominant Protestant denomination when they were in the second grade. The seven- and eight-year-old members of the stronger church group stoutly asserted their faith by pulling the pigtails of these two girls, who several times cried with no one to comfort them. But as the youngsters moved toward adolescence, something else came into the picture: these two girls were clever and pretty and the manly boys who once took so dim a view of them began to take a second look, and the girls became popular. Not all girls, of course, can count on a pretty face to bring them out of isolation. But as a result of many circumstances the youngster who receives a low popularity rating as a child is not necessarily destined to be an outcast or an unhappy person in later years. Some children who are conspicuously shy, for example, seem to find a comfortable place for themselves in later life (Morris *et al.*, 1954).

[7] Studies by Cunningham (1951) and Riley (1953) report interesting illustrations of what teachers can discover when they look beneath the sociogram and endeavor to help individual children.

A sociogram (as illustrated on page 209) is revealing as far as it goes, but it provides only the first step in an endeavor to understand the children whose position it records. When we ask, "What does it mean from the standpoint of the individual child?" we raise a host of intricate questions. As a general proposition, it seems obvious that the youngster who stands high in social acceptance is well off and the child who stands low, or is actively rejected, is certainly not in a comfortable spot. However, to assess the situation of an individual child we need more than a sociogram. We must look both at the child and at the group standards by which he is being judged. A child who is not accepted by his peers may have qualities which, in a larger view, are admirable. He may have qualities that children in one group will reject but which, in another group, would be admired. An example of this is given in an account by Hollingworth (1926) of a child who was unusually bright. When in a class consisting mainly of children of average intelligence, this boy was practically cut off from the social life of the group. But when transferred to a class which included bright children, he was warmly appreciated. The rejected "Perfessor" in one social set became an accepted pal in another.

In considering this case we might ask: If the boy was as bright as all that why wasn't he sensitive to the social climate in the average class and smart enough to pass himself off as a "regular guy"? The answer may be that he was unwilling or unable to change his ways in order to become socially well-adjusted.

Some youngsters (and adults) do have a knack for tailoring their behavior to the standards of the group. In one instance, a bright boy who had "skipped a grade" was able to blunt the sharp edge of rejection in his new group by pretending to be like the rest. Occasionally, for example, he would deliberately misspell a word after two or three of the bigger children had failed to spell it. He would rather receive a reproof from the teacher than hostile glances from his classmates. Similar tactics were used by a boy (mentioned in Chapter Nine) who adopted a "dialect" of poor grammar to conform to the speech habits of other children in the community. In knuckling down to the standards of his peer group, this boy, like the one who deliberately misspelled words, knowingly paid a price in order to avoid the discomfort of being a social misfit. In many instances, of course, children are not able or willing to pay such a price, especially if it involves a severe conflict of values. A child from a home that is high or low in socioeconomic status is likely to meet some conflicts in standards if his peers come from homes differing from his own. In one investigation (Pope, 1953) it was noted, for example, that fighting and restlessness were less acceptable to the boys of high socioeconomic background than to those of lower socioeconomic status and that a child who was known as a good student was less likely to lose favor in the eyes of boys of high socioeconomic status than of boys of low socioeconomic status.

If we could look beneath the surface of group behavior into the lives of the individual children we probably, in every instance, would find a complicated drama. At the high end of the scale of social acceptance, there are youngsters who are comfortable with the group and also comfortable within themselves. But a high standing in the group may be bought at great cost. Wittenberg and Berg (1952), in a moving account, have pointed out how a youngster can achieve popularity by surrendering personal integrity. If such a surrender is not made knowingly (as in the two illustrations above) but in a blind effort to win approval, the child who stands high in the sociometric scale may be in a sorrier plight than the one who stands low.

A child with strong interests of his own and with a sturdy regard for his own rights will not be as concerned about the impression he makes on others as a youngster who has little confidence in himself and whose sense of his own worth is completely at the mercy of what others think of him. So if a child with independent interests is relatively low on the scale of acceptance over a period of time this may simply mean that he has the strength as time passes, to follow his own bent. However, there probably are few who are so strong as to be unaffected by disapproval from the group. And it is likely that a child who has been rejected by his peers—whether because of unfortunate personality traits or because of qualities which are unappreciated at the time by the group (such as being bright and a good learner)—will move into adult life with a trace of bitterness.

Rivalry, cooperation, and competition

Cooperation and competition have many elements in common, and activities which outwardly appear to be competitive or cooperative may spring from a variety of motives. Competition usually denotes a struggle or contest in which one individual seeks to equal or excel another, or to secure objects, recognition, prestige, attainments, or honors also sought by others. Cooperation involves mutual action on a common enterprise toward a common goal.

Competition and cooperation are in some respects opposites, but this is not always the case, for it often happens that both are parts of a larger project. Many competitive games involve a great deal of cooperation just as many cooperative ventures entail a good deal of competition. Children compete vigorously in a game of baseball, for example, but without a great deal of cooperation they would not come together in the same place for the same purpose or follow the rules of the game.

Competition and cooperation both provide the growing child with opportunities to discover his resources and to test his abilities. When he races another child he is not necessarily just trying to assert his superiority —he is perhaps also testing himself.

COMPETITION

When they enter elementary school most children in our culture are launched on a competitive career, although they differ greatly in the intensity of their competitiveness. They differ also in their choice of competition. In an unpublished study the writer and his associates recorded the number of times each child in several classrooms took part in "free" class discussion. In every class there were several children who competed for a chance to be heard and each class contained one or two highly competitive youngsters who monopolized a large share of the discussion consistently from day to day. In several classes, one or two children managed regularly to be heard as often as all the other class members combined. Some children were choosy in selecting their competitors. In one class, two boys consistently out-talked all others in the room. One day, one boy was absent and the research team expected that the other—now having the field to himself—would really have a talk-fest. But this did not happen. Instead, he was strangely silent. On the next day, when the classmate was back in school, both sounded forth again. It appeared that these two boys were not competing with the rest of the class or the teacher by demanding so much attention; they were using the class situation to compete with each other.

COMPETITION AS A MOTIVATING INFLUENCE IN SCHOOL

While the school is not the primary source or cause of competitiveness, it is apparent that most schools encourage and exploit competition, notably in connection with assignments which need "extraneous" motivation—assignments which in themselves are uninteresting and rather meaningless to many of the pupils. In most schools, academic learning and competition are joined as though "you can't have one without the other." This combination is fortunate when it produces a zest for learning but not when it places a higher premium on the amount than on the meaning of what is learned. Competitiveness also strongly emphasizes the speed with which intellectual operations can be performed, as though education were preparing students for an intellectual horse race. Competitiveness in school sometimes approaches the ridiculous. The writer witnessed an exhibition of sharp competitiveness in an avowedly progressive school: The youngsters were competing with each other trying to expose the evils of competition!

Children face conflicting pressures bearing on cooperation and competition: They are urged to cooperate, and some schools have an entry in the report card for marking the child's cooperativeness. Yet in the same schools they are also under great pressure to compete. All children to some degree face the problem of how to be cooperative within a competitive structure and how to assert their competitiveness within a cooperative structure.

Selection of areas of competition. A child's competitiveness is influenced by many conditions in the social situation and, as time goes on, by his need to measure himself against others, to support his self-evaluation by equalling or excelling others.

Some children seem to compete in almost every sphere of their lives; while others specialize, staking out areas in which they will vie with others; still others seem to resign from competition. After being reminded again and again that he cannot successfully compete with others in reading or spelling a youngster may give up his efforts to compete in these subjects. He may seem lacking in the desire to excel, and his report card may even include such statements as "Is not well-motivated," "Does not work up to capacity." Such a youngster, however, may at the beginning have felt the competitive pressure just as keenly as those who were successful and his sting of defeat may have been just as intense as the others' glow of victory. Evidence of a tendency to select only certain areas in which to compete appears in findings at the adolescent level that show low or zero correlations between academic grades and success in athletics. While a low correlation may mean there is little basic relationship between potential academic and athletic ability, it probably also means that individual youngsters have chosen to center their efforts in one field and not the other.

VALUES OF COOPERATION AND COMPETITION

The values of cooperation are obvious. An atmosphere of genuine cooperation is likely to be more relaxed, friendly and pleasant than an atmosphere of intense competition. In a cooperative setting a child can express and enjoy the strong potentialities for "positive" human feelings that he and all children possess; he has more opportunity to savor the joys of companionship and to escape, for a time, from the lonely prison in which an individual resides when he regards all other creatures as his rivals. Here we are speaking of "genuine" cooperation: cooperation which, while containing an element of self-interest (as most human endeavors do), also possesses a strong surge of spontaneity.

Competition affects a child as a member of a competitive society and as an individual. As a member of society, a child benefits from the competitiveness of others when, for example, under the spur of competitive drives, scientists discover new medicines, or inventors develop useful products, or industrial enterprises open up new resources of wealth and employment He also benefits if members of his social group, in competition with a hostile group, band together to protect themselves from being annihilated In naming these benefits we do not imply that equal or greater benefits might not flow from cooperation rather than competition. We merely state that a person's competitive efforts may bring advantages to others even if he himself is more bent on achieving individual glory than on serving the general welfare.

From an individual point of view, competition has both healthy and unhealthy connotations.

HEALTHY ASPECTS OF COMPETITION

As we have already noted, competition serves many useful purposes in the child's development. In countless practical situations the competing child serves as a pacemaker, an aid to the process of self-discovery. The pace and performance of others often set a standard which the youngster can achieve and enjoy. He may, for example, discover that he can get his homework out of the way more effectively than he had thought, get dressed in less time than was his custom, endure and enjoy the water of a cold stream which otherwise he would not plunge into, draw upon reserves of strength in his work and play.

In competing with others outside the home a youngster may get a truer view of some of his qualities than he previously had. This is especially valuable if a youngster has previously underrated himself in comparison with an older sibling, or if ambitious parents have set before him a standard that he could never live up to.

Moreover, competition (especially in a cooperative setting) can give zest to many enterprises which are useful (or at least required) but which, in themselves, would be rather boring. Whether we like it or not, competition is one of the main props, and in some cases *the* major prop, in our educational system.

UNHEALTHY ASPECTS OF COMPETITION

Competition also has its unhealthy side. Very often, the competitiveness of older children is not tied to a process of self-discovery or to adventures in group relations, but has instead a kind of driven quality.

Competition is unhealthy if the child's self-regard depends on his ability to outdo others. It is unhealthy if the child has a tendency to regard himself as inferior unless he can prove his superiority to all comers.

Peer Relationships in Later Childhood **217**

Competitiveness has a sick quality if the child is vindictive, gloating over his rivals and relishing their defeat. It also has a morbid quality if the child, when he fails to win, feels bitter toward himself (or others), has vengeful fantasies, or feels that he has to grit his teeth and train hard solely to prove he can win, even though the contest itself has little or no value to him. This would be the case, for example, if a child seeks to be elected to a class office, or to head a committee, not because he likes the job or feels he can contribute something, but simply to show that he can win the job.

Competitive pressures are unhealthy if they force a judgment of failure on those who do not, of their own accord, have a compulsion to compete. An enterprising child who enjoys reading may doubt his own promptings when he notices that the reading class is conducted like a contest.

A child may become so convinced that it is important to surpass others that this motive pervades all his actions. He is like a college student whose only interest in taking a course is to get another A. A competitive standard may result in a kind of private moral surrender, even though, in public, it brings him high honor. (According to testimony in a study of teachers currently conducted by the writer it appears that, in individual cases, even a Phi Beta Kappa key may not stand for *philosophia biou kybernētēs*—philosophy, the guide of life—but instead, may symbolize compulsive competitiveness.)

Competitive standards become especially onerous when persons who adopt them for themselves also try to impose them on others.

Standards used in evaluating students in a competitive system usually are narrow and arbitrary. The paths to glory are likely to be laid out by adults who themselves have tried to win competitive success along these paths. The more a competitive program caters to a limited range of abilities the more it tends artificially to reward only a few.

The results of a narrow competitive standard are strikingly shown at graduation time in some schools when a few selected children march self-consciously again and again to the stage to receive prizes and awards while the other children are expected to applaud politely.

In the academic program of most schools, the road to competitive success (or defeat) is largely verbal. Even the child who has an outstanding aptitude for painting, music, or mechanics is likely to get a low mark if he does not know the right *words*.

> A boy who had outstanding mechanical ability got poor grades in a mechanics course because his reading and spelling abilities were below average. No one in the class surpassed him in taking generators and carburetors apart, repairing them, and putting them together again. But this didn't count in his favor because in the written examination he misspelled "generator" and "carburetor."

When we use a purely verbal approach, based on the competitive bias of academic people with "verbal" minds, we are likely to put a stigma of failure on a child who, if judged by other criteria, would be marked as a success.

Competition and callousness. When children are judged according to narrow competitive standards, they are not respected for their basic humanity but rather for their ability to outdo others. Competitive standards give little, if any, recognition to the child who—though not the first to cross the finish line—entered the race under a great handicap. Yet if gameness were the criterion, he should get the prize. Competitive standards give a medal to the winner of the oratorical contest but they ignore the one who, in joining the contest, scored a magnificent triumph over his shyness, even though he did not surpass someone else's skill.

If, on Commencement Day, it were possible to show a film depicting the struggle each student had gone through, the heights each had scaled, and the difficulties each had overcome, and a jury, viewing it were asked to draw up an honor roll, the jury would probably select many names that are not among those listed on the printed program. Many names would appear which, by ordinary competitive standards, would go "unwept, unhonored, and unsung." It is perhaps even more likely that as the members of the jury came to know the drama of each child's life they would refuse to single out any one for mention above the rest. According to this view, the more fully we appreciate another's struggle the less desire we have to triumph over him or to profit (through taking first place) from the fact that he was in the second or last place. John Greenleaf Whittier caught some of this spirit in the poem, "In School Days," when the girl says to the boy ("As if a fault confessing"):

> "I'm sorry that I spelt the word:
> I hate to go above you,
> Because,"—the brown eyes lower fell,—
> "Because, you see, I love you!"

Conflicts between older children

Open fighting and squabbling usually decline from the preschool period into the elementary-school years, although most children continue to have occasional battles and some children maintain continuing feuds. Many factors, both in the child and in the environment, contribute to a decline in open combat. The child's increased understanding of property rights eliminates many conflicts on that score. With time, the child gains more understanding of other children, what he can expect from them, what they will tolerate from him, and what might happen to him if he is combative. Increasingly, also, the child understands and accepts the unwritten rules and codes of group behavior which children impose upon one another.

The decline in combativeness is probably more apparent than real, however, for there may not be a corresponding decline in feelings of hostility. The youngster learns to conceal or disguise his feelings. He learns many techniques for avoiding or repelling persons who offend him and for seeking out persons who are congenial.

Toward the end of the preschool years, and more especially during the school-age period, some children claim they are interested in fighting as a sport. Some boys assert with pride and with a smile that they "like to fight," and one of the things many boys will claim when asked how boys differ from girls is that "boys fight, but girls don't fight much." In many seemingly playful combats, however, there is likely to be more than a sheer sporting interest. Fighting may spring from many motives, including maladjustments of various kinds, but it also is part of a child's experimentation in social living and a means of testing his powers and exploring his status with his group.

Frequently, in groups of children who have known one another for some time, the members of the group come to recognize a hierarchy of dominance, with a child at one extreme whom all the children, by mutual consent or through bitter experience, look upon as the best fighter and who had better be left alone, and at the other extreme a noncombative child whom no one fears.

Teasing, bullying, and disguised hostility. Teasing and scurrilous nicknames are much used in children's efforts to discipline or hurt one another. In some ways, teasing is a more serious sign of emotional stress than outright fighting. When a child fights, it often (but not always) means that he is acting on the spur of the moment: Someone bothered him and he struck back, and then the episode is over. When a child is a chronic teaser he expresses a kind of ill will that has carried over from the past. This is especially true if he goes out of his way to tease someone who is not bothering him and has no intention to do so. An interesting sequence in teasing behavior in a summer camp is described by Osborne (1937).

> When first introduced into the camp, a child was the butt of much teasing and bullying, partly because of certain "babyish" traits. As he continued in camp, he changed his ways, but while in the process of becoming adjusted to the group he went through a stage when he in turn teased and bullied other children. Thus he seemed to express some of the hostility that had been aroused in him by the teasing he had received. As time went on and as the child's poise and ability to get along in the group improved, he stopped being a tease and a bully.

Influence of socioeconomic status
on the child's social development

Many practical aspects of a child's upbringing are influenced by his family's socioeconomic status. Sooner or later, also, a child's conception of his role in society will be influenced by his family's social, educational and economic background.

The bearing of socioeconomic status on children's upbringing is discussed in several contexts in this book, so only a brief overview will be offered in this section.

CIRCUMSTANCES CONNECTED WITH SOCIOECONOMIC STATUS

Children of low socioeconomic status who live in crowded quarters in a poor neighborhood feel the pinch in many ways. Crowding creates many frictions from which children in more spacious quarters are spared. Children in crowded homes are less likely than those in more affluent homes to be shielded from the raw facts of life. With less privacy they are more likely to come in contact with the processes of birth, illness, death, family worries, and quarrels. If the family is large, or if both parents are working, children may also be required to assume responsibility for their own care and safety at an early age.

In one study (Jersild *et al.*, 1949) parents in poor economic circumstances, in describing their relationships with their children, gave more emphasis to the physical aspects of child care (such as physical discomforts, physical health) than did parents of higher status. Wealthier parents gave more emphasis to psychological aspects of child care (such as personality traits).

In the past, parents of low socioeconomic status had more children, on the average, than parents of higher status (in recent years the difference has narrowed).

Even if the father and mother of a large family are devoted to their children they will have less time to give to each. There will be more distractions, more calls upon their energy, less money for baby-sitters or vacations which might provide the children with an outing and the parents with some respite.

In comparisons between children of lower and higher socioeconomic status it has been found that those of lower status are, on the average, more openly aggressive and more punitive in their moral attitudes, more likely to become delinquent, more likely to have fears of a superstitious nature and also fears of certain concrete dangers (such as beatings, drunks, "bad guys," rats, illness without money to pay doctors' bills). While children in poorer neighborhoods mention many fears from which those in better neighborhoods are spared, children in both groups have many "irrational" fears (this subject is discussed in Chapter Twelve).

In some poor neighborhoods a child may be encouraged to be a fighter, although subject to certain rules (Davis, 1944). However, various segments of the population differ in this respect and it cannot be said that, as a general rule, parents of lower socioeconomic status tolerate aggressiveness more than parents of higher socioeconomic status (Sears et al., 1954; Markley, 1958).

In weighing the meaning of conduct in relation to socioeconomic status it is necessary to consider both the overt behavior and the emotional undertones. The difference between people in the lower and middle social ranks may be more a difference in mode of expression than in intensity of feeling. In some areas, for example, "lower-class" boys, until prohibited, have been found to carry knives with them to school, presumably as weapons. To a middle-class teacher this is a horrible practice. The wound that might be inflicted by a lower-class boy can be severe, but the hurts inflicted by the sarcasm of a middle-class teacher (who would not think of using a knife) can also be very severe.

Child-rearing practices and attitudes. In many of the earlier studies dealing with child-rearing practices and attitudes it was concluded that middle-class parents were, on the whole, more demanding, more ambitious, and less easy-going than lower-class parents. For many years it has been accepted as a truism that middle-class parents insist more on cleanliness, are more rigid in the handling of children's weaning and toilet training, more intolerant of aggressiveness, more prudish about sex, and allow children less freedom to roam about in the community. Many writers, while describing the "lower-class" child as one who, in many ways, has a rough time, have also portrayed him as enjoying more freedom than his peers in the middle-class. This picture has not been confirmed in recent studies. Sears and his associates (1957) found, for example, that middle-class mothers were generally more permissive and less punitive in dealing with their children than were working-class mothers. Working-class mothers were, if anything, more severe in toilet training and they pushed the child to complete his training more than did the middle-class mothers. Working-class mothers were less likely to allow their young children to wander about the community without supervision. They were less lenient toward sex behavior and toward aggression. Other recent studies, which dispute the view that the child of lower socioeconomic status is under less pressure, include investigations by Maccoby and Gibbs (1954) and by Markley (1958). Markley makes the reservation, however, that middle-class parents perhaps apply subtle pressures which they themselves do not recognize or report.

In a discussion of differing findings in this area, Havighurst and Davis (1955) state that as we learn more about social conditions in the United States "it becomes clear that one should not attempt to generalize concerning child-rearing to an entire social class in one part of the country, even if it is a representative sample."

Attitudes toward education. Parents in higher socioeconomic groups more often than those in lower groups expect that their children will continue their education through high school and go on to college. According to one point of view (Hollingshead, 1949) parents of middle or higher socioeconomic status are also more in favor of the sort of education schools usually provide and more sympathetic toward the overall idea of schooling than parents of lower status. However, recent research casts some doubt on this theory. Sears and his associates (1957) noted that while middle-class, better educated families took it for granted that their children would go to college this did not mean that they were putting more pressure on the school achievement in the earlier grades than did the working-class families. How pressures of this sort affect the ideas an individual child acquires about what he *should* do as a child and what he might look forward to as an older person would require a study of the youngsters themselves.

Delinquency and socioeconomic status. The delinquency rate is frequently higher in the lower than in the higher socioeconomic groups. One reservation with regard to the meaning of this statistic is that youngsters of higher socioeconomic status who perform delinquent acts are more likely to be protected and less likely to be brought to court than children of lower income groups. However this may be, a youngster living in a community in which the delinquency rate is high certainly faces a different social situation than one living in a community where the rate is low. The former is more exposed to the influence of delinquent companions. He may feel that he cannot count on the protection of his parents or of the community when he does something wrong. He may even develop a cynical attitude toward policemen and toward the idea of law and justice. In one class which the writer visited in a school in a "delinquency area" most of the members, in connection with a discussion of cops, claimed that they knew policemen who were crooked or unfair or brutal or otherwise unsuited to be respected upholders of the law. It should be added, however, that a large proportion of these youngsters also said that they knew other cops who were "okay." Many young people themselves seem to recognize the social pressures that prevail in an underprivileged "delinquency area."

AWARENESS OF SYMBOLS OF SOCIAL POSITION

In time the child becomes aware of the symbols of social position, such as a professional man's brief case and white collar and the laborer's overalls. This kind of awareness develops somewhat slowly, according to a study by Stendler (1949a). First-grade children showed little awareness of their own social class position. First-graders described their families as rich more often than fourth-graders, but even in the fourth grade some children were not as clearly aware of the economic position of their families as of other symbols of social status. At the eighth-grade level, no child in the lower economic group described his family as rich, and many of the children were reluctant to answer the question.

Children in the first grade were not only inclined to rate themselves as rich, but they also rated a large proportion of their classmates as rich. In naming children who had "lots of money" they showed little agreement with adults. At the fourth-grade level, and even more at the sixth- and eighth-grade levels, the children were much less naive and, at the two upper levels, they could rate with high accuracy (as measured against the judgment of well-informed adults) the financial status of any ten classmates named at random.

The features in his environment which a child notices are not always those which an adult would recognize as signs of socioeconomic status. What is physically near the child is not necessarily psychologically near to him in the sense that he notices and comments on it (Estvan, 1952). In a study by the writer and Tasch (1949) it was found that children living under conditions of poor housing were less likely to mention housing as an unpleasant feature of their environment than children whose living quarters were comparatively good.

Children tend to describe their circumstances as being in a middle position between poverty and wealth (Stendler, 1949). Children from wealthier homes, by saying they are "in-between," tend to understate their financial circumstances, while children from poorer homes tend, at least in relative terms, to overstate their condition. Adults similarly tend to identify themselves as belonging somewhere in the middle social class (Cantril, 1946).

Many children become more distinctly aware of status differences during adolescence as they develop an interest in dating and begin to think about their vocational future. At this time the disadvantage of living on the wrong side of the tracks, and the advantage of coming from a "good" family, may be brought home to a young person quite sharply. The status of a child's family obviously has had an important effect on his ideas and attitudes concerning himself if he is ashamed of his home or lacks confidence in his manners and his ability to mingle freely with others.

Boy-girl relationships

When a young child begins to enter into social relations with other children, distinctions between boys and girls are not likely to be very noticeable. Boys and girls play together and enjoy the same activities. Even at the preschool level, however, some distinctions and differences appear. Boys tend to be more active in their play, although differences within each sex group are larger than differences between the two sexes. At the ages of three and four boys enter into a larger number of conflicts than do girls and are more likely to resort to hitting. In a mixed group, boy-boy and girl-girl conflicts are likely to be more frequent than boy-girl conflicts. At the preschool level, especially after the age of two years, boy-boy and girl-girl friendships are likely to be more numerous than friendships between a boy and a girl. However, even though children prefer playmates of their own sex, there is a good deal of interplay, and at this age a child is not likely to be disturbed if he is in a group in which all other members are of the opposite sex.

Differences between the average boy and girl are referred to in several sections of this book. Some of these are reflected in their social behavior. Girls are somewhat superior in early language development. They tend from an early age to show more interest in people and in social relationships, while boys show relatively more interest in things and in mechanical contrivances.

In many respects, boys are the weaker of the two sexes, at least during the first years of life. Infant mortality among them is somewhat higher, and they are slower in their growth as measured by skeletal development. More boys than girls have speech defects and reading difficulties. Usually "problem behavior," including delinquency, is found in boys far more often than in girls.

Differences between boys and girls are probably more apparent in their public behavior than in the privacy of their inner lives. When projective procedures (briefly described in Chapter Fifteen) are used to explore feelings and fantasies, both boys and girls display far more hostility and emotional turmoil than they reveal in their overt conduct (Frank et al., 1953; Symonds, 1949). The direct consequences of a boy's behavior are usually more apparent: When a boy is aggressive, for example, he prompts others to defend themselves or to direct aggression against him. On the other hand, the standards imposed on girls are, in many ways, more strict than those imposed on boys. At the adolescent level, for example, girls are judged more severely than boys for various forms of misconduct (including stealing and sex behavior). It has even been found that homicide is considered a more serious crime if committed by a girl even though the victim killed is equally dead whether his life was taken by a boy or a girl.

SEX STEREOTYPES

From a very early age boys and girls are nudged or urged into living up to their particular sex role. Early in life they begin to hear what a "real" girl or a "real" boy would or should do. They are dressed differently, receive different toys, and somewhat different instructions as to what is "nice" and what is forbidden.

The stereotyped notion of a "real" boy or a "real" girl deals mainly with superficial aspects of conduct. The male role is usually represented by a robust figure, less inclined to weep than a female, less sentimental, more "practical," less capable of tenderness, more richly endowed with physical courage. According to this stereotype, a man can "take it"; he should be able to grin even though he is sad or afraid. Actually, there is no good reason to believe that boys are more robust emotionally, less moved by fear, stronger in the face of danger, less capable of tenderness, more inclined than girls to be ruled by reason instead of sentiment.

SOCIAL DISTANCE BETWEEN THE SEXES

"Social distance" between the sexes, which can be noted as early as the age of two or three, becomes more conspicuous at the elementary-school level (Koch, 1944). At the late preschool and elementary-school levels boys express a greater preference for boys and girls for girls. This preference for members of the same sex increases up to the high-school level and then decreases.

The cleavage between the sexes can be observed in almost any situation where boys and girls gather together for free, unsupervised play. But it can also be observed that under adult leadership girls and boys enjoy many activities in common, even though, when left to themselves they tend to segregate.

ROMANTIC INTERESTS OF BOYS AND GIRLS

It is not usually until they reach the teens that boys and girls begin to date and let it be known that they are "going steady," but many children show a romantic interest in the opposite sex long before adolescence. Public signs of such interest appear in scribblings, such as, "Charlie loves Mabel," in the sending of valentines and notes, in the behavior of the boy who loiters after school to walk his girl friend home, in the eagerness some children show for folk dancing or social dancing (if the climate of opinion in the school or community in which they live permits). Many adults have tender memories of childhood "sweethearts," and recall the surges of emotion they went through, ranging from delight to jealousy and grief, during their childhood romances.[8]

Prejudice

Great numbers of children, while yet very young, are exposed to influences that produce prejudice. In a study by Ammons (1950) evidence of active prejudice was found as early as four years.

Prejudice is a bias held against an individual because he is a member of a certain group. It is a form of prejudgment, a tendency to generalize an attitude of disfavor. This means that a person belonging to a group against which there is a prejudice is regarded with misgiving, and perhaps with distrust or hostility, not because of his *individual* qualities but because he belongs to a *group* against which a stand has been taken.

Prejudice is a sickness within the society. It has three unhappy aspects: It is damaging to those against whom there is prejudice; it is an unhealthy condition within the person who is prejudiced; and it creates difficulties for the total social group.

EMOTIONAL ASPECT OF PREJUDICE

Persons who are conspicuously prejudiced are more likely than unprejudiced persons to be anxious, insecure, and burdened with veiled hostility.[9] Their values are more probably based on the authoritarian standards imposed by others than on personal convictions of their own. Unfavorable attitudes toward others are sometimes accompanied by rejecting attitudes toward oneself. In one study it was noted that Negro children who expressed positive feelings about themselves also expressed more positive feelings toward other Negroes and toward whites than did children who were least positive in their attitudes toward themselves (Trent, 1953).

Prejudice sometimes is a form of displaced anger by which a troubled person seeks to resolve or evade his grievances by fixing the blame on a scapegoat.

Prejudice and inner conflict. A conflict (open or thinly disguised) is likely to arise between the older child's prejudices and the moral principles he is taught. For example, he may attend a church where he is

---

[8] For a discussion of amorous sentiments in children see Grant (1948).

[9] For references bearing on this matter, see Adorno *et al.*, 1950; Gough *et al.*, 1950; Ammons, 1950; Harris *et al.*, 1950; Frenkel-Brunswik, 1951; and Harding *et al.*, 1954.

told he should love others as he loves himself, but such a belief does not fit well with the idea of hating (or at least disliking and distrusting) the people he is prejudiced against (or barring them from his church!). So there is conflict between his prejudices and the values he is supposed to embrace. The young child is not likely to be aware of this; the older person is likely to dull the sharp edge of conflict, or to dismiss it, by justifying and rationalizing his attitudes. To defend or to avoid facing an untenable position he will find reasons for not feeling friendly toward the people he is prejudiced against. He may carry his self-justification so far that he persuades himself that he actually is not prejudiced.

As children grow older and better informed, more able to reason and to weigh the pros and cons of problems, they do not automatically re-examine the prejudices they began to acquire in their less-informed youth. The ability to think incisively on new problems (especially those not emotionally toned) may exist side by side with remnants of childish attitudes. Prejudices, firmly entrenched in what has come to be known as the logic-tight compartments of the mind, are hard to dislodge. As a result, bright children may be just as irrationally prejudiced as dull children, and adults with brilliant minds may be as childish in their prejudices as adults who are stupid.

It is easy to support a prejudice, at least on a superficial level, for in every large group of people there are some who are mean and unpleasant; one needs only to notice the meanness of some people in the group and overlook similar meanness in people of other groups. Such grounds for prejudice are rather shaky. But the same is true of any kind of reasoning undertaken to support an emotional bias and a foregone conclusion. Others who do not happen to share the prejudice (or who have prejudices of their own to keep in a good state of nourishment) may not be taken in by a certain person's justification of his prejudice but, for the time being, it is enough that *he* is convinced of its merit.

EMOTIONAL CONSEQUENCES OF PREJUDICE

When a chlid is treated unkindly or unfairly because he is a member of a group against which there is a prejudice he cannot help feeling hurt and angry. This is a natural response to unkindness, but it may be a seed from which he derives a set of prejudices of his own. When a person against whom there is a prejudice reacts by becoming prejudiced, the member of the minority group will have the most difficulty. Members of a minority not only have to bear the grievances of the majority group, but they also lack the strength to retaliate in kind.

A moving account of the problems and emotional difficulties faced by people because of their membership in a minority group has been offered by Goff (1949) who interviewed 150 Negro children in two cities. Among the difficulties faced by the children (as seen and interpreted by them) because of their race were disparagement, ridicule, and other aggressive and hostile acts. Consider, for example, this situation:

> A Negro girl stood in line, eagerly waiting her turn to receive a doll which a storekeeper had advertised would be given free to any girl who came to the store. When she finally reached the counter she was told she could not have a doll—the dolls were only for white girls.

In Goff's study, almost half of the children said they had suffered from feelings of self-belittlement such as shame, hurt feelings, embarrassment, and the like. Girls seemed to smart more severely than boys under what they regarded as rude and humiliating treatment.

A child who is the victim of prejudice faces a tough predicament. As a member of a minority group it is dangerous for him to use against others the weapons they use against him. If he is aggressive he invites attack. If he turns the other cheek the result may be further abuse. If, as he grows older, he becomes resigned to the fact that the doors of opportunity are closed he runs the risk of being called lazy and shiftless. If he tries to assert himself through the usual channels of competition for position, wealth, or power he runs the risk of being called "pushy" or unscrupulous. In the meantime he may be denied even the solace of sharing his troubles with others. In studies of minority groups it has been noted that parents may be deeply concerned about prejudice but evade the issue when it is brought up by their children (see Goodman, 1952; and Weaver, 1955).

When a person is the victim of prejudice, one of the ironic turns of fate is that he will sometimes turn the prejudice against himself or his own group. This occurs when a member of minority group A, unable to retaliate against offending members of majority group B, "takes out" his anger against himself or his own people.

Communication of prejudice.   Children may become prejudiced because of a firsthand unpleasant experience, but prejudices are usually transmitted to them through the attitudes shown by their elders. Other things being equal, a child will tend to be favorably disposed toward other people, no matter what group they belong to, and he will be disposed against people whom his elders dislike even though he has no significant firsthand experience with them. Many children express unfavorable views toward minority groups in America even though they have had little or no contact with members of the groups (Radke *et al.*, 1950).

One way in which prejudice is communicated is through "stereotypes." Many stereotypes which are unfavorable to this group or that are passed on carelessly and unthinkingly in everyday life in the form of jokes and speech habits, or cartoons.

Prejudice as a barrier to communication.   Prejudice tends to block emotional communication between people and to reduce a person's emotional communication with himself. Groups which are prejudiced against each other tend to lose sight of the fact that people in the rejected group are also human beings with the same sensitiveness, the same fears and grievances, the same desire to be accepted, the same bitter revulsion against being rejected as they themselves possess. If one person is prejudiced against another, the first tends, in effect, to dehumanize the other person; this means that by the same process and to the same extent he dehumanizes himself. The deeper a prejudice, the less room there is for compassion.

Influence of
adult direction and management

In everyday life, one can repeatedly observe the way in which children's social reactions to one another can be influenced by the kind of direction they receive from adults who are in charge of the group. A teacher may betray her attitude toward a child and, in effect, let other children understand that it would be all right for them to attack a child of whom the teacher disapproves (Fite, 1940).

Children respond more favorably to an adult who identifies himself with their concerns and is pleasant in his dealings. This can be observed repeatedly in everyday life, and it has been amply confirmed in research studies. For example, when children and older persons describe the qualities of teachers whom they like best or dislike most they give less emphasis to academic matters than to more personal aspects of the teacher's personality. Similarly, it has been noted that children working with an adult who is democratic and who establishes a cordial personal relationship with children, are likely to be more constructive, to show less strife, and to be more responsible than when with an adult who has autocratic tendencies.[10]

Adults as peers

Association with peers is essential to a child's full development. Parents and teachers, however chummy they may be, cannot fully take the place of a child's peers in

---

[10] See Lewin, Lippett, and White (1939); and Thorndike (1941).

the child's development as an independent person. Although some adults have a great talent for spontaneous fellowship with children, they are more likely to be able to play the part of peers in some areas of experience than in others. A forty-year-old father may, for example, be able to plunge into a game of hide-and-seek with his six- and eight-year-old children with such abandon that he is as good as any other playmate. But he is just a hindrance to twelve-year-olds who like to mix romance with their hide-and-seek. A fifty-year-old man who still has a boyish enthusiasm for collecting stamps may lose himself in a common activity of search and barter and subtle communication with a stamp-collecting child of eight or ten or twelve, but the same adult will probably be quite unwelcome as a visitor in a lean-to which boys have built in the woods. A parent may even enter into a relationship in which he plays the role not simply of a child but of a child who is younger and more inadequate than his child. This occurs, for example, if a boy of eight or ten happens to understand mechanical things better than his father and patiently helps the father learn the workings of a new machine.

In the school, as in the home, it is possible to break down some of the barriers between the adult and the child and to find a common meeting ground. If the adult is genuine, spontaneous, and free to expose his humanity, he can find more in common with children and the children can find more in common with him. People who differ greatly in age are quite similar when viewed from the standpoint of their emotional needs and concerns. If an adult can accept himself as a person who is sometimes anxious and who as a child was sometimes deeply afraid, he can better appreciate the difficulties of a child of six or eight or eighteen who is afraid to trust himself in a new situation or who fears rejection and rebuke from his peers. Similarly, the adult who is able to appreciate and to accept the implications of his own struggle for independence will better be able to appreciate the child's struggle.

In day-to-day relationships there are innumerable occasions when the young and the old can communicate their understanding of each other. A parent or teacher who perceives that his child is angry or anxious can often let the child know that he appreciates the struggle he is undergoing. He can do this by means of a glance, or by noticeably keeping his mouth shut. He can do it by a kind of understanding patience which allows the child to express his annoyance (even though to a neighbor it seems far out of proportion) or to voice his grievances (even though those against whom the child complains may have an even greater cause for feeling abused).

This kind of communication is not necessarily carried on by words. Indeed, silence is often the deepest kind of communication between an adult and a child.

Recommended Readings

Readings in Social Psychology, edited by Eleanor E. Maccoby, Theo-
dore M. Newcomb, and Eugene L. Hartley (3rd edition, 1958) contains excellent reviews of literature pertaining to various aspects of
social behavior. Roger C. Barker and Herbert F. Wright in *Midwest
and Its Children* (1954) present a very interesting, detailed picture of
the many avenues through which children move as they enter the social
world. The books of readings edited by Wayne Dennis (1951), William
E. Martin and Celia Burns Stendler (1954), and Jerome M. Seidman
(1958), referred to in earlier chapters, contain numerous original
studies dealing with the socialization process.

PART THREE

Emotional Development

The Meaning of Emotion
Love, Joy, Sensuality, Humor

CHAPTER ELEVEN   To understand a child we need to know as much as possible about four dimensions of his experience: his overt actions, his private thoughts, his feelings, and his motives. When a child knows and tells what he thinks, feels, and wants, and acts accordingly, these four dimensions are merged into one. But frequently he fails to reveal his thoughts and feelings and sometimes they are quite contrary to his words or his actions. This happens when the "reason" he gives for his conduct is not the one he really has in mind, when he covers his disappointment with a smile, or when he is frightened but acts as though he were angry.

It is important to try to understand a child's feelings, for it is through them that he has the most intimate experience of the tang and taste of his existence as a person. This dimension of

a child's experience—his feelings—becomes less perceptible to others as he grows older. An older child is better able than a younger one to "speak his mind" but he is also better able to retreat into silence. He is better able to suit his actions to his impulses, but also better able to assume a façade.

The meaning of emotion

Emotion means a state of being "moved." Outwardly it shows itself in laughter or tears. Inwardly it includes three qualities of experience which sometimes are clear and sometimes blurred. First, it involves *feeling*, such as jubilation or depression or anger or fear. Second, it includes an *impulse* toward some kind of action, such as an impulse to hit, or to run, or to seek and prolong a pleasurable event. Third, on the subjective side, emotion involves *awareness* or *perception* (although often not at all in clear detail) of what it is, or what it might be, that produces these impulses and feelings.

As we have said, these feelings and impulses and the intellectual perception of what has produced them may or may not be well defined in one's experience. Many common emotional conditions, such as anxiety, are not clearly defined in the perceptions of the person who is emotionally aroused.

Early emotional reactions

In Chapter Three, we noted that at the time of birth emotional behavior is not very precise or well differentiated. Moreover, the child is undisturbed by many conditions that will arouse him as he matures.[1]

As a child grows older his expressions of emotion become more clearly distinguishable. For example, when adult judges were asked to identify pictures taken of a ten-month-old child when he was exposed to conditions that usually arouse fear, astonishment, satisfaction, anger, and the like, their identifications were more accurate than could be expected by chance. The sounds an infant uses to express emotion also become more definite after a time.

The role of needs, drives, motives, goals

Whether or not a child will be aroused emotionally by a happening depends on what he has at stake.

---

[1] Bonsfield and Orbison (1952) have presented a theory of emotional development based on the assumption that the infant's emotional capacities are limited because his cortex is undeveloped and also that he is relatively lacking in the endocrine products which sustain some of the physiological responses to stress.

Emotion is likely to be aroused by anything that furthers or threatens his motives and plans, anything that blocks or promotes activities he desires to carry out, or anything that helps or hinders his hopes and aspirations. As a result, the same external event can produce varied effects. A child who is poised for action will be angered when someone holds him tightly, but if he is in a mood to be cuddled he will enjoy being held.

To list all the drives that make a person subject to emotion would be an impossible undertaking, for while some are "original," common to all persons, and quite obvious (such as the drive to obtain food when hungry), others have been influenced by learning and past experience and may be unique (such as a certain child's desire to collect the stubs of theater tickets). Yet it is possible to specify groups of motives that come into play.

Some drives are associated with *primary needs* of the organism, such as the need for food, for drink, for air, for rest and sleep, for protection against heat or cold, and for protection of bodily tissue against damage through bruises and punctures. Connected with many of these needs are cravings of varying intensity, such as a thirsty person's craving for water.

In addition, human beings, in common with other creatures, have a drive to use their energies. For example, the child has a drive to creep and walk, to venture and explore.

Another category of motives includes those involved in a child's relations with other people: his desire for company, his need to belong, to be accepted, to have a place, and to have status with his own age group. These desires vary with different children, and are of course very much influenced by learning and experience.

In addition, there are almost countless varieties of motives of a more optional character that are described by such everyday terms as interests, wishes and desires, wants, and hopes.

Among the most prominent concerns underlying emotion as a child grows older are those connected with his desire to maintain his self-esteem and to protect and assert the ideas and attitudes he has formed regarding himself.

INTERWEAVING OF EMOTION AND OTHER ASPECTS OF DEVELOPMENT

The development of emotions during infancy and childhood is interwoven with other aspects of development. As a child's senses become more acute, as his capacities for discrimination and perception mature, and as he moves forward in this or that phase of his development, the range of events which arouse emotion grows wider and wider. With the growth of the child's understanding and imagination the things that affect him emotionally become increasingly involved with symbols and fancies, with abstract plans and values.

One outstanding consequence of the interweaving of emotional and other aspects of growth is that the same external stimulus may induce not only quite different but also apparently opposite emotional reactions as the child moves from one phase of development to the next. At one phase, the infant smiles when spoken to, even though the voice is "angry"; but a similar angry voice can later produce fear, and, still later, annoyance. Similarly, an infant who at one point smiled at strangers may later show fear and, still later, view strangers with interest and curiosity. The youngster who merrily grabs and bangs a toy at eight months may, at about twelve months slam it down in anger if he fails to figure out how it works, or if he tries to take it apart and does not succeed.[2] During the next phase, he may show signs of pleasure when he discovers how the toy works. At a later phase, when the toy is no longer a challenge to his hands or his wits, it neither attracts or offends him. At still a later phase, when he is aware of what is "mine" and "thine" he may hand the toy to another child or angrily snatch it away if another child tries to possess it, as though the toy, although no longer alluring in itself, is still valued as a piece of property. In this chapter and the two that follow we will note many other illustrations of the changing emotional reactions that occur in connection with the child's motor, intellectual, and social development.

Concealment and suppression of feeling

In early infancy, as we have noted, a child's expression of emotion is rather aimless and not very precise, and then as he grows older he is able to show his emotion in more clearly defined ways. But from early childhood forces are at work that induce him to moderate or blunt his expressions of emotion and to conceal his feelings. The discipline most children receive from others figures importantly in inducing them to restrain their show of emotion and to conceal their "true" feelings. We might ask, however, is the curbing of outbursts of emotion to some degree a *developmental* as well as a *cultural* phenomenon? We can observe that some animals (dogs, for example) are less given to yelping, whinning, or crying when they are older than when they were younger. (It may be, of course, that the older dog is not more stoical but has less to whine about.) More directly to the point, it has been observed that children, while yet very young, show

---

[2] An interesting study of changing nuances in a child's emotional reactions has been reported by Meili (1957).

an ability to muffle or modify their show of emotion. Meili (1947) observed, for example, that between the middle of the first and the second year of life, some children would "swallow" their crying, seemingly fight back their tears, when a toy was taken way from them. At about this time also he noted seemingly forced or affected laughter, and laughing or smiling that seemed to express embarrassment rather than pleasure. When a child who is frustrated comes forth with an "artificial" laugh instead of a show of temper, he may be trying to be polite, as a result of the training he has received. But something within the child's own development probably also has intervened: with added mental growth he might now perceive the frustration as a challenge to his wits and not just as something that provokes his anger by thwarting his wishes.

Pressures from others leading to concealment of emotion.   At first from his parents and brothers and sisters, and later from others, the child receives reminders that he should calm down, not get angry, not be afraid. He is told, in effect, not only to conceal his emotion but even to avoid having emotion: There is "nothing to be afraid of"; "you better not get sore at me"; "there is nothing to cry about or to laugh at." There are many pressures on children to drive emotion underground. Children learn to disguise their feelings, to hide them, to express them in devious ways.

"DON'T CRY!"

Pressure on children to play false with their feelings, and thus in time to play false with themselves, appears noticeably in connection with feelings springing from grief, sorrow, pain, or anxiety so acute that the individual is helpless and feels like breaking into tears.

It is natural for a child to cry when hurt, to sob when in distress, to weep when lonely, to shriek with fright, and to scream in anger if he is helpless in his rage and there is nothing else he can do in his helplessness.

But many adults and many older children recoil when they see another person cry. Some become anxious at the sight of tears and the sound of weeping. So from an early age, quite apart from their own natural course of development (which leads to changes in the use of crying), children are constrained not to let their feelings show by crying. They also are under pressure to conceal feelings that might cause them to cry, and to guard against such feelings.

The writer recalls a newspaper story about a baby who fell out of a window several stories high and when the mother rushed out to pick up the child, mercifully alive and crying lustily, she said: "Don't cry." As though a child should fall from a skyscraper to earn the right to cry! Actually, when the mother said, "Don't cry," she was not giving a command but expressing her own agitation, yet it is noteworthy that it took this form. From the child's point of view such an admonition might sound as though there is something bad about crying.

When people say to children, "Don't cry," the reason may be that crying arouses in them buried recollections and banished impulses, going back to the time when they would like to have cried in anger, or screamed with fear, or wept out of a feeling of hurt or loneliness and helplessness. It is hard for the older person to endure a reminder of these old and buried hurts, and the harder it is the more anxious he will be when another cries.

When a child is asked to keep from crying he is being asked to bury something of himself, to conceal rather than to express and to face his impulses and his feelings at the moment when they occur. And thereby we encourage him to go astray in his development. If an older person wishes to understand a child's emotions and to help him cope with the conditions that arouse emotion it is necessary to encourage the child to face feelings rather than to falsify them or run away from them. But to do this requires courage on the adult's part, the courage to permit a child to allow his feelings to show and the courage to face feelings that are aroused within himself when the emotions of someone else appear in raw form.

It is necessary, of course, for a child as he grows older to learn to set limits on his emotional outbursts. He shouldn't laugh in church and he had better not laugh at his teacher. For his own good and the safety of others he must learn not to rend and destroy when he is angry. Children are required to curb their impulses (especially their anger) even in a therapy situation where the aim is to encourage them to reveal their feelings. However, (so the writer believes) the pressures placed on children to conceal their feelings go far beyond what is necessary for the child's own good or the welfare of others.

HIDDEN CURRENTS OF FEELING

As a consequence of the suppression of an outward display of emotion there usually is a wide disparity between an older child's actions and his inner state. Even among nursery-school children, there is a marked difference between the person who appears in public and the hidden person who harbors feelings quite different from those he puts on display. At the adolescent level, most children have become so adept in acting the role they are supposed to play that there is a sharp difference between the "outer" and "inner" dimensions of their lives. There is the visible scholar who goes through the academic motions; and there is the invisible scholar, preoccupied with personal concerns that are a world removed from the "academic" man (or woman) who appears in the classroom or the "organization" man (or woman) who goes through the social rituals prescribed by the group. At the adult level, the difference between what is revealed and what is concealed is likely to be even more marked, so marked, according to a study now being conducted by the writer and Allina, that persons who are long-time "friends" and professional colleagues are, in many ways, complete strangers to one another. One reason for this strangeness is that in the natural course of development a growing person wants to protect his privacy. But another reason is that in our educational system we usually try to promote all kinds of learning except knowledge of our own feelings and the feelings of others. As a consequence, when we try to understand the emotional life of a child we seek a kind of knowledge which most of us, in our discipline at home and at school, have been trained assiduously *not* to acquire. Therefore, it is difficult for us to fathom a child's feelings; but two circumstances come to our aid. One is that many children, if properly approached, are not only willing but pathetically eager to reveal feelings which they usually keep hidden. The writer has frequently found, for example, that youngsters will disclose to a friendly inquirer joys and fears which they have not mentioned to their parents or teachers or playmates. In doing so, they usually are better able to tell what they are afraid of than to tell why they are afraid; but the information is revealing as far as it goes.

Affection

Since we have discussed affection in several earlier parts of this book, notably in Chapter Seven, we will touch on only a few aspects of the subject in this section.

In his relations with his parents a child craves affection and, in time, he seeks to bestow it. The normal child as an infant and as a preschooler is more inclined to be friendly than unfriendly. As was noted in Chapters Three and Nine, friendly responses far outnumber unfriendly ones in the child's relationships with adults when he is an infant and later in his dealings with other children outside the home. At the elementary-school level, children show their need for affection in their great desire to be accepted by their peers and in the emphasis they give to the qualities of kindness when they describe teachers whom they like best.

ORIGINS OF AFFECTION

According to one theory affection is something the child acquires; according to another, affection is inherent in a human being's "original nature."

According to the first view, love is learned: A youngster becomes attached to persons or things by virtue of the satisfaction they bring him, the role they play in gratifying his elemental needs. Briefly put, he loves his mother because he loves his milk. According to the second view, love is not a by-product or after-thought but as basic a feature of human nature as legs are an original part of the body. This view is stated by Montagu (1953) who says: "The most important thing to realize about the nature of human nature is that the most significant ingredient in its structure is love."

In one sense, the question we have raised is academic, for whether the need for receiving and giving affection is original or acquired it eventually plays a powerful role in a child's life. In another sense, however, it is not academic, for it touches on a basic issue in the philosophy of human growth. Our view of human potentialities is quite different if, for example, we assume that it is at least as natural for a child to love as to hate.

Pleasures, joys, and satisfactions

The joys of childhood are as many and varied as the scope of children's activities. Most obvious as a source of pleasure is anything that gratifies an appetite or desire—food, drink, warmth, and pleasant physical contacts. Also quite apparent are the joys children derive from free and unimpeded activity.

Activity pleasure. The infant appears to be having a pleasant time as he coos and gurgles, exercises his voice, kicks, manipulates convenient objects with his hands, ventures into creeping and crawling and walking. As he grows older, he gains pleasure from an increasing range of activities. Whether the child gets as much pleasure from his activities as his shouts, laughter, and eagerness seem to express we have no way of knowing for sure. But it is apparent that, like a healthy puppy who frisks playfully, the child draws satisfaction from being active of his own accord. There is a kind of spontaneity in much of a young child's activity that flows from the total economy of his organism as distinguished from the press of demands from the external environment.

Zestful ventures. From infancy the child is on the go. He ventures, he gets into difficult situations, he often welcomes excitement. He sometimes seems to get a thrill out of "play" with emotions which, in themselves, are not pleasant. He plays with anger as he tests the patience of his parents and the forebearance of his peers. He "plays" with fear, returning of his own accord to situations that are somewhat frightening to him, but not completely overwhelming. In many ways a child "asks for trouble." If he feels secure he is likely to take chances, and he will laugh and shout with glee as he successfully scales a hurdle, overcomes a difficulty, or gets out of a tight spot.

"Pleasures of the mind." Among the pleasures a child experiences as he grows older are those that occur when he satisfies his curiosity and applies his mind to intellectual tasks. Many children are extremely happy when they first discover they are able to read. And even arithmetic has charms. One seven-year-old child described the happiest day of her life as the day "I learned to take away!" (the day she learned to subtract).

Joy in self-discovery. Prominent among the joy-producing experiences in a child's life are those that give him a new perception of himself, a new glimpse of his ability, a broadened view of his capacity to "take it," to stand up to a difficulty, to handle a troublesome problem. Many children discover such satisfactions in the process of overcoming their fears, a process by which they gain freedom from a threat and also a greater realization of their strength. In one of his studies the author had the good fortune over a stretch of several days to watch a child (aged about three) who was trying to overcome a fear of high places. The youngster had made an inclined plane with a board, one end resting on the ground, the other on a high box. Again and again he started to walk up the board, at first venturing only a few steps, then a few more. When finally he succeeded in going the whole way he stood on top of the box and let forth a shout of triumph such as Beowulf might have made after slaying a dragon.

Table 11 summarizes some of the joys of childhood as expressed in the terms children themselves use, or broad categories based on such terms. Younger children expressed their joys frequently in the language of gifts, holidays and festivities, games and sports, and visits or special contacts with people. This language reveals more concerning the objective nature of the enjoyable event than concerning its subjective meaning, for often it appeared (but was not literally stated) that the joy stemmed not from the gift alone (or the visit, and the like), but had a deeper meaning. For example, in many of these accounts of "one of my happiest days" children mentioned gifts which in themselves were not particularly valuable (when a teacher reverses the usual order of things and gives an apple to a pupil, the apple has a value far beyond that of the fruit itself). To many children, a gift is far more than just another material possession: It is a symbol of acceptance, a token of good will. It may be a gesture of forgiveness, an expression of confidence. A thoughtful person gives not simply the gift he bears in his hand but also something of himself.

In view of this, many of the happy circumstances listed in Table 11 should be regarded as symbols, the objective media through which deeper subjective meanings are communicated.

(The values represent percentage of children giving one or more responses
in each category.)

Description	Grades 1-3 Ages 6-9		Grades 4-6 Ages 9-12		Grades 7-9 Ages 12-15		Grades 10-12 Ages 15-18	
	363 Boys	331 Girls	309 Boys	343 Girls	282 Boys	290 Girls	159 Boys	171 Girls
Receiving or having or otherwise enjoying material things, gifts, toys, money, living quarters	8.7	8.1	10.4	7.2	10.1	4.5	5.6	3.1
Holidays, festive occasions, birthdays, Christmas, etc.	39.1	40.5	32.4	38.9	6.3	10.1	0.6	6.5
Sports, games, hiking, hunting, bicycling, etc.	10.2	6.4	9.1	5.5	12.4	5.8	13.0	7.3
Going to miscellaneous places of recreation, going to camps, traveling, going to resorts, to parks	9.6	9.0	10.1	11.4	9.7	13.9	30.2	6.9
Self-improvement, success in school, educational opportunity, evidence of vocational competence, getting a job	2.4	2.3	2.9	1.9	4.8	4.1	13.6	15.9
Happenings connected with school, including last day, end of school, going to a certain school	3.6	3.4	5.4	4.3	14.0	11.1	7.0	5.4
Relationship with people (explicitly described), companionship, being with certain friend, return home of relatives, etc.	7.7	15.9	8.0	15.8	10.5	22.0	8.7	19.9
Residing in, moving to, a certain city or community	1.3	1.0	0.8	2.9	0.9	2.9	1.4	5.0
Benefits befalling others, or mankind in general, including end of war	0.6	0.8	3.2	2.8	2.2	2.6	7.9	9.7

* Reproduced, by permission, from A. T. Jersild and R. J. Tasch, *Children's Interests.* Bureau of Publications, Teachers College, Columbia University, 1949. The table omits several categories, including hobbies, movies and radio programs, art activities, and so forth, mentioned by only small percentages of children.

Boredom

The term "boredom" covers a variety of "negative" experiences in which the individual is marking time with nothing stimulating or challenging to absorb his attention. Boredom involves an absence of the "activity pleasure" described above. Although boredom is very common, it has received little attention in psychological research. In everyday speech it is revealed by such expressions as "nothing ever happens around here" and "feeling fed up." Being "tired" often denotes boredom rather than fatigue, and even "pain" often has this connotation, especially if the pain is located, euphemistically, in the neck.

A study of boredom would no doubt reveal that much of the mischievousness and misbehavior of children springs from a desire for action. Children will court danger or even severe punishment in order to stir up some "excitement." Similarly, mishaps and minor tragedies may be welcomed as a break in the monotony of life, as when a child dances with delight when the family car is stuck in the snow or when he learns that a bat has gotten into Grandma's bedroom, or that a beetle has crept into the bosom of Auntie's blouse. Many adults also, of course, go to great lengths to relieve boredom. Boredom sometimes is a precursor of anger as, for example, when a child is not allowed simply to be inattentive or to leave but is forced to listen to long lectures or to stay at the table until others are finished.

Boredom at school. Children's boredom frequently centers in the school. The bored ones include children who are not challenged by what is taught, either because it is too easy or because it has little or no meaning for them. Even children who do well at school usually welcome a holiday to relieve the monotony. In the study from which Table II is taken it was noted that the children seldom expressed any great liking for school but, on the contrary, more often expressed dislike, and more children mentioned the last day or closing of school than mentioned an actual school event when describing the happiest day of their lives. Of course, a child's pleasure or boredom with school will vary greatly from child to child and from school to school. It would be impossible to arrange matters in school so that everything occupying a child's time is scaled and varied to continue to challenge his growing abilities.

Boredom in everyday life. Many activities of daily life, both during childhood and adult years, consist of chores one must learn to take in stride. Failure to accept this fact leads to dissatisfaction, and the situation is even worse when everything in the day's activities becomes a matter of uninteresting routine. This problem is likely to be more acute in adult years, after the individual is pretty well established and finds that his daily round of duties no longer challenges his powers. Regardless of the importance of his duties in the larger scheme of things, he may find them boring; and he may develop, as many adults do, a sense of futility accompanied by a search for remedies that will either dull the senses or excite them. Much worse, of course, than the condition of boredom in an adult who has an occupation is the plight of an able-bodied person who has no occupation.

Chronic and pervasive boredom of the sort sometimes found in adults is not likely to occur in a child, because so much still lies ahead and he is constantly meeting new experiences. The frontiers of his world are still open. But the child and his activities have a definite bearing on the adult problem because the resources for satisfaction through activity which an adult possesses in his thirties and beyond are much influenced by his training and experiences as a child. Many adult hobbies and avocations first began to flower early in childhood; then, perhaps, they may have been dormant for a time through adolescence and youth, only to grow again in later years. Indeed, activities and skills, which a child exercised only because he had to may, in later years, be revived with enthusiasm; this happens, for example, when a person who worked in the garden reluctantly as a child, later as an adult, picks up a spade and hoe and goes joyfully to work.

Boredom with self. An important aspect of boredom which may manifest itself at the adult level but which is likely to be an outgrowth, at least in part, of the individual's childhood and youth, is the boredom a person feels with reference to himself. He does not like to be alone with himself. He becomes restless when left with his own thoughts. He seeks distraction, excitement, work, play, anything, in preference to his own company. Perhaps we should not call this boredom, although it often goes by that name. Another way of putting it is that a person so afflicted feels "the itch," a constant urge to "go places and do things." Such a person is the opposite of the god who is content to sit through eternity in solemn contemplation of his navel. A person who bores easily would probably soon tire of contemplating his navel, and it is also likely that other parts of his anatomy, generally viewed as more interesting than the navel, would not hold his attention very long.

When a person is thus bored it may be a sign that he is not at ease with himself. It may mean that he does not like his own thoughts, or relish the memories that arise when he is unoccupied, and that he is made uneasy by these reveries. Perhaps it is his conscience that troubles him—thoughts of deeds done or left undone, thoughts of self-condemnation. When this is the case, and the person flees from himself into a whirl of activities that focus his attention on external things, it is likely that he is not just bored but anxious. Often at school, when a child is bored it is not because there is nothing for him to do; he may even be behind in his lessons. Rather, what seems to look like boredom and a lack of interest may be the restlessness that goes with an inner conflict, a conflict arising between various impulses and needs and demands that the child places upon himself; a conflict between an impulse to work and a feeling of grievance against the teacher who is *making* him work against his will; a conflict between the need to exert effort and an expectation that such a person as he should be able to succeed without exerting much effort.

Emotional ramifications
of sexual development

As noted in Chapter Four, experiences that influence a person's emotional reactions to sex go back to infancy. Some of Freud's theories (1930, 1933, 1938a, 1938b) relating to sexuality in infancy and various phases of sexual development in early childhood have been discussed in Chapters Four and Seven.

According to Kinsey and his associates (1953) there are children, both male and female, who are "quite capable of true sexual response" prior to adolescence. Some writers take issue with the theory of infantile sexuality, claiming that erotic behavior does not have the same quality in a child as in an adult. In one sense, this claim is correct, for clearly a six-month-old infant or a four-year-old child is "immature" both sexually and emotionally as compared with an adult who is capable of begetting a child and of having parental sentiments. However, regardless of whether a child's sexuality is similar to that of a mature person from a *biological* point of view it is obvious that the sexuality of a child is important from a *psychological* point of view. When children reveal sensitivity in the genital area, or show an interest in sex play and become aware of attitudes of other children or of adults relating to sex, they are undergoing experiences which can have a significant bearing on their own attitudes and behavior.

Sex interests of older children. As they move into the preschool years and beyond, many children conceal their interest in sex from the eyes and ears of adults, but a large proportion of children, if not all, are interested in one way or another. All normal children eventually become curious about reproduction and the form of their curiosity or the kind of information they seek is likely to vary as they mature.

Tables 12 and 13 show the results of a study by Hattendorf (1932) in which parents were interviewed on what questions their children asked about sex.

TABLE 12	CLASSIFICATION OF QUESTIONS WITH RESPECT TO SEX ASKED BY 1797 BOYS AND GIRLS AGED TWO TO THIRTEEN YEARS AS REPORTED BY PARENTS [*]		
	Question	Number	Percentage
	Origin of babies	722	40.9
	Coming of another baby	256	14.5
	Intra-uterine growth	42	2.4
	Process of birth	183	10.4
	Organs and functions of the body	209	11.9
	Physical sex differences	226	12.7
	Relation of the father to reproduction	92	5.2
	Marriage	36	2.0

[*] K. W. Hattendorf: "A Study of the Questions of Young Children Concerning Sex: A Phase of an Experimental Approach to Parent Education," *Journal of Social Psychology* (1932), 3:37-65.

Sex experiences and practices. During elementary-school years a large proportion of children have experiences relating to sex, such as observing the sex behavior of animals or people, or being exposed to the advances of older children or adults, undertaking sex play in private, or entering into sex play with their peers. In a study of boys by Ramsey (1943) it was found that 72.6 per cent of the boys who were questioned had had experience with masturbation by the age of twelve. No physical damage was reported in connection with these experiences but boys did report many fears and much worry. In this same study, about a third of the boys reported that they had attempted heterosexual intercourse before adolescence. In their studies of female sex behavior, Kinsey and his associates (1953) found that about 14 per cent of the females in their sample recalled that they had reached orgasm prior to adolescence through masturbation or sexual contacts with other children or with adults. They surmise that, in addition, there might be many others who had had the experience without recognizing its nature. In a study by Landis, Landis, and Bolles (1940) over half of a group of normal single women aged fifteen to thirty years and almost half of a group of normal married women aged twenty-two to thirty-five years reported that their first experience with sex aggressions had occurred prior to puberty, ranging from exploration of their bodies by a boy of their own age to sexual advances by an older boy or adult.

Such findings as the foregoing should not be regarded as typical for all communities or for different sections of the population. There are large variations in sex behavior as in all other matters. The study by Kinsey and his associates (1948) of sexual behavior in males shows, for example, that persons from various socioeconomic groups and from families with differing educational backgrounds vary decidedly in their sex practices, particularly before marriage. Yet, such findings as these, while dealing with only a very limited aspect of sex behavior, impressively show that a large proportion of preadolescent children have experiences with physical aspects of sex which go beyond a passive, academic interest in the subject.

TABLE 13	RANK OF INTEREST FOR 856 QUESTIONS OF CHILDREN TWO TO FIVE, 707 QUESTIONS OF CHILDREN SIX TO NINE, AND 191 QUESTIONS OF CHILDREN TEN TO THIRTEEN YEARS CLASSIFIED IN EIGHT GROUPS *

| | Age in Years | | |
Classification	2 to 5	6 to 9	10 to 13
Origin of babies	1	1	2
Coming of another baby	4	2	1
Intra-uterine growth	7	7	8
Process of birth	5	3	5
Organs and functions	3	4	3
Physical sex differences	2	4	6
Relation of father to reproduction	6	6	4
Marriage	8	8	7

* Ibid.

THE CONCEPT OF THE "LATENCY PERIOD"

In discussions of sexual development, some writers speak of a "latency period," which extends roughly from about the age of five to the beginning of adolescence. According to the theory of latency, the child faces certain hurdles in his early sexual development—the "oral" and "anal" phases, and the need to resolve the Oedipus situation (as noted in Chapters Four and Seven) and another hurdle when sex takes on a new urgency at the time of puberty. The intervening time is referred to as a period of latency because during this period, according to Freudian theory, there is no new decisive stage or phase of sexual development. When viewed in the context of this theory, "latency" has a special meaning. But when viewed in the light of empirical studies of children's interests and actions during this period "latency" cannot be taken literally. In a large number of children, interest in sex during this period is not latent or inactive or held in abey·ance but is distinctly manifest and active (as can be seen from findings by Ramsey, Kinsey, and Hattendorf, cited above).

Many children, according to their own accounts, have impressions or experiences relating to sex and have discussed the topic with other children before they have received much information from their parents or from other responsible sources (Goudy, 1957). This is not surprising since adults differ greatly in their ability or willingness to "face the facts of life." However, even when parents (or teachers) are free to discuss sex with children in their care, a youngster is likely to desire to discuss sex with his peers. In the usual course of things, sex eventually is an aspect of life which people share most intimately with peers rather than with the older generation. Even after a child receives sex instruction from an adult, he is interested in exploring the subject with his peers. There will probably be matters of interest connected with sex which a ten-year-old does not especially care to discuss with Dad, just as Dad has interests which he does not discuss with Grandpa.

Observations based on twenty-five years of work in the area of sex education with twelve-year-old boys (Goudy, 1957) indicate that there are aspects of a boy's sex education and of his search for understanding which cannot be met solely by academic instruction from adults. Many boys from good homes, who are destined to be excellent fathers some day, go through a phase during which they have "bull sessions." While such sessions may not add anything important to the knowledge a boy already has acquired about the facts of reproduction, apparently they help him to explore his role as a young male.

Laughter and humor

Among the many appealing human qualities of an infant are his smiles and his laughter. The first ap-pearance of laughter was noted in one study at twelve weeks when the experimenter bent over the child and made a chirruping sound (Washburn, 1929). Babies also laugh at other playful actions, such as peek-a-boo, sudden reappearances from under the table, tickling, and rhythmical hand clapping. Most effective in producing laughter was the "threatening-head" stimulus: While holding the child's hands, the experimenter shook her head playfully from side to side and then ducked rapidly, until her head was in contact with the center of the child's body, whence it was immediately withdrawn again. Laughter in response to this action appeared at sixteen weeks.

As the months go by, most children laugh eagerly in response to a bit of horseplay. Frequently, too, a baby's laughter is aroused by an anticipated pleasure, as when he is being dressed to go out in his carriage or for a ride in a car. Many babies before the age of one year laugh in sympathy with the banter of others, even though they cannot directly take part in it. Laughter also occurs in connection with the baby's own adventures.

THE YOUNG COMIC

Just when a typical child acquires a "sense of humor" is hard to tell, but it is apparent that some babies have what might be called a sense of the comic well in advance of the time when they are able to express their humor through language. An illustration of the comic touch is given in Chapter Fifteen in the account of an eleven-month-old baby who made several false starts toward a forbidden garbage pail (while the mother was looking on) laughing at what seemed to be a merry game of "Let's Pretend."

LAUGHTER AND PLAY

As the child grows older he laughs mostly during his active social contacts with others. The child is more likely to laugh with friends than with strangers. Among children as among adults laughter is often an expression of good will, but even very early in childhood laughter may express "nervousness" or embarrassment (when, for example, the youngster seems both eager and apprehensive and gives a smothered laugh).

LAUGHTER DURING PRESCHOOL YEARS

At the preschool level laughter often occurs in connection with some form of physical activity (Ding *et al.*, 1932), but it also appears in many other contexts. When the laughter of runabout children is examined in the light of some of the theories that have been proposed to explain laughter of adults several interesting observations have emerged (see Justin, 1932; Ding *et al.*, 1932; Kenderdine, 1931; and Wolfenstein, 1954). Among the situations found to produce laughter at the preschool level are surprise, defeated expectations, incongruity, another's smile, sudden relief from strain, playful give and take, and sudden feelings of superiority or degradation. In a large collection of records of young children's laughter while at play, laughter seldom occurred as a form of derision or an expression of superiority because of another's coming to grief, or of vindictiveness (Ding *et al.*, 1932). As children grow older, however, their laughter or "favorite jokes" often express what seem to be underlying feelings of aggression. Laughter or humor is frequently associated with forbidden things, such as reference to sex or elimination.

Love, Joy, Sensuality, Humor   **251**

The development of humor is interrelated with other aspects of development (Laing, 1939; Omwake, 1939). When a child is able to appreciate relationships in size and space he is able to laugh at incongruities which he did not notice before, such as Junior's small cap on Papa's big head. When he has attained command of language he may find it humorous when a younger child makes mistakes similar to his own mistakes at an earlier age (like singing "Me muvver and fahver were Irish"). As he gains in understanding, he appreciates word play, which is sometimes slightly off-color, such as:

> *Question:* Why did the ram fall over the cliff?
> *Answer:* He didn't see the U-turn.

At the elementary-school level and beyond a great proportion of children's humor, at least as represented by "favorite jokes," deals with topics that are slightly if not entirely taboo. Many of these jokes support Freud's view (1938) that jokes express motives or impulses which have been suppressed and would be condemned if expressed in a more direct way. Some jokes, however, do not so clearly illustrate this view. While jokes have a comic flavor they often deal with themes that are not basically comical. The undertone of seriousness appears when children, through jokes, express envy, or give a ridiculous turn to a common human predicament, or play with desires under the guise of foolishness. In joking about the foibles of others, or about his own, the child may be trying to make light of his own difficulties. In this respect, joking, as described by Wolfenstein, is "a bit of humble heroism, which for the moment that it succeeds provides elation, but only for the moment."

Older children, like adults, frequently use humor in a hostile way by making someone the butt of a joke. But they also use humor in a friendly way to share their feelings with others. A joke may have a hidden bite, based upon something significant to the joker, but it will, of course, fall flat if it does not also touch upon something significant to the one who hears or reads it. When the other person enjoys the joke and laughs he is, in effect, saying: "I feel that way, too." Accordingly, while humor sometimes expresses malice, it also often voices a form of compassion.

In the writer's collection of children's jokes, there is a large number that bear in one way or another on sex. Many of these jokes are sprinkled with uncensored four-letter words. Sometimes, however, the youngster will play with the subject of sex more subtly, as in the U-turn joke mentioned above.

Forbidden material relating directly to elimination and indirectly to sex may come out in a relatively guarded way as in the following:

> A French woman went to an American store to buy a rug.
> *Storekeeper:* Is this all right?
> *Woman:* Oui, oui.
> *Storekeeper:* Oh, yes, but don't do it on my new rug.

Humor that plays with the theme of hostility is also quite prominent in children's "favorite jokes." The humor may lie in making another person seem foolish, as in the following:

> *Jim:* How much is 5Q plus 5Q?
> *Tim:* 10Q.
> *Jim:* You're welcome.

Some jokes have the effect of placing another person in an inferior position:

> Two motorists met on a bridge that was too narrow for both cars to pass. One motorist said, "I never back up for an idiot." The other said, "That's all right, *I* always do."

Humor containing an element of hostility may also be directed by proxy at other children or parents or authority figures. Some of these jokes run in cycles. The writer's collection of children's favorite jokes include many of the so-called "sick-sick-sick" jokes.

> "Mom! Mom! Dad's running across the lawn!"
> "Shut up, kid, and re-load."

> "But Mom, I don't want to go to Europe."
> "Don't talk. Keep swimming."

A sophisticated brand of humor occurs when a person is able to make a quip about himself (such as in the following exchange between two adults):

> *A:* "I admire your modesty."
> *B:* "I'm glad, for I have so much to be modest about."

Humor of this kind has a rueful quality yet it also has a deeper significance, for it means that a person, for the moment, is casting aside his pretenses and is viewing himself objectively. Such humor was expressed by a slightly over-weight child who said with mock seriousness: "What I really need is six banana splits with lots of whipped cream."

HUMOR AS RELATED TO SELF-APPRAISAL

Most children eventually like to think of themselves as having a sense of humor, and a number of them will take great pains to discover what they can do to make people laugh and how to gauge timing and emphasis to bring out the comic in what they have to say. In a study by the writer, in which youngsters wrote little essays on what they liked and disliked about themselves, there were many who said they were pleased about having a sense of humor, but no child admitted or expressed regret about being without a sense of humor. In this respect children resemble older persons. In a study by Allport (1937) college students were asked to estimate their sense of humor. Ninety-four per cent replied that it was as good or better than the average.

Recommended Readings

The author's chapter on "Emotional Development" in the *Manual of Child Psychology*, edited by Leonard Carmichael, explores some historical and theoretical aspects of emotion that are not touched upon in the present volume. *The Meaning of Love*, edited by Ashley Montagu (1953), discusses the nature and role of affection. Martha Wolfenstein's *Children's Humor: A Psychological Analysis* (1954) gives an interpretation of motives underlying humor. Part VII of Wayne Dennis's *Readings in Child Psychology* (1951) contains six articles on various aspects of emotional development.

Fear and Anxiety

CHAPTER TWELVE   Fear exists so generally in contemporary life that our time has been called the "age of anxiety." The present age is probably no more fear-ridden than earlier periods in history; instead, we perhaps recognize the inroads of fear more clearly and acknowledge them more openly than we did in the past. In the folklore of many countries, one mark of a hero was that he was without fear; such a hero probably never existed.

From an early age all children are more or less troubled by fear, and some are so afraid that their freedom of action is seriously impaired. Adults, too, are often afraid, and many of them struggle with apprehensions that are rooted in their childhood fears. No one who is alert to currents in his own life and to circumstances in the world in which he lives can be without fear.

255

While some people will not acknowledge their fears, realistic adults accept the fact that fear has had, and still has, an important place in their lives.

In this chapter we will first review age trends in children's fears and worries as revealed by information obtained from parents and teachers and from children themselves. As we will note more particularly at a later point, the term "fear" is used in everyday speech to denote a variety of apprehensions, ranging from acute fear of obvious dangers (such as a snarling dog) to a more complicated kind of uneasiness (such as worry about reciting in class or fear of being hit by a tornado, even though at the moment the weather is calm).

During infancy, a child's fears arise in response to happenings in his immediate environment. As he grows older, the range of his fears grows wider. As he acquires the ability to dwell opon his past and to anticipate his future, a large number of fears pertain to distant dangers, forebodings of what the future may bring, and apprehensions concerning his own impulses and what he has done or might do.

Origins of fear

In an earlier day, there were theories that many of our fears were instinctive, such as fear of animals, of the occult, of death, of large bodies of water. Later a theory was advanced that there are only two original "natural" fear stimuli, namely, loud noises and sudden displacement or loss of support (Watson, 1924a, 1924b). This account was quite simple and quite inadequate. The circumstances that give rise to so-called "unlearned" fears in the infant include not only noises and loss of support, but any intense, sudden, unexpected, or novel stimulus, or any condition which demands some kind of adaptation for which the organism is unprepared. Moreover, whether or not a certain stimulus will evoke fear depends not only on the nature of the stimulus but also on the condition of the individual who is responding and the total setting in which the stimulus occurs. A jolt or loud noise, for example, may arouse fear when a child is with an unfamiliar person but not when a familiar person is near.[1]

THE ROLE OF MATURATION

The young infant is unaffected by many happenings that will frighten him at a later time when his capacities for perception and discrimination have matured. An example of this was given in the discussion of fear of

---

[1] English (1929) and Valentine (1930, 1946) give illustrations of the difficulty of predicting when a child will be afraid.

strangers in Chapter Nine. Gesell's (1929) account of the response of infants at different ages to confinement in a small pen offers a further illustration. At ten weeks, the child may be completely complaisant in this situation; at twenty weeks, he may exhibit mild apprehension, and at thirty weeks, his response to the same situation "may be so vigorously expressed by crying that we describe the reaction as fear or fright." As the child matures, new things affect him by virtue of his keener perceptions, and fear is likely to arise when the individual knows enough to recognize the potential danger in a situation but has not "advanced to the point of a complete comprehension and control of the changing situation" (Jones and Jones, 1928).

Changes with age in fear responses appeared impressively in a study in which a large, active, harmless snake was set free in an enclosure with persons of various ages. Children up to the age of two years showed no fear of the snake; children aged three and four tended to be cautious and hesitated to approach or touch the snake; definite signs of fear were displayed more often after the age of four and were more pronounced in adults than in children (Jones and Jones, 1928).

The important role played by maturation in children's fear is brought out by findings that a child who is precocious or advanced in his development may be afraid of events that do not disturb other children until they are older (Holmes, 1935). A bright two-year-old, for example, may show fear of a strange room or of a snake that does not disturb the child of average mental ability until later.

Changing susceptibility to fear is interwoven with many other aspects of the child's development. With the development of the child's imaginative abilities, his fears become increasingly concerned with imaginary dangers. With the development of competitiveness and awareness of status come fears of ridicule or loss of prestige. The wider the scope and range of a child's understanding, the more he is able to recognize possibilities of disaster, and the more versatile he becomes in fitting his apprehension into varied images and lines of thought. This does not mean, necessarily, that the child becomes more and more afraid, for with a gain in strength and understanding the child is better able to handle some of the situations that once made him afraid.

THE ROLE OF LEARNING

Fears are also influenced by learning. By virtue of a painful experience, or of having been startled or overwhelmed, a child may "learn" to fear something that did not disturb him earlier.

This learning may be quite direct, specific, and restricted: A child is bowled over by a dog and later fears that dog. Again, the effects may be more general: The child may fear not only the dog that hurt him but all dogs and, perhaps, he may be on guard, as never before, whenever he sees any four-footed animal. Similarly, he may not only be afraid when he sees a dog but he may also be apprehensive when he passes the yard where he knows a dog is kept, even though no dog is in sight.

The process by which fear is acquired may involve indirect or intermediate steps. For example, a child who had been knocked down but not seriously injured by an automobile was still quite wrought up when he went to bed, and then he had a bad dream. Thereafter he was afraid of going into his bedroom when it was dark. Through the dream, the accident and its emotional effects had been placed, so to speak, in the setting of darkness. Once a child is frightened, his fear may thus "spread" to many other things and conditions.

The essential element when such a "spread" takes place is the fact that something left him in a state of apprehension or fear. The conditioning process does not in itself create a new fear but provides an object or circumstance (other than the one that frightened him in the first instance) with which his fright becomes associated.

CHANGES WITH AGE IN THE EXPRESSION OF FEAR

As children grow older, there is a decrease in the number of occasions per day or week when they exhibit overt signs of fear, such as crying, trembling, or clinging to an adult. However, this does not mean that there is a corresponding decline in the role of fear in the child's everyday life. The decline in open expression occurs, in part, because of the child's tendency to display less emotion as he grows older. It is partly associated also with changes in the character of the dangers which the child fears: Fears formulated in terms of imaginary dangers or apprehension concerning misfortunes that might occur, seldom express themselves in sudden starts, cries, or fleeing. Imaginary fears leave nothing to flee from, for the child who does both the fearing and the imagining cannot physically run away from himself.

Disguises of fear. Expression of fear may assume innumerable forms and occur in countless disguises, ranging from an obvious show of fear to a show of complete confidence, and from extremely good and compliant conduct to stubbornness, resistance, unwillingness to "see the point," and outright rebellion and defiance that look more like anger than like fear.

By virtue of the premium that is placed on not being afraid, or not revealing that he is afraid, the child may be driven to the point that one of his fears is the fear of showing fear.

The following paragraphs illustrate how children conceal their fears.

A girl of three-and-a-half years asked her mother to fetch a doll that had been left in a room separated by a hallway from the rest of the house, and she kept insisting violently after the mother had suggested that she get it herself. The mother then suspected what the matter was and said, "I'll hold the door while you get it." At this the girl ran happily to the room and got the doll. The mother remembered that the child had been frightened previously by the slamming of a door in this hallway, and now, instead of admitting that she was afraid, she was trying to commandeer her mother. Some other adult might have thought the girl was an unreasonable child, not a frightened child.

A girl of seven, two nights in succession, after having been put to bed, insisted that she had to go downstairs because she had forgotten to bring a blanket for her doll and asked her mother to go with her since she did not like to go alone. On the second night her mother, thinking that the girl was merely trying to delay her bedtime, refused to accompany her, so finally she had to go by herself. She hurriedly went all the way to the basement where she got the blanket; then she went on another quick errand on the first floor, and then returned to bed. A few minutes later she revealed that her reason for going downstairs was to make sure that the front door was locked. On some previous nights she had anxiously asked whether the front door was locked. She was using the "forgotten" doll blanket as a device for making sure that the door was locked.

A boy of ten had earned two passes to a circus, but after attending the afternoon performance he said he did not care to go again, and so he gave his remaining pass to his brother. It was not until some time later that he happened to reveal that on his way out of the circus grounds he had been threatened and chased by two older boys who belonged to the circus, and that he did not go to the show again because he was afraid.

A child may be so embarrassed by the fact that he is or has been afraid that he will deny his fears. An interesting observation regarding children's freedom to acknowledge fear appeared in a study by Kraus (1956) in which children were studied as they moved from kindergarten into the elementary-school grades. When entering kindergarten, many children openly displayed fear while others (many of whom probably also were apprehensive) did not. When questioned in the *second* grade about how they felt when they first entered school few children said they had been distressed. However, when questioned in the *fifth* grade many of these same children (including youngsters who had openly shown fear and others who had not) admitted they had been "scared." Apparently, fifth graders were able to look back tolerantly and acknowledge weaknesses which they had had as "little kids," but which they would not admit at the second grade.

The disguise a child uses for his fears becomes especially troublesome if, instead of getting him out of trouble, it gets him into more trouble. A child may be so frightened at the thought of being laughed at in class that he will act dumb rather than recite and risk making a mistake. As a result, he may get a scolding from a teacher who would be willing to help him if she suspected he was afraid. To understand the child who is afraid, we must be alert to such disguises, although no adult can expect to be all-knowing.

Parents and teachers may assume that a child is quite free from fear when actually he is afraid of many things. Several instances of this were observed in a study by the writer and his associates. Needless to say, the concealment of fear makes it more difficult for adults to help a child. But when adults openly or subtly encourage children to hide their fears it is not simply because the adults are deliberately being stupid. The reason may be that adults are disturbed by signs of fear in a child. A frightened child is in many ways a threatening child, threatening because he presents a problem which the adult may be unable to solve. Moreover, the fact that a child is afraid may be a sign to the parent that he has failed (as though any parent could bring up a child completely free from fear!). When an adult tries to dismiss the problem by telling the child there is nothing to be afraid of he is, in effect, encouraging the child not to reveal his fears.

Open and hidden aspects of fear. When we try to understand a child's fear we must recognize that there is usually more than appears on the surface. There may be both a manifest and a hidden content. Two children say they are afraid of dogs, but to one the "dogs" may be two real dogs on his street that are an actual menace, while to another child "dogs" is almost a manner of speech, for he is uneasy in the presence of any dog, or at the thought of meeting a dog, even when repeated experiences tell him that this or that dog is perfectly harmless. When he says he is afraid of dogs, he tells the truth and yet not the whole truth, for it is what the dog symbolizes rather than the external danger which the dog actually represents that bothers him. The fear named by the child may represent both an external threat and an internal disturbance—this is especially noticeable when children mention fears that have little or no basis in reality, such as when a child says he is afraid of ghosts, or when a child with an excellent record at school says he is afraid he will fail.

Age trends in "fears"

Figure 3, which is based on information obtained from parents, shows trends in children's openly expressed fears between birth and six years of age. There is a decline with age in fears in response to certain tangible and immediate situations, such as specific objects, noises, falling and danger of falling, strange objects and persons; and an increase with age in fear of such things as imaginary creatures, the dark, and being alone or abandoned. Figure 3 shows the results obtained when a tally of one only was given in the case of each child who exhibited *one* or *several* fears of a given category. The relative frequency of various fear categories would be different if each additional item in a given category received a new tally, such as three tallies under "Animals" if a child mentions lions, tigers, and wolves (Pratt, 1945).

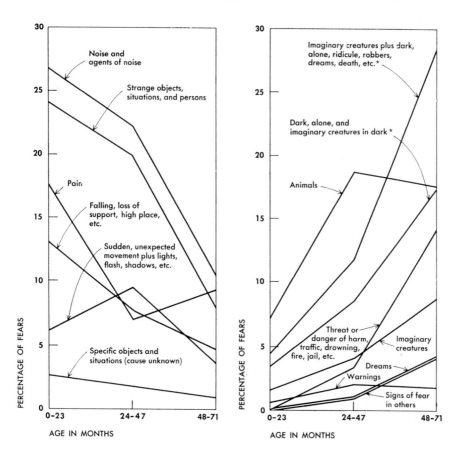

FIGURE 3 *Relative frequency of fears in response to various situations reported by children or observed in children by parents or teachers. The data include 146 records of observation of children for periods of 21 days (31, 91, and 24 at the respective bi-yearly levels), combined with occasional records of 117 additional children (27, 67, and 23 at the respective levels). Adapted from* Children's Fears *by A. T. Jersild and F. B. Holmes,* Child Development Monographs, *1935, No. 20, by permission of the publishers. Starred items represent the cumulative tally of two or more categories that also are depicted separately.*

Table 14 shows findings obtained in a study by Holmes (1935) in which the following semi-experimental situations were used to investigate children's fears:

1. *Being left alone.* A concealed observer watches the child as he is left alone in the experimental room when the experimenter leaves with the excuse that she has to get her handkerchief in another part of the building.

2. *Falling boards.* The child is asked to walk across two inclined boards so arranged that, as the child steps from one to the other, one board suddenly tilts and gives way a distance of two inches.

3. *A dark room.* The child is asked to retrieve a ball seemingly inadvertently thrown by the experimenter into a long, narrow, dark passageway.

4. *A strange person.* Standing in the child's path as he seeks to reach a box of toys is a woman rakishly dressed in a long gray coat, large black hat, and black veil that obscures the features of her face.

5. *High boards.* The child is asked to walk across a plank raised by degrees to elevations of from about two to six feet from the floor.

6. *A loud sound.* While the child is playing a sound is suddenly produced by sharply striking an iron pipe with a hammer.

7. *A snake.* The child is asked to pick a toy out of box which contains a live snake, two feet long.

8. *A large dog.* The child is asked to go and pat a dog that is brought in on a leash.

		FEARS SHOWN BY CHILDREN AT YEARLY AGE LEVELS
		FROM 24 TO 71 MONTHS
TABLE 14		IN VARIOUS EXPERIMENTAL SITUATIONS *

	Percentage of Children Showing Fear			
Situation	*24-35 months*	*36-47 months*	*48-59 months*	*60-71 months*
1. Being left alone	12.1	15.6	7.0	0
2. Falling boards	24.2	8.9	0	0
3. Dark room	46.9	51.1	35.7	0
4. Strange person	31.3	22.2	7.1	0
5. High boards	35.5	35.6	7.1	0
6. Loud sound	22.6	20.0	14.3	0
7. Snake	34.8	55.6	42.9	30.8
8. Large dog	61.9	42.9	42.9	. . .
Total	32.0	30.2	18.1	4.5

* From F. B. Holmes, "An Experimental Study of the Fears of Young Children," in A. T. Jersild, and F. B. Holmes, *Children's Fears*, Child Development Monographs (New York: Teachers College, Columbia University, 1935), No. 20, Pt. III, pp. 167-296. Reproduced by permission.

The experimental situations were not designed to frighten the child (except that he might be startled by the noise and the inclined board), but rather to confront the child with a situation into which he could choose to enter and participate or from which he was free to withdraw and retreat. Observers recorded the children's behavior, and the presence or absence of "fear" was determined according to carefully formulated criteria. The number of children at each yearly age level ranged from twelve to forty-five, with the smallest numbers at sixty to seventy-one months.

The results shown in Table 14 indicate a trend toward a decrease with age in fear of the situations employed in the study. At the five-year level only the snake aroused signs of fear. Even the dark room did not produce overt symptoms of fear to five-year-olds (but undoubtedly the presence of an adult accounted for this; for, according to their own reports, many children of this age are afraid of dark places, especially when they are alone). At earlier levels the number of children who were afraid of the dark room in the experiment was considerably larger than the number of children who were reported by their parents as being afraid of the dark.

Age trends in fears of older children. Changes with age in the fears reported by children have been found also as children move through middle childhood and into the teens. Angelino and his associates (1956) asked groups of youngsters from nine to eighteen years old to "list the fears and worries you think persons of your own age-group have."

There was, on the whole, a *decline* in fears relating to personal safety (including attacks from others, accidents, storms). There was also, in general, a decline in fear of animals. On the other hand, fears pertaining to school (including worries about grades, fears of teachers, stage fright) showed, in general, an *increase* from age nine to about age twelve and a slight but uneven decline thereafter. There was also, on the whole, an increase of fears pertaining to social relationships and in fears classified as "economic and political" (including worries about money, allowances, getting jobs, the possibility of war, menacing conditions in the world).

FEARS ASSOCIATED WITH GUILT,
REMORSE, AND UNDERLYING INSECURITY

Many children have fears of punishment or feelings of guilt or remorse about past misdeeds. In a study of fifth- and sixth-grade children in which a list of "worries" was presented, it was found that a large proportion of children checked items having to do with punishment, being scolded, "making parents sad," telling lies, and doing wrong.

A tendency to be apprehensive, even though no specific fear can be named or identified, often exists in shy children and withdrawn children. Pritchard and Ojemann (1941) found that children who were rated "insecure" by their teachers exhibited a greater tendency to be apprehensive than did children rated as emotionally "secure."

"Fears" as compared with worst happenings. A large proportion of the fears children report are expressed in terms that are different from prosaic

day-to-day hurts and threats. This is illustrated in Table 15 by a comparison between accounts given by school-age children of their fears and of the "worst thing that ever happened" to them. Less than 2 per cent of the "worst happenings" involved dangerous experiences with animals, but almost 14 per cent of the "fears" pertained to animals (mainly remote animals such as wolves, lions, and gorillas).

TABLE 15	COMPARISON OF CHILDREN'S DESCRIPTIONS OF THEIR FEARS AND OF THE "WORST THING THAT EVER HAPPENED TO THEM" *

(Abridged results, based upon interviews with 398 children aged 5 to 12 years)

	Percentage Naming Event	
Event Described	Actual "Worst Happenings"	Fears
Bodily injury, falling, illness, traffic accident, operations, hurts and pains, etc.	72.7	12.8
Attack or danger of attack by animals	1.8	13.7
Contacts with, or activities of, criminals, kidnappers, burglars, bad characters, etc.	1.3	8.0
Being alone, in dark, in strange place, being lost, and dangers associated with being alone, darkness, etc.	2.3	14.6
Death, loss, removal of relatives, being abandoned by relatives	5.0	1.4
Contacts with, or activities of, or dangers from supernatural agents, ghosts, witches, corpses, mysterious agents or events	0.0	19.2
Scolding, embarrassment, being teased, ridiculed, etc.	5.5	3.4
Remaining categories	12.4	26.9

* From A. T. Jersild, F. V. Markey, and C. L. Jersild, *Children's Fears, Dreams, Wishes, Daydreams, Likes, Dislikes, Pleasant and Unpleasant Memories*, Child Development Monographs (New York: Teachers College, Columbia University, 1933), No. 12, 172 pp. Reproduced by permission.

The fears of children (and of adults) usually go far beyond the statistical probabilities of disaster. In a study by the writer and associates (1941) it was noted that in a school system in which the percentage of failure or nonpromotion was less than two, the percentage of children who said they "worried" about the possibility of not being promoted was about fifty. We will have more to say about "fears" of this sort in the discussion of anxiety later in this chapter.

Fears that persist

Although many fears wane and seem to disappear, a large proportion of childhood fears persist in one form or another into adult years.

In a study of childhood fears as recalled by adults (Jersild and Holmes, 1935), it was found that of 804 fears reported, over 40 per cent still persisted into adult years. This percentage cannot, of course, be accepted without reservation, since an adult's recall of childhood fears probably will be influenced by his present apprehensions and he would be likely to forget many passing fears that had waned. Yet, according to the testimony of adults, there is a large carry-over of childhood fear into later years. Of the fears described as "still persisting," about 27 per cent were also described as being the "most intense" fears recalled from childhood, and 28 per cent were described as being the "earliest recalled" fears.

Among the fears that show the largest carry-over into later years are fears of animals; of bodily harm through such dangers as fire, illness, drowning; and of dangers associated with the supernatural, with the dark, and with being alone. Many of the continuing fears probably reflect anxieties such as are discussed later in this chapter.

Some special conditions of fear

Fear of strange things, conditions, and circumstances. As we have seen, many of the fears of children are reactions to something strange, new, and unfamiliar. Throughout childhood and throughout life the growing person is confronted by new people, unfamiliar surroundings, new ideas, new features in his own development (as at adolescence), new discoveries concerning himself and his limitations. In the normal process of growth, the child frequently stands at the threshold of the unknown; this may give him pause or may induce fear, but when all goes well, the strange recedes into the realm of the familiar. But sometimes a child (or an adult) stands at the threshold of something new and is unable to cross it.

The new is particularly frightening if it calls not simply for a bit of inspection and study but threatens to confront a person with an unwelcome discovery concerning himself (such as the discovery that some of his judgments are prejudices). The concepts of hostility and anxiety are among the unfamiliar ideas that are frightening to some older children and adults, especially when they begin to suspect that these concepts also apply to them.

Fear of the dark. This fear is frequently reported by children and by adults. There is something dangerous about the dark, both in what it represents in reality and in what it symbolizes. In the dark we usually are less powerful than when we can see; we might stumble or lose our way. Darkness also signifies that we are out of sight, and that others are out of sight, so it means psychologically that we are cut off from others. Darkness is an added menace when a child is already frightened, for his imagination can supply what he cannot see, and he can people the darkness with dangers that reside within himself.

Fear of solitude, abandonment, loneliness, death. Many children (perhaps all) have had momentary experiences of being abandoned: The mother may be in another room, out of sight and out of earshot; on a walk the parent may have moved out of view; in a crowd the child may have found himself completely surrounded by strangers. Such an experience, even if brief and quite unintended, may be very frightening, but the child is likely soon to recover from his fright when his parents make their appearance.

Fear of abandonment does not arise only from the physical fact of being abandoned. A child can be abandoned, psychologically, if threats and punishments are held over him in a manner that says he cannot count on his elders to protect him. In the studies by the writer and his associates referred to in this chapter, many children reported cruel instances of having been threatened in this way.

When the writer was a child one form of abandonment some children had to face (and probably still do today) was the threat of death and hell fire connected with religious instruction. When the threat of hell is held over a child as a punishment for his sins, it is as though he were being consigned to outer darkness. The picture of a hell from which there is no escape, a hell located out of reach of his parents (who probably are going to heaven anyway, and between the two there is a vast gulf) presents about as black a prospect of abandonment as any child can imagine. Such a frightful place is not wholly imaginary from the child's point of view if his elders have told him that there is such a place.

For children who have thus been frightened, death may become a symbol of their unworthiness and of the means by which the threat of abandonment is achieved. According to this view, death is the ultimate in loneliness and isolation. With such teaching and with a child so taught that he extracts the gloomiest elements from such teaching, religious symbols come to stand for despair rather than hope, a conviction of being damned rather than of being saved. The child can only extract a gloomy view of himself from what he is taught, and the rejection implicit in it.

This is the way a six-year-old told about his fear of being abandoned:

> His mother had told him that because he had been bad (he had quarreled with his sister) a time would come when he would not be able to move the hand that struck his sister. The mother then described what happened to a neighbor's child. This child died, the mother said, and he was placed in a coffin. But his hand remained outside the coffin, and no one could put it inside. The lid of the coffin could not be closed until a priest had struck the hand and then it slipped into the coffin. Meanwhile, his mother said, everyone talked about this child, and laughed and laughed, *and this may also happen to you."*

If a child feels abandoned he has a tendency, through his imagination, to fill the empty space. Unfriendly characters move in and appear in his fears. When a child is in the dark, isolated, separated, and alone (in a psychological sense), the characters who invade his fears often are evil ones: threatening ghosts, dead people, walking corpses, "bad guys," kidnappers, and so on. These companions are, to him, pregnant with potential harm. The pathetic thing about a child who is afraid in his solitude, alone with his troubled emotions, is that he will people his world with these cadavers and spectral creatures as though it were better to have a corpse for company than to have no companionship at all.

Factors contributing to susceptibility to fear

Weakness and physical disability. Actual weakness in the face of the demands of every day life is an obvious condition underlying fear. Anything that weakens a child, such as illness or physical disability, makes him more defenseless.

When children are ill, or have an accident, or suffer from a physical disability there often is a subtle interweaving of guilt and fear. It has been observed, for example, that children who are hospitalized after an accident or in order to undergo an operation not only are likely to be apprehensive about what might happen to them but also, very frequently, feel that it is their fault that they are sick (Gips, 1956). Likewise, physically disabled children see themselves as having more fears and feelings of guilt than able-bodied children (Cruickshank, 1951).

It is not difficult to understand why such an intermingling of guilt and fear should occur. After a child has repeatedly been warned to be careful, it is not surprising that he should feel it is his own fault if he breaks a limb (he was not careful enough). Similarly, if he must have a tonsillectomy or appendectomy, it requires only a little stretch of the imagination to see that he might have avoided the need for an operation if he had lived right.

Even more drastic afflictions, such as polio or cerebral palsy, are likely to arouse feelings of fear tinged with guilt in parents or in children, or both (Roe, 1952). As noted in an earlier chapter, mothers during pregnancy sometimes fear that their child will be deformed, as though they were to be punished for their misdeeds. When adults view physical impairments as a punishment, something for which they are to blame, it is not surprising that children suffering from a physical disability sooner or later also adopt the attitude that someone is at fault—and that *someone* may be one of the others or it may be themselves.

Disparagement. Anything that lowers the child's confidence in himself, or involves him in situations where he is insecure, or threatens him with failure, conflict, remorse, self-disparagement, temptations, or other disturbances in his own view of himself or in his demands and expectations upon himself will increase his susceptibility to fear.

The disparagement that leads a child to distrust himself may be fed in many ways. He may be given impossible standards to attain. Reminders of his unworthiness are constantly being given to a child if almost everything he does is wrong. He meets a steady stream of disparagement at school if he happens to be one of the millions who is daily reminded that he falls short.

Vicarious dangers. At the present time children are being exposed more than ever before to vicarious fear stimulation in the form of sensational newspaper stories, the speedy communication of catastrophe, exciting movies and radio and television programs. Although children's fears may be activated by these factors, the fears of children today, as reported by themselves, do not differ substantially from the fears of children of a generation ago, as reported by adults in their recollections. More important than any specific form of excitement is the undertow of factors leading to insecurity, and the threats that prevail from one generation to the next.

Influence of example. Adults may have a distinct influence on a child's fears through the example set by their own fears. By obvious or subtle manifestations of their fears, adults may not only suggest to the child the presence of danger but also weaken the child's conviction of security in their protection. In a study by Hagman (1932), a correlation of .67 was found between the gross number of children's fears and the gross number of mothers' fears, as reported by the mothers. A study by John (1941) of children's reactions to wartime events, such as an air raid, likewise emphasizes the influence of adult example.

As long as fear prevails in the society in which they live, there probably is no way to spare children from the example of fear set by others. In some situations it is possible, however, to bring fear out into the open, to acknowledge it and share it. If an adult and child, during a storm, are frightened by the lightning, thunder, and the roaring wind, even so simple a statement as "Gee, that scared us both, I guess" may help to relieve the tension. According to statements made to the author by teachers who supervised air raid drills during tense times in World War II, many children were noticeably less disturbed if a teacher was able openly to acknowledge that she and everyone else was startled by the shriek of the sirens. In many situations it appears that the courage to admit fear helps to strip away some of the sinister qualities of a secret terror.

Anxiety

Anxiety is interlinked with the development of a growing child's ideas and attitudes pertaining to himself. As the child grows older much of his anxiety, whatever may have been its roots, is tied to the choices and conflicts that arise in the management of his life. He faces a predicament when he has an urge to venture into the unknown, but he also has a need to cling to the familiar; when he seeks independence and yet finds comfort in being dependent; when he has an impulse to resist but also to comply. There is a conflict within himself when he feels anger toward his parents when they thwart him but also feels affection for them; or when he is lured by temptation, yet is restrained by his conscience. As he grows older, anxiety is likely to occur when impulses from within or reminders from without threaten to undermine a cherished view of himself.

There are many theories of anxiety, as we will note below, but in an older child or an adult one prominent fact stands out—anxiety is often linked to the contending *possibilities* that are open, or seem open, to a human being. When Hamlet said, "To be or not to be," he was at odds with himself, torn between two possibilities, and his words were those of an anxious man.

According to one definition, anxiety is a painful uneasiness of mind, a kind of apprehension or foreboding concerning an impending or anticipated ill. There are many other definitions of anxiety as distinguished from fear and writers are not fully agreed on what the definition should be. There is fairly common agreement in regarding anxiety as a response to a threat to the self or to the "ego." According to one concept "anything which endangers self-realization produces anxiety" (Goldstein, 1952). According to another definition, anxiety arises when an essential value, or what a person feels to be an essential value, is threatened.

Objective and subjective aspects
of fear and anxiety

The main distinction that has been made between fear and anxiety (a distinction we will adhere to in this discussion) is that fear is a response to an *objective* danger while anxiety is wholly or in large part a response to a *subjective* danger.

Fears and phobias. When a person walking on a narrow plank high above ground hears a cracking sound and sees the plank give way under his weight he faces tangible danger. The apprehension he feels is fear. Something beyond an objective danger is involved, however, if a person dreads the thought of being in a high place—such as the fifth floor of an apartment house—even though intellectually he *knows* that the building will not collapse. The apprehension he feels is quite out of proportion to the danger. There is something in him, as distinguished from the physical menace which confronts him, that produces his distress. He has what is known as a phobia, which is one form of anxiety.

Many of the "fears" described in the preceding pages of this chapter have the characteristics of a phobia. When a child says he is afraid of ghosts, or is beset with a fear of kidnappers, the ghosts and the kidnappers are not the sole source of his distress—they are, instead, symbols of something that is sinister, symbols through which he expresses a condition of uneasiness or foreboding that resides within him.

FURTHER DISTINCTIONS BETWEEN FEAR AND ANXIETY

There are several characteristics of "fear" that suggest the existence of anxiety. We may suspect a state of anxiety if a child's apprehensions are decidedly out of proportion to the danger, as when, for example, he feels as terrified by a friendly little puppy as by a snarling dog. We may suspect that anxiety prevails if "fear" seems completely "irrational" according to any reasonable standard: if, for example, a child is afraid of crocodiles even though there is no possibility that there are any about, or worries about the possibility that there might be fire in the cellar even though he has made a dozen inspections in trying to assure himself that there is no fire. We may suspect that there is anxiety if a "fear" persists contrary to repeated assurance that it is groundless—as, for example, when a child who has always been successful in giving reports in class continues to suffer from stage fright, or when one who has always earned high marks faces each new examination as though he were on the brink of disaster.

Inner conflicts as a source of anxiety.   One condition that leads to anxiety is a state of inner conflict, especially a conflict in which there are hidden or unrecognized elements. A conflict denotes a condition of dividedness and disharmony within the self. Conflict may arise, for example, when a child is angry at his parents and has an impulse to hurt them, but this impulse goes counter to his love for them. Similarly, when a child is tempted to take something that is forbidden, the temptation conflicts with his loyalty and desire to obey. Again, disharmony involving a kind of dividedness within the self occurs when a child feels guilty: he is his own accuser—it is as though a part of him (the conscience he has acquired) is condemning another part of him. There is also a state of dividedness within the self when a child as he *is* is out of kilter with what he feels he *should be.* Such a dislocation is likely to be especially troublesome if the child has adopted standards that are beyond his reach. For example, if a youngster at the age of three believes that he should always be able to control his bladder but then, due to his immaturity, fails to do so—ideally he should be dry, but actually he is wet. Or if a youngster has a high ideal of obedience but simply can't live up to it, or of generosity beyond what he can sustain, or of being "reasonable" but unavoidably does things that are unreasonable.

Conflicts such as these provide the soil from which anxiety may grow, but they do not necessarily produce a state of anxiety.

In day-to-day life children as well as adults face many conflicts which they manage to handle without serious distress. There is conflict when a child would like to take cookies from the cookie jar, but has been told not to; or when he is supposed to do his homework but would rather go out and play. When there is a conflict between alternatives which a person is fully aware of, and he then knowingly and deliberately makes a choice, he may not feel completely at ease about the choice he makes, but he is not necessarily in a state of anxiety: if he decides to take the cookies, he runs the risk of being found out and punished, and he may fear punishment—but this fear may vanish when he has been discovered and forgiven or when the danger of being discovered is past.

Unrecognized conflicts as related to anxiety.   However, a different situation prevails if the issue involves deeper conflicts which the child is unable or unwilling to face openly. More may be involved in the child's conflict about the cookies than a clash between his desire to eat and his desire to obey his mother. The inner battle between wanting the cookies and wanting to obey his mother may be part of a larger and more disturbing battle if, for example, the youngster does not just desire the cookies, but, without facing the fact, also feels a grievance against his mother, and stealing cookies is one way to take revenge; or if taking the cookies means that his brother, a bitter rival, will be deprived of his share. The conflict becomes far more than just a skirmish in the pantry if the temptation to take the cookies threatens to do violence to deep-seated attitudes the child has formed regarding himself. If he has acquired a stern conscience, with a need to see himself as an upright character, the taking of the forbidden cookies may, to him, mean the difference between strength and weakness; for him, the little act of thievery is—in a sense—shaking the foundations of the self. In such an event, the temptation to take the cookies is not just an isolated threat. Even if his mother forgives him, he may not be able to forgive himself. He is vulnerable. He may be frightened by an impulse which, in itself, does not mean much but which, as a sign of weakness, means a great deal. In the meantime, the more he takes his high standards for granted, or in other words, the less conscious he is of seeking to preserve an image of righteousness which he does not have the strength to sustain, the more likely he is to be anxious.

Fortunately, most children are made of stuff so sturdy that they are not shattered by filching a cookie or two. Yet there probably are few children who have not filched things and felt disturbed about it. Probably every child, according to his own view, has either been a thief, at least on a small scale, or has been tempted to become one. It probably is no coincidence that many children, in describing their "fears," mention thieves, robbers, kidnappers, and other "bad guys" who take what does not belong to them. When a child says he is afraid of thieves he is perhaps indirectly, without knowing it, saying that he is afraid of himself.

If we examine some other fears and worries reported by children we see that many of these might readily represent a form of anxiety connected with conflicts pertaining to themselves. Take, for example, the fear of examinations or the worry about not being promoted which many children express: Many complicated conflicts are at work in such worries. A child who has always managed to pass his tests has little objective reason to be apprehensive; yet there may be a subjective basis for it. If he has been admonished to study hard, and accepts the idea that he should but then often does not study hard, it means that he has been remiss according to his own standards. He perhaps feels a bit guilty about his lack of study and has an unrecognized feeling that he deserves punishment. According to this train of thought, the child who has groundless worries about not passing is punishing himself. But in explaining his worry he ascribes it to the objective test situation rather than the test he is undergoing within himself.

The youngster who worries about grades, even though he has always done well at school, may be vulnerable (and anxious) in other ways. For example, he may earn good marks not because he is interested in learning but because he has chosen academic work as the arena in which to compete with others. He may see himself as the ideal scholar, and to succeed in scholarly competition is important for his self-esteem. When facing an examination he has much at stake: the chance that he might get a 90 (instead of a 95) is more "dangerous" to his self-esteem than a mark of 75 might be to another student. Accordingly, when he "worries" about a test, the worry is completely groundless in the eyes of others, but the worry, as a form of anxiety, is well grounded from the point of view of his position. The more he stakes his worth on his need to be the top dog, without recognizing that this is the image he desperately needs to protect, the more vulnerable he will be.

Differing "fears" linked to similar anxieties. Many of the specific "fears" children report are, in a sense, an outcropping, an objective way of expressing an underlying anxiety. In keeping with this, fears which seem quite different may have much more in common than appears on the surface. For example, an adolescent boy of high socioeconomic status says he is afraid of getting a low mark and a boy of low socioeconomic status says he is afraid he can't raise money to pay the next installment on his automobile. The fears are different but they may spring from the same basic source. One boy stakes his self-esteem on grades; the other on the rather insecure foundation of being known as a hot-rodder. From a practical point of view there is, of course, a great difference between a scholar and a hot-rodder. But from a psychological point of view each is anxious about himself; each is involved in basically the same struggle—to preserve a cherished image of himself.

PERCEPTIONS, FEELINGS,
AND IMPULSES ASSOCIATED WITH ANXIETY

When we try to understand the meaning or to detect the signs of anxiety it is helpful to take account of the three elements which we mentioned earlier in our discussion of emotion, namely, *perception* of the exciting event, *feeling*, and *impulse*.

Perception of the anxiety-producing event. In a relatively straightforward emotional experience, a person can perceive, either at the time or as an after-thought what it was that stirred him: it was a loud noise that frightened him; it was someone's elbow in his ribs that angered him, and so forth. When anxiety is aroused, the perception of what provoked it frequently is not clear. For example, when an anxious child is violently disturbed by a minor criticism, he perceives the criticism as the "cause" of his distress; but he may not perceive that the criticism hit him so hard because it touched a sore spot in him—a long-standing grievance, perhaps, or a need to be admired by everyone.

"Feelings of anxiety." In a relatively elemental emotional state, a child feels pleased when someone gives him a gift, feels angry when thwarted, and frightened when attacked by a bully. In a condition of anxiety, however, the feelings often are not so clear. An anxious person sometimes feels distress that has the quality of fear—ranging from terror to a mild and vague form of apprehension. But other feelings also occur. The "feeling tone" of anxiety may be anger, rather than fear. If a little criticism arouses a torrent of anger, the anger is a very real experience, but a person might better ask, "Why did that make me so anxious?" rather than "Why did that make me so angry?"

Anxiety comes through in other feelings: a feeling of depression, or a feeling of grief (which may be a feeling of being aggrieved), or a feeling of being irritable, edgy, out of sorts. It may be experienced in a kind of numbness or emptiness of feeling, such as occurs when a person is deeply moved and yet says, "I don't know what it is I feel."

Impulse. In an uncomplicated emotional response to an objective happening, the impulse usually is quite direct and clear. In joy there is an impulse to savor and prolong the joyful event, in anger an impulse to attack, in fear an impulse to flee. When anxiety prevails, however, a wide variety of impulses comes into play. These impulses, and the actions that flow from them, fall under two headings: First, there are the actions a person takes in expressing anxiety that already has been aroused; secondly, there are actions to ward off, to evade or blunt the edge of a happening that might produce anxiety.

Actions which flow from impulses connected with anxiety cover a vast range and include many paradoxes and inconsistencies. A very competitive child who has a great need to bolster his self-esteem by vying with others may plunge into the fray, vigorously contending with all comers; on the other hand, his need to be superior may be so strong that he cannot tolerate the idea of losing, so instead of being active he may be immobilized, standing on the sidelines. Again, if he is anxious about his sexual impulses he may "act out" his desires or, going to the opposite extreme, build up a rigid code of conduct to protect himself from a painful struggle between temptation and his conscience, or he may vacillate between these two kinds of conduct. If he is anxious because of a conflict between a desire to conform and a desire to rebel, he may do both, or go to one extreme or the other.

The measures taken to ward off the arousal of anxiety likewise take many forms. A person may seek protection from allowing thoughts to arise that would be disturbing to him by building up an elaborate rationale. He may convince himself that he does not care; or he may endeavor to *externalize* his conflict by attributing all his troubles to others rather than to difficulties that reside within him. One means of avoiding reminders of conflict (which is probably more common at the adult level but which can also be seen at times in children) is to try to deal with an emotional issue as though it were entirely an intellectual one. For example, a person who has a personal problem relating to sex might seek to deal with it in a completely impersonal way, showing concern, say, with the facts of reproduction, or scientific theories about the role of sex in human behavior, or anthropological information about sex conduct in other cultures, meanwhile carefully trying to side-step his own personal concerns.

One of the ironies of our culture (and other cultures, too, apparently) is that while anxiety is very prevalent we use our educational system to raise the evasion of anxiety to a high art. From such evidence as we have, we can prudently conclude that there probably is no school child, no college student or professor (or no reader of this book) who is not anxious to some degree. The human situation is such that there probably is no way to avoid anxiety. Anxiety thrives on the predicaments of human existence, but is not relieved by evasion. The academic program and the academic mind are geared to evasion when, in our educational program, we teach children to know about almost everything except about the intimate strivings and conflicts which concern themselves. We evade anxiety (or seek to evade it) when we avoid the personal implication of knowledge and emphasize only the impersonal, objective facts.

Even psychology, the scientific discipline which deals with the most intimate operations of the "psyche" can be used as an instrument for evading anxiety. It is so used when we approach psychology only as an academic subject with no concern about the distinct *personal* meanings it might have for *us*. In the study of anxiety, for example, we lose the personal meaning if we become so absorbed in theories and definitions that we manage to evade the question: In what ways was I an anxious child? In what ways am I an anxious adult? And what might I do to understand the meaning of this question and to face it?

We do two important things when we raise questions such as these. We acknowledge the existence of anxiety, and we alert ourselves to detect its symptoms and consequences in ourselves and in others. At present, there is no simple formula for understanding anxiety or for "curing" it; yet a willingness to accept the concept of anxiety and to look for signs of it means that we can be wiser and more humane than if we simply close our eyes. When we seek to understand the inroads of anxiety in the lives of children we will be in a better position to inquire into the plight of the child who is "nervous," restless, or constantly on the go as if seeking to escape from himself; we will be in a better position to inquire into the condition of the child who has nightmares and other signs of inner stress, or the child who is constantly getting himself into trouble by being extremely rebellious, aggressive, or defiant. The concept of anxiety is also helpful when we try to understand the child who seems unable to learn because of an "emotional block" or the child who is exceedingly cautious or withdrawn, shrinking from asserting himself as though it was dangerous even to try, or the child who is frequently "absent," as though personal problems absorb so much of his energy that he has no strength left for dealing with the practical demands of everyday life.

THEORIES OF ANXIETY

Theories of anxiety range from those which stress age-old predicaments that confront all human beings to those which give especial emphasis to particular problems or areas of stress.[2] Kierkegaard over a century ago anticipated many of the concepts that recently have received much attention in psychological thought, notably in discussions of anxiety in relation to the concept of the self. One of Kierkegaard's themes dealt with the decisions, possibilities, and alternatives which (according to him) man faces in choosing to be or not to be himself (". . . even what one might call the poorest personality is everything when he has chosen himself; for the great thing is not to be this or that but to be oneself.") (Kierkegaard, 1949b).

Among the more noteworthy recent writings dealing with the origins of anxiety are those of Freud, Horney, and Sullivan.

Freud's accounts of anxiety draw attention especially to two conditions. First, the young child's helpless dependence on the love and care of his parents makes him vulnerable to "separation anxiety." Freud speaks of anxiety as arising in a child in a situation of being left alone, being in the dark (and thus separated), or finding himself with a stranger instead of the person to whom he clings (the mother). These situations, according to Freud, are reducible to one, namely, the loss of the loved person.

Secondly, according to Freud, anxiety will arise when a child, without being conscious of the nature of his predicament, is beset by an unresolved conflict between his need for "instinctual" gratification and the conditions in his environment that forbid such gratification. In his book, *The Problem of Anxiety*, Freud gives an account of little Hans, who has become a classical character. Hans was anxious—he had a phobia of horses, which arose, according to Freud's account, from the fact that Hans had an unresolved Oedipus complex. Hans had a desire to possess his mother and to replace his father. He felt jealousy toward his father, but he also loved him; he felt hostile toward his father but he also feared retaliation.

---

[2] For discussions of anxiety, see Freud (1936); Horney (1937, 1939, 1945, 1950); Sullivan (1947, 1948); Hoch and Zubin (1950); Tillich (1952); May (1950); May, Angel, and Ellenberger (1958); and W. Lowrie's translations of Kierkegaard's *Sickness Unto Death* (1951).

To escape from this painful situation, Hans's hostility was "detoured" from his father to horses. The phobia of horses was painful, but it was less painful than to center his hostility and fear on his father. Hans was not consciously aware of the process by which he had substituted fear of a horse for fear of his father.

In their accounts of anxiety, both Sullivan and Horney, in common with Freud (although in somewhat different language), emphasize the child's dependence and helplessness and the difficulties he faces if there is a disturbance in his relationships with persons who are important to him—leading to a disorder in his relationships with himself.

According to Horney's theories, a chronic condition of anxiety develops when a child has to build a defense against an environment that is unreliable, unjust, and harsh, an environment he does not have the power to change, which undermines his ability to grow in reliance upon himself. He is not simply frightened in this or that particular of his life, but the environment as a whole is a menace, threatening his individuality and interfering with his opportunity to develop his potentialities as a person. Such a forbidding environment exists when a child is unloved and is treated without consideration. According to Horney's account, a child tries to find "solutions" to such predicaments, but these "solutions" may only lead to further trouble. Harsh treatment provokes hostility, but it is dangerous for a child to express hostility against the people on whom his life and everyday care depend. While he feels hostile toward them he also needs their help, and so conflicting influences are at work. Instead of fighting and freely expressing his anger he must, for his own safety, resort to other measures. His solutions take the form of defenses and stratagems. But these stratagems, although developed out of necessity, may take a turn that leaves the child at odds with himself.

Sullivan's theory of anxiety emphasizes the concept of interpersonal relationships, which has been mentioned in several earlier sections of this book. The child's self, according to Sullivan, is at first made up of "reflected appraisals": His feelings and attitudes pertaining to himself are determined by the feelings and attitudes others have toward him (and these are an expression of the feelings and attitudes others have toward themselves). Accordingly, the offspring of an anxiously self-rejecting parent faces the danger of becoming an anxiously self-rejecting child. Sullivan's theory of empathy as a means of communication between a parent and a child, and as a vehicle through which the young child of an anxious mother becomes anxious, is discussed in Chapter Four.

All three of the theories discussed above emphasize anxiety-producing conditions that arise in a child's life after he is born, but they do not touch on one important question: Is there something in the nature of children that makes some of them more susceptible to anxiety than others? As noted elsewhere in this book, children within the same home, begotten and reared by the same parents, differ greatly from birth onward in their emotional response.

In extreme instances, one child moves into adolescence and adulthood so anxious that he becomes mentally ill, while his brothers and sisters do not. The findings reported by Kallman (cited in Chapter Two) are pertinent here, for they deal with a form of mental illness (schizophrenia) which has been regarded as representing or being a means of escaping from extreme anxiety. The chances that this illness will afflict both members of a pair of identical (one-egg) twins are many times greater than the chances that it will afflict both members of a pair of fraternal (two-egg) twins, or both members of a pair of siblings. Does this mean that an anxious mother who (according to Sullivan's theory communicates her anxiety to her children) usually conveys an equally destructive amount of anxiety to them when she is rearing identical twins but in most instances conveys an *unequal* amount of her anxiety to her children when they are fraternal twins or siblings? The answer may be "yes," but a more plausible answer is that to explain the great variations in anxiety among human beings it is necessary not only to consider the mother's anxiety and other conditions in the child's environment that are anxiety-producing but also the conditions within the individual that make him susceptible or resistant to anxiety.

DEFENSES AGAINST ANXIETY

Anxiety, whatever may be its origin, is a painful state, and when it prevails a person is likely to use various ways of coping with it as best he can. In doing so, he faces the possibility of getting into a worse jam than before.

Horney (1945-1950) has given an account of ways of dealing with anxiety. This account leaves many questions unanswered, yet it describes ways of behaving which can be observed in everyday life. Horney describes three major "strategies" which an anxious person can adopt in dealing with a threatening world: he can move *with* people by being meek, compliant, and self-effacing; he can move *against* others by being aggressive, competitive, and seeking to control others; or he can move *away* from others by being withdrawn, detached, and aloof. These "strategies" may not appear in "pure" form. In describing them, Horney does not assume that these represent three distinct personality types, nor does she assume that any of these forms of behavior is, in itself, a sign of anxiety: In the normal course of events there are times when a person spontaneously competes or complies or remains aloof. However, according to Horney, when used as "strategies" in dealing with anxiety these ways of behaving are not spontaneous, but become a compulsive means of self-defense.

When a child resorts to such ways as these he undertakes to play a role in order to play safe. But any such stratagem he adopts and any role or combination of roles he assumes, other than acting "natural," so to speak, is likely to involve conflict. Instead of being spontaneous, he adopts a "front," and it is burdensome to maintain a front. If he uses compliance as a solution there are times when, according to his spontaneous tendencies, he would like to rebel. If he seeks to relieve his anxiety by playing a competitive role there are times when this role becomes burdensome. If his front is detachment, it will be threatened whenever he has an impulse to have a close relationship. Such conflict is unpleasant, and so, according to Horney, the growing child who has gotten into this fix adopts tactics to support, defend, and rationalize the measures he has taken, and this further complicates things. What emerges is a distortion of the self through which the child achieves a precarious unity in his style of life. He may even succeed in arriving at an uneasy conviction that his stratagems are the ideal thing. He may be able to convince himself that his compliance is not a weakness but a fine streak of gentleness and generosity; that his aggressiveness and competitiveness are not a defense against weakness but a mark of strength; or that his tendency to withdraw from close relationships with others and to remain detached is not a way of playing safe but a sign of a rugged ability to "go it alone." If he does this, he is, in Horney's account building an "idealized self" which is false—a "pseudo-self"—but which he strives to preserve and defend.

He is likely to become anxious when anything threatens to undermine or expose the front he has assumed. Anxiety which at first arose in the child's relationships with others now arises from tendencies within himself. According to this line of thought, anxiety arises when anything threatens this "neurotic solution," represented by the superstructure of ideas, concepts, habits, and attitudes built around early attempts at protecting the self from harm (Gershman, 1950).

Values of fear and anxiety

In assessing the value of fear it is necessary first to recognize that fear is important for self-preservation. Fear may take many foolish turns, but a creature totally without fear would probably not live very long. A rabbit who gets scared and runs away has a chance to live another day, and even the rabbit who scares nine times out of ten when there is really no danger will be better off than a rabbit who happened not to be scared the one time in ten when there *was* something to be afraid of. In the lives of children and adults, as in the lives of rabbits, there are many false alarms, but nature has endowed her creatures with fear to alert them to alarms that might not be false.

Any condition that mobilizes an individual's energies and puts him on the alert in the face of danger is obviously of tremendous value as a protection.

According to physiological findings, during acute emotional stress, glandular products are released into the blood stream, resulting in an increase in heart rate and blood pressure, a larger supply of available sugar, quicker coagulation of the blood and, in general, greater physical efficiency for meeting an emergency by fighting or fleeing (Cannon, 1929). However, often in modern life an issue which one fears cannot be solved by fighting or fleeing. A worried student cannot pass a hard examination by outrunning his instructor or by throwing him out the window. Most of the emergencies in modern life call for quick wits rather than for strong fists. And many of the apprehensions a child has concerning himself and his relations with others are not based on conditions which an extra spurt of physical energy can solve.

Several years ago the writer and an associate undertook an experiment which dealt indirectly with the effects of psychological changes associated with emotional excitement on efficiency. Through injections of adrenalin most of the physiological reactions described above were artifically induced. At the height of the physiological effects various tests were administered. The tests showed that in the state of excitement there was an increase in physical strength and in speed of movement, but there was little or no gain in performing simple mental tasks, and, if anything, there was a loss in performing somewhat more complex intellectual tasks (Jersild and Thomas, 1931).

Findings in studies of children and adults who, according to their own self-ratings have a high or low degree of "manifest anxiety" [3] appear, on the whole, to be in accord with the results obtained in the study just cited. In one such study (Castaneda, McCandless and Palermo, 1956b), an apparatus containing a series of electrical push buttons which activated a series of lights was used, and children were instructed to learn which button turned off which light. Simple as well as complex button-light combinations were used. In this study (as in earlier studies of adults) it was found that children who were in the "high-anxious" group performed better than "low-anxious" children on simple learning tasks but did more poorly on more complex tasks. In another study, manifest anxiety scores of children in the fourth, fifth, and sixth grades were correlated with academic achievement as measured by standardized tests. (McCandless

---

[3] A children's form of a "manifest anxiety scale" developed by Castaneda, McCandless, and Palermo (1956a), is an adaptation of a scale which Taylor (1953) devised for measuring "manifest anxiety" in adults.

et al., 1956). The correlations ranged from zero to −.74, and in thirteen of the correlations there was a statistically significant *negative* correlation between manifest anxiety and achievement. Children with higher anxiety scores not only showed poorer achievement, on the whole, than children with lower anxiety ratings, but they also tended to show the poorest performance in the more complicated academic skills.

In a study by Phillips and others (1959) tests differing in difficulty and complexity were administered to children who also were given the Manifest Anxiety Scale and a test of intelligence. The tests ranged from one in which children simply had to put three pencil dots in each one of a series of circles as quickly as possible to tests of vocabulary requiring more complex forms of verbal ability. Children with higher manifest anxiety did not consistently perform more poorly on the complex than on the simple tests, but in connection with practically all of the measurements there was a negative correlation between scores on manifest anxiety and performance on the tests. On the other hand, in all instances there was a positive correlation between intelligence and performance on the tests.

From everyday observation it appears that some people perform much better when they are "keyed up" than others do. The tensions connected with anxiety seem to operate almost as a tonic for some and as a depressant for others. Other factors also are at work. A person who is already being taxed to the utmost will probably have less tolerance for added anxiety than one who has what might be called a large margin of free energy. The effects of stress may even be quite specific. For example, a child whose abilities in reading and in learning verbal materials is considerably higher than his ability in arithmetic may be able to carry on under stress in a reading assignment but not be able to do so in an arithmetic assignment. In general, however, a high degree of fear or anxiety is more likely to be a hindrance than a help in dealing with complex intellectual tasks. Certainly there is little basis for assuming that a policy of playing on a child's fears by threats of punishment and failure will help him to reach higher levels of academic achievement or contentment.

Helping children to deal with fear

Many apprehensions wane as the individual has a chance gradually to face and to cope with the feared situation. In one study (Slater, 1939) it was noted that most children during the first day of nursery school showed some signs of apprehension, but there was a marked decline in uneasiness after the first day.

> An interesting observation was that the degree to which a child openly revealed his concern on his first visit did not indicate how well or how soon he would adjust to the new situation: ". . . children who cried loudest

on their first morning might often be the happiest later on, whereas some who were tearless on their first morning sometimes continued for days to be rather solemn and none too happy." The youngster who is most free to express his feelings when he is troubled may be the one who is best able to come to grips with his trouble. Kraus (1956) observed that beginners in kindergarten who most openly showed distress made, if anything, a better adjustment to school as time went on than those who seemed outwardly calm.

PRACTICAL STEPS USED BY PARENTS IN DEALING WITH FEAR

When an adult notices that a child is afraid his impulse usually is to say or do something. If a child is acutely frightened he will, of course, try to comfort and protect the youngster. However, in dealing with lingering fears it is important for an adult to bide his time, to study the child, the nature of the fear, and the context in which it occurs.[4] The first principle in dealing with fear is that we should not look simply at the specific symptoms but try to discover the conditions underlying fear. This is essential especially in coping with fears that are rooted in a state of insecurity and conflict. When such a condition prevails, the elimination of one "fear" may quickly be followed by other fears.

Among the methods parents employ in dealing with children's fears (as reported to interviewers in a study by the writer and Holmes, 1935b), the following were described as probably doing more harm than good:

1. Consistently ignoring fear.
2. Ridiculing or punishing the child for being afraid.
3. Forcing the child into the feared situation.

Parents were able sometimes to help children to cope with fear when they used the following methods:

   1. Explaining the situation, trying to convince the child there is nothing to be afraid of. This method sometimes helps if the explanation actually touches on the reason for the child's fear, but it probably does more harm than good if the "explanation" means, in effect, that it is foolish for the child to be afraid.
   2. Setting an example of fearlessness. Such an example, among other things, may bolster the child's assurance in the protection of another person and help him realize that there is nothing to be afraid of. In many situations the example of fearlessness set by other children is helpful. A child will frequently follow other children into activities he would be afraid to undertake if he were alone, such as entering a "haunted" barn, or wading or jumping into a stream.
   3. Trying to effect "positive reconditioning" by presenting the feared stimulus with an attractive or benign stimulus. This method is likely to

---

[4] For studies dealing with overcoming fear see Hagman (1932); Holmes (1936); Jersild and Holmes (1935b); and Jones (1924).

work best if the feared event can be incorporated into a larger setting that is reassuring.

4. Helping the child by degrees to gain confidence in his ability to deal with feared situations. This method, according to parents, frequently is helpful. In an experimental test of this procedure, Holmes (1936) found that of twenty children in a nursery-school group, fourteen were initially afraid to enter a strange, dark room to recover a ball which had rolled into this room while the experimenter and the child were playing with it in an adjoining, lighted room. The children were then familiarized with the place, and after relatively few sessions, thirteen of these fourteen children went into the room without hesitation, turned on the light, and recovered the ball. In the company of a reassuring adult they had learned to cope at least with this practical situation, although the experimenter could not be sure that they would be unafraid of the dark in a different situation.

Another series of experiments dealt with two children who were afraid to walk the length of a plank that was raised above the ground. After eight brief sessions, over a period of about a month, one child, who at first had clung to the experimenter and had whined and protested that she would fall and get hurt, cheerfully walked back and forth the length of a board raised six feet above the ground as though enjoying her victory over fear. She performed the same feat when the apparatus was moved to the playground. Another child also made progress, but less rapidly and then he relapsed. This occurred at a time when his nurse left the household and his mother was in the hospital having a baby. The whining and infantile responses which he showed in the fear experiment were similar to behavior he showed at home. The procedure of simply helping the child to deal directly with a specific feared situation did not suffice to overcome a fear that apparently was interwoven with other emotional difficulties.

An active approach aimed at improving the child's confidence in himself may be helpful even in dealing with fears of imaginary dangers. One child was afraid of an imaginary dog, which hounded him, troubled him when he was alone, and haunted him in dark places. His mother, aiming to help him, first watched the child in his make-believe play, and then gradually joined the child in games of "Let's Pretend." Gradually, also, she began to introduce the imaginary dog into the make-believe play. In time, the child took the dog with him into closets and elsewhere, all as part of the play pattern, and eventually he no longer appeared to be bothered by the dog.

The value of the technique of helping the child to cope directly with his fears no doubt comes more from companionship with an adult than from the specific methods used by the adult. The child's burden of fear is being shared. He is being told, in effect, that he need not be ashamed of being afraid and that he is not, at least for the time being, defenseless and alone.

Another value of helping a child to cope in an active way with a feared situation is that through it the youngster may get a changed conception of his own abilities. When a child, for example, has become able to go by himself to a remote part of the house he once feared he has not just overcome an external danger but he has overcome an internal weakness. If he now goes confidently to a place he once feared he is, to that degree, a changed person.

ENCOURAGEMENT OF CHILDREN'S OWN EFFORTS
TO OVERCOME FEAR

Adults can sometimes help a child by encouraging him in his own efforts to cope with his fears. Children frequently make such an effort, sometimes by facing a feared situation directly, sometimes by bringing it into their make-believe play. (Examples of this use of make-believe are given in Chapter Fifteen. An illustration of a child's triumph over fear of a high place is given in Chapter Eleven.)

INQUIRY INTO UNDERLYING CAUSES

The idea that we should try to look into the conditions underlying fear obviously is more easily said than done. Even highly trained professional psychotherapists often find it a baffling, difficult, and time-consuming job. An adult will find it especially difficult to deal with a child's fears which are related to his own. Moreover, as we have noted, a "fear" may be the child's way of giving a name or tangible reference point to a disturbance that is much more complicated than the fear appearing on the surface. Besides, even if a child's fear is a burden, he is likely to resist facing it if the fear is a screen for attitudes pertaining to himself which are even more disturbing than the particular fear which he reports (this would be the case if, for instance, a child's fear of robbers is rooted in a conflict about his own impulse to steal). With fear, we deal not just with one segment of emotion but with the whole network of emotions and strivings that permeate human experience.

Even though there are very real limits to what a parent or teacher or friend can do to understand or to help a frightened child, any humane thing that one can do is well worth the effort. A child who has severe persisting fears is a tortured child. He deserves at least as much compassion as a child who is physically ill. Moreover, there are many elements in this kind of situation that make the endeavor to help such a youngster hopeful and potentially rewarding.

As we have seen in earlier sections, fear thrives on unresolved anger, so to understand fear we need to look for and face the inroads of rage. Fear also thrives on rejection, failure, and weakness, so we need to face the impact of these conditions as best we can. There is an affinity, too, between fear and loneliness, for the child who keeps his fears concealed keeps a lonely vigil. It is remarkable to observe, in working with children and adults, how great a relief a frightened or anxious person can derive simply from discovering that others, too, are anxious and afraid and that he is not alone.

When an adult seeks to help a child cope with fear he needs above all to have an accepting attitude, the kind of attitude that enables him to watch, to listen, and to wait. This means he will avoid breezy assurances such as, "There really is nothing to be afraid of." Such a statement is false: A child isn't afraid just for the sport of it. An accepting attitude is essential to give the child the freedom to reveal his fears, especially those that he has learned to disguise or those he is ashamed to disclose.

To help the child, the adult needs to maintain, as well as he can, an accepting attitude toward the child and also toward himself. Such acceptance means he will try not to expect too much of himself, or to blame himself for being slow and obtuse, or for not finding a quick solution. He will be on guard against the guilt and self-reproach aroused in him by the theories of fear and anxiety which accuse him of being the source and author of his child's fears. The idea of acceptance has a homiletic sound, but it is very practical, and it is especially needed in order to combat the aura of condemnation with which the subject of fear is so often surrounded. If an adult feels guilty about each sign of fear in his child this condition is more likely to discourage him rather than help him in his endeavor to cope with fear.

Even though children often have strong defenses against revealing their fears, many are eager to share the burden of their fear with someone else whom they trust. The child who has the freedom to unburden himself already has, to that extent, done something to cope with fear. He has surmounted some of the guilt, shame, and self-reproach with which fears are often enmeshed. He has surmounted the cruel notion that it is shameful to be afraid.

Even when children feel free to confide in others, they will still have difficulty in bringing fears out into the open and in coming to grips with the conditions underlying them. Certainly no child or adult could be expected, by sheer dint of thought, to relive conditions under which fear arose and to illuminate the unconscious or unrecognized forces that might underlie fear. However, even this situation is not as hopeless as it might seem, for three reasons: (1) Dealing with the conscious elements of fear is helpful as far as it goes. (2) In exploring the conscious elements of a child's fear, an adult may get an inkling of the unconscious elements, such as the relationship between fear and punishment, fear and guilt, fear and the expectations that a person puts upon himself when he is trying to live up to a picture of what he cannot be. (3) In tracing and trying to understand a fear rooted in the past it is impossible to go back and relive the past, but to the extent that a child's present fears are linked to experiences of the past (and most of them are) the past still lives in the present.

Recommended Readings

The most enlightening writings on anxiety reflect a scholarly effort to understand this condition and they also reveal something about the personal preoccupations of the authors. The accounts have much in common, for all deal with predicaments and conflicts imbedded in human existence. The theme of separation or alienation from self or from others is expressed in varying language and with varying emphases by three outstanding psychoanalytic writers: Sigmund Freud, *The Problem of Anxiety* (1936); Karen Horney, *Our Inner Conflicts* (1945); and Harry Stack Sullivan, *The Meaning of Anxiety in Psychiatry and in Life* (1948). This theme has also been discussed by writers with a background in philosophy and religion: Sören Kierkegaard, *The Sickness Unto Death* (referred to in Chapter Six); and Paul Tillich, *The Courage To Be* (1952). Rollo May's *The Meaning of Anxiety* (1950) reviews findings regarding children's fears and theories of anxiety and then, wisely, discusses issues that are in need of further investigation. *Anxiety*, edited by Paul H. Hoch and Joseph Zubin (1950), contains contributions by a number of distinguished writers.

Anger and Hostility

CHAPTER THIRTEEN   Through the impetus of anger the child asserts himself, gives a sharp edge to his demands and retaliates against those who thwart him or hurt him. Anger, like fear, is an instrument for dealing with a threatening environment. In anger the child takes action against the threat while in fear he retreats from it.

A child's capacity for anger is essential for his self-preservation, but to get along comfortably with others he must also acquire a prudent degree of self-control. One of the most difficult tasks a child faces in his development is maintaining his ability to become angry while managing his anger so that it does not cause more trouble than it cures.

An angry child is usually an unpleasant child, and even when he is too weak to hurt us we are likely to view his anger as an affront to our pride.

Consequently, children are reared as though the eleventh and greatest Commandment were "Thou shalt not show anger, nor even feel it." Yet if we would understand children we need, as far as possible, to penetrate the meaning of their anger. To do this, we must take stock of our own anger, including our tendency to counter the child's anger with our own, or to blame ourselves for his anger.

Sooner or later a child's anger is likely to involve him in conflict of a two-fold nature: conflict *with others* who object to his anger, or are threatened by it; and conflict *within himself* by reason of the fact that the healthy child's impulse to feel and express anger goes counter to other strong impulses, such as those connected with affection and fear. Partly as a consequence of this two-fold conflict, there is a complicated interplay between anger that is fully experienced and openly expressed, and covert anger that ranges through a child's fantasies. Further, partly by reason of this conflict the child who at first directed his anger against other persons and things may, in time, become the object of his own rage. This happens when he becomes excessively self-reproachful and, as we say, "kicks himself."

Sources and expressions of anger

Anger can be aroused in young children by forcible restraint, interference with movement, blocking of activities that are in progress, or anything that thwarts a child's wishes. The younger the child, the more his anger will turn upon an interference with his physical needs and activities. As he grows older, the conditions that cause anger include anything that interferes with his possessions, or thwarts his plans, purposes, expectations, and his rights as he sees them, and by criticisms or fault-finding that are an attack on ideas he has concerning himself.

Anger, like fear, is influenced by factors of both learning and maturation. As we noted in Chapter Three, during the first few days of life such interferences as having his arms pinned momentarily to his sides or having his nostrils closed, so that breathing is prevented for a moment, do not especially arouse the ire of an infant. When the infant does protest, his movements are likely to be uncoordinated and display no clear pattern of rage. As he grows older, he becomes more responsive to interference.

After the child's capacities expand, learning plays an increasingly important role in determining how he will express his rage and the conditions that excite him.

Throughout childhood, however, there are great individual differences in the irascibility and violence of children. Even in early infancy, children differ in the intensity of their demands for food or attention, and in the severity of their anger when demands are not met. Children differ not only in their response to thwarting from others but also in their tendency to become angry in connection with activities of their own. When seeking, for example, to put a spoon in his mouth and failing because he makes a broadside approach, one child shows anger, another not.

CHANGES WITH AGE IN THE EXPRESSION OF ANGER

As the infant grows older his expressions of anger become less random and more directly aimed at something or someone. Before the age of one year a child's outbursts are not well designed to remove obstacles or to attack an enemy. The most frequent single expression of anger in early childhood is crying, but this diminishes with age. By the age of four almost half of a child's outbursts are likely to be aimed at the object of his wrath (Goodenough, 1931b). Accompanying this change is an increase in retaliative behavior apparently aimed at securing revenge for an injury. Threats make their appearance between the ages of two and three and increase in frequency thereafter.

Indirect forms of retaliation and attack include such activities as over-turning furniture and engaging in acts previously forbidden: One child of three, when angry, sucked his thumb conspicuously, although thumb-sucking was not his usual habit. Other indirect forms of aggression are raucous laughter and the refusal to speak. One child voiced resentment toward her mother by remarking "I wish I had a mother like Mary's." In some cases, children express their anger by attacks upon themselves; for example, a child was observed to bite himself when angry. Aftereffects of anger are more frequent and prolonged in children over the age of four than in children under four (Goodenough, 1931b).

In showing anger children sometimes go to extreme lengths such as holding their breath or vomiting or banging their heads against a hard surface. At about four some children resort to such threats as running away, chopping off the offender's head, or chopping his house to pieces. Many youngsters go through a period of threatening to kill when angered. In expressing anger, a child will frequently vary the nature of his outburst under different circumstances. He is more likely, for example, to cry at home than at school (Ricketts, 1934) and to hit and kick when angered by another child than when angered by an adult.

ANGER DIRECTED AGAINST SELF

Even when quite young children show a good deal of anger directed against themselves. In addition to the physical self-punishment (biting self, head banging) mentioned above, children sometimes express anger against themselves in words, such as "I hate myself" or "I feel like killing myself," or use milder terms, such as "That's just like me" (when they make a mistake or have an accident).

The concept of self-hate is not a pleasant one, but it is useful in understanding adults, and it is essential in understanding children. This concept is illustrated by different forms of self-disparagement such as "running oneself down," variations of the phenomenon of masochism, by proneness to accidents, and by a compulsive tendency to get into trouble.

Factors contributing to susceptibility to anger

Many circumstances that make a child more susceptible to anger have been described by Goodenough (1931b) who made a study of anger with the cooperation of a number of parents. Children are more disposed to anger after a restless night, or when recovering from an illness, or when tired or hungry. A good rule is not to start an argument before mealtime. A few mouthfuls of food may do more to settle a dispute than the best logic emanating from an empty stomach. Late afternoon, before dinner, is a time when many adults are especially disposed to be angry, although others favor the time before breakfast. It would help if such persons could realize that a soft-boiled egg, like a soft answer, will turn away wrath.

Outbursts of anger are likely to increase when there are visitors, especially when they overstay their welcome. Also there is likely to be more anger if there are more than two adults in the household.

Parents whose children show many outbursts of anger strive to calm them by coaxing and soothing more frequently than parents whose children show less anger (Goodenough, 1931b). This difference gives us a clue to many angry outbursts. When a child gets what he wants, his anger is successful; but if he fails to get what he wants, his anger is abortive and he will have less reason to resort to anger as a means of solving a problem another time.

Boys tend to show anger more openly than girls in the home. This is in keeping with other findings indicating that boys also are more openly aggressive outside the home. Mothers seem to be more at a loss in dealing with an angry boy than in dealing with an angry girl.

Anger is more likely to occur in homes where parents are over-anxious and concerned with whether the child's behavior is "good" or "bad" than in homes where parents are tolerant and capable of looking upon the child objectively. Anger is often provoked by parents who nag and recriminate instead of viewing each anger episode as a thing of the past when it is over. Consistency in methods of discipline appears to be a more important factor than the strictness or lenience of the disciplinary procedures used.

Some methods, such as bribery and letting the child have his own way, may bring an outburst to an end but may also pave the way for future outbursts (Goodenough, 1931b).

The level of the child's abilities and, in time, his ideas of what to expect of himself will have an important bearing on whether or not a situation is potentially frustrating. When he is able, or thinks he is able, to walk by himself on rough ground, he may be angry if someone tries to take his hand, whereas earlier, when this feat was beyond what he expected of himself, he was glad to take a hand or to be carried (and even later, when the rough terrain is no longer a challenge, he again may be quite glad to hold a hand or to get a lift).

CARRYOVER OF RESENTMENT OF AUTHORITY

As noted in Chapter Four, the discipline children receive from those in authority—at first from their parents and later from their teachers and other adults—often produces anger. Adults are thwarting a child's intentions in an annoying way when they lay down rules, refuse to yield to all of his demands and limit his freedom. Even when discipline is most essential and administered in the most reasonable manner, it may provoke a feeling of being abused.

Anger arises even in situations in which an adult is doing his utmost to help a child. It has been noted, for example, that children who are sick sometimes react to the care they receive as though it were a kind of assault. An enema, a hypodermic injection, a dentist's drill may provoke anger even when they are essential for the child's welfare.

A child's resentment of authority in the home or school sometimes leaves a lasting mark on his behavior if he continues during adult years to "take out" his anger against authority figures (as described in Chapter Seven).

We can see evidences of reactions to the father figure (using him now as our main symbol of authority) in many reactions of older persons in everyday life. For example, when a student is extremely sensitive to mild criticism from his instructor—reacting to a helpful suggestion as though it were an affront—it is likely that he is showing a carry-over of resentments from an earlier period of his life.

A continuing revolt against authority figures also appears when an older person is chronically opposed to anyone who stands as a symbol of authority, be he an elected official, the congenial dean of a college, the head of a department, or the president of a corporation. The reaction sometimes takes the form of trying to outwit anyone who is in authority, or taking sides with one who is regarded as an underdog.

Attitudes toward the "father (or mother) figure" are complicated by the fact that a devoted parent is one who forbids and also one who is kind and lovable—he is, in a sense, both a good father and a bad father. When adults attach resentments and loyalties carried over from childhood to authority figures they vary considerably in their views as to who is the good father and who is the bad one. In a political campaign, for example, a "father figure" who is regarded as a villain by one person may be a hero to another (who happens to fix his resentment on the opposing candidate). As a result, an outstanding public character (notably in the political field) who has a host of admirers is also likely to have many detractors. Long-standing resentments also are attached to causes and symbols that carry labels reminiscent of parent-child relationships. Labels such as "Big," "Little," and "Small" have meanings beyond mere size. When one person resents "Big Business" another "Big Labor" and a third "Big Government" they choose different targets but each is reacting to something Big and this reaction may be colored by the feelings a little child has for or against a big father. (The association between bigness and fatherliness is openly expressed when "Big Government" is also referred to as "Paternalistic Government.")

SUPPRESSION OF OVERT SIGNS OF RAGE

As a rule, the child has no sooner acquired the ability to stage a good performance of rage than he must begin to learn how to suppress it. Through social restraints and partly through his own discovery he learns not to kick, hit, destroy, or attack by other physical means when his ire is aroused. Studies of anger in adults (by Richardson, 1918, Gates, 1926, and Meltzer, 1933) show how far this learning extends by the time a person reaches maturity. In several hundred occasions of anger described by adults, there were only a few good fights. Although an adult learns to smother most of his violent expressions, this does not mean that his anger is disposed of; he may still have a strong impulse to do physical injury to the offender or to scream or swear or make a scene. As H. S. Sullivan has said, it is easier to swallow anger than to digest it.

DEVIOUS MANIFESTATIONS OF ANGER

A frequent substitute for a physical show of anger is the use of language in the form of sneers, innuendoes, gossip, and the like. The angry person can also resort to indirect methods of vanquishing the object of his rage, such as belittling his opponent, overcoming him in competition, rejoicing in his misfortunes, plotting against him, or imagining situations that will bring sorrow to him. Children sometimes imagine themselves as dead, secretly relishing the tears that wet the cheeks of the sorrowing persons who have abused them.

In extreme cases, anger is expressed in the form of active revolt, vandalism, thievery, and other antisocial acts. A child may also discover that he can "get another's goat" by using bad words, by using ungrammatical speech, or by mannerisms and little acts which in themselves are relatively harmless but which cause irritation.

Friendliness as a front for anger.   In trying to suppress his anger an older person may display just the opposite sentiments. Instead of showing hostility toward a person whom he basically dislikes, he may show friendliness and appear to be very concerned about the welfare of this person.

Such a cloak of friendliness may be assumed quite deliberately, as when a person "goes out of his way to be nice" to a person he doesn't like. When children are old enough to understand some of the polite disguises for aggressiveness they may be able to take this line. Again, a display of unusual friendliness may be a delayed reaction to anger, an attempt at atonement. A mother may not suspect, for example, how enraged her child was when she refused him permission to go swimming until he comes, an hour or so later, penitently bringing her a flower or a glass of cold water or some other token of regard. Here, the process may be quite open, with no significant deception of self or others. However, there is a self-deception if a youngster covers his anger with a set of polite manners, and, as he moves into adult years, uses them more and more as a habit without recognizing that he is acting a part. In this way, a person may be elaborately polite in meeting people, even though secretly he has no use for them or even despises them.

In most social circles a polite facade frequently conceals attitudes ranging from unconcern to deep dislike and even hatred. In the usual superficialities connected with parties, teas, receptions, and other gatherings the masquerade goes on unrevealed, except at times when ill will breaks through in the form of gossip.

This duplicity may be innocent enough from a psychological point of view (just as it is perhaps inescapable from a social point of view). But it results in a psychological disturbance when: (a) the person who wears the mask of friendliness does so indiscriminately, unaware of his real feelings toward others and unable to distinguish between hollow and sincere relationships or (b) he becomes convinced (although perhaps never thoroughly) that the friendly person he appears to be is not a pose but is his "real" self. The disturbance may be concealed, but it may also become so severe that anger breaks through the controls that have been placed upon it. Such a break-through occurs, for example, when the "politest boy in town" commits a crime.

Finding a scapegoat.   When a person is not free to direct his aggressive impulses toward the person or circumstances that provoked him, he may succeed in directing them toward someone or something else. The child who has been angered by his parents, but who does not dare to strike back at his parents, may, for example, "Take out" his anger on a brother or sister.

Change in quality of performance. Anger is sometimes expressed by a change in the quality of the child's performance. One response may be to show restless and aimless forms of behavior. Another response may be to leave the situation: The child will walk away, if free to do so. Even when confined, in the flesh, to the annoying situation he may try to absent himself psychologically, as when he finds the arithmetic too difficult and sits through the class period without paying attention to what is going on or goes through the motions of spelling but misses every word. The child may remain bodily in the situation but he is psychologically withdrawn. Instances of withdrawal of this kind occurred in a study of frustration by Seashore and Bavelas (1942). One at a time the children were asked to draw a man, but as soon as a child had completed a drawing the experimenter, without taking further notice of it, gave the child another piece of paper and asked him to draw another man, and so on, one drawing after the other. As one trial followed another, many of the children gave less and less time to the drawing. A child who devoted seven or eight minutes to his first drawing or two might, several trials later, dash off a drawing in a few seconds. As one trial followed the next, the children's drawings deteriorated.

The change in quality of performance in response to frustration may also take the form of regression—the child backslides and behaves in a more childish or infantile manner.[1]

Considerations
in dealing with anger in children

In this chapter we have already touched upon many practical considerations connected with the problem of anger. In its primitive form anger is an aid to self-defense. The child is on the alert to protect himself when he is angry, and this emotion can serve as a corrective in parent-child relationships. For example, the anger aroused in parents by a child who continually seems to expect too much and demand too much may lead the parents to examine themselves and their child-rearing policies and their own rights.

A child's anger, like an adult's, usually means that there is an annoyance

---

[1] For accounts of loss of constructiveness, regression, and other forms of lowered quality of performance in frustrating situations see Barker, Dembo, and Lewin (1941); Keister (1937); and Updegraff and Keister (1937).

immediately at hand, and this annoyance may call attention to a condition that can, and should be, remedied. In addition, since anger is not only a surface manifestation but also has roots in the child's experience, the grownup faces not simply an immediate problem but also a larger opportunity and challenge when a child gets angry. In a mood of anger, a child, like an adult, draws aside the curtain behind which he normally conceals himself. The child's anger can provide a significant clue to his motives and to currents in his emotional life which otherwise would go unnoticed.

Anger may be a sign of strength as well as weakness. A child's anger may be genuine, healthy, and noble. It is healthy for a child to become angry or at least to feel anger when someone abuses him, takes advantage of him, or violates his integrity. It is healthy for him to show anger when people whom he loves are under attack, or when someone tries to attack his loyalties, or when someone tries to abuse a weaker person for whom he feels responsible. We should probably be more concerned about the child who seems to have lost his capacity for anger than about the one who seems too often to lose his temper.

A child's anger, like the anger of an adult, is a sign of weakness when it is not suited to the occasion, when it is not directed against the real source of difficulty, or when it creates more difficulty for him. We may suspect that the child's anger springs from difficulties in his own internal life when he is very demanding, quick to take offense, or ready to fly off the handle over petty matters.

When a minor setback acts like a fuse to set off an open show of anger, or provokes rage that is kept under control but betrays itself by little signs, we may suspect that a child is not only struggling with the problems that beset him in his day-to-day life but is also involved in a larger struggle, complicated by attitudes of vindictiveness which have arisen in his earlier experiences. If an adult can understand a child's anger he has gone a long way toward understanding the child and toward understanding himself.

It is difficult to deal wisely with an angry child because a display of anger is likely to arouse anger in the person against whom it is directed. Few parents or teachers are so robust that they are immune to this tendency, and it is helpful to recognize this and not feel guilty about it. However, when an episode of anger is over and feelings have calmed down, it is possible for an adult to try to look at the child's anger from a larger point of view: What can be learned from it? Why was the child so angry? What touched him off? Why are his feelings so raw and sensitive on the issue that aroused him? Was he perhaps striving anxiously to protect his pride? What weakness might the anger-provoking circumstance threaten to expose? What might this flare-up of anger reveal concerning the expectations he places on himself or on others? What long-standing grievance might he be harboring?

Jealousy

Complex feelings and impulses are usually involved in jealousy. In introspective accounts of jealousy offered by adults (Gesell, 1906) anger was most frequently mentioned, including feelings of hatred and vengeful thoughts. Feelings of self-pity, as well as dejection, mortification, fear, and anxiety, were also mentioned by many persons. The most frequent combination was anger, self-pity, and grief.

Expressions of jealousy. Many specific examples of the behavior of jealous children have been described in studies of sibling rivalry (Sewall, 1930; Foster, 1927; Neisser, 1951). A four-year-old boy, at first well-disposed toward his baby sister, became aroused when a blanket which had been his was used to cover her; thereafter, he would hit her if the two were left alone together. In an extreme case, a five-year-old child who had the whooping cough was told by the doctor that if he coughed near his baby sister she might become sick, and "then you won't have a baby sister any more." Thereafter, he was caught several times in the act of coughing into his sister's face.

Some children express jealousy through their make-believe and wreak vengeance by proxy. In a study that used a "housekeeping game" to investigate children's make-believe, one three-year-old child took the "baby" doll, placed it on the "stove," and earnestly told the "baby" that it would have to sit there and burn and burn. This child was found to be acutely jealous of a younger sibling (Markey, 1935).

A jealous child sometimes reverts to earlier infantile habits. For example, when a new baby arrives, an older child who for some time has achieved bladder control at night may revert to bed wetting or frequently call his parents at night to take him to the toilet. He may seek extra help and attention in connection with eating, dressing, and other activities. Apparently as a bid for attention, he may exhibit fears that did not appear at an earlier time and that, in effect, represent a plea for sympathy and attention (although such pleas can easily be misinterpreted). Again, he may become more affectionate than was his wont, or meek and submissive and very obedient.

As a child grows older, his expressions of jealousy show varied forms such as: tattling and lying; swaggering or assuming a conspicuous attitude of nonchalance; vindictive plans; and fantasies in which the child plays the role of a martyr or a conquering hero. Neisser (1951) has described many instances of resentment in disguise.

Conditions precipitating jealousy. Sometimes parents unwittingly discriminate against one child by showing greater admiration for another child in the family. It is only human for adults to prefer some traits and characteristics to others, and in the process one child may get the notion that he does not rank as high in his parents' estimation as does his brother or sister. Where there are children differing in age, sex, interests, and abilities it is impossible for parents always to treat the youngsters in a way that seems fair to all. It is likely that all siblings near each other in age will exhibit symptoms of jealousy at some time or another.

The coming of a new baby into the home often marks the beginning of symptoms of jealousy; but in many cases the child who becomes jealous does not show this attitude until the new arrival is a year or two old.

Many parents take great pains to "prepare" an older child for the advent of a new baby, but they cannot anticipate with certainty the effect a new arrival will have on them or on their other children. Moreover, parents, who after all are human beings, cannot possibly achieve a thorough and perfectly rational balance in the handling of their children. An effort to "think out" and to weigh the merits of every practice used in the rearing of children might only confuse matters.

Competitive relations between siblings are sometimes stimulated by visitors who call attention to the fact, say, that George, although a year younger, is just as tall as his brother, Jim; or who gush over Mildred's curls in the presence of sister Janet, whose hair is straight. It often happens that an older child who used to be noticed by callers is especially neglected and slighted when they come to see a newly arrived baby. It would be a good rule if visitors who come bearing gifts at such a time would bring their gifts to the older child rather than to the new baby (particularly since the presents mean nothing to him anyhow).

When notably jealous children are singled out for special study and compared with children who are not so jealous, the findings do not lead to any sweeping generalization that would account for the difference. Jealousy is often entangled with other symptoms of emotional difficulty, however. Among the characteristics observed more frequently in jealous than in non-jealous children in a study by Foster (1927) were selfishness, pugnacity, a special attachment to one parent, and fears. A higher proportion of the jealous children exhibited sleep disturbances, enuresis, nail biting, thumb sucking, hyperactivity, destructiveness, and excessive demands for attention. Where there are many other difficulties of this kind, aggressive expressions of jealousy may be simply one feature of a more pervasive problem.

The link between jealousy in early childhood and a jealous disposition in later years has not been traced adequately in scientific studies. Children normally lose their more obvious symptoms of jealousy as they grow older and become absorbed in interests outside the family. On the other hand, some children maintain a jealous attitude into mature years, not only toward members of their own family, but sometimes even more toward their associates in daily life.

Among adults, the degree of jealousy a person exhibits frequently bears little relationship to his relative status or power as compared with others. The person who has "arrived" and has achieved the outward semblance of success will sometimes begrudge the recognition bestowed upon an underling, much as a big hound bristles when his master pets a forlorn poodle. A person who was intensely jealous of a younger sibling may, as far as he can see, have outgrown this jealousy, but traces of these earlier bitter experiences may remain, even though jealousy is no longer shown toward the brother. An attitude of jealousy persists in an adult, for example, if he feels hurt when another gets recognition or wins good fortune. His feelings may also express themselves in the way he takes sides against some people in his environment who represent, psychologically, objects of jealousy similar to what his brother represented when he was younger.[2]

Recommended Readings

Florence Goodenough's *Anger in Young Children* (1931) contains a wealth of information about children's anger as perceived and reported by their parents. *Children Who Hate* by Fritz Redl and David Wineman (1951) gives a vivid and revealing account of children who had difficulty in managing their aggressive impulses. Although this book deals with an exceptional group of children, it contains many insightful glimpses into the working of hostility in the lives of normal children and adults. The relationship between hostility and anxiety is discussed by Freud and Horney in books cited in preceding chapters. The interplay between love and hostility is discussed in books listed at the end of Chapter Fifteen. Elton B. McNeil's "Psychology and Aggression" (1959) is a richly documented and thought-provoking account of the sources and ramifications of aggressive impulses and the dangers inherent in unresolved hostility.

---

[2] Hilgard (1951), in a study referred to in the discussion of rivalry in Chapter Seven, has offered an interesting account of the way in which the rivalries a mother experienced as a child might, if not resolved, be re-enacted in her relations with her children.

PART FOUR

Expanding Horizons

Mind in the Making

CHAPTER FOURTEEN   Signs of mental growth are apparent to others from the time when a child is born; but his mind is not at the beginning able to establish a record of its own making. As we will note more particularly later in this chapter, most of us have only sketchy memories of what happened during the first three or four years of childhood. In later childhood and adolescence we move more knowingly from one act to the next in the drama of our lives. But much that occurred at the beginning of the drama is beyond the reach of our recollection.

While this lack of recall of our own past complicates the task, there are ways of studying the young child's mental development. We can observe him, and, when he is able to talk, listen to what he says. This approach is simple, but it must be used guardedly, for what we observe will not depend on the child alone but on circumstances in our own lives that influence what we will look for, what we will notice and ignore, and how we will interpret what we see and hear.

Writers on the mental growth of the young child differ considerably in their views—so much so that we may wonder whose mind is being portrayed—the child's or the writer's? We find, at one extreme, the view that the child's mind is a *tabula rasa*, a blank slate (he begins from scratch!); at the other extreme, the view that even at birth the child's psyche is richly endowed with the substance of human experience. This second view was discussed briefly in Chapter Three.

When we study the mental growth of children what we observe will be influenced by our own attitudes and ideas. This underscores a principle that is set forth in many places in this book: When we seek to understand the mental processes of others it is valuable to be as aware as we can of our own mental processes.

Early signs of awareness

At birth or very soon thereafter the child responds to impressions borne in upon him through his sense organs—he responds to light, to sound, to bodily contact, and to the taste and smell of things. Apparently he also experiences sensations from within his own body. He cries when he is hungry, becomes restless and irritable when he has "gas on his stomach," and settles down in his cradle comfortably when he is dry and well-fed. When an infant has the ability to *sense* and to *feel* he possesses two of the elements of which mind is made.

Soon after birth, he shows another essential attribute of the mind: The ability to respond to cues—to respond to a part of a past total stimulus situation as he once did to the total situation. We see this when the child who previously stopped crying only when picked up and held to his mother's breast now ceases his crying when his mother touches his cheek, or when he hears the sound of the door latch as his mother enters his room. The touch, the sound, which were earlier but a feature of the total situation of being fed now (for the moment at least) have the quieting effect that originally was produced only when he actively was fed. A process of *association* has occurred, so that now a part of a situation functions for the whole. Here, in rudimentary form, is a situation analogous to what happens when a driver applies the brakes upon seeing a red light: The light is a symbol of danger and of society's laws. Even though no visible danger lies ahead, and no one orders him to stop, the driver stops.

A further property of the mind appears when the child not only responds to cues or signals in the external environment (such as the click of the door latch) but employs symbols of his own. This occurs, for example, when he forms an impression, retains it in the form of an idea or image, "sees" a dog in his dreams or in his imagination plays with a dog that isn't there. In time, the child's mind becomes a treasury of symbols, enabling him to encompass the present, to relive his past, to project himself into the future. He becomes able in his thoughts to deal with countless circumstances of life without actually encountering them in the flesh. By the use of symbols the child is able, in a sense, to detach himself from the world and yet manipulate it by means of thoughts and fantasies.

To deal with the world through the medium of symbols, several developments are necessary. The child must become able to *discriminate*, to be sensitive to the qualities of the events that impinge on his sense organs—the distinct properties of the sights and sounds and other sensations.

He must be capable of perception—able not only to experience the raw impressions brought to him through his senses, but also to recognize or interpret what these signify. In the process of perception, traces of past experience give meaning to a present experience. The aftereffects of past experiences may be subtle and unnoticed or they may, in time, be retained as conscious *memories,* so clearly defined that an episode of the past can be recalled and reviewed in a detailed way.

MIND, MILK, AND MOTHERING

While we cannot know the exact nature of an infant's mental life, it is apparent that there is a close interplay between his intellectual processes and his bodily needs and activities. When a hungry baby begins to make sucking movements as soon as his mother touches his cheek he is showing the beginnings of a form of perception; we might say that he has the germ of an idea. In this display of mental activity, the workings of his mind are linked to his need for milk. As he grows older, much of his mental activity and his exploration of the world takes place in connection with his need for bodily activity.

Many of a child's first signs of taking notice, perceiving similarities and differences between persons and things, venturing into new forms of mental activity, and using language take place in a setting in which he is being watched and cared for by a person who is significant in his life.

INTERMINGLING OF INTELLECTUAL AND EMOTIONAL

In the child's early life there is reason to believe that the emotional and intellectual aspects of experience are more closely bound into one than will be the case later on. True enough, as long as a person lives his intellect and his emotions are closely linked. But as the child matures, the linkage is not so consistently obvious or direct. The person who as a baby had his desires and perceptions centered on milk is able, as an adult, to write a treatise on milk even though now, as the saying goes, he never touches the stuff.

EXPANDING RANGE OF OBSERVATION AND MANIPULATION

A child begins very early in life to explore and to experiment with things that do not serve his need for food or bodily comfort. He observes and manipulates things as though to do this were rewarding in itself. The mind has an impulse to feed itself.

Tests during the first years of life show that some of the earliest signs of mental growth appear in connection with this impulse to explore. Even before the age of one month, for example, the typical baby, in a notable study by Bayley (1933b) would fix his gaze momentarily on a ring that was placed before him. At 1.2 months the child showed "prolonged regard" for the ring. At 2.9 months he would manipulate the ring if it was brought into contact with his hand. At three months he reached for it, and about a month later he closed in upon it. He showed "sustained inspection" of the ring at about six months, and during the seventh he secured the ring by pulling at the string to which it was attached. Why should he bother about a ring? It satisfies no bodily hunger or thirst, and we might expect him to reach not for the ring but for the adult hand that holds it. Yet he is interested in this impersonal object, and, as other items in Bayley's inventory show, he is interested in a great many other impersonal things. This interest is linked to his endeavors to examine his environment.

In time, the child examines the form and the texture of things, follows the movements of objects, pursues these with his gaze, fingers the parts of an object—such as a bell, and fits forms together. This impulse to investigate is pronounced in infancy and early childhood, and in later years it carries the youngster into many areas of knowledge.

Mental growth as revealed by the development of language

Language is a unique accomplishment of human beings and it represents perhaps the highest form of behavioral development. It is also interlinked with bodily functions necessary for survival; the organs of speech are the organs involved in breathing, eating, and food getting.

There are parallels, too, between language development and motor development: The child begins to babble at about the time he becomes able to sit alone; he speaks his first word at about the time he becomes able to stand alone. The development of language is also tied to the development of his teeth. And, as we have noted in earlier chapters, a child's early progress in speech formation is related to emotional factors, notably to the affection and attention he receives from adults.

EARLY VOCALIZATIONS

During the first two or three weeks of life a child's vocalizations include cries of varying pitch, quality, and loudness. He produces also a number of other sounds, such as grunts, yawns, sighs, an "inspirational crow," and, of course, sounds connected with coughing, sneezing, and belching. During the early days of life many of the sounds uttered by the infant are the aspirate *h* sound (Irwin, 1947a, 1947b). McCarthy (1952a) regards these sounds as possibly linked to the young child's gasping for breath.

The child's earliest vocalizations do not include many sounds which later will appear. Vowel sounds predominate in the child's earliest vocalizations. During the first days of life certain consonant sounds appear while others occur seldom, if at all, until later in the child's development.

EARLY FORMS OF COMMUNICATION

A child uses many utterances in communicating with others long before he acquires the ability to articulate precise words. The median child in one study (Shirley, 1933a) was credited by the examiner with his "first word" at about sixty weeks, but the babies babbled to the examiner at twenty-five weeks, and many of the mothers reported babbling at a considerably earlier age. Inflections and intonations similar to those found in adult speech were also noted in advance of the "first word." Among these expressive utterances were "squeals of delight, strong grunts of pain or disgust, grunts with the rising inflection of a question, guttural barking growls that reminded the examiner of a dog worrying a bone, shouting and calling to attract attention, and calling in scolding or warning tones."

The child usually understands many words and inflections before he himself can use the words. If he has learned to wave in response to "bye-bye," he may similarly respond to "my-my" or even "pooh-pooh," if these words are spoken in the same tone of voice. According to Bühler (1930), the average child reacts to a change in the tone of an adult's voice at two months (as when an adult, hidden behind the child, first speaks in a normal tone and "then suddenly begins to growl" or begins to emit falsetto tones), and distinguishes between angry and friendly talking at six months.

Gesture language, such as pointing, reaching, and movements indicating rejection, aversion, or acceptance, frequently serves as a means of communication long before the child can express himself in words.

THE "FIRST WORD"

As we have seen, much language development has taken place before the baby speaks his "first word." It is difficult to spot the first word. A child may use a certain sound to convey a definite meaning even though that sound cannot be found in any dictionary. For example, one child used the expression "oi-yoi" to ask for water and for no other purpose. The expression functioned as a word even though a stranger would not know what it meant. On the other hand, a child might use an utterance that sounds like a word without apparently intending to use it as a word. Because of ambiguities of this sort, one mother may credit her child with a "first word" where another would not. In the study by Shirley, cited above (in which the children were somewhat above the average of children in the general population), the first comprehensible word was spoken in the examiner's presence at a median age of sixty weeks, but most of the mothers reported that the babies had a vocabulary of two or three words at fifty-two weeks. Twenty-five per cent of the children spoke their first comprehensible words in the presence of the examiner by the age of forty-seven weeks, and 25 per cent had not yet reached this accomplishment by the age of sixty-six weeks. The age at which the first word appeared varied from eight months or less to well over two years.

CONTENT OF CHILD'S EARLY VOCABULARY

Nouns are likely to be most numerous among children's "first words," but there is also a sprinkling of verbs, adverbs, and adjectives. Pronouns usually appear later.

For a long time after he begins to use a few words the child continues to babble and to use a good deal of incomprehensible speech, and during the months immediately following the appearance of articulate words, additional new words may be rather slow in coming.

In a study of the size of vocabularies at different ages, Smith (1941) found an average vocabulary of three words at twelve months, nineteen words at fifteen months, and twenty-two words at eighteen months. At two years the average number of words spoken by children in the study was 272. The averages at later levels follow: 896 words at three years; 1,540 words at four; 2,072 at five; and 2,562 at six (based on only nine subjects). Such vocabulary counts as these are instructive even though they cannot be regarded as establishing a norm for children in general.

Decline in incomprehensible speech. As the child adds more and more words to his repertoire his unrecognizable or incomprehensible utterances begin to decline. However, his ability to pronounce words clearly enough for a stranger to understand them may lag considerably behind the development of a rather large vocabulary. Frequently a child will continue for a time to use a large number of words that can be understood only by members of his family who are familiar with his way of talking.

Spontaneous revision of language habits. The development of language provides many illustrations of the principle of developmental revision of habits as set forth in Chapter Two. In his own good time, if provided with a suitable model, the child will correct his earlier mispronounciations even though no adult is hounding him. Most children who for a time say "free," because that is the best they can do, eventually say "three," and so it is with countless other words. In spite of a great amount of self-correction, however, many children show faulty articulation of certain speech sounds after entering the elementary grades.

Misunderstanding due to faulty articulation. While a child's articulation is still inexact there must be many times when his elders strike him as rather stupid people. Often he will repeat himself over and over, without being understood. For example: A father noticed that there was a dog in the nursery school attended by his three-year-old daughter, and on their way home he asked her about it:

> *Father:* What is the name of the dog at your school?
> *Child:* Way.
> *Father:* Way?
> *Child:* No, Way.
> *Father:* Did you say Way?
> *Child:* No. (*Angrily*) I said WAY!
> *Father:* (*suddenly catching on*) Oh, you mean *Ray?*
> *Child:* Yes, that's what I said.

In a similar vein:

> *Mother:* (*to two- and three-year-old Peggy and Marian*) Oh, look, there's a monkey wearing a red coat!
> *Peggy:* Oh, yook!
> *Marian:* Don't say yook, say wook.

A difference between perceptual and language development appears in the following exchange between two three-year-olds:

> *Joan:* (*picking up a yellow crayon*) This is green and this (*picking up a purple crayon*) is red.
> *Mildred:* No, this is lellow and that one is pulpel.

Development of phrases and sentences. Whn a child first begins to "talk," single words are likely to predominate (although a string of sounds with varying inflections that resemble sentences may be noted before that time). Single words frequently are intended to serve as sentences. As McCarthy has pointed out (1933), the word "mama," with varying inflections and gestures, may mean "mama give me," or "mama look," or "there is mama."

Even the single words thus used are likely to be short ones. Up to the age of two years, one-syllable words constituted about 70 per cent of all the comprehensible words spoken by all the babies in the study by Shirley cited earlier. For several years many youngsters continue to shorten words by dropping a syllable or two so that "inspect" is " 'spect," "conductor" is " 'ductor," and a neighboring "Missus" with four children is a maiden "Miss."

Some of the children in Shirley's study began to use phrases and sentences shortly before the age of eighteen months, but such combinations of words were relatively infrequent before the age of two years. When sentence formation did appear it was noted that children frequently repeated a sentence over and over. One child, for example, at sixty-six weeks, repeated "Wha's dat?" seventeen times during an examination and used only two other sentences.

The increase with age in number of words per remark has been measured with considerable care in several studies. The averages in different studies agree quite closely when based upon a substantially normal or representative selection of children. The average length per remark is considerably higher, however, in the case of bright children. In one of the studies (McCarthy, 1930), in which an analysis was made of fifty consecutive remarks made by each of twenty children at each half-yearly age level from eighteen to fifty-four months (the children were selected from various socioeconomic groups; the average IQ's at the various half-yearly age levels ranged from 103 to 112), it was found that the average number of words per remark increased from 1.2 at eighteen months to 4.6 at fifty-four months. In another study of brighter children, observed mainly on the nursery-school playground and primarily when conversing with one another, the corresponding averages at eighteen months and fifty-four months were 3.7 and 9.5.

As the child's development proceeds there is an increase in the use of sentences that are structurally complete with nouns, verbs, and other parts of speech. There is also an increase in the use of complex and compound sentences, although, throughout the preschool period, simple sentences are far more common than sentences containing dependent or coordinate clauses (Fisher, 1934).

During this period of development, the increase in the child's language repertory is, of course, associated with the development of his mental abilities in general. Among other things, there is an increased use of inflections and verbs, of the past tense (which is infrequent at the age of two years), and of the future tense.

Beyond the nursery-school level, the child's language activities become increasingly complex and they assume increasing importance in connection with the child's schooling. In his reading, and to a lesser extent in his writing, he eventually uses an enormous number of words which he seldom or never uses in speech. His language activities soon become saddled with the need for many associated learnings—spelling, grammar, punctuation, sentence formation, paragraphing.

Increased understanding of word meanings. A child's mastery of language develops not only by adding "new" words but also by an increased understanding of the connotations of "old" words. Many terms that the child uses have relatively little meaning to him, as compared with the meaning intended by the writer or the teacher. Quite a few words have several meanings (for example, the word *run*), which may vary considerably in difficulty. A person's vocabulary as measured by the number of words for which he knows at least one meaning is likely to differ from his vocabulary as measured by the number of words for which he knows all or several meanings (Thevaos, 1951).

Vague meanings. In connection with their schoolwork, many children in the elementary grades meet and use many words without a clear notion of their meaning. In one study it was found that less than 40 per cent of the children below the eighth grade were able to give "reasonably correct" definitions of such terms as "colonists," "taxation," "minister" (ambassador), and "constitution" (Scott and Myers, 1923).

Children's varying levels of understanding are illustrated in an unpublished study by the writer. Among other things, the children were asked to tell what is meant by a strike. To some children, the term was associated only with the verb *to hit*, but most of the children in the fourth through the sixth grades had other associations with the term. Some of them answered little more than: "It's when people break windows and throw stones at the police"; or "It's when people walk outside a shop with signs on their backs with words like 'unfair' on them." These answers, it can be observed, indicate that the child has a notion that a strike means conflict of some sort. Still more comprehension was revealed in an answer such as, "It's when the workers and the bosses have an argument and the workers stop working." At a higher level of understanding the child not only mentioned the fact of a dispute and described the parties to the dispute but also described the issues involved, such as demands for more pay or shorter hours. At a still higher level of comprehension a few children not only described what happened in a strike and the issues that might be involved but also discussed steps that might be taken to terminate a strike and the possible effects on the employer's business or on the cost to the consumer if the strikers won.

Mental and social orientation of the young child as revealed by his language

Once a child has begun to talk, his language development reflects his mental processes, his interests, and his orientation to the material and social world in which he lives.

"I" and "you."   When pronouns appear, various forms of "I" predominate. In a study by Smith (1931) of children aged two to five years, "I" had a frequency of 2,543, as compared with a score of 955 for "you." "I" is especially frequent as compared with other pronouns at the earlier age levels, and it continues to show a high frequency of use throughout the preschool period (and from that point onward, too); but as children advance in age during preschool years, there also is an increase in other forms, such as "we," "you," "she," and "it." Table 16 summarizes the number of times various pronouns were used at half-yearly age levels in the spontaneous speech of two- and three-year-old children (above average in IQ), as recorded during observation of the children on a nursery-school playground.

| TABLE 16 | FREQUENCY OF VARIOUS PRONOUNS IN CHILDREN'S CONVERSATIONS * |

Age in Months	24-29	30-35	36-41	42-47
Number of Children	11	11	11	11
Total Words Spoken During Period of Recording	13,124	22,016	46,624	64,352
Pronouns Used:				
I (my, me, etc.)	1,442	2,991	5,692	5,753
you (your, -self)	94	468	1,770	2,372
we (our, us, etc.)	28	177	406	881
he, she (him, her, etc.)	33	187	437	698
it (it's, -self, etc.)	155	567	1,206	1,485
they (their, them, etc.)	24	58	139	266

* Adapted from A. T. Jersild and R. Ritzman, "Aspects of Language Development: The Growth of Loquacity and Vocabulary," *Child Development* (1938), 9:243-259. Reproduced by permission.

The relatively high frequency of the first-person pronoun in the speech of young children is not difficult to understand. A child's own impulses and desires, activities, pleasures, and pains are more vivid and closer to him than is his comprehension of the personalities and concerns of other people. The prime position held by his own concerns is evident in the child's language—not only through his frequent use of "I" but also through the content and tone of his remarks, questions, and demands. However, from the time he begins to talk, the very fact that he expresses himself at all bespeaks a certain degree of sociability and adaptation to other persons. This point has been emphasized in a study by Fisher (1934) of the content of children's spontaneous speech on the playground. When comprehensible remarks were analyzed according to three categories—self as subject: "I want to be first"; other person as subject: "Mary is coming along"; and thing as subject: "The carriage goes there"—it was found that slightly over one-third of the remarks were of the first-named type. However, while a child's remarks are heavily studded with "I's," there is also a vein of sociability running through them, for they are usually addressed to another person.

One investigator (Piaget, 1932), working with French-speaking children in Europe, distinguishes between "egocentric" and "socialized" speech. In "egocentric" speech there is no endeavor to interchange ideas, to consider the other person's point of view; rather, it is a form of "collective monologue" or "pseudo-conversation." In "socialized" speech, on the other hand, the talker really addresses the listener, considers the other person's viewpoint, and tries to communicate ideas and to share meanings. According to Piaget, young children think and act more egocentrically and share one another's thoughts much less than do adults. One conclusion in Piaget's earlier work was that there is little in the nature of a meeting of minds and of ability to take account of another person's point of view until about the age of seven or eight years. Many other investigators, however, have noted that children are capable of "socialized speech" well before the age of seven or eight (McCarthy, 1946). "Socialized" language in children as young as three or four has been noted by many observers. In general, however, the less mature a child the more limited he will be in understanding or joining in another's point of view.

FACTORS IN THE
DEVELOPMENT AND ACQUISITION OF LANGUAGE

Learning and growth. Changes associated with maturation, as distinguished from practice, play an important role in early language development as we have seen in Chapter Two. It is obviously through a process of learning, however, that a child becomes proficient in his use of language.

Language as related to socioeconomic status and age of associates. Various studies have shown that children of higher socioeconomic status surpass those of lower status in such matters as length of sentences used, frequency of questions, and vocabulary. This difference may be due in part to a higher level of intelligence, but it seems reasonable to assume that children living in homes with a higher socioeconomic level (which usually means a higher educational level) would have advantages even if the factor of intelligence were equalized. There is evidence that children who associate primarily with adults are more precocious in their language development than children who associate mainly with children.

Language of twins and "singletons." Twins have been found to progress less rapidly in their language development from two to five years of age than "singletons" (Day, 1932a, 1932b, and Davis, 1937). Apart from hereditary or congenital factors that might account for this, the phenomenon is probably due in part to environmental factors. Twins seem to be able to communicate with each other by using fewer words than would be required to communicate the same meanings to someone else. Facial expressions, gestures, single words, cryptic murmurings, and the like, which each has learned to understand through close companionship with the other, take the place of conventional words and sentences.

Sex differences. In several investigations girls have been found to surpass boys in many aspects of early language development, such as amount of talking, number of different words used, and use of sentences. The amount of the difference between boys and girls has varied in different studies, and exceptions to a tendency toward superiority of girls have been noted. McCarthy (1953) has discussed the ways in which a girl may have an advantage in language development because she has more access to common interests with the mother than a boy has. At the elementary-school level there usually are far more boys than girls with reading difficulties, but factors in addition to language development as such are involved in this.

Language and intelligence. A positive relationship is usually found between language ability and mental ability, as measured by standard intelligence tests. But since the understanding and use of words play so large a role in many intelligence tests it is difficult to determine just what this relationship means. Does the child earn a good score on a verbal intelligence test because he has a good command of a language or does he have a good command of language because he has good intelligence? Probably it works both ways. The relationship is not so high that early language development can be used to predict later intelligence, except within broad limits.

Bilingualism.   Many children in this country and throughout the world are called upon to adjust to two different languages. Bilingualism poses a problem, both for children whose parents commonly use a foreign language in the home, and—to a lesser extent—for educators who must determine when foreign languages should be introduced into the school curriculum.

As communication between the various peoples of the world continues to expand, it seems likely that learning two or more languages will, for many persons, become commonplace and not merely the fulfillment of a formal academic requirement (as it so often has been in the past).

The ways in which children are called upon to acquire two different languages vary decidedly. A child who lives in a home or community where two languages are spoken is likely, through practical necessity, to become familiar with both, even though he is also likely to become more fluent in one than in the other. There are many interesting combinations of binguality: a child may be able to understand and use both languages; he may be able to speak both, but able to write only one; he may be able to understand both, but able to speak only one.

A youngster who has to acquire two different languages will probably, during early childhood, make slower progress in each than he would make if he were acquiring only one language (Smith, 1931, 1935, 1949).

In a study in which children of native-born American parents were compared with children of foreign-born parents, no reliable differences were found between the two groups in average intelligence or in age-grade status (Arsenian, 1937). In a study of matched children at the preschool level Darcy (1946) found that bilingual children did relatively much better on a "performance" test of intelligence (Adkins Object-Fitting Test) than on a test which involves greater use of language (the Stanford-Binet).

Anastasi and Cordova (1953) found that Puerto Rican children who had suddenly been required to cope with an all-English school situation "insulated" themselves by becoming rather passive and apathetic in their attitudes. This apparently also contributes, in part, to a lower than average performance on mental tests (see Spoerl, 1944).

Somewhat more difficult to probe are the effects bilingualism may have on a child's social and emotional adjustments. A child from a foreign-language background is likely, in some situations, to be teased and cut off from the group. Even when he is not singled out by his peers, the child himself may be self-conscious about his background and language, and may be timid (or sometimes overassertive) when called upon to express himself, especially if he is in the process of transition from one tongue to another, still uses accents and speech forms from the foreign language, or still "thinks" in a foreign language.

The problems faced by children who come from one language background and then are forced at school to learn another are different from those faced by youngsters whose mother tongue is the prevailing language but who take up a foreign language as a school subject. Observers report that children of elementary-school age show a remarkable facility for learning a new language if it is introduced in a "functional" way (such as combining the learning of the French names for common plants with a trip to the fields or combining the learning of the words on a French menu with a meal in a French restaurant). If a youngster is going to be required some time in school to learn a foreign language he probably will have an advantage (especially in learning the correct accent) if he is introduced to the language *before* rather than after he reaches the teens. However, the classical method of teaching a foreign language in school is almost as far removed from the "natural" way in which children acquire the use of a language as anything could be. Nothing in the educational program is more grotesque than a conventional introductory course in a foreign language. If children at home were required to learn their mother tongue in the same way that languages are commonly taught at school many of them might never learn to speak adequately.

Children's questions

Once a child has learned to talk he begins to ask a vast number of questions. He asks questions mainly to satisfy his curiosity, but many other motives come into play such as a desire to establish social contact, or to receive attention, or to gain reassurance, solace, or help (Coan, 1939). Children also use persistent questioning as a form of resistance or as a means of expressing resentment. And questioning sometimes occurs as a general outflow of language spoken for its own sake without apparent expectation of an answer. One of the means a child uses to practice his language is to raise questions.

An increase with age in the proportion of questions in children's language in their play with one another has been noted in observations of nursery-school children (from 2 to 15 per cent in a study by Fisher, 1934). One observer, who recorded a child's language at home, noted that questions occurred at the rate of thirty-one per hour at thirty-eight months (Brandenburg, 1915), and another observer noted that questions comprised 2 per cent of a child's language at two years and about a fourth to a fifth at ages three to eight years. It is clear that a youngster, if given the chance, will raise a staggering number of questions during a week or month.

The questions raised by children vary according to their language abilities and interests. Thus, when a child is in the "naming stage" in his language development he is likely to ask many "what" questions to learn what things are and to acquire names for them. The youngster likewise goes through a "Who is that?" period during which he wants to know the names of all people who pass by. Such questions usually precede "why" questions which deal with causal relations in everyday happenings or with reasons for another's behavior.

In an analysis of 3,650 questions asked by seventy-three children aged three to twelve years, as recorded by parents, 87.8 per cent of the questions seemed to arise from something in the immediate situation, as distinguished from questions about remembered or remote events (which constituted 10.8 per cent; 1.4 per cent could not be accounted for). A novel occurrence was more likely to provoke a long series of logically related questions than an ordinary situation, but the latter also frequently provoked such a series of questions. Boys asked more questions involving causal explanations than did girls, while girls exceeded boys in questions regarding social relations (Davis, 1932).

The following illustrations of questions asked by preschool children (above average in intelligence) are from data collected by Rust in a study of the growth of children's concepts.[1]

The following conversation began after the child (who was four and a half years old) had been told a story about a six-year-old girl:

Child: I'm four, aren't I?
Mother: Yes, four years.
Child: What's a year?
Mother: (*Explains.*)
Child: Is that a long time?
Mother: Quite a long time.
Child: How long?
Mother: It's hard to explain, but it is a lot of days, 365, and that's many.
Child: Well, but how long?
Mother: Well, well, you know when it was Christmas.
Child: Oh, yes, and I had a tree, and once I had a tree in the corner and once I had it on the table.
Mother: Well, that was twice, and it takes a year to have a Christmas. You see we have Christmas, then the time between that Christmas and the time between the next is a year.
Child: Well, that's a very long, long time. When I was very small we had a Christmas. Is a year a birthday?
Mother: Well, you have one birthday, then the time between is called a year, then you have the next birthday.

---

[1] M. M. Rust, *The Growth of Children's Concepts of Time, Space, and Magnitude,* unpublished (Teachers College, Columbia University). Reproduced by permission.

Child: Yes, three then four—then five— Say, how old are you?
Mother: Thirty.
Child: How did you stretch up?

This turn in the conversation appeared to suggest another line of questions to the child. She immediately continued:

Child: When I'm thirty will I be a mother?
Mother: If you have a baby you will.
Child: Do all womans have babies?
Mother: No.
Child: Why?
Mother: Some are not strong enough, some are too busy doing other things—some . . .
Child: Well, in three or six weeks when I'm thirty, I shall have a baby— Where do babies come from?
Mother: Seeds.
Child: Where do the seeds come from?
Mother: The father and the mother.
Child: Where does the father keep his?
Mother: They're in his body.
Child: Oh, is he keeping them warm same as the mother does the baby?
Mother: He doesn't have them there to keep them warm, but because they belong there.
Child: Well, when I'm six weeks I'll marry you because you're so cute.
Mother: But— (*Father comes in.*)
Child: Hello, Daddy. Did you buy me something? (*No further questioning.*)

The following questions and comments of a four-year-old child deal in part with concepts of time:

Child: Is this today?
Teacher: Yes, why?
Child: Well, is tomorrow tomorrow?
Teacher: Yes.
Child: Well, Sunday is my birthday.
Teacher: Do you know what date that is?
Child: Yes, it's March 5 and I will be four years old. That's this many (*counts down four buttons on his coat*).
Teacher: That is right, Frank.
Child: Some day I will be this old (*stretches out his arms at full length*).

The problem of time was the subject of the questions of another child, aged four and a half.

Child: What time is it?
Mother: 6:30.
Child: What means that?
Mother: What do you mean?
Child: What means 6:30?

Mother:	Well, when it's evening it means time for you to think of bed and time for me to get dinner.
Child:	How long is 6:30?
Mother:	Just one minute, then it is 6:31.
Child:	Is a minute big?
Mother:	No, very short.
Child:	Just a little bit like this? (*Demonstrates with finger and thumb and a tiny pinch.*)
Mother:	I'll show you with my watch.
Child:	(*Watches watch for a minute or two, then speaks.*) Do you like me, Mummy? (*Dismisses subject of time.*)

The same child, on another occasion, ended a series of questions concerning the days of the week with the query, "Where does time go?"

Many of the questions raised by young children are difficult if not impossible to answer. Sometimes an adequate answer would go beyond the child's comprehension or willingness to listen (for example, an answer to this question by a three-year-old: "Where is the people in the TV set?" or "What makes the subway run?"). Sometimes the adult is at a loss how to put his answer (for example, if the question asked is: "Who made God?").

Children's questions may spring from motives more pressing than intellectual curiosity. There may be fear, worry, or uneasiness. A child who has been frightened by an animal may ask about any new thing that he sees, "Has it got a mouf? Does it bite?" The child of a mother who works away from home a good deal may ask, repeatedly, on seeing an unaccompanied adult or a child, "Where is his mamma?" A three-year-old boy raised many questions after the slaughter of two pigs that had been reared by his father since they were little. "Why did you butcher Blackie and Whitie?" (the pigs). When told (as he had been told repeatedly beforehand) that pigs are butchered for meat when they are big and fat, he asked, "Will me and—(naming his sister) be butchered when we are big?" On later days he asked such questions as, "Do people close their eyes when they are dead?" After one such question, he asserted firmly, "When I be dead I won't close my eyes and I'm going to run around." (In this remark he seems to show resistance to the idea of death.) Apparently it was the idea of death rather than the demise of the two particular pigs that bothered him, for he later identified parts of the pigs at the table and ate with great relish.

The following (also from Rust) is another example of a child who was puzzled about death:

Child (four and a half years old): Mummy, what means a dead mother?
Mother: A woman that has died and does not walk or talk any more.
Child: But what will the children do?

Mother: Well, if a mother should die, the father would take care of them and maybe an aunt.
Child: Will you be a dead mother some day?
Mother: Why yes, though I don't expect to be for a long time.
Child: A *very* long time?
Mother: Yes.
Child: But I don't want you to die; I want you here like this.
Mother: Well you will probably be quite grown-up before that happens.
Child: A *long* time?
Mother: Yes.
Child: But what *means* dead, mummy?
Mother: Well, your heart stops beating and you lie still without breathing.
Child: And what do you do with the talking part—you know, the inside talk?
Mother: I'm not sure, but some people think you live in another world and, of course, some don't.
Child: I guess we do (*excitedly*). Yes! And then you die in a *long,* long time—a *very* long time, and then I die and we both hug each other and then you won't have any wrinkles— Oh, look at that cute pussy? Isn't she darling? (*Runs off.*)

Often a child will continue to repeat a question after an adult has given an answer. Such repetition may be aimed at getting attention, but it may also mean the child is still troubled. To answer a child's question it is, of course, first necessary to understand the question. Sometimes the meaning of a question is not obvious. If an adult would understand the more elusive questions he must prepare to be sympathetic, patient, and genuinely interested. Some questions cannot be understood without knowledge of what has gone before in the child's life. For example, a child might ask again and again during an afternoon, "Are you going to put the car in the garage?" This repetition becomes more understandable if the parent realizes that the question really means, "Are you going to stay home or are you going out this evening?"

In trying to fathom the meaning of a child's question it is well, on the other hand, not to read too much into his inquiry. An example of this occurred in a home in which there was a two-and-a-half-year-old girl who had just received a new rubber doll. She held it up for both her father and mother to see, saying, "See my baby?" Then she said, "Where baby come from?" The father thought the child was asking her first question about the origin of babies, but before he could gather his wits to give an answer worthy of this great occasion the mother simply said, "Woolworth's." This answer suited the child perfectly, for all she apparently wanted to know was whether the doll had been bought by her parents in the store or had been mailed to her as a gift.

Capacity for attention and concentration

As a child grows older he normally acquires increased ability to give sustained attention to an intellectual task. Except in response to urgent physical demands, the infant's concentration span usually is brief. When he fixes his eyes on an object his regard is likely to be fleeting at first and then to lengthen with time. Of course, the span of concentration is no unitary ability, for it will vary in different situations and it depends not simply on the child's energies but upon his interests and motives. For example, as we have noted in earlier chapters, at a certain phase of his development a child will concentrate at length on walking, or on repeating certain sounds, but his attention might flit hither and yon in other activities.

An exact measure of how the attention span increases with age is almost impossible to obtain, for results vary with different children and in different situations. It is possible, however, to trace the rise in duration of attention in some situations. In one study children were shown a jack-in-the-box and asked to watch it until it was opened. The experimenter timed each child until he looked away. On the average, children at the age of four kept their eyes fixed on the object for eight seconds; at five years the average was seventeen seconds; and at six years, twenty-eight seconds (Miles, 1933). In a somewhat different approach, children were timed in a task such as taking colored paper disks out of a box and laying them in rows across a table. On the simplest task the average duration of attention ranged from a little over eight minutes at three years to a little over nine minutes at five years (the differences between three-, four-, and five-year-olds were not significant, and there were large individual differences).

Another approach to measuring children's interest span has been through observation of the amount of time they spend on a project, without interruption or turning to something else, during their free play. In studies such as these great variations have been found, although an increase with age in staying power has been noted.

While children, as a rule, become willing as they grow older to concentrate their attention for longer periods of time on tasks assigned to them, they vary greatly in their persistence. From about the second year of life until they enter school, the time they devote to a project on their own accord is likely to be more closely related to the strength of their interest in the particular thing they are doing than to their age (see Moyer and Gilmer, 1955).

Childhood memories

With the development of memory the child becomes able to retain a past impression and to revive it, without having to relive the original experience. Through his memories an older child keeps a record, as it were, of his own history. The childhood memories of an adult form a bridge between his present and the view he has of his past; and an adult also draws on his childhood memories when he tries to interpret the experiences of children.

In this section we will first consider some of the earliest evidences of remembering, then we will go on to discuss the nature and meaning of the memories that come to mind when older children and adults try to recall the events of their earlier years.

EARLY SIGNS OF REMEMBERING

During the first few years of life children remember a vast number of happenings from day to day which they do not recall some years later in telling their earliest memories.

An early sign of the ability to remember appears when the child ceases crying at the sound of someone's approach or adjusts himself to being lifted on seeing a particular person. Other evidences, such as the ability to discriminate between familiar and unfamiliar objects and persons, come later. We see signs of remembering when a child keeps his attention fixed upon an object that has disappeared from sight, or turns his attention back to a task that has been interrupted some moments before.

The following shows how a child is able to retain and to act upon a past impression (without having any recollection, as a young adult, that the happening took place).

> A girl aged ten-and-a-half months, while visiting her grandparents, watched as her father hid a cookie under the cushion of a sofa. The girl then was taken from the room for three minutes. When she returned she immediately crept to the sofa, lifted the cushion and got the cookie. Some weeks later when she again visited her grandparents she again went to the sofa as though expecting to find a cookie and she whimpered and was apparently disappointed at not finding any. The child clearly was "remembering," and acting out an expectation built on past experiences.

Such remembering takes place on a tremendous scale in the early months and years of life, before a person begins to formulate the memories that persist into later years.

EARLY MEMORIES

The "early memories" of a person's life—the events from early childhood that he is able to recall as an older child or adult—are significant both from a personal and a scientific point of view. (If the reader has not already speculated about his childhood memories, it would be interesting, before going on, to make a brief written record of some of the earliest happenings he can recall.) If a written record were made of the experiences of early life it would fill many volumes, but usually what we ourselves remember runs to only a few paragraphs or pages.[2]

TIMING OF EARLY MEMORIES

There have been claims stating that individual persons have recollected happenings that occurred early during the first year of life, even extending as far back as the day of birth. Before such claims could be accepted, however, further verification would be required.

In one study (Dudycha and Dudycha, 1933) reports were obtained from college students concerning the earliest experiences they could remember, and then an effort was made through the help of parents and others to verify memories and the age at which the remembered incidents occurred. The average age referred to in these earliest memories was three years and seven months. Four per cent of the earliest memories dated back to the first year of life, 19 per cent to the second, 37 per cent to the third, 38 per cent to the fourth and 2 per cent to the fifth.

In another study (Waldfogel, 1948) college students were asked to record "all the experiences of which they had any knowledge or recollection up to the time of their eighth birthday" and to state as accurately as possible, within the nearest year, the age at which the remembered experience occurred. They were given eighty-five minutes to write their reports and later another eighty-five minute period. At one extreme was a person who reported only 10 memories and at the other extreme one who reported 137; the average number of memories was about 50. Relatively few of the experiences that were recalled extended back to the third year or earlier. There was an increase in memories attributed to the fourth year and a still larger number assigned to the fifth year.

DEVELOPMENTAL FACTORS
LIMITING RECALL OF EARLY EXPERIENCES

There are many conditions that make it difficult for a young child to formulate his experiences in such a way that he could recall them in later years.

---

[2] For reviews of studies of early memories see Thompson and Witryol (1948), and Charry (1959).

First, we may note that what an adult remembers is often, to a large degree, an abstraction—an image or *idea* of what happened. The young child tends to think in concrete terms. He does not possess what has been called "the abstract faculty" to the same degree as an older person, and this circumstance limits his recall of early experiences.

Second, in childhood as in later years, the events most likely to be recalled have an *emotional* content, yet it is difficult to revive this emotional content. We can observe this when an adult, for example, gives his recollections of an automobile accident. He can give a vivid picture of the physical events that struck his senses, what he saw and heard, but it is more difficult to relive or vividly portray the terror that he felt (although he can now repeat calmly that he was "scared to death"). He can tell of the sharp pain he felt, but the memory of pain is usually a memory of the idea of pain rather than a renewal of the pain itself. It is probably more difficult for a young child than for an adult to abstract and recall the intellectual picture or idea of an experience which was predominantly an emotional experience.

Third, in the mental operations of older children and adults *language* is a very important tool, but the young child is lacking in the ability to formulate his experiences by way of "inner speech" or by way of the kind of language that is used when a person communicates something to others. There is an interesting parallel between the course of language development and the amount recalled from early childhood (Waldfogel, 1948).

Fourth, the younger the child the less likely it is that an experience will be linked to a large network of ideas, and this would limit his recall. Most of our day to day and year to year recollections as older persons are associated with the patterns of our thoughts, including our plans and purposes, our notions of what preceded and what followed, what was the cause and what might be the effect, and so forth. Except for highly unusual and striking happenings, we are most likely to remember the things that fit significantly into the framework of our thought. The young child also has his plans and his beginning notions of cause and effect, but it is likely that many of the experiences that befall him are not so clearly interwoven with a larger context of thinking.

So far we have touched upon reasons why, from a developmental point of view, the memories a child is able to tuck away and recall when he is older are rather scanty. But we still face another question: Why, in view of the thousands of things the child might remember does he single out some events and not others? This question leads to a consideration of other aspects of early memories and the conditions which might influence them.

EMOTIONAL QUALITY OF EARLY MEMORIES

Emotional experiences encompassing the whole range of human feeling are imbedded in our early memories. Joy is an emotion that appears frequently, representing about 30 per cent of the total in one study (Waldfogel, 1948), and fear was next frequent. Other commonly named emotions are anger, grief, and excitement. In an analysis of *earliest memories only*, fear was the most frequent emotion, followed by joy and anger; other emotions recalled were wonder (awe), and sorrow and disappointment (Dudycha and Dudycha, 1933). While it may be easy enough to label a certain early memory as one of joy or fear or some other emotion, closer examination is likely to reveal a very complex emotional content. This point will be illustrated later in this discussion.

"MEMORY OPTIMISM" AND "MEMORY PESSIMISM"

Some persons recall a larger proportion of unpleasant than of pleasant happenings, but the "memory optimists" tend to outnumber the "pessimists." In one of the studies cited above about 50 per cent of the memories were pleasant, 30 per cent unpleasant and 20 per cent neutral (Waldfogel, 1948). Pleasant memories are also likely to predominate when older persons record recollections from their recent lives, say, the past two or three weeks. In a study by the writer (one of many investigations dealing with this theme) college students not only recalled more pleasant than unpleasant events from a recent period in their lives but also, when asked three weeks later to give an account of this same period, they had forgotten relatively more of the unpleasant than of the pleasant events cited in their first reports (Jersild, 1930).

MEMORIES FROM CHILDHOOD AS COMPARED WITH CHILDHOOD BEHAVIOR AS VIEWED BY OTHERS

An interesting approach to the study of early memories is to compare what an adult recalls about his childhood with records of his actual behavior (at least as interpreted at the time by others). This approach was used in a study of 50 adults, with an average age of twenty-six years, who had been observed while they were young children (Jayaswal, 1955). In a nursery school and later in other settings the behavior of these adults had been rated on an Ascendance-Submission scale. Now, as adults, they were asked to rate themselves on an adaptation of that scale, checking those items on the scale which they recalled as descriptive of them when they were children not more than six years old. These self-ratings revealed that in 52 per cent of the cases the recall of childhood behavior (as seen by others) was inaccurate and unreliable; in 32 per cent of the cases the recall was partially inaccurate; and in 18 per cent of the cases the older persons' recall of their childhood corresponded to their behavior as observed at the time.

Why, we might ask, did these adults do so poorly in recalling childhood characteristics which, according to observers at the time, were clearly evident? Part of the answer is that this behavior took place at a time of life which adults ordinarily do not remember very well. But other factors were probably at work, too. Even at the time, many of these adults, as children, probably did not perceive their behavior in the same light as it was perceived by adult observers. An "ascendant" child who barges into things, asserts himself, aggressively demands to be seen and heard, may not see himself as being particularly pushy. (Even an ascendant "adult" who charges into a group meeting, monopolizing most of the discussion, may not see himself as he appears to others.) Whether a child (or an adult) is "ascendant" or "submissive" he may be so absorbed in his need for attention or in his fear of asserting himself that he is quite unaware of the objective aspects of his behavior. When older persons do not remember certain aspects of their behavior as children the reason may be that, from their view of things, there wasn't anything in particular to remember. A neat example of this appeared in a report of early memories from which an example is cited later in this chapter. A woman who recalled the episode of polishing her grandfather's shoes at the age of four was, at that early age, able to read, an accomplishment which to her parents was important and pleasing. Yet she had no later recollection of this achievement. Here we touch upon an aspect of childhood experience which we have discussed earlier in this book, namely, that the nature of a child's experience cannot be judged simply by noting what he openly does, or by what others openly do to him, or by what others perceive in him: The nature of the experience depends in part on his own perception of what is taking place and on the importance, to him, of what happened.

CONDITIONS THAT INFLUENCE FORGETTING
AND FACILITATE RECALL

Since pleasant memories quite commonly outnumber unpleasant ones, should we conclude that more pleasant happenings actually occurred or that children have a tendency to blot out the unpleasant? And, if the latter is the case, do children differ from older persons in this respect? In considering the memory fragments an adult recalls from childhood as compared with all that he might conceivably recall Freud (1938a) says "we can only ask ourselves in amazement" why just this or that particular detail should escape oblivion.

According to Freud (1938b) during the first years of life there is a kind of blotting out of memory, a "peculiar amnesia which veils from most people (not from all) the first years of their childhood, usually the first six or eight years." While the particular detail that is recalled might not be important in itself, it represents something significant. Freud speaks of early memories as "screen memories" in the sense that the particular event recalled is a disguise behind which there lies something more important. The important latent or hidden meaning may be represented "in the memory by something that seems quite trivial." Freud implies that most people (although not all) need the help of an analyst in order to uncover memories and the meaning of the memories hidden behind the screen.

Whether we agree or disagree with Freud's views in this matter, it seems that the usual person does not commonly try to penetrate very deeply into the meanings of his or her early memories. A moderately intelligent person with an interest in exploring his own mind (or in exploring another's) can probably go considerably farther than people usually go. By a process of free association, "letting the mind go," it is possible to start with a fragment of memory and then to bring forth many other memories and many additional thoughts and feelings connected with the fragment. In the process, a person may discover that a particular early memory takes on a different meaning, or takes on several added meanings. Here are some examples, from a study by the writer, of additional ideas that emerged when persons were asked to make only a brief and limited effort to go beyond the details they gave at first in reporting a distinct early memory. (The interviewer's questions are given in parentheses.)

I remember a very happy time I once had with my grandfather when I was about four years old. I polished his shoes and he was very pleased with me. (*Anything else?*) When I think back to that time I also remember that I was vying with my brother with a feeling that I could never match him. He got a lot of praise from my grandfather and maybe that made grandfather's praise for me mean so much. (*Anything else?*) As I think of it now, I was getting praise for being a very good girl, not for being a bright and witty person like my brother, and I guess the praise I got was like triumph in the midst of defeat. At any rate, I do know that it has been hard for me to feel the confidence in myself that I really have a right to feel. (*Any further thoughts?*) Yes, a memory of something I don't remember except in a sketchy way. When I was four I was able to read; I definitely know this because my family moved to another place when I was four and I was able to read before we moved. I don't remember how or when I learned—just the fact that I was able to do it.

I remember being terribly afraid of a steam threshing rig, especially the engine, the clanking noise, the big wheels with iron treads, the deep marks the wheels made in the road, and the whistle and the smoke. (*Any other thoughts or feelings about it?*) Yes, this fear is connected in my mind with a fear of death and punishment. The smoke and noise remind me of the first idea I had about hell, full of flames and horrible sounds.

And the man who ran the rig, he was called "The Thresher"; when I think of that I think of a thrashing, getting a beating from my father for being bad. (*Anything else?*) Yes, the great joy I felt several years later on a farm at threshing time when I was able to walk right up to the machine and touch it without being afraid.

I remember being terribly embarrassed at a wedding when I had a bowel movement in my pants. I had on a new white suit. I stayed out behind a grove of trees. I don't remember how it ended. (*Any other thoughts or feelings?*) Now, as I look back, I wonder how this happened. I couldn't manage the buttons but I guess I was ashamed to go and ask my mother for help.

In these examples, further thought not only led to additional material, but even the emotional quality of the early memory as first formulated, underwent a change. One of the "pleasant" memories brought back a recollection of sibling rivalry and a feeling of inadequacy, which was somewhat painful; this led to another memory (being able to read at an early age), which somehow had little feeling attached to it—though ordinarily we might expect this to be a pleasant recollection. The memory of fear of a threshing rig was interwoven with a kind of foreboding and guilt and topped off with a recollection of a feeling of triumph. A memory of shame was left dangling with a note of reproach against the mother. If those who reported these memories explored further, other emotional qualities, both open and hidden, might be revealed. A large complex of thought and feeling would probably be disclosed in connection with most of the memories of early childhood if we could delve into the background out of which they arose.[3]

INFLUENCE OF PRESENT MOODS
AND PERSONALITY TRENDS ON RECALL OF THE PAST

What we remember from the past is influenced not only by what actually happened but also by the manner in which a past event was in keeping with a person's mood at the time or with his present mood and outlook on life (Adler, 1937; Kadis, 1957). According to this theory, the one who has a cheerful view of life would be more likely to remember happy experiences, and the one who feels that life has treated him unjustly would remember grievances, and so on.

In one study of college students it was found that those who rated themselves as "insecure," reporting feelings of isolation or rejection or uniqueness, reported more unpleasant childhood memories than did "secure" persons who, as college students had a tendency toward opti-

---

[3] Author's note to readers who followed my earlier suggestion of briefly jotting down some of their own early memories: You might find it interesting at odd moments to let your mind play around with these memories, noting whether a particular memory leads to other currents of feeling and thought, as in the examples above.

mism, happiness, and self-acceptance (Purcell, 1952). Insecure persons described significantly more of their memories as being unpleasant than did the secure persons. Low but positive correlations have also been found between the percentage of unfavorable childhood memories reported by older children and the extent to which they rate themselves unfavorably on a test of personal adjustment (Pattie and Cornett, 1952).

The relationship between a person's present view of himself (as measured by his response to a personality test) and his tendency to take a somewhat similar view of his past (as indicated by his childhood memories) is not so close that a record of a person's early memories can be used as a reliable measure of his personality in the present. Yet the fact that there is some correspondence between present ratings and recollections of the past suggests that the particular events which a person recalls from an earlier period of his life may be biased in keeping with his present frame of mind.

In interpreting a person's recall of his past it is important to bear in mind that a relationship of this kind may exist. In keeping with this, a four-year-old child who already feels unfairly treated may remember a scolding which another child would forget. A person who in childhood or later has felt anxious about sex may recall sex experiences which another might not recall. A parent who feels guilty about his performance as a parent may remember, with a twinge of self-accusation, episodes in his dealings with his children which another parent would neither regret nor remember.

It is especially important to consider the fact that a person's present state of mind may have an influence on what he reports about his own or another's past when we try to reconstruct a child's history, or a parent's account of his child at a time of stress. Frequently it is during a time of special stress, *after* a misfortune has occurred—such as trouble at school, or a delinquent act, or severe mental disturbance—that professional workers question a child or his parents about his past. The story a child tells about himself when he is in a state of distress might differ in significant ways from what he ordinarily would tell. The same may hold true when parents are questioned at a time when they are especially anxious about a child. If they feel defensive or guilty, or feel a need to place the blame on others or on themselves, the "facts" they report may be selected and colored accordingly.

There are two further considerations concerning the nature of what people remember from the past. One is that what a person selects to report may be influenced by the views of the person to whom he is reporting. A person telling about his past to a psychologist who emphasizes the importance of sex in personality development may come forth with a good deal of material about sex, while a person recounting his past to one who emphasizes the importance of sibling relationships may come forth with a good deal of material pertaining to that topic (Bach, 1952). The tendency to suit what is said to what a person believes the other person expects to hear may play curious tricks even in connection with "memories" that are reported a few months apart. During group therapy sessions with adults, Bach made a recording of what members of the group actually reported as "memory statements" about attitudes and experiences relating to parents, siblings, and childhood sex experiences, and these statements were transcribed on cards. After the elapse of some time the subjects were given packs of cards containing memory statements and were asked to sort out those that applied to them and those that did not. In this sorting 25 per cent of the statements which, according to actual recordings various individuals had reported as their own personal memories, were placed in a pile representing statements which were now considered false or as not touching upon their past lives.

RESIDUAL EFFECTS OF EARLY EXPERIENCES

Before we proceed to our final summary of this discussion of early memories, one further statement should be added, namely that even though a person connot distinctly remember a childhood experience, it may still leave a residue in his mind. An example of the manner in which impressions can leave their mark on a child is shown in an interesting study by Burtt (1932, 1937, 1941). Passages from Sophocles in the original Greek were read to a child (who had no other contact with Greek) when he was no more than fifteen months old; twenty lines were read to him daily for a period of three months, and at the end of each period a new selection was read. This reading was continued until the child was three years old. When he was eight and a half years old, the same passages, as well as new ones, were read to him; but he was now required to memorize the lines. To commit to memory new passages that never before had been read to him required an average of 435 repetitions, while an average of only 317 repetitions was needed for passages that had been read to him when he was a baby. Thus he showed the effect of past impressions, even of material that had been read to him between the ages of fifteen and eighteen months.

Again, when this child was fourteen years old, he undertook to memorize Greek passages, some of which had been read to him before the age of three and some of which were new. This time, the difference between the effort required to learn "old" and "new" material was appreciable but much decreased. A final check was then made when the child was eighteen years old. At this age no difference was apparent in the number of repetitions required to master new and old passages.

We have seen that memories from early life, and memories from later periods of life leave large areas of experience unrecalled and are influenced not only by what happened in the past but also by present moods and needs. How, then, can we assess the meaning of early memories and how can we employ them in understanding the childhood of others or in seeking to understand our own childhood? Several answers suggest themselves.

First, while it is true that early memories are fragmentary and sometimes seem trivial, it also is apparent that many of these memories can be verified as accounts of actual happenings. Moreover, a large proportion of these happenings had a strong emotional impact: great joy, grief, intense fear in a situation that actually threatened the child's well-being. A full record of a person's experience would probably disclose many other joyful or frightening or grief-producing experiences which are not recalled, but this does not deny the significance of those that are remembered.

Second, even the memories that do not faithfully reflect the past have a meaning. They do not spring from nowhere. If we could examine them, we would probably discover that they fit into a picture which a person already had formed of himself when he was young, or had formed later, and wishes to maintain. So the memories may provide an important clue to understanding an individual's personality.

Third, the fact that the particular memories a person brings forth from his past may be influenced by later circumstances in his life tells us that we cannot reconstruct an individual's personality development by a literal interpretation of what he tells about his childhood. But this, again, does not detract from the importance of the memories that come forth. It means that instead of regarding them as stagnant pools in the graveyard of the past we must view them as currents in the continuing and changing stream of life. The personality of any human being is in the making, and in a process of remaking, as long as there is life. Circumstances that arise at any period of life may also give new meaning and substance to what has happened in the past. And the past is also being shaped and reshaped by the underlying hope or despair in a person's outlook on what the future might bring.

Fourth, while we must recognize that memories from childhood usually consist of only a few sketchy fragments we can also recognize that the capacity for remembering is not necessarily limited to these fragments. As noted earlier in this chapter, a person may be able, by a process of free association, to enlarge on them. One thought leads to another, and one memory may call forth many others. In this process, a person may see a particular memory in a new light, and get a new glimpse into the contents of his own mind and into the making of the mind of a child.

From experimentation to planning

Many youngsters who ultimately will prove to be adept at abstract thinking and abstract planning begin their thinking, as it were, by way of their hands and feet. In building a boat or a wooden shelf they combine thinking with fingering. They do not lay out a careful plan or make exact measurements in advance for each piece. Instead, they are likely to proceed to cut, saw, fit, and hammer as they go. As a result, many pieces are discarded, and shelves are of unequal length or width. If something so advanced as the fitting of a door with hinges is undertaken, two hinges may on first trial be so attached that they operate in opposition of each other.

This is the time when the young carpenter seems to waste good lumber, the young painter seems to waste good paint. But actually the waste is in many ways similar to the spills a youngster goes through when learning to ride a bicycle. Many children go through a phase of wanting to construct, and even to create or improvise with things before they have reached the phase in which they can give careful thought to dimensions, measurements, and proportions. To punish a child or to give him materials only on condition that he thinks before he acts and measures before he saws may simply discourage him from further effort.

The way in which the young child's curiosity and efforts to understand the world about him are linked with his total activity as a person has been observed by Almy (1949):

> The learning of younger children so obviously involves activity. They pull the covers off all the pots and carefully fit them on again; they climb to the top of a chest to discover the contents of a basket they can barely see from below; they sort out enough knives, forks, and spoons to set the family supper table; they dig out recently planted seeds to see what has happened to them; they unscrew the loose bolts on their tricycles. With each episode they acquire a little more understanding of the world in which they live.

Often, however, the efforts of the eager little scholar get a serious setback when he begins to go to school (which is supposed to be the seat of learning). As Almy puts it, "In many first grades, however, there is not only little opportunity to move about and explore, but the materials provided actually offer the child less chance to feel, touch, taste, take apart, and put together than he has in his own kitchen or backyard."

Recommended Readings

Jean Piaget has written the most thought-provoking books on children's reasoning. Among his earlier works are *Judgment and Reasoning in the Child* (1928) and *The Language and Thought of the Child* (2nd edition, 1932). Later works include *The Origins of Intelligence in Children* (1952), *Play, Dreams and Imitation in Childhood* (1951), *The Construction of Reality in the Child* (1954), *The Growth of Logical Thinking from Childhood to Adolescence: An Essay on the Construction of Formal Operations* (1958).

A thorough review and discussion of children's acquisition of language can be found in Dorothea McCarthy's "Language Development in Children" (1954).

The World
of Fantasy and Dreams

CHAPTER FIFTEEN   Through make-believe, daydreams, and other imaginative activities the child is able vastly to extend the reaches of his world. In his imagination he leaps beyond boundaries of time and space, and he performs feats beyond the limits of his actual strength.

A child's imagination plays an important role in all aspects of his development. In the intellectual sphere, he is able through his imagination to experiment and explore, to work with ideas without being bound by the rules of logic. In the emotional sphere, he can give play to desires, fears, hopes, and aggressive impulses. He frequently uses his imagination in his social development, for much of his play with other youngsters takes place in make-believe settings. And there is interaction also between a child's imaginative activity and his motor development: Many

important motor skills are acquired or are practiced in play activities that have a high imaginative content, such as doll play and housekeeping. Make-believe also often supplies the plot or purpose when the child practices such motor activities as climbing, swinging, or riding a bicycle.

Early manifestations

The child's ability to imagine appears at least as early as his ability to talk, and some children enter into complicated imaginative ventures before they are able to talk. A child of eleven months, who was observed by the author, provides an example of imaginative behavior preceding the ability to talk.

> In the course of her creepings about the house this child discovered the garbage pail and she also discovered that she was not supposed to pry into it. Once, as her mother was watching, she started to creep across the kitchen floor toward the pail. When her mother gave a warning sound the child stopped for a moment, then crept a short distance, then looked up at her mother, laughing heartily. Again she made a false start and again she looked up, laughing merrily. She obviously was getting great sport out of this game of pretending to go to the garbage pail while her mother looked on. This episode occurred several months before she combined two or more words in her speech.

Another early sign of imaginative activities appears when children imitate older persons. At ten months, for example, a child went through the motions of "telephoning" with a toy phone belonging to his older sister. Similarly, a child about a year old went through such motions as "feeding" a doll and putting on Daddy's hat while dragging his briefcase toward the door.

Make-believe becomes more apparent after a child learns to talk. Findings at the preschool level show that imaginative play increases during the period between two and four years. In one study in which records were made of children's language it was found that 1.5 per cent of children's remarks at twenty-four to twenty-nine months of age were imaginative in character; at forty-two to forty-seven months the percentage of imaginative remarks was 8.7 (Burnham, 1940). In another study, in which language as well as overt behavior was recorded, there was a sixfold increase in frequency of imaginative episodes from two and a half years to four years (Markey, 1935).

Themes of make-believe

In addition to changes in the amount of make-believe activity, there are changes in the themes with which children deal. In one study (Markey, 1935) it was observed that much of the imaginative activity of children under the age of three fell into three categories: (1) personification, such as talking to inanimate objects; (2) make-believe use of materials, such as calling a slide a train, drinking out of an empty cup; and (3) participation in make-believe situations, such as in a game of putting out a fire or taking a bath. At the age of three and over, make-believe uses of materials were among the most typical imaginative activities. But after the age of three and a half years, longer make-believe situations were devised, including complicated dramatic play. The younger child most frequently engages in imaginative activity revolving around specific materials which he can see and touch, but the older preschool child frequently throws himself into make-believe situations in which he himself supplies the setting, the necessary equipment, and the drama in which it is used. He uses and enjoys treasures which no Midas could supply, and, young as he is, he anticipates that great faculty that older persons have for building a world *as if* which differs from the world *as is,* yet sometimes comes close to telling what is yet to be.

Emotional content of make-believe

A child's imaginings, which are often quite extravagant, reflect his emotional life. The school-age child who has only a dime in his pocket is a millionaire in his daydreams. The young cowboy has not one horse but a whole herd (although he would probably be glad to exchange all his make-believe horses for one real little pony). A youngster expresses affection and sympathy through make-believe—for example, in the "mothering" a girl provides for her dolls. Fear, anger, and aggressive impulses are also expressed in this way.

Aggressive impulses are prominent in the imaginings of young children. This was brought out impressively in a study by Griffiths of five-year-old children. These children were observed at play and their imaginings were also studied through their drawings, stories they told, the responses they gave to ink-blots and to an "imagery test" (the child was asked to cover his eyes with his hands and then was asked to tell what he could see). "Crude and brutal imagery" occurred not only in the records of children from poor and overcrowded homes but also in those from better homes.

MAKE-BELIEVE AS A KIND OF THINKING

Through the use of his imagination the child is able to build large thoughts out of fragments, and use these fragments in a flexible way. A wagon with which he plays is now a car, now a train, now a ship, now a lunch counter in a restaurant. He can manipulate ideas which he only partly grasps. For example, he knows the names of certain cities where relatives live or through which he and his parents have recently traveled, but then, in connection with imaginary boat play, he can visit these cities, going by boat from a city on the seacoast to another city that lies far inland. A trip between two cities 500 miles apart requires less time than a trip between adjacent towns. And even though the voyage is by water, there is nothing to prevent him from stepping off and making little side trips on foot, for when he steps off the water becomes dry land. Such ventures seem quite illogical and may even seem to be a retreat from reality, yet it is important to recognize that the child has made a journey of the mind, an ambitious one at that; and he has made it in the only way that would be possible for him.

Through make-believe a child is able to experiment and explore without being bound by a pre-determined logic. Examples of this appear when children are in the beginning stages of drawing. If certain lines and colors that have been put together resemble a flower it is easy to give the product a logical structure by calling it a flower.

Through make-believe a youngster can substitute one rationale for another. A five-year-old girl who had visited her grandmother in the city was inspired to make a colored drawing of her grandmother's apartment house. She first made a good representation of an eight-story apartment building. Then, in the process of putting a street into the drawing, she happened to run the lines of the street through the fourth floor so that the lower floors were buried below ground level. This apparently was not in keeping with the original theory of the drawing and so, it being impossible to erase the crayoned street, the youngster changed the theory of her drawing. She shaded the entire portion below the fourth-floor level. She added little insect-like creatures, both in the floors under the ground and above the ground. Then she triumphantly displayed the drawing as the "home of the ant-killers." (The insect-like creatures were ants.) In experimenting with lines and relationships she had produced a striking drawing. From the point of view of a literally-minded architect, the drawing would be regarded as a failure, but the youngster, by supplying a new name and rationale, converted it into an artistic success.

MAKE-BELIEVE AS A MEANS OF DEALING WITH EMOTIONAL PROBLEMS

In an imaginary setting a child can come to grips with personal problems which, in real life, are too hard for him to handle.

Make-believe as a means of coping with fear. A two-and-a-half-year-old child who was frightened whenever she saw a dog on the street often at home went through a game in which she would get down on all fours, bark, growl, and head toward her mother saying, "I'm going to bite you." When she came close to her mother, she would say in a comforting tone, "I'm a good dog. I'm not going to bite you, Mama, I will kiss you." Then she would proceed to lick her mother's stockings with a great show of affection. It was as though she were transforming a threatening dog (or mother!) into a friendly creature and "proving" to herself that there was nothing to fear. After several episodes in which the child had played the part of a dangerous dog, suddenly turned friendly, the youngster took to using similar words on the street. While holding her mother's hand, she would say about a dog—very much in the same tone as she had used in her play—"Mama, he's a good dog. He doesn't bite me." She still stayed close to her mother, but there was now less fear in the manner in which she clutched her mother's hand and in her tone of voice than when the fear of dogs was first observed.

Another example of the use of make-believe as a means of coping with fear appeared in the behavior of a four-year-old girl who had a fear of a bogey man. She sometimes faced this fear on an imaginary level by getting her two-year-old brother to play the role of a bogey man; she would put a white towel over his head and he would sit by as she called him a bogey man. As part of the game the four-year-old then would take to her heels to escape from the bogey man. The youngster's intention, it seemed, was to confront her fear within the safety of a make-believe situation. This was not at first an easy task. It was noted several times that the fleeing which began in fancy ended in earnest—she seemed to become genuinely afraid of the bogey man she had created. But as time went on, the bogey man seemed to become less menacing. Here is one example of how the work of development is accomplished through play.

A further illustration of make-believe as a means of facing fear is supplied by a boy who was afraid of crossing streets for fear he might be run over by a motor car (Griffiths, 1935). He played incessantly with toy cars, pushing them around and causing "accidents" to occur. In this harmless way he gradually overcame his fear and "gained a sense of power" over the object he had feared (Griffiths, 1935). According to Griffiths, "It can often be observed that children who are afraid of some object, like that very object more than any other as a miniature toy." In this instance, the boy's passion for toy motors was no mere accident. Through his make-believe play with them he was attending to some very serious personal business. An example such as this probably provides the key for explaining many of the toys children choose (including instances when a child who has received many presents concentrates on a toy which, from an adult's point of view, is not the most attractive one).

Make-believe as an outlet for aggression. Children also often use make-believe to deal with irritations, to take action against conditions that annoy and thwart them in real life. The way they dispose of such problems is sometimes rather drastic; if children were suddenly to translate their fantasies into action there would be a great deal of carnage. In the study by Markey, cited above, children were provided with small pieces of kitchen equipment and a "family" in the form of dolls and were encouraged to play a housekeeping game. One boy proceeded to lay hands on the dolls. He called them bad babies, put them on the toy stove, and said, "You've got to be dead. You've got to stay on there for three weeks." Then he proceeded to break the house down and to beat the dolls, talking while he did so about the burning of the bad babies in the imaginary fire. The school records of this child revealed that he was very jealous of a baby brother and, at home, had shown delight at the baby's squirming and crying when his nose was being cleaned, just as now, in the imaginary situation, he seemed to relish the thought of watching the wretched baby burn. Although the records in this case were not complete, it seems reasonable to conjecture that the boy came closer to grips with his antagonism to his brother by showing his hostility in a make-believe setting than he would come if he had not dared to express this hostility even in his fantasies.

Another child, aged about three years, began to "make supper for the little girls"; she opened the icebox and said, "Dolly dear, we *always* leave the icebox door open." This child's mother explained that, to keep the youngster from raiding the icebox at home, it had become necessary to tie a heavy wire around it; and one night the mother had discovered the child trying unsuccessfully, while muttering angrily to herself, to open the icebox. In her doll play the child not only solved the problem of the icebox but seemed also to express anger toward her mother.

Escape by way of the imagination from an unpleasant situation appeared also in the case of a child of four-and-a-half years who announced to her mother: "I'm inventing a new paint for the bathtub. It will take twelve years to dry, and you can't use the bathtub for twelve years."

FACING THE FUTURE THROUGH FANTASY

Imaginative activity enables a child to anticipate an event before it actually occurs. This ability to borrow what is yet to be augments the child's powers but it also exposes him to difficulties. Just as he can savor future pleasure and success he also, in anticipation, can taste fear and trouble. The toddler may feel delight at the prospect of taking a walk when he sees his mother bring his wraps from the closet, but his delight is diminished when, similarly in anticipation, he dreads a ride on the elevator which he fears. When he is in the park he may feel depressed when he sees that his mother is preparing to take him home, for now, still eager to taste the excitement of the outside world, he can anticipate the unwelcome prospect of having to leave.

As a child becomes older, this ability to anticipate both the good and the ill appears in more complicated forms. The life of the older child is lived with much reference to the future. The expectation that the work of the present will pay off in the future can give meaning to a chore which in itself is rather unrewarding. The image of future fulfillment will, for example, sustain some children through long periods when they practice a musical instrument, or laboriously assemble materials to build a raft.

The capacity to work for deferred goals, based in part on a dream of what is yet to be, is prominent in the later high-school years and at the college level. Students spend years preparing for a profession and accept the academic chores that are assigned even though many of these assignments at the time have little or no meaning in themselves.

To have expectations of what is to happen in the future a person must be able to imagine. Unless a child can imagine he cannot know what it is to hope. As children grow older and approach adolescence their ability to build their labors on a hoped-for future gives substance to the present. Through such imagining an older child is able to endure more easily the hurt and unpleasantness he finds in the real world in which he resides. For example, a boy who is nearing his teens and feels that his lot is not a good one may, in his imagination, picture the time when he will be able to move out of his present environment and make his own way into a better world.

MAKE-BELIEVE UNDERCURRENTS
IN SEEMINGLY UNREASONABLE BEHAVIOR

The fact that a child is able through his imagination to endow the happenings of everyday life with a drama of his own making sometimes adds undercurrents to his behavior that are difficult for others to understand. If a child seems to be unduly unreasonable, or takes offense at a minor thwarting, the reason may be that in his fancy he has built vivid expectations which now are thwarted. So, for example, a four-year-old who has looked forward to going on a shopping trip with his mother may show extreme anger and disappointment when the mother is unable at the moment to make the trip. In his fancy he not only has made the trip several times but he may also have built elaborate plans and experiences around what he expected his mother to buy. The fact that the trip simply had to be postponed does not minimize the child's disappointment.

An eight-year-old boy who sometimes had been permitted to stay up late enough at night to listen to a certain radio program became violently angry one evening when told that he could not listen that night. His father gave what he thought was a good reason, but the boy accused his father of rank injustice. Later the father learned that his announcement that the boy could not listen to the program did not simply mean that he would be deprived of the pleasure of following a show for a half hour; instead it meant that what amounted to a little plan of the boy's life had been broken. All during the day the child had been pointing toward the program in his make-believe play. He had taken the part of one of the characters. He was counting on living with this character and with the other characters on the program that evening. He was also counting on this experience as an especially enjoyable feature in a make-believe enterprise that could be continued after the program was over.

In this example the father happened to discover how much the deprivation meant, and thus was better able to understand the behavior of his child. No doubt situations analogous to this, many of them perhaps less violent in nature, occur repeatedly without being detected in the everyday lives of children.

As can be seen, the play of a child's imagination provides one clue among many to childhood behavior that frequently in the eyes of adults seems unreasonable and perverse. In both of the examples above the adults acted according to what to them were good and sufficient reasons. The children, on their part, responded in terms of what to them were powerful reasons. In many situations, such as these, the issue does not involve the position of one who is right opposed to someone who is wrong. Rather, each may be right in the light of his own experience and wishes.

Uses of make-believe in social relationships

Often when two or more young children play with one another they are held together by a make-believe activity. Make-believe can also supply the basis for play between children who are several years apart in age. Thus two sisters or brothers, an eight-year-old and a three-year-old, might play at a game of being parent and child, doctor and patient, captain and engineer on a boat, although there are few if any activities of a more prosaic character that would keep the two together (unless an adult entered into the activity with them). Make-believe is thus one of mother's greatest helpers.

Make-believe activities provide a setting in which children are better able to tolerate and enjoy one another than in a realistic setting. A six-year-old may be annoyed when in real life her two-year-old sister cries easily, or needs help with her clothes, or spills her food. Now, in a make-believe setting, in which she is the mother and the two-year-old is the baby, the same six-year-old not only accepts but may even encourage babyish behavior of this sort. Likewise, the younger child who resents the bossing of an older sibling may, in a make-believe role as a pupil or a baby, cheerfully obey orders and even accept punishment from the older sibling. In a make-believe setting with other children, a child often will accept restraints and deprivations which he would resent if they were imposed by a well-liked adult. Thus, when told by an older child who is the "teacher" that he must sit very still, a young child may remain quiet for a relatively long time; and when at a "birthday party" he may be Spartanlike in waiting until all imaginary guests are served before he begins to eat.

Often, of course, reality intrudes upon such idyllic scenes, especially if the demands within the imaginary setting becomes too taxing. For example, a four- or five-year-old in a cops-and-robbers game with an older child will rebel if required to be "dead" for an unendurable period of time. Even so, it appears that it is often in a make-believe setting, in play with other children, that youngsters for the first time achieve feats of self-restraint, patience, perseverance at a task, good manners, and the like, which adults constantly are trying to promote.

Daydreams and fantasies

Toward the end of the pre-school period and throughout later years, much of a child's imaginary activity takes the form of private fantasies and daydreams as distinguished from the acting out which appears in make-believe play. These fantasies variously serve as a means of wish-fulfillment, riddance, escape, compensation, revenge, vicarious adventure, and excitement, and they may provide a means for the exercise of many interests and ideas. In many of these daydreams, the child plays dramatic and heroic roles that are more remote from everyday happenings than the make-believe activities of an earlier age.

Daydreams continue throughout life. The themes involved and the extent to which the individual indulges vary as different life situations arise, and at times the daydreams may range from the abandonment of sheer fancy to an ordered procession of ideas. Such enterprises are related to the individual's everyday problems and desires.

Even though the imaginings of an older child are not bound by the facts of experience, some of his make-believe is likely to have more logical coherence than it had at an earlier age. In the process of achieving a semblance of plausibility, an undertaking that begins as a fanciful daydream may end as a form of businesslike problem solving. Thus, an eight-year-old boy rides, in his fancies, jauntily over the western range on a fine horse, ready for combat with horse thieves, coyotes, or Indians. As the plot unfolds, his activities become increasingly complex. He has a trusty rifle and a belt of ammunition at the start; but when he stops to camp, he needs materials for making a fire, cooking utensils, and what not, so he finds it necessary to pretend that he had an extra pack horse with him from the beginning. As the drama goes on, he may find himself so burdened with equipment, horses, and other paraphernalia that the job of planning and ordering things in the daydream becomes somewhat arduous. This tendency for a daydream to bog down under its own weight as it calls for more and more ingenuity and "thinking" frequently occurs in adults, spoiling what might otherwise have been a fine time.

Imaginary companions

An especially interesting form of imagery in childhood is the "imaginary companion." [1] This phenomenon, if it appears at all, is likely to occur some time between the ages of three and ten years, more probably during the earlier than during the later years within this range. It is difficult precisely to define an imaginary companion since the difference between this imagined character and what occurs in an ordinary play of imagery apparently is a difference mainly in degree. The label "imaginary companion" is commonly applied to an imagined creature or thing that is unusually vivid and that has quite stable characteristics as long as it lasts.

The character may be a person, an animal, or an object. In some cases it is almost as vivid as an hallucination. Although it is a figment of the child's mind, it may assume for a time what seems to be an independent reality. An example of such vividness appears in the following: A girl of four screamed a warning to her father as he was in the act of sitting down on a sofa. When questioned she reported that her imaginary playmate (a monkey) was having a sick spell and had just soiled the cushion on which her father was about to sit.

The imaginary companion may appear in many forms, with varying degrees of vividness, and like other imaginative enterprises it may serve a variety of purposes. One purpose it serves, as the name implies, is to provide the child with a companion. The companion can be endowed with characteristics which the youngster desires but does not find in his associates in real life. However, the phenomenon cannot be explained

---

[1] For studies of imaginary companions, see Hurlock and Burnstein (1932); Svendsen (1934); Ames and Learned (1946).

simply on the theory that it is a child's means of meeting a need for agreeable companionship. For one thing, the companions described by some children seem to be rather disagreeable. Again, a child may describe several companions varying in congeniality.

Many motives other than a desire for companionship are served by the imaginary character. The character may possess powers and virtues which the child lacks; he may have many privileges the child himself is denied; he may have the courage or the boldness to do things which the child himself would like to do. An imaginary companion can also serve as a basis for excusing or defending the child's conduct or his demands. One child with an entire imaginary family (father, mother, and two children) would try to excuse himself from various tasks by claiming that one of his companions had a stomach-ache and needed his attention. Another boy had an imaginary uncle who always allowed children to do what they wanted; this boy threatened to call the imaginary uncle to come and hit people who did not do what the boy wanted. These items illustrate only a few of the ways in which the imaginary character, like other forms of make-believe, takes care of a variety of tasks.

Incidence of imaginary companions. Several studies have shown that a rather large proportion of young children have imaginary companions, but it is difficult to determine the exact number, for several reasons. One difficulty is that children differ in the extent to which they reveal their "companions." When a youngster openly "plays" with a companion, and clearly, over a period of time, is dealing with a creature that has stable characteristics and a definite name, there is little doubt that he has an imaginary companion. However, the situation is not so clear if a child only refers in passing to what might be a companion. One four-year-old boy, for example, frequently mentioned a character named "John Trot," but never openly went through the motions of playing with him and never described "John Trot" in clear terms. In this instance, there was something resembling an imaginary playmate, but the boy's parents could not be sure.

When an older child brings certain characters into his daydreams again and again—as happens when he has fantasies of a "continued story" type, stretching over a period of months or even years—it is difficult to tell whether these qualify as imaginary companions. On the one hand, he may not tell anyone else about them. On the other hand, even if he does tell about them it is not easy to determine whether these imaginary creatures have a quality of seeming "real" or are just convenient characters which he can round up and then lay aside, much as a writer of fiction constructs characters to suit the purpose of his story.

Estimates of the proportion of persons who have (or have had) imaginary playmates have ranged from about 15 to close to 30 per cent. In one investigation (Ames and Learned, 1946) of 210 children who had been studied at the Yale Clinic of Child Development (including over a hundred who had been enrolled in a guidance nursery), 21 per cent of the children exhibited "imaginary companions and other imaginative phenomena." The authors add: "Probably the incidence is higher than this. Frequently, we believe, parents are not aware of these phenomena." In another group of children (Svendsen, 1934), 13 per cent appeared to have imaginary companions. In a study in which adults described their childhood experiences (Hurlock and Burnstein, 1932), 31 per cent of the women and 23 per cent of the men reported that they remembered having imaginary playmates. In a study by the writer and associates (1933) in which several hundred children were interviewed, almost a third of the youngsters described imaginary creations that seemed to have "fairly definite and stable characteristics," but more direct and intimate observations would be needed to establish an exact figure. Ames and Learned state that imaginary companions and related phenomena appear in many, although not in all, children "as a natural developmental phenomena characteristic of the age period from 2½ to 4½ years, and perhaps persisting secretly considerably beyond that age."

Personality traits of children with imaginary companions. Imaginary companions, in common with other imaginative constructions, appear in children with a wide range of personality traits. We cannot assume that having an imaginary playmate is, of itself, a sign of either a healthy or an unhealthy trend in a child's development. This goes counter to the opinion of some adults who seem to view imaginative behavior as harmful. The child who has an imaginary companion may be timid and withdrawn, or just the opposite. He may have obvious emotional difficulties or he may be managing his emotions very well. According to Ames and Learned, "We definitely do not find imaginary companions only in timid or lonely children or in those exhibiting personality difficulties." Similarly, Hurlock and Burnstein did not find marked general or unique differences between adults who had had companions and those who had not. About the only thing of a general nature that can be said is that a bright child is more likely to have imaginary companions (or at least to disclose them) then a child below average in intelligence. Each child employs his companions in his own way to satisfy his own particular needs, and there are youngsters who, in time of need, use their companions in a constructive way and then give them up when the need no longer exists.

Girls seem to have imaginary companions more often than boys, but this may reflect a cultural rather than a genuine developmental difference. According to a study by the writer and associates (1933) there is reason to believe that boys have as much need for make-believe outlets as girls. However, boys are not as openly encouraged to reveal their fantasies. We encourage girls to give play to their fancies in doll play, but boys do not have a similar imaginative outlet to which they can freely and unashamedly turn. Boys are, it is true, permitted, as miniature he-men, to play cops-and-robbers and to commit carnage with their toy guns. When a boy mows down Indians and outlaws he does have a chance to act out his aggressive impulses; but the girl, in her doll play, can project a far greater flow of feelings, including anger at the child who is being "spanked," worry over the one who is "sick," sympathy for the baby who is "crying," concern for the baby who is tired.

Themes in daydreams of older children

In the study by the writer and associates (1933) referred to above, 400 children, aged five to twelve, were asked in interviews to describe their daydreams and imaginary companions. Over 30 per cent of the daydreams reported dealt with amusements, play, or some form of diversion. Specific mention of some form of self-glorification—of prestige or playing a superior or heroic role—was made in 19 per cent of the cases; many children also reported daydreams about specific objects which they wished to possess.

In this study the less intelligent children were more frequently unable to describe make-believe activity than the more intelligent. Also, younger children and less intelligent children of all ages reported a larger proportion of daydreams dealing with specific objects and amusements than did the older and more intelligent. The brighter the child, the more likely he is to entertain daydreams with a plot.

Other forms of vivid imagery and association of images

In addition to ordinary make-believe, special forms of imagery can be observed in some children. People differ in the vividness of their images; at one extreme are those who seem to have difficulty in forming a clear image of an absent event, while at the other are individuals who report images almost as vivid as the event itself.

A phenomenon known as *synaesthesia* also occurs in some children of school age (and perhaps at an earlier time), as well as among adults.[2] A

---

[2] For an interesting account of a case of synaesthesia persisting over a period of years, see Hollingworth and Weischer (1939).

sensation from one sense modality has associated with it images from another modality. In "colored hearing," the individual reports, for example, that bass tones look blue and high soprano tones look pink. Or the synaesthesia may take the form of colors associated with certain names, as when a child of six reports that Mildred, her friend, is blue and Margaret is yellow, the number "17" is pink, and the word "rush" is gray. Tones likewise may accompany words, according to the testimony of those who report this phenomenon; thus, "paper" brings an association of soprano tones, "piazza" carries a tinkling sound, and so on.

The origin of this phenomenon is difficult to trace. Undoubtedly, experiences in the past have resulted in a more than usually vivid association between different sense impressions, so that the recurrence of one now revives the other; but this conjecture does not reveal why some individuals have such an association of images while others do not.

Children's dreams

Children's dreams, like their waking fancies, draw upon the materials of actual experience, but often the events and emotional elements in a dream are so diverse that it is difficult to trace them to their source.

EARLY SIGNS OF DREAMING

It is likely that many children dream before they are able to remember or describe their dreams. Stern (1926), who made an intensive study of the development of a child, states that dreaming possibly begins as far back as the child's first year. The first sign of dreaming may occur when a child screams in his sleep, or awakens in apparent fright, or makes sucking movements, or throws out his arms, or smiles while asleep. The age at which the first signs of dreaming appear, as reported by parents, varies considerably with different children.

Some children, as well as adults, say they never dream, but they may simply have forgotten their dreams. Laboratory studies have shown that if a sleeper is promptly awakened when he shows signs of dreaming he may be able to report dreams on the spur of the moment, even though he ordinarily does not remember any dreams in the morning after a night's sleep. To detect whether a sleeping person might be dreaming an apparatus has been used which records an increase in the sleeper's eye movements (Dement et al., 1957, 1958). In a large proportion of instances when sleepers were awakened after showing rapid eye movements they were able to recall dreams. There is reason to believe that practically all people dream, even those who say they never dream.

Some children when they first begin to dream seem to confuse the dream with reality not only while still asleep and dreaming, but also, at least momentarily, on awakening. Thus, as a child emerges from sleep he may look around searchingly and say, "There was a pony here; where did he go?"

Available evidence suggests that younger persons dream more than older ones (Ramsey, 1953). It is possible also that the dreams of children are more forthright and less camouflaged than those of older persons. Dreams containing an element of violence or fear are more likely to cause a young child than an older child to awaken. Similarly, wishes and desires seem to appear more openly in the dreams of young children. In dreams, as in waking life, the emotions of a younger child are likely to "show through" more than those of an older person. It probably would be a great help in understanding children (and adults) if somehow it were possible for an adult student of dreams to have the dreams of a child.

Terror dreams. The extent to which unpleasant dreams occur and some of the symptoms and conditions associated with them have been described in a study (Foster and Anderson, 1936), conducted in coopera-

TABLE 17	EVIDENCES AND FREQUENCIES OF UNPLEASANT DREAMS EXHIBITED BY 519 CHILDREN, AS REPORTED BY PARENTS WHO KEPT RECORDS FOR A SEVEN-DAY PERIOD [*]		
Age in Years	*1-4*	*5-8*	*9-12*
Number of Children	*81*	*215*	*223*
Average Frequency per Week of Various Evidences of Unpleasant Dreams:			
Moans during the night	.81	.57	.17
Comes to adult	.18	.16	.05
Reports bad dream in the morning	.21	.42	.26
Any evidence of bad dreaming	.93	.71	.39
Percentage of Children Having Some Unpleasant Dreams During the Week	43.0	39.2	22.2
Subject Matter of Bad Dreams (Percentages):			
Personal difficulties	26.7	33.3	54.5
Difficulties of friends, pets	13.3	6.3	18.2
Animals (probably strange or fearful)	40.0	15.9	9.1
Strange or bad people	6.7	20.6	13.6
The unknown, dark, etc.	6.7	7.9	.0
Loss of property	.0	4.6	.0
Impersonal dangers	6.7	9.5	.0
Miscellaneous	.0	1.6	4.5

* Adapted from J. C. Foster and J. E. Anderson, "Unpleasant Dreams in Childhood," *Child Development* (1936), 7:77-84. Reproduced by permission.

tion with a large number of parents who kept records of their children's dreams for a seven-day period. The parents and children in this study represented all socioeconomic levels but included a larger number of persons of high socioeconomic status than is found in a normal sampling of the population. Some of the findings revealed by a classification of the parents' reports are summarized in Table 17.

THE DREAM AS RELATED TO THE DREAMER

While some dreams almost seem to copy experiences of everyday life there are many dreams that seem to be quite unreal. Yet no matter how foreign and bizarre a dream may seem, it is something that originated within the dreamer. Every image in the dream, however strange—every emotion, however gratifying or horrible—every impulse, however noble or savage—every sensation of pleasure and of joy, however sweet or colored with guilt—arises out of the reservoir of the dreamer's own thoughts and feelings. The frightful monster that threatens to devour the child, leaving him screaming and in a state of panic, was not thrust upon him by someone else; it is his own creation. The angry creatures who threaten to attack him and the terrifying beasts that pursue him are his creatures. The desires that are gratified in his dreams are his own desires. The high place to which he ascends and the pit to which he descends are heights and depths within him. The good deeds he performs, the struggles he undertakes, the fortune he finds, the tenderness he shows, and the love he receives in his dreams embody something within him. The events that occur in a dream may be unreal in the sense that happenings are combined which have never been so combined during waking moments. But the substance of the dream is not unreal, it arises out of the substance of the dreamer's life.

Each dream contains a message that might reveal something about the experiences of life from which it springs. For this reason a study of dreams can be very instructive in connection with a person's efforts to understand himself and in his efforts to understand a child. The view that dreams have meanings, although the meanings often are disguised and difficult to untangle, stems largely from the pioneer work of Freud.[3] Freud's theories about the manifest and the latent or disguised elements of the dream, the symbolism of the dream, the relationship between dream and desire and between the dream and currents in a person's life which he does not consciously recognize or admit in his waking thoughts, have given a powerful impetus to those who are seeking to uncover the hidden reaches of man's mental life.

---

[3] See Freud's *The Interpretation of Dreams* (1956; originally published in 1900). Studies of dreaming have been reviewed by Ramsey (1953) and DeMartino (1955).

Projective methods

Projective methods include a variety of procedures that enable a child (or adult) to reveal his perception of things, his fantasies, thoughts and feelings, without speaking directly about himself. The assumption underlying these procedures is that a person's interpretation of what he hears or sees is determined not only by the objective nature of the stimulus situation but by subjective factors within himself. For example, when asked to tell what he sees in a somewhat blurred picture of two children facing an adult one child might say, "There is a father and two boys and they are planning a trip"; another might say, "There are two boys and the father is scolding them." We cannot conclude from these responses alone just what the attitudes of these two boys toward their fathers might be. But we can assume that it is not solely the picture itself but something within the children that led one to see a friendly father and another an angry father.

The following brief account describes projective methods that have been widely used. The descriptions are sufficient to enable a reader to experiment with the methods in an informal way, but for a full account of ways of using the methods and precautions that are necessary in interpreting the responses, the reader is referred to the footnote references.[4]

Play techniques. The use of play situations in the study of children is illustrated by the doll family referred to earlier in this chapter. In devising a play situation, it is possible to use a great variety of materials: dolls that might be interpreted as representing parents, siblings, or playmates; toys and equipment that might be used in make-believe play; fragile things that might be handled carefully or destroyed; household scenes (such as a kitchen, bedroom, or bathroom).[5]

Drawing and painting. Drawing or painting under free or quasi-controlled conditions provides the child with an opportunity to express fantasies and moods (Alschuler and Hattwick, 1943). The child's choice of a theme for his drawing may reveal something about his concerns, and in many studies it has also been assumed that various themes and particular

---

[4] For earlier discussions and some of the later reviews of techniques that involve an interpretation of imaginative productions, see Frank (1939); Lerner *et al.* (1941); Murphy and Horowitz (1938); White (1945); Abt and Bellak (1950); Anderson and Anderson (1951); Goodenough and Harris (1950); and Symonds (1949).

[5] See, for example, the Driscoll Playkit (1952); also Bach (1945); Erikson (1940); and Axline (1947). There is a further discussion of the manner in which children reveal themselves in their play in Chapter Nineteen.

aspects of a drawing symbolize particular desires and conflicts of various kinds. One variation of this procedure is finger painting, which has been described by Shaw (1934), and another is an analysis of drawing of the human figure (Machover, 1949). Claims concerning the extent to which a child (or an adult) unknowingly reveals himself are difficult to confirm, but a study of children's art has large promise as a means of studying children. Sometimes, also, a drawing that the child has made can serve as a point of departure for discussion of what he is concerned about.

Response to pictures. The way in which a child describes, interprets, or tells a story about pictures that he sees may provide a good deal of information about him. In the use of this procedure it is assumed that what a child sees in a picture or reads into it might reveal something about his own attitudes, his desires, his hopes, and his fears. Among the most widely used sets of pictures are those contained in the *Thematic Apperception Test* (Murray, 1937) and in the *Children's Apperception Test* (Bellak and Bellak, 1949-1950).

Story completion. Here again the assumption is that the way in which a child (or adult) completes a story might reveal something about his inner life. Unfinished stories have been used to study children's punitive attitudes (offering them an opportunity, for example, to end a story about a child who has committed a misdeed by punishing him, or excusing him). They have been used to study children's attitudes toward their parents (for example, the story tells that a child has just heard that one of his parents and one of his friends have been in an accident: the story might be completed by having the child go to help his father or to help his friend).

The Rorschach test. The Rorschach test material consists of a set of cards each one of which contains an enlarged "ink blot"; the ink blots vary in contour and include some that are in black and white and others that are multicolored. On being shown each ink blot the person is asked to tell what it might be or what it looks like. There are standard directions for administering the test and very elaborate directions for interpreting the results.[6]

---

[6] For discussions of the Rorschach test see Beck (1937); Klopfer (1956); Klopfer and Kelley (1946); Krugman (1940); Rorschach (1937); Ames *et al.* (1952); Blum *et al.* (1954); and Halpern (1953). (An ink-blot resembling one of the Rorschach cards can be made as follows: fold a piece of paper down the middle, making a sharp crease; open the paper and place a drop of ink at the center of the crease, then close the fold again, as before. Place the paper on a hard surface and stroke from the crease outward until the ink has spread as far as it will go.)

Many questions arise when we try to interpret children's responses to projective situations. Frequently there is a marked difference between a child's responses to a projective situation, his overt behavior and what he tells about himself.[7] For example, in doll-play a youngster may treat a "baby" violently, suggesting that he is fiercely jealous of a younger sibling; in his actual conduct, however, he treats his sibling quite gently; and if we question him he may say that he likes his younger sibling. Similarly, one youngster may be very aggressive in a projective situation but say, when questioned, that a child should not hit another child; still another youngster who gives an aggressive projective response may say that all children hit one another and that it is quite all right for him to hit.

When such discrepancies occur we face the question: Which is the truest measure of a child's state of mind: his overt action, his verbal report, or his projected response? This question cannot be answered categorically in the abstract. A projective technique should provide the most revealing information if it is so designed that it enables the child to react spontaneously, to let down his guard, and to "act out" thoughts and feelings he ordinarily would not talk about or openly express in his behavior. But without further evidence we cannot assume in advance that a certain projective method will give a truer picture of a child than is revealed by his overt conduct or by a series of skillfully conducted interviews.

A child's projected reaction may give a clue to an attitude which can be confirmed by closer observation of his behavior and by questioning. For example, we may discover that the youngster who treats a baby sibling violently in a doll-play situation also in his everyday conduct betrays resentment toward his sibling, not by openly hitting him but in more subtle ways (such as excluding him from his play or by tattling or by luring him into misbehavior).

Recommended Readings

Ruth Griffiths' *Imagination in Early Childhood* (1935) is a rich source of information concerning the fantasy life of young children. Two publications based on studies of adolescents that have important implications for understanding the fantasy life of persons at all age levels are Percival M. Symonds' *Adolescent Fantasy* (1949) and a

---

[7] McElvaney (1958) has reviewed findings dealing with the similarities and discrepancies between children's projective responses and observations or ratings of their overt behavior.

monograph by Lawrence K. Frank and his associates, *Personality Development in Adolescent Girls* (1953). Books dealing with the content of dreams and efforts to interpret their meaning include Sigmund Freud's classic work, *The Interpretation of Dreams* (1950 translation), and a paperback volume by J. A. Hadfield, *Dreams and Nightmares* (1954). Calvin S. Hall presents an account of dreams in a paperback book entitled *The Meaning of Dreams* (1959). Projective techniques have been discussed by Harold H. Anderson and Gladys L. Anderson in *An Introduction to Projective Techniques and Other Devices for Understanding the Dynamics of Human Behavior* (1951) and by Lawrence E. Abt and Leopold Bellak in *Projective Psychology* (1950).

Reasoning
and Concept Formation

CHAPTER SIXTEEN   When a child reaches elementary-school age, he is capable of most of the intellectual operations an adult can perform. He can recollect the past and plan for the future. Within the limits of his experience and information he uses both inductive and deductive reasoning, although he is not always able to express his reasoning in words. He is able to imagine and can manipulate countless symbols without actually having to handle the physical material these symbols represent. But he still has a long way to go in his intellectual development.

During the elementary-school years the child will show a marked increase in his knowledge and general information, as one would expect. He will become better able to deal with the abstract. He will gain in ability to deal with affairs in the world that do not directly touch his every-

day life. He will fall in with the academic concern about what is impersonal and remote. He will show an increasing capacity for intellectual teamwork, for understanding and discussing the ideas and viewpoints of others, and for joining with them in the give-and-take of group discussion. He will be able to deal with more complex problems and plans and will gain added ability to concentrate his attention on intellectual tasks.

The growing world

By the age of six the world in which the child dwells has expanded far beyond the cradle, but his thoughts, plans, and interests still are restricted mainly to things that are near in time and space. The ensuing years bring a great expansion.

AWARENESS OF PEOPLE

One form of expansion appears in the child's awareness of people in the world at large. An example of this change appears when children name the persons whom they admire. In one study, in the age range from six to eight, 58 per cent of the characters named by the children as heroes and ideals belonged to the immediate everyday environment of the children. At the age of twelve about a third belonged in this category. Only about one-third of the persons named by the younger children were historical or public characters—people not in the child's immediate environment; at the age of twelve almost two-thirds of the characters were in this category (Hill, 1930).

WIDENED RANGE OF RESPONSE TO WORLD AT LARGE

The child's intellectual life expands also through an increased interest in happenings in the world outside his own immediate day-to-day existence. Table 18, based on a study of what children said during free discussion periods in the classroom, illustrates this.

One conspicuous change, as we can see, is a decided drop from the second to the sixth grade in discussion of topics relating to a child's own personal activities and experiences. At the second grade, 61 per cent of all contributions dealt with personal activities and experiences as contrasted with 18 per cent at the sixth grade.

There was a corresponding increase from the second to the sixth grade in contributions dealing with world and domestic news, and with activities of people other than the child himself. A change also appeared in the extent to which children were preoccupied with events they had directly witnessed, whether or not they themselves were the main actors in an event. At the second grade most of the topics or items of information discussed by the children dealt with matters that had actually happened

Subject and Source	62 Second-graders	54 Fourth-graders	45 Sixth-graders
Subject Matter Content:			
Personal activity	61%	41%	18%
Animals	10	7	8
Books, radio, movies	7	13	6
Current happenings in world at large	18	29	60
Miscellaneous	4	10	9
Medium of Acquisition:			
Personal presence	83	52	25
Reflection	1	15	18
Other media (books, magazines, radio, theater, personal conversation)	16	31	56
Unknown	0	2	1

* Adapted from H. V. Baker, *Children's Contributions in Elementary School General Discussion*, Child Development Monographs (New York: Teachers College, Columbia University, 1942), No. 29, pp. 32-33. Reproduced by permission.

in their lives or in their presence (83 per cent of contributions fell in this category). At the sixth grade, however, only about one-fourth of the contributions dealt with matters that the children had become aware of through personal experience or direct contact.

When older children deal more than the younger ones with world affairs and with events unrelated to their day to day experience many of them probably are simply conforming to what is expected in school. It is likely that most of these youngsters in their out-of-school conversations concentrate more on topics that are of immediate practical and personal concern than on the problems of the Middle East or on the natural resources of Alaska (the same probably also holds true for their teachers). The findings do not indicate how much meaning the news items pertaining to world affairs have for the children but they do indicate that the youngsters are at least able to handle the formal academic aspects of such topics.

INCREASED CAPACITY FOR GENERALIZING

During the elementary-school years and beyond, the child acquires increased ability to use general and inclusive categories of thought. This ability to think in terms of the more inclusive concepts is illustrated when children express their wishes. A younger child might wish, for example, for a football, a football helmet, a football suit, while an older child, instead of devoting three wishes to different objects might wish for money to buy a football outfit and still have two wishes left. In one such study, in which children aged five to twelve were asked to name three wishes, the responses were tabulated under a number of headings including one that represented wishes for specific material objects and another that included wishes for general benefits for self and others. The percentages are shown in Table 19.

TABLE 19	PERCENTAGE OF CHILDREN WHOSE FIRST WISH WAS FOR SPECIFIC THINGS OR FOR MORE GENERAL BENEFITS IN THE AGE RANGE FROM FIVE TO TWELVE *

(Other categories not reproduced bring the total at each level to 100 per cent.)

Type of Wish	Age Groups				IQ Groups		
	5-6	7-8	9-10	11-12	120 and above	100-119	80-99
Specific material objects and possessions	55.	48.	26.	14.	23.3	38.3	47.9
General benefits for self and others	8.	14.	22.	27.	25.6	17.1	8.3

* Adapted from A. T. Jersild, F. V. Markey, and C. L. Jersild, *Children's Fears, Dreams, Wishes, Daydreams, Likes, Dislikes, Pleasant and Unpleasant Memories*, Child Development Monographs (New York: Teachers College, Columbia University, 1933), No. 12, 172 pp. Reproduced by permission. This version omits comparisons between boys and girls and between school groups that are included in the original table.

Children's reasoning

On his fifth birthday a boy proudly told his parents: "I am five years old and you can weason with me now." His pronunciation was poor, but his claim, if true, was profound. One of our most treasured human possessions is the ability to reason, to take a thoughtful view of things, to recognize relationships, to draw correct inferences and arrive at logical conclusions. One of the crowning achievements of the mind occurs when a person through reasoning gains new insights into the workings of the world in which he lives. Another great achievement occurs when a person, child or adult, is able to accept a reasonable conclusion even if it goes contrary to his personal desires and cherished beliefs. The first of these achievements adds to man's ability to deal with his physical and social environment. The second adds to his effectiveness in dealing with the affairs of his inner life.

Many investigators of children's thinking have been influenced by the work of Piaget, a Swiss investigator, and by Piaget's conclusions, the first of which were published several decades ago.

In tests made by Piaget and others, experiments such as the following have been used: The child is shown a glass full or partly full of water and some pebbles and is asked to predict what will happen if the pebbles are dropped into the glass, and then, after the pebbles have been inserted, to give an explanation of what did happen. He is asked to predict what will happen or to explain what has happened when a lighted candle is covered by a glass jar; when weights are attached to the extended arms of flexible metal bars differing in form, length, or thickness; when a lightweight or heavyweight object is placed in water, such as a toothpick (which floats) or a nail (which sinks). Tests of children's ideas of cause and effect have included questions such as: What makes the wind move? What makes the clouds move? In tests of children's ability to reason or to see things from the point of view of another person a proposition such as the following has been used: If you are Henry and there are two other boys in your family, Peter and John, how many brothers do you have? How many brothers does Peter have?

In his writings Piaget has set forth the view that there are stages in children's thinking, and in his earlier experiments he maintained that up to about the age of seven or eight years a child: (1) tends to reason only in terms of isolated or particular cases; (2) is incapable of a genuine argument; (3) feels no need for verification or logical justification; (4) has difficulty in making generalizations or deductions; (5) has difficulty in reasoning from the point of view of another person or from the point of view of a general proposition. He has also maintained that it is not until about the age of eleven or twelve years that a child typically is able to make pure deductions or master the logical concept of cause and effect.

Several investigations dealing with children of kindergarten age and upward have indicated that children at any age level vary greatly in their reasoning ability and many of them are able to reason about cause-and-effect relationships earlier than the children described by Piaget. In one such study (Deutsche, 1937), a number of experiments were performed (such as the candle and the glass jar). There was an increase in the children's scores at each successive age level. The types of answers covered a wide range, but at no age did the children's answers fall into any single type. A child might handle a problem that touched upon matters on which he was informed quite effectively and then give a naive answer to another problem. Children's ability to solve the problems was more closely related to their school experience than to chronological or mental age.

Numerous studies of children's concepts (reviewed by Russell, 1956; and by Lee and Bingham, 1959) have shown that children show an improvement in most areas of thinking as they become older and move on in their schooling. According to most of the studies, the improvement is more likely to be continuous than to show distinct phases or stages. Development moves in general from the more simple to the more complex, from the concrete to the abstract.

It has been noted that young children's explanations of some phenomena often are naive and self-contradictory. When pressed, they may resort to animistic or magical answers. A child is giving an animistic explanation, when, for example, he is asked, "Why does an icicle fall to the ground?" and answers, "Because it wants to." He seems to endow the icicle with a life and will of its own. However, reasoning that seems to be animistic may be more a manner of speaking than a manner of thinking. When a child speaks of an object as being alive he does not necessarily mean that it is able to see or think or have a will of its own (Klingensmith, 1953). He may be using the term "alive" or an equivalent term to denote activity rather than life: e.g., a clock is alive in the sense that it ticks. In everyday speech children hear many animistic expressions: the motor that was dead has "come to life"; this is a "live wire"; the wind is "sighing"; this is a "stubborn knot." Moreover, when adults are called upon to deal with wholly unfamiliar material they also frequently give answers that are animistic or even mystical. In one study (Oakes, 1947), thirty-five college faculty members were faced with a number of experiments which demonstrated certain principles of physics and were asked to predict what would happen and to give an explanation of what did happen. The answers ranged from precise explanations to what have been regarded as typically "childish" answers. Twenty-three comments made by eighteen different adults bordered on the mystical and magical: "It's a long time since I studied any science. Maybe nature has changed a little," or "It seems a bit unfair that the iron doesn't get there first."

When a child is questioned about various conditions over a period of time it is likely that the nature of his answers will change. Findings on this point have been reported by Dennis (1942). At the age of six years and two months his daughter gave much the same kind of answers as do adults to a variety of questions about the nature and cause of things. However, many of the answers that she gave before the age of three were of a different character. At the earlier age some of her explanations were more on the side of magic than of physical cause and effect. She said, for example, "I move the sun when I go up and down." Also she seemed to believe that she could make the auto run by blowing the horn. At this earlier age, some of her answers also had an anthropomorphic touch (such as, a daddy-man makes daddies, candy is made by a candyman). These observations suggest that there may be a stage during which children think in prelogical, magical, or animistic terms. We need more convincing evidence than is now at hand, however, in order to substantiate this point.

Many findings indicate that nonlogical or logical thinking is not an either-or phenomenon. The same child, at a given time, will exhibit both varieties of thinking. One three-year-old girl for example, when asked, "What makes the wind blow?" answered, "It blows itself." When asked, "What makes a car run?" she answered, "The motor." The second answer is the more acceptable one from an adult point of view, yet it probably meant little more to her than did the first. In any event, the two answers do not seem to represent two different kinds of thinking but, rather, the best explanation the child was able to supply at the moment.

Generally speaking, the younger the child, the more his thoughts tend to center on immediate events and problems as distinct from more remote concerns. He deals more with the concrete than with the abstract. Illustrations of this were noted during bombings in World War II: the younger child, responding more on a *perceptual* level, would react to the danger and damage wrought by a particular air raid; but the older person would also view a raid as an ominous sign that the enemy had broken through and might do so again. In the same way, the younger child is more likely than the older one to deal with specific attributes of things rather than with a general scheme of classification (as when he defines apple as "round" or "something to eat" rather than as a "kind of fruit").

Inductive reasoning

In a study by Burt (1919) tests were made of the ability of English children at various age levels to reason inductively—that is, from the particular to the general—and their ability to handle arguments that proceed by eliminating in succession each of a number of alternative hypotheses except the right one. There were differences between the older and the younger children in abiilty to handle problems of varying difficulty and complexity but there was no evidence that the reasoning processes of the younger children of elementary-school age differed in kind from the reasoning processes of older children.

At seven years, for example, children could solve this problem:

> Tom runs faster than Jim; Jack runs slower than Jim: Who is the slowest, Jim or Jack or Tom?

At eight years, the children solved a problem, such as this, which likewise called for elimination of untenable hypotheses:

> I don't like sea voyages, and I don't like the seaside. I must spend Easter either in France, or among the Scottish Hills, or on the South Coast. Which shall it be?

It was not until a later age, near the end of the elementary-school period, however, that the children were able to solve a problem calling for the discovery of a general rule from a number of particular instances, such as:

> One pound of meat should roast for half an hour; two pounds, three-quarters of an hour; three pounds, one hour; eight pounds, two-and-a-quarter hours; nine pounds, two-and-a-half hours. From this, can you discover a simple rule by which you can tell from the weight of a joint how long it should roast?

ABILITY TO REASON
FROM THE STANDPOINT OF AN ABSTRACT PROPOSITION

Children show an increase with age in their knowledge of and ability to deal with the abstract. In time, most children are able not only to apply a general proposition which they know or believe to be true but also are able to reason in terms of a hypothesis which for the time being is supposed to be true. Eventually, a large proportion of people are able to reason from the standpoint of a proposition that assumes what is contrary to what they regard as fact ("If Columbus had not discovered America, it is likely that. . . .").

Some persons eventually achieve, with varying degrees of success, the ability to reason in terms of a proposition that goes contrary to their wishes, although this is not an easy task. The writer observed an example of this in a fifth-grade discussion of current events prior to World War II. A boy reported his current event in the form of a question: "There will be no war if the president of what country gives in to Hitler's demands?" At the time, Hitler was making demands on Czechoslovakia, and the idea behind the boy's question was that if the Czechoslovakian government yielded Hitler would not start a war. When no one else ventured an answer, the boy himself answered that if the president of Czechoslovakia yielded to Hitler there would be no war. But many children protested that this answer was wrong. When the teacher let the children debate the issue, it was apparent that most members of the class were arguing the merits of Hitler's demands and not the substance of the boy's question. The class argument was: What right has Hitler to ask for this territory? How would you like it if you were a Czechoslovakian? and so on. The boy who first raised the issue maintained that he was not arguing the merits of the demands, he was simply arguing that *if* the Czechoslovakians yielded there would be no war between Czechoslovakia and Germany. When a vote was taken almost every pupil in the class voted that the boy who had presented the proposition had lost the debate.

OTHER DIFFERENCES
BETWEEN THE REASONING OF OLDER AND YOUNGER PERSONS

Various studies have shown that when older and younger persons are confronted with a similar problem some of the older ones usually are more deliberate in their procedure, turning the matter over in their minds, whereas children are more likely to forge ahead in overt trial and error. Also, as we might expect, adults are likely to reach a conclusion or correct answer more quickly and to see the point more readily. On all these points there are, of course, large individual differences both among children and adults.

The more mature person also is better able to perceive the inevitable and to accept objective facts. For example, at the age of two-and-a-half a child may ask for more prunes and then reply, when told that there are no more, "Yes there are, because I want some." At the age of five or six the child is less likely to insist that there actually are some prunes in the kitchen and more likely to express disappointment or to blame his mother for not buying a large enough supply.

PRECAUTIONS ADULTS NEED TO CONSIDER
IN TRYING TO UNDERSTAND CHILDREN'S THINKING

When we, as adults, try to understand or try to promote a child's ability to deal with a problem in a thoughtful way it is important to consider both the problem and the solution from the child's point of view. We get a distorted view of a child's thinking if we examine it only in terms of the logic of an educated adult. Children may have a good practical grasp of the idea of cause and effect in their own sphere of activities even though they cannot phrase the idea in logical terms. A five-year-old child, for example, has a spill on his tricycle when one wheel goes over the edge of an inclined board on which he is riding. The next time he avoids the edge, or daringly explores how close he can come to the edge without toppling over. His actions here show a practical grasp of cause and effect. Similarly, a youngster applies many scientific principles in his everyday actions, as when he uses a stick to pry a stone out of the ground (the principle of the lever) or props up a plank so that he can push his wagon from the ground onto the porch (the principle of the inclined plane). But he probably would have difficulty in phrasing the principles involved.

If, instead of examining what the child does in dealing with problems within his own domain we ask him to solve problems he has not had an opportunity to explore or if we ask him to explain a happening in abstract terms we are likely to find that his judgment is faulty, and that his reasoning seems different from that of an older person. We might, for example, come to him with the following problem, which has been used in studies of children's thinking: Here are two sheets of paper of the same size. I will crumple one into a ball while the other stays flat. Which will reach the floor first if both are dropped at the same time? The child may be able to answer correctly if he has had experience with this sort of thing. If not, he probably will feel obliged to answer and just give a guess. After the papers have dropped, and one lands before the other, we could ask the child: Why did the crumpled sheet reach the ground first? His answer, from an adult point of view, may be quite illogical (even some college students would fumble before giving an answer in proper scientific terms). The youngster who used good practical judgment with his wagon and tricycle would probably make a sorry showing when quizzed according to the logic of an adult scientist. From this we can conclude that a five-year-old child does not know as much as a college professor of physics; but we cannot conclude that the thinking processes of the two are basically different.

In order to study children's thinking it is necessary for an adult to try to wrench himself free, as far as possible, from the deposits of years of experience, and to look at children in their own habitat. A well-known story offers a parable that bears on this:

> A valuable horse had strayed and the wise people of the village went on searching parties, but they all failed to find the horse. Then the village idiot volunteered, and soon he came back with the horse. He was asked, "How did you find him?" And the "idiot" replied, "I just figured where I would go if I were a horse."

The moral here is not that one must be a horse to study the mind of a horse, but, rather, that to study the "horse-sense" of either a horse or a child we need to test him within the framework of his own world. When an adult inquires into children's thinking he is undertaking a project that is in many ways as much a test of his own mentality as of the child's.

When children respond to tests of their reasoning ability many factors other than "pure reason" come into play. One child may be interested in one problem but bored by a second. Another child may be challenged by almost any kind of questioning. One youngster may feel that he ought to come up with some kind of an answer while another is more free simply to say he doesn't know. One youngster may try to face the problem that is put to him directly, another may try to figure out what the adult questioner has in mind. A youngster may give a straightforward response or answer with his tongue in cheek—offering any answer that comes to mind because he thinks he should have some sort of reply or persisting in an answer even if he has doubts about it. An example of a tongue-in-cheek answer appeared in a study by the writer (referred to later in this chapter) of children's concepts. One series of questions was designed to find whether children knew the difference between mammals and non-mammals. A ten-year-old boy went out on a limb by insisting that only cows have milk for their young. When asked how a puppy gets its food he said that puppies need milk, "So you have to have a cow." The same answer, "You have to have a cow" was given when he was questioned about a baby horse, and a baby camel. However, he was uneasy about his answers, so when he was asked, "What about a baby elephant?" he exploded with, "Oh, let him eat hay!"

Many illustrations of the fact that an inquiry into children's thinking may be as much a test of the adult's ingenuity as of the child's have been noted in a study by Almy (1959). A youngster may give a dead-pan answer to a question when secretly he wonders why it was asked. One series of questions in Almy's study dealt with children's ideas concerning what is and what is not alive. (The child is shown a live mouse, a wind-up toy, and other things, and as each is shown he is asked, "Is this alive?") After being questioned, one girl quietly went to her teacher and said, "Miss _____ must be very stupid." "Why?" "She doesn't even know that a clock is not alive."

The problem facing an adult when he tries to explore the mind of a child was underscored by a remark made by one investigator who had labored several months on a study of children's thinking. When asked what conclusion he had reached, he said ruefully: "I don't know whether I was really testing children's capacity for thinking or my own capacity for thinking, but I am convinced that children have a great capacity for pulling a professor's leg."

Children's information and concepts

Inquiries into the "content of children's minds" before and after they enter the first grade give an interesting picture of what children know and do not know. Almost all children are informed on some topics while only a few possess items of information which most educated adults take for granted. Tables 20 and 21 give a few illustrative findings. The first of these tables is based in part on carefully conducted studies of kindergarten children in Minneapolis, Minnesota, in 1928 and again, with some modifications, in 1954-1955.

The influence of television was especially noteworthy in the 1954-1955 results. Two prominent television personalities (Howdy Doody and Arthur Godfrey) were identified by considerably more children than the

TABLE 20	SELECTED RESULTS OF INFORMATION TEST ADMINISTERED TO 100 CHILDREN, AGED 5 YEARS AND 4 MONTHS TO 6 YEARS

(The values show the percentage of children who answered each question correctly. Some of the items and questions have been abbreviated in the present table.)

Test Items	Percentage Answering Correctly
Local Points of Interest: °	
Tell me the name of a Minneapolis newspaper	85
What is the name of a lake in Minneapolis?	27
What is the Mississippi?	78
What is the Great Northern?	39
Time and Number:	
How many pennies in a dime?	22
What time of year do flowers grow outdoors?	99
How many eggs in half a dozen?	12
What time or what o'clock is it at noon?	30
How many pennies in a nickel?	37
Animals, Birds, and Insects:	
How many legs has a horse?	100
From what are little chickens hatched?	63
What do bees make that we eat?	59
A baby dog is called a puppy; what is a baby cow called?	26
Plants and Flowers:	
What do apples grow on?	97
What color is wheat when it is ripe?	35
What do we call the part of the plant underground?	32
What do we eat that grows on vines?	29
Occupations and Industries:	
Who makes money by cutting hair?	96
What does a plumber do?	60
What is butter made from?	40
Where does coal come from?	32
Simple Mechanics:	
What do you see on the ground that trains run on?	98
What is the brake on an automobile for?	55
How are trees made into boards?	19
What is a thermometer for?	50
Current Topics and Miscellaneous: †	
What is a helicopter?	47
Who is Dwight D. Eisenhower?	51
Who is Harry Truman?	12
Who is Howdy Doody?	96
Who is Arthur Godfrey?	83

* The first six sections of this table are adapted from C. A. Probst, "A General Information Test for Kindergarten Children," *Child Development*, 1931, 2:81-95.

† The last section of this table is adapted from M. C. Templin, "General Information of Kindergarten Children: A Comparison with the Probst Study After 26 Years," *Child Development*, 1958, 29:87-96. The original tables report separate scores for boys and girls and for different occupational groups. For an earlier study of children's information, see Hall (1891).

president of the United States or the former president (who also made television appearances, but not so frequently). In the 1954-1955 results, differences between boys and girls and between children of higher and lower socioeconomic status were not as large as in 1928.

The answers children give when their information is tested often yield many clues to the flow of a child's thoughts, as illustrated by the following replies in the study cited above: A carpenter fixes carpet sweepers or repairs cars; the Great Northern is the North star; butter is made from buttermilk or butterflies make it; plants, seeds, and flowers are manufactured in the Ford plant; a plumber plumbs, pulls out plums, or sells plumbers; beans grow in gardens but bees make them. The source of incorrect answers may be obscure, as when a child asserts that a man who raises corn or wheat is called a "bachelor" (Probst, 1931).

A further brief sampling of children's information concerning certain topics is shown in Table 21. This table is based on results obtained by the writer during the 1940's in a study of about 500 children, aged eight to twelve years, most of whom were pupils in public schools in New York City. The younger children were interviewed; the older ones wrote their answers on individual test blanks. The percentages shown in this table might be different if a similar study were made today or if rural rather than urban children were questioned.

On many of the items in Table 21 the percentage of children who answered correctly would no doubt be considerably lower if guesses were eliminated. On some items, the percentage of correct answers is not much larger than could be expected by chance.

Certain comparisons, not reproduced in the table, showed large differences between brighter and duller children. In one public school, the children in two bright classes were correct on 67 per cent of the questions concerning directions (e.g., If you go up the Hudson River do you go north? south? east? west?) as compared with a score of only 28 per cent in the case of older children in four classes of less intelligent children. The difference between the bright and dull children was not so large, however, in answers to questions which they could not so readily answer on the basis of everyday observation (such as the question on where watermelons grow).

SOME EXAMPLES OF MISCONCEPTIONS

Practically all adults can recall from their own childhood many erroneous impressions, false beliefs, and misinterpretations of words and phrases. These misconceptions throw some light on the difficulties children have in incorporating the ideas presented to them by others.

Mistaken beliefs frequently arise by chance or through the solemn

TABLE 21

PERCENTAGE OF CHILDREN IN GREATER NEW YORK
CHOOSING CORRECT ALTERNATIVE ANSWER
OR SUPPLYING CORRECT ANSWER TO VARIOUS ITEMS
OF AN INFORMATION TEST

(Abridged and adapted from an unpublished study by the writer.)

Percentage of Children Giving Correct Answer

Test Item	Age 8	Age 9	Age 10	Age 11	Age 12 *
The sun rises in the: (a) east; (b) north; (c) west; (d) south	54	51	63	66	71
The moon sets in the: (a) east; (b) north; (c) west; (d) south	29	40	35	50	49
Up the Hudson River is: (a) east; (b) north; (c) west; (d) south	29	50	59	54	65
To the Rocky Mountains is: (a) east; (b) north; (c) west; (d) south	10	34	53	59	70
A boy walks a mile in about: (a) 1 hour; (b) 2 hours; (c) 25 minutes; (d) 5 minutes	27	44	58	52	47
Which is bigger, a corn plant or a wheat plant?	54	58	66	77	77
Which is bigger, a duck or a goose?	92	84	91	89	79
Which of the following is known as: (a) a President; (b) an actor; (c) a prizefighter:					
Hoover?	45	66	76	84	95
Roosevelt?	93	97	96	99	100
Joe Louis?	79	92	96	98	95
Clark Gable?	87	96	98	98	100
From what animal do we get:					
Bacon?	41	51	67	63	65
Beef?	48	48	62	74	78
Pork?	32	65	84	92	91
Does a mother . . . . have milk for her baby? †					
Elephant?	18	16	23	18	20
Wolf?	19	19	28	32	20
Goat?	69	81	90	91	93
Do the following grow: (a) on vines; (b) in the ground; (c) on trees; (d) on bushes:					
Watermelons?	10	17	45	48	45
Carrots?	65	80	73	91	93
Apples?	98	96	99	99	98
Which of the following comes from: (a) an animal; (b) a mine; (c) a plant; (d) the air:					
Linen?	29	50	69	68	83
Salt?	30	44	74	82	85
Sugar?	44	58	75	82	80
Cotton?	42	75	87	90	92
Leather?	63	68	82	92	80
Coal?	64	82	94	96	92
Wool?	89	93	95	93	94
Meat?	92	100	91	99	100

* The twelve-year-olds were not as representative as the younger children, since they included no pupil above the sixth grade.

† Introductory item: A mother cow has milk for her baby, but a mother hen does not. Does a mother . . . . have milk for her baby?

testimony of a playmate. Unless a child, through somewhat bitter experience, has learned to distrust others, he is prone to accept as true anything told to him that is not contradicted by his own experience or by some higher authority. Here are some of the things believed by one child: A swallowed hair will turn into a worm; a swallowed apple seed may sprout in the stomach; a withered spot on the lawn or in the pasture means that the ground is hollow underneath and, if one lands on such a spot hard enough, he may sink all the way to China; the devil comes when people whistle.

Misconceptions may likewise arise through malicious remarks made by adults concerning individuals against whom they are prejudiced. Such remarks are often elaborated on by children and passed along to others. Thus, a boy of nine believed that members of a certain small religious denomination could spit blood whenever they wanted to and that children would catch a bad disease by using a toilet that was used by members of another denomination.

Faulty perception of a word may lead to confusion. At the dinner table a boy devoutly closed his eyes and folded his hands when his mother said, "Now we are to have pears" ("pears" at the time, was his pronunciation of the word "prayers"). A boy, after finishing his bedtime prayer said, "Mama, I want to say the wort prayer." After some questioning it became clear: He wanted the prayer used by his older sister, "Our Father Who'rt in heaven." A boy in a geography class, hearing his teacher discuss "the earth as a whole," was so lost in thought trying to picture the earth as a hole that he failed a few moments later to answer a question put to him by his teacher and got a sharp rebuke for not paying attention.

Many of the more obvious misconceptions involve misinterpretation or lack of understanding of words and phrases. Thus a child was overheard giving this version of the pledge of allegiance to the flag: "I pledge a legion to the flag of the Republic of Richard Sands; one nation and a vegetable with liberty and justice to all." Another sang: "Long train run over us" ("Long to reign over us"); and another patriotically intoned: "I love thy rots and chills" ("rocks and rills"). After a moment's hesitation on a line in "The Night Before Christmas," a child came forth with: "I rushed to the window and vomited (threw up) the sash." One youngster for several years patriotically sang, "the grandpas we watched were so gallantly screaming."

Children may be able to deliver the right answers without actually knowing the meanings of the words they are using. For instance, a girl came home from school and excitedly announced that she now knew where hens lay their eggs: "They lay their eggs on the average." Her teacher had told the class that hens, in the laying season, lay one egg a day, *on the average.*

UNDERSTANDING OF ACADEMIC TERMS AND CONCEPTS

In their school work children are often called upon to use ideas in large relationships when they have little understanding of the underlying meanings of the individual terms and ideas (Scott and Myers, 1923). As we have seen, a child may correctly give the name of a colony, of an explorer, and so on, and yet be unable to clearly state just what an explorer or a colony *is*. On a test, a child may be able correctly to identify Benjamin Franklin as a *minister* to France, but still wonder why we sent a *clergyman,* with a big wig and tight breeches, over to preach to the Frenchmen. A child may fail for a long time to see any relationship between the taxes he reads about in his history class and the extra penny he pays as sales tax in making a small purchase.

UNDERSTANDING OF ABSTRACTIONS AS ILLUSTRATED BY CARTOONS

In a study by Shaffer (1930), ten newspaper cartoons were presented to approximately 150 children in each grade from four through twelve, and the children were asked to write an answer to the question, "What does this cartoon mean?" It was noted that a large proportion of responses in grades four and five were descriptions of the cartoon, without interpretation. At the later grade levels interpretations which recognized the symbolic nature of the picture predominated.

CONCEPTS OF TIME, SPACE, AND MAGNITUDE

Through concrete experience in the day's routine, a child has opportunities gradually to formulate notions of what is meant by a minute or a day, although much confusion often prevails, partly because of vagueness in adult usage (such as "Just a minute" which sometimes stretches to an hour). As with adults, a child's awareness of time will be influenced by how his time is occupied: time spent in waiting is long, and a twenty-minute lesson may seem almost interminable, while a similar recess period spent in play seems short.

Young children refer to the present before they refer to the future, and deal with the future before they seem to have clear ideas about the past (Ames, 1946). The word "today" was used by children in one study at about twenty-four months, "tomorrow" at thirty months, and "yesterday" at thirty-six months (Ames, 1946).

Children's ideas of historical time, in terms of decades, centuries, or epochs are likely to be quite hazy until they are well along in school. Even in high school some youngsters have difficulty in grasping concepts of duration and sequence in connection with historical events and movements. In one study (Oakden and Sturt, 1922), children's ideas of degrees of antiquity were measured by such means as having them arrange the names of well-known historical personages in order of their remoteness in the past and having them respond to pictures denoting customs and costumes representing different historical periods. Concepts of historical time held by children were found to be rather hazy until about the age of eleven years. Some children, of course, acquire ideas of time considerably earlier than others.

Undoubtedly, much that a child is exposed to in history lessons, or in units on Ancient Egypt, or on the Early American Indian (not to mention units in geology dealing with the age of the earth!) is lost upon him as far as time relations are concerned. In one fifth-grade class, the children were discussing the Appalachian Mountains, and the teacher took the opportunity to question them on what they had retained from previous discussions of the age of the earth. The question, "How old do you think those mountains are?" stumped the group, until a hardy youngster answered, "I think those mountains came there at about the same time as the Pilgrim Fathers."

DISCREPANCIES BETWEEN CONCEPTS
CHILDREN ARE TAUGHT AND WHAT THEY LEARN

Many studies have shown that a large proportion of children at junior-high-school age and below have relatively little understanding of many topics relative to historical or contemporary social, economic, and political affairs, which are frequently emphasized in textbooks. In many schools there is a great discrepancy between what the teachers try to teach and what the pupils learn.

We might ask: What is the reason for this discrepancy? Although we lack a complete answer there are two factors that especially deserve attention: To promote effective learning, it is essential (1) to scale the subject matter to the child's level of mental maturity and (2) to present the subject matter in such a way that the child can test and grasp its meaning in the light of his own experience.

UNDERSTANDING AS RELATED TO MATURITY LEVEL

First, a word with respect to scaling to maturity level. Findings from numerous studies show that children's ability to grasp subject matter in the areas commonly known as the "social studies" depends in part upon a process of maturing and upon experiences associated with the fact of growing older. Children's knowledge in these areas does not increase in proportion to the length of time devoted to them (Eaton, 1944). We have no assurance, for example, that a child who has studied history in school since he entered fourth grade will have a significantly more profound grasp of historical concepts at the end of the sixth grade than a child of similar mental ability who first began to study history when he entered the sixth grade. Neither can we be sure that conditions in the general environment surrounding the child will substantially alter the pattern of his concept formation. We might expect that in the excitement of wartime, for example, children would have a deeper appreciation of the meaning of current events than during peacetime. Actually, findings from a number of studies indicate that children's understanding of wartime happenings is substantially similar to their understanding of peacetime affairs (Kimmons, 1915-1916). In a study conducted with children in the New York City area in 1940 while World War II was in progress (Preston, 1942), 62 per cent of children aged nine and ten did not know that the British Navy was larger than the German Navy, and 52 per cent did not know that the German Air Force was stronger—at the time—than the British Air Force. Both of these facts were crucial to an understanding of the war situation and both facts were constantly being stressed in the news and in adult conversation.

Various other lines of evidence further illustrate the fact that the understanding of certain concepts depends not upon concentrated study or vivid experiences alone but upon impressions that accumulate in the process of becoming older. A study by Pistor (1940) deals with the development of time concepts. A time-concept test was given to two groups of sixth-grade pupils, aged ten, eleven, and twelve years. One group had previously, in the fourth and fifth grades, received systematic training in both history and geography and during the sixth grade the concept of historical time was taught to them in quite an intensive fashion. The children of the other group had received training primarily in geography alone, with only incidental attention to historical matters.

When tested early in the seventh grade, both groups showed a substantial gain over the scores earned before they began their work in the sixth grade. However, the average scores of the two groups of children were practically equal. Special emphasis on time concepts in one case, and absence of special attention to such concepts in the other, had not produced any significant differences.

ACADEMIC ABSTRACTIONS
AS DISTINGUISHED FROM PERSONAL MEANINGS

When we study the child from a developmental point of view and then look at the kind of subject matter he is required to learn at school we can observe many contrasts. In our educational system we have a passion for asking children to lift themselves by their own boot-straps out of the world in which they live into a world of academic abstractions. The child who is still trying to find a place for himself in the present is asked to study about the remote past. The child who is preoccupied with problems in his current social life is asked to study the rise and fall of ancient civilizations. The child who has only a hazy notion of the geography of his own township is asked to bound the nations of Europe and to give a learned discourse about the Rock of Gibraltar.

The youngster who is deeply immersed in competition with his fellows, and perhaps not even half aware of what this competitiveness means, is diverted from his own situation into a study of competition between nations for the world's trade. The child who sees prejudice and racial discrimination practiced before his eyes is asked to side-step this situation while studying about the misfortunes of subjugated people ten thousand miles away.

All these excursions from his own homeland into the fields of academic scholarship would be well justified if the child thereby stretched and exercised the muscles of his mind. But we have little reason to believe that the mind is strengthened by abandoning the reality of what is immediate and moving into regions that are remote.

Actually, the personal and the academic need not be so divorced from each other. Every subject or skill taught at school could have a personal meaning. History, for example, is the study of the acting out of motives and emotions such as arise in the life of every child: courage and cowardice; anger and fear; strivings for possession and power; loyalty and love; spite and vindictiveness; struggles for independence and freedom. History tells of the pioneers, but each child, in his own way, is a pioneer. It tells about Napoleon, but there are Napoleonic tendencies in everyone. History tells of Lincoln's tears as he spared the life of a deserter and also tells how Lincoln sent armies into slaughter; on a small scale, in one way or another, each person faces conflicts such as those Lincoln had to face. Literature, likewise, deals with sentiments, motives and moods, and with predicaments that occur in the personal drama of a child's own life. Biology, similarly, touches on areas that are or might be of intimate concern to the learner, including his curiosity about sex. But when a teacher tries to tap the personal significance of a school subject he needs to do something more than to repeat the conventional academic motions. It is essential for him not only to master the intellectual content of the subject he teaches but also to be alert to the emotional meanings his subject might have for his students.

Interplay of thinking and feeling

In childhood, as in adult years, a person's thinking is greatly influenced by his feelings and emotional needs. Emotion can be both an aid and a hindrance to fruitful thinking. It is an aid when a person, spurred by affection or desire or anger or fear, plunges into new areas of thought and uses his mind to solve problems in a realistic way. It is a hindrance when a person, instead of taking a thoughtful view of things, uses his reasoning to shield himself from facing reality. This occurs, for example, when a child over-indulges in "wishful thinking" or looks for evidence to support his anger while ignoring evidence of good will. It is not children alone but also scholarly adults whose thinking is distorted by their emotions. According to Murphy (1945), "the towering genius of the great scientist often lapses into childish babbling as he turns to problems in which his personal desires give structure to his thought."

What a person hears or what he perceives in a written account is likely to reflect the attitudes he already has. Also, materials that are in keeping with a person's firmly held attitudes are likely to be more easily learned or retained than materials that are opposed to his attitudes.

The attitudes that already prevail show through prominently when people are confronted with ambiguous material from which they can infer or into which they can inject their own bias. In a study by McKillop (1952) children were asked to respond to biased but more or less plausible statements about communism and about racial relationships. When the passages and the questions were so phrased that there were no right answers, but, rather, an opportunity for the children to express judgments of their own, the children revealed their attitudes more clearly than when the information was specific and the questions quite definite.

Every child (as well as adult) is strongly tempted at times to use thought as a servant of desire rather than of truth, to use it to rationalize a grievance, and to put a false face on his emotional problems. But the comfort a person derives from using his ability to think as a means of evading reality is likely to be short-lived. In the discussion of anxiety in Chapter Thirteen we noted examples of the way in which a rationalized "solution" can create more problems than it solves. When a child uses his mind to deceive himself it is unfortunate but he can hardly be blamed; everybody else does it! However, this does not mean that his mind is so constituted that it necessarily must be used as an instrument of self-deception.

When children (in common with adults) seem rather naive with regard to their motives and disinclined to take a look at themselves we cannot assume that they lack the capacity for self-inquiry. Very little has been done by our educational system to discover children's capacity for self-inquiry or to help them to cultivate it.

Recommended Readings

The books named at the end of Chapter Fourteen are also appropriate for this chapter. In addition, the following briefer writings are recommended: Lawrence Kubie's "The Forgotten Man of Education" (1954a); and "Some Unresolved Problems of the Scientific Career" (1954b); W. Edgar Vinacke's "Concept Formation in Children of School Ages"; and Chapter 11 in Jerome M. Seidman's *The Child: A Book of Readings* (1958).

Measuring and Predicting Intellectual Growth

  In this chapter we will consider the abilities that are measured by intelligence tests, the conditions that influence their development, and the personal characteristics of children who possess these abilities to a high or low degree.

A child's intelligence profoundly influences the way he is regarded by others. At school, the bright child who applies his wits is praised and viewed by his teachers as a success. The dull child frequently feels the sting of failure. In life's adventure, a child has a big advantage if he is bright. But high intelligence is not always an unmixed good. The bright child is better able to foresee and to plan happy possibilities, but he is also better able to anticipate misfortune. He is able to set high goals, but his aspirations may be so high that he can never attain them.

Definitions of intelligence

Authorities in the field of mental testing differ in their definitions of intelligence. Some define intelligence solely as a cognitive or intellectual operation, the ability to think abstractly, to deal with symbols, to perceive relationships, to reason, to reach correct generalizations. Some include in their definition not only the ability to reach solutions that are true from a purely intellectual point of view but also in the ability to reach solutions that are correct from a social point of view.

Thorndike's account of the nature of intelligence (1927) names a variety of operations including attention, retention, recall, recognition, selective and relational thinking, abstraction, generalization, inductive and deductive reasoning. Stoddard (1943) offers this definition: "Intelligence is the ability to undertake activities that are characterized by (1) difficulty, (2) complexity, (3) abstractness, (4) economy, (5) adaptiveness to goal, (6) social value, and (7) the emergence of originals, and to maintain such activities under conditions that demand a concentration of energy and a resistance to emotional forces." This definition, with its reference to social value and resistance to emotional forces, goes beyond the purely abstract, cognitive aspects of intellectual activity.

Intelligence tests

The typical intelligence test consists of a number of concrete tasks yielding, in the aggregate, a total score. Tests designed for children are scaled to children's capacities at various maturity levels. Thus a young child may be asked to fit blocks of varying shapes (round, square, triangular) into corresponding depressions in a board, to repeat numbers that are spoken to him, to name objects or to identify pictures of objects. An inventory of mental growth in infancy and early childhood developed by Bayley (1933b) includes such items as response to sounds, giving sustained attention to an object, and securing a ring by pulling a string to which it is attached. Tests of older children include measures of vocabulary, ability to solve problems of various kinds, immediate memory, speed of learning, ability to understand and interpret the meanings of written passages, to make deductions or inductions from observed facts, and so forth.

THE STANFORD-BINET SCALE

The best-known individual intelligence test is the Stanford-Binet scale, an instrument originated by Binet and subsequently revised and improved by Terman and later by Terman and Merrill (1937). This scale consists of test items graded in difficulty from the age of two upward. Each item can be scored as passed or failed. There are six test items at each half-yearly level from two years through four years, and six test items at each yearly age level thereafter up through age fourteen. After these follow tests for the "average adult" and "superior adult" levels.[1] The items at any age level represent tasks that the normal child of that age has been able to perform successfully.

A child's performance on the scale can be scored in terms of *mental age*. Thus, if he passes all the tests up to and including the third year and fails all tests beyond that point, he has a mental age of three years. If he succeeds on tests beyond the three-year level, he receives credit for each such success. Each of the twelve tests at the two-, three-, and four-year levels counts as one month of mental age; and each of the six tests at later yearly levels counts as two months of mental age. Thus, if a child passes all tests up to and including three years, plus four of the twelve tests at four years, he is credited with a mental age of three years, four months, which means that his mentality is equal to that of the average child of three years and four months.

The intelligence quotient. To obtain an index of the child's brightness, when the Stanford-Binet scale is used, the *mental age* is divided by the *chronological age* and the result multiplied by 100 to yield a value known as the *intelligence quotient*. Thus a normal or average three-year-old child will have a mental age of three, a chronological age of three, and an IQ of 100. If the same child earns a mental score of four years, his IQ is 133; if he does no better than the normal two-year-old, his IQ is only 67.[2]

OTHER TYPES OF INTELLIGENCE TESTS

The Stanford-Binet test is administered to one child at a time. There are other individual tests and also tests applicable to older children and adults that can be administered to several persons in a group simultaneously. Among the intelligence tests widely used with children is the WISC —Wechsler Intelligence Scale for Children (Wechsler, 1949, 1950a, 1950b, 1951).

---

[1] This statement refers to the 1937 revision. An earlier revision included tests from the age of three upward, with six tests at each age level. For a discussion of intelligence tests, steps involved in constructing tests and in determining their effectiveness, see Thorndike and Hagen (1955).

[2] When the test is used with adults, the value representing chronological age does not become higher as the person becomes older; instead, an upper limit of fifteen years is set. Thus, a man of thirty with a mental age of twelve has an IQ of 80.

Consistency and reliability
of intelligence ratings

Bayley (1933b) and others have shown that intelligence scales designed for children below the age of three are less reliable than scales designed for older children. Many difficulties arise in testing a child before he has learned to talk and to understand spoken language. With young children it is more difficult than at later levels to segregate the more strictly mental from the motor, social, and emotional forms of response. The young child's response is also likely to be more variable than the older child's.

Infant tests, in their present form, do not give an accurate prediction of a child's intelligence. The younger the child, the less certain we are that his score gives an indication of his probable IQ in later years, although even in early infancy a markedly subnormal or a markedly superior rating may have significance for the future.

A young child's ratings on *consecutive* tests, near in time, are likely to show a good deal of resemblance, but the longer the interval between two tests, the lower the resemblance is likely to be. Bayley found, for example, a positive correlation [3] of .57 between average scores at one to three

---

[3] Two examples of a correlation coefficient are given below. The first shows the correlation between IQ ratings based on two separate tests; the second, the correlation between IQ and strength of grip. In these examples, one of the simplest methods of correlation, known as the "rank-difference method," is used. It can be applied when there are only a small number of cases. Only seven cases are included here; this number is large enough for illustrative purposes but too small for ordinary statistical work.

The rank difference correlation coefficient is expressed by the symbol ρ. The formula used in the present case is:

$$\rho = 1 - \frac{6 \times \text{sum of } D^2}{N(N^2 - 1)}$$

The illustrations show that the subjects' scores must first be ranked. D represents the difference between the same subject's rank in the two tests; N, the number of cases.

Individuals Tested	IQ Test I	Rank	IQ Test II	Rank	D	D^2	IQ Test I Rank	Strength of Grip in Kgm.	Rank	D	D^2
Albert	80	7	79	7	0	0	7	22	6	1	1
Henry	90	6	95	4	2	4	6	28	3	3	9
John	104	3	110	3	0	0	3	20	7	4	16
Peter	95	5	92	6	1	1	5	30	2	3	9
Palmer	140	1	135	1	0	0	1	26	4	3	9
Robert	120	2	125	2	0	0	2	34	1	1	1
Walter	100	4	94	5	1	1	4	24	5	1	1

months and at four to six months, and a correlation of .42 between scores at one to three and seven to nine months. As the interval increased, the correlations decreased, so that there was practically a zero correlation between scores at one to three months and scores beyond the age of twelve months. However, as children grow older the scores usually become more stable.

Many factors contribute to the lack of consistency in young children's ratings on consecutive tests: different rates of growth; irregularities in rate of growth; changes in adjustment to the test situation; and the likelihood that the various functions measured by the test mature at different rates.

According to Bayley's findings, differences between children become greater with advancing age, and there is also a greater spread in the performance of individual children on a given examination (as when a child of eighteen months performs at a level of a two-year-old on some parts of the scale and no better than the average child of eighteen months on other parts).

Theoretically, we might expect less consistency in rate of mental growth during the earlier years. The young child is progressing rapidly; new abilities are emerging at different rates and are being consolidated. At six or seven years the child is still maturing rapidly, but his gains from year to year consist more of added competence in using his existing capacities than in the emergence of new abilities.

$$N = 7 \qquad \text{Sum of } D^2 = 6$$
$$N^2 - 1 = 48 \qquad 6 \times \text{sum of } D^2 = 36$$
$$N(N^2 - 1) = 336$$

$$\rho = 1 - \frac{6 \times \text{sum of } D^2}{N(N^2 - 1)}$$

$$= 1 - 36/336$$

$$= +.89 \text{ (between the first and second test of IQ)}$$

$$\text{Sum of } D^2 = 46$$
$$6 \times \text{sum of } D^2 = 276$$

$$\rho = 1 - 276/336$$

$$= +.18 \text{ (between first IQ test and strength of grip)}$$

In the first example, there is a high degree of correspondence between the children's IQ's on Tests I and II. Each child maintains about the same rank on both tests. If each child kept exactly the same rank on both tests, there would be a perfect correlation of +1.00. If there were no consistency at all between scores on the first and second tests, the correlation would be 0. If there were a complete reversal of ranks, the correlation would be −1.00. For practical purposes, we would be able to make a fairly accurate estimate of what a child's rating on Test II would be if we knew his relative standing on Test I.

In the second example, we find a positive but low correlation between IQ and strength of grip. On the basis of the figures in this example, there is a likelihood that a child with a high IQ will also tend to be above rather than below average in strength of grip. But the correspondence is so small that, if we tried to estimate his score in one test on the basis of our knowledge of his score on the other, our estimate would be little more than a guess.

Age at Earlier Test	Interval Between Test and Retest							
	Less than 4 months	4 to 9 months	10 to 15 months	16 to 21 months	22 to 29 months	30 to 41 months	42 to 53 months	Over 53 months
Under 4 months	.57	.33	.10	−.03	−.09			
4- 9 months	.77	.53	.49	.23	.16	.46	.00	
10-15 months	.78	.66	.50	.45	.33			.55
16-21 months	.76	.68	.51	.44	.38	.41	.25	.33
22-29 months	.82	.74	.68					.43
30-41 months	.87	.68	.66	.49	.57	.57	.56	.66
42-53 months	.81	.65	.72	.71	.66	.63	.63	.41
54-65 months			.76		.73			

TABLE 22 — COMPOSITE OF TEST-RETEST CORRELATIONS FROM SEVERAL STUDIES OF INFANT AND PRESCHOOL GROUPS *

* From R. L. Thorndike, " 'Constancy' of the I.Q.," *Psychological Bulletin* (1940), 37, p. 173. Reproduced by permission of the American Psychological Association.

The lower predictive value of tests at the preschool than at the school-age level is not due entirely to irregularities in the growth pattern or to imperfections in the measuring instruments. As in infancy, so to a lesser but important degree at the preschool level, the reliability of test results depends upon the tester's success in winning the child's cooperation. Resistance or fear on the child's part may interfere with the test. The young child is less likely to recognize the importance (from the adult's point of view) of doing things according to the letter of the tester's instructions, and his interest may turn to features of the test that don't count. Also, a child who has learned to conform to directions will have an advantage over a child who has not learned to do so.

Constancy of mental test scores beyond the preschool level. As we have noted above, there is a relatively high degree of consistency in intelligence-test ratings from year to year at the school age and beyond. Children have approximately similar IQ's on successive tests if no significant changes in their circumstances have intervened (such as illness, emotional maladjustment, or transfer to a different environment).

It should be emphasized in passing that when psychologists speak of the "constancy" of the IQ they do not at all imply that the IQ will remain precisely the same from year to year. Rather the concept implies a high degree of probability (not certainty) that fluctuations will be relatively small in a majority of cases. Indeed, because of the variables involved in measuring the complex operations that constitute intelligence, it is improbable that a child would obtain precisely the same score on two equivalent forms of the same test, even if they were administered on successive days. In discussing results obtained with the best known of all individual tests for children (the Stanford-Binet scale), Terman some years ago pointed out that the chances were one in two that the IQ might increase as much as six points or decrease as much as four points; the chances of an increase of twelve points or a decrease of eight points were one in five; the chances of shifts larger than twelve points were considerably smaller but still impressive.

Goodenough (1940) estimates that in tests of a group of 500 children under the best conditions, at least 100 may be expected, on retests, to show changes in IQ of as much as ten points; changes of as much as fifteen points may be expected in about twenty-five instances, and four or five children may shift as much as twenty points. Goodenough points out that there may be even greater fluctuations if the tests are not administered by workers of equal competence or if comparisons are based upon results of different types of tests. In view of such fluctuations, a child's IQ on a test at a given time should not be regarded as a fixed value to be used once and for all in classifying a pupil or in guiding his work at school.

A child's score on an intelligence test will be inaccurate if the child, by reason of unique circumstances in his environment, is at a disadvantage on certain test items. Thus, a child who seldom has a chance to use money is at a disadvantage on test items dealing with the names and values of coins. Similarly, the score earned by a bilingual child may not represent his true ability. If a test involves questions that are better suited to the experience of one group than another (as, for example, urban as compared with rural, or isolated mountaineer, or Indian reservation groups), it will yield misleading results.

Limits of intellectual growth

The abilities measured by intelligence tests increase on the average from year to year during childhood and the yearly increase continues, but at a lower rate, during the late teens. In a review of earlier findings and from an analysis of the retest scores made by approximately a thousand persons, still in school, R. L. Thorndike (1948) concludes that the ability to achieve on a standard type of paper-and-pencil test of intelligence continues to increase until age twenty and probably beyond.

The influence of nature
and nurture on intellectual ability

It has been said that hered-
ity determines what a person *can* do while the environment determines
what he *does* do; also that heredity provides the potentialities while the
environment determines how well these will be realized. These statements
emphasize the importance of both heredity and environment, but they
oversimplify the situation, for whether a child happens to be richly or
poorly endowed he is not just a passive bystander: He takes an active
role himself in seeking, selecting, and using, or avoiding and rejecting
what his environment offers to him.

One of the most widely used means of studying the influence of heredity
and environment has been to measure the resemblances between blood
relatives: parents and children, siblings and twins. Another approach has
been to study the resemblances between children and their foster parents
as compared with resemblances between children and their own parents.

The method of statistical correlation, yielding what is called a correlation coefficient—which we discussed earlier in this chapter—has been
applied in such studies.

RESEMBLANCES BETWEEN PARENTS AND CHILDREN
AND BETWEEN SIBLINGS

In a study in 1903, Pearson compared certain physical characteristics of
parents and children and found correlations of about .50. When he compared certain of their mental characteristics, he found about the same
correlations. Pearson made a historic conclusion that physical and mental
characteristics in man are inherited within broad lines in the same manner
and with the same intensity. Later investigations have, in the main, supported this generalization.

In a large number of studies during the past decades correlations of
about .50 have been found in comparisons between the intelligence of
fathers and their children and between mothers and their children. Positive correlations ranging around the .50 mark have likewise been found
between the intelligence of siblings living in the same environment.

In a review of findings in this area Jones (1954) points out that this
correlation of about .50 between the intelligence of siblings is so well
established that if a study reports a lower correlation we probably should
suspect that there was something faulty in the method of the study or
that the sampling is not typical.

While a correlation of +.50 is very respectable, it falls far short of a
"perfect" correlation of +1.00. Actually, even if heredity, or the environ-

ment, were the one and only factor in determining intelligence, a correlation of +1.00 between fathers or mothers and their children could not be obtained unless fathers and mothers had exactly the same intelligence level or had an identical influence on their children's environment. It is, of course, very unlikely that fathers and mothers would be identical in intelligence or in the nature of their relationships with their children, and whatever either parent contributes to the heredity of a child reflects not only what is measurable in the parent's own make-up, but also hereditary influences that are latent and not apparent.

When we study parent-child resemblances in intelligence it is important to take account of the age level of the children at the time when the intelligence tests are administered. In long-term studies it has been found that the similarity in intelligence between parents and children is quite low when based on measurements of children before the age of three years. This does not mean that the young child is less influenced by heredity than the older child. It means, rather, that tests of a very young child do not measure the same abilities as are measured in an older person or that they do not give as trustworthy a measure of his potentialities as tests applied at a later age level.

> In a study by Honzik (1957), children were first tested at the age of 21 months and then were tested again several times until they had reached the age of 14 or 15. Two measures were used to get an approximate indication of the intelligence of the mothers: ratings by members of a research team, and the number of years of schooling the mothers had completed. (The correlation between the two ratings was .73.) At 21 months the correlation between the intelligence of the children and ratings of the abilities of the mothers were close to zero. However, on tests of the children from age 7 to the age of 14 or 15, the correlation between the children's scores and the ratings of the mothers' intelligence were near or somewhat above .50. In a similar study by Bayley (1954) it was likewise found that the correlation between children's mental test scores and the education of parents was near zero during the first fifteen months but reached the level of .60 or more when the children were in their teens.

RESEMBLANCES BETWEEN TWINS

Correlations between the intelligence of identical twins (also called uniovular or monozygotic twins) who have presumably developed from the same fertilized ovum have ranged from the upper .70's to about .90. When identical twins are so similar in intelligence, to what extent might this be due to a similar environment? One way of getting a partial answer is to compare twins who have been brought up together in the same home with twins who have been separated and brought up in different homes. Newman, Freeman, and Holzinger (1937) found that twins who had received about the same amount and kind of education were, on the whole, more alike in IQ than twins who differed considerably in this respect. This is in keeping with findings which show that schooling makes a difference in intellectual development. However, identical twins reared apart still, as a group, were more alike than siblings reared in the same home. This does not mean that the twins are precisely similar in their behavior. As noted elsewhere in this book, there are differences between twins classed as "identical" in vigor and enterprise even from the time of birth. Even if the environment is the "same" in the sense that their parents make every effort to treat them alike, it does not necessarily follow that they will respond in the same fashion in what they take from the environment.

THE INTELLIGENCE OF FOSTER CHILDREN

Foster children share the home environment but not the immediate heredity of the family in which they are reared, so it is instructive to compare resemblances between foster children and foster parents with resemblances between blood relatives living in the same home.

In interpreting the resemblance between parents and foster children it is important to recognize that placement agencies try to "fit the child to the home." As a result, a child might resemble his adopted parents quite apart from any influence they may have had upon him (Leahy, 1935). In a study by Leahy (1935) in which this factor was taken into account, it was found that the correlation between "own" parents and their children ranged considerably higher (clustering around .50) than correlations between foster parents and children (clustering around .20). In an earlier study, Burks (1928) found that the correlations between parents and their own children were considerably higher than the correlations between children and foster parents. A higher estimate of the effect of the environment was given by Freeman and his associates (1928).

A series of studies of foster children by Skodak and Skeels is especially interesting because the investigators followed the development of a number of adopted children from infancy to adolescence. In their latest investigation Skodak and Skeels (1949) were able to locate and re-test 100 foster children who had been placed for adoption at the age of 6 months. The average age of the children at the time of the first test was 2 years and 2 months; they were tested again at 4 years and 3 months, at 7 years, then again at an average age of 13 years and 6 months. Test scores were available for 63 of the true mothers of these children. The tests were administered to the mothers at a time that could not be regarded as favorable since each of the mothers had recently conceived and given birth to a child whom she could not keep as her own.

The correlation between the scores of the true mothers and the foster children on the first test was zero; on the second .28; on the third .35; on the fourth .38 (based on a 1916 revision of the Stanford-Binet test) and

.44 (based on the 1937 revision of the Stanford-Binet test). In other words, at about the time of adolescence, the correlation between scores of the children who had lived in foster homes and the scores earned by their own mothers—from whom they had been separated since infancy—came close to the parent-child correlations that have been found in tests of children who have spent all their lives with their own parents. On the other hand, correlations between the intelligence of the foster children and the educational status of the foster parents, with whom they had spent most of their lives, hovered around zero.

In commenting on the results of her own long-term study of children living with their original parents and the findings in the Skodak-Skeels study, Honzik says that "the finding that parent-child resemblances in ability follow the same changes in the two studies, even though the true parents did not rear the children in the Skeels-Skodak group, suggests that the existing relationship is largely due to genetic factors which tend to become manifest in the child during the later preschool years." According to Honzik, the fact that the resemblances between children and their biological parents are not substantially greater if children are reared by their own parents than if they are reared by foster parents, and the further fact that there was no relationship between foster children's mental test performance and the foster parents' ability as measured by educational status indicate that "parental education *per se* is not an environmentally important factor and that the obtained parent-child correlations reflect individual differences which are genetically determined" (1957).

IMPLICATIONS FOR PARENTS

Findings that show a considerably higher relationship between the intelligence of children and their true parents than between the intelligence of adopted children and the educational level of their foster parents have implications for parents in general and also for those who are thinking of adopting a child, or already have adopted children. For people who are thinking of adopting a child, the findings in the nature-nurture studies show that in many instances children from an unpromising family background turn out to be bright. But the findings do not offer anything approaching a guarantee that an adopted child is likely to have good or high intelligence by virtue of the fact that his foster parents are bright and well-educated.

For parents in general, the findings emphasize this simple fact: While it is important for parents to encourage a child's intellectual development as well as they can, it is also important that they recognize that there are limits to what they can do. If a child turns out to be as bright as his parents wanted him to be, they have reason to be pleased; but if he does not they should guard against blaming themselves, or him, or others.

While the evidence shows that heredity plays an important role in determining mental ability, there remains a tremendous amount of leeway in the way in which a child can use his potential ability.

HEREDITY AND LEARNING ABILITY IN LOWER ANIMALS

Striking evidence concerning the relationship between heredity and the ability to learn has come from studies of selective breeding in rats. In one study, beginning with 142 rats, Tryon (1940) kept a record of the number of errors the rats made in running a maze (a rat was charged with an error each time he entered a blind alley). Then the "brightest" of the rats (those with the fewest errors) were bred with the brightest and the dullest with the dullest, and this selective breeding was continued for several generations. In the eighth generation the scores made by the two groups of rats on the maze were radically different; the averages were far apart and the dullest in the bright group performed almost as well as the brightest in the dull group. In later generations the bright rats continued to be far superior, on the average, to the dull, but the difference between the two groups did not become progressively greater.

We might ask whether, from a rat's point of view, an animal who makes few errors in solving a man-made puzzle is brighter than one who makes many errors. But this question does not negate the finding that the ability required to run the maze was influenced to a marked degree by selective breeding.

Effect of schooling
on intellectual development

To what extent is a child's intelligence influenced by the amount, kind, and timing of the schooling he receives? If a child's intelligence test scores vary according to the schooling he has received, does this mean that intelligence tests are largely a measure of the skills and performances a child has learned? Or does it mean that through his schooling the child not only has learned specific things but also that his mind has become better equipped to deal with new intellectual tasks than it would be if he had gone to a different school or had not gone to school at all?

INFLUENCE OF NURSERY-SCHOOL EXPERIENCE

Many studies have raised the question as to whether attending nursery school is likely to raise a child's IQ above the level it would reach had he not gone to nursery school. The findings here have varied.

In studies conducted by Wellman and her associates at the University of Iowa, children who attended nursery school showed gains in IQ. In several other studies, children have shown little or no change in IQ. The reported average gains following a year in nursery school, in studies in which gains have appeared, have not been large compared with the differences between the IQ's of children in the population at large. In one of Wellman's studies (1932), average gains of about six to eight points were noted between fall and spring tests.

Olson and Hughes (1940) found that nursery-school children from privileged backgrounds did not differ significantly in their intellectual growth from non-nursery-school children of similar backgrounds; and children who attended nursery school an average of over two hundred days did not differ significantly from children who, on the average, had attended only about half as many days. They point out, however, that the home nurture of these children was perhaps of such a character that the nursery school could add little to it. They suggest also that different results might be obtained if studies were made of children who suffer from deprivation in the home environment and for whom the nursery school might provide intellectual nurture more in keeping with their potential achievement.[4]

The findings do not promise that a child from a "good" home environment is likely to show a substantial rise in IQ if sent to nursery school. (He may, of course, gain in other ways, as has been shown in studies of the effects of nursery-school experience on children's social adjustments, habits, and skills.)

One of the most interesting studies of the effects of the nursery-school environment (Skeels, Updegraf, et al., 1938) was undertaken in a large orphanage. The orphanage provided meager stimulation and limited opportunities, and the children were deficient in many ways; they lacked imagination in using play material, and were backward in their social skills, their ability to work effectively with others, and in their motor skills. A number of these children were assigned to an experimental group while others, matched in age and ability, served as a control group. Both groups remained in the orphanage, but during several hours of the day the experimental group attended a nursery school that was established in the institution. The children who attended nursery school for a period of about twenty months showed an average gain of 4.6 points in IQ. Many individuals showed large gains. In the meantime, the children in the control group during this period showed an average loss of 4.6 points in IQ. (As noted in a more detailed account of this study in Chapter

---

[4] For other studies and comments on studies dealing with the effects of nursery-school or kindergarten experience on intelligence, see Goodenough and Maurer (1940), a report of an experiment by McCandless dealing with very bright children (reported in Wellman, 1934), and other studies reported in the *Thirty-Ninth Yearbook* of the N.S.S.E. (1940).

Seven, the gains made by the nursery-school children in other aspects of their development and behavior were in many ways more impressive than the improvements in their IQ's.)

In studies of older children, gains in intelligence have been noted in children after they have been transferred from institutions to foster homes or after they have moved from one community to another offering better educational opportunities. In one study (Klineberg, 1935, 1938), Negro children who had come to New York from the South with their families and who had lived longer periods in the North earned higher average scores than those who had arrived more recently. A Philadelphia study reports results that are, in the main, in keeping with those reported by Klineberg (Lee, 1951).

Another study which indicates that problems associated with a child's cultural background may adversely affect his response to an intelligence test has been reported by Anastasi and Cordova (1953), who gave intelligence tests to Puerto Rican children, most of whom had learned to speak Spanish and then had to learn English. The test performance of the children was below the norm. They appeared to have little or no desire to excel in a competitive intellectual situation, and they showed a lack of interest in the relatively abstract and intellectual content of the test. This reaction to the testing situation was apparently related to a rather passive and unresponsive attitude toward school, brought about in part, so it seemed, by the fact that the children had been thrust into an exclusively English-speaking environment at a time when they knew little English.

It does not appear that large changes in IQ can be expected simply by sending children who already have reasonably good educational opportunities to relatively superior elementary schools (Thorndike et al., 1940) or by transferring children from regular classes to special "opportunity" classes. Pritchard, Horan, and Hollingworth (1940) studied 111 children of below-average intelligence and socioeconomic status who were transferred from their regular classrooms in the New York public school system to special classes in a school that was designed to provide an optimal educational environment. The children derived many benefits from the school, but there was no significant change in the pattern of their mental growth as measured by standard intelligence tests.

EFFECTS OF SCHOOLING BEYOND THE ELEMENTARY LEVEL

Apart from the question, "Would a different school make a difference in a child's intelligence?" is the question, "Would dropping out of school entirely make a difference?" Findings in a study by Lorge (1945) bear on the second question. A number of boys who were first tested in 1921-1922 when they were in the eighth grade were retested, twenty years later, in 1941. During the intervening twenty years the young people had continued their schooling for varying lengths of time; some had gone no farther than eighth grade while others had gone beyond high school. The youngsters were now grouped in terms of highest grade completed by 1941 and in terms of intelligence test scores earned in 1921. In a large number of comparisons, it was found that higher scores were earned by those who had gone on to complete higher grades in school. The farther persons went in their schooling (as measured by *highest grade completed*, not number of years of school attended) the higher their scores tended to be as compared with their original ratings in 1921.

Such findings as these do not mean, however, that intelligence rises in proportion to amount of schooling or that people with equal schooling will have equal intelligence. In spite of gains in scores of many (but not all) individuals who continued their schooling in Lorge's study, there was a high degree of correspondence between scores obtained twenty years apart (correlations of .62 and .64 respectively on the two instruments that were used at the time of the final test). Gains were relative to initial scores. Some children whose scores were among the highest on the first test and who went no farther than the eighth grade earned decidedly higher scores twenty years later than did children initially in lower brackets who successfully completed two, three, or four grades in high school.

In passing, it may be re-emphasized that the value of schooling cannot be measured simply by "before-and-after" mental tests. The opportunities a school affords may have an effect on the child's everyday habits and skills, and his social and emotional adjustments, quite apart from any gains in IQ. There may be gains also in the child's "functioning intelligence," in the effectiveness and the ways in which he puts his intelligence to everyday use, even if there are no demonstrable gains in his intelligence quotient as measured by mental tests.

Family and socioeconomic status and intelligence

In general, children of higher socioeconomic status have been found to have a higher average level of intelligence than children of lower status. These differences are not so apparent while children are still quite young, and, needless to say, individual differences within each occupational group are a good deal larger than the differences between the average scores of different groups.

These questions arise: To what extent is the higher average intelligence of children in the "upper" occupational levels due to a better environment? To what extent is due to heredity? To what extent is the difference only an apparent one because of faults in the testing instruments? A precise answer cannot be given to these questions. A child's environment obviously can have an important influence on his performance on an intelligence test, but it is also possible that the native abilities of a child's parents played a part in determining their occupational status. Other things being equal, we might expect, in a competitive society, that the hereditary endowment of a child's parents will have an important bearing on the vocation they choose and on their ability to "get ahead." However, the "other things" are far from "equal" if, for example, a child is reared in circumstances which do not foster his potentialities, or do not encourage the kind of learning and verbal ability that is measured by intelligence tests.

Exceptional children

The label "exceptional" is commonly applied to children who differ notably from the average. Among them the outstandingly bright ones are referred to as *gifted* children. Those who possess outstanding aptitudes in music, the arts, mechanics, and other areas are usually referred to as *talented*. The exceptional ones who are distinctly below average in mental ability are labelled *mentally retarded* or *deficient*. Those who suffer from special disabilities, such as brain damage, blindness, or other impairments are referred to as *handicapped* children.

The exceptional child clearly stands out as different from others, yet he is still a child. To understand him, we must appreciate the humanity he shares with ordinary human beings, and also assess the qualities that set him apart.

GIFTED CHILDREN

Children with IQ's of 120 or 125 or above are described as "superior." They represent from 5 to 10 per cent of the population. Among the superior ones are the "gifted" with IQ's of 135 or 140 and above; and the "extremely gifted" with IQ's of 170 or 180 or above. The "gifted" group constitutes approximately 1 to 3 per cent of the total population.

PERSONAL CHARACTERISTICS

Children with high intelligence are usually above rather than below average in many other characteristics, but it is in the intellectual field that their qualities are especially outstanding (Dunlap, 1958; Terman and

Oden, 1940; Wilson, 1953). A gifted child is likely to be curious and to ask many questions when he is young and to push into many areas of knowledge as he grows older. He is likely to be adept in the use of language, and many gifted children at an early age acquire a large vocabulary and an awareness of subtle shades of word meanings.

Gifted children frequently excel in reading. Many learn to read before entering school, and shortly thereafter plunge into materials designed for older children and adults. Many of the anecdotes about gifted youngsters deal with their appetite for reading, and barriers they encounter in trying to satisfy this appetite. One fourth-grade child in a small school had read and re-read everything in sight, including a set of encyclopedias and the books used by children in upper grades. When the school acquired a huge, unabridged dictionary, he proceeded to devour it, standing as he read— for he was not allowed to bring it to his desk. Judy, a second-grader, (described by Dunlap, 1958) came home from school one day with seven library books recommended by her teacher. When the teacher telephoned in the evening to explain that she was trying to encourage Judy to get a taste for the normal interests of her age-group, the mother exclaimed, "Oh, Judy read all seven books for you this afternoon so she could finish *Green Pastures* before bedtime."

Among other outstanding accomplishments of many gifted children is an ability to remember, to learn from past experience, and to use foresight in planning for the future. Also, they are frequently far above average in the maturity of their moral judgments.

Brightness and astuteness in responding to tests. A person who is able to earn a high score on an intelligence test is also likely to be more clever than the average person in responding to other forms of tests. Some gifted persons have a knack of anticipating the questions a teacher will ask on an examination and the kinds of answers he expects. This knack comes in handy at the high-school and college level. One bright student earned a mark of 99 on the first examination he took in a college course, and a glowing public tribute from the instructor. This student had deftly slanted all the answers on his examination to support the bias of the instructor, even though he disagreed with the instructor's point of view. (He was practicing what Hollingworth, in her classic work on the gifted, described as the art of "benign chicanery.")

The knack for figuring out the right or expected answer has undoubtedly colored the findings obtained in studies of the moral attitudes and emotional adjustment of gifted persons. A person who "knows the score" can, for example, give a "mature" answer on a test of moral judgment, and the "correct" answer on a test of politeness, social intelligence, civic responsibility, or neuroticism whether or not the answer expresses his personal attitudes or convictions. Even with this reservation, however, the weight of evidence indicates that gifted persons are more likely to be above than below average in character, responsibility, respectability, and conformity to what society regards as proper ways of behaving.

Discrepancies between brightness and academic achievement. While bright children, on the average, do superior work at school there are many individual exceptions to this rule. In a review of studies of the relation between intelligence test scores and academic success, Thorndike and Hagen (1955) state: "Viewing all the hundreds of correlations that have been reported, a figure of .50 to .60 might be taken as fairly representative." The correlations are somewhat higher at the elementary-school level (in the neighborhood of .70) and then drop to about .60 in high school and about .50 in college.

From a review of the literature by Goldberg, Gotkin, and Tannenbaum (1959) it is evident that many bright children do not use their superior ability to earn high grades. There probably are several reasons for this: Some children undoubtedly are bored; some have poor work habits; some are deterred by emotional problems; probably also (although this has not been explored adequately) many of them consciously or unconsciously feel that much of what is prescribed in the academic program is meaningless from a personal point of view.

When we try to assess the relationship between brightness and academic achievement, we must not only take into account the habits and attitudes of the individual student, but also consider the climate of opinion that prevails in his group, and the attitudes other children have toward scholarship. As children move from the elementary grades into high school it appears that high academic achievement is viewed much more favorably by their teachers than by their classmates. A study by Tannenbaum (1959) offers interesting findings about the values children assign to studiousness at the high-school level. Tannenbaum asked 615 eleventh-graders (305 boys and 310 girls) to record their attitudes toward hypothetical high-school students with various combinations of the following characteristics: brilliance, studiousness, and participation in athletics. The ratings are shown in Table 23.

As can be seen in Table 23, the student described as athletic consistently received a much higher rating than the one who was nonathletic. Brightness alone did not seem to be a decisive factor, for although the lowest rank was given to the student described as brilliant-studious-nonathletic, the highest rank was given to the one described as brilliant-nonstudious-athletic. The brilliant or average *nonstudious*-athletic person was regarded more favorably than the brilliant or average *studious* person. In this study, higher ratings were given to the athletic than to the nonathletic person by boys and by girls, by young people in a number of different communities, by students of higher as well as lower intelligence, and by students whose parents were in the upper as well as the lower educational brackets. Preliminary results in a study of younger children by Tannenbaum and his associates indicate that the studious pupil is likely to be viewed with more favor by his classmates at the elementary-school level than at the high-school level, yet the findings in Table 23 suggest that he cannot count on continued favor in the eyes of his classmates as he moves into the high-school grades.

TABLE 23 | AVERAGE RATINGS MADE BY 615 ELEVENTH-GRADERS OF THE SOCIAL ACCEPTABILITY OF EIGHT HYPOTHETICAL STUDENTS *

Hypothetical Student	Average Rating	Rank in Acceptability
Brilliant—Nonstudious—Athletic	28.35	1
Average—Nonstudious—Athletic	26.11	2
Average—Studious—Athletic	24.20	3
Brilliant—Studious—Athletic	23.75	4
Brilliant—Nonstudious—Nonathletic	11.78	5
Average—Nonstudious—Nonathletic	10.65	6
Average—Studious—Nonathletic	8.44	7
Brilliant—Studious—Nonathletic	2.20	8

* From A. J. Tannenbaum, *A Study of Verbal Stereotypes Associated with Brilliant and Average Students,* 1959. Unpublished Ph.D. Dissertation, Teachers College, Columbia University. Reproduced by permission.

According to the findings in Tannenbaum's study, the stereotype of the studious high-school student is, comparatively, not a favorable one. This raises many questions. Are high-school students perhaps envious of a classmate who works hard? Are they reflecting attitudes prevailing in the adult population? When they give such a relatively low rating to the student who takes his work seriously are they perhaps expressing disenchantment with school and even a growing rebellion against what the school claims to offer them? Further research would be required to answer these questions. Whatever the reasons underlying the results shown in Table 23 may be, these findings are consistent with trends in other studies which show that many children become less enthusiastic about the academic program as they move from elementary school into high school.

Brightness and undisclosed personal problems. Partly because of their higher intelligence, gifted children may be able to conceal personal problems from the eyes of their teachers. Many of them come from middle or high socioeconomic backgrounds in which there is less openly expressed emotional reaction than is found among children of lower socioeconomic status. In a study of 100 children with IQ's ranging from 150 to over 180, Gallagher and Crowder (1957) report that 20 per cent of the youngsters had emotional problems sufficient to cause personal difficulties; but usually the children managed not to bring these to the surface in a manner that was irritating to their teachers or so obvious that the teachers would rate them as emotionally maladjusted.

As a group, gifted children are likely to be named as the preferred companions of their classmates more often than children of average or below average intelligence (Miller, 1956; Gallagher and Crowder, 1947). However, Gallagher and Crowder (1957) found that a "sizable minority" had difficulties in their social relationships.

GIFTEDNESS AND ATTITUDES TOWARD SELF

Since brains are a great asset, the gifted child has a great potentiality for developing a realistic conception of himself and a healthy attitude toward his worth. He is more likely than the average child to win success and praise at school. He has a better than even chance in competition with others. His family is more likely to be of middle or high than low socioeconomic status and thus he avoids the stigma of being born on the wrong side of the tracks (there are, of course, many exceptions to this). He is potentially better able than those who are less richly endowed to take a thoughtful view of things, to plan, and to avoid the penalties of foolish actions. Theoretically, also, he should be able to use his superior intelligence in dealing with predicaments which lead to fear, anger, or unresolved grievances. In addition, his greater ability to deal with moral questions (at least on an intellectual level) should permit him to take a reasonable view of his conduct and to avoid a burden of irrational guilt.

Actually, however, high intelligence does not guarantee insight or healthy self-esteem. While gifted children generally rate higher than below-average children in tests of emotional adjustment, it has not been found that they uniformly rate themselves high in their own regard. In a study in which junior-high-school students rated themselves there was a zero correlation between their scores on a lengthy scale of self-acceptance and their scholastic standing (Spivack, 1956). This probably means that many bright children with high marks gave themselves rather low ratings. While there are many advantages in being bright there are also hazards, especially in the emotional and social spheres.

A keen mind can be used as an instrument of self-knowledge or for self-deception. The person who is brilliant but anxious may use his intellect in an effort to blunt his anxiety or to run away from it. According to Kubie (1954), even brilliant scientists may apply their intellects to evade rather than to face important issues in their personal lives.

Partly by reason of his brightness, a child may meet with disapproval from others, especially if they envy him, or if he is restless, or demanding because of unmet needs, or is sensitive to slights that another child might not notice, or sees possibilities of danger which another youngster would not perceive. A bright child also faces the possibility of being rejected by other children when he uses words they do not understand and pursues interests they cannot share. He even faces the possibility of being rejected by some of his teachers, especially if a teacher feels threatened by his superior mind, or sees his yawns and boredom as an affront to her authority. He is likely to meet many irksome restraints because so many rights and rewards that go with growing up are linked to chronological age rather than mental age. If he remains with his own age group, he may be a misfit, but if he casts his lot with children (or adults) similar to him in mental age, but bigger and stronger, he may be more of a misfit.

While the bright child has many opportunities to experience the favorable self-regard that goes with high achievement he is also likely to face many situations in which he is reminded, perhaps painfully, of his limitations. Such reminders arise, in part, from the fact that a bright child is usually somewhat uneven in his development. The correlation between intelligence and bodily size is positive, but low; the correlation between intelligence and athletic ability is also low; and so is the correlation between mental ability and popularity.

AWARENESS OF BRIGHTNESS

One of the ironies in the experience of some bright children is that they regard themselves as being rather stupid. Such a self-estimate may arise from the way in which they are judged by others or from the fact that they fail to measure up to the high standards they set for themselves. A man who had graduated from college with high honors and little effort was asked, "You must have been a bright child, did you know that?" The answer: "No. The marks on my report card, especially in 'deportment,' never seemed to be high enough to suit my father."

When a bright youngster at school is in a group consisting of other bright children he is likely to use them as a yardstick in assessing himself and if he compares himself with the ablest members of the group he may feel that he falls short of what he should be. A bright youngster in a bright group may also fail to meet the teacher's standards. (The author, in reading the appraisals a professor had made of a number of bright college students, noted that one girl was described as having an "ordinary mind." As compared with her fellow-students this girl was not outstanding, but as compared with young women in the total population she had an exceptionally good mind.)

In a classic study by Terman and his associates, the careers of a thousand gifted persons who first had been studied as children were followed into adult years (Terman, 1925; Terman and Oden, 1940, 1959). Almost 90 per cent of the boys and 85 per cent of the girls had attended college, and although these gifted children were, on the average, nearly two years younger than their classmates, about three times as many of them graduated with honors. About two-fifths of the boys and one-fifth of the girls had earned half or more than half of their expenses as undergraduates.

Of those who had completed their training and could be classed as employable less than 1 per cent were unemployed in 1936, even though this was a period of widespread unemployment. The moral record of the group was found to be "well above that of the generality." At least half of the boys were launched upon promising careers in 1936, and several of them were already nationally or internationally known.

While a large majority of these young people made superior records in college, some did not. Of those who did not do well, the poor college records were not due to lack of ability, but to various other factors, such as lack of interest, maladjustments of various kinds, or deliberate neglect of college studies in favor of other activities. Many of those who did not do well in college apparently underestimated the amount of effort necessary to make a good record by virtue of the small amount of study required to earn good grades prior to college.

An interesting conclusion in Terman's study was that an IQ in excess of 140 or 150 added little to achievement in early adult years. Above this level, adult success seemed to be determined by social adjustment, emotional stability, and the drive to accomplish. This does not mean, the investigators state, that the potentiality for achievement is the same for individuals with an IQ of 150 as for persons with even higher IQ's. Rather, the more probable interpretation, according to Terman and Oden, is that we have not learned how to bring the highest gifts to fruition and how best to guide the personality development of those who are extremely bright.

The fact that a person's achievement and excellence as a person does not depend on intelligence alone appears in an account by Hollingworth of exceedingly bright persons with IQ's of 180 or more (1942). A person with such towering intelligence may perform spectacular feats and yet, for lack of well-balanced personal qualities, his achievements as an individual or his contribution to society may be mediocre.

The gifted persons, whom Terman and his associates first studied when they were children and later as young adults, were studied (Terman and Oden, 1959) again in "mid-life" (between the ages of forty and fifty). The superior children, with few exceptions, were superior adults. They excelled the average to the greatest extent in intellectual ability, scholastic accomplishment, and vocational achievement. They excelled the average also in physical health, and their mortality rate was below average. A smaller proportion of these persons than in the general population had been delinquents or alcoholics. Apart from this, however, they did not differ greatly from the general population in the extent to which they had encountered personal difficulties.

On the basis of information concerning their personal adjustment, supplied by the gifted persons themselves and by others, they were classified according to three categories, as follows:

1. "*Satisfactory adjustment.*" Essentially normal; not necessarily perfectly contented or without difficulties but able to cope adequately with life's problems as they arose and possessing desires, emotions, and interests that were compatible with the social standards and pressures of this group; 68.8 per cent of the men and 65.9 per cent of the women were classed in this category.

2. "*Some maladjustment.*" In this category were persons with "excessive feelings of inadequacy or inferiority, nervous fatigue, mild anxiety neurosis, and the like." These were persons who definitely had problems but were able to handle them without "marked interference with social or personal life or achievement." Persons whose behavior was noticeably odd or freakish, but without evidence of serious neurotic tendencies, were also included in this group. Over a fifth of the gifted persons were in this "Some maladjustment" category (22.3 per cent of the men and 25.1 per cent of the women).

3. "*Serious maladjustment.*" These people were judged to have "serious maladjustment": (a) persons who had shown "marked symptoms of anxiety, mental depression, personality maladjustment, or psychopathic personality" and "nervous breakdown," but whose condition was not so severe that they went to hospitals for the mentally ill; and (b) those who at some time had had "a complete mental breakdown requiring hospitalization." Eight and nine-tenths per cent of the gifted men and 9 per cent of the women at middle age were in this "serious maladjustment" group (about two-thirds were in category 3a and about one-third in 3b).

The findings in this classic study of gifted children indicate that unusually high intellectual ability is more likely to insure that a person will make important achievements and win success in the eyes of the world than to protect him from misfortunes in the more intimate and personal dimensions of his private life.

The story of gifted children told by Terman and his associates is dramatic but it leaves many questions unanswered. If, from the beginning, this research had combined measurements of public achievement and expressed attitudes with careful attention to the ideas and attitudes these gifted children held regarding themselves as they moved from childhood into adulthood it would have added greatly to our understanding of human development.

EDUCATION OF THE GIFTED

Although gifted children are very resourceful in finding ways of putting their abilities to work, they cannot themselves create an environment that will bring out their full potentialities. Hollingworth estimated that in the ordinary elementary-school situation children of 140 IQ waste half of their time and those above 170 IQ waste practically all their time!

In one case described by Hollingworth (1939), the most tangible results of a girl's brightness was an increase in the amount of laundering her mother had to do because the teacher, to keep her occupied, asked her to clean the blackboards and erasers while the other children were working at their lessons.

Hollingworth also described a ten-year-old boy with an IQ of 165 who was referred as a problem: "Not interested in schoolwork. Very impudent. A liar." His trouble was by no means lack of interest. The teacher had resented the boy's superior knowledge and had given him a "raking-over" before the whole class. A friendly counselor to whom the boy was telling his troubles suggested that he should learn to be more tolerant. But the child was so filled with resentment that when told "One of the first things to learn in the world is to suffer fools *gladly*," he heard only the word "suffer" and replied, "Yes, that's it. That's what *I* say! Make 'em suffer. Roll a rock on 'em." As the conversation proceeded, however, this boy was "straightened out on the subject of who was to do the suffering. He agreed to do it himself." In another instance, the epithet, "Perfesser," was thrown at a ten-year-old child, of IQ 175, when he tried to discuss events of medieval history.

The children in Hollingworth's experiment were able to cover the regular elementary-school course requirements in less than half their time and were able to push far ahead into projects with which the average child, and even the average adult, usually does not become familiar. Hollingworth has emphasized that a program of intellectual training represents only a part, however, of the bright child's needs. In addition, he needs training and adequate opportunities to develop wholesome attitudes toward himself and toward others and to achieve competence as a social being.

Many expedients have been used in an effort to help gifted children realize their potentialities (Dunlap, 1958; Passow, 1958). These include:

1. *Keeping the youngster with his age-mates but giving him extra opportunities or assignments.* This procedure is sometimes referred to as "enrichment." If the child is a "self-starter" with an appetite for extra work this arrangement may work out quite satisfactorily. However, snags may arise if the extra work requires supervision from a teacher who has little extra energy or time to give to individual pupils.

2. *Rapid promotion, also called "acceleration."* This gives the youngster a chance to be with pupils more nearly similar to himself in mental age, but it also has the disadvantage of placing him with children who are likely to be bigger and, in some ways, more socially and emotionally mature than he. If a child is exceptionally bright he may have to be "skipped" as many as three or four grades if he is to be placed with pupils similar to him in mental age.

3. *Special classes on a full-time or part-time basis.* With this arrangement bright children are grouped together and participate in a program especially designed for them. This plan seems to have worked out well in school systems that are large enough to make special provisions and to provide able teachers.

As Hollingworth pointed out, provisions for gifted children should not simply emphasize academic work but also give attention to the youngsters' social and emotional development. As much attention as possible, in such a program, should be given to human values, character development, and experiences that might help a growing child to achieve a balance between his intellectual and emotional growth. To do this presents both a challenge and a problem, especially in view of the fact that the typical educational program even for ordinary children is geared more to promote academic learning than to give attention to the social and emotional dimensions of children's lives. In the writer's opinion, as we discover how to develop an educational program that will help the bright child to make the fullest use of his resources we are likely to discover procedures that will be valuable also for children who are average or below normal. The farther we go in helping youngsters to realize their possibilities the more similar, rather than different, programs for the bright and the average are likely to be, not with respect to the amount that is taught, but in the essential aim and approach.

Children with lower than average IQ's

Children whose mental ability is below average range from those who are able to gain some benefit from regular school attendance (although they are likely to have difficulties) to those whose handicap is so severe that they are classed as mentally deficient.

The youngsters who stand highest in the mentally backward group are frequently referred to as "slow learners." According to a survey by Johnson (1958), the slow learners include the 15 to 17 per cent of school children who cannot quite "keep up" and who usually do the poorest work in the regular classroom. Among the youngsters in the lowest segment of the mentally retarded group are those who in the past have been classed as "feeble-minded." According to one definition, the "feeble-minded" or mentally deficient category includes youngsters with an IQ below 70.

A child who suffers from severe mental deficiency presents a special problem both to society and—more especially—to his family. If such a child is born into a family in which there are other children with normal intelligence, as frequently occurs, the whole family faces a heavy burden. By reason of guilt or compassion or a combination of both, parents may go to great expense and trouble to get medical aid for the youngster when he is young and to protect him as he grows older. If urged, for the good of the total family situation, to place him in an institution they face an agonizing conflict. When the child is young his parents go through an anxious period when they begin to sense, but perhaps refuse to admit, that their child is defective. As the youngster grows older many parents have forebodings about the future and about what might happen to the helpless child if they should die. In the meantime the child's brothers and sisters, even if they are basically good-hearted, may feel that their whole family is under a cloud, or feel that *their* rights are being sacrificed in favor of the unfortunate sibling. The label "mental deficiency" or "feeble-mindedness" covers a great amount of human tragedy.

SLOW LEARNERS

Slow learners usually have difficulty in meeting ordinary school requirements, but many of them have potentialities for "essentially normal" emotional, social, physical, and motor development (Johnson, 1958). Sooner or later, however, many of these youngsters encounter emotional difficulties. A large proportion of "trouble makers" in school are youngsters with low intelligence. But their troublesomeness does not arise primarily because of a special bent for getting into difficulty; the trouble springs largely from the kinds of demands made on them. If pressure is put on slow learners to keep pace with others in the conventional curriculum, to learn faster than their ability permits, or to learn in a setting in which they soon realize that others are much better than they, it is difficult for them to avoid feeling that they are not much good. They especially face difficulties if they are taunted by other children, referred to as "dopes," or are lashed by the sarcasm of impatient teachers. Yet within the limits of their ability they—like all children—enjoy the thrill of achievement. Unless they have acquired deep grievances, they are as eager for acceptance and affection as anyone else. In common with all other human beings they know the meaning of fear and taste the bitterness of anger. Many of them also are likely to be rather lonely people, for when other children in a regular classroom pick out their companions, they are less likely to pick the slow learners than their more intelligent peers. The slow learners did not choose the poor heredity or poor environment that produced their inability to do well at school. Yet they are likely to feel that from the point of view of the school, and from their point of view, it is they who failed to make the grade.

EDUCATION OF THE SLOW LEARNER

The main goals in an educational program for slow learners are much the same as those that should prevail in an educational program for *all* children, namely, to help the youngsters as far as possible to use their resources and to develop the skills and the attitudes that will enable them to achieve a healthy regard for themselves, to learn to live productive lives, and to become useful members of society. In describing the education of the mentally handicapped, Johnson lists three areas that are especially important: (1) personal or emotional adjustment, (2) social adjustment, (3) economic adjustment. He places personal and emotional growth first on the ground that this is fundamental if the children are to achieve social competence in an occupation and in their social relationships with other people. Among the basic needs which education must seek to meet, according to Johnson, are opportunities which will enable slow learners to participate in worthwhile activities; to feel that they are valuable contributing members of the group; to be accepted for what they are; and to experience success in the performance of worthwhile activities. Since it is difficult and sometimes impossible for mentally handicapped children to meet these needs in a regular classroom situation, many schools have made provision for special classes.

Recommended Readings

Measurement and Evaluation in Psychology and Education, by Robert L. Thorndike and Elizabeth Hagen (1955) is recommended to those who are interested in studying the nature and results of tests of mental ability and achievement. *Education of Exceptional Children and Youth*, edited by William M. Cruickshank and G. Orville Johnson (1958), contains excellent chapters dealing with the characteristics of children with exceptional abilities or handicaps and educational programs that have been established to meet the needs of these children.

Leta S. Hollingworth's *Gifted Children: Their Nature and Nurture* (1926) is a pioneer work in its field. Miriam L. Goldberg, Lassar G. Gotkin, and Abraham J. Tannenbaum have made a valuable compilation of research in a report entitled *Cultural, Social and Personal Factors Influencing Talent Fruition* (1959). Several references to Lewis M. Terman's outstanding long-term studies of gifted children and youth are listed in the bibliography at the end of this book. The most recent volume in this series is *The Gifted Group at Mid-Life: Thirty-five Years' Follow-up of the Superior Child* by Terman and Melita H. Oden (1959). Several sections in the books of readings edited by Wayne Dennis (1951) and Jerome M. Seidman (1958) discuss the measurement of intelligence.

Moral Development and Religion

CHAPTER EIGHTEEN From their earliest years children come under the influence of moral values and obligations. They are reminded of what is approved and not approved, what is right and what is wrong. When they become able to understand language, and even before, they are constantly confronted with *oughts* and *shoulds*.

A child's moral code eventually consists of his ideas of right and wrong, his convictions about his responsibilities and about what he should or should not do or be, and the values and standards by which he judges the worthiness or unworthiness of his thoughts and actions. Ideas of right and wrong are imbedded in the daily thought and conduct of all persons, even those who claim to be least governed by moral standards. The moral teachings that pervade a child's upbringing profoundly affect his ideas and attitudes about himself. When we as adults study the child's moral development we are, in a sense, inquiring into ourselves, for each standard we apply in judging the child expresses a moral assumption of our own.

Trends and directions in moral development

The work of Piaget (1932) has greatly influenced the study of children's moral development. He described certain qualities of children's moral judgments during various periods of childhood. Piaget gives an illuminating account of the thinking that underlies children's moral judgments, although his conclusions concerning the characteristics of children's moral judgments at one particular age level as compared with the next have not generally been confirmed by other investigators (Bloom, 1959).

Among the important developments that mark a change from what is generally regarded as less mature to more mature moral conduct are the following:

> A shift from morals based on specific rules to more general conceptions of what is right and wrong.
> A shift from moral conduct that is primarily a response to external demands toward a moral code that is based on internal standards which the child has adopted as his own.
> An increased ability to perceive rules of the game as rules based on mutual respect and mutual consent rather than on arbitrary edicts.
> An increased ability and willingness, in judging the acts of others, to take account of the circumstances in which these acts occur and of the motives and intentions underlying them, instead of judging them according to inflexible standards. For example, a young child may voice the opinion that to steal is to steal and all stealing is bad. When he is a bit older he will view the stealing of an apple by a hungry child as a less serious offense than the stealing of an apple by a well-fed adult.

In his account of the development of moral judgment, Piaget makes a distinction between moral "realism" and "relativism." The moral "realist" is literal in his interpretation of rules. He applies the letter rather than the spirit of the law (as when he equally condemns the two apple-stealers mentioned above). He judges the seriousness of an act according to its practical consequences (for example, the *accidental* spilling of a pitcher full of milk is a more serious offense than the *intentional* spilling of a cupful). Further, according to the concept of moral realism, duty is a strict matter of obedience. What is right is *heteronomous* (subject to laws imposed by others) as distinguished from being *autonomous* (subject to the individual's own judgment and his right to make decisions and allowances). Moral realism also prevails if a person not only judges the seriousness of an act according to the arbitrary letter of the law but also according to the severity of the punishment that is applied (a "moral realist" might, for example, regard a child who is slapped for whispering in class as a more serious offender than a youngster who is mildly reprimanded for smashing a window).

As children grow older many of them shift from rigid judgments to a more thoughtful recognition of individual motives and intentions, but children at any particular chronological age vary greatly in their ideas concerning what is right and wrong. They vary also in their ideas of justice (Durkin, 1959a, 1959b).

Even within the same child (or adult), the process of moral development is likely to be uneven. The child may apply general rules in some areas of conduct but not in others, act according to principles of his own in connection with some of his conduct and according to external demands in connection with others. A youngster who would not think of stealing a nickel might have no scruples about raiding a strawberry patch. One who strictly observes the rules of honesty may simply go through the motions of observing the rules of generosity. If we made a detailed examination of the moral ideas and attitudes of children and adults we would probably find a complex mixture of mature and immature standards.

Important factors other than age which influence moral judgments are *intelligence, social background,* and *emotional disposition.* These factors will be discussed in a later section of this chapter.

Changes with age in children's regard for various virtues and moral values

Several studies have indicated that as children grow older their concept of what is right and wrong, their ideas concerning what is praiseworthy or blameworthy, and the importance they attach to various conventional virtues correspond more and more closely to the judgments of adults. In one study in this area (Lockhart, 1930) children in the fourth grade were compared with adults (graduate students and lawyers) in their attitudes toward certain laws. Twenty laws were selected and various circumstances were described which provided motives for disobeying a law, such as the saving of a human life when to do so would violate a law. On the whole, the responses of the fourth grade children were quite similar to those of the adults.

Some children are able at an early age to phrase some of their ideas of right and wrong in rather mature terms. This is illustrated in a study by Harrower (1934), who questioned children aged about six to eleven years concerning their ideas of cheating, as follows: "Why must you not copy from your neighbor? What do you think about cheating?" Children from homes of relatively high educational and socioeconomic status most frequently answered to this effect: "It doesn't do any good," or "One can't learn that way." Children from a poorer environment more frequently gave such answers as "Cheating is forbidden. It is naughty. It is a lie. It is unfair."

In this study, Harrower also questioned children concerning their ideas of punishment. They were told a tale about two boys, Peter and Tommy, who were playing together. Peter had a lovely new engine and Tommy had a boat. Naughty Tommy suddenly kicked Peter's engine and smashed it. Now, what should be done with naughty Tommy? Should he be "smacked" (appeal to authority and a *retaliatory* concept of punishment), should his own boat be broken up (the idea of *reciprocation*—an eye for an eye), or should he be made to save up his pocket money until he can buy Peter a new engine (the idea of equity, *restitution*, or making amends)? In response to these questions, a majority of the poorer children, in the age range from six to eight years, gave the authoritarian answer: "Smack him." At eight to eleven years: a majority of the poorer children gave the third type of answer: "He should make up for the damage." A large majority of children from more privileged homes, both at the age range from six to eight and from eight to eleven, gave the answer that Tommy should replace the toy that he had broken. In both groups and at both age ranges, the "eye-for-an-eye" (break his toy) type of answer occurred relatively infrequently.

In appraising a child's moral concepts, as in appraising his concepts in any area, the answer a child gives to a direct question may fail to reveal the extent of his understanding.[1] This is especially likely if he is being called to account for a misdeed or if a question puts him on the defensive. He may answer evasively, giving any reply that seems expedient, and sometimes his replies will be inconsistent; this is also likely to be the case with adults.[2]

Younger children as well as adolescents quite consistently give a high rating to certain virtues or values. They usually ascribe greater importance to proprieties of the more conventional sort than to moral attitudes which reflect loyalty and fellow-feeling for others. It has been found, for example, that children are likely to rate honesty and politeness as being more praiseworthy than kindness and generosity (Thompson, 1949, 1952). Even at the senior-high-school level it has been noted that such virtues as honesty and sportsmanship receive a higher rating than kindness and charity (Mitchell, 1943). It appears that many children and adolescents

---

[1] An extensive review of literature dealing with morals and character development has been prepared by Jones (1946).

[2] A study by Carmichael describes the behavior of children when called to account for past irregularities (1930).

in expressing their moral beliefs, accept familiar cultural stereotypes without inquiring very deeply into what these stereotypes might mean to them in a personal way (Taba, 1953). It has also been noted that children may profess a certain social value, such as the idea that a person should be considerate, and yet apply it unequally in their relationships with others. Foshay and Wann (1954) found that children who stood high in social acceptance in the group to which they belonged were more likely to be considerate toward children who also stood high in acceptance than toward children who did not. "... considerateness tended to be directed toward social equals, and to be withheld from social inferiors."

HONESTY

In view of the fact that many children seem to regard honesty as the most important moral virtue it is instructive to examine some of the findings in an outstanding study of children's honesty and deceit conducted about thirty years ago (Hartshorne and May, 1928). A number of tests were applied, so devised that it was possible to detect whether children had cheated or had given truthful or deceptive answers. It was found that older children were slightly more deceptive than younger ones. This is interesting since several studies have shown that older youngsters are quite as likely as younger ones to regard honesty as being especially praiseworthy. In general, there was no outstanding difference in the deceptiveness of boys and girls. Brighter children were, on the whole, more honest than duller children. Children who showed symptoms of emotional instability (as measured independently by a standard test) showed a greater tendency to be deceptive than those who were better adjusted emotionally. When children were classified into four occupational levels, according to socioeconomic status of their parents, those at the highest level deceived the least; those at the second and third highest levels, progressively more; and those at the lowest level, the most.

Children belonging to the same family resembled each other more in honesty and deceptiveness than children matched at random. But the authors of the study believe it is possible that children would vary in deceptiveness even if all were brought up under similar conditions.

There was a positive relationship between cheating and low marks in school deportment.

Children who were friends, even though not members of the same class, showed more than a chance resemblance in the amount of cheating. Children who cheated less tended to be less suggestible. Children in the care of a teacher who was able to stimulate cooperation and good will cheated less than those who were taught under a more conventional and rigid routine. Children who were members of organizations purporting, as one of their aims, to teach honesty, cheated about as much as nonmembers.

The findings in this study indicate that there seems to be no generalized, uniform trait that can be labeled "honesty" which characterizes the child's behavior in all situations. The child who lies, steals, or cheats in one situation may be quite without guile in another; he may be a brazen cheater when given a chance to copy in a test and be completely honorable in an athletic contest.

But the fact that cheating is quite specific does not mean it occurs by chance. When a child cheats there is a motive underlying his behavior— he has something at stake, a desire or purpose. One situation may be seen as an important challenge to win or to succeed by hook or by crook, and another may not. A child may undertake one activity with a desire to learn and to correct his mistakes (and in keeping with this, let his errors be known so that he can get help in learning), whereas, in another situation in which he desires only to "get by," he may cheat if that shortens or eases the task. Accordingly, a child may seem inconsistent in his tendency to cheat when his behavior is viewed from the standpoint of the external situation, and yet his tendency to cheat or to be honest may be consistent when viewed in the light of his own motives.

GENEROSITY

In a further investigation, Hartshorne and May (1929) used objective methods to study generosity and the readiness to serve others. Willingness to give up ice cream for the sake of helping someone else, to vote money (which each child actually received) to charity, to surrender attractive objects (in a kit which each child received as a present), to prepare materials for children in a hospital, and to work as hard for the group as for oneself were among the items that were tested. In this study, as in the study of deceit, it was found that the intercorrelations between the various tests were positive but low. Although it is probable that a child who is generous in one situation will show the same tendency, rather than the opposite, in another situation, one cannot with any degree of confidence predict from a single episode just what his behavior in general will be. No consistent changes in the readiness to serve others were observed with relation to age. Bright children were somewhat more cooperative than normal and dull children; but the relationship between generosity and intelligence was low, as compared with the correlation between honesty and intelligence.

Relationship of morals to the child's view of himself

There is a deep-seated interrelationship between the growing child's moral development and his ideas and attitudes pertaining to himself. The verdicts of "good" or "bad" which he receives from others are likely to have an important influence on his view of himself as someone who is good or bad. And, as we have noted above, in the course of his upbringing, all or nearly all of the impulses that arise within himself receive a stamp of moral approval or disapproval. There is a strong moral undertone in a child's attitude toward himself when he begins to formulate his ideas and aspirations, and he faces a moral conflict if the ideal he strives to live up to includes many *oughts* and *shoulds* which go beyond anything he can ever hope to achieve or attain.

MORALS AND THE DEVELOPMENT OF CONSCIENCE

The child's conscience consists of the sum total of moral ideas, standards, and values by which he judges what is right or wrong and holds himself accountable for what he does and for what he is and what he should strive to be. The conscience is sometimes referred to by other terms, such as "acquired moral needs," or "internalized standards," or the "super-ego." The child's conscience includes not only his awareness of the goodness or blameworthiness of his conduct and character but also a sense or feeling of obligation to act, think, and feel in a way that is in keeping with his conception of what is right or wrong. When a person applies the ideas and attitudes that comprise his conscience he is, in effect, standing in judgment upon himself. Through his conscience, a person approves or disapproves of his actions whether or not someone else is there to blame or praise him, to punish or reward.[3]

In everyday language we use many expressions to describe a person's conscience when we say, for example, that it is "weak" or "strong" or "severe," "easy," or "overactive." We observe also that people differ in the ways in which their consciences operate when we say, for example, that one person is "fighting it out with his conscience" while another's conscience is a "wee, small voice that reminds him that someone may be watching," or we say of one person that "he follows the dictates of his conscience" and of another that his conscience does not prevent him from doing what he regards as wrong but simply prevents him from enjoying it.

ADVANTAGES OF FIRM MORAL CONCEPTS

The child who has established a firm set of moral standards has many advantages unless his standards are so demanding that they lead to fruitless feelings of guilt. He is spared from the need to struggle each time he faces an opportunity to do something which goes counter to his code. If he has accepted a certain code of honesty he does not have to wrestle with his conscience each time he passes the fruit stand. If he has taken

---

[3] For a discussion of conscience and conflict and references to some other writings in this area see Allinsmith (1957).

a moral stand against cheating he will not have to spend time and energy in laying schemes for cheating in an examination. (Even this often has a great practical advantage, for the work involved in contriving a safe and effective method of cheating may be more laborious than preparing for an examination honestly.) If he has standards of duty, responsibility, industry and thrift, which operate automatically it is not necessary for him again and again to calculate what he should do, what he might get away with, whether or not he should finish his job or whether or not he should spend his savings each time he sees an attractive object. As he grows older his moral values are especially helpful as he lays plans for the future and sets up the goals he desires to attain.

In the older child, a reasonably firm set of moral standards will be of value in his dealings with others. If he associates with youngsters whose standards differ from his own he is bound to face difficulties, for it is hard for any young person to cling to his values when they differ from those of his peers. However, he will be less vulnerable than the youngster who does not know his own mind and is constantly choosing and judging according to the example set by others rather than according to convictions of his own.

DISADVANTAGES OF AN OVERLY-SEVERE CONSCIENCE: GUILT

An important aspect of the interrelationship between moral development and the development of attitudes toward self arises in connection with the condition of guilt. Guilt may be a kind of thoughtful remorse or regret through which a person reviews his past and from which he can learn either to mend his ways or that the remorse is unfounded. But guilt can also arise in a less thoughtful or rational form, involving a kind of self-accusation which leads nowhere and profits no one; such guilt is a merciless kind of self-condemnation. A youngster carries a heavy burden of guilt when he continues to reproach himself for deeds which all others would gladly forgive, or if he condemns himself for having qualities which no one would deplore and over which he has no control. A state of guilt prevails when the child, in seeking to live up to impossible standards, repeatedly pronounces an adverse judgment against himself. He is the accuser and the accused, the prosecutor, judge, and jury.

If we could study the ramifications of guilt, we would probably discover that they extend into many reaches of a child's life which ordinarily are hard to understand. If we could penetrate into this area we probably would find that many of the seemingly irrational fears that burden children's lives are interfused with guilt. One child expressed this thought when he was asked "Why are you afraid?" and answered, "Because I am bad." The interplay between guilt and fear has frequently been noted in clinical studies of individual children, but it has not been investigated in a systematic way in groups of normal children. It is not unlikely (so the writer believes) that a systematic study in this area would reveal that as children grow older the punishment inflicted on them by others is far less severe than the punishment they inflict upon themselves. One characteristic sometimes found in an older child with a heavy burden of guilt is that he is able to forgive others for shortcomings which he is unable to forgive in himself.

Environmental and personal factors that influence moral standards and conduct

INFLUENCES FROM THE HOME AND OUTSIDE THE HOME

As we might expect, it has been found that the young child's moral judgments and his ideals are greatly influenced by the standards that prevail in his home. As the child grows older his moral judgments are increasingly influenced by the standards he meets outside the home. In naming the persons whom they especially admire (and probably feel inclined to emulate) younger children usually mention parents and relatives while children in middle-childhood and adolescence mention persons outside the home, including historical characters, heroes and heroines in fiction, and prominent contemporary figures such as athletes, movie stars, and government officials (Hill, 1930; Havighurst et al., 1946). It has also been found in comparisons between ten-year-olds and sixteen-year-olds that as children move from middle-childhood into adolescence, the influence of the family becomes less important and social relationships outside the home become relatively more important in determining a child's character, such as his reputation for honesty, moral courage, loyalty, responsibility, and friendliness (Brown et al., 1947).

MORALITY AND INTELLIGENCE

A child's intelligence has an important bearing on the *cognitive* aspects of moral development. Numerous investigations have shown that children and adolescents of high intelligence are likely to make a better showing than less intelligent youngsters on tests of moral judgments and attitudes. This finding is open to many interpretations. The more intelligent individuals are better able to understand the rules they have been taught, to appreciate the meaning of these rules, and to perceive the situations in which they apply. We may also expect that the brighter child is better able to appreciate the kind of moral conduct which is likely to lead others to condemn him or approve him. Further, the more intelligent person (regardless of his basic moral convictions) can better afford, in many situations, to conduct himself in a morally upright way. In competing with others, for example, and meeting the ordinary demands of life the more clever and resourceful he is the more assured he can be of winning his way without trickery or shady practices. He also is more clever in giving a plausible explanation or excuse if he is called to account for conduct that is questionable.

But a positive correlation between intelligence and professed moral concepts and attitudes cannot be taken completely at face value. A youngster who gives the correct answers on a test of moral knowledge and moral attitudes does not thereby reveal the extent to which he will carry such knowledge and attitudes into action. Moreover, in many situations, a bright person is better able than a dull person to observe the proprieties even if his intentions are questionable from a moral point of view. A bright child who hurts another youngster by a biting remark is usually not regarded as having committed as great a moral offense as a dull child who physically hurts another youngster.

MORAL STANDARDS AS RELATED TO SOCIAL BACKGROUND

The relationship between socioeconomic status and attitudes and actions that have moral implications has been touched on in other sections of this book. Briefly, findings have indicated that children of lower socioeconomic status are, on the average, more authoritarian in their judgments; they recommend more severe punishment for misconduct (Dolger and Ginandes, 1946); and they also commit moral offenses which get them into trouble relatively more often (as seen in the fact that the delinquency rate is higher in the lower socioeconomic groups).

When children of lower socioeconomic status are found on some counts to have a poorer moral record than children of higher socioeconomic status many influences are at work, including such factors as the effects of poverty and neglect, lower average level of intelligence, differences in the standards or examples that are set before them, and a tendency among persons of lower status to lay down rules of conduct in an arbitrary way rather than to discuss the pro's and con's of what constitutes good moral behavior.

There are many interesting paradoxes in the relationship between socioeconomic status and moral attitudes and conduct. On the one hand, in some lower socioeconomic groups the standards seem, if anything, to be more severe than those prevailing in upper socioeconomic groups. Standards of modesty and obedience to authority, for example, are especially strict among some lower groups, and, as noted above, members of lower socioeconomic groups tend to prescribe more severe punishment for misconduct. On the other hand, many forms of conduct that are generally disapproved in the higher socioeconomic groups prevail relatively more frequently in the lower groups, including truancy, fighting, sexual misconduct, stealing, and vandalism. From this we might infer that the child who is subjected to rigid rules and the threat of punishment is likely, if anything, to be less morally upright than the youngster for whom the rules of conduct and threats of punishment are not so severe. However, we are dealing here with a very complicated psychological situation that cannot be explored simply by a statistical comparison between groups. We face enigmas which have confronted us elsewhere in this book. One child who is brought up strictly turns out to be a fine moral character, while another does not. A youngster who has been reared in a very permissive moral atmosphere turns out to be a splendid character, while another runs into trouble. Two youngsters—one from the slums and the other from the best section of the community—acquire fine moral characters. Even within the same home much the same kind of moral training may lead to a high degree of conformity in one child and a great amount of rebellion in another.

An interesting comparison of the moral judgments of children differing in social origins was made in a study by Liu (1950) of fifty-two New York City Chinese-American children and fifty-two children of American-born parents. Both groups were of relatively low socioeconomic status. Liu concluded that the Chinese-American children showed more respect for adult authority than did the non-Chinese, but they were also more mature in their moral judgments. According to Liu, the Chinese-American children's greater respect for authority does not necessarily mean they are subservient; instead, the close family ties and the well-defined roles of Chinese-American children give them more freedom to assess responsibility and to judge an act from the point of view of the motive or intention underlying it. For example, more children in the Chinese-American group than in the other said that a girl who accidentally cut a *little* hole in her dress while playing with scissors, after she had been forbidden to use the scissors, was committing a more serious moral offense than a girl who accidentally cut a *large* hole in a dress while cutting out a picture which she thought her mother would especially like.

MORAL ATTITUDES AS RELATED TO EMOTIONAL DEVELOPMENT

Moral development is closely interrelated with a child's *emotional* development. His capacity for *affection* influences the way he will respond to the moral teachings of his elders (Zucker, 1943). A child's moral conduct is also likely to be influenced by *fear:* fear of punishment, fear of the consequences of not conforming to the standards of his group, and fear also of impulses arising within himself which go counter to other impulses that he harbors. There is also a close interrelationship between moral development and *anxiety.* Many of the dilemmas faced by an anxious person who is in conflict within himself represent moral issues of what is right or wrong or what he should or should not do. Moral conduct is also linked to the child's capacity for *anger*, notably when his anger is regarded by others as morally wrong or when he commits a misdeed springing from an impulse to rebel or to punish or to take revenge.

There is an interplay between children's emotional adjustment and their moral standards or attitudes. Children who earned favorable ratings on emotional adjustment were compared (by Shumsky, 1956) with children of similar socioeconomic status who were rated as emotionally maladjusted. When passing judgement on various acts, the children rated as emotionally maladjusted tended more than the well-adjusted group to judge acts in terms of their consequences rather than in terms of the intentions underlying the acts. They also tended more often to assume that misbehavior would be punished, to suggest punitive methods of discipline, and to judge the goodness or badness of an action according to authoritarian standards laid down by others.

A child who is burdened with emotional difficulties apparently does not have as much freedom as a more serene child to develop ideas of his own concerning what is right and wrong. He is less able to make allowances for human frailty and, in his misery, he is more likely than a happy child to be punitive rather than compassionate in passing judgment on the misdeeds of others.

Some problems encountered in children's moral training

Many circumstances complicate the moral training of children. The growing child faces conflicting impulses within himself, and he also is likely to face many conflicting influences and pressures in his social environment. In time a youngster cannot help but notice the numerous discrepancies between what his elders preach and what they practice. Moreover, what he is taught at home may clash with the model set before him outside the home. He may be admonished at home that he should never fight and then discover in the nursery school or kindergarten that nearly all the children do fight. If his family belongs to a certain socioeconomic group while the school which he attends is dominated by another socioeconomic group, many inconsistent pressures bear upon him.

Even within the home he may notice that his parents apply different standards to boys than to girls or that his parents differ in their views concerning the seriousness of various forms of misconduct and the importance of various moral values.

As a member of a younger generation he comes under influences which may be different from those that molded his parents, and if there are grandparents in the home further complications arise. In a study dealing in part with moral codes Pressey and Jones (1953) computed the percentage of persons who marked various actions as "wrong" in recent years as compared with some decades ago. Many "borderland acts" were less frequently marked as "wrong" in 1943 and 1953 than in 1923. Among the items which were less often regarded as wrong at the later dates were smoking, flirting, the use of slang, extravagance, visiting poolrooms, and playing craps. In the 1953 survey older adults marked more items wrong than did younger adults. Apparently this does not mean that present-day older adults are becoming increasingly conservative with age; instead, older adults are probably still expressing the attitudes they acquired when they were young. The older people in 1953 "marked about the same number as young people in the decades when these adults were young." According to this study, during the past two or three decades there has been a trend toward less condemnation of certain freedoms in sex-social relationships and social amusements. The trends indicate a general decrease in social taboos, although "there seems to be no lessening in social responsibility." In this study, as well as in a study by Jones (1959) in which attitudes and interests expressed by ninth-grade children in the 1930's were compared with the responses of ninth-graders two decades later it appears that young people today have a more permissive attitude toward many aspects of conduct and that younger people now are demanding certain rights (such as the use of lipstick by girls) at an earlier age than was true twenty or more years ago. Such changes do not necessarily mean a radical change in the moral climate, but we can reasonably assume that in particular homes children are now demanding certain rights, pleasures, and privileges which their parents or grandparents did not feel a right to demand when they were young. This may cause a certain amount of conflict and tension in these homes.

Another factor that complicates the moral upbringing of children is the considerable amount of confusion existing in the adult world over the proper standards and the proper kind of discipline. In earlier chapters we have drawn attention to this in noting the conflict between "authoritarian" and "permissive" methods of child-rearing. Some parents, teachers, and public figures openly advocate corporal punishment, others condemn it, while still others are uncertain about whether and how to punish and how severe or lenient a child's discipline should be.

Of all the complications confronting a child in his moral development the most significant is probably the discrepancy between the words and deeds of those who have charge of his upbringing. Most children, for example, profess that cheating is bad and most teachers say it is bad for pupils to cheat, but many adults do not themselves hesitate to cheat when they take examinations. When a child condemns cheating and yet cheats he is showing much the same disparity between word and deed as is shown by his elders.

There may be a discrepancy even on a purely verbal level between what children are taught to regard as good and their translation of this into something concrete. In connection with a study by the writer and his associates (1933) a number of children were asked, among other things, what they would do if they had a lot of money. In one of the schools in the study, in which there was a considerable amount of emphasis on moral values, a large percentage of the children stated that they would use the money for the good of others, and many of them described ambitious philanthropic ventures. When, at a later time, the interviewer casually asked each of a number of these children what he would do if he found a quarter on the way home it did not occur to any child that he might begin the work on a small scale with a small sum. It is likely that much the same result would emerge if adults were questioned in a similar way.

Even in connection with the more intellectual and abstract aspects of moral training children are exposed to inconsistent pressures. We noted above that the morally more mature child is supposed to judge acts not simply in terms of the practical consequences but in terms of motives and intentions and extenuating circumstances. Yet a good deal of the moral training children receive is in terms of "moral realism" as described on an earlier page. When a mother, for instance, says reprovingly, "you spilled it," when a child accidentally spills milk, his action is being judged in terms of its practical consequences. In the school, likewise, a child is, in effect, being taught to view morality as something arbitrary if he is forced to follow rules without understanding the reasons behind them. He is, in effect, taught to make a literal interpretation of the rules when he observes that a bright child is praised while a slow learner is scolded as though his lack of ability were a moral offense. Likewise, he is being encouraged to judge the seriousness of misconduct according to the severity of the punishment it provokes when he notes, for example, that a prudish principal suspends a boy from school when he overhears the boy use a "bad word" which the youngster and all of his pals use in their everyday conversation.

Moral assumptions underlying child-rearing and child psychology

To guide or understand the moral development of a child it is necessary to take account of the moral climate of the adult world in which he lives and of the moral assumptions on which adult standards are based. We cannot study children or deal with them unless we operate in terms of certain open or unexpressed moral assumptions. In the education children receive at school there are many underlying moral assumptions although frequently these are not made explicit. For example, when an adolescent with low verbal abilities, but possessing a bent for mechanics, is not allowed to graduate from high school unless he passes a course in history, this youngster is being punished by failure and punishment is based on a moral assumption.

Even in the most rigidly scientific approach to a study of the psychology of childhood (or of adulthood) moral values are explicitly or implicitly assumed. As soon as we favor one kind of interpretation of human behavior and not another, or one idea or habit or attitude rather than another we are applying a moral standard. When we set up criteria of "maturity" or "adjustment" or "efficiency" or "self-fulfillment," we are assuming some kind of a standard or value as a measuring rod. This is a rather simple proposition, and yet it is worth emphasizing, for often it seems to be assumed that psychology should be free of moral assumptions. The further we go in studying children and principles of development that might guide us in understanding children and in rearing them, the more important it is to examine the moral assumptions underlying the problems we study and the conclusions we reach.

There have been many assumptions of value throughout this book. They are tied to the concept of self-realization. According to this concept, life has value. The greatest value in a human life, such as we are concerned about when we follow a child from his conception until the end of his mortal span, is the living of that life. The growing person who realizes life and its possibilities most fully is one who is able to draw to the fullest extent, within the limits set by his heredity and circumstances, on the capacities and resources that go with life.

One moral attribute of a life so lived, when viewed from within, is that it has integrity, a quality that might be called "trueness to self" in the sense that the individual, whether his talents be great or small, is as genuine and authentic as a human being in his circumstances can be.

Religion

Religion plays a large part in the lives of most people in one way or another. All children in such a culture as ours are influenced by religious practices, ideas, and beliefs, whether or not they receive formal religious instruction. The tendency of children is to accept, rather than to reject, what they hear and read, especially if it ties in with their own desires and interests, and as long as they meet with no direct contradictions. Parents who do not provide religious instruction sometimes discover that a child through his conversation with others and his reading has accepted many religious beliefs, and occasionally a child whose parents disavow religion may even acquire the habit of praying quite regularly for a time.

Factors influencing the meaning of religious teachings. A child's religious ideas and images will, of necessity, be influenced by his experiences in everyday life. This fact presents a practical issue to parents and teachers who endeavor to give religious instruction. If the instruction is to be genuine, it must not merely come by way of verbal precepts but must be interpreted also by the practical example set by the child's elders. A child's image of God the Father may include a blend of details from pictures he has seen and Bible stories he has heard. The image may vary from time to time, including now a kindly expression, now a wrathful countenance. His conception of the attributes of a fatherly God will be influenced, perhaps imperceptibly, by his experience of the attributes of his own father or of others in a paternal role. His ideas of sin will be influenced by his experiences of grief or remorse through having caused distress to other persons, and by experiences of regret flowing from hostility or fear aroused by the treatment he has received as a consequence of having disobeyed someone in authority. His ideas of forgiveness will be influenced by his own experience of being forgiven by his elders. The idea of forgiveness will be a difficult one for him to grasp if in his relations with others he finds it impossible to confide or confess his troubles and must bottle up his feelings of guilt and fears of retribution.

The younger the child, the more his ideas in matters of religion, and in other matters, will be built upon his own concrete experiences. These are likely to be elaborated by fantasies. His ideas may be influenced by a multitude of conditions, such as the physical appearance, atmosphere, furnishings, the odors and echoes of the church or synagogue; the confinement of movement imposed upon him if he must sit quietly longer than is agreeable to his limited attention span; the kindliness or austerity of those who give him religious instruction.

From early childhood through the elementary-school years, numerous religious concepts will have relatively little meaning to a child in the abstract, and a problem in religious education is how to translate religious concepts into terms that are meaningful.[4] Misconceptions through failure to understand the terms that are used can be seen when the child, for example, comes home and tells his mother about Jesus' twelve bicycles (disciples), or is puzzled by "the consecrated cross-eyed bear" (the consecrated Cross, I'd bear). Children also are confused at times by de-

---

[4] For an account of children's and adolescents' understanding of religious terms and concepts, see Bose (1929), Harms (1944), Franzblau (1934), and Ross (1950).

nominational differences, and frequently they have difficulty in distinguishing between the form and intended substance of religious observances.

In a brief passage, Murphy (1937) has tried to construct a picture, from the child's point of view, of the way Jesus is sometimes presented. Children are likely to learn of Him, "not as an ideal grown-up who helped people, but as a little baby whose mother put him in a straw thing in a barn instead of a crib, and to whom queer-looking men in striped gowns brought presents no baby could use. They learn, too, that there was a bad king, with a ferocious face, of whom the baby's mother was afraid, so that she had to take him a long way from home, riding on an animal that is not seen in the city, nor even in the zoo."

Interest in the Bible.   Children's interest in Biblical characters and scenes and in different portions of the Bible have been studied (by Dawson, 1900) in an investigation conducted many years ago in a New England community. Since results of such a study are likely to be influenced by the religious background and affiliations of the children, and might also vary over a period of time, the findings cannot be regarded as typical for all children who have had religious training, but the general trends are noteworthy.

Up to eight or nine years the children expressed most interest in accounts of the birth and childhood of Jesus and in stories concerning the childhood of such characters as Moses, Samuel, Joseph, and David. From nine to thirteen or fourteen years, portions of the Old Testament, especially the historical books, had greatest appeal. At about the age of fourteen, and from then until twenty years (the upper age level in the study), interest in the historical sections receded and there was an increased interest in the Gospels. Dawson also shows "age curves" for other portions of the Bible. From the age of about ten through adolescence, poetic sections of the Bible appeal to numerous children, although the number who chose these sections was considerably smaller than the number who selected the historical books and the Gospels. Books of prophecy received a few votes from the age of twelve and onward. The Proverbs and doctrinal sections received relatively little mention until about the adolescent period and then were preferred by relatively few children. At all ages, children expressed more interest in persons than in other elements of the Bible.

Children's prayers.   One of the many aspects of childhood religion that adults have difficulty in understanding from the child's point of view is prayer. In teaching the child to pray, parents may become involved in many pitfalls, as when they teach the child to approach God as though

He were an absentminded magician, given to granting any thoughtless petition addressed to Him. The idea of praying to a higher power is usually accepted quite readily by children, who, in their experiences, frequently have occasion to be reminded of their own limitations and unfulfilled desires. The desires that lie back of the child's frequent "I wish" or "If only I had" and which he realizes vicariously in his own make-believe can readily be translated into the petition: "Please give." It is considerably easier, of course, to lead a child to petition that his passing desires be granted than to petition that he be helped to have desires and aspirations of the kind that should be granted and the determination to carry out these aspirations. The same, to be sure, holds true also of adults.

Although the "pennies-from-heaven" type of prayer is easier to learn— and also readily leads to some perplexity when the pennies are not forth-coming—it has been observed that children who receive religious instruc-tion can, at a relatively early age, learn to voice prayers more in keeping with theological interpretations of the purpose of prayer. Frequently a child will recite prayers that he has been taught without understanding what they mean and then proceed to express prayers of his own in less conventional language. In a study by MacLean (1930), it was found that a large proportion of children in primary Sunday-school classes described prayer in terms of "talking to God," with emphasis more frequently upon such factors as help in doing right, avoiding wrong, help in "trying harder to get the things we want," and thanksgiving than upon requests for concrete gifts. Children in the junior and intermediate classes likewise carried out this emphasis. In response to a questionnaire, 95 per cent of the children expressed agreement with the statement: "When I talk to God, I often find out what is right for me to do"; 90 per cent expressed agreement with the statement: "God answers prayers mostly when we do our best to answer them ourselves"; and 85 per cent agreed: "God won't give us anything we ask for, but He knows what is best for us and gives us that." In this group of Sunday-school children, 6 per cent expressed agreement with the statement: "It doesn't do a fellow any good to pray."

Sherrill (1939) cites the case of a five-year-old child (who must have been somewhat precocious) who was overheard to pray: "Father in Heaven, help me to be kind and good, . . . to know what's what; help me to know what is good and what is bad, and what is poison and what is not poison, and what is right and what is wrong. Amen." [5]

A child may also be moved to voice thanksgiving, as in the case of an eight-year-old boy who, while walking homeward after having delivered milk to a neighbor on Christmas Eve, with snow under foot and a clear

---

[5] Adapted from L. J. Sherrill. *The Opening Doors of Childhood* (New York: Mac-millan, 1939), 193 pp. Reproduced by permission.

sky above, and with keen anticipation of a good dinner and gifts to come, turned his eyes skyward and exclaimed: "Gosh, God, you're good—and help everybody to be happy like me!"

Effects of religious training. The influence of religious training on children has not been studied at all in a systematic manner. In the general literature of psychology there are miscellaneous findings dealing, for example, with such points as the honesty of children who have attended Sunday school and of children who have not (as measured by tests that give the children an opportunity to cheat), the generosity of such children (again as measured by limited test situations), the degree of "liberal-mindedness" (as defined by the investigator) of members of various religious denominations and of nonmembers, the religious affiliations of delinquents, and so forth. Such studies, do not, on the whole, show that youngsters who regularly receive religious instruction are significantly more honest or humane than those who don't. The available studies in this area, however, have dealt with the problem in a manner that is limited and inconclusive.

This problem is difficult to explore in a scientific way, especially since many ends sought by religious instruction reside in the subjective realm of faith, hope, and charity and since the objective good works of religion are supposed to be done with a minimum of fanfare. It is very difficult to measure the "inward" aspects of religious convictions and commitments, the attitude of religious devotion, and the attitudes of humility and compassion which many religions stress.

Even if measurement of outward and visible signs of an inward religious orientation were possible, it would be difficult to find a control group with which to compare the religiously trained individual, since religious influences are deeply imbedded in the culture and there is a large degree of overlapping between the morals and virtues that are promoted under religious and nonreligious auspices. By reason of this large overlap between the kind of training and influence brought to bear upon technically religious and nonreligious individuals, it is difficult adequately to measure the effects of religious training even on the more commonplace expressions of moral conduct.

Apart from this overlap on many points between those who have formal religious affiliations and those who do not, there also are large variations in the religious influences brought to bear upon children who technically receive religious instruction. One child may be required to attend religious services by parents who never themselves attended; another attends with his entire family. In one case the religious practices of the child's elders may be quite perfunctory, while in another case they occupy an important place in the family's everyday activities. One child's attention may be centered only upon some of the formalities and externals of religion while another's may be impressed by the feeling and concern his elders invest in their religion. Thus there may be a decided psychological difference between the experiences of two individuals whose religious background, as measured by the criterion of training and church attendance, appears to be similar.

Even more difficult to measure are the subtle and indirect influences. In her study of sympathy, Murphy (1937) reports an incidental observation concerning the relation of the behavior of young children to the religious background of the children's parents. The influences of the church were difficult "to detach from the deepest personality characteristics of the parents who had been identified with it [the church]." Among the children in the Murphy study, there were eight whose parents had been or who were then identified with the church. With one exception, the children were less aggressive than the median child in the group as a whole. In some of these children, the observers noted manifestations of gentleness and considerateness that seemed to indicate that patterns of kindness had become deeply assimilated by the families to which the children belonged. These observations, obviously, are not presented as conclusive; other children of other parents who profess a religious faith might not conform at all to this trend. But the observations are suggestive in pointing the way toward a line of study to discover some of the subtler ways in which a religious background in the home might be reflected in the everyday behavior of children.

A study of the effects of religious instruction would not only have to cover such ground as the foregoing, it would also have to appraise the more subjective phenomena denoted by such terms as peace of mind, relief from guilt feelings, a disposition to be forgiving and patient, and faith and hope as contrasted with despair.

RELIGION AND SELF-REALIZATION

In our earlier discussion of moral development in this chapter, we referred to two ideas that also have implications for the discussion of religion—namely, the concepts of self-realization and integrity.

There are many parallels between the psychology of self-realization and psychological features of a religious view of life. In the process of realizing himself, a person will draw upon his capacity for entering into relationships with other people; the religious person will draw on similar capacities as he joins with others in his devotions. In realizing himself a person will draw upon his capacity for love; the idea of love is also central to most religious faiths. He will draw upon his capacity for realizing the joys and hurts, fears and hopes, struggles and disappointments, pains and gratifications associated with the venture of living which we in this book have referred to as compassion; most religions adjure their followers to be compassionate.

When we examine the concept of integrity as it relates to religion we deal with an area in which the growing person faces difficulty and confusion in the life about him, just as is true in the moral sphere. In the religious sphere there is a vast discrepancy between what is publicly subscribed to and what is privately embraced, between what is professed and what is realized as a matter of genuine conviction and commitment. Ross (1950) in a study of the religious attitudes of young people estimates that while about three-fourths of those who were questioned assented to various orthodox religious beliefs and doctrines only about 16 per cent seemed to show the kind of firmness of belief, zest, and security of conviction which might be expected in a genuinely religious person. In a Foreword comment on Ross' findings, Allport (1950) speaks of the same paradox: Belief in God is almost universal; prayer is widely used; and there is a friendly estimate of the church, and a widely expressed conviction that man needs religion. Yet there is at the same time, in Allport's words, a "ghostly quality" about these attitudes. Many religious teachings are unclear to those who profess them, and their bearing on people's everyday lives is vague.

These observations, in the writer's opinion, touch upon a condition of confusion which faces children in our society. Whether or not the proportions mentioned in this study between those who give lip service and those who speak from genuine conviction are precise is not so important. The fact that there are dislocations of this sort is the important consideration, and it is not in the religious sphere alone that these exist, for we can find large gaps between what is assented to and what is realized as a genuine kind of personal involvement also in politics, in the teaching profession, in scientific bodies, and in all spheres and walks of life. We see the same lack of integrity when a politician, claiming to serve the public good, appeals now to the cupidity of this group, now to the passions of that, solely to exploit their unhealthy grievances in order to get votes. We see it when a scientist, supposedly devoted solely to the logical pursuit of truth, steps out of his role and passes judgments on others in a very unscientific and emotional way.

Such dividedness, such a schism between the official pose and the personal life that is lived, is, of course, a commonplace. As the saying goes, "Such is life. What more can you expect?" Certainly it is true that such is life. The kind of dislocation here discussed can be found to some degree in the lives of all. So no one is fitted to sit in judgment upon others. Only an arrogant person would deem himself fit to cast the first stone. However, this does not free the child from the confusion and inconsistency he faces in connection with his upbringing. Nor does it free any adult from the implications of the struggle that is involved.

Recommended Readings

Jean Piaget's *The Moral Judgment of the Child* (1932) is an important book which has served as a stimulus to a large number of studies of moral development. Vernon Jones' "Character Development in Children—An Objective Approach" (1954) includes a thoughtful review and discussion of studies of children's moral ideas and attitudes. Dilemmas in the adult world which directly or indirectly influence the moral climate in which children are reared have been discussed by Karen Horney in *The Neurotic Personality of Our Time* (1937), by Erich Fromm in *The Sane Society* (1955), and in Part I of *Existence*, edited by Rollo May (1958). Issues facing parents and religious leaders who are seeking to help young people grasp the personal meaning of religion have been discussed by Abraham N. Franzblau in *Religious Belief and Character Among Jewish Adolescents* (1934), David E. Roberts in *Psychotherapy and a Christian View of Man* (1950), and Murray G. Ross in *Religious Beliefs of Youth* (1950).

Children's Interests

CHAPTER NINETEEN   This chapter will discuss selected aspects of children's interests, since almost all the chapters in this book have considered, in one way or another, the activities children undertake of their own accord.

As we have noted in an earlier section, the young child seeks to exercise and put to use his growing abilities and powers. Just as "fish gotta swim, birds gotta fly," so the young child uses his voice, his limbs, his mental machinery, and all his equipment. He spontaneously watches, handles things, creeps, walks, vocalizes, explores, asks questions, and is on the go, and as he grows older, he enters into many complex undertakings of his own choosing. His early interests are a feature of the larger dynamic pattern of his growing capacities and powers.

Generally speaking, the younger the child is, the more will the things he chooses to do give an indication of what he *can* do or can *learn to like* to do. (There are exceptions to this, of course.) Thus, while still too immature to walk, the child does not show an interest in walking, and efforts to coach him or force his progress are of little avail, but later he is eager to walk. Similarly, before the age of two a child shows little spontaneous interest in dressing himself, handling buttons, and so forth, but later insists on doing these things.

Throughout the period of growth, a child's interests are closely related to his abilities, but as he grows older the interests he *might* acquire are more numerous than those he does acquire. The older child's choices are increasingly influenced by opportunities that happen to come his way and by habits he has carried over from the past.

Play

A child's play is a serious occupation. It is through play that much of the work of childhood is done. Play is a self-chosen medium whereby a youngster tries himself out, not simply in fantasy by way of daydreams, but actively in the flesh. Through play a child moves from the known into the untried and unknown.

CHARACTERISTICS OF PLAY

Apart from being a self-chosen undertaking, play has several other characteristics and purposes.

Risk. At the beginning of any new play experience there often is an element of risk, as when a child seeks to climb, to ride a bicycle, or to swim. In many of their play activities children deliberately make conditions somewhat more hazardous than is necessary. This can be seen in coasting, sledding, climbing, and also in conventional games. For example, in ball play, the game not only becomes more complicated as the children grow older, but there is a shift from a soft to a hard ball which is violently thrown and which might cause an injury if it is clumsily handled.

Repetition. Another important element in play is repetition. Repetition gives a child the chance to consolidate the skills that the game calls for, and as he becomes more and more adept he gains freedom to improvise, to create innovations of his own. Even though children in their play sometimes seem to be doing the same thing over and over again, the repetition may be very far from static. If the child, for example, has learned the elementary motor skills in running and dodging, he has freedom to develop strategy, to try to anticipate the moves of his playmates, and to deal with them. Moreover, after repetition has enabled them to master a basic skill, children often go on to develop this into a more complicated movement. This has been observed, for example, in children's rhythmical activities (Christiansen, 1938).

Play as a means of problem solving. A youngster, while playing, may be hard at work when his play is linked to a persisting problem in his everyday life. Play of this kind has been noted in Chapter Fifteen in the account of how a child, in coping with his fears, plays a bogey man game, or selects a toy (such as a little truck) which, on a miniature scale, represents an object he fears.

Play as a vehicle for other intentions. A relatively simple play activity can become the vehicle for a more complicated intention; this is seen in the play of boys and girls as they reach adolescence. Adolescent boys and girls often resort to very "childish" play, such as running and chasing and hitting: through this play they are making advances to one another. Even a coltish forty-year-old man and a kittenish forty-year-old woman sometimes make their first tentative steps toward getting acquainted by means of childish play activities at parties and picnics.

Much more is involved in play than appears on the surface. An observer may think it rather childish for a fourteen-year-old boy or a forty-year-old man to go through the motions of making four-year-old passes at members of the opposite sex, unless he is aware that these childish motions express a serious drama.

Play as a guarded means of self-assertion. Through play children can express their needs in relative safety, as when a child who desires affection cuddles up to another person in a game. They can experiment with what is forbidden, as when they play with sex, or exercise, within "the rules of the game," a desire to hit and punish. In their play children can also act out and try out various roles—the role of being the baby, the mother, the teacher—and, in the process, express openly by outcries and actions some feelings with regard to these roles that otherwise might be forbidden. In this way, a child's play serves as a revealment to others and to himself. A child, in playing a role, may express a need to hurt others. He may submit to pain and thus express or imply a desire to punish himself. He may reveal a desire for being dominant or submissive, a desire for greater freedom or for security.[1]

---

[1] For accounts of the sources, functions, and uses of play, see Hartley (1952); Hartley, Frank, and Goldenson (1952a and 1952b); Harris (1950); Mitchell and Mason (1948).

Play as a permissible form of expressing forbidden impulses. Many of the play activities of children (and the professional sports of adults) provide a socially accepted outlet for impulses that would be forbidden if they appeared in raw form. A child in a housekeeping game punishes other children in a manner that would not be permitted outside a play setting. The young football player charges into another youngster with a violence that would be punished if it occurred outside the field. The prizefighter mauls and slugs, and gives the spectators a vicarious chance to maul and slug with a vengeance which would put everyone in jail if it happened outside the ring. In the old "post-office" games, and in more recent versions of "spin the bottle" and other games, a boy can kiss a girl without being set down as a wolf and a girl can kiss a boy without being called boy-crazy.

Play and self-revealment. In a play setting a child will reveal desires, fears, grievances, and other disturbing conditions; this is the basis for play therapy. In the process of play a child may be able not only to formulate and reveal but also to "work through" and to receive help in working through problems that are supremely important in his private life.

CHANGES IN PLAY ACTIVITIES

For a time during childhood there is an increase in the number of playthings that appeal to children and in the number of play activities in which they take part; then, as they grow older, there is a decrease with age in the number of their activities (Lehman and Witty, 1927b, 1930). Older children also engage in more solitary games.

Among the games that are dropped with advancing age are many that consist to a large degree of gross muscular coordination (such as tag, dodging, pom-pom-pull-away, run sheep run). Many of the movements involved in these activities are incorporated into the more complex games that appear at later levels. Another form of play that diminishes sharply with increasing age is play of a make-believe sort, such as cowboys and Indians, cops and robbers, house, and doll-play.

The decline with age is not limited, however, to make-believe games and simple physical enterprises, for there is a high degree of mortality among games that require considerable skill and coordination. As children advance toward adolescence many of them become spectators rather than participants. Much of the activity stressed in their own games and many of the activities stressed in directed play periods at school fall into disuse. One of the activities most widely emphasized in recreational and physical-education programs, for example, is baseball; yet, after the elementary years, large numbers of children seldom play baseball.

Influence of play space and available materials. It might be maintained that play activities and games have served their purpose if they are sufficient to the time and age level at which they flourish. But children's play is not influenced solely by their own spontaneous interests, for the environment in which their interests are learned is to a large extent controlled by adults.

One practical problem connected with children's play is the provision of play space and recreation centers. This problem is not solved simply by giving the children a large amount of space and equipment, for many children, while making use at times of available space, will also be interested in playing on the streets and congregating where adults are going about their affairs. An indication of this tendency is provided in a study by Reeves (1931), based on a survey of street play in a large number of cities. Reeves found that a large proportion of the children (boys more than girls) were simply "hanging around" on the streets during their free time; on the average, less than half of the children who were in the streets were actively playing, and only a small proportion played organized games. The percentage of children on the streets bore little relationship to the amount of open play space available in the city.

The extent to which children frequent the streets when play space is available varies according to the attractions afforded by the playgrounds. In some instances it has been observed that children are more likely to go to a playground if there is an able adult supervisor in charge. In the case of younger children, it has been found that children who for a long time have attended nursery school and kindergarten frequently become bored with repetitious play activities and look to adults for ideas and stimulation. A child's ability to master and enjoy a performance may exceed his ability to invent or improvise a performance that will serve as a proper challenge to his powers.

Children's interests

When children are asked to reveal their interests, they not only mention things they like to do but many will also, if given a chance, reveal that they are bored with many of the things they are supposed to be interested in.

Tables 24 and 25 present some of the results obtained in a series of studies in which children were asked, among other matters, to tell what they "liked best" and "disliked most" in and out of school.

In describing what they liked best at school, pupils of junior- and senior-high-school age less often mentioned academic subjects than did the younger children; on the other hand, the older pupils more often

TABLE 24 | RESPONSE OF PUPILS TO THE ITEM, "WHAT I LIKE BEST IN SCHOOL." THE VALUES REPRESENT PERCENTAGE OF PUPILS GIVING ONE OR MORE ANSWERS IN EACH CATEGORY *

	1-3	4-6	7-9	10-12	1-6		7-12	
Grade								
Age	6-9	9-12	12-15	15-18	6-12		12-18	
					Boys	Girls	Boys	Girls
No. of Pupils	544	452	372	230	497	499	281	321
1. School plant and facilities	.6	0	.3	0	.6	0	.4	0
2. Games, sport, gym, recess, etc.	7.0	2.9	30.6	33.9	6.0	4.2	27.4	35.8
Games, play, playground sports	6.4	.7	2.4	7.4	4.0	3.6	6.8	2.2
Gym, physical education	.2	.9	27.2	26.1	.4	.6	19.6	33.0
Recess, lunch, "free time"	.7	1.3	1.1	1.7	1.6	.4	2.5	.3
Other	0	0	.3	0	0	0	.4	0
3. Parties, dances, etc.	0	1.3	1.1	.9	0	1.2	1.1	.9
4. Academic subjects, information on various topics	77.8	85.3	57.3	45.7	78.5	84.4	49.5	55.8
Numbers, arithmetic, math.	27.2	33.0	26.1	13.5	30.2	29.4	25.6	17.4
Spelling	8.4	23.0	9.1	0	13.1	17.0	5.3	5.9
Reading, language arts, writing	41.7	29.2	18.0	19.1	33.2	38.9	11.0	24.9
Nature study, science	1.1	4.2	5.6	13.9	1.4	3.6	11.7	6.2
Health	0	.4	0	0	.4	0	0	0
Social studies, community, world affairs, peoples, industry, biography, conservation, etc.	1.1	10.6	6.4	8.7	5.0	5.8	7.1	7.5
Miscellaneous	.2	0	5.1	2.2	.2	0	1.1	6.5
5. Arts, fine and dramatic	12.5	10.4	9.4	12.2	10.9	12.2	10.3	10.6
Graphic and plastic	11.8	7.5	3.8	.4	9.8	9.8	2.8	2.2
Music	.7	3.1	5.1	12.2	1.0	2.6	7.1	8.4
Dramatics	0	.9	1.1	.9	.4	.4	1.1	.9
6. Mechanical and industrial arts, shopwork, etc.	0	0	9.4	7.4	0	0	18.1	.3

TABLE 24 (*continued*)

	1-3 6-9	4-6 9-12	7-9 12-15	10-12 15-18	1-6 6-12		7-12 12-18	
Grade / Age					497 Boys	499 Girls	281 Boys	321 Girls
No. of Pupils	544	452	372	230				
7. Domestic arts	0	0	3.8	4.8	0	0	.4	7.5
8. Personal self-improvement, vocational, self-understanding:								
Intellectual, improve mind	0	0	0	4.3	0	0	.4	2.8
Knowledge of human nature	0	0	0	1.7	0	0	.7	.6
Religious, moral improvement	.4	.4	.3	0	.2	.6	0	.3
"Commercial," typing, etc.	0	0	0	3.9	0	0	.4	2.5
9. Special successes, awards	0	0	0	.9	0	0	.4	.3
10. Self-government, forums, discussion	0	1.3	.8	.9	.6	.6	.7	.9
11. Monitor duties	.6	.2	0	0	.2	.6	0	0
12. School privileges, requirements, discipline, management	.9	.2	1.1	.9	.4	.8	1.1	.9
13. People Pupils (other than 3)	2.4	6.0	3.5	8.3	3.0	5.0	3.2	7.2
Teachers	.9	1.1	1.3	8.3	1.0	1.0	1.8	5.9
Boy-girl friendships	1.5	5.1	1.1	0	2.0	4.2	.4	.9
14. Miscellaneous	0	.4	.8	1.3	.2	0	1.1	.9
15. No response, unintelligible	1.3	2.6	3.0	2.2	2.4	1.4	3.9	1.6

* From A. T. Jersild and R. Tasch, *Children's Interests* (New York: Teachers College, Columbia University, 1949). Reproduced by permission. Since a child received a tally of one for one or several items in a given category or subcategory, the cumulative total in the subcategories may exceed the value shown for the main category. This table *illustrates* children's interests at school, but it is not presented as *typical*. See wide variations between groups in Table 25.

mentioned sports, industrial and mechanical arts, intellectual self-improvement, vocational preparation, and relations with other persons of their own age. The fact that children's responses are determined to a large degree by what the school offers is shown in Table 26. School *D* was equipped with a variety of gymnasium facilities, a swimming pool, good facilities in the fine arts, and opportunities for shop work. Undoubtedly that is why the children in this school mentioned these activities so provided relatively more often, and academic subjects relatively less often, than did children in some of the other schools. The influence of unfavorable neighborhood conditions is reflected in the responses of children in School *C,* which was situated in an overcrowded community in which there was a good deal of violence and crime. The children in this school, it can be noted, were much more preoccupied with *people* and characteristics of people in naming what they disliked most than were children in the other schools. (This preoccupation with "bad" people was even more pronounced in reports concerning what the youngsters disliked most in their lives outside of school.)

From such studies as the one cited in tables 24, 25, and 26 and in other investigations, the following findings and interpretations have emerged.

When children express their interests, wishes, likes, and dislikes, or what it is in their lives that pleases them most, or has given them the

		PERCENTAGE OF CHILDREN GIVING RESPONSES IN VARIOUS LIMITED SELECTED CATEGORIES, WHEN REPORTING WHAT THEY LIKED BEST AND WHAT THEY DISLIKED MOST AT SCHOOL *			
TABLE 25					

	996 Pupils in Grades 1-6 (Ages 6-12)		602 Pupils in Grades 7-12 (Ages 12-18)	
Subjects Mentioned	Like Best	Dislike Most	Like Best	Dislike Most
Games, sport, gym, recess, etc.	5.1	5.4	31.9	2.8
Academic information, subjects	81.4	42.7	52.8	46.2
Art	11.5	4.8	10.5	3.2
Mechanics, shop, domestic art	0	.2	12.8	3.7
People	4.0	4.6	5.3	15.1
Pupils	1.0	4.1	4.0	7.0
Teachers	3.1	.2	.7	8.0
Other	0	.2	.7	.8

* Adapted from A. T. Jersild and R. Tasch, *Children's Interests* (New York: Teachers College, Columbia University, 1949). Reproduced by permission.

TABLE 26 | PERCENTAGE OF CHILDREN IN GRADES 4, 5, AND 6 IN VARIOUS SCHOOLS GIVING RESPONSES IN SELECTED, LIMITED CATEGORIES WHEN INDICATING WHAT THEY LIKED BEST AND DISLIKED MOST IN SCHOOL *

	Like Best (by Schools) †				Dislike Most (by Schools)			
	A	B	C	D	A	B	C	D
Games, play, sports, recess, gym	3.5	2.6	19.0	51.1	1.4	6.8	4.5	2.3
Academic information	79.0	89.0	50.0	34.1	60.1	48.9	39.0	41.5
Art	10.5	10.4	15.0	21.0	6.3	4.9	5.0	11.9
Mechanics, shop, domestic arts	0	0	1.0	8.0	0	0	1.0	1.7
People	7.0	5.5	6.0	4.5	2.1	8.7	23.0	8.5
Pupils	.7	1.3	0	1.7	1.4	7.8	14.5	4.0
Teachers	7.0	4.2	6.0	2.8	0	.3	9.0	6.2
Other	0	0	0	0	.7	.6	0	0
Unintelligible, no response	3.5	2.3	3.5	2.3	23.8	27.8	15.5	15.9

* *Ibid.*
† Schools *A*, *B*, and *C* are public schools. *A* is in a mid-western city, *B* in a southern city, *C* in one of the most congested and unfavorable neighborhoods in New York City, *D* is a private school in New York City. Included in this study were 176 pupils from school *A;* 368 from school *B;* 200 from *C;* 176 from *D*.

greatest thrill, they give a great deal of emphasis to people and relationships with people.

Older children's interests are influenced to a great degree by what happens to be available in their environment for them to get interested in. To a large degree, they like what they have learned to like (subject to their ability and maturity level). This means that the interests children report tell more about what they have had a chance to learn to like than about what they might learn to like, if given the opportunity. There is a large element of chance in the interests children at a given level in a given school report.

Declining interest in academic content. Many children, as they move through the school grades, show a decline in interest in the school's academic program. In many communities there is a decline with age in educational morale. No doubt there are many reasons for this. One contributing factor is the competition of other interests. As children near adolescence, for example, the social contacts they can establish during nonacademic periods (lunch time, after-school hours) appeal to many of them more than does what is offered in class. In the case of many children, however, it seems that the decline with age in enthusiasm for what the school offers springs from the fact that the content of the curriculum seems academic, arbitrary, and remote from their concerns.

Interest in self-understanding.   In the study represented in the foregoing tables it was noted that many of the older children, with little encouragement from the school, showed an interest in various forms of self-understanding and self-improvement, and yet it was not apparent that these youngsters could see any relation between what they were asked to learn at school and their own desire for self-improvement. Probably there is a need not only to re-examine what is offered but also to interpret more clearly how the lessons the children are asked to learn from day to day actually do or might fit in with their own desire to grow.

Discrepancy between academic content and personal interests.   In the study cited above and in several other studies it has been found that the material children are taught in their social studies classes is relatively unpopular as compared with some other subjects. In theory, one might expect this subject to be potentially the most interesting in the academic program. And when children state what they would like to learn about many of them refer to topics which ordinarily would fall under the heading of the social studies (such as history, but not as commonly taught). One difficulty apparently, in teaching the social studies, is that teachers and textbooks present the material more from an adult, academic point of view than from the point of view of problems and human strivings which children can understand.

Overlap between interests displayed in and out of school.   In most of the communities included in the study cited in Table 24, there was relatively little overlap between the things children reported they were occupied with at school and the things that interested them most outside of school.

Relation of children's interests to later interests.   Various studies have shown that the interests adults possess, and in turn help their children to acquire, are considerably influenced by the interests and skills the adults happened to acquire when they were children. Failure to acquire interests in childhood may leave lifelong gaps. There are many indications that the range of children's interests is quite restricted compared with the interests they might, with help, acquire.

When adults were asked (in the study cited above) to speak about the interests they developed as children and the interests which they now, as adults, wished they had acquired, many expressed regret about having given so much time to conventional sports, such as baseball, which have little utility for later life, except for the spectator. They regretted having not spent more time in cultivating interests which they could more readily enjoy as adults, such as music.

Many people move into adult years possessing potential resources for activity and enjoyment which never were cultivated and which never will be. This does not imply that the more interests a young person acquires the more contented he will be as an adult. The person who becomes interested in ten things is not necessarily better off than the person who acquires an interest in only five things, or two. Many interests may represent weakness rather than strength, a tendency to be diffuse, and a lack of conviction in any chosen line of activity. However, other things being equal, the more interests a child has at least an opportunity to taste or to acquire, the more chance he will have to hit upon some interests that are suited to his particular gifts. By developing interests in keeping with his particular abilities a child is helped to realize himself, and through this process he probably also can be helped to acquire a wholesome idea of his own worth.

Television, movie, and radio interests

The average child devotes many hours to television programs, and many youngsters who have access to television sets also spend time in listening to the radio. Surveys of television interests have not been as complete as the surveys of radio habits that were made during the past thirty years or so. However, it seems that many of the findings concerning children's radio interests appear even more emphatically in studies of children's television interests, tastes, and habits.

In surveys of children's radio interests some years ago it was estimated that in the elementary-school age range the average child spent about one-seventh of his waking hours listening to the radio. In studies of television viewing, the amount of time spent by the average child has been estimated as ranging from around 14 to as much as 20 hours a week, and some children spend as much as eight or ten hours a day in watching television (studies in this area have been reviewed by Banning, 1955). Counting Saturdays and Sundays as well as weekdays, there are many youngsters who spend at least as much time during the week at the radio or television set as they spend in school.[2]

By adding the visual element, television not only gives added interest to many children's programs of adventure and other popular themes but also gives a graphic and meaningful portrayal of many subjects in the social and natural sciences and in reports of current events.

---

[2] For surveys and discussions of children's television interests, see Dunham (1952); Maccoby (1951); Marx (1953); Seagoe (1952); Shayon (1951); Witty (1950, 1951, 1952); and Coffin (1955).

It appears that programs dealing with "Western" themes, cowboys, the frontier, cops and robbers, crime and mystery, and interplanetary communication have as much appeal in television as they did in radio. Dramas of family life, quiz shows in which contestants can win money and other prizes, and musical "variety" shows that are especially popular with adults are also popular with children. If anything, however, television caters to a larger fund of interests which both adults and children have in common than is true of the radio; for example, "adventures in science," deep-sea explorations, portrayals of distant people in their native habitats. Television, to an even greater extent than radio, frequently offers entertainment which an entire family can share. Occasionally, it gives youngsters a pleasant opportunity to instruct their elders (for example, a child who spends much time with television may be quicker than his parents in detecting who is the "bad guy" in a crime show).

Television and radio programs present problems in many homes, especially in connection with the daily routine, interference with mealtime, interference with homework, and with bedtime schedules. Television presents practical problems of home management and of sharing and of consideration for various members of the household.

The clashes of interest that occur in the home because of television probably do not give rise to any particularly new issue in the relationship between siblings or between parents and children. But a very appealing television program can precipitate a sharp clash within families when children would like to listen at mealtime or postpone their homework or postpone their bedtime.

As has been true for several decades in connection with the radio, parents and educators raise many questions and quite a few eyebrows with regard to the emotional and moral content of what is portrayed on television. While it is probably true that television has not added any particularly new form of temptation or novel kind of emotional threat, it must be recognized that a televised dramatic scene can have a far more intense emotional impact, especially by playing on children's feelings of vindictiveness and fear, than stories that they read or hear.

In appraising the influence of television programs it is difficult to establish a cause and effect relationship. When it is found, for example, that children who are doing below-average work at school spend more time viewing television than those who are doing well at school, the reason may be that the programs interfere with homework or it may be that the youngsters who are not succeeding at school would spend their time on something else even if they had no television to watch. In one study it was found that children who spent six hours or more viewing television programs did poorer school work than other youngsters, but they had done poorly in school before their families acquired a television set (Greenstein, 1954). Likewise, we cannot assume that children will become more aggressive as a result of viewing programs in which there is fighting (Albert, 1957). However, the clever forms of persuasion used in many of the commercials seem to make a strong impression on some youngsters.

When children in large numbers prefer programs that adults question there may be right and wrong on both sides. Adults are likely to judge a program in terms of their own adult point of view. A program that seems trashy to a sophisticated adult may still be suitable for a child, just as a child's pants may fit him well even though they don't fit his father. There is another aspect to this, however: The fact that a child is interested in a program does not necessarily mean that the program fills a "need." Moreover, parents have grounds for bitter complaint, not against the child but against those producing the show, if a program takes advantage of a child's lack of knowledge and discrimination and plies him with distortions and humbug, or is false from an emotional point of view. A basic question of moral responsibility is raised, for example, when television programs use crime themes on a vast commercial scale and prove, in effect, that crime *does* pay (at least for advertising purposes), while offering an unrealistic picture of the sordid circumstances that often surround crime and the personal anguish and tragedy it frequently entails.

Reading interests

The beginnings of an interest in reading appear in the young child's manipulation of books, his interest in looking at pictures, and his desire for storytelling and being read to. Many children enjoy being read to even before they can understand the words—apparently the flow of sound and the changes in facial expression and vocal inflection attract their attention (and the reading is no doubt all the more attractive if they are nestled in the lap of the one who reads). Children thus show an interest in one feature or another of the total reading situation before the age of two years and even before they are a year old. Reading interests emerge out of experiences that go back to early infancy. A study by Almy (1949) shows how experiences related to reading are interwoven with the child's contacts and relationships with others long before he actually begins to read.[3]

When the child himself has learned to read, his reading activities and interests show certain age trends, but there are large individual differ-

---

[3] For discussion of reading interests and factors that influence interest, progress, and the development of ability in reading, see Ephron (1953); Gates (1949); and Russell (1949a, 1949b).

ences at each age level. Among trends that have been noted are the following: Prior to the age of five many children show a fondness for simple factual stories, rhymes and jingles, and stories illustrated by pictures that can be discussed with an older person.

In a survey of the reading interests of over two thousand kindergarten children, based on ratings by teachers of over 400 books read to the youngsters, the following preferences were found: studies of what "actually happened" liked by 67.5 per cent of the children; "could happen," 73.4 per cent; "fanciful," 75.9 per cent; and "nonsense tales," 42.2 per cent (Cappa, 1956). According to these results, kindergarten children prefer stories "sprinkled with a slight bit of unrealism," yet it can be seen that the "did happen" and "could happen" stories stand practically as high as those in the fanciful category.

The reading interests of children during the primary- and elementary-school period differ widely, depending in part on such factors as differences in intelligence, available materials, and the encouragement supplied by the child's associates and his elders. At the primary-school level children like surprise and plot. Stories about animals have a good deal of appeal from early childhood through the elementary grades. There is no evidence that children at the primary-school level are in an "age of pure fancy" or that legends and folk tales, as a class, are the most interesting materials.

With increasing age comes an increased interest in robust adventure, especially in the case of the boys. During the elementary years, girls show more interest than boys in stories of home life and domestic happenings; girls show an earlier interest than boys in romance, and girls show a greater interest than boys in tranquil social situations while boys lean more toward aggressive action (Vandament and Thalman, 1956).

In a study of children in the fourth, fifth, and sixth grades, Lazar (1937) found that the following elements had considerable appeal: adventure, action, excitement, thrills, mystery, realism, suspense, child life, humor-mischief, animal life and nature, sportsmanship and bravery, sports, airplanes and other inventions. Toward the junior-high-school and the high-school age, an increasing number of children show an interest in history, biography, and in books and magazine articles dealing with the social and natural environment. Girls show more interest than boys in sentimental fiction of the adult type, but both boys and girls are likely cheerfully to digest fictional materials that distort reality and deal with impossible situations. In addition to such trends, there is an increased taste for humor, and there is likely also to be some reading in connection with hobbies, how to make things, and the like. As children reach the junior-high-school level they are increasingly interested in reading about children and teen-agers (Rudman, 1955).

It has been found that about 90 per cent of children between the ages of eight and thirteen frequently read comic books, and many youngsters read five or six such books each week (Witty and Sizemore, 1954).

In a study by R. L. Thorndike (1941), children's reading interests were investigated by means of a list of fictitious (but very plausible) titles, accompanied by brief annotations such as the following:

> *Bowser the Hound.* Bowser went hunting rabbits with his master. What happened when they met Jimmy Skunk instead?
>
> *King of the Gangs.* How Slick McCoy made himself king of the underworld. A story of gangs and gang warfare.
>
> *The Ghost Ranger of Lonesome Valley.* Why were cattle always disappearing from Lonesome Valley? Who was the shadow that carried them away?
>
> *Me and My Job.* What different jobs are really like. What to think about in picking out your job.
>
> *Cupid Takes a Holiday.* Joan and Fred had always been good friends— just good friends and nothing more. Then Fred went away to college. When he came back he found a different Joan.
>
> *History of the Lutheran Church.* The story of the Lutheran church, from the time of its beginning up to the present.

The list included both fiction and nonfiction with such topics as adventure and mystery involving boys and girls, animals and fairies, romance, sports, and hobbies, self-improvement, history, and travel. Boys and girls showed more differences in their preferences than did old or young or bright or dull children of the same sex (within the age range from 10 to 15 years). There were, however, differences between bright and dull children. The brighter children (with a median IQ of about 125) had interests resembling those of mentally slower children (median IQ about 92) who were two or three years older. This greater maturity of the reading interests of the brighter children appeared not simply (or even predominantly) in connection with scholarly or bookish topics but in connection with other topics, such as mystery and adventure. Within the same sex there were some titles that differed widely in popularity at different age levels, but there were many titles that appealed both to the youngest and the oldest children in the study. Of the ten titles that had the highest appeal for average ten-year-old boys, five were still among the top ten titles at the fifteen-year-old level.

In the sphere of reading interests, as in connection with other interests, we cannot assume that children's choices are entirely "free" or a sure sign of their "natural" inclinations. Children learn what they are supposed to be interested in, in reading as in other matters. Once they begin to read, their interests in reading are likely to be influenced by the content of what they are given to read. It has been observed, for example, that reading materials are more or less loaded with emphases that encourage boys to develop somewhat different interests than girls and to develop different ideas as to what boys are like (Child, Potter, and Levine, 1946). Seward and Harris (1951) have also shown, by way of further example, that children's reading materials sometimes place children in unrealistic situations in which they imitate adults.

INTEREST IN FACT AND FANCY

In their reading, children are both romanticists and realists. They read fiction that deals with situations that are not only impossible but absurd, and also read solid discussions of travel, natural history, biography, descriptions of other lands and people, and similar topics. Although children are thus quite catholic in their tastes, they are likely to exercise some critical powers in going from one kind of reading matter to another. If they have sought out a book that deals with actual happenings, they like to have a truthful and informative account, although they may prefer treatment of the dramatic and unusual to a systematic treatment of all phases of a topic.

That children prefer straightforward, factual material in books dealing with science and that adults may be quite mistaken in their judgment as to the probable appeal of a book has been shown by Williams (1939). Among other things, children in his study were not much influenced by the color and design of a book's cover or by general features of format. The content is what interested them most, and they wanted informative content—new information, explanations of how animals live and how things work—rather than rhapsodies about the glories of nature and the wonders of the subject under treatment. Many objected strenuously to devices that some authors inject to appeal to children, such as personification, glowing introductory essays that reflect the author's enthusiasm but tell no facts, or the device of having an indulgent adult enter into conversation with a child as a means of injecting both a human and an informative quality. Also it was noted that children would read books representing a wide range of "reading difficulty." If interested in the topic, a reader of eighth-grade ability would dip into a book of fourth-grade difficulty, and a poorer reader would delve into books that were above his reading level as measured by an achievement test. The important consideration was the child's interest in the subject and his ability to get the general flow of ideas from the context and the pictures, even if he failed to understand a large number of individual words.

In this study, adults were also asked to rate the books that the children had used and commented on. First, they were told to rate them in terms of their own reactions, on a scale ranging from most liked to least liked; then they were asked to rate the same books in terms of their judgment as to how well the *children* would like them. The interesting finding was that there was more correspondence between *adults' preferences* and children's preferences than between *adults' judgment* as to what the children would like and what the children actually did like. Broadly speaking, it would appear that a good guide for adults to follow in selecting books for a child in the field of science, assuming that they are choosing from a general area that appeals to the child and that they show some regard for his reading ability, is to select books which they themselves find most interesting. On the other hand, a study by Rankin (1944) of children's interest in fiction shows that some children's books selected by adult reviewing committees as especially outstanding have not been popular with children. Among factors that seem to lower a book's popularity are a large proportion of descriptive matter, whimsy, and scenes and customs foreign to a child's background. The children reported that their choices of books for leisure-time reading were influenced more by librarians than by teachers but, far more, by recommendations of other children.

A difference between children's "read-about interests" and their "ask-about interests" was noted in a study by Rudman (1955) who obtained information from several thousand children and parents and from several hundred teachers and librarians. In answer to the question, "If someone were to give you a book as a present what would you want it to be about?" children in grades four through eight named interests such as those described in studies referred to above. However, when asked, "If a good friend could answer any question you asked, what would you ask about?" children expressed many concerns that seldom were mentioned in accounts of their reading interests. In the upper elementary- and junior-high-school grades many children raised questions regarding ethics, values, and religion. "Ask-about" questions pertaining to personal problems—notably boy-girl relationships and vocations—increase "dramatically" as children approach puberty, but children apparently do not look upon available reading materials as a means of finding answers to their personal problems.

Recommended Readings

An inventory of children's interests entitled "What I Like to Do," containing 294 items, has been prepared by Louis P. Thorpe, Charles E. Meyers, and Marcella Ryser Sea (1954) for use with children in grades four through seven. An accompanying "profile folder" shows the percentage of children in grades four, five, and six who have expressed an interest in each of the items in the instrument. A number of research studies dealing with children's favorite occupations, their reading and TV interests are cited in the text.

Personality —
A Final View

In this chapter we will take a final view of developments in the child's personality as he moves into adolescence toward adult life. We will briefly examine the dimensions of a child's personality and circumstances that influence the course of his growth. We will also consider the values according to which children assess their worth, problems that follow them from childhood into later years, and conditions in our culture that help or hinder young people in realizing their potentialities.

By personality we mean the sum-total of an individual's properties as a distinct and unique human being. The outer dimensions of personality include an individual's measurable characteristics, his physique, talents and abilities, and the qualities of temperament and disposition that are observable in his public conduct. The inner

dimensions comprise an individual's drives, the total system of ideas and attitudes that constitute his awareness of himself, and the unrecognized or unconscious tendencies that have an important bearing on his feelings, thoughts, and actions.

Interplay between heredity
and environment in personality development

A child's personality is the product of an interplay between influences in the environment and forces of heredity that have been described in earlier chapters in this book. As we have seen, the effects of both heredity and environment are apparent in the child's physical and intellectual development (and especially in the more extreme forms of mental impairment and personality disorder). The effects of both also appear in the aspects of an individual's personality commonly referred to as temperament and disposition. According to Shirley (1933b) personality has its physiological basis in the structure and organization of the nervous system and of the physical-chemical constitution of the body as a whole. Gesell (1928) states that a person's "basic developmental tempo, trend and temperament are mainly inherent individual characteristics." However, it is also apparent from studies of the effects of the environment, notably a very adverse environment, that the circumstances of a child's life can profoundly influence his personality development no matter what his heredity may be. The interacting forces of heredity and environment are difficult to assess. In studies of a number of children, Bühler (1952) noted that some youngsters developed unexpectedly well even though they had an unfavorable heredity background and there were other children "whose mothers were close and warm" but who were unable to respond to affection "and disintegrated in spite of their mother's devotion."

Each child's personality emerges from a complex biological system and a complex field of social forces. The factors influencing the course of a child's development are so intricate that two children are likely to differ from one another even if both seem to have the "same" heredity and, while they are babies, seem to share the "same" environment. A study by Blatz and Millichamp (1937) of the Dionne quintuplets from the time they were twelve to thirty-six months old illustrates the complexity of early personality development. An examination of the biological characteristics of the five sisters led to the conclusion that they were "identicals" —derived from a single fertilized egg. As babies they looked so alike that a casual observer could not tell their faces apart; yet they showed small variations in form of the face, ears, teeth, and other characteristics. When their behavior was closely observed from the twelfth to the thirty-sixth month it was also noted that they differed in their social behavior—in the number of social contacts they initiated and received, in aggressiveness, in their skill in manipulating material, in their efforts to gain attention. The differences between them made a difference in the response they elicited from one another. It appeared, for example, that one of the girls, in seeking to attract attention, stimulated one of her sisters to become aggressive in *her* efforts to satisfy a "need for an audience." On the basis of their observations of the quintuplets, Blatz and Millichamp make this interesting statement: "The environmental characteristics most influential in moulding an individual are those which result from the individual's own response to his social environment."

Almost from the time of birth babies differ in temperament and disposition. Distinct individual differences are frequently noted by mothers who have reared two or more children, and such differences have also been described in considerable detail in research studies of infants as noted in earlier chapters (see Shirley, 1933b; Burlingham, 1952).

Infants vary in the extent to which they are active or inactive, fussy or placid, quick or slow to respond. They differ in the vigor of their demands for food, in the intensity of their reaction to sounds, contacts, and other stimuli. Some are easily awakened while others continue to drowse. When aroused, some quickly subside while others keep going. Some seem to be especially sensitive to wet diapers, rashes, and other irritations while others are not. Early in life babies differ in their responsiveness to human contact. Some are cuddly, easily comforted when handled or held, others seem to be less responsive, less eager to be held, and more difficult to soothe.

When babies show distinct marks of individuality at a very early age it is difficult to tell whether they were "born that way" or whether, at a very early age, they have acquired certain ways of responding because of the way in which they are handled by their mothers. It is clear, however, that babies in the care of the same person frequently differ greatly in their reactions to this person. This was noted by Berezin (1959) in a study of babies cared for by twenty-two boarding mothers while awaiting adoption. Through direct observation, information supplied by a psychologist, and records kept by the adoption agency, Berezin obtained ratings of the temperamental qualities of the boarding mothers and of the infants. The mothers perceived distinct individual characteristics in the babies in their care. Five of the mothers studied were each caring for three infants. These five mothers saw each of the three babies in her care as having his own unique characteristics. Boarding mothers rated high or low in such qualities as activity tempo or sensitivity or tension did not show any consistent tendency to rate their babies high or low with respect to these qualities, but gave a variety of ratings. One mother, for example, who rated high in expression of affection, in responsiveness, and in sensitivity, was observed while caring for three infants almost identical in age (aged ten and eleven weeks). According to her perception, these infants differed in their disposition, their needs and demands and, as a consequence, her child-care practices varied with each one.

Consistency and change
in predominant personality traits

Children not only show individual characteristics in infancy, but as they grow older they are more likely to remain "true of type" than to change to a marked degree. In observations of twenty-five babies during the first two years of life Shirley (1933b) found that the children showed a high degree of consistency in the general pattern of their behavior from month to month. Their behavior changed as they matured but there were always "identifying earmarks." A given form of behavior "waned and lapsed, only to be supplanted by another that apparently was its consistent outgrowth." For example, one baby was distinctive at an early age for his "timorous crying"; this crying waned, but then he exhibited "apprehensive watching" and, at a later age, showed a similarly timorous trend by hiding behind his mother and by reluctance to play and talk in the presence of a visitor. Shirley (1933b) gives a further example of two infants, one of whom remained consistently the most irritable and the other the least irritable among the youngsters in her group even though, during the course of the study, both of the children showed a decrease in irritability, in common with children in the group as a whole.

When the babies in Shirley's study reached the age of seventeen a new assessment was made of their personality traits by Neilon (1948). Judges were asked to match the two-year-old personality descriptions with descriptions of the same children at seventeen. The two personality descriptions were in most instances so much alike that the judges were able to match them far more accurately than could be expected by chance; however, the two-year-old and the seventeen-year-old personality sketches of some of the children were so unlike that the judges either disagreed in their judgment of them or matched them incorrectly.

In a later study, Shirley (1941) gives a detailed description of two boys who were reared quite differently by their mothers and yet retained their individuality. The mother of one of the boys seemingly tried to keep him a baby, sought to prolong his attachment to her, and appeared anxious about practical details of his everyday care. Yet by the age of six this boy, according to Shirley, had grown into "an independent, objective little boy ... a person in his own right." His mother, through her lack of firmness and her inability to pursue a consistent course of action, had left her baby "to grow up on the shifting sands of insecurity," and the boy "therefore had to build his own foundation of security." He did this by means of different techniques at different times. He gained attention at first by crying, later by refusing to eat, and then as time passed, his methods took a more mature form. At six he appeared to be a well-adjusted and quite self-sufficient person. It would, of course, require more than one case study to establish how far a child can go in building "his own foundations of security." The boy might not have been able to assert himself so effectively if his mother, instead of being over-zealous, had neglected him or actively rejected him. However, this boy, in common with many children who have been studied less intensively, supports Shirley's theory that each child has a "tough core" of temperamental qualities.

In a study by McKinnon (1942), children were first observed in a nursery school and then were followed through the first two elementary grades. At the nursery-school age the youngsters were classified into four groups on the basis of the most prominent characteristics of their social behavior: "conforming," "invasive," "withdrawn," and "cautious." Ten of the sixteen children continued from the age of three to the age of eight or nine to remain in the same classification. The changes that occurred were in the direction of "conforming." Changes consisted primarily in building upon characteristics that previously were manifested rather than in doing an about-face or in the tacking on of something strange or new. One child, for example, changed from predominantly "invasive" behavior at three to "conforming" behavior at eight, but the underlying direction of his behavior remained much the same: At both ages he was very eager to be noticed by other children. At three his techniques were crude and produced many conflicts, but at eight he had acquired more effective techniques.

Impressive evidence bearing on the stability of certain personality tendencies from year to year has been reported by Stott (1957) who studied the conduct of over a hundred youngsters during a period of approximately twelve years. The first assessment of these children was made while they were in nursery school, and later the children were observed in recreational clubs which they attended. The children were rated on a scale of "ascendance-submission" (ranging from extreme bossiness to "dependent ineffective submissiveness"). Stott found that "persistence of pattern was far more frequent than change." Eighty-two per cent of the children "showed no consistent direction of change." When changes did occur they were temporary in most instances, with subsequent return to the earlier pattern. Some children continued, in later years, to display the characteristics they had shown at the beginning of their nursery-school experience even though considerable effort had been made by teachers and other members of the staff to change them. "Many aspects of each child's personality did change in the sense of becoming more mature, and marked changes in overall social behavior occurred. But even with these changes in capacity to function and modifications of patterns of functioning, the fundamental qualities of his person and of his functioning remained to give him uniqueness and individuality among his play peers."

The foregoing studies deal primarily with the degree of consistency children show in their public behavior—in the objective dimensions of personality that were mentioned at the beginning of this chapter. To assess the full meaning of this behavior we would also need information concerning the subjective meanings and motives underlying it. Similar overt behavior may have different subjective meanings: One child who is "withdrawn" may be apathetic or afraid, another may be "withdrawn" in the sense that he makes few contacts with other children and yet has vigorous interests which he pursues in a solitary way. However, the fact that a child who is withdrawn at one stage of his social development is more likely to remain that way than to become a joiner is still significant, whatever the motives underlying his behavior might be.

When a child has a certain personality trait he takes a hand in shaping his environment. The youngster who happens to have a genial disposition is more likely to get a friendly response than the one who is not genial. The genial child thus helps to preserve his geniality. An overly-aggressive child is likely to arouse counter-aggression and add fuel to his aggressive impulses. When a youngster's characteristics thus influence his environment, he is, in a sense, establishing conditions that help to perpetuate these characteristics (Davitz, 1958).

Findings showing that a child's predominant social characteristics are tenacious does not, of course, mean that his behavior remains unchanged. Whatever may be the pattern of his individuality he is likely to move along with developmental trends. A child who was timorous at three is likely to show it openly, but if he is still timorous at twelve he may have many disguises for this trait. The youngster who was openly (but not obnoxiously) aggressive at three is likely at twelve to express his aggressiveness in a more mannerly way.

Further, evidence indicating that personality traits are rather persistent does not rule out the possibility that radical changes will occur in individual children. Nor does it mean that we can accurately predict an adult's personality from our knowledge of his childhood characteristics. Changing demands and fortunes of life can bring out characteristics that were not apparent before. Among the factors that can have this effect are illness, success or failure at school, finding or losing a close friend, and the pattern of a child's development when he reaches adolescence. At any juncture of life a person may meet circumstances that impair his effectiveness or provide an opportunity for him to show previously undisclosed facets of his make-up. A youngster who does well at school may, for example, acquire a degree of independence and self-confidence he did not show during preschool years. On the other hand, a youngster who was self-confident and friendly as a preschooler but who is unable to hold his own in the elementary grades may take a new turn in his personality development, such as a tendency toward "nervousness" or withdrawal or an effort to gain attention by showing off. Forces operating in a child's life in and out of school may have quite differing effects on the manifest aspects of a child's personality; this can be observed in children who display problems at school but not at home, or have problems at home but not at school (Kraus, 1956).

> A child's personality is not static and, therefore, a radical change in his style of life may occur, but it is important to recognize that he is more likely to be consistent than to change. When we notice certain characteristics in an older child we can be quite certain that he has had them for a long time. This means that when we try to get a child to change his ways, as often we do in the guidance of children, we are asking him to modify a strongly established pattern. It is very unlikely that we can convert the compliant child into a rebel or transform the self-assertive youngster into a self-effacing one. When an older child has traits that create difficulties for him it is wiser to help him to gain insight into the nature and consequences of his conduct and to change his manner of expressing a strongly established trait than to require him to reconstruct his personality. The over-compliant child is benefitted, for example, if we can help him to become aware of the nature of his operations, to discover areas of achievement in which he can assert himself, to recognize and be on guard against those who take advantage of his compliance, and to recognize the nature of the feelings of grievance that arise when he has allowed others to impose upon him.

RELATION OF CHILDHOOD CHARACTERISTICS TO ADULT TRAITS

When we say "the child is father of the man" we express a widely held belief that characteristics established during childhood provide the foundation for an individual's adult personality. This is a reasonable assumption, both from a hereditary and environmental point of view. The qualities a person has *inherited* do not change as he grows older; and habits, attitudes, and traits he has *acquired* at any stage of his development will have a powerful influence on his style of life as he moves into the next stage. However, in the process of development from infancy to old age there is great variation in what individuals do with their inherited resources or limitations and in the ways they adapt their acquired characteristics to the changing demands of life.

Evidence regarding the persistence of childhood characteristics into adult years comes, in the main, from two sources: (1) case studies of adults who were not observed as children but whose childhood characteristics and experiences are *inferred* or *reconstructed* from what they or others tell about their earlier lives; and (2) *longitudinal* studies of individuals whose characteristics have been assessed during phases of their development from childhood into adult years. Obviously, the longitudinal approach can yield the most authentic information if the investigator, from the beginning, is wise enough to identify and to appraise significant aspects of personality.

In a study by Jayaswal (1955a, 1955b) a new assessment was made, at an average age of twenty-six, of fifty-six persons who had been rated by observers on an Ascendance-Submission scale while attending nursery school. The adults rated themselves on a portion of a personality inventory (the Guilford-Martin) which "was assumed to fit quite well the definition of ascendance-submission" used in the original study. According to one method of treatment (statistical correlation) there was no significant relationship between the self-rating of the young adults and the ratings others had made of their behavior when they were in nursery school. When an "individual case approach" was used in treating the data it was found that ". . . in some individuals the tendency to be ascendant or submissive persists, in others varying degrees of change in one direction or the other take place as they grow toward adulthood."

An adequate test of the ways in which a person's childhood characteristics persist into adult years requires more incisive information than is supplied by other's ratings of his overt behavior when he was a child and self-ratings on a personality inventory when he is an adult. According to Jayaswal, "Only the intensive longitudinal study of individual cases can reveal the factors which underlie persistence or change."

The influence of a child's characteristics on his way of life as an adult depends not simply on whether a childhood trait has persisted but also on the way in which he manages, as he grows older, to live with this trait. This is shown in a study by Morris et al. (1954) of fifty-four adults who 16 to 27 years previously had been referred to a child guidance clinic. As children they were classed as "Internal Reactors." This classification included "Those showing predominantly shy, withdrawn, fearful or anxious behavior, those who are tending to develop neuroses, or those who are bothering themselves rather than others." As adults these people continued to be "quiet and retiring" and they tended to choose jobs of a sheltered type in which "security on the job is greatly emphasized over

TABLE 27 | PERCENTAGE OF BOYS AND GIRLS IN A POPULATION OF 2,893 WHO MENTIONED ITEMS IN VARIOUS CATEGORIES OF SELF-DESCRIPTION IN REPORTING "WHAT I LIKE ABOUT MYSELF" *

Grade	Elementary Grades						Junior High School						High School						College			
	IV		V		VI		VII		VIII		IX		X		XI		XII		Fresh. & Soph.		Jr. & Sr.	
Sex	B	G	B	G	B	G	B	G	B	G	B	G	B	G	B	G	B	G	B	G	B	G
Number	220	206	147	142	171	172	96	77	134	151	170	204	151	157	112	124	137	122	50	50	50	50
Category																						
1. Physical Characteristics and Appearance	15	19	22	30	12	30	14	13	29	42	23	35	25	37	17	19	15	20	40	28	20	38
2. Clothing and Grooming	16	27	12	26	12	28	14	12	13	25	13	23	17	11	10	15	9	6	10	34	24	20
3. Health and Physical Soundness	6	2	8	8	7	5	8	0	8	5	4	3	5	5	8	2	4	2	4	0	6	0
3x. Bodily Pleasures	3	3	1	1	1	1	2	1	2	2	2	0	1	0	3	1	1	2	0	0	2	0
4. Material Possessions	3	4	3	1	1	2	5	0	1	1	1	0	0	1	1	0	2	0	0	0	2	0
5. Animals and Pets	4	2	1	1	4	6	5	1	1	1	5	1	1	2	1	2	0	1	0	8	2	4
6-7. Home and Family	18	24	7	13	14	16	11	9	13	11	7	7	5	6	4	10	4	5	0	2	4	4
8. Recreation: Enjoyment of	15	10	7	4	18	10	13	5	15	5	7	3	8	5	8	6	4	3	28	2	6	6
9. Ability in Sports, Play	13	9	20	6	24	9	13	4	16	7	10	5	17	5	11	6	8	2	14	18	8	8
10. School: Ability in School; Attitudes Toward, etc.	21	33	13	17	23	21	19	29	21	27	15	12	11	8	12	6	9	9	26	22	16	18
11. Intellectual Abilities	5	3	6	6	8	3	4	4	7	7	8	6	6	11	14	9	12	9	14	26	34	36
12. Special Talents (Music, Arts)	14	11	14	17	16	20	8	23	16	18	8	11	12	11	14	14	13	12	24	16	22	28
13. Just Me, Myself	11	6	7	5	15	9	9	8	14	13	11	10	21	27	19	9	17	11	78	72	12	8
13x. Personality, Character, Inner Resources, Emotional Tendencies	23	19	20	13	24	28	37	35	35	36	29	39	36	38	31	30	35	45	74	82	78	94
14. Social Relationships and Attitudes	20	22	22	29	22	38	38	51	37	50	34	52	42	43	51	46	42	61	4	2	76	86
15. Religion	4	2	1	0	4	2	0	1	1	5	1	1	1	3	2	2	1	4	6	8	0	2
16. Independence, Self-Help	5	2	3	2	1	2	2	0	4	2	6	0	5	0	8	7	6	2	6	2	12	2
16x. Privacy	1	0	3	1	1	2	3	1	1	1	2	2	0	4	2	1	1	1	0	2	0	4
17. Attitude Toward World	1	0	4	1	1	1	3	1	2	0	1	1	2	1	0	2	4	2	0	2	16	4
18. No Response	2	4	4	3	4	4	6	3	1	3	7	6	5	10	5	12	16	3	2	2	0	0

* Reproduced, in abridged form, with permission, from A. T. Jersild, In Search of Self, Bureau of Publications, Teachers College, Columbia University, 1952. Approximately forty subcategories in the original table are not reproduced.

448

increasing opportunities and competitiveness." But most of them had managed to develop in their own way at their own pace with "generally satisfactory results." (As adults, approximately two-thirds were rated as "satisfactorily adjusted," about one-third as "marginally adjusted" and only two were considered sick—an outcome that compares favorably with adults in the population at large.) In most instances, these persons evidently had learned to live with their shyness, and some appeared to have compensated for their shyness, rather than attempting to change it.

As can be seen from what has been said so far in this chapter, the evidence from studies of children does not provide a simple formula for explaining characteristics that help or hinder a child in dealing with life's opportunities and demands. Each individual's personality emerges from a vast network of forces residing within and outside himself. The student of child psychology who accepts this truism will not have an easy answer to the riddle of life. But he is likely to be somewhat wiser, more humble, and far more considerate in his view of others and of himself than the person who claims to possess the secret of human existence.

Children's assets as viewed by themselves

Table 27 gives a summary of the kinds of ideas children express when they are asked to describe the qualities they admire in themselves. It is based on compositions written by young people of elementary, high-school, and college age on the theme, "What I Like About Myself." Compositions of this sort touch only lightly on children's views about themselves (a thorough investigation would require more intensive study), yet they bring out some matters of considerable interest.

At all ages, for example, a large proportion of young people, without any leading questions, evaluated themselves in terms belonging to the category of "Personality traits, character, inner resources, and emotional tendencies." Likewise, a large proportion at all ages appraised themselves in terms falling under the category "Social relationships and attitudes." This last-named category included mention of their attitudes toward others as well as the attitudes of others toward them. Children of elementary-school age pointed with pride to their homes and family life more often than did the older subjects.

According to the results in this study, many of the criteria young people use in judging themselves at any level tend to stand out prominently at all levels. The standards by which young people judge themselves are not scaled according to age or developmental stages, or in the manner of subjects taught at school.

TABLE 28 | PERCENTAGE OF BOYS AND GIRLS IN MAIN POPULATION OF 2,893 WHO MENTIONED ITEMS IN VARIOUS CATEGORIES IN REPORTING "WHAT I DISLIKE ABOUT MYSELF" *

	Elementary Grades						Junior High School						High School						College			
	IV		V		VI		VII		VIII		IX		X		XI		XII		Fresh. & Soph.		Jr. & Sr.	
Grade / Sex / Number	B 220	G 206	B 147	G 142	B 171	G 172	B 96	G 77	B 134	G 151	B 170	G 204	B 151	G 157	B 112	G 124	B 137	G 122	B 50	G 50	B 50	G 50
Category																						
1. Physical Characteristics and Appearance	11	16	17	30	17	41	17	26	24	48	32	53	27	44	13	32	10	30	12	20	8	12
2. Clothing and Grooming	4	10	7	5	4	9	2	8	4	7	3	10	1	3	3	2	4	2	0	0	2	0
3. Health and Physical Soundness	2	3	3	4	5	2	4	1	4	1	6	2	3	3	0	6	1	2	6	2	0	2
3x. Bodily Pleasures	4	4	4	1	2	2	4	0	3	1	4	3	1	3	2	1	3	3	0	2	0	0
4. Material Possessions	0	0	1	1	1	1	0	0	1	1	0	0	0	0	1	0	1	0	0	0	0	0
5. Animals and Pets	2	1	0	1	0	1	2	0	0	0	1	1	0	0	0	1	1	0	6	6	2	6
6-7. Home and Family	17	19	9	9	11	21	8	10	7	14	11	11	7	8	4	15	6	6	6	6	2	0
8. Recreation: Enjoyment of	5	1	1	1	4	2	3	0	2	0	2	0	2	1	2	1	1	1	0	0	2	4
9. Ability in Sports, Play	4	4	7	1	10	6	3	1	7	5	7	3	5	2	7	0	5	0	0	2	0	0
10. School: Ability in School; Attitudes Toward, etc.	22	22	18	23	32	27	31	27	26	34	36	24	25	17	27	15	15	23	36	10	14	16
11. Intellectual Abilities	1	1	3	2	6	4	5	8	7	4	5	4	7	4	11	10	8	9	8	2	4	4
12. Special Talents (Music, Arts)	9	10	5	4	9	15	4	10	7	11	2	6	5	7	5	10	5	6	12	8	6	8
13. Just Me, Myself	1	2	4	3	5	5	0	1	1	6	4	9	4	6	2	9	6	8	0	0	0	0
13x. Personality, Character, Inner Resources, Emotional Tendencies	37	38	37	32	44	48	53	43	51	57	55	65	44	55	51	67	58	72	84	90	72	94
14. Social Relationships and Attitudes	16	14	15	18	15	20	13	22	22	28	16	26	25	25	18	30	24	25	52	58	50	48
15. Religion	0	0	3	0	1	1	1	0	1	1	1	0	1	2	2	1	0	1	4	0	6	0
16. Independence, Self-Help	0	0	0	0	1	1	2	1	4	4	5	3	3	2	8	2	9	4	12	12	18	10
16x. Privacy	0	0	0	0	1	0	1	0	0	0	0	0	0	0	0	0	0	0	2	2	0	0
17. Attitude Toward World	0	0	0	0	0	0	0	4	0	1	0	0	0	0	1	1	1	1	0	0	0	2
18. No Response	10	5	5	5	3	5	5	1	4	1	1	1	11	12	14	4	16	4	0	8	8	0

* Reproduced, in abridged form, with permission, from A. T. Jersild, *In Search of Self*, Bureau of Publications, Teachers College, Columbia University, 1952.

Children's shortcomings
as viewed by themselves

Table 28 shows results ob-
tained when young people from the fourth grade through college wrote
compositions on the subject, "What I Dislike About Myself." Again it
appears that certain categories of self-evaluation, notably those referring
to personality, character, and emotional tendencies, and those pertaining
to social attitudes and relationships with other people, are mentioned
quite frequently at all levels.

However, there are some differences between the details mentioned in
the "Like" and "Dislike" descriptions. For example, from 6 to 30 per cent
of the young people deplored their tendency to become angry or to lose
their temper as something they disliked about themselves (the subcategory
covering this is not reproduced in Table 28). On the other hand, the
percentage of young people in the various groups who spoke favorably
of their ability to manage their anger ranged from zero to six. The young
people mentioned inability to control anger as a fault more often than
they mentioned control of anger as an asset. In a similar manner, upwards
of 18 per cent of the young people in some groups deplored their tendency
to be afraid when they described their unfavorable characteristics, but
no more than 3 per cent of the young people in any of the groups described
their ability to cope with their fears as a favorable trait. These findings
are in keeping with what we noted in earlier chapters concerning the
influences at home and at school that induce growing children to reproach
themselves for being angry or afraid.

EXPERIENCES AT SCHOOL AS RELATED TO SELF-EVALUATION

Experiences at school and attitudes toward school figure prominently
in children's evaluations of themselves. Roughly about one-fourth of the
children in the study cited above made reference to the school in telling
about what they liked or did not like about themselves. (The proportion
would have been larger, of course, if they had been asked specific questions about their experiences at school instead of being asked to write
on the general theme of what they liked or disliked about themselves.)
At practically all levels (except at college) experiences at school were
mentioned more often as a source of self-disparagement than as a source
of self-esteem. According to the children's own accounts, life at school
does more to weaken than to strengthen their assurance of personal worth.

Why is this? To answer this question would require a more intensive
inquiry than the one just cited. Such an inquiry would probably show in
many instances that experiences at school are mentioned as a source of

self-disparagement even though the school is not the primary source. A youngster who is not living up to his *own* expectations may, for example, phrase his self-reproach by saying he is not living up to the *school's* expectations. However, a more intensive inquiry would also reveal, so the writer believes, two major conditions at school that hinder children from acquiring healthy attitudes of self-regard.

One condition is that schools constantly impress upon large numbers of children the idea that they are not much good. Children who are lacking in the intellectual aptitudes that are praised in most schools meet failure and rejection on a vast scale. Schools expose some children endlessly to situations in which the teacher and the school administration know in advance that they will fail.

Another condition within the school that hinders pupils from acquiring a healthy regard for their worth is the educational policy of encouraging the child to learn about almost everything except the most important thing: himself. We will have more to say on this subject later in this chapter.

Children's problems as viewed by themselves and others

A large proportion of children, according to their own accounts, have "problems" and according to the judgment of others, many youngsters move from childhood into adolescence and adult years with severe personality disorders.

EXTENT OF PERSONALITY DISORDERS

When we ask "What is the proportion of children who suffer from personality disorders?" the answer depends on the standards we apply. According to a perfectionist standard, we could label children as "maladjusted" if they have persisting fears, grievances, or guilt feelings or if (as they grow older) they feel that there is a discrepancy between what they are and what they ought to be. By this criterion, practically all children would be regarded as being somewhat maladjusted. At the other extreme, we might class as maladjusted only those so seriously disturbed that they have to be placed in an institution for the mentally ill. Under conditions now prevailing, it has been estimated that one child in every ten who lives to be seventy-five years old will be hospitalized for mental illness (Goldhamer and Marshall, 1953). This is a somber statistic. It would be smaller if we do not count those whose illness is associated with other evidences of deterioration in old age. But the percentage would be larger if we included not only those who are hospitalized but also the unhospitalized persons who are so disturbed that they withdraw from life through invalidism and complete dependence on others.

Estimates of the percentage of children who suffer from personality disorders have varied, depending on the criteria of adjustment that have been applied and the nature of the information that has been gathered. In a survey by Ullman (1952) of ninth graders, the teachers identified 8 per cent of the children as likely sooner or later to have serious problems of adjustment. This percentage is smaller than that obtained when ratings by teachers are supplemented by other sources of information. Many youngsters who have serious emotional difficulties manage to do good work at school and are not regarded by their teachers as "problem" children (Pilzer, 1952; Harris, 1952). In a study by Rogers (1942a) of over 1500 elementary-school children, several criteria of maladjustment were applied: truancy; distinctly unfavorable ratings by classmates; unfavorable ratings by teachers and visiting observers or on an adjustment inventory; non-promotion; information that labelled a youngster as a "misfit" by virtue of differing from the group in reading ability, mental ability, or age. A child was regarded as "seriously maladjusted" if he was in the "maladjusted" category according to four or more of the criteria that were applied. By this standard, 12 per cent of the pupils were seriously maladjusted, and 30 per cent gave evidence of being poorly adjusted, but not to a degree that would place them in the seriously maladjusted group.

A large proportion of young people at the adolescent and late adolescent level have personal problems, and many of these are very serious (Frank et al. 1953). Heath and Gregory (1946) found that 92 per cent in a group of 259 male college sophomores had personal problems. These young men were selected to represent a "normal" and "healthy" sampling of Harvard College sophomores; they did not include boys who sought help of their own accord. Seventeen per cent of the college boys had "urgent or acute" problems as judged by a research staff consisting of a physician, several psychiatrists, a psychologist, and a social case-worker (who interviewed practically all of the families of the young men as well as the young men themselves).

PERSONALITY PROBLEMS AS REVEALED BY SELF-RATINGS

When children describe or rate themselves on personality tests, or on scales dealing with specific facets of their emotional lives, it commonly is found that the "normal" or typical child has many problems. In a section of one test (California Test of Personality Adjustment, Thorpe et al. 1942, 1953) dealing with "personal adjustment," a child, in rating himself, might obtain a score ranging from 90 (best possible adjustment) to 0 (poorest adjustment). When several thousand children from the kindergarten through the tenth grade rated themselves on this test, their median score was about 67. This means that half of the children described themselves as having either symptoms or a leaning toward the maladjusted side in marking approximately one-fourth of the items.

A few further findings may be cited. In a test of "manifest anxiety" devised for adults (Taylor, 1953), the *least* anxiety a person could report was 0, the most was 50. In a test of about two thousand college students the average anxiety score was about fifteen. Among the one-fifth of the population recording themselves as *least* anxious, the highest anxiety score was 7; and among the one-fifth who described themselves as *most* anxious, the lowest anxiety score was 21.

In a test of "manifest anxiety" adapted to children (Castaneda *et al.* 1956), 50 per cent of the children marked 16 of 42 items as problems which prevailed in their own lives.

In a study by the writer and his associates (Jersild *et al.* 1941), a large proportion of children (ranging close to 50 per cent) "worried" about a number of conditions at home or at school. In all computations except one, "worries" relating to school outnumbered worries relating to life outside the school.

IMPLICATIONS OF FINDINGS
RELATING TO PERSONALITY PROBLEMS

One thing is clear from the foregoing studies (and many others that could be named): The normal or typical child, according to his own account, or according to the judgments of others, is beset by many problems, and according to statistics on mental illness and ratings by clinical psychologists about one child in ten is seriously disturbed or destined to become so. These findings raise challenging questions. Is a person in a "normal" state of mental health a troubled person? Actually, there is little agreement among psychiatrists or psychologists as to how mental health should be defined, although most would probably agree that children rated as severely maladjusted do not possess it.

In the present scheme of things it is inevitable that some children will have difficulties. Among these are children with poor heredity; children with low intelligence who are destined to be "misfits" in our present school systems; youngsters who face an uphill struggle due to a variety of conditions such as brain damage, poverty, broken homes, neglect, harsh home conditions. But many individuals suffer from personal difficulties even though the odds seem to be in their favor, as shown by findings (reviewed in Chapter Seventeen) concerning the lives and careers of gifted children. Most of these gifted children came from environments that were above average, and their native abilities gave them a great advantage in school and in competition for jobs after they left school. Yet, according to the information they and others supplied, over a fifth of them in their forties (22.3 per cent of the men and 25.1 per cent of the women) suffered from "some maladjustment," including such difficulties as "excessive feelings of inadequacy or inferiority, nervous fatigue, mild anxiety neurosis and the like." And almost one in ten (8.9 per cent of the men and 9 per cent of the women) suffered from "serious maladjustment."

According to these results, it is not just the disinherited or under-privileged who bear a heavy burden of distress. Mild or acute personality disorders run through all segments of society.

In work with parents and teachers the writer has observed that evidence about the difficulties children face is quite unwelcome and disturbing to some adults. It is not surprising that adults should recoil when they get reminders of the burden borne by children. Many adults were themselves once in the ranks of the troubled children. Such reminders are also disquieting if the adult suspects that perhaps one of his own children would have to answer if a roll call were taken of the troubled ones.

When we face the fact that large numbers of children (and adults) struggle with problems ranging from worries, anxiety, and hostile attitudes to severe personality disorders we face these questions: Is so much distress inevitable? Are we *tapping* or *blocking* the resources for health that human beings possess?

There is no way of ridding life of adversity, but in the writer's judgment far more could be done than is being done to help children face the rigors of life in a more realistic and effective way. The growing child strives to make use of his powers. He possesses a large capacity for self-repair. Most children who have "problems" possess an impulse to grow, and this impulse, and the potential of health behind it, is far more important than the disorders that appear. But if children are to use this impulse and to realize this potential it is necessary to help them rather than to put barriers in their way.

Knowledge of self, acceptance of self, and mental health

According to the position taken in this book, human beings, from an early age have a greater capacity for taking a thoughtful and realistic view of the affairs of their inner lives than we have commonly assumed in our psychological theories and our educational practices. Throughout this book self-understanding and self-acceptance have been emphasized as important concepts for promoting healthy growth and healthy relationships between the child and others.

Each child is deeply immersed in the psychological issues that influence his way of life. Each, in his way, is a psychologist. From early infancy, without being deliberate about it, he acquires ideas and attitudes about himself and others. These are woven into the pattern of his life. They may be true or false, healthy or unhealthy. With most children the development of these ideas and attitudes is left largely to chance, but it is not necessary that this should be so.

Children's potentialities for self-understanding are usually neglected while other aspects of their training are being pushed. They must hasten to learn about Mother Goose and the habits of beavers, the Gold Rush, the Dark Ages, and the amendments to the Constitution. They memorize the dates of bygone wars and the names of distant stars. But human motives and the inner life of man are largely ignored in formal education from nursery school through college.

A policy of encouraging children to evade rather than to face their personal concerns is deeply imbedded in our culture and strongly entrenched in our educational system. Even in schools that claim to deal with the "whole child," and with children's "basic needs and concerns," a wide gulf often exists between the child's most pressing preoccupations and the things emphasized in the course of study. An example of this appeared in an informal offshoot of a study of children's interests conducted by the writer and his colleagues (cited in Chapter Nineteen). When children were asked in the usual manner to tell about their "interests," what they would "like to know more about," they mentioned the conventional things, ranging from games, arts, crafts and athletics to the subject matter of literature, arithmetic, history, and the like. In a small section of the study we questioned children a bit more deeply and found that practically all of them were troubled with fear. Yet it did not occur to a single child to express the idea that the subject of fear was one that the school might be concerned about. Other studies, notably at the adolescent level, have shown that nearly all children harbor grievances and attitudes of hostility. But the barriers against self-scrutiny are usually so high that it would require an exceptionally bold youngster to bring up the subject of the *personal* meanings of hostility even when the class is studying evidences of human hostility as revealed by the cruelty, warfare, and bloodshed recorded in history books.

When elementary-school children (as well as high-school and college students) avoid an inquiry into the personal dimensions of their existence, they are conforming to a standard set for them by others. They have learned to take for granted that the educational program does not subscribe to the principle that "the proper study of mankind is man." Yet many youngsters who studiously conform to impersonal academic expectations are pathetically eager, if given a little encouragement, to explore their personal concerns.

A person's search for knowledge of self has many facets: a willingness to examine the experiences through which he perceives the objective dimensions of his personality; a willingness to explore the bases of his conception of his properties as a person—his conception of who and what he is; and an inquiry into the standards according to which he evaluates his worth.

Self-understanding consists of recognizing facts and in realizing the significance of these facts. It has the meaning of *knowing* as in Socrates' "Know thyself"; it has the meaning of consciousness of one's own being, such as is implied in Macmurray's (1935) statement that "Until we know ourselves we cannot be ourselves."

SELF-UNDERSTANDING AND SELF-ACCEPTANCE

A child whose personality development is proceeding in a healthy way acquires realistic attitudes of self-acceptance. Among the marks of a self-accepting attitude in a child are the following: He is able to live fairly comfortably with his own emotions. He is willing as he grows older to assume responsibility for himself. He regards himself as someone who is worthy even though he obviously is not perfect. He has a healthy regard for his own rights and he stands up for them. As he moves toward adulthood he accepts the limitations of his nature without feeling abused or severely blaming himself or others to such an extent that he is barred from using such resources as he has. He is able to draw on his capacities for thinking, feeling, and entering into friendly relationships with others. The self-accepting person uses his abilities, without having a compulsion to underrate them or to reach for the impossible. The more he can live *as is* the less he needs to behave *as if* (Wenkart, 1954).

Self-acceptance and knowledge of self both involve a process of facing the facts and conditions of life, favorable as well as unfavorable, as candidly and as fully as possible. Self-acceptance is something very different from smugness or self-righteousness. (We stress this point because the question often arises.) There are some who look askance upon the concept of self-acceptance as though a self-accepting child might lose his enterprise and become resigned to faults and lacks which he actually might be able to overcome. Self-acceptance has no such connotation.

Self-acceptance and understanding of self are closely associated. To accept himself, the growing person must be aware of himself. To accept his limitations he must be able to recognize them. Self-acceptance, in other words, requires awareness and perception. But the child's ability to become aware of himself will be influenced by the way he feels about himself, and the way he feels about himself will depend, in part, on the way others feel about him and encourage him in the process of self-discovery.

According to the conception of self-acceptance a child is "successful" in his development if he is making constructive use of his capacities whether he happens to be the brightest child in the community or one of the dullest, the handsomest or one of the ugliest, the tallest and best built or the puniest and most ungainly. By the same token there is defeat in the process of development if a child, whether he is talented or humbly endowed, draws only to a small extent upon his intellectual and emotional resources even though he is quite successful by external standards and seems to meet most of the common standards of "adjustment." [1]

SELF-ACCEPTANCE, SELF-CRITICISM, AND CONFORMITY

As he grows older, a child's ability to accept and to benefit from criticism and to make a critical appraisal of himself is an important feature of a self-accepting attitude. To develop this ability it is necessary for him to be with people, at home, or at school, or somewhere, who can help him to become aware of his strengths, his faults and his limitations without rejecting him. A self-accepting person does not relish criticism, but he does not hold himself above it. He is better able than the self-rejecting person to consider its worth, and act on it, rather than to feel angry, guilty, or dismayed about it. A self-accepting child in the upper elementary grades will have some ability to judge whether his teacher's criticism of him is reasonable, and to profit from it. But a self-rejecting child is likely to feel anxious and angry even when the teacher's criticism is quite reasonable.

As noted in a study by Taylor and Combs (1952) cited in Chapter Six, "better-adjusted" children accepted a larger number of derogatory statements as applying to them than did those rated as poorly adjusted. The greater a child's over-all confidence in himself is, the better he can afford to face the fact that he is an imperfect human being.

The child who is self-accepting has freedom to cultivate his own interests without being a slave to every fad or expectation that confronts him. In simple terms this means, for example, that on a cold day a boy's first impulse will be to put on a warm coat as he sets out for school rather than to hesitate, or set out without a coat, because in his crowd of boys it is regarded as "sissy" to be warmly dressed.

---

[1] Sören Kierkegaard emphasized the concept of self-realization in these terms: "As an heir, even though he were heir to the treasure of all the world, nevertheless does not possess his property before he has come of age, so even the richest personality is nothing before he has chosen himself, on the other hand even what one might call the poorest personality is everything when he has chosen himself; for the great thing is not to be this or that but to be oneself" (*Either/Or*, Vol. II; Princeton: Princeton University Press, 1949b, pp. 149-50, translated by Walter Lowrie).

The person who claims to have a favorable attitude toward himself is likely to express a favorable rather than a condemning attitude toward others. One who, for example, claims that he is, on the whole, reasonably generous, fair-minded, and able to accept criticism is likely to say that other persons, on the whole, also have these qualities. The findings pertaining to the relationship between acceptance of self and acceptance of others have been obtained largely in studies of adolescents and adults, but they are significant for child psychology and therefore we will discuss them briefly in this section.[2]

The relationship between self-acceptance and acceptance of others has been phrased in many ways. According to Fromm, we cannot love others unless we have a healthy love of ourselves. Kierkegaard stated that in judging another person one reveals what one is oneself. In the same vein, Sullivan has maintained that as one judges oneself so one will judge others. Nietzsche expressed the relationship between self-blame and blame of others by warning that we should fear him who hates himself because we shall become the victims of his revenge.

Although sages and researchers have concluded that love of self and love of others go together (and self-hate and hate toward others, likewise), there are many facets of this relationship that need to be more deeply explored. A common procedure in psychological studies of self-acceptance and self-rejection has been to rely on the assertions a person makes regarding himself. Self-rejection has also been assessed by measuring the discrepancy between what a person says he *is* with his views concerning what he *ought* to be (his "ideal" self), (Jervis, 1958).

As noted in Chapter Six, a person's account of himself and his attitudes toward others will depend on his candor and his insight. The same answer from two persons may have quite different meanings. One might maintain that he is a generous person, and that he is neither hostile nor anxious, and similarly say that most people are generous and free of hostility and anxiety. Another might say that he has a selfish streak, that he harbors anxiety and hostility and so do most other persons. On the surface it appears that the former is self-accepting and accepting of others, and that the latter is self-rejecting and rejecting of others. But the seemingly rejecting one is not necessarily so. When he *recognizes* and *admits* that he and others have selfish motives, hostile impulses, and anxious

---

[2] Writings bearing on this topic include the following: Trent (1953), Sheerer (1948), Phillips (1951), Eastman (1956), Berger (1952), Fey (1954, 1955), Jervis (1958).

moments, he is perhaps more realistic in facing his own humanity and better able to feel compassion for the humanity of others than the one who feels impelled to see himself and others as creatures free of human frailties.

Since the commonly used tests of acceptance of self and of others do not, in themselves, measure the candor or insight of those who are being tested the results cannot be taken at face value. However (so the writer believes), if authentic measurements could be made we would find that as a child approaches maturity there is an intimate relationship between acceptance of self and acceptance of others, and between rejection of self and rejection of others. This relationship is not built upon an attitude of easy optimism or shallow cynicism. Rather, it is rooted in something more substantial, something best expressed by the word *compassion*.

COMPASSION

This section does not deal specifically with children, nor is it documented with empirical findings. But the writer wishes to include it for, in his judgment, compassion is an essential feature of mental health, emotional maturity, and acceptance of self and others.

To be compassionate a person must draw, as far as he is able, upon all his resources, his ability to have a feeling of fellowship with all that is glorious and sordid in the human situation, the noble things, the comic, the tragic, the wells of sorrow and the currents of joy. To do this, a person must endeavor to realize the meaning and quality of his own emotions in such a manner that he can be compassionate with himself.

Often we think of compassion as a kind of pity, a sort of readiness to commiserate with another who is in a bad plight. But compassion means more than to grieve with those who weep. It means more than to rejoice with those who are happy. It means an ability to enter into the meaning of any of a vast range of emotions. To be compassionate with one who is angry we must draw upon our own capacity for anger, and what we can learn from our own rage—the rack and grind of it; the bitter gall of it; the spite and vindictiveness that often go with it.

To be compassionate with one who is frightened, we must be able to draw upon our own experiences of fear. These go back to our infancy and extend through the entire span of our lives. To be compassionate with those who are afraid we must be willing, in effect, to say: Fear was a companion of my childhood and it has been my companion ever since. Fear has been at my side at times when I have cried and trembled, at times when I showed anger instead of apprehension, at times when I chose not to do what I might have done, saying to myself, "I am not afraid—I just don't care."

To be compassionate with one who is happy we must draw upon our own experiences of happiness—the joy of being accepted, the pleasure of achievement, the triumphant feeling of having overcome a weakness, the ecstasy of loving and being loved or anticipating what it might mean to be loved, and the uprush of gladness that comes with the giving or receiving of kindness. Unless a person has realized some of his potentialities for happiness he will have nothing on which to base his appreciation of another's gladness. For this reason, some persons find it harder to be compassionate with those who are joyful than with those who are in distress.

To be compassionate represents a high level of maturity, according to the concept here presented. To achieve it one must have compassion for oneself. As long as a person blames himself for being anxious, or feels contempt for himself because he is subject to anger, or unworthy of being happy, or reproaches himself for feeling weak and unable to face all his problems alone, he will be so absorbed in his own shortcomings and so preoccupied with self-reproach that he will not be capable of feeling compassion for someone else.

In defense of pride

Although the child's developing selfhood is an ever-changing phenomenon, children (and adults) also resist reminders that go counter to any attitude or ideas they already have formed concerning themselves. They often try to preserve their pride and self-picture even when these are false and burdensome.

Many of the methods a person can use in defending a vulnerable position within himself have been referred to by Freud and his followers as defenses of the ego. Such defenses, when used by a child or an adult, not only divert him from his real problem, but they also quite often divert others from the real problem. A person's defense against self-discovery may take many forms, such as: avoidance by denial; shifting the blame to others; assuming an attitude of self-righteousness; converting a weakness into an appearance of strength; taking flight into academic arguments and intellectual definitions as a means of avoiding the *personal* meaning of what he reads or hears.

Emotion, self-acceptance, and mental health

When we try to help a child to realize his potentialities it is essential not only to promote his physical and intellectual development but also to foster his emotional development.

Mental health depends, to a large degree, on emotional health. Unfortunately, many adults who conscientiously safeguard children's physical health and spare no expense in furthering their intellectual development give little heed to children's emotional well-being. Children usually receive prompt attention when they show signs of physical distress; but when they show signs of emotional distress they often are admonished to conceal their emotions. At school, a child with a fractured limb is far more sure of getting sympathetic help than a child with fractured feelings. In most communities, the sums budgeted for school buildings and the conventional academic program vastly exceeds the sums devoted to children's emotional welfare.

In a community known to the writer the school board, while recommending hundreds of thousands of dollars for a new building, removed from the annual budget an item of a few thousand dollars to cover the salary of a psychologist who had demonstrated an exceptional talent for helping children to come to grips with their emotional problems. While eliminating the psychologist, the school board also failed to budget any money or encourage any provisions that might help the classroom teachers to become more competent in dealing with the children.

One result of attitudes of this sort is that teachers in many schools must enter into their search for understanding of children and of themselves as though it were a luxury, an extra task, rather than an essential feature of their professional work.

If children are to acquire emotional health it is necessary for parents and teachers to allow children to show and examine their emotions. Only through such a policy is it possible to undestand the child and to help him to understand and accept himself in a realistic way. It is essential, of course, both at home and at school to set limits beyond which a child must not go in expressing his emotions, especially his anger. But schools go far beyond this need for setting limits when they emphasize academic learning and the outward forms of social conformity to such an extent that children's emotional development is not only ignored but actually impaired.[3]

An emotional outburst *as such* probably has little or no value for a child, but something significant can take place when feelings are shown or "released" in an atmosphere where learning is encouraged. When a child, in a setting in which self-discovery is encouraged, has a chance to express his feelings he not only may be able to get a clearer view of them but he also may make the discovery (surprising to some children) that he can have pretty intense feelings without being rebuked.

---

[3] It is essential to give attention to children's emotions to help them to achieve their fullest intellectual development (if not for other and far more compelling reasons). Recent writings have emphasized that academic disabilities often, if not always, are closely tied to emotional difficulties. (See Ephron, 1953).

A classroom teacher who has been trained in the usual fashion is not a psychotherapist and should not pretend to be, but the school situation offers teachers many opportunities for exploring and applying many of the concepts underlying psychotherapy and psychoanalysis. The procedures used in group therapy as described, for example, by Slavson (1943, 1947), and by Hinckley and Herman (1951), and in therapeutic relationships as described by Rogers (1942b, 1951), and Allen (1942) have many implications for teachers. Snygg and Combs (1949) and Combs and Snygg (1959) have discussed implications of the concept of the self for education. The writer and his associates, in cooperation with several hundred teachers, have explored the emotional currents within themselves which teachers must face whenever they seek to understand children's emotions or help children to understand their emotions (Jersild, 1952; 1955; Jersild and Helfant, 1953). In a current study, the writer and Allina (1959) are assessing the effects of psychotherapy and psychoanalysis on teachers' personal lives and professional work as perceived by over a hundred teachers who have undergone therapy or analysis.

An important consequence of freedom to express feeling may be that children are relieved from some of the burden of secrecy which many of them bear. Children live in an isolated and lonely world when they must struggle to keep their emotional difficulties hidden from others. A child is afraid of corpses, for example, but he harbors this fear within the privacy of his life as a guilty secret. When he is free to tell of this fear he has, in a sense, not only confessed but thrown himself on the mercy of others. When the confession does not bring shame and ridicule upon him he can relax a bit, and perhaps not feel so strong a need to hide within himself. Moreover, when a child has the courage to reveal something about his feelings, under the eye of a watchful and considerate teacher, other children may find that they have the courage to do so, too. When this happens all may discover that they are not alone in their troubles: They are not queer, for others have exactly the same troubles, or worse ones. Fears and anxieties and grievances are not banished simply by realizing that others also are anxious and angry. Far from it. But when a frightened child feels free to express his fright and is struck by the fact that others also are afraid, at least a small dent has been made in the vicious chain of fear and blame through which a child becomes alienated from others and from himself.

The same line of thought applies also to hostility and the consequences of hostility. It is in an interpersonal setting that most of the resentments a child harbors arise, and if he can bring them out into an interpersonal setting there is a chance that they might be resolved.

To have access to his feelings it is necessary for a child to experience the actual feelings rather than just talk about them. To talk about joy, fear, or hate in intellectual terms is similar to talking about a steak instead of tasting and chewing it. This fact stands out when one observes that children often feel guilty (as adults often do) even though they have openly confessed and made a clean breast of some transgression or other. The confession, which represents what they can grasp intellectually and express verbally, may not represent the real psychological issue or the real emotional content. So a child may continue to feel badly, even though he has been assured that God has forgiven him and that no human being will hold his faults against him. Jimmy confesses, for example, that he stole a dime from Johnny's desk, and then Johnny forgives him, and his teacher and parents and pastor forgive him, but he still feels guilty. He feels guilty because the act of confession and the gift of forgiveness did not touch upon his real problem. He stole, it is true, but his real trouble is not that he is a thief. Perhaps he stole because he feels envious of Johnny who always has spending money—but it was theft, not envy, that he confessed, and by being absolved of theft he did not become free of envy.

Or he stole the dime, let us say, to buy candy to bribe a big boy next door into liking him; so he stole because he was lonely, not because he was a thief. But after the theft has been forgotten and forgiven he may still be as lonely as ever.

Perhaps he stole to buy candy for another boy who might tell on him because Jimmy had been involved in sex play with him. In that event it was a sexual conflict that made him so frightened he became involved in theft.

After the theft had been forgiven by others Jimmy might be no nearer than before in solving his fear or his loneliness or his conflicts regarding sex. But if a situation were provided in which an adult, for the time being at least, was not interested in getting Jimmy to inform against himself, or to promise to live a new life, or to put his trouble into one nice verbal package, but was interested in letting Jimmy reveal some of the drama of his feelings something very significant might take place. If the teacher could allow Jimmy to ramble on in talking about himself, or to react and express his feelings (or remain silent) now in one context, now in another, it is likely that the teacher would get glimpses now and then of what really was troubling Jimmy. And Jimmy might himself begin to let drop little hints of his fear, his loneliness, his guilt relating to sex, and out of this and their common search both might come to a clearer grasp of Jimmy's struggle.

There are ramifications of this kind of exploration that go far beyond the province of this book, and so we leave the topic with only a few summary statements.

To grow in understanding of what is important in his life and in the life about him, a child must be encouraged to make the most important discovery of all: himself. To discover himself and his resources, and to grow in knowledge of himself, it is essential for him to have a chance to test the reaches and limits of his abilities and to draw upon his feelings and face their impact and meaning. To face his feelings, he needs freedom to experience them and he needs freedom to reveal them, if not to others, then at least to himself.

When we as adults seek to help children to find themselves we must also seek to understand the issues that arise in our own personal lives. The major concerns of childhood continue into adult years. So when we try to enter a child's world we are not invading a strange land. We are homeward bound.

Recommended Readings

Mary M. Shirley's *The First Two Years: A Study of Twenty-Five Babies, Volume III, Personality Manifestations* (1933b) is one of the most informative, crisp, and readable inquiries into early personality development. Among the outstanding books dealing with general theories of personality are Gordon Willard Allport's *Personality* (1937) and Gardner Murphy's *Personality: A Biosocial Approach to Origins and Structure* (1947). Personality development is discussed in many contributions included in the books of readings, earlier referred to, by Dennis (1951), Martin and Stendler (1954), and Seidman (1958). In a section of the *Collected Studies of the Dionne Quintuplets*, William E. Blatz, D. A. Millichamp, and M. W. Charles (1937) give a fascinating account of personality differences shown by the Dionne sisters between 12 and 36 months.

Bibliography
and Author Index[1]

Abernethy E. M., 1936, *Relationships Between Mental and Physical Growth.* Monographs of the Society for Research in Child Development, 1, No. 7. Wash., D. C.: National Research Council. **107**

Abt, L. E., and L. Bellak, 1950, *Projective Psychology.* N. Y.: Knopf. **348, 351**

Adler, A., 1937, "The Significance of Early Childhood Recollections," *International Journal of Individual Psychology,* 6, 484-493. **326**

Adorno, T. W., E. Frenkel-Brunswik, D. J. Levinson, and R. N. Sanford, 1950, *The Authoritarian Personality.* N. Y.: Harper. **227**

Albert, R. S., 1957, "The Role of Mass Media and the Effect of Aggressive Film Content upon Children's Aggressive Responses and Identification Choices," *Genetic Psychology Monographs,* 55, 221-285. **435**

Aldrich, C. A., C. Sung, and C. Knop
   1945a, "The Crying of Newly Born Babies: I. Community Phase," *Journal of Pediatrics,* 26, 313-326. **48**
   1945b, "The Crying of Newly Born Babies: II. The Individual Phase," *Journal of Pediatrics,* 27, 89-96. **48**

Allen, F., 1942, *Psychotherapy with Children.* N. Y.: Norton. **463**

Allen, L. *See* Macfarlane, J., 1954.

Allina, E. *See* Jersild, A. T., 1960.

Allinsmith, W., 1957, "Conscience and Conflict: The Moral Force in Personality," *Child Development,* 28, 469-476. **407**

Allport, G. W., 1937, *Personality.* N. Y.: Holt. **254, 465**

Almy, M. C.
   1949, *Children's Experiences Prior to First Grade and Success in Beginning Reading.* Contributions to Education, No. 954. N. Y.: Bureau of Publications, Teachers College, Columbia Univ. **330, 435**
   1959, *Ways of Studying Children.* N. Y.: Bureau of Publications, Teachers College, Columbia Univ. **11**
   1959, "Children's Thinking," unpublished manuscript. **362**

Alschuler, R. H., and L. A. Hattwick, 1943, "Easel Painting as an Index of Personality in Preschool Children," *American Journal of Orthopsychiatry,* 13, 616-626. **348**

Amatora, M., 1954, "Similarity in Teacher and Pupil Personality," *Journal of Psychology,* 37, 45-50. **167**

Amatruda, C. S. *See* Gesell, A., 1945.

Ames, L. B.
   1940, "The Constancy of Psycho-Motor Tempo in Individual Infants," *Journal of Genetic Psychology,* 57, 445-450. **19**
   1946, "The Development of the Sense of Time in the Young Child," *Journal of Genetic Psychology,* 68, 97-125. **367**
   1952, "The Sense of Self of Nursery School Children as Manifested by Their Verbal Behavior," *Journal of Genetic Psychology,* 81, 193-232. **117**

---

[1] The numbers in bold-faced type refer to pages in the text in which an author's work is mentioned.

Ames, L. B., and J. Learned, 1946, "Imaginary Companions and Related Phenomena," *Journal of Genetic Psychology,* 69, 147-167. **341, 343**

Ames, L. B., J. Learned, R. W. Metraux, and R. N. Walker, 1952, *Child Rorschach Responses, Developmental Trends from Two to Ten Years.* N. Y.: Hoeber. **349**

Ammons, R. B., 1950, "Reactions in a Projective Doll-Play Interview of White Males Two to Six Years of Age to Differences in Skin Color and Facial Features," *Journal of Genetic Psychology,* 76, 323-341. **227**

Anastasi, A., and F. A. Cordova, 1953, "Some Effects of Bilingualism upon the Intelligence Test Performance of Puerto Rican Children in New York City," *Journal of Educational Psychology,* 44, 1-19. **313, 386**

Anderson, G. L. *See* Anderson, H. H., 1951, 1954.

Anderson, H. H.
  1937a, "Domination and Integration in the Social Behavior of Young Children in an Experimental Play Situation," *Genetic Psychology Monographs,* 19, 343-408. **157**
  1937b, "An Experimental Study of Dominative and Integrative Behavior in Children of Preschool Age," *Journal of Social Psychology,* 8, 335-345. **157**

Anderson, H. H., and G. L. Anderson
  1951, eds., *An Introduction to Projective Techniques and Other Devices for Understanding the Dynamics of Human Behavior.* N. Y.: Prentice-Hall. **348, 351**
  1954, "Social Development," in *Manual of Child Psychology,* 2nd ed., edited by L. Carmichael, pp. 1162-1215. N. Y.: Wiley. **198**

Anderson, H. H., and H. M. Brewer, 1945, *Studies of Teachers' Classroom Personalities: I. Dominative and Socially Integrative Behavior of Kindergarten Teachers.* Applied Psychology Monographs, No. 6. Stanford, Calif.: Stanford Univ. Press. **157**

Anderson, H. H., J. E. Brewer, and M. F. Reed, 1946, *Studies of Teachers' Classroom Personalities: III. Follow-up Studies of the Effects of Dominative and Integrative Contacts on Children's Behavior.* Applied Psychology Monographs, No. 11. Stanford, Calif.: Stanford Univ. Press. **157, 167**

Anderson, J. E.
  1936, "Child Development and the Interpretation of Behavior," *Science,* 83, 245-252. **43**
  1954, "Methods of Child Psychology," in *Manual of Child Psychology,* 2nd ed., edited by L. Carmichael, pp. 1-59. N. Y.: Wiley. **10**
  See also Foster, J. C., 1928, 1930, 1936.

Angel, E. *See* May, R., 1958.

Angelino, H., J. Dollins, and E. V. Mech, 1956, "Trends in the Fears and Worries of School Children as Related to Socio-economic Status and Age," *Journal of Genetic Psychology,* 89, 263-276. **263**

Appel, M. H., 1942, "Aggressive Behavior of Nursery School Children and Adult Procedures in Dealing with Such Behavior," *Journal of Experimental Education,* 11, 185-199. **190-191**

Arsenian, S., 1937, *Bilingualism and Mental Development.* Contributions to Education, No. 712. N. Y.: Bureau of Publications, Teachers College, Columbia Univ. **313**

Ausubel, D. P., 1958, *Theory and Problems of Child Development.* N. Y.: Grune and Stratton. **33, 170**

Ausubel, D. P., E. E. Balthazar, I. Rosenthal, L. S. Blackman, S. H. Schpoont, and J. Welkowitz, 1954, "Perceived Parent Attitudes as Determinants of Children's Ego Structure," *Child Development,* 25, 173-183. **144**

Axline, V. M., 1947, *Play Therapy.* Boston: Houghton Mifflin. **348**

Bach, G. R.
  1945, *Young Children's Play Fantasies.* Psychological Monographs, 59, No. 2. Evanston, Ill.: American Psychological Assoc. **348**
  1952, "Some Diadic Functions of Childhood Memories," *Journal of Psychology,* 33, 87-88. **328**

Baker, H. V., 1942, *Children's Contributions in Elementary School General Discussion.* Child Development Monographs, No. 29. N. Y.: Teachers College, Columbia Univ. **202, 353-354**

Baldwin, A. L., 1949, "The Effect of Home Environment on Nursery School Behavior," *Child Development,* 20, 49-62. **157**

Baldwin, A. L., J. Kalhorn, and F. H. Breese
  1945, *Patterns of Parent Behavior.* Psychological Monographs, 58, No. 3. Evanston, Ill.: American Psychological Assoc. **157**
  1949, *The Appraisal of Parent Behavior,* Psychological Monographs, 63, No. 4. **157**

Balthazar, E. E. *See* Ausubel, D. P., 1954.

Banning, E. I., 1955, "Social Influences on Children and Youth," *Review of Educational Research*, 25, 36-47. **433**

Barker, R., T. Dembo, and K. Lewin, 1941, *Studies in Topological and Vector Psychology: II. Frustration and Regression*. University of Iowa Studies in Child Welfare, 18, No. 1. Iowa City: Univ. of Iowa Press. **294**

Barker, R. G., and H. F. Wright, 1954, *Midwest and Its Children*. Evanston, Ill.: Row Peterson. **199-200, 232**

Bavelas, A. *See* Seashore, H. G., 1942.

Bayley, N.

    1933a, *The California First Year Mental Scale*. University of California Syllabus Series, No. 243. Berkeley, Calif.: Univ. of California Press. **107**

    1933b, "Mental Growth During the First Three Years," *Genetic Psychology Monographs*, 14, 7-92. **304, 374, 376-377**

    1935, *The Development of Motor Abilities During the First Three Years*. Monographs of the Society for Research in Child Development, No. 1. Wash., D. C.: National Research Council. **99-100, 102**

    1949, "Consistency and Variability in the Growth of Intelligence from Birth to Eighteen Years," *Journal of Genetic Psychology*, 75, 165-196. **376**

    1954, "Some Increasing Parent-Child Similarities During the Growth of Children," *Journal of Educational Psychology*, 45, 1-21. **95, 381**

    See also Rheingold, H. L., 1959.

Beach, F. A., and J. Jaynes, 1954, "Effects of Early Experience upon the Behavior of Animals," *Psychological Bulletin*, 51, 239-263. **24**

Beasley, W. C., 1933, "Visual Pursuit in 109 White and 142 Negro Newborn Infants," *Child Development*, 4, 106-120. **44**

Beck, S. J., 1937, *Introduction to the Rorschach Method: A Manual of Personality Study*. Research Monograph of the American Orthopsychiatric Association, No. 1. Menasha, Wisc.: American Orthopsychiatric Assoc. **349**

Behrens, M. L., 1954, "Child Rearing and the Character Structure of the Mother," *Child Development*, 25, 225-238. **128**

Bell, R. Q. *See* Schaefer, E. S., 1955.

Bellak, L., and S. S. Bellak, 1949-55, *Children's Apperception Test*, rev. ed., ages 3-10. C.P.S. Co., P. O. Box 42, Gracie Station, N. Y. C. **349**

Bellak, L. *See also* Abt, L. E., 1950.

Bellak, S. S. *See* Bellak, L., 1949-55.

Benezet, L. P., 1935, "The Story of an Experiment," *Journal of the National Education Association*, 24, 241-244; 301-303. **21**

Benjamin, E., 1942, "The Period of Resistance in Early Childhood, Its Significance for the Development of Problem Children," *American Journal of Diseases of Children*, 63, 1019-1079. **150**

Berezin, D., 1959, "An Inquiry into the Temperamental Differences of Infants Noted by Their Boarding Mothers in Adoption Studies," unpublished Doctor of Education dissertation, Teachers College, Columbia Univ. **442-443**

Berger, E., 1952, "Relation Between Expressed Acceptance of Self and Others," *Journal of Abnormal and Social Psychology*, 47, 778-782. **459**

Beyer, E. *See* Lerner, E., 1941.

Bibace, R., H. Caplan, A. Hughes, and M. S. Rabinovitch, 1958, "Prematurity and Perceptual-Motor Functioning," A Preliminary Report, Montreal Children's Hospital and McGill University. Research Canadian Mental Health Grant No. 604-5-51. **53**

Biber, B., 1934, *Children's Drawings; From Lines to Pictures*. N. Y.: Bureau of Educational Experiments. **105-106**

Biehler, R. F., 1954, "Companion Choice Behavior in the Kindergarten," *Child Development*, 25, 45-51. **209**

Bienstock, S. F. *See* Jersild, A. T., 1935.

Bingham, A. *See* Lee, D. M., 1959.

Blackman, L. S. *See* Ausubel, D. P., 1954.

Blatz, W. E., and D. A. Millichamp, 1937, "The Mental Growth of the Dionne Quintuplets," University of Toronto Studies, Child Development Series, No. 12, in Blatz, W. C., *et al., Collected Studies of the Dionne Quintuplets*. Toronto, Canada: Univ. of Toronto Press. **52**

Blatz, W. E., D. A. Millichamp, and M. W. Charles, 1937, "The Early Social Development of the Dionne Quintuplets," University of Toronto Studies, Child Development Series,

No. 13, in Blatz, W. C., *et al., Collected Studies of the Dionne Quintuplets.* Toronto Canada: Univ. of Toronto Press. **52, 441-442, 465**

Blau, L. R. *See* Blau, T. H., 1955.

Blau, T. H., and L. R. Blau, 1955, "The Sucking Reflex: The Effects of Long Feeding vs. Short Feeding on the Behavior of a Human Infant," *Journal of Abnormal Social Psychology,* 51, 123-125. **69**

Bloom, L., 1959, "A Reappraisal of Piaget's Theory of Moral Judgment," *Journal of Genetic Psychology,* 95, 3-12. **402**

Blum, L. H., 1950, "Some Psychological and Educational Aspects of Pediatric Practice: A Study of Well-Baby Clinics," *Genetic Psychology Monographs,* 41, 3-97. **77**

Blum, L. H., H. H. Davidson, and N. D. Fieldsteel, 1954, *A Rorschach Workbook.* N. Y.: International Univ. Press. **349**

Boll, E. S. *See* Bossard, J. H. S., 1957.

Bolles, M. M. *See* Landis, C., 1940.

Bonney, M. E.
    1943a, "The Constancy of Sociometric Scores and Their Relationship to Teacher Judgments of Social Success and to Personality Self Ratings," *Sociometry,* 6, 409-424. **209**
    1943b, "The Relative Stability of Social, Intellectual, and Academic Status in Grades II to IV, and the Interrelationships Between These Various Forms of Growth," *Journal of Educational Psychology,* 34, 88-102. **209**

Bonney, M. E., and E. L. Nicholson, 1958, "Comparative School Adjustments of Elementary School Pupils With and Without Preschool Training," *Child Development,* 29, 125-133. **193, 197**

Bonney, M. E., and J. Powell, 1953, "Differences in Social Behavior Between Sociometrically High and Sociometrically Low Children," *Journal of Educational Research,* 46, 481-495. **210**

Bonsfield, W. A., and W. D. Orbison, 1952, "Ontogenesis of Emotional Behavior," *Psychological Review,* 59, 1-7. **236**

Bose, R. G., 1929, "Religious Concepts of Children," *Religious Education,* 24, 831-837. **415**

Bossard, J. H. S., and E. S. Boll, 1957, "Child Behavior and the Empathic Complex," *Child Development,* 28, 37-42. **166**

Bostock, J., 1951, "Enuresis and Toilet Training," *Medical Journal of Australia,* 2, 110-113. **85**

Boyd, W. C., 1953, *Genetics and the Races of Man.* Boston: Little, Brown. **33**

Brandenburg, G. C., 1915, "The Language of a Three Year Old Child," *Journal of Genetic Psychology,* 22, 89-120. **314**

Breese, F. H. *See* Baldwin, A. L., 1945.

Bregman, E. O. *See* Thorndike, E. L., 1927.

Brewer, H. M. *See* Anderson, H. H., 1945, 1946.

Brown, A. W., J. Morrison, and G. B. Couch, 1947, "Influence of Affectional Family Relationships on Character Development," *Journal of Abnormal Social Psychology,* 42, 422-428. **409**

Brown, E. W. *See* Lerner, E., 1941.

Brown, S. C. *See* Isaacs, S., 1941.

Bruch, H.
    1947, "Psychological Aspects of Obesity," *Psychiatry,* 10, 373-381. **77**
    1952, *Don't Be Afraid of Your Child.* N. Y.: Farrar, Straus & Young. **153, 167**

Bühler, C.
    1930, *The First Year of Life.* N. Y.: John Day. **59, 62, 63, 172, 305**
    1933, "The Social Behavior of Children." in *A Handbook of Child Psychology,* 2nd rev. ed., edited by C. Murchison, pp. 374-416. Worcester, Mass.: Clark Univ. Press. **122, 175, 198, 201**
    1952, "The Diagnostic Problem in Childhood Schizophrenia," *Nervous Child,* 10, 60-62. **441**

Burchinal, L. G., G. R. Hawkes, and B. Gardner, 1957, "The Relationship Between Parental Acceptance and Adjustment of Children," *Child Development,* 28, 65-77. **161**

Burchinal, L. G. *See also* Hawkes, G. R., 1956.

Burks, B. S., 1928, "The Relative Influence of Nature and Nurture upon Mental Development: A Comparative Study of the Foster Parent-Foster Child Resemblance and True Parent-True Child Resemblance," National Society for the Study of Education. *Nature and Nurture,* Twenty-seventh Yearbook, Part I., pp. 219-316. Bloomington, Ill.: Public School Publishing Co. **382**

Burlingham, D.
    1952, *Twins: A Study of Three Pairs of Identical Twins.* N. Y.: International Univ. Press. **63, 128, 164-165, 442**
    See also Freud, A., 1944.
Burnham, M. P., 1940, "Imaginative Behavior of Young Children as Revealed in Their Language," unpublished Doctor of Philosophy dissertation, Columbia Univ. **333**
Burstein, M. *See* Hurlock, E. B., 1932.
Burt, C.
    1919, "The Development of Reasoning in Children," *Journal of Experimental Pedagogy,* 5, 68-77; 121-127. **358-359**
    1940, "The Incidence of Neurotic Symptoms Among Evacuated School Children," *British Journal of Educational Psychology,* 10, 8-15. **84**
    1941, "The Billeting of Evacuated Children," *British Journal of Educational Psychology,* 11, 85-98. **140**
Burtt, H. E.
    1932, "An Experimental Study of Early Childhood Memory," *Journal of Genetic Psychology,* 40, 287-295. **328**
    1937, "A Further Study of Early Childhood Memory," *Journal of Genetic Psychology,* 50, 187-192. **328**
    1941, "An Experimental Study of Early Childhood Memory: Final Report," *Journal of Genetic Psychology,* 58, 435-439. **328**
Buruss, G. *See* Morris, D. P., 1954.

Caille, R. K., 1933, *Resistant Behavior of Preschool Children.* Child Development Monographs, No. 11. N. Y.: Teachers College, Columbia Univ. **194**
Calkins, L. A. *See* Scammon, R. E., 1929.
Cannon, W. B., 1929, *Bodily Changes in Pain, Hunger, Fear, and Rage,* 2nd ed. N. Y.: Appleton-Century. **280**
Cantril, H., 1946, "Identification with Social and Economic Class," in *Twentieth Century Psychology,* edited by P. L. Harriman, pp. 146-152. N. Y.: Philosophical Library. **224**
Cape, J. *See* Sontag, L. W., 1935.
Cappa, D., 1956, "Types of Storybooks Enjoyed by Kindergarten Children," *Journal of Educational Research,* 49, 555-557. **436**
Carmichael, A. M., 1930, "The Behavior of Six-Year-Old Children When Called Upon to Account for Past Irregularities," *Journal of Genetic Psychology,* 38, 352-360. **409**
Carmichael, L., 1954, "The Onset and Early Development of Behavior," in *Manual of Child Psychology,* 2nd ed., pp. 60-185. N. Y.: Wiley. **10, 37, 63, 254**
Castaneda, A., B. R. McCandless, and D. S. Palermo
    1956a, "The Children's Form of the Manifest Anxiety Scale," *Child Development,* 27, 317-326. **280, 454**
    1956b, "Complex Learning and Performance as a Function of Anxiety in Children and Task Difficulty," *Child Development,* 27, 327-332. **280-281**
Castaneda, A. *See also* McCandless, B. R., 1956a, 1956b; Palermo, D. S., 1956.
Challman, R. C., 1932, Factors Influencing Friendships Among Preschool Children," *Child Development,* 3, 146-158. **178**
Champney, H., 1941, "The Measurement of Parent Behavior," *Child Development,* 12, 131-166. **157**
Charles, M. W. *See* Blatz, W. E., 1937.
Charry, J. B., 1959, "Childhood and Teen-Age Memories in Mentally Ill and Normal Groups," unpublished Doctor of Philosophy dissertation, Teachers College, Columbia Univ. **321**
Chein, I. *See* Harding, J., 1954.
Child, I. L., E. H. Potter, and E. M. Levine, 1946, *Children's Textbooks and Personality Development; An Exploration in the Social Psychology of Education.* Psychological Monographs, 60, No. 3. Wash. D. C.: American Psychological Assoc. **438**
Child, I. L. *See also* Whiting, J. W. M., 1953.
Chittenden, G. E., 1942, *An Experimental Study in Measuring and Modifying Assertive Behavior in Young Children.* Monograph of Society for Research in Child Development, 7, No. 1. Wash., D. C.: National Research Council. **191**
Christiansen, H., 1938, *Bodily Rhythmic Movements of Children in Relation to Rhythm in Music.* Contributions to Education, No. 736. N. Y.: Bureau of Publications, Teachers College, Columbia Univ. **22, 425**

Clark, K. B., and M. K. Clark, 1940, "Skin Color as a Factor in Racial Identification of Negro Preschool Children," *Journal of Social Psychology,* 11, 159-169. **122**
Clark, M. K. *See* Clark, K. B., 1940.
Clark, W. W. *See* Thorpe, L. P., 1942-53.
Clements, E. M. B., 1953, "Changes in the Mean Stature and Weight of British Children over the Past Seventy Years," *British Medical Journal,* No. 4841, Oct. 17, 892-902. **97**
Coan, L., 1939, "Children's Questions." A paper presented in a class at Teachers College, Columbia Univ. **314**
Cobb, M. V. *See* Thorndike, E. L., 1927.
Coffin, T. E., 1955, "Television's Impact on Society," *American Psychologist,* 10, 630-641. **433**
Coghill, G. E.
    1929, *Anatomy and the Problem of Behavior.* N. Y.: Macmillan. **37**
    1936, "Integration and Motivation of Behavior as Problems of Growth," *Journal of Genetic Psychology,* 48, 3-19. **37**
Coleman, R. W., E. Kris, and S. Provence, 1953, "The Study of Variations of Early Parental Attitudes," in *The Psychoanalytic Study of the Child,* vol. 8, pp. 20-47. N. Y.: International Univ. Press. **128**
Combs, A. W., and D. Snygg, 1959, *Individual Behavior: A Perceptual Approach to Behavior,* 2nd ed. N. Y.: Harper. **126, 463**
Combs, A. W. *See also* Snygg, D., 1949; Taylor, C., 1952.
Conn, J. H., 1940, "Children's Reactions to the Discovery of Genital Differences," *American Journal of Orthopsychiatry,* 10, 747-755. **88, 120**
Connor, R., H. F. Greene, and J. Walters, 1958, "Agreement of Family Member Conceptions of 'Good' Parent and Child Roles," *Social Forces,* 36, No. 4, 353-358. **144**
Constantinou, K. *See* Pasamanick, B., 1956.
Cordova, F. A. *See* Anastasi, A., 1953.
Cornett, S. *See* Pattie, F. A., 1952.
Couch, G. B., *See* Brown, A. W., 1947.
Cox, F. N., 1953, "Sociometric Status and Individual Adjustment Before and After Play Therapy," *Journal of Abnormal Social Psychology,* 48, 354-356. **210**
Crandall, J., and A. Preston, 1955, "Patterns and Levels of Maternal Behavior," *Child Development,* 26, 267-277. **157, 163**
Crowder, T. *See* Gallagher, J. J., 1957.
Cruickshank, W. M., 1951, "The Relation of Physical Disability to Fear and Guilt Feelings," *Child Development,* 22, 291-298. **267**
Cruickshank, W. M., and G. O. Johnson, eds., 1958, *Education of Exceptional Children and Youth.* Englewood Cliffs. N. J.: Prentice-Hall. **399**
Cunningham, R., 1947, "How to Construct a Sociogram," Horace Mann-Lincoln Institute of School Experimentation, Bureau of Publications, Teachers College, Columbia Univ. **206**
Cunningham, R., A. Elzi, J. A. Hall, M. Farrell, and M. Roberts, 1951, *Understanding Group Behavior of Boys and Girls.* N. Y.: Bureau of Publications, Teachers College, Columbia Univ. **206, 212**
Cushing, H. M., 1934, "A Tentative Report of the Influence of Nursery School Training Upon Kindergarten Adjustment as Reported by Kindergarten Teachers," *Child Development,* 5, 304-314. **193**

Dahms, L. *See* Walters, J., 1957.
Damann, V. T., 1941, "Developmental Changes in Attitudes as One Factor Determining Energy Output in a Motor Performance," *Child Development,* 12, 241-246. **100**
Dann, S. *See* Freud, A., 1951.
Darcy, N. T., 1946, "The Effect of Bilingualism upon the Measurement of the Intelligence of Children of Preschool Age," *Journal of Educational Psychology,* 37, 21-44. **313**
Davidson, H. H. *See* Blum, L. H., 1954.
Davidson, K. S., S. B. Sarason, F. Lighthall, R. R. Waite, and I. Sarnoff, 1958, "Differences Between Mothers' and Fathers' Ratings of Low Anxious and High Anxious Children," *Child Development,* 29, 155-160. **144**
Davis, A.
    1944, "Socialization and Adolescent Personality," National Society for the Study of Education. *Adolescence,* Forty-third Yearbook, Part I, pp. 198-216. Chicago: Univ. of Chicago Press. **222**
    See also Havighurst, R. J., 1955.

Davis, C. M.

1928, "Self-Selection of Diet by Newly Weaned Infants," *American Journal of Diseases of Children,* 46, 743-750. **73-74**

1931, "Self-Selection of Diets: An Experiment with Infants," *The Trained Nurse and Hospital Review,* 86, 629-634. **74**

1933, "A Practical Application of Some Lessons of the Self-Selection of Diet Study to the Feeding of Children in Hospitals," *American Journal of Diseases of Children,* 46, 743-750. **73-74**

1935, "Choice of Formulas Made by Three Infants Throughout the Nursing Period," *American Journal of Diseases of Children,* 50, 385-394. **73**

Davis, E. A.

1932, "The Form and Function of Children's Questions," *Child Development,* 3, 57-74. **315**

1937, *The Development of Linguistic Skills in Twins, Singletons with Siblings, and Only Children from Age Five to Ten Years.* Institute of Child Welfare Monograph Series, No. 14. Minneapolis: Univ. of Minnesota Press. **312**

Davitz, J. R.

1955, "Social Perception and Sociometric Choice of Children," *Journal of Abnormal & Social Psychology,* 50, 173-176. **210**

1958, "Contributions of Research with Children to a Theory of Maladjustment," *Child Development,* 29, 3-7. **445**

Dawson, G. E., 1900, "Children's Interest in the Bible," *Journal of Genetic Psychology,* 7, 151-178. **417**

Day, E. J.

1932a, "The Development of Language in Twins: I. A Comparison of Twins and Single Children," *Child Development,* 3, 179-199. **312**

1932b, "The Development of Language in Twins: II. The Development of Twins: Their Resemblances and Differences," *Child Development,* 3, 298-316. **312**

Debus, R. L., 1953, "Aggressive Behavior in Young Children," *Forum of Education,* 11, 95-105. **185, 186, 189**

del Solar, C. F. *See* Jersild, A. T., 1949.

DeMartino, M. F., 1955, "A Review of the Literature on Children's Dreams," *Psychiatric Quarterly Supplement,* 29, 90-101. **347**

Dembo, T. *See* Barker, R., 1941.

Dement, W., and N. Kleitman

1957a, "Cyclic Variations in EEG During Sleep and Their Relation to Eye Movements, Body Motility, and Dreaming," *Electroencephalography and Clinical Neurophysiology,* 9, 673-690. **345**

1957b, "The Relation of Eye Movements During Sleep to Dream Activity: An Objective Method for the Study of Dreaming," *Journal of Experimental Psychology,* 53, 339-346. **345**

Dement, W., and E. A. Wolpert

1958a, "Relationships to the Manifest Content of Dreams Occurring on the Same Night," *Journal of Nervous and Mental Disease,* 126, No. 6, 568-578. **345**

1958b, "The Relation of Eye Movements, Body Motility, and External Stimuli to Dream Content," *Journal of Experimental Psychology,* 55, No. 6, 543-553. **345**

Dennis, M. G. *See* Dennis, W., 1940.

Dennis, W.

1938, "Infant Development Under Conditions of Restricted Practice and of Minimum Social Stimulation: A Preliminary Report," *Journal of Genetic Psychology,* 53, 149-157. **19-20, 175**

1939-1940, "Infant Reaction to Restraint: An Evaluation of Watson's Theory," *Transactions of the New York Academy of Sciences,* Ser. II, 2, 202-219. **51**

1942, Piaget's Questions Applied to a Child of Known Environment," *Journal of Genetic Psychology,* 60, 307-320. **357**

1949, "Historical Beginnings of Child Psychology," *Psychological Bulletin,* 46, 224-235. **10**

1951, ed., *Readings in Child Psychology.* N. Y.: Prentice-Hall. **11, 93, 154, 232, 254, 400, 465**

1959, "Causes of Retardation Among Institutional Children," Hectographed. Brooklyn College, Brooklyn, N. Y. **20, 137**

Dennis, W., and M. G. Dennis, 1940, "The Effect of Cradling Practices Upon the Onset of Walking in Hopi Children," *Journal of Genetic Psychology,* 56, 77-86. **20**

Dennis, W., and P. Najarian, 1957, *Infant Development Under Environmental Handicap.* Psychological Monographs, 71, No. 7. Wash., D. C.: American Psychological Assoc. **138-139**

Despert, J. L.
  1944, "Urinary Control and Enuresis," *Psychosomatic Medicine,* 6, 294-307. **86**
  1946, "Anxiety, Phobias, and Fears in Young Children with Special Reference to Pre-natal, Natal, and Postnatal Factors," *Nervous Child,* 5, 8-24. **46**

Deutsche, J. M., 1937, *The Development of Children's Concepts of Causal Relations.* Minneapolis: Univ. of Minnesota Press. **356**

Dillon, M. S., 1934, "Attitudes of Children Toward Their Own Bodies and Those of Other Children," *Child Development,* 5, 165-176. **87-88**

Ding, G. F., and A. T. Jersild, 1932, "A Study of the Laughing and Smiling of Preschool Children," *Journal of Genetic Psychology,* 40, 452-472. **251**

Dixon, J. C., 1957, "Development of Self Recognition," *Journal of Genetic Psychology,* 91, 251-256. **119**

Dolger, L., and J. Ginandes, 1946, "Children's Attitude Toward Discipline As Related to Socioeconomic Status," *Journal of Experimental Education,* 15, 161-165. **410**

Dollins, J. *See* Angelino, H., 1956.

Dorr, M. *See* Havighurst, R. J., 1946.

Driscoll, G. P., 1952, *Driscoll Playkit.* N. Y.: Psychological Corp. **348**

Dudycha, G. J., and M. M. Dudycha
  1933a, "Some Factors and Characteristics in Childhood Memories," *Child Development,* 4, 265-278. **321, 323**
  1933b, "Adolescents' Memories of Preschool Experiences," *Journal of Genetic Psychology,* 42, 468-480. **321, 323**

Dudycha, M. M. *See* Dudycha, G. J., 1933a, 1933b.

Dunham, E. C., 1955, *Premature Infants.* N. Y.: Hoeber. **53**

Dunham, F., 1952, "Effect of Television on School Achievement of Children," *School Life,* 34, 88-89. **433**

Dunlap, J. M., 1958, "The Education of Children with High Mental Ability," in *Education of Exceptional Children and Youth,* edited by W. M. Cruickshank and G. O. Johnson, pp. 147-188. Englewood Cliffs, N. J.: Prentice-Hall. **388, 389, 396**

Dunnington, M. J., 1957, "Behavioral Differences of Sociometric Status Groups in a Nursery School," *Child Development,* 28, 103-111. **209, 210**

Durkin, D.
  1959a, "Children's Acceptance of Reciprocity as a Justice-Principle," *Child Development,* 30, 289-296. **403**
  1959b, "Children's Concepts of Justice: A Comparison With the Piaget Data," *Child Development,* 30, 59-67. **403**

Eastman, D., 1956, "Self-Acceptance as a Factor in Marital Adjustment," unpublished Doctor of Philosophy dissertation, Teachers College, Columbia Univ. **459**

Eaton, M. T., 1944, *A Survey of the Achievement in Social Studies of 10,220 Sixth-Grade Pupils in 464 Schools in Indiana.* Bulletin 20, No. 3. School of Education, Univ. of Indiana. Bloomington, Ill.: Bureau of Cooperative Research and Field Service, Indiana Univ. **368**

Eckhardt, B. C. *See* Landreth, C., 1943.

Eichorn, D. H., 1959, "Two-Generation Similarities in Weight, Height and Weight/Height During the First Five Years." Reported at the Twenty-fifth Anniversary Meeting, Society for Research in Child Development, National Institutes of Health, Bethesda, Md., March, 1959. **96-97**

Eissler, R. S., A. Freud, H. Hartmann, and M. Kris, eds., 1958, *The Psychoanalytic Study of the Child.* N. Y.: International Univ. Press. **11**

Ellenberger, H. F. *See* May, R., 1958.

Elzi, A. *See* Cunningham, R., 1951.

English, H. B., 1929, "Three Cases of the Conditioned Fear Response," *Journal of Abnormal and Social Psychology,* 24, 221-225. **256**

Ephron, B. K., 1953, *Emotional Difficulties in Reading.* N. Y.: Julian Press. **435, 462**

Erikson, E. H., 1940, "Studies in the Interpretation of Play," *Genetic Psychology Monographs,* 22, 557-671. **348**

Escalona, S., 1945, "Feeding Disturbances in Very Young Children," *American Journal of Orthopsychiatry,* 15, 76-80. **49**

Estvan, F. J., 1952, "The Relationship of Social Status, Intelligence, and Sex of Ten- and Eleven-Year-Old Children to an Awareness of Poverty," *Genetic Psychology Monographs*, 46, 3-60. **224**

Ezekiel, L. F., 1931, "Changes in Egocentricity of Nursery School Children," *Child Development*, 2, 74-75. **194**

Farrell, M. *See* Cunningham, R., 1951.

Fauquier, W., 1940, "The Attitudes of Aggressive and Submissive Boys Toward Athletics," *Child Development*, 11, 115-125. **108**

Feldman, W. M., 1920, *The Principles of Ante-Natal and Post-Natal Child Physiology, Pure and Applied*. N. Y.: Longmans, Green. **52, 68**

Fenichel, O., 1945, *The Psychoanalytic Theory of Neurosis*. N. Y.: Norton. **71, 86**

Fey, W. F.
1954, "Acceptance of Self and Others, and Its Relations to Therapy-Readiness," *Journal of Clinical Psychology*, 10, 269-271. **459**
1955, "Acceptance of Others and Its Relation to Acceptance of Self and Others: A Revaluation," *Journal of Abnormal and Social Psychology*, 274-276. **459**

Fieldsteel, N. D. *See* Blum, L. H., 1954.

Fisher, M. S., 1934, *Language Patterns of Preschool Children*. Child Development Monographs, No. 15. N. Y.: Teachers College, Columbia Univ. **308, 311, 314**

Fite, M. D.
1940, "Aggressive Behavior in Young Children and Children's Attitudes Toward Aggression," *Genetic Psychology Monographs*, 22, 151-319. **186, 191, 230**
See also Jersild, A. T., 1939.

Fitz-Simons, M. J., 1935, *Some Parent-Child Relationships As Shown in Clinical Case Studies*. Contributions to Education, No. 643. N. Y.: Bureau of Publications, Teachers College, Columbia Univ. **134-135**

Flemming, C. W. *See* Thorndike, R. L., 1940.

Forbes, H. B. *See* Forbes, H. S., 1927.

Forbes, H. S., and H. B. Forbes, 1927, "Fetal Sense Reaction: Hearing," *Journal of Comparative Psychology*, 7, 353-355. **34**

Foshay, A. W., and K. D. Wann, *et al.*, 1954, *Children's Social Values: An Action Research Study*. N. Y.: Bureau of Publications, Teachers College, Columbia Univ. **405**

Foster, J. C., and J. E. Anderson, 1936, "Unpleasant Dreams in Childhood," *Child Development*, 7, 77-84. **346, 347**

Foster, J. C., F. L. Goodenough, and J. E. Anderson
1928, "The Sleep of Young Children," *Journal of Genetic Psychology*, 35, 201-218. **78-79**
1930, *The Sleep of Young Children*. Institute of Child Welfare Monograph Series, Circular No. 4. Minneapolis: Univ. of Minnesota Press. **78-79**

Foster, S., 1927, "A Study of Personality Make-Up and Social Setting of Fifty Jealous Children," *Mental Hygiene*, 11, 53-77. **183, 296, 297**

Frank, L. K.
1939, "Protective Methods for the Study of Personality," *Journal of Psychology*, 8, 389-413. **348**
See also Hartley, R. E., 1952a, 1952b.

Frank, L. K., R. Harrison, E. Hellersberg, K. Machover, and M. Steiner, 1953, *Personality Development in Adolescent Girls*. Monographs of the Society for Research in Child Development, 16, No. 53. New Orleans: Child Development Publications of the Society for Research in Child Development. **225, 351, 453**

Franzblau, A. N., 1934, *Religious Belief and Character Among Jewish Adolescents*. Contributions to Education, No. 634. N. Y.: Bureau of Publications, Teachers College, Columbia Univ. **415, 422**

Freeman, F. N., K. J. Holzinger, B. C. Mitchell, *et al.*, 1928, "The Influence of Environment on the Intelligence, School Achievement, and Conduct of Foster Children." National Society for the Study of Education. *Nature and Nurture*, Twenty-seventh Yearbook, Part I. 103-217. Bloomington, Ill.: Public School Publishing Co. **382**

Freeman, F. N. *See also* Newman, H. H., 1937.

Frenkel-Brunswik, E.
1951, "Patterns of Social and Cognitive Outlook in Children and Parents," *American Journal of Orthopsychiatry*, 21, 543-558. **227**
See also Adorno, T. W., 1950.

Freud, A., 1955, "Safeguarding the Emotional Health of our Children—An Inquiry into the Concept of the Rejecting Mother," *Child Welfare*, 34, 1-4. **134**

Freud, A., and D. Burlingham, 1944, *Infants Without Families.* N. Y.: International Univ Press. **177-178**
Freud, A., and S. Dann, 1951, "An Experiment in Group Upbringing," *The Psycho-analytic Study of the Child,* vol. 6, pp. 127-168. N. Y.: International Univ. Press. **176-177, 198**
Freud, A. *See also* Eissler, R. S., 1958.
Freud, S.
1930, *Three Contributions to the Theory of Sex.* Nervous and Mental Diseases Monograph Series, No. 7. N. Y.: Nervous and Mental Disease Publishing Co. **70, 86, 247**
1933, *New Introductory Lectures on Psycho-Analysis,* trans. W. J. H. Sprott. N. Y.: Norton. **247**
1936, *The Problem of Anxiety.* N. Y.: Norton. **46, 276, 277, 286, 298**
1938a, *A General Introduction to Psychoanalysis.* N. Y.: Garden City. **247, 324-325**
1938b, *The Basic Writings of Sigmund Freud,* edited by A. A. Brill. N. Y.: Modern Library. **70, 71, 86, 141-142, 247, 324-325, 461**
1938c, "Wit and Its Relation to the Unconscious," in *The Basic Writings of Sigmund Freud,* translated and edited by A. A. Brill, pp. 633-803. N. Y.: Modern Library. **252**
1950, *The Interpretation of Dreams,* translated by A. A. Brill. N. Y.: Modern Library. **347, 351**
Freudenberg, E., 1921, "Der Morosche Umklammerungsreflex und das Brudzinkische Nackenzeichen als Reflexe das Säuglingsalters," *München med. Wchnuschr.,* 68, 1646-1647. **43**
Fries, M. E., 1947, "The Child's Ego Development and the Training of Adults in His Environment," in *The Psychoanalytic Study of the Child,* vol. 2, pp. 85-112. N. Y.: International Univ. Press. **86**
Fromm, E.
1947, *Man for Himself.* N. Y.: Rinehart.
1955, *The Sane Society.* N. Y.: Rinehart. **422**

Gardner, B. *See* Burchinal, L. G., 1957; Hawkes, G. R., 1956.
Gardner, G. M. *See* Landreth, C., 1943.
Gallagher, J. J., and T. Crowder, 1957, "The Adjustment of Gifted Children in the Regular Classroom," *Exceptional Children,* 23, 306-312, 317-319. **392**
Gates, A. I.
1928, "The Nature and Limit of Improvement Due to Training," National Society for the Study of Education. *Nature and Nurture.* Twenty-seventh Yearbook, Part I, pp. 441-460. Bloomington, Ill.: Public School Publishing Co. **21**
1949, Chairman, Yearbook Committee. National Society for the Study of Education. *Reading in the Elementary School,* Forty-eighth Yearbook, Part II. Chicago: Univ. of Chicago Press. **435**
Gates, A. I., and A. W. Scott, 1931, "Characteristics and Relations of Motor Speed and Dexterity Among Young Children," *Journal of Genetic Psychology,* 39, 423-454. **107**
Gates, A. I., and G. A. Taylor, 1926, "An Experimental Study of the Nature of Improvement Resulting from Practice in a Motor Function," *Journal of Educational Psychology,* 17, 226-236. **21**
Gates, G. S.
1923, "An Experimental Study of the Growth of Social Perception," *Journal of Educational Psychology,* 14, 449-462. **203**
1925, "A Preliminary Study of a Test for Social Perception," *Journal of Educational Psychology,* 16, 452-457. **203**
1926, "An Observational Study of Anger," *Journal of Experimental Psychology,* 9, 325-336. **292**
Gershman, H.
1950, "The Problem of Anxiety," *American Journal of Psychoanalysis,* 10, 89-91. **279**
See also Goldstein, K., 1952.
Gesell, A.
1906, "Jealousy," *American Journal of Psychology,* 17, 437-496. **296**
1928, *Infancy and Human Growth.* N. Y.: Macmillan. **62, 257, 441**
1929, "The Individual in Infancy," in *The Foundations of Experimental Psychology,* edited by C. Murchison, pp. 628-660. Worcester, Mass.: Clark Univ. Press. **257**
Gesell, A., and C. S. Amatruda, 1945, *The Embryology of Behavior.* N. Y.: Harper. **52, 54**
Gesell, A., and F. L. Ilg
1937, *Feeding Behavior of Infants.* Philadelphia: Lippincott. **43, 68, 72, 73, 75, 82**
1943, *Infant and Child in the Culture of Today.* N. Y.: Harper. **59, 93**

Bibliography and Author Index   **475**

Gesell, A., and H. Thompson
    1929, "Learning and Growth in Identical Infant Twins: An Experimental Study by the Method of Co-Twin Control," *Genetic Psychology Monographs*, 6, 1-124. **21**
    1934, Infant Behavior. N. Y.: McGraw-Hill, **63**
Gibbs, P. K. *See* Maccoby, E. E., 1954.
Gilmer, B. V. *See* Moyer, K. E., 1955.
Ginandes, J. *See* Dolger, L., 1946.
Gips, C., 1956, "How Illness Experiences Are Interpreted by Hospitalized Children," unpublished Doctor of Education dissertation, Teachers College, Columbia Univ. **267**
Goff, R. M., 1949, *Problems and Emotional Difficulties of Negro Children*. Contributions to Education, No. 960. N. Y.: Bureau of Publications, Teachers College, Columbia Univ. **229**
Goldberg, M. L., L. G. Gotkin, and A. J. Tannenbaum, 1959, Cultural, Social and Personal Factors Influencing Talent Fruition. Mimeographed report. Horace Mann-Lincoln Institute of School Experimentation, Teachers College, Columbia Univ. **390, 400**
Goldenson, R. M. *See* Hartley, R. E., 1952a, 1956b, 1957.
Goldfarb, W., 1943, "The Effects of Early Institutional Care on Adolescent Personality," *Journal of Experimental Education*, 12, 106-129. **140**
Goldhamer, H., and A. Marshall, 1953, *Psychosis and Civilization*. Glencoe, Ill.: Free Press. **451**
Goldman, B. *See* Jersild, A. T., 1939.
Goldstein, K., P. Hoch, R. May, K. Horney, F. A. Weiss, and H. Gershman, 1952, "Neurotic Anxiety—A Panel Discussion," *American Journal of Psychoanalysis*, 12, 89-95. **269**
Goldstein, K., and Scheerer, M., 1941, *Abstract and Concrete Behavior: An Experimental Study with Special Tests*. Psychological Monographs, 53, No. 239. Evanston, Ill.: American Psychological Assoc. **140**
Goodenough, F. L.
    1931, *Anger in Young Children*. Institute of Child Welfare Monograph Series, No. 9. Minneapolis: Univ. of Minnesota Press. **289-291, 298**
    1940, "New Evidence on Environmental Influence on Intelligence," National Society for the Study of Education. *Intelligence: Its Nature and Nurture*, Thirty-ninth Yearbook, Part I, 307-365. Bloomington, Ill.: Public School Publishing Co. **379**
Goodenough, F. L., and D. B. Harris, 1950, "Studies in the Psychology of Children's Drawings. II, 1928-1949," *Psychological Bulletin*, 47, 369-433. **348**
Goodenough, F. L., and K. M. Maurer, 1940, "The Mental Development of Nursery-School Children Compared with that of Non-Nursery School Children," National Society for the Study of Education. *Intelligence· Its Nature and Nurture*, Thirty-ninth Yearbook, Part II, 161-178. Bloomington, Ill.: Public School Publishing Co. **385**
Goodenough, F. L. *See also* Foster, J. C., 1928, 1930.
Goodman, M. E., 1952, *Race Awareness in Young Children*. Cambridge, Mass.: Addison-Wesley. **229**
Gotkin, L. G. *See* Goldberg, M. L., 1959.
Goudey, E., 1957, "Sex Education of Fifteen Hundred Twelve-Year-Old Boys," unpublished Doctor of Education dissertation, Teachers College, Columbia Univ. **252**
Gough, H. G., D. B. Harris, W. E. Martin, and M. Edwards, 1950, "Children's Ethnic Attitudes: I. Relationship to Certain Personality Factors," *Child Development*, 21, 83-91. **227**
Gough, H. G. *See also* Harris, D. B., 1950.
Grant, V. W., 1948, "A Major Problem of Human Sexuality," *Journal of Social Psychology*, 28, 79-101. **227**
Green, E. H.
    1933a, "Friendships and Quarrels Among Preschool Children," *Child Development*, 4, 237-252. **178, 187**
    1933b, "Group Play and Quarreling Among Preschool Children," *Child Development*, 4, 302-307. **174, 178**
Greenberg, P. J., 1932, "Competition in Children: An Experimental Study," *American Journal of Psychology*, 44, 221-248. **185**
Greene, H. F. *See* Connor, R., 1958.
Greenstein, J., 1954, "Effect of Television upon Elementary School Grades," *Journal of Educational Research*, 3, 161-176. **435**
Gregory, L. W. *See* Heath, C. W., 1946.
Griffiths, R., 1935, *Imagination in Early Childhood*. London: Kegan, Paul. **143-144, 334, 336, 350**

Hadfield, J. A., 1954, *Dreams and Nightmares*. London: Penguin Books. **351**

Hagen, E. *See* Thorndike, R. L., 1955.

Hagman, E. P., 1933, *The Companionships of Preschool Children*. University of Iowa Studies in Child Welfare, 7, No. 4. Iowa City: Univ. of Iowa Press. **178**

Hagman, R. R., 1932, "A Study of Fears of Children of Preschool Age," *Journal of Experimental Education*, 1, 110-130. **268, 281**

Hall, C. S., 1959, *The Meaning of Dreams*. N. Y.: Dell. **351**

Hall, G. S., 1891, "The Contents of Children's Minds on Entering School," *Journal of Genetic Psychology*, 1, 139-173. **363**

Hall, J. A. *See* Cunningham, R., 1951.

Hallowell, A. T., 1940, "Aggression in Saulteaux Society," *Psychiatry*, 3, 395-407. **169**

Halpern, F. C., 1953, *A Clinical Approach to Children's Rorschachs*. N. Y.: Grune and Stratton. **349**

Halverson, H. M.
   1931, "An Experimental Study of Prehension in Infants by Means of Systematic Cinema Records." *Genetic Psychology Monographs*, 10, 107-286. **99**
   1940, "Genital and Sphincter Behavior of the Male Infant," *Journal of Genetic Psychology*, 56, 95-136. **52, 87**

Hamilton, E., 1955, "Emotional Aspects of Pregnancy: An Intensive Study of Fourteen Normal Primiparae," unpublished Doctor of Philosophy dissertation, Teachers College, Columbia Univ. **38-39**

Handel, G. *See* Hess, R. D., 1956.

Harding, J., B. Kutner, H. Proshansky, and I. Chein, 1954, "Prejudice and Ethnic Relations," in *Handbook of Social Psychology*, edited by G. Lindzey, vol. 2, pp. 1021-1061. Cambridge, Mass.: Addison-Wesley. **227**

Harms, E., 1944, "The Development of Religious Experience in Children," *American Journal of Socoiology*, 5, 112-122. **415**

Harris, D. B.
   1950, "How Children Learn Interests, Motives and Attitudes." National Society for the Study of Education. *Learning and Instruction*, Forty-ninth Yearbook, Part I, pp. 129-155. Chicago: National Society for the Study of Education. **425**
   1952, "Intellective Functions: Children," in *Progress in Clinical Psychology*, edited by D. Brower and L. E. Abt, vol. I, pp. 26-45. N. Y.: Grune and Stratton.
   1956, "Child Psychology and the Concept of Development," Mimeographed Presidential Address, Division of Developmental Psychology, American Psychological Assoc. **28**
   1957, editor and contributor, *The Concept of Development*. Minneapolis: Univ. of Minnesota Press. **29**

Harris, D. B., H. G. Gough, and W. E. Martin, 1950, "Children's Ethnic Attitudes: II. Relationship to Parental Beliefs Concerning Child Training," *Child Development*, 21, 169-181. **227**

Harris, D. B. *See also* Goodenough, F. L., 1950; Seward, B., 1951.

Harrison, R. *See* Frank, L. K., 1953.

Harrower, M. R., 1934, "Social Status and the Moral Development of the Child," *British Journal of Educational Psychology*, 1, 75-95. **403-404**

Hartley, E. L. *See* Maccoby, E. E., 1958.

Hartley, R. E., 1952, *Growing Through Play: Experiences of Teddy and Bud*. N. Y.: Columbia Univ. Press. **425**

Hartley, R. E., L. K. Frank, and R. M. Goldenson
   1952a, *Understanding Children's Play*. N. Y.: Columbia Univ. Press. **425**
   1952b, *New Play Experiences for Children: Planned Play Groups, Miniature Life Toys, and Puppets*. N. Y.: Columbia Univ. Press. **425**

Hartley, R. E., and R. M. Goldenson, 1957, *The Complete Book of Children's Play*. N. Y.: Crowell. **111, 425**

Hartmann, H. *See* Eissler, R. S., 1958.

Hartshorne, H., and M. A. May
   1928, *Studies in the Nature of Character, Vol. I: Studies in Deceit*. N. Y.: Macmillan. **405-406**
   1929, *Studies in the Nature of Character, Vol. II: Studies in Service and Self-Control*. N. Y.: Macmillan. **406**

Hattendorf, K. W., 1932, "A Study of the Questions of Young Children Concerning Sex: A Phase of an Experimental Approach to Parent Education," *Journal of Social Psychology*, 3, 37-65. **248, 249, 250**

Hattwick, B. W., 1936, "The Influence of Nursery School Attendance upon the Behavior and Personality of the Preschool Child," *Journal of Experimental Education*, 5, 180-190. **193**

Hattwick, L. A. *See* Van Alstyne, D., 1939; Alschuler, R. H., 1943.

Havighurst, R. J., and A. Davis, 1955, "A Comparison of the Chicago and Harvard Studies of Social Class Differences in Child Rearing," *American Sociological Review,* 20, 438-442. **223**

Havighurst, R. J., M. Z. Robinson, and M. Dorr, 1946, "The Development of the Ideal Self in Childhood and Adolescence," *Journal of Educational Research,* 40, 241-257. **409**

Hawkes, G. R., L. G. Burchinal, B. Gardner, and B. M. Porter, 1956, "Parents' Acceptance of Their Children," *Journal of Home Economics,* 48, 195-200. **129**

Hawkes, G. R. *See also* Burchinal, L. G., 1957.

Heath, C. W., and L. W. Gregory, 1946, "Problems of Normal College Students and Their Families," *School and Society,* 63, 355-358. **453**

Heiliger, L. *See* Updegraff, R., 1937.

Helfant, K. *See* Jersild, A. T., 1953.

Hellersberg, E. *See* Frank, L. K., 1953.

Henry, A. F., 1957, "Sibling Structure and Perception of the Disciplinary Roles of Parents," *Sociometry,* 20, 67-74. **144**

Hermann, L. *See* Hinckley, R. G., 1951.

Herrick, V. E., 1945, "Teachers' Classroom Personalities," *Elementary School Journal,* 46, 126-129. **167**

Hess, D., and G. Handel, 1956, "Patterns of Aggression in Parents and Their Children," *Journal of Genetic Psychology,* 89, 199-212. **161**

Highberger, R., 1955, "The Relationship Between Maternal Behavior and the Child's Early Adjustment in Nursery School," *Child Development,* 26, 49-61. **161**

Hildreth, G. *See also* Thorndike, R. L., 1940.

Hilgard, J. R.
1932, "Learning and Maturation in Preschool Children," *Journal of Genetic Psychology,* 41, 36-56. **21**
1933, "The Effect of Early and Delayed Practice on Memory and Motor Performances Studied by the Method of Co-Twin Control," *Genetic Psychology Monographs,* 14, 493-567. **21**
1951, "Sibling Rivalry and Social Heredity," *Psychiatry,* 14, 375-385. **183, 298**

Hill, D. S., 1930, "Personification of Ideals by Urban Children," *Journal of Social Psychology,* 1, 379-392. **353, 409**

Hinckley, R. G., and L. Hermann, 1951, *Group Treatment in Psychotherapy: A Report of Experience.* Minneapolis: Univ. of Minnesota Press. **453**

Hoch, P. *See also* Goldstein, K., 1952.

Hoch, P. H., and J. Zubin, eds., 1950, *Anxiety.* N. Y.: Grune and Stratton, **276, 286**

Hoefer, C. *See* Kawin, E., 1931.

Hollingshead, A., 1949, *Elmtown's Youth.* N. Y.: Wiley.

Hollingworth, H. L. 1927, *Mental Growth and Decline.* N. Y.: Appleton-Century. **25**

Hollingworth, H. L. and V. Weischer, 1939, "Persistent Alphabetical Synthesis," *American Journal of Psychology,* 52, 361-366. **344**

Hollingworth, L. S.
1926, *Gifted Children: Their Nature and Nurture.* N. Y.: Macmillan. **213, 396, 400**
1939, "What We Know About the Early Selection and Training of Leaders," *Teachers College Record,* 40, 575-592. **396**
See also Pritchard, M. C., 1940.

Holmes, F. B.
1935, "An Experimental Study of the Fears of Young Children," in Jersild, A. T., and F. B. Holmes, *Children's Fears,* pp. 167-296. Child Development Monographs, No. 20. N. Y.: Teachers College, Columbia Univ. **257, 261-263**
1936, "An Experimental Investigation of a Method of Overcoming Children's Fears," *Child Development,* 7, 6-30. **281-282**
See also Jersild, A. T., 1935a, 1935b.

Holmes, T. H. *See* Stewart, A. H., 1954.

Holzinger, K. J. *See* Freeman, F. N., 1928; Newman, H. H., 1937.

Honzik, M. P., 1957, "Developmental Studies of Parent-Child Resemblance in Intelligence," *Child Development,* 28, 215-228. **381**

Honzik, M. P., and J. P. McKee, 1959, "Social Behavior Traits in Relation to Certain Physical and Functional Characteristics in Young Children." Reported at the Twenty-fifth Anniversary Meeting, Society for Research in Child Development, National Institutes of Health, Bethesda, Md., March, 1959. **69**

Honzik, M. P. *See also* Macfarlane, J., 1954.

Hooker, D., 1943, "Reflex Activities in the Human Fetus," in *Child Behavior and Development*, edited by R. G. Barker, J. S. Kounin, and H. F. Wright, pp. 17-28. N. Y.: McGraw-Hill. **31**

Horan, K. M. *See* Pritchard, M. C., 1940.

Horney, K.
    1937, *The Neurotic Personality of Our Time*. N. Y.: Norton. **125, 276, 422**
    1939, *New Ways in Psychoanalysis*. N. Y.: Norton. **86, 125, 276**
    1945, *Our Inner Conflicts*. N. Y.: Norton. **125, 126, 277, 278, 279, 286, 298**
    1950, *Neurosis and Human Growth*. N. Y.: Norton. **125, 126, 278**
    See also Goldstein, K., 1952.

Horowitz, E., 1935, "Spacial Localization of the Self," *Journal of Social Psychology*, 6, 379-387. **120**

Horowitz, R.
    1939, "Racial Aspects of Self-Identification," *Journal of Psychology*, 7, 91-99. **122**
    See also Murphy, L. B., 1938.

Hughes, B. O. *See* Olson, W. C., 1940; 1943; 1944.

Hunt, J. M., 1941, "The Effects of Infant Feeding-Frustration Upon Adult Hoarding in the Albino Rat," *Journal of Abnormal Social Psychology*, 36, 338-360. **23**

Hunt, J. M., H. Schlosberg, R. L. Solomon, and E. Stellar, 1947, "Studies of the Effects of Infantile Experience on Adult Behavior in Rats: I. Effects of Infantile Feeding-Frustration on Adult Hoarding," *Journal of Comparative Physiological Psychology*, 40, 313-320. **23**

Hurlock, E. B., and M. Burstein, 1932, "The Imaginary Playmate: A Questionnaire Study," *Journal of Genetic Psychology*, 41, 380-392. **341, 343**

Huschka, M., 1942, "The Child's Response to Coercive Bowel Training," *Psychosomatic Medicine*, 4, 301-308. **86**

Ilg, F. L. *See* Gesell, A., 1937; 1943.

Inhelder, B. *See* Piaget, J., 1958.

Irwin, O. C.
    1932, "Infant Responses to Vertical Movements," *Child Development*, 3, 167-169. **51**
    1947a, "Infant Speech: Consonantal Sounds According to Place of Articulation," *Journal of Speech Disorders*, 12, 397-401. **305**
    1947b, Infant Speech: Consonantal Sounds According to Place of Articulation, *Journal of Speech Disorders*, 12, 402-404. **305**

Isaacs, S.
    1933, *Social Development in Young Children*. N. Y.: Harcourt, Brace. **87, 198**
    1936, *The Nursery Years*. N. Y.: Vanguard Press. **46**

Isaacs, S., S. C. Brown, and R. H. Thouless, eds., 1941, *The Cambridge Evacuation Survey*. London: Methuen. **140**

Itkin, W., 1955, "Relationships Between Attitudes Toward Parents and Parents' Attitudes Toward Children," *Journal of Genetic Psychology*, 86, 339-352. **161**

Jack, L. M., 1934, "An Experimental Study of Ascendant Behavior in Preschool Children," in Jack, L. M., E. M. Manwell, I. G. Mengert, *et al.*, *Behavior of the Preschool Child*, pp. 7-65. University of Iowa Studies in Child Welfare, 9, No. 3. Iowa City: Univ. of Iowa Press. **192**

Jackson, E. B., and G. Trainham, eds., 1950, *Family Centered Maternity and Infant Care*. Report of the Committee on Rooming-in. Conference on Problems of Infancy and Childhood. N. Y.: Josiah Macy, Jr., Foundation. **41**

Jackson, P. W., 1956, "Verbal Solutions to Parent-Child Problems," *Child Development*, 27, 339-349. **144**

James, W., 1890, *Principles of Psychology*, 2 vols. N. Y.: Holt. **116, 126**

Jaynes, J. *See* Beach, F. A., 1954.

Jayaswal, S. R.
    1955, "Adult Recall of Early Memories," *Uttara Bharati*, July, 69-74. **323-324**
    1955a, "Early Childhood and Adult Personality," *Manasi*, 1, 12-15. **447**
    1955b, "Ascendance-Submission in the Preschool Child and in His Adult Personality," *Dissertation Abstracts*, 15. **447**

Jenkins, L. M., 1930, *A Comparative Study of Motor Achievements of Children at Five, Six, and Seven Years of Age.* Contributions to Education, No. 414. N. Y.: Bureau of Publications, Teachers College, Columbia Univ. **103-104**

Jennings, H.
1950a, "Sociodrama as Educative Process," in *Fostering Mental Health in Our Schools.* 1950 Yearbook. Wash., D. C.: Association for Supervision and Curriculum Development, a department of the National Education Assoc. **207**
1950b, "Sociometric Grouping in Relation to Child Development," in *Fostering Mental Health in Our Schools.* 1950 Yearbook. Wash., D. C.: Association for Supervision and Curriculum Development, a department of the National Education Association. **207**

Jensen, K., 1932, "Differential Reactions to Taste and Temperament Stimuli in Newborn Infants," *Genetic Psychology Monographs,* 12, 361-479. **42, 45**

Jersild, A. T.
1931, "Memory For the Pleasant as Compared With the Unpleasant," *Journal of Experimental Psychology,* 14, No. 3, 284-288. **323**
1932, *Training and Growth in the Development of Children.* Child Development Monographs, No. 10. N. Y.: Teachers College, Columbia Univ. **22**
1952, *In Search of Self.* N. Y.: Bureau of Publications, Teachers College, Columbia Univ. **448, 450, 463**
1954, "Emotional Development," in *Manual of Child Psychology,* 2nd ed., edited by L. Carmichael, pp. 833-917. N. Y.: Wiley. **254**
1955, *When Teachers Face Themselves.* N. Y.: Bureau of Publications, Teachers College, Columbia Univ. **11, 91, 463**

Jersild, A. T., and E. Allina, 1960, *The Effects of Psychotherapy and Psychoanalysis as Perceived by Teachers* (in progress). **91, 145, 463**

Jersild, A. T., and S. F. Bienstock, 1935, *Development of Rhythm in Young Children.* Child Development Monographs, No. 22. N. Y.: Teachers College, Columbia Univ. **22**

Jersild, A. T., and M. D. Fite, 1939, *The Influence of Nursery School Experience on Children's Social Adjustments.* Child Development Monographs, No. 25. N. Y.: Teachers College, Columbia Univ. **188, 193, 195**

Jersild, A. T., B. Goldman, and J. Loftus, 1941, "A Comparative Study of the Worries of Children in Two School Situations," *Journal of Experimental Education,* 9, 323-326. **454**

Jersild, A. T., and K. Helfant, 1953, *Education for Self-Understanding.* N. Y.: Bureau of Publications, Teachers College, Columbia Univ. **463**

Jersild, A. T., and F. B. Holmes
1935a, *Children's Fears.* Child Development Monographs, No. 20. N. Y.: Teachers College, Columbia Univ. **261, 265**
1935b, "Methods of Overcoming Children's Fears," *Journal of Psychology,* 1, 75-104. **282-283**

Jersild, A. T., and F. V. Markey, 1935, *Conflicts Between Preschool Children.* Child Development Monographs, No. 21. N. Y.: Teachers College, Columbia Univ. **186**

Jersild, A. T., F. V. Markey, and C. L. Jersild, 1933, *Children's Fears, Dreams, Wishes, Daydreams, Likes, Dislikes, Pleasant and Unpleasant Memories.* Child Development Monographs, No. 12. N. Y.: Teachers College, Columbia Univ. **203, 264, 343, 344, 365**

Jersild, A. T., and R. Ritzman, 1938, "Aspects of Language Development: I. The Growth of Loquacity and Vocabulary," *Child Development,* 9, 243-259. **310**

Jersild, A. T., and R. J. Tasch, 1949, *Children's Interests.* N. Y.: Bureau of Publications, Teachers College, Columbia Univ. **244, 428-429, 430**

Jersild, A. T., and W. S. Thomas, 1931, "The Influence of Adrenal Extract on Behavior and Mental Efficiency," *American Journal of Psychology,* 43, 447-456. **280**

Jersild, A. T., E. S. Woodyard, and C. F. del Solar, 1949, *Joys and Problems of Child Rearing.* N. Y.: Bureau of Publications, Teachers College, Columbia Univ. **99, 130, 132, 221**

Jersild, C. L.   See Jersild, A. T., 1933.

Jervis, F. M., 1958, "The Meaning of a Positive Self-Concept," unpublished Doctor of Philosophy dissertation, Teachers College, Columbia Univ. **459**

Johnson, G. O.
1958, "The Education of Mentally Handicapped Children," pp. 189-226, and "Guidance for Exceptional Children," pp. 611-647, in *Education of Exceptional Children and Youth,* edited by W. M. Cruickshank and G. O. Johnson. Englewood Cliffs, N. J.: Prentice-Hall. **398**
See also Cruickshank, W. M., 1958.

Johnson, H. M., 1933, *The Art of Block Building.* N. Y.: John Day. **105**

Jones, A. W.   *See* Pressey, S. L., 1955.

Jones, H. E.
1949, *Motor Performance and Growth.* Berkeley, Calif.: Univ. of California Press, **24, 107, 108, 211**
1954, "The Environment and Mental Development," in *Manual of Child Psychology,* 2nd ed., edited by L. Carmichael, pp. 631-696. N. Y.: Wiley. **380-381**
Jones, H. E., and M. C. Jones, 1928, "Fear," *Childhood Education,* 5, 136-143. **257**
Jones, M. C.
1924, "The Elimination of Children's Fears," *Journal of Experimental Psychology,* 7, 383-390. **281**
1959, "A Comparison of the Attitudes and Interests of Ninth Graders Over Two Decades," from the Twenty-Fifth Anniversary Meeting of the Society for Research in Child Development, National Institutes of Health, Bethesda, Md. **413**
See also Jones, H. E., 1928.
Jones, T. D., 1939, *The Development of Certain Motor Skills and Play Activities in Young Children.* Child Development Monographs, No. 26. N. Y.: Teachers College, Columbia Univ. **101-103**
Jones, V., 1954, "Character Development in Children—An Objective Approach," in *Manual of Child Psychology,* 2nd ed., edited by L. Carmichael, pp. 781-832. N. Y.: Wiley. **404, 422**
Justin, F., 1932, "A Genetic Study of Laughter Provoking Stimuli," *Child Development,* 3, 114-136. **251**

Kadis, A., 1957, "Early Childhood Recollections As Aids in Group Psychotherapy," *Journal of Individual Psychology,* 13, 182-187. **326**
Kagan, J., 1956, "The Child's Perception of the Parent," *Journal of Abnormal Social Psychology,* 53, 257-258. **144**
Kahn, M. W.
1951, "The Effect of Severe Defeat at Various Age Levels on the Aggressive Behavior of Mice," *Journal of Genetic Psychology,* 79, 117-130. **23**
1954, "Infantile Experience and Mature Aggressive Behavior of Mice: Some Maternal Influences," *Journal of Genetic Psychology,* 84, 65-75. **23**
Kalhorn, J. *See* Baldwin, A. L., 1945.
Kallman, F. J., 1953, *Heredity in Health and Mental Disorder.* N. Y.: Norton. **17, 18, 29, 33, 278**
Kantrow, R. W., 1937, *An Investigation of Conditioned Feeding Responses and Concomitant Adaptive Behavior in Young Infants.* University of Iowa Studies in Child Welfare, 13, No. 3. Iowa City: Univ. of Iowa Press. **55**
Kawi, A., and B. Pasamanick, 1959, *Prenatal and Paranatal Factors in the Development of Childhood Reading Disorders.* Monographs of the Society for Research in Child Development, 24, No. 4. Lafayette, Ind.: Child Development Publications. **36**
Kawi, A. *See also* Pasamanick, B., 1956. **36**
Kawin, E., and G. Hoefer, 1931, *A Comparative Study of Nursery School vs. a Non-Nursery School Group.* Chicago: Univ. of Chicago Press. **193**
Keisler, E. R., 1953, "A Distinction Between Social Acceptance and Prestige Among Adolescents," *Child Development,* 24, 275-283. **211**
Keister, M. E.
1937, "The Behavior of Young Children in Failure: An Experimental Attempt to Discover and to Modify Undesirable Responses of Preschool Children to Failure," *Studies in Preschool Education.* University of Iowa Studies in Child Welfare, 14, No. 346. Iowa City: Univ. of Iowa Press. **294**
See also Updegraff, R., 1937.
Kelley, D. McG. *See* Klopfer, B., 1946.
Kenderine, M., 1931, "Laughter in the Pre-School Child," *Child Development,* 2, 228-230. **251**
Kerlinger, F. N., 1953, "Behavior and Personality in Japan: A Critique of Three Studies of Japanese Personality," *Social Forces,* 31, 250-258. **168, 169**
Kerstetter, L. M., and J. Sargent, 1940, "Reassignment Therapy in the Classroom," *Sociometry,* 3, 293-306. **207**
Kierkegaard, S.
1944, *The Concept of Dread,* trans. W. Lowrie. Princeton, N. J.: Princeton Univ. Press. **126**
1949, *Either/Or,* trans. W. Lowrie. Princeton: Princeton Univ. Press. **458**

1951, *Sickness Unto Death,* trans. W. Lowrie. Princeton: Princeton Univ. Press. **126, 276, 286**

1954, *Fear and Trembling* and *Sickness Unto Death,* trans. W. Lowrie. Garden City, N. Y.: Doubleday Anchor. **126, 286**

Kimmins, C. W., 1915-1916, *An Experimental Investigation of Young Children's Ideas of Causality.* Studies in Psychology and Psychiatry, 6. No. 2. Wash., D. C.: Catholic Univ. of America. **369**

King, F. J. *See* Phillips, B. N., 1959.

Kinsey, A. C., W. B. Pomeroy, and C. E. Martin

1948, *Sexual Behavior in the Human Male.* Philadelphia: W. B. Saunders. **248, 249, 250**

1953, *Sexual Behavior in the Human Female.* Philadelphia: W. B. Saunders. **247, 250**

Kleitman, N. *See* Dement, W., 1957a, 1957b.

Klineberg, O.

1935, *Negro Intelligence and Selective Migration.* N. Y.: Columbia Univ. Press. **386**

1938, "The Intelligence of Migrants," *American Sociological Review,* 3, 218-224. **386**

1953, "Cultural Factors in Personality Adjustment of Children," *American Journal of Orthopsychiatry,* 23, 465-471. **170**

Klingensmith, S. W., 1953, "Child Animism: What the Child Means by 'Alive'," *Child Development,* 24, 51-61. **357**

Klopfer, B., 1956, *Development in the Rorschach Technique.* Yonkers, N. Y.: World Book. **349**

Klopfer, B., and D. McG. Kelley, 1946, *The Rorschach Technique.* Yonkers, N. Y.: World Book. **349**

Knop, C. *See* Aldrich, C. A., 1945a, 1945b.

Koch, H. L.

1935, "An Analysis of Certain Forms of So-Called 'Nervous Habits' in Young Children," *Journal of Genetic Psychology,* 46, 139-170. **87**

1944, "A Study of Some Factors Conditioning the Social Distance Between the Sexes," *Journal of Social Psychology,* 20, 79-107. **178, 226**

Koppitz, E. M., 1957, "Relationships Between Some Background Factors and Children's Interpersonal Attitudes," *Journal of Genetic Psychology,* 91, 119-129. **162**

Kraft, R. M. *See* Trainham, G., 1945.

Kraus, P. E., 1956, "A Longitudinal Study of Children," (mimeographed), Board of Education. N. Y.[2] **152, 200, 259, 381, 446**

Kris, E. *See* Coleman, R. W., 1953; Eissler, 1958.

Krugman, M., 1940, "Out of the Inkwell: The Rorschach Method," *Character and Personality,* 9, 91-110. **349**

Kubie, L. S.

1954a, "The Forgotten Man of Education," *The Goddard Bulletin,* 19, No. 2. **372**

1954b, "Some Unresolved Problems of the Scientific Career," *American Scientist,* 42, 104-112. **372, 393**

Kutner, B. *See* Harding, J., 1954.

Lacan, J., 1953, "Some Reflections on the Ego," *International Journal of Psychoanalysis,* 34, 11-17. **120**

Lafore, G. G., 1945, *Practices of Parents in Dealing with Preschool Children.* Child Development Monographs, No. 31. N. Y.: Teachers College, Columbia Univ. **156, 159-160, 370**

Laing, A., 1939, "The Sense of Humor in Childhood and Adolescence," *British Journal of Educational Psychology,* 9, 201. **252**

Lakin, M., 1957, *Personality Factors in Mothers of Excessively Crying (Colicky) Infants.* Monographs of the Society for Research in Child Development, 22, No. 1. Wash., D. C.: National Research Council. **49**

Landis, A. T. *See* Landis, C., 1940.

Landis, C., A. T. Landis, M. M. Bolles, *et al.,* 1940, *Sex in Development.* N. Y.: Hoeber. **248**

Landreth, C., G. M. Gardner, B. C. Eckhardt, and A. D. Prugh, 1943, "Teacher-Child Contacts in Nursery Schools," *Journal of Experimental Education,* 12, 65-91. **198**

Lasko, J. K., 1954, "Parent Behavior Toward First and Second Children," *Genetic Psychology Monographs,* 49, 97-137. **133**

Laughlin, F., 1953, "A Study of the Peer Status of Sixth and Seventh Grade Children," unpublished Doctor of Education dissertation, Teachers College, Columbia Univ. **209, 210, 211**

---

[2] This report was supplemented by a personal communication from Dr. Kraus.

Lazar, M., 1937, *Reading Interests, Activities and Opportunities of Bright, Average, and Dull Children.* Contributions to Education, No. 707. N. Y.: Bureau of Publications, Teachers College, Columbia Univ. **436**

Leahy, A. M., 1935, "Nature-Nurture and Intelligence," *Genetic Psychology Monographs,* 17, 236-308. **382**

Learned, J. *See* Updegraff, R., 1937; Ames, L. B., 1946, 1952.

Lecky, P., 1945, *Self-Consistency: A Theory of Personality.* N. Y.: Island Press. **124, 126**

Lee, D. M., and A. Bingham, 1959, "Intellectual Processes," *Review of Educational Research,* 29, No. 2, 185-196. **357**

Lee, E. S., 1951, "Negro Intelligence and Selective Migration: A Philadelphia Test of the Klineberg Hypothesis," *American Sociological Review,* 16, 227-233. **386**

Lehman, H. C., and P. A. Witty
1927, *The Psychology of Play Activities.* N. Y.: Barnes. **426**
1930, "A Study of Play in Relation to Pubescence," *Journal of Social Psychology,* 1, 510-523. **426**

Leider, I. H. *See* Stewart, A. H., 1954.

Le Masters, E. E., 1957, "Parenthood as Crisis," *Marriage and Family Living,* 19, 352-355. **133**

Lerner, E., L. B. Murphy, J. L. Stone, E. Beyer, and E. W. Brown, 1941, *Methods for the Study of Personality in Young Children.* Monographs of the Society for Research in Child Development, 6, No. 30. Wash., D. C.: National Research Council. **348**

Leuba, C., 1933, "An Experimental Study of Rivalry in Young Children," *Journal of Comparative Psychology,* 16, 367-378. **185**

Levin, H. *See* Sears, R. R., 1957.

Levine, E. M. *See* Child, I. L., 1946.

Levinson, D. J. *See* Adorno, T. W., 1950.

Levy, D. M.
1928, "Fingersucking and Accessory Movements in Early Infancy," *American Journal of Psychiatry,* 7, 881-918. **87**
1937, "Thumb or Finger Sucking from the Psychiatric Angle," *Child Development,* 8, 99-101. **69**
1940, "Control-Situation Studies of Children's Responses to the Difference in Genitalia," *American Journal of Orthopsychiatry,* 10, 755-763. **88**
1943, *Maternal Overprotection.* N. Y.: Columbia Univ. Press. **135, 136**

Levy, J., and R. Monroe, 1938, *The Happy Family.* N. Y.: Knopf. **153**

Lewin, K., R. Lippitt, and R. White, 1939, "Patterns of Aggressive Behavior in Experimentally Created 'Social Climate,'" *Journal of Social Psychology,* 10, 271-299. **230**

Lewin, K. *See also* Barker, R., 1941.

Lewis, S. J., 1937, "The Effect of Thumb and Finger Sucking on the Primary Teeth and Dental Arches," *Child Development,* 8, 93-98. **69**

Lighthall, F. *See* Davidson, K. S., 1958.

Lilienfeld, A. M. *See* Pasamanick, B., 1955a, 1955b, 1956; Rogers, M. E., 1955.

Lippitt, Ronald. *See* Lewin, K., 1939.

Lippitt, Rosemary, 1941, "Popularity Among Preschool Children," *Child Development,* 12, 305-332. **177**

Liu, C. H., 1950, "The Influence of Cultural Background on the Moral Judgment of Children," unpublished Doctor of Philosophy dissertation, Columbia Univ. **411**

Lockhard, E. G., 1930, "The Attitude of Children Towards Certain Laws," *Religious Education,* 25, 144-149. **403**

Loftus, J. J. *See* Jersild, A. T., 1941.

Lorge, I., 1945, "Schooling Makes a Difference," *Teachers College Record,* 46, 483-492. **387**

Maccoby, E. E., 1951, "Television: Its Impact on School Children," *Public Opinion Quarterly,* 15, 421-444. **433**

Maccoby, E. E., P. K. Gibbs, *et al.,* 1954, "Methods of Child-Rearing in Two Social Classes,' in *Readings in Child Development,* edited by W. E. Martin and C. B. Stendler, pp. 380-396. N. Y.: Harcourt, Brace. **222, 223**

Maccoby, E. E., J. M. Newcomb, and E. L. Hartley, 1958, *Readings in Social Psychology,* 3rd ed. N. Y.: Holt. **232**

Maccoby, E. E. *See also* Sears, R. R., 1957.

Macfarlane, J., L. Allen, and M. P. Honzik, 1954, *A Developmental Study of the Behavior Problems of Normal Children Between Twenty-One Months and Fourteen Years.* Berkeley: Univ. of California Press. **66, 77, 78, 80-81, 84, 200**

Machover, K.
  1949, *Personality Projection in the Drawing of the Human Figure: A Method of Personality Investigation*. Springfield, Ill.: C. C. Thomas, **349**
  See also Frank, L. K., 1953.
MacLean, A. H., 1930, *The Idea of God in Protestant Religious Education*. Contributions to Education, No. 410. N. Y.: Bureau of Publications, Teachers College, Columbia Univ. **418**
Mallay, H. *See* Reynolds, M. M., 1933.
Mangham, C. A. *See* Stewart, A. H., 1954.
Markey, F. V.
  1935, *Imaginative Behavior in Preschool Children*. Child Development Monographs, No. 18. N. Y.: Teachers College, Columbia Univ. **296, 333-334, 337**
  See also Jersild, A. T., 1933, 1935.
Markley, E. R., 1958, "Social Class Differences in Mothers Attitudes Toward Child Rearing," unpublished Doctor of Philosophy dissertation, Teachers College, Columbia Univ. **157, 222**
Marquis, D. P.
  1931, "Can Conditioned Responses Be Established in the New-Born Infant?" *Journal of Genetic Psychology*, 39, 479-492. **55**
  1941, "Learning in the Neonate: The Modification of Behavior Under Three Feeding Schedules," *Journal of Experimental Psychology*, 29, 263-282. **52, 55-57**
Marshall, A. *See* Goldhamer, H., 1953.
Marshall, H. R., and B. R. McCandless, 1957, "Relationships Between Dependence on Adults and Social Acceptance by Peers," *Child Development*, 28, 413-419. **210**
Marshall, H. R. *See also* McCandless, B. R., 1957.
Martin, C. E. *See* Kinsey, A. C., 1948, 1953.
Martin, K. L., 1952, "Handedness: A Review of the Literature on the History, Development, and Research of Laterality Preference," *Journal of Educational Research*, 45, 527-533. **109**
Martin, W. E., and C. B. Stendler, 1954, *Readings in Child Development*. N. Y.: Harcourt, Brace. **11, 93, 154, 198, 232, 465**
Martin, W. E. *See also* Harris, D. B., 1950.
Marx, H. L., ed., 1953, *Television and Radio in American Life*. N. Y.: H. W. Wilson. **433**
Mason, B. S. *See* Mitchell, E. D., 1948.
Maudry, M., and M. Nekula, 1939, "Social Relations Between Children of the Same Age During the First Two Years of Life," *Journal of Genetic Psychology*, 54, 193-215. **173**
Maurer, K. M. *See* Goodenough, F. L., 1940.
May, R., 1950, *The Meaning of Anxiety*. N. Y.: Ronald Press. **276, 286**
May, R., E. Angel, and H. F. Ellenberger, eds., 1958, *Existence: A New Dimension in Psychiatry and Psychology*. N. Y.: Basic Books. **276, 422**
May, R. *See also* Goldstein, K., 1952.
McCandless, B. R., and A. Castaneda, 1956a, "Anxiety in Children, School Achievement, and Intelligence," *Child Development*, 27, 379-382. **280-281**
McCandless, B. R., A. Castaneda, and D. S. Palermo, 1956b, "Anxiety in Children and Social Status," *Child Development*, 27, 385-391. **280-281**
McCandless, B. R., and H. R. Marshall, 1957, "Sex Differences in Social Acceptance and Participation of Preschool Children," *Child Development*, 28, 421-425. **210**
McCandless, B. R. *See also* Castaneda, A., 1956a, 1956b; Palermo, D. S., 1956; Marshall, H.R., 1957.
McCarthy, D.
  1930, *The Language Development of the Preschool Child*. Institute of Child Welfare Monograph Series, No. 4. Minneapolis: Univ. of Minnesota Press. **308**
  1933, "Language Development," in *A Handbook of Child Psychology*, rev. ed., edited by C. Murchison, pp. 329-373. Worcester, Mass.: Clark Univ. Press. **308**
  1952, "Factors That Influence Language Growth: Home Influences," *Elementary English*, 29, 421-428. **312**
  1952a, "Organismic Interpretation of Infant Vocalizations," *Child Development*, 23, 273-280. **305**
  1953, "Some Possible Explanations of Sex Differences in Language Development and Disorders," *Journal of Psychology*, 35, 155-160. **312**
  1954, "Language Development in Children," in *Manual of Child Psychology*, 2nd ed., edited by L. Carmichael, pp. 492-630. N. Y.: Wiley. **305, 331**
McElvaney, M. E., 1958, "Four Types of Fantasy Aggression in the Responses of 'Rebellious' and 'Submissive' Children to the Driscoll Playkit, Structured by Parental-Demand and

Neutral Studious Stress," unpublished Doctor of Philosophy dissertation, Teachers College, Columbia Univ. **350**

McFarland, M. B., 1938, *Relationships Between Young Sisters As Revealed in Their Overt Responses.* Child Development Monographs, No. 23. N. Y.: Teachers College, Columbia Univ. **184, 185**

McGraw, M. B.
    1935, *Growth: A Study of Johnny and Jimmy.* N. Y.: Appleton-Century. **21, 22**
    1937, "The Moro Reflex," *American Journal of Diseases of Children,* 54, 240-251. **43**
    1939, "Later Development of Children Specially Trained During Infancy: Jimmy and Johnny at School Age," *Child Development,* 10, 1-19. **22**
    1940, "Neural Maturation as Exemplified in Achievement of Bladder Control," *Journal of Pediatrics,* 16, 580-590. **83, 85**

McGuire, C.
    1953, "Family and Age-Mates in Personality Formation," *Marriage and Family Living,* 15, 17-23. **166**
    See also Phillips, B. N., 1959.

McKee, J. P. *See also* Honzik, M. P., 1959.

McKillop, A. S., 1952, *The Relationship Between the Reader's Attitude and Certain Types of Reading Response.* N. Y.: Bureau of Publications, Teachers College, Columbia Univ. **371**

McLendon, P. A. *See* Simsarian, F. P., 1942, 1945.

McNeil, E. B., 1959, "Psychology and Aggression," *Journal of Conflict Resolution,* 3, No. 3. **298**

Mead, G. H., 1934, *Mind, Self and Society.* Chicago: Univ. of Chicago Press. **126**

Mech, V. *See* Angelino, H., 1956.

Meili, R., 1957, "Anfänge Der Karakterentwicklung," *Beitrage Zur Genetische Characterologie,* Hans Huber, Bern and Stuttgart. **238**

Meltzer, H., 1933, "Students' Adjustments in Anger," *Journal of Social Psychology,* 4, 285-309. **292**

Mengert, I. G., 1931, "A Preliminary Study of the Reactions of Two-Year-Old Children to Each Other When Paired in a Semi-Controlled Situation," *Journal of Genetic Psychology,* 39, 393-398. **176**

Merrill, M. A. *See* Terman, L. M., 1937.

Metraux, R. W. *See* Ames, L. B., 1952.

Meyers, C. E. *See* Thorpe, L. P., 1954.

Miles, K. A., 1933, "Sustained Visual Fixation of Preschool Children to a Delayed Stimulus," *Child Development,* 4, 1-5. **319**

Millard, C. V., 1940, "The Nature and Character of Pre-Adolescent Growth in Reading Achievement," *Child Development,* 11, 71-114. **21**

Miller, R. V., 1956, "Social Status and Socioempathic Differences Among Mentally Superior, Mentally Typical, and Mentally Retarded Children," *Exceptional Children,* 23, No. 3, 114-119. **392**

Millichamp, D. A. *See* Blatz, W. E., 1937.

Mitchell, B. C. *See* Freeman, F. N., 1928.

Mitchell, C., 1943, "Do Virtues and Vices Change?" *School and Society,* 57, 111-112. **404**

Mitchell, E. D., and B. S. Mason, *The Theory of Play,* rev. ed. N. Y.: Barnes. **425**

Monroe, R. *See* Levy, J., 1938.

Montagu, A., ed., 1953, *The Meaning of Love.* N. Y.: Julian Press. **242, 254**

Moreno, J. L.
    1934, *Who Shall Survive?* Wash., D. C.: Nervous and Mental Disease Publishing Co. **205**
    1954, "Old and New Trends in Sociometry: Turning Points in Small Group Research," *International Social Science Bulletin,* 17, 179-193. **205**

Morris, D. P., E. Soroker, and G. Buruss, 1954, "Follow-up Studies of Shy, Withdrawn Children: I. Evaluation of Later Adjustment," *American Journal of Orthopsychiatry,* 24, 743-754. **212, 447-448**

Morrison, J. *See* Brown, A. W., 1947.

Moyer, K. E., and B. Von Haller Gilmer, 1955, "Attention Spans of Children for Experimentally Designed Toys," *Journal of Genetic Psychology,* 87, 187-201. **319**

Mummery, D. V., 1954, "Family Backgrounds of Assertive and Non-assertive Children," *Child Development,* 25, 63-80. **161**

Murphy, G.
    1945, "The Freeing of Intelligence," *Psychological Bulletin,* 42, 1-19. **371**
    1947, *Personality: A Biosocial Approach to Origins and Structure.* N. Y.: Harper. **465**

Murphy, L. B., 1937, *Social Behavior and Child Personality*. N. Y.: Columbia Univ. Press. **181-182, 193, 417, 420**

Murphy, L. B., and R. Horowitz, 1938, "Projective Methods in the Psychological Study of Children," *Journal of Experimental Education*, 7, 133-140. **348**

Murphy, L. B. *See also* Lerner, E., 1941.

Murray, H., 1953, "The Sociometric Stability of Personal Relations Among Retarded Children," *Sociometry Monographs*, 28, 31. **209**

Murray, H. A., 1937, *Thematic Apperception Test*. Cambridge, Mass.: Harvard Psychological Clinic, Harvard Univ. **349**

Mussen, P. H. *See* Sewell, W. H., 1952; Thurston, J. R., 1951.

Myers, G. C. *See* Scott, F., 1923.

Najarian, P. *See* Dennis, W., 1957.

Neisser, E. G., 1951, *Brothers and Sisters*. N. Y.: Harper. **183, 296, 297**

Nekula, M. *See* Maudry, M., 1939.

Nelson, A. K. *See* Pratt, K. C., 1930.

Nesbitt, M., 1943, "Student and Child Relationships in the Nursery School," *Child Development*, 19, 143-166. **198**

Newcomb, J. M. *See* Macoby, E. E., 1958.

Newman, H. H., F. N. Freeman, and K. J. Holzinger, 1937, *Twins: A Study of Heredity and Environment*. Chicago: Univ. of Chicago Press. **381-382**

Newton, N. R., 1951, "The Relationship Between Infant Feeding and Later Behavior," *Journal of Pediatrics*, 38, 28-40. **71**

Nicholson, E. L. *See* Bonney, M. E., 1958.

Northway, M. L.
  1936, "The Influence of Age and Social Group on Children's Remembering," *British Journal of Psychology*, 27, 11-29. **210**
  1944a, "Children With Few Friends," *School*, 32, 380-384. **210**
  1944b, "Outsiders; A Study of the Personality Patterns of Children Least Acceptable to Their Age Mates," *Sociometry*, 7, 10-25. **210**

Oakden, E. C., and M. Sturt, 1922, "Development of the Knowledge of Time in Children," *British Journal of Psychology*, 12, 309-336. **368**

Oakes, M. E., 1947, *Children's Explanations of Natural Phenomena*. Contributions to Education, No. 926, N. Y.: Bureau of Publications, Teachers College, Columbia Univ. **357**

Oden, M. *See* Terman, L. M., 1940, 1959.

Ojemann, R. *See* Pritchard, E., 1941.

Olson, W. C.
  1943, "The Meaning of Growth," *Michigan Education Journal*, 20, 462-463. **21**
  1959, *Child Development*, 2nd ed. Boston: Heath. **21, 29**

Olson, W. C., and B. O. Hughes
  1940, "Subsequent Growth of Children With and Without Nursery-School Experience." National Society for the Study of Education. *Intelligence: Its Nature and Nurture*, Thirty-ninth Yearbook, Part II, 237-244. Bloomington, Ill.: Public School Publishing Co. **385**
  1943, "Growth of the Child as a Whole," in *Child Behavior and Development*, edited by R. G. Barker, J. S. Kounin, and H. F. Wright, pp. 199-208. N. Y.: McGraw-Hill. **21**
  1944, "Concepts of Growth—Their Significance to Teachers," *Childhood Education*, 21, 2-12. **21**

Omwake, L., 1939, "Factors Influencing the Sense of Humor," *Journal of Social Psychology*, 10, 95-104. **252**

Orbison, W. D. *See* Bonsfield, W. A., 1952.

Orlansky, H., 1949, "Infant Care and Personality," *Psychological Bulletin*, 46, 1-48. **71**

Osborne, E. G., 1937, *Camping and Guidance*. N. Y.: Association Press. **220**

Palermo, D. S., A. Castaneda, and B. R. McCandless, 1956, "The Relationship of Anxiety in Children to Performance in a Complex Learning Task," *Child Development*, 27, 333-337. **280-281**

Palermo, D. S. *See also* McCandless, B. R., 1956b.; Castaneda, A., 1956a, 1956b.

Parten, M. B., 1932, "Social Participation Among Preschool Children," *Journal of Abnormal and Social Psychology*, 27, 243-269. **174**

Pasamanick, B., F. K. Constantinou, and A. M. Lilienfeld, 1956, "Pregnancy Experience and the Development of Childhood Speech Disorders," *American Medical Association Journal of Diseases of Children,* Feb., 91, 113-118. **36**

Pasamanick, B., and A. Kawi, 1956, "A Study of the Association of Prenatal and Paranatal Factors With the Development of Tics in Children," *Journal of Pediatrics,* Vol. 48, May, 596-601. **36**

Pasamanick, B., and A. M. Lilienfeld

    1955a, "The Association of Maternal and Fetal Factors With the Development of Cerebral Palsy and Epilepsy," *American Journal of Obstetrics and Gynecology,* Vol. 70, July, 93-101. **36**

    1955b, "Association of Maternal and Fetal Factors With the Development of Mental Deficiency: I. Abnormalities in the Prenatal and Paranatal Periods," *Journal of American Medical Association,* Vol. 159, Sept., 155-160. **36**

Pasamanick, B., M. E. Rogers, and A. M. Lilienfeld, 1956, "Pregnancy Experience and the Development of Behavior Disorder in Children," *American Journal of Psychiatry,* Vol. 112, Feb., 613-618. **36**

Pasamanick, B. *See also* Rogers, M. E., 1955; Kawi, A. A., 1959.

Passow, A. H., 1958, "Enrichment of Education for the Gifted," *Education for the Gifted.* National Society for the Study of Education. *Fifty-seventh Yearbook,* Part II, pp. 193-221. Chicago: Univ. of Chicago Press. **397**

Pattie, F. A., and S. Cornett, 1952, "Unpleasantness of Early Memories and Maladjustment of Children," *Journal of Personality,* 20, 315-321. **327**

Pearce, D. *See* Walters, J., 1957.

Pearson, K., 1903, "On the Inheritance of the Mental and Moral Characters in Man, and Its Comparison with the Inheritance of the Physical Character," *Journal of the Anthropological Institute,* 33, 179-237. **380**

Phillips, B. N., F. J. King, and C. McGuire, 1959, "Studies on Anxiety: I. Anxiety and Performance on Psychometric Tests Varying in Complexity," *Child Development,* 30, 253-259. **281**

Phillips, E. L., 1951, "Attitudes Toward Self and Others: A Brief Questionnaire Report," *Journal of Consulting Psychology,* 15, 79-81. **459**

Piaget, J.

    1928, *Judgment and Reasoning in the Child,* trans. M. Gabain. N. Y.: Harcourt, Brace. **331, 356**

    1932a, *The Language and Thought of the Child,* 2nd ed., trans. M. Gabain. N. Y.: Harcourt, Brace. **311, 331**

    1932b, *The Moral Judgment of the Child.* London: The Free Press. **402-403, 422**

    1951, *Play, Dreams and Imitation in Childhood,* trans. C. Gattegno and F. M. Hodgson. London: Wm. Heineman in association with the New Education Fellowship. **331**

    1952, *The Origins of Intelligence in Children,* trans. M. Cook. N. Y.: International Universities Press. **331**

Piaget, J., and B. Inhelder, 1958, *The Growth of Logical Thinking From Childhood to Adolescence; An Essay on the Construction of Formal Operations,* trans. A. Parsons and S. Milgram. N. Y.: Basic Books. **331**

Pilafian, G. J. *See* Trainham, G., 1945.

Pilzer, E., 1952, "Disturbed Children Who Make a Good School Adjustment," *Smith College Studies in Social Work,* 22, 193-210. **453**

Pistor, F., 1940, "How Time Concepts Are Acquired by Children," *Educational Method,* 20, 107-112. **21, 369**

Pomeroy, W. B. *See* Kinsey, A. C., 1948, 1953.

Pope, B., 1953, "Socio-economic Contrasts in Children's Peer Culture Prestige Values," *Genetic Psychology Monographs,* 48, 157-220. **213-214**

Porter, B. M.

    1954, "Measurement of Parental Acceptance of Children," *Journal of Home Economics,* 46, 176-182. **129**

    See also Hawkes, G. R., 1956.

Potter, E. H. *See* Child, I. L., 1946.

Powell, J. *See* Bonney, M. E., 1953.

Pratt, K. C.

    1945, "A Study of the 'Fears' of Rural Children," *Journal of Genetic Psychology,* 67, 179-194. **261**

    1954, "The Neonate," in *Manual of Child Psychology,* 2nd ed., edited by L. Carmichael, pp. 215-291. **42, 45, 63**

Pratt, K. C., A. K. Nelson, and K. H. Sun, 1930, *The Behavior of the Newborn Infant.* Columbus: Ohio State Univ. Press. **42, 45**

Pressey, S. L., and A. W. Jones, 1955, "1923-53 and 20-60 Age Changes in Moral Codes, Anxieties, and Interests, as Shown by the 'X-O Tests'," *Journal of Psychology,* 39, 485-502. **413**

Preston, A. *See* Crandall, J., 1955.

Preston, R. C., 1942, *Children's Reactions to a Contemporary War Situation.* Child Development Monographs, No. 29. N. Y.: Teachers College, Columbia Univ. **369**

Preyer, W., 1888, *The Mind of the Child.* N. Y.: Appleton. **63, 118**

Pritchard, E., and R. Ojemann, 1941, "An Approach to the Measurement of Insecurity," *Journal of Experimental Education,* 10, 114-118. **263**

Pritchard, M. C., K. M. Horan, and L. S. Hollingworth, 1940, "The Course of Mental Development in Slow Learners Under an 'Experience Curriculum,' " National Society for the Study of Education. *Intelligence: Its Nature and Nurture,* Thirty-ninth Yearbook, Part II, 245-254. Bloomington, Ill.: Public School Publishing Co. **386**

Probst, C. A., 1931, "A General Information Test for Kindergarten Children," *Child Development,* 2, 81-95. **362-364**

Proshansky, H. *See* Harding, J., 1954.

Prout, C. T., and M. A. White, 1956, "The Schizophrenic's Sibling," *Journal of Nervous and Mental Disorders,* 123, 162-170. **162**

Provence, S. *See* Coleman, R. W., 1953.

Prugh, A. D. *See* Landreth, C., 1943.

Purcell, K., 1952, "Memory and Psychological Security," *Journal of Abnormal Social Psychology,* 47, 433-440. **327**

Pyle, S. I. *See* Sontag, L. W. 1935.

Radke, M., J. Sutherland, and P. Rosenberg, 1950, "Racial Attitudes of Children," *Sociometry,* 13, 154-171. **229**

Ramsey, G. V.
    1943, "The Sexual Development of Boys," *American Journal of Psychology,* 56, 217-233. **248**
    1950, *Factors in the Sex Life of 291 Boys.* Ann Arbor, Mich.: Edward Bros. **248**
    1953, "Studies of Dreaming," *Psychological Bulletin,* Vol. 50, No. 6. 432-455. **346, 347**

Rankin, M., 1944, *Children's Interests in Library Books of Fiction.* N. Y.: Teachers College, Columbia Univ. **439**

Read, G. D., 1953, *Childbirth Without Fear,* rev. ed. N. Y.: Harper. **41**

Redl, F., and D. Wineman, 1951, *Children Who Hate.* Glencoe, Ill.: Free Press. **298**

Redl, F. *See also* Sheviakov, G., 1956.

Reed, M. F. *See* Anderson, H. H., 1946.

Reeves, W. R., 1931, "Report of Committee on Street Play," *Journal of Educational Sociology,* 4, 607-618. **427**

Reynolds, M. M., 1928, *Negativism of Preschool Children.* Contributions to Education, No. 288. N. Y.: Bureau of Publications, Teachers College, Columbia Univ. **149-151**

Reynolds, M. M., and H. Mallay, 1933, "Sleep of Young Children," *Journal of Genetic Psychology,* 43, 322-351. **80**

Rheingold, H. L., 1956, *The Modification of Social Responsiveness in Institutional Babies.* Monographs of the Society for Research in Child Development, 21, No. 2. Lafayette, Ind.: Child Development Publications. **59**

Rheingold, H. L., and N. Bayley, 1959, "The Later Effects of an Experimental Modification of Mothering," *Child Development.* **137-138**

Richards, T. W. *See* Sontag, L. W., 1938.

Richardson, R. F., 1918, *The Psychology and Pedagogy of Anger.* Educational Psychology Monographs, No. 19. Baltimore, Md.: Warwick and York. **292**

Ricketts, A. F., 1934, "A Study of the Behavior of Young Children in Anger," in Jack, Manwell, Mengert, *et al., Behavior of the Preschool Child,* pp. 159-171. University of Iowa Studies in Child Welfare, 9, No. 3. Iowa City: Univ. of Iowa Press, **292**

Rigney, M. G., 1952, "Practices of Teachers in Dealing with Preschool Children," unpublished Doctor of Philosophy dissertation, Columbia Univ. **197-198**

Riley, P., 1953, "An Evaluation of the Use of Selected Sociometric Devices in a Study of Adolescent Group Behavior," unpublished Doctor of Education dissertation, Teachers College, Columbia Univ. **209, 212**

Ripley, H. S. *See* Stewart, A. H., 1954.

Ritzman, R. *See* Jersild, A. T., 1938.

Roberts, D. E., 1950, *Psychotherapy and a Christian View of Man.* N. Y.: Scribner. **422**
Roberts, L. J., 1935, *Nutrition Work with Children,* 2nd ed. Chicago: Univ. of Chicago Press. **75**
Roberts, M. *See* Cunningham, R., 1951.
Robinson, M. Z. *See* Havighurst, R. J., 1946.
Roe, H., 1952, "Psychological Effects of Having a Cerebral Palsied Child in the Family," unpublished Doctor of Philosophy dissertation, Teachers College, Columbia Univ. **268**
Rogers, C. R.
  1942a, "A Study of the Mental Health Problems in Three Representative Elementary Schools," *A Study of Health and Physical Education in Columbus Public Schools.* Monographs of the Bureau of Educational Reasearch, No. 25. Columbus: Ohio State Univ. Press. **453**
  1942b, *Counseling and Psychotherapy: Newer Concepts in Practice.* Boston: Houghton, Mifflin. **126, 463**
  1951, *Client-Centered Therapy: Its Current Practice, Implications, and Theory.* Boston: Houghton, Mifflin. **463**
Rogers, M. E., A. M. Lilienfeld, and B. Pasamanick, 1955, "Prenatal and Paranatal Factors in the Development of Childhood Behavior Disorders," *Acta Psychiatrica et Neurologica Scandinavica, Supplementum* 102 (Copenhagen). Baltimore, Md.: Johns Hopkins Univ., School of Hygiene and Public Health. **37, 53**
Rogers, M. E. *See also* Pasamanick, B., 1956.
Rorschach, H., 1937, *Psychodiagnostik. Methodik und Ergebnisse eines wahrnehmungsdiagnostischen Experiments,* 3rd ed. Berlin: Huber. **349**
Rosenberg, P. *See* Radke, M., 1950.
Rosenthal, I. *See* Ausubel, D. P., 1954.
Ross, M. G., 1950, *Religious Beliefs of Youth.* N. Y.: Association Press. **416, 421, 422**
Roth, M., 1950, "Intra-Family Resemblances in Personality Characteristics," *Journal of Psychology,* 30, 199-227. **161**
Rudman, H. C., 1955, "The Information Needs and Reading Interests of Children in Grades IV through VIII," *Elementary School Journal,* 55, 502-512. **436, 439**
Russell, D. H.
  1949a, *Children Learn to Read.* Boston: Ginn. **435**
  1949b, "Reading and Child Development," National Society for the Study of Education. *Reading in the Elementary School,* Forty-eighth Yearbook, Part II, pp. 10-32. Chicago: Univ. of Chicago Press. **435**
  1956, *Children's Thinking.* Boston: Ginn. **357**
Rust, M. M.
  "The Growth of Children's Concepts of Time, Space and Magnitude," unpublished, Teachers College, Columbia Univ. **315-318**
  1931, *The Effect of Resistance on Intelligence Test Scores of Young Children.* Child Development Monographs, No. 6. N. Y.: Teachers College, Columbia Univ. **152**

Sandin, A. A., 1944, *Social and Emotional Adjustments of Regularly Promoted and Non-Promoted Pupils.* Child Development Monographs, No. 32. N. Y.: Teachers College, Columbia Univ. **207**
Sanford, R. N. *See* Adorno, T. W., 1950.
Sarason, S. B. *See* Davidson, K. S., 1958.
Sarbin, T. R., 1952, "A Preface to a Psychological Analysis of the Self," *Psychological Review,* 59, 11-22. **117**
Sargent, J. *See* Kerstetter, L. M., 1940.
Sarnoff, I. *See* Davidson, K. S., 1958.
Sartre, J. P., 1956, *Being and Nothingness,* trans. H. E. Barnes. N. Y.: Philosophical Library. **29**
Scammon, R. E., and I. A. Calkins, 1929, *The Development and Growth of the External Dimensions of the Human Body in the Fetal Period.* Minneapolis: Univ. of Minnesota Press. **31, 52**
Schaefer, E. S., and R. Q. Bell, 1955, "Parental Attitude Research Instrument (PARI)," unpublished preliminary draft, National Institutes of Mental Health, Bethesda, Md. **157**
Schaltenbrand, G., 1925, "Normale Bewegungs- und Lage-Reaktionen bei Kindern," *Deutsch. Ztschr. f. Nervrnh.,* 87, 23-59. **43**
Scheerer, M. *See* Goldstein, K., 1941.
Schlosberg, H. *See* Hunt, J. M., 1947.
Schpoont, S. H. *See* Ausubel, D. P., 1954.

Scott, A. W. *See* Gates, A. I., 1931.

Scott, F., and G. C. Myers, 1923, "Children's Empty and Erroneous Concepts of the Commonplace," *Journal of Educational Research*, 8, 327-335. **309, 367**

Scott, J. P., 1957, "The Genetic and Environmental Differentiation of Behavior," in *The Concept of Development*, edited by D. Harris, pp. 59-77. Minneapolis: Univ. of Minnesota Press. **23**

Sea, M. R. *See* Thorpe, L. P., 1954.

Saegoe, M. V., 1952, "Children's Television Habits and Preferences," *Quarterly of Film, Radio, Television*, 6, 143-152. **433**

Sears, P. S., 1951, *Doll Play Aggression in Normal Young Chiiren: Influence of Sex, Age, Sibling Status, Father's Absence*. Psychological Monographs, 65, No. 6. Wash., D. C.: American Psychological Assoc. **190**

Sears, R. R., E. E. Maccoby, and H. Levin, 1957, *Patterns of Child Rearing*. Evanston, Ill.: Row, Peterson. **157-158, 168, 170, 222**

Sears, R. R., and G. W. Wise, 1950, "Relation of Cup Feeding in Infancy to Thumb-Sucking and the Oral Drive." *American Journal of Orthopsychiatry*, 20, 123-138. **71**

Seashore, H. G., and A. Bavelas, 1942, "A Study of Frustration in Children," *Journal of Genetic Psychology*, 61, 279-314. **294**

Seidman, J. E., ed., 1958, *The Child: A Book of Readings*. N. Y.: Rinehart, **11, 93, 111, 154, 232, 372, 400, 465**

Senn, M. J., ed., "Transactions of the Conference on Problems of Infancy and Childhood." N. Y.: Josiah Macy, Jr., Foundation.

Sewall, M., 1930, "Two Studies in Sibling Rivarly: I. Some Causes of Jealousy in Young Children," *Smith College Studies in Social Work*, 1, 6-22. **183, 296**

Seward, B., and D. B. Harris, 1951, "The Reading Ease, Human Interest Value, and Thematic Content of *St. Nicholas Magazine;* A Study of Children's Literature," *Journal of Educational Psychology*, 42, 153-165. **438**

Sewell, W. H., 1952, "Infant Training and the Personality of the Child," *American Journal of Sociology*, 58, 150-159. **161**

Sewell, W. H., and P. H. Mussen, 1952, "The Effects of Feeding, Weaning, and Scheduling Procedures on Childhood Adjustment and the Formation of Oral Symptoms," *Child Development*, 23, 185-191. **71**

Shaffer, L. F., 1930, *Children's Interpretation of Cartoons*. Contributions to Education, No. 429. N. Y.: Bureau of Publications, Teachers College, Columbia Univ. **367**

Sharpe, E. F., 1950, "Planning for Stability," in *On the Bringing Up of Children*, 2nd ed., edited by J. Rickman, pp. 1-30. N. Y.: Robert Brunner. **46**

Shaw, R. F., 1934, *Finger Painting*. Boston: Little, Brown. **349**

Shayon, R. L., 1951, *Television and Our Children*. N. Y.: Longmans, Green. **433**

Sheerer, E. T., 1949, "An Analysis of the Relationship Between Acceptance of and Respect for Self and Acceptance of and Respect for Others in Ten Counseling Cases," *Journal of Consulting Psychology*, 13, 169-175. **459**

Sherman, M., 1930, "Afternoon Sleep of Young Children: Some Influencing Factors," *Journal of Genetic Psychology*, 38, 114-126. **80**

Sherrill, L. J., 1939, *The Opening Doors of Childhood*. N. Y.: Macmillan. **417**

Sheviakov, G., and F. Redl, 1956, *Discipline for Today's Children and Youth*, new revision by S. K. Richardson. Wash., D. C.: Washington Assoc. for Supervision and Curriculum Division of National Education Assoc. **93**

Shirley, M. M.
1931, *The First Two Years: A Study of Twenty-Five Babies, Vol. I. Postural and Locomotor Development*. Institute of Child Welfare Monograph Series, No. 6. Minneapolis: Univ. of Minnesota Press. **63, 97, 111**
1933a, *The First Two Years: A Study of Twenty-Five Babies, Vol. II. Intellectual Development*. Institute of Child Welfare Monograph Series, No. 7. Minneapolis: Univ. of Minnesota Press. **60-61, 63, 305-306, 308**
1933b, *The First Two Years: A Study of Twenty-Five Babies, Vol. III. Personality Manifestations*. Institute of Child Welfare Monograph Series, No. 8. Minneapolis: Univ. of Minnesota Press. **63, 172, 175, 441, 442, 443, 465**
1938, "Development of Immature Babies During the First Two Years," *Child Development*, 9, 347-360. **54, 55**
1939, "A Behavior Syndrome Characterizing Prematurely-Born Children," *Child Development*, 10, 115-128. **54**
1941, "Impact of Mother's Personality on the Young Child," *Smith College Studies in Social Work*, 12, 15-64. **128, 443-444**

Shoben, E. J., 1949, "The Assessment of Parentai Attitudes in Relation to Child Adjust-ment," *Genetic Psychology Monographs,* 39, 103-148. **157**

Sillman, J. H., 1951, "Thumb-Sucking and the Oral Structure," *Journal of Pediatrics,* 39, 424-430. **69**

Simsarian, F. P., 1948, "Self-Demand Feeding of Infants and Young Children in Family Settings," *Mental Hygiene,* 32, 217-225. **69, 73**

Simsarian, F. P., and P. A. McLendon
1942, "Feeding Behavior of an Infant During the First Twelve Weeks of Life on a Self-Demand Schedule," *Journal of Pediatrics,* 20, 93-103. **52, 72**
1945, "Further Records of the Self-Demand Schedule in Infant Feeding," *Journal of Pediatrics,* 27, 109-114. **52, 73**

Sizemore, R. A. *See* Witty, P. A., 1954.

Skeels, H. M., R. Updegraff, B. L. Wellman, and H. M. Williams, 1938, *A Study of En-vironmental Stimulation: An Orphanage Preschool Project.* University of Iowa Studies in Child Welfare, 15, No. 4. Iowa City: Univ. of Iowa Press. **139, 385**

Skeels, H. M. *See also* Skodak, M., 1949.

Skodak, M., and H. M. Skeels, 1949, "A Final Follow-Up of One Hundred Adopted Chil-dren," *Journal of Genetic Psychology,* 75, 85-125. **17, 382-383**

Slater, E.
1939, *II. Types, Levels, and Irregularities of Response to a Nursery School Situation of Forty Children Observed with Special Reference to the Home Environments.* Monographs of the Society for Research in Child Development, 4, No. 2. Wash., D. C.: National Research Council. **105-106, 281-282**
1953, "Genetic Investigations in Twins," *Journal of Mental Science,* 99, 44-52.

Slavson, S. R.
1943, *An Introduction to Group Therapy.* N. Y.: Commonwealth Fund. **463**
1947, ed., *The Practice of Group Therapy.* N. Y.: International Universities Press. **463**
1952, *Child Psychotherapy.* N. Y.: Columbia Univ. Press. **463**

Smalley, R. E., 1930, "Two Studies in Sibling Rivalry, Pt. II. The Influence of Differences in Age, Sex, and Intelligence in Determining the Attitudes of Siblings Toward Each Other," *Smith College Studies in Social Work,* 1, 23-40. **183**

Smith, M. E.
1931, "A Study of Five Bilingual Children from the Same Family," *Child Development,* 2, 184-187. **310, 313**
1935, "A Study of the Speech of Eight Bilingual Children of the Same Family," *Child Development,* 6, 19-25. **313**
1949, "Measurement of Vocabularies of Young Bilingual Children in Both the Languages Used," *Journal of Genetic Psychology,* 74, 305-315. **313**

Smith, M. K., 1941, "Measurement of the Size of General English Vocabulary Through the Elementary Grades and High School," *Genetic Psychology Monographs,* 24, 311-345. **306**

Snygg, D., and A. W. Combs, 1949, *Individual Behavior.* N. Y.: Harper. **463**

Snygg, D. *See also* Combs, A. W., 1959.

Solomon, R. L. *See* Hunt, J. M., 1947.

Sontag, L. W.
1941, "The Significance of Fetal Environmental Differences," *American Journal of Obstetrics and Gynecology,* 42, 996-1003. **35**
1944a, "Differences in Modifiability of Fetal Behavior and Physiology," *Psychosomatic Medicine,* 6, 151-154. **35**
1944b, "War and the Fetal Maternal Relationship," *Marriage and Family Living,* 6, 3-4, 16. **35**

Sontag, L. W., S. I. Pyle, and J. Cape, 1935, "Prenatal Conditions and the Status of Infants at Birth," *American Journal of Diseases of Children,* 50, 337-342. **35**

Sontag, L. W., and T. W. Richards, 1938, *Studies in Fetal Behavior: I. Fetal Heart Rate as a Behavioral Indicator.* Monographs of the Society for Research in Child Development, 3, No. 4. Wash., D. C.: National Research Council. **34-35, 52**

Sontag, L. W., and R. F. Wallace
1934, "Preliminary Report of the Fels Fund: Study of Fetal Activity," *American Journal of Diseases of Children,* 48, 1050-1057. **35**
1935, "The Movement Response of the Human Fetus to Sound Stimuli," *Child De-velopment,* 6, 253-258. **35**

Soroker, E. *See* Morris, D. P., 1954.

Spitz, R. A.
1949, "Autoerotism, Some Empirical Findings and Hypotheses on Three of Its Mani-

festations in the First Year of Life," in *Psychoanalytic Study of the Child,* edited by A. Freud *et al.,* vol. 3/4, pp. 85-120. N. Y.: International Univ. Press. **87**

1951, "The Psychogenic Diseases in Infancy: An Attempt at Their Etiologic Classification," in *Psychoanalytic Study of the Child,* vol. 6, pp. 255-275. N. Y.: International Univ. Press. **137**

Spivack, S. S., 1956, "A Study of a Method of Appraising Self-acceptance and Self-rejection," *Journal of Genetic Psychology,* 88, 183-202. **392**

Spock, B. M., 1946, *The Common Sense Book of Baby and Child Care.* N. Y.: Duell, Sloan and Pearce. **93**

Spoerl, D. T., 1944, "The Academic and Verbal Adjustment of College Age Bilingual Students," *Journal of Genetic Psychology,* 64, 139-157. **313**

Stagner, R., 1944, Studies of Aggressive Social Attitudes: III. The Role of Personal and Family Scores," *Journal of Social Psychology,* 20, 129-140. **140**

Stanger, M. *See* Thorndike, R. L., 1940.

Steiner, M. *See* Frank, L. K., 1953.

Stellar, E. *See* Hunt, J. M., 1947.

Stendler, C. B.
  1949, *Children of Brasstown.* Urbana: Univ. of Illinois Press. **121, 224**
  See also Martin, W. E., 1954.

Stern, W., 1926, *Psychology of Early Childhood.* N. Y.: Holt. **345**

Stewart, A. H., I. H. Weiland, A. R. Leider, C. A. Mangham, T. H. Holmes, and H. S. Ripley, 1954, "Excessive Infant Crying (Colic) in Relation to Parent Behavior," *American Journal of Psychiatry,* 110, 687-694. **49**

Stoddard, G. D., 1943, *The Meaning of Intelligence.* N. Y.: Macmillan. **374**

Stone, J. L. *See* Lerner, E., 1941.

Stott, L. H., 1957, "Persisting Effects of Early Family Experiences Upon Personality Development," *Merrill-Palmer School Quarterly,* Spring, Vol. 3, No. 3, Detroit. (Special Issue, Seminar on Child Development.) **444-445**

Strayer, L. C., 1930, "Language and Growth: The Relative Efficacy of Early and Deferred Vocabulary Training Studied by the Method of Co-Twin Control," *Genetic Psychology Monographs,* 8, 209-319. **21**

Sturt, M. *See* Oakden, E. C., 1922.

Sullivan, H. S.
  1947, *Conceptions of Modern Psychiatry.* Wash., D. C.: William Alanson White Psychiatric Foundation. **65, 122, 126, 276, 277, 287**
  1948, *The Meaning of Anxiety in Psychiatry and in Life.* N. Y.: William Alanson White Institute of Psychiatry. **276, 277, 286**
  1953, *The Interpersonal Theory of Psychiatry.* N. Y.: Norton. **65**

Sun, K. H. *See* Pratt, K. C., 1930.

Sung, C. *See* Aldrich, C. A., 1945a, 1945b.

Sutherland, J. *See* Radke, M., 1950.

Svendsen, M., 1934, "Children's Imaginary Companions," *Archives of Neurology and Psychiatry,* 32, 985-999. **341, 343**

Symonds, P. M.
  1938, "A Study of Parental Acceptance and Rejection," *American Journal of Orthopsychiatry,* 8, 679-688. **135**
  1949, *Adolescent Fantasy.* N. Y.: Columbia Univ. Press. **225, 348, 350**

Taba, H., 1953, "The Moral Beliefs of Sixteen-Year-Olds," in *The Adolescent: A Book of Readings,* edited by J. Seidman, pp. 315-318. N. Y.: Dryden Press. **405**

Tannenbaum, A. J.
  1959, "A Study of Verbal Stereotypes Associated with Brilliant and Average Students," unpublished Doctor of Philosophy dissertation, Teachers College, Columbia Univ. **390-391**
  See also Goldberg, M. L., 1959.

Tasch, R. J. *See* Jersild, A. T., 1949.

Taylor, C., and A. W. Combs, 1952, "Self-Acceptance and Adjustment," *Journal of Consulting Psychology,* 16, 89-91. **124, 458**

Taylor, G. A. *See* Gates, A. I., 1926.

Taylor, J. A., 1953, "A Personality Scale of Manifest Anxiety," *Journal of Abnormal Social Psychology,* 48, 285-290. **280, 454**

Templin, M. C., 1958, "General Information of Kindergarten Children: A Comparison With the Probst Study After 26 Years," *Child Development,* 29, 87-96. **362-364**

Terman, L. M., 1916, *The Measurement of Intelligence.* Boston: Houghton Mifflin. **375**

Terman, L. M., and M. A. Merrill, 1937, *Measuring Intelligence.* Boston: Houghton Mifflin. **375, 379**

Terman, L. M., and M. Oden
1940, "Status of the California Gifted Group at the End of Sixteen Years." National Society for the Study of Education. *Intelligence: Its Nature and Nurture.* Thirty-ninth Yearbook, Part I, pp. 67-89. Bloomington, Ill.: Public School Publishing Co. **389, 395**
1959, *The Gifted Group at Mid-Life: Thirty-five Years' Follow-up of the Superior Child.* Stanford University Genetic Studies of Genius, Vol. 5. Stanford: Stanford Univ. Press. **395-396, 400, 455**

Thalman, W. A. *See* Vandament, W. E., 1956.

Thevaos, D. G., 1951, "The Influence of Semantic Variation on Word Difficulty, with Consequent Effects on Vocabulary Estimates and Frequency-Difficulty Variations," unpublished Doctor of Education dissertation, Teachers College, Columbia Univ. **309**

Thomas, W. S. *See* Jersild, A. T., 1931.

Thompson, G. G.
1944, *The Social and Emotional Development of Preschool Children Under Two Types of Educational Program.* Psychological Monographs, 56, No. 258. Evanston, Ill.: American Psychological Assoc. **193, 196**
1949, "Age Trends in Social Values During Adolescent Years," *American Psychologist,* 4, No. 7. **404**
1952, *Child Psychology.* N. Y.: Houghton Mifflin. **404**
1959, "Developmental Psychology," in *Annual Review of Psychology,* edited by P. R. Farnsworth, pp. 1-42. Palo Alto, Calif.: Annual Reviews. **11**

Thompson, G. G., and S. L. Witryol, 1948, "Adult Recall of Unpleasant Experiences During Three Periods of Childhood," Journal of Genetic Psychology, 72, 111-123. **321**

Thompson, G. G. *See also* Witryol, S. L., 1953.

Thompson, H.
1954, "Physical Growth," in *Manual of Child Psychology,* 2nd ed., edited by L. Carmichael, pp. 292-334. N. Y.: Wiley. **111**
See also Gesell, A., 1929, 1934.

Thorndike, E. L., 1913, *Educational Psychology, Vol. II. The Original Nature of Man.* N. Y.: Teachers College, Columbia Univ. **128**

Thorndike, E. L., E. O. Bregman, M. V. Cobb, E. S. Woodyard, *et al.,* 1927, *The Measurement of Intelligence.* N. Y.: Teachers College, Columbia Univ. **374**

Thorndike, R. L.
1940, " 'Constancy' of the I.Q.," *Psychological Bulletin,* 37, 167-186. **378**
1941, *Comparative Study of Children's Reading Interests.* N. Y.: Bureau of Publications, Teachers College, Columbia Univ. **437**
1948, "Growth of Intelligence During Adolescence," *Journal of Genetic Psychology,* 72, 11-15. **379**

Thorndike, R. L., C. W. Flemming, G. Hildreth, and M. Stanger, 1940, "Retest Changes in the I.Q. in Certain Superior Schools." National Society for the Study of Education. *Intelligence: Its Nature and Nurture,* Thirty-ninth Yearbook, Part II, pp. 351-361. Bloomington, Ill.: Public School Publishing Co. **386**

Thorndike, R. L., J. J. Loftus, and B. Goldman, 1941, "Observation of Excursions in Activity and Control Schools," *Journal of Experimental Education,* 10, 146-149. **230**

Thorndike, R. L., and E. Hagen, 1955, *Measurement and Evaluation in Psychology and Education.* N. Y.: Wiley.

Thorpe, L. P., W. W. Clark, and E. W. Tiegs, 1942-53, *California Test of Personality.* Los Angeles: California Test Bureau. **453-454**

Thorpe, L. P., C. E. Meyers, and M. R. Sea, 1954, *SRA Profile Folder for 'What I Like To Do': An Inventory of Children's Interests.* Chicago: Science Research Assoc. **439**

Thouless, R. H. *See* Isaacs, S., 1941.

Thurston, J. R., and P. H. Mussen, 1951, "Infant Feeding Gratification and Adult Personality," *Journal of Personality,* 19, 449-458. **71**

Tiegs, E. W. *See* Thorpe, L. P., 1942-53.

Tillich, P., 1952, *The Courage To Be.* New Haven, Conn.: Yale Univ. Press. **29, 276, 286**

Trainham, G., G. J. Pilafian, and R. M. Kraft, 1945, "A Case History of Twins Breast-Fed on a Self-Demand Regime," *Journal of Pediatrics,* 27, 97-108. **73**

Trainham, G. *See also* Jackson, E. B., 1950.

Trent, R.
1953, "The Correlates of Self-Acceptance Among Negro Children," unpublished Doctor of Education dissertation, Teachers College, Columbia Univ. **227, 459**

1957, "The Relationship of Anxiety to Popularity and Rejection Among Institutionalized Delinquent Boys," *Child Development,* 28, 379-384. **210, 227**

Tryon, R. C., 1940, "Genetic Differences in Maze Learning," *National Society for the Study of Education,* 39th Yearbook, Part I, 111-119. **384**

Tucker, L. E., 1937, *A Study of Problem Pupils.* Contributions to Education, No. 720. N. Y.: Bureau of Publications, Teachers College, Columbia Univ. **211**

Ullmann, C. A., 1952, *Identification of Maladjusted School Children. A Comparison of Three Methods of Screening.* Public Health Monograph, No. 7. Wash., D. C.: Government Printing Office. **453**

Updegraff, R., L. Heiliger, and J. Learned, 1937, "Part III: The Effect of Training Upon the Singing Ability and Musical Interest of Three-, Four-, and Five-Year-Old Children," *Studies in Preschool Education.* University of Iowa Studies in Child Welfare, 14, No. 346, Iowa City: Univ. of Iowa Press. **22**

Updegraff, R., and M. E. Keister, 1937, "A Study of Children's Reactions to Failure and an Experimental Attempt to Modify Them," *Child Development,* 8, 241-248. **294**

Updegraff, R. *See also* Skeels, H. M., 1938.

U. S. Children's Bureau Publication
1955, *Infant Care,* No. 8, rev. ed. Wash., D. C.: U. S. Govt. Printing Office. **93**
1956, *Your Child from One to Six,* No 30, rev. ed. Wash., D. C.: U. S. Govt. Printing Office. **93**

Valentine, C. W.
1930, "The Innate Bases of Fear," *Journal of Genetic Psychology,* 37, 394-420. **256**
1946, *The Psychology of Early Childhood,* 3rd ed. London: Methuen and Co. **256**

Van Alstyne, D., and L. A. Hattwick, 1939, "A Follow-Up Study of the Behavior of Nursery School Children," *Child Development,* 10, 43-70. **195-196**

Vandament, W. E., and W. A. Thalman, 1956, "An Investigation into the Reading Interests of Children," *Journal of Educational Research,* 49, 467-470. **436**

Vinacke, W. E., 1954, "Concept Formation of Children of School Ages," *Education,* 74, May, 527-534. **372**

Waite, R. R. *See* Davidson, K. S., 1958.

Waldfogel, S., 1948, "The Frequency and Affective Character of Childhood Memories," *Psychological Monographs,* 62, No. 291. **322-323**

Walker, R. N. *See* Ames, L. B., 1952.

Wallace, R. F. *See* Sontag, L. W., 1934, 1935.

Walters, J., D. Pearce, and L. Dahms, 1957, "Affection and Aggressive Behavior of Preschool Children," *Child Development,* 28, 15-26. **176**

Walters, J. *See also* Connor, R., 1958.

Washburn, R. W., 1929, "A Study of the Smiling and Laughing of Infants in the First Year of Life," *Genetic Psychology Monographs,* 6, 397-539. **250**

Watson, G. B., 1957, "Some Personality Differences in Children Related to Strict or Permissive Parental Discipline," *Journal of Psychology,* 44, 227-249. **158, 160-161**

Watson, J. B.
1924a, *Behaviorism.* N. Y.: People's Institute. **256**
1924b, *Psychology from the Standpoint of a Behaviorist.* Philadelphia: Lippincott. **256**

Watson, J. B., and R. R. Watson, 1928, *Psychological Care of Infant and Child.* N. Y.: Norton. **168**

Watson, R. R. *See* Watson, J. B., 1928.

Weaver, E., 1955, "How Do Children Discover They Are Negroes," *Understanding the Child,* 24, 35-41. **229**

Wechsler, D.
1949, *Wechsler Intelligence Scale for Children Manual.* N. Y.: Psychological Corp. **375**
1950a, "Cognitive, Conative, and Non-Intellective Intelligence," *American Psychologist,* 5, 78-83. **375**
1950b, "Intellectual Development and Psychological Maturity," *Child Development,* 21, 45-50. **375**
1951, "Equivalent Test and Mental Ages for the WISC," *Journal of Consulting Psychology,* 15, 381-384. **375**

Weiland, I. H. *See* Stewart, I. H., 1954.

Weischer, V. *See* Hollingworth, H. L., 1939.

Weiss, F. A. *See* Goldstein, K., 1952.

Welkowitz, J. *See* Ausubel, D. P., 1954.
Wellman, B. L.
    1932, "The Effect of Preschool Attendance Upon the I.Q.," *Journal of Experimental Education,* 1, 48-69. **384-385**
    1934, "Growth in Intelligence Under Differing School Environments," *Journal of Experimental Education,* 3, 59-83. **385**
    1937, "Motor Achievements of Preschool Children," *Childhood Education,* 13, 311-316. **107**
    See also Skeels, H. M., 1938.
Wenger, M. A., 1936, *An Investigation of Conditioned Responses in Human Infants.* University of Iowa Studies in Child Welfare, 12, No. 318. Iowa City: Univ. of Iowa Press. **56**
Wenkart, A., 1955, "Self-Acceptance," *American Journal of Psychoanalysis,* 15, 135-143. **456**
White, M. A. *See* Prout, C. T., 1956.
White, R. *See* Lewin, K., 1939.
White, R. W., 1945, "Interpretation of Imaginative Productions," in *Personality and the Behavior Disorders,* edited by J. McV. Hunt, Vol. I, pp. 214-251. N. Y.: Ronald Press. **348**
Whiting, J. W. M., and I. L. Child, 1953, *Child Training and Personality: A Cross-cultural Study.* New Haven, Conn.: Yale Univ. Press. **168, 170**
Wickens, C. *See* Wickens, D. D., 1940.
Wickens, D. D., and C. Wickens, 1940, "A Study of Conditioning in the Neonate," *Journal of Experimental Psychology,* 26, 94-102. **56**
Williams, A. M., 1939, *Children's Choices in Science Books.* Child Development Monographs, No. 27. N. Y.: Teachers College, Columbia Univ. **438**
Williams, H. M. *See* Skeels, H. M., 1938.
Wilson, F. T., 1953, "Some Special Ability Test Scores of Gifted Children," *Journal of Genetic Psychology,* 82, 59-68. **389**
Wineman, D. *See* Redl, F., 1951.
Wise, G. W. *See* Sears, R. R., 1950.
Witryol, S. L., and G. G. Thompson, 1953, "A Critical Review of the Stability of Social Acceptability Scores Obtained with the Partial-rank-order and the Paired-comparison Scales," *Genetic Psychology Monographs,* 48, 221-260. **209**
Witryol, S. L. *See also* Thompson, G. G., 1948.
Wittenberg, R. M., and J. Berg, 1952, "The Stranger in the Group," *American Journal of Orthopsychiatry,* 22, 89-97. **214**
Witty, P. A.
    1950, "Children's Parents' and Teachers' Reactions to Television," *Elementary English,* 27, 349-355. **433**
    1951, "Television and the High School Student," *Education,* 72, 242-245. **433**
    1952, "Children's Interest in Comics, Radio, Motion Pictures, and Television," *Educational Administration and Supervision,* 38, 138-147. **433**
Witty, P. A., and R. A. Sizemore, 1954, "Reading the Comics: A Summary of Studies and an Evaluation," *Elementary English,* 31, 501-506. **437**
Witty, P. A. *See also* Lehman, H. C., 1927, 1930.
Wolf, T. H., 1938, *The Effect of Praise and Competition on the Persisting Behavior of Kindergarten Children.* Institute of Child Welfare Monograph Series, No. 15. Minneapolis: Univ. of Minnesota Press. **185**
Wolfenstein, M.
    1953, "Trends in Infant Care," *American Journal of Orthopsychiatry,* 33, 120-130. **167**
    1954, *Children's Humor: A Psychological Analysis.* Glencoe, Ill.: Free Press. **251, 254**
Wolpert, A. *See* Dement, W., 1958a, 1958b.
Woodyard, E. S. *See* Thorndike, E. L., 1927; Jersild, A. T., 1949.
Wright, B. A., 1942, "Altruism in Children and the Perceived Conduct of Others," *Journal of Abnormal and Social Psychology,* 37, 218-233. **176**
Wright, H. F.
    1956, "Psychological Development in Midwest," *Child Development,* 27, 265-286. **200**
    See also Barker, R. G., 1954.

Zazzo, R., 1948, "Images du Corps et Conscience de Soi. Matériaux pour L'Etude Expérimentale de la Conscience," *Enfance,* I, 29-43. **119**
Zubin, J. *See* Hoch, P. H., 1950.
Zucker, H. J., 1943, *Affectional Identification and Delinquency.* Archives of Psychology, No. 286. N. Y.: Archives of Psychology. **140, 411**

Subject Index

A

Abandonment, fear of, 266-267 (*see also* Separation, Rejection, Institutional care)

Abstract thinking, 367, 369-370 (*see also* Reasoning, Symbols)

Academic achievement, of gifted children, 390-391 (*see also* School)

Acceleration of gifted children, 397

Acceptance:
by parents, 129-132
by peers, 204-207
consequences of, 133-134
in dealing with fear, 285
of others and self-acceptance, 131, 457-459
(*see also* Love, Affection)

Achievement, as related to intelligence, 393

Adjustment:
later, of shy children, 447
to school, 282
varying degrees of, 152
(*see also* Problem behavior, Personality)

Adult attitudes:
toward aggressiveness, 186
toward children's problems, 462
(*see also* Parent-child relationships)

Adult practices:
as related to aggressiveness in children, 190-191
influence of, 230

Adults, as peers, 231 (*see also* Parent-child relationships)

Affection, 129, 241 ff. (*see also* Love, Acceptance)

Affinities between children, 173

Aggressiveness:
adults' attitudes toward, 157, 190-191
as stimulus to counteraggression, 445

Aggressiveness (*cont.*):
cultural differences in expression of, 169
in children's make-believe, 334, 337-338
relation to socioeconomic status, 221-223
self-perception of, 163
to television, 435
(*see also* Anger, Fights and quarrels, Hostility, Prejudice)

Ambivalence:
toward children, 131-132
toward parents, 142-145
(*see also* Anxiety)

Amnesia, of early years, 324-325

"Anal phase," 86

Anatomical differences, awareness of, 119

Anger, 49-50, 238, 287-298
component of jealousy, 296
relation to fear, 258, 283
relation to mental health, 463
(*see also* Grievances)

Animistic thinking, 357-358

Anoxia, 36

Anticipation:
as a feature of development, 25-26
of future, through fantasies, 337-338

Anxiety, 255 ff., 454
acknowledgment of, 163, 459
as related to boredom, 246
hereditary factors in, 278
in parents, 48, 98, 163
influence on early memories, 327
self-rating of, 454
theories of, 269, 276 ff.

"Appeasing" parents, 156

Archaic behavior trends, 27-28

Artistic activities, 105

Ascendance-submission, 323 ff., 444 ff.

Aspiration level, 123

Asymmetry in development, 106-107, 393

Athletic ability, and self-evaluation, 447 ff.
Attachment of children to parents, 141-143
Attention span, 319 ff.
Attitudes, of parents, 127 ff. (*see also* Acceptance, Rejection, Parent-child relationships)
Authority figures, attitudes toward, 291
Autonomous moral judgments, 402
Awareness:
    of anxiety and hostility, 162-163
    of emotional expressions, 203
    of others, 59, 60-61, 353
    of self and others, 117-122, 302-303
    of symbols of social class, 224

B

"Baby-party" technique, 173
Bed-going ritual, 81-82
Bed-wetting, 82-86
Behavior:
    organization of, 36-37
    problems in school, 200
Belonging, desire for, 204 (*see also* Acceptance)
Bible, interests in, 417
Bilingualism, 313-314
Birth, ordeal of, 40-41
Bladder control, 82-86
Block-building, 106
Body-image, 118-119
Boredom, 245-246
Bowel control, 83-85
Boy-girl relationships, 224-226
Brain damage, 36
Breast-feeding, 71
Brightness, 213, 343, 388 ff. (*see also* Intelligence)
Bullying, 220

C

Callousness, and competition, 219
Cartoons, interpretation of, 367
Cause and effect relationships, understanding of, 356 ff., 360-361
Cephalocaudal direction of growth, 31
Cerebral palsy, 36
Character, as related to oral and anal drives, 70-71, 86 (*see also* Moral development, Personality)

Cheating, 405-406
Chewing, 72
Child-rearing, and socioeconomic status, 222-223
Choice, awareness of, 5-6
Chromosomes, 32
Climbing, 99
Coercive control, 157
Colic, 48
Comics, interest in, 437
Communication (*see* Language development)
Companionship, 178
Companions, imaginary, 341-344
Compassion, qualities of, 460-461
Competition, 183 ff., 214 ff.
    as defense against anxiety, 278-279
    unrecognized aspects of, 125
Compliance:
    as defense against anxiety, 277 ff.
    as disguise of fear, 258
Concentration, 319 ff.
Conception, 4
Concepts:
    formation of, 352 ff.
    of religion, 416 ff.
    of time, 315-316, 367 ff.
    (*see also* Thinking, Reasoning)
Conditioned responses in early infancy, 54-57
Conflict:
    and moral development, 407-408
    as related to prejudice, 227
    as source of anxiety, 271
    between children, 185 ff., 219-220
Congenital factors, 35-36, 164
Conscience, 406-407
Consistency:
    in mental test performance, 376 ff.
    in personality traits, 443 ff.
    in sociometric ratings, 211
Constancy:
    of IQ, 376 ff.
    of personality trends, 443 ff.
"Cooperating" parents, 156 ff.
Cooperation, 176 ff., 215-216
Correlation method (*illustration*), 376-377
Creeping, 19, 97
"Critical phase," 23-25
Crying:
    as response to aggressiveness, 189
    differentiation of, 62-63
    in newborn, 49-50
    suppression of, 239
Culture:
    influence on child-rearing, 167 ff.

Idealized self, as related to anxiety, 279
Ideals and heroes, 409
Ideational and emotional aspects of early memories, 322
Illness:
    emotional response to, 267
    in relation to anger, 290
Imaginary activities, as a means of coping with fear, 283
Imaginary companions, 341-344
Imaginary dangers, 260 ff.
Imagination, 333 ff.
    as outlet for anger, 292
    as related to emotion, 237-238
    fear, 257, 267
    (see also Fantasies, Dreams)
Impulse:
    as a component of emotion, 236
    as related to anxiety, 274
Independence, as related to parental practices, 160 (see also Self-assertion)
Individual differences in patterns of growth, 20
Individuality:
    as shown in response to treatment by others, 122-123
    constancy of, 443 ff.
    early evidences of, 18, 164, 442
    influence of on parental practices, 128-129, 164
    (see also Personality)
Individuation, 36
Inductive reasoning, 358-359
Infancy, developments during, 57-63
Information, children's, 362 ff.
Initiative, as related to parental practices, 160
Insecurity:
    and fear, 263
    as related to early memories, 327
Insight, as related to self-assessment, 459
Institutional care, effects of, 136-140
Intellectual ability, and self-evaluation, 447 ff.
Intellectual activity, as a source of pleasure, 243
Intellectual development, 301 ff.
    as related to humor, 252
    effects of maturation on, 20
    influence of deprivation on, 139-140
Intellectual growth, limits of, 379-380
Intellectual teamwork, 202
Intelligence:
    measurement and prediction of, 373 ff.
    of bilingual children, 312

Intelligence (cont.):
    relation to generosity, 406
    relation to honesty, 405
    relation to language development, 312
    relation to moral judgment, 402 ff., 409
    role in self-evaluation, 373
Intelligence quotient, 375
Interest span, duration of, 319
Interests, 423 ff.
    as related to growing capacity, 99-100
    in sex, 247-248
    of gifted children, 389
    romantic, 226-227
Interpersonal relationships, 65, 122
    as related to anxiety, 277
    influence of, on reported early memories, 327-328

J

Jealousy, 296 ff.
Jokes, 251-252
Joy, 242 ff.
Justice, ideas of, 402-403

L

Language development, 304-314
    early evidences of, 64
    influence of deprivation on, 139
    misunderstanding of, 365-366
    relation of, to early memories, 322
Latency period, 249-250
Latent content:
    of dreams, 347-348
    of early memories, 324
    (see also Subjective and objective aspects)
Laughter, 62-63, 250 ff.
Leadership, 178
Learning:
    and growth, 18 ff.
    as related to aggressiveness and anger, 191, 288
    effect of anxiety on, 276, 280-281
    fear, 257-258
    in infancy, 54-58
    in lower animals, 384
    influence of early impressions on, 328
    language development, 309, 311

Learning (*cont.*):
  love, 241-242
  (*see also* Environment)
Learning difficulties, role of anger in, 294
Likes and dislikes, 430 ff.
Locomotion, 97-98
  influence of maturation on, 19
Logical thinking, 356-359 (*see also* Concepts, Reasoning)
Loneliness, 180, 266, 463
Longitudinal study, findings in, 17 ff., 55, 76, 80, 83, 95, 96, 99, 101 ff., 119, 137 ff., 165, 172, 176, 195, 382-383, 442-444, 447-449
Love, 241 ff. (*see also* Acceptance)
Love objects, 177
Loyalties within the group, 176-177

M

Make-believe (*see* Imagination, Fantasies)
Maladjustment, 452 ff.
Manifest anxiety, 280-281
Manifest content (*see* Dreams, Fantasies, Subjective and objective aspects)
Manipulation, 60-61, 304 (*see also* Prehension)
Marasmus, 137
Masturbation, 87, 248
Maternal deprivation, 176-177
Maturation, 18-22
  and language development, 307, 311
  as related to anger, 288
  role of, in fear, 256-257
  understanding of concepts, 368-369
Maturity:
  emotional, as related to compassion, 460-461
  individual differences in, at birth, 51-52
Meaning, personal aspects of, 275
Memories, early, 320 ff.
  influence of later experiences on, 162
Memory, 303, 320 ff.
  "optimism" and "pessimism" of, 323
Mental deficiency, 397-398
  role of brain damage in, 36
Mental development, 54, 301 ff.
  and moral development, 401 ff.
  as related to motor, 106-107
  (*see also* Perception, Thinking)
Mental health, 452 ff.

Mental illness:
  extent of, 452
  role of heredity in, 17
Methods of dealing with fear, 281 ff.
Methods of studying children, 4, 6-9, 356
  as related to fear, 260, 262
  precautions in, 9, 360-361
  projective, 348 ff.
  sociometric, 206-208
  (*see also* Longitudinal study, Self-assessment)
Methods of studying parents, 162-164
Mirror image, recognition of, 119
Misconception:
  examples of, 364-365
  of religious concepts, 416
Moods, as related to recall of earlier experiences, 326-328
Moral attitudes, of gifted children, 389-390
Moral conduct, influence of religion on, 419
Moral conflict, as related to prejudice, 227-228
Moral development, 401 ff.
Moral issues:
  in children's questions, 439
  relating to television, 435
Moral judgment, 402-404
Moral realism, 413
Moral standards, changes in, 412
Mothering, 46-48
  and early mental development, 303
  by way of make-believe, 334
  effects of lack of, 136-140
  (*see also* Deprivation)
Motives:
  as expressed in children's daydreams, 342
  in cheating, 406
  in children's fights and quarrels, 187
  influence of, on attention span, 319
  role of, in emotion, 236-237
  (*see also* Emotion, Subjective and objective aspects)
Movies, interest in, 433-434

N

"Natural" and acquired aspects of social behavior, 175
Natural phenomena, understanding of, 356-357
Nature and nurture, influence of, 380 ff.
  (*see also* Heredity, Environment)

Needs and demands:
in early childhood, 64 ff.
role of, in emotion, 236-237
underlying fantasies, 333 ff.
"Negative" responses in infancy, 58,
147 ff. (*see also* Anger, Grievances)
Negativism, 147 ff.
Neglect, consequences of, 136 ff.
Neonate, 42 ff.
Nervousness, as symptom of anxiety,
275
Neurotic solutions, 279
Newborn child, characteristics of, 42 ff.
Nursery school, effects of, 139, 192-197,
384-385

O

Objective dimensions of child's world,
6-7 (*see also* Subjective and objec-
tive aspects)
Oedipal phase, 141-142, 164, 249, 267-
277
Oral activities (*see* Sucking)
Oral eroticism, 70-71
Original nature, 242 (*see also* Heredity)
Orphanage children, 138-139, 385
Overprotection, 135-136

P

Pain, sensitivity to, at birth, 48
Painting, as a projective technique, 348
Paranatal injuries, 36
Parent-child relationships, 16, 46-48,
127-170
as related to anger, 290, 295
jealousy, 297
motor development, 98
religious training, 416-417
(*see also* Anxiety, Discipline, Punishment, Sexual development)
Parent-child resemblances in:
fear, 268
intelligence, 16, 380 ff.
physical characteristics, 16, 95-97
Parental attitudes and rivalry, 183
Parental behavior patterns, 154 ff.
Parental example, as related to fear, 282
Parents, substitute, attitudes toward,
204
Participant observer, 7-8
Peer relationships, 168, 170-232

Peers:
as substitute parents, 176-177
influence of, on child, 168
(*see also* Social development)
Perception:
as related to anxiety, 273-274
early memories, 226-227
emotional development, 237
influence of emotion on, 371
role of, in emotion, 236
sympathy, 181
Perception of:
child by parent, 161, 442-443
characteristics of others, 201
early childhood as compared with objective records of, 323-324
feelings of others, 203
own roles by parents, 162
parent by child, 144 ff., 161
Perceptual component of self, 95, 116
(*see also* Body-image)
Perceptual level of thinking, 358
Permissiveness, 157, 158, 160-161
Persisting fears, 265
Personal and academic concerns, discrepancy between, 368-369
Personality:
as expressed by motor activities, 107-
108
as influenced by nursery-school experience, 196-197
as related to jealousy, 297
as related to parental practices, 160-
161
Personality adjustment:
and admission of weakness, 124
of gifted children as adults, 454
(*see also* Maladjustment)
Personality development, 18, 164,
440 ff.
influence of bilingualism on, 313
influence of parents on, 161-162
(*see also* Parent-child relationships)
Personality problems, 452 ff. (*see also*
Anxiety, Hostility, Jealousy)
Personality traits:
of children with imaginary companions, 343-344
reflection of in parental practices,
127 ff.
relation of to early memories, 326-
328
Phenomenal self, 124-125
Phenotype, 33-34
Phobia, 270
Physical care, emotional meanings of,
64-67 (*see also* Mothering)

Physical disability, as related to fear, 267
Physical growth, 95-97
Physiological accompaniments of emotion, 280
Pictures, use of, as a projective method, 349
Play, 242, 251, 424 ff. (*see also* Fantasies)
Play techniques, 191, 348
Pleasantness, incidence of in early memories, 323-324
Pleasure, 242 ff.
Popularity, 206-209
"Positive" and "negative" responses, 58, 176, 182
Possessions, conflicts regarding, 187
Postural control, 59-60
Practice, effect on rate of development, 18-22
Prayers, 417-418
Pregnancy, psychology of, 38-40
Prehension, 60, 74, 99
Prejudice, 212, 227-229
Premature child, 25, 52-54
Prenatal development, 31-32, 34-40
Prestige, as factor in social acceptance, 211
Pride, defense of, 461
Principles of development, 12 ff.
Privacy, protection of, 241
Problem behavior:
    as related to elimination, 85-86
    in fantasy, 335 ff.
    in feeding, 76-78
    in sleep, 80
    persistence of, 211
Problem solving:
    through fantasy, 335 ff.
    through play, 425
Problems, children's, as viewed by themselves and others, 452 ff.
Projective methods, 348 ff.
Proximo-distal direction of development, 31, 99
"Psychological habitat," 199
Psychotherapy, implications for education, 463
Punishment, 91-93
    ideas of, 404-405, 410-411

Q

Questioning, 314 ff.
Questions, personal, 439

R

Racial identification, 121-122
Radio, interest in, 433-434
Rationalization, 371 (*see also* Prejudice, Idealized self, Defenses of self)
Reaching, 60
Reading disability, role of brain damage in, 36
Reading interests, 435 ff.
    of gifted children, 389
Realism, as a mark of acceptance, 132
Reasoning, 352 ff.
    as an aspect of fantasies, 335
Rebellion, 152 (*see also* Resistance)
Recall (*see* Memory)
"Reflected appraisals," 121
Reflexes, 43-44
Regression, 294
Rejection:
    as related to anxiety, 277
    by parents, 133 ff.
    by peers, 204-209, 393
    consequences of, 136-137
    of parents by children, 131-132
"Relativism," moral, 402
Reliability of mental tests, 376 ff.
Religion, 415 ff.
Remembering (*see* Memory)
Remorse (*see* Guilt)
Resistance to parents, 147 ff., 150
Restlessness, during sleep, 81
Restraint, effects of, 51
Ridicule, fear of, 257
Risk:
    as a feature of development, 14
    as related to play, 424
Rivalry, 181, 183 ff., 185, 214 ff. (*see also* Jealousy)
Rorschach test, 349
Rules, as related to teamwork, 201-202

S

Satisfactions, 242-243
Scapegoat, 163, 293
Schizophrenia, 17, 278
School:
    apprehensions regarding, 281
    attitudes toward, 245
    boredom in, 245
    competition in, 215 ff.
    effect of, on self-evaluation, 450

School (cont.):
  influence of, on personality, 446
  interests relating to, 427-430
  maladjustment in, 453
  response to first experience with, 200
  vague concepts in, 309-310
  (see also Education, Nursery school)
Schooling, effect on intelligence, 384 ff.
"Screen memories," 325
Self:
  as target of anger, 289-290
  attitudes toward as related to training
    in bladder control, 83-85
  boredom with, 246
  defenses of, 461
  definition of, 115
  development of, 4-5, 116 ff.
  origins of, 115-126
  (see also Anxiety, Guilt, Conflict,
    Conscience, Idealized self)
Self-acceptance:
  and mental health, 455
  as related to acceptance of others,
    129 ff., 457-459
  as related to pregnancy, 39-40
Self-appraisal, 123
  and brightness, 392-393
  and handedness, 110
  and humor, 253
  as related to competition, 217-218
  influence of candor on, 459
  moral aspects of, 406-407
Self-assertion, 121
  as related to motor development, 98
  in relationships with parents, 148 ff.
  through play, 425
Self-awareness, 117 ff., 393
Self-confidence, as related to fear, 283
Self-criticism and self-acceptance, 458
Self-deception, 292, 392
Self-defeating actions, 275
Self-demand, 72-75, 79-80
Self-discovery:
  as influenced by peers, 174
  as related to care of children, 66-67
  joys of, 243
Self-effacement, 279
Self-esteem, 236, 273
Self-evaluation, 449-451
Self-evasion, 275
Self-fulfillment and pregnancy, 38
Self-glorification, in make-believe, 344
Self-help in eating, 75
Self-knowledge, 455 ff.
Self-perception, 145-146
Self-perpetuating traits, 211, 445
Self-preservation, role of anger in, 287

Self-rating of adjustment, 453-454
Self-realization:
  as related to anxiety, 269
  as related to religion, 420-422
Self-regard, effect of rejection on, 136
Self-rejection, 277
Self-repair, 26, 139-140
Self-revealment:
  as related to fear, 259
  through play, 426
Self-understanding:
  and understanding of others, 7-8, 10,
    66-67
  facets of, 369-370
Sensitivity, feature of acceptance, 129
Separation:
  effects of, 136 ff.
  fear of, 266-267
Sex:
  as related to anxiety, 275
  as related to humor, 251
  references to, in early memories, 327
Sex differences, 224
  awareness of, 88
  fantasies, 343-344
  hazards of birth, 36-37
  in aggressiveness, 190
  language development, 312
Sex education, 250
Sex stereotypes, 226
Sexual development, 70-71, 86-87, 247-
  248
Shyness, 212, 447-449
Sibling relationships:
  as portrayed in make-believe, 337
  projective techniques, 350
  references to, in early memories, 328
Sibling rivalry, 183-184, 296 ff.
Siblings, resemblances between, in in-
  telligence, 380
Sight, capacity for, in newborn child, 44
Singing, effects of training on, 22
Sisters, relationships between, 181
Skills, influence on social behavior, 192
Sleep, 77-81
Slow learners, 398-399
Smell, sense of, 45
Smiling, 59, 61-62, 172, 175
Social acceptance, 205-209, 391-392
Social adjustment, importance for slow
  learners, 399
Social behavior, and fantasies, 339-340
Social class, awareness of, 121
Social development, 59 ff., 170-232
  as revealed by language, 310-311
  influence of deprivation on, 137-139
Social origins of individual, 15